CONVEYANCING MANUAL

A J McDONALD BA LLB WS
Solicitor, Emeritus Professor of Conveyancing
University of Dundee

Park Place Publishing 1986

CONVEYANCING MANUAL by Professor A J McDonald

© Professor A J McDonald

1st edition 1982
2nd edition 1983
    reprinted with minor amendments 1984
3rd edition reset 1986

ISBN 0 947641 06 8 paperback

Published by PARK PLACE PUBLISHING (DUNDEE) LIMITED, 11 Whitehall Street, Dundee DD1 4AE.

Typed on a Digital Word Processor by THORNTON OLIVER, WS, Dundee.

Typeset and printed by HARLEY & COX (PRINTERS) LIMITED, 4 Shaftesbury Road, Dundee DD2 1UL utilising Advanced Communication Interface between the Digital Word Processor and Computerised Film-setting equipment.

PREFACE TO THE THIRD EDITION

With the cut back in Universities in 1981/82, I agreed to accept early retirement on the footing that no new apppointment would be made, so creating a significant financial saving to the University. The inevitable implication was, however, that, both in the Degree and in the Diploma Conveyancing Courses existing staff had to shoulder a substantial additional teaching burden.

With a view to easing that burden and possibly as a first stage towards re-thinking the teaching of this and other subjects in the Degree and Diploma Courses, I agreed to revise, amalgamate, and edit my Lecture Notes for both Degree and Diploma Courses in this single volume which, for ease of reference, I have simply called a Conveyancing Manual.

Keeping these points in view, I would emphasise to the reader that this volume is intended purely as an introductory Student Text Book and is not an exhaustive treatment of the subject. On the other hand, if the Student emerges from his Diploma Course thoroughly familiar with everything contained in this Volume, he will be well equipped to cope with most of the Conveyancing problems encountered in day to day practice.

By producing notes in this form, I think it will be possible for both Degree and Diploma Lecturers in Conveyancing to cut down substantially on the lecture content by referring simply to the Notes, and expanding in lectures only on those points in the Notes and in my Case Notes which may cause particular difficulty to the Student.

As indicated in the Preface to my published Case Notes, when Walker's Principles were first published, we re-organised our Conveyancing Degree Course in Dundee (later divided into the Degree and Diploma Courses) on the lines of Book 5 of Walker's Principles; and Book 5 of Walker's Principles is the standard text for the Course. These Notes must therefore be read along with Walker's Principles and cannot be taken in isolation, because a lot of material is omitted as being fully and adequately dealt with in that text. The Student should bear this in mind when using this Volume.

For simplicity of treatment and ease of reference, these notes follow exactly the pattern of the Case Notes and the Subject Headings are the same throughout. For the same reason, case references in these Notes are kept to the minimum, on the understanding that the student will constantly refer to and read the relevant Case Notes in relation to each topic in the Notes in this Manual.

These Notes, Walker's Principles, and the Case Notes must therefore be taken together as the common body of knowledge which the Conveyancing Student should digest and absorb in his two years of Degree and Diploma study on the Practice of Conveyancing.

The practitioner may find this Volume useful but I have not to any extent attempted to produce a practitioner's work; and any practitioner using these Notes must clearly understand that they are designed as a Student Text Book only. On the other hand, taken together with the Case Notes and Walker's Principles, they may serve as a convenient starting off point in the solving of particular problems.

As an aid to the Student and perhaps more usefully for the practitioner, I have included a fairly extensive Reading List, sub-divided into Chapter Headings corresponding with the treatment of the subjects in these Notes.

I am indebted to Mr. D. J. Hogarth, Director of Studies in the Diploma of Legal Practice in Dundee for revising and substantially rewriting the Section on Town & Country Planning in Heading 4.2; to Miss E.M. Wilson and Mr I. T. Innes, both Solicitors with Perth and Kinross District Council, for revising the remaining material on statutory controls on the use of land in Section 4.2, and the Chapter on Compulsory Purchase in heading 7.2.6.

The whole of Chapter 7.5. was also contributed by Mr. D. J. Hogarth for the Diploma Class in Dundee.

Chapter 9 — is a collection of contributions from myself, Mr. Stewart Brymer in my own Office; Mr. W. T. Fraser, Advocate, Aberdeen; and Mr. Ken Swinton, Solicitor, Dundee.

The Table of Statutes and the Index was compiled entirely by Mr Gordon Brough, an Assistant in my own office, who also spotted more than 300 typographical errors in the text of the First Edition.

I am greatly indebted to all these contributors for their respective efforts.

I am also greatly indebted to my Secretary, Mrs. Dunn, for organising the production of the whole of this volume on my firm's Word Processor; and for the processor staff, in particular Mrs. Hay, Mrs. Joiner, Miss Mackie and Miss Gray, for inputting the material in its present form; and for putting in quite a lot of overtime in the process.

By the combined skill and enthusiasm of Mrs. Dunn and Mr. G. E. Panton of Messrs Harley & Cox, Printers, Dundee the whole text was then transferred by some magical process from my firm's word processor to the computerised film-setting equipment of Messrs Harley & Cox to be printed by them in its new format.

Finally, I am greatly indebted to Mr. Tom Winsor and Mr. Martin Collins, then Assistant and Trainee respectively in my professional office, for slogging their way through the whole of the First Edition, comparing the print with my somewhat scruffy and not altogether legible Notes — a task which they undertook entirely in their spare time.

This Third Edition has been revised and updated to 30.6.85. It now includes a Digest of Cases. To that extent it is, I hope, an improvement on the Second Edition but otherwise remains basically the same.

Any suggestions for further improvement or amendment would be welcome.

Dundee
July 1985

A. J. McDonald

CONVEYANCING MANUAL

CONTENTS

TABLE OF STATUTES

DIGEST OF CASES

Where the name of the case is in *italic type,* there is a case note in the published Case Notes, either under that reference, or under the reference in brackets at the end of the note. Thus:

'1.2.1 *Stuart* 12 R 610. Signature illegible; touched up; stamp' is digested in the Case Notes at 1.2.1 But:

'1.2.36 *McNeill* 1973 SLT (Sh.Ct) 16. Signatures on reverse page. (See 1.2.13)' is digested in the Case Notes at 1.2.13, not at 1.2.36.

Where the name is not in italic type, there is no published Case Note in the Second Edition of the Case Notes published in 1984.

1.2 Authentication

Form of signature

1. *Stuart* 12 R 610. Signature illegible; touched up; stamp.
2. Donald 1926 SLT 103. Partial signature and mark invalid.
3. Draper 1954 SC 136. Signature by christian name on a testamentary letter valid.
4. *Rhodes* 1972 SLT 98. Signature 'Mum' on a testamentary letter.
5. Morton 1908 SC 171. Signature by mark on a testamentary nomination invalid.
6. Brown 15 R 511. Signature on erasure valid.
7. *Gardner* 5 R (HL) 105. Signatures on last page, initials on preceding pages.
8. *Lowrie's* JF 1972 SLT 159. Signature by initials.
8a. Elwick Bay Shipping Co. Ltd. 1982 SLT 62. Signature 'Pro General Manager' not equivalent to signature of General Manager.

Whether deed subscribed

9. *McLay* 1950 SC 149. Holograph will subscribed, clause added below signature.
10. Robbie 1959 SLT (Notes) 16. Holograph will; signature in margin. Invalid.
11. *Fraser's Exix.* 1931 SC 536. Holograph will subscribed, clauses added below signature.
12. Baird's Trs 1955 SC 286. Signatures on reverse page. Invalid. c.f. 1.2.13.
13. *McNeill* 1973 SLT (Sh. Ct) 16. Signatures on reverse page valid.
14. *Ferguson* 1959 SC 56. Writing on first page, signatures on third.

Authentication of alterations

15. Munro 7 M 250. Essential word interlined but not authenticated; whole deed invalidated.
16. Gollan 1 M (HL) 65. Inessential words on erasure not authenticated; whole deed not invalidated.
17. *Cattanach's Tr.* 11 R 972. Inessential words on erasure not authenticated.
18. *Pattison's* Trs 16 R 73. Will altered in testator's own hand.
19. *Manson* 1948 SLT 196. Alterations by testator to copy will.
20. Thomson's Trs 1956 SC 217. Alterations by testator to copy will, duly authenticated; effective to revoke the Will.

Attestation

21. Allan & Crichton 1933 SLT (Sh. Ct) 2. Witness signing 'Mrs. Bernard'; invalid.
22. Young 1910 SC 63. Allegation that witness did not see deed signed, nor hear acknowledgement — onus of proof.

23. *Forrests* 1907 SC 1240. Allegation that witness did not see deed signed nor hear acknowledgement — onus of proof.
24. Baird's Tr 11 R 153. Allegation that witness did not see deed signed nor hear acknowledgement — onus of proof.
25. *Walker* 1916 SC (HL) 75. Witness signing after death of granter.
26. Murray 6 F 840. Witness signing ex intervallo. Valid; but c.f. 1.2.25.

The testing clause

27. *Blair* 23 R (HL) 36. Operative words inserted in testing clause invalid.
28. Gibson's Trs 1931 SLT 22. Holograph provision in testing clause held valid in special circumstances.
29. McDougall 2 R 814. Names in testing clause written on erasure did not invalidate.

Informality of execution

30. Addison 2 R 457. Omitted testing clause may be added later; 1874 Act S.39 petition probably unnecessary.
31. Thomson's Trs 6 R 141. Witnesses' designations omitted.
32. *Elliot's Exors* 1939 SLT 69. Witnesses' designations omitted.

Alterations not authenticated

33. Grieve's Trs 1917 1 SLT 70. Parties inaccurately designed; not sufficient to invalidate; S.39 petition not necessary.
34. *Simsons* 10 R 1247. Writing in pencil.
35. McLaren 3 R 1151. Deed on several sheets signed on last page only; curable under S.39.
36. *McNeill* 1973 SLT (Sh.Ct) 16. Signatures on reverse page. (See 1.2.13)
37. Baird's Trs 1955 SC 286. Signatures on reverse page.
38. *Walker* 1916 SC (HL) 75. Defective solemnities. (See 1.2.25)
39. *Hynd's Tr.* 1955 SC (HL) 1. Defective solemnities.

Ex facie probativity and personal bar

40. Baird's Tr 11 R 153. Latent defect in probativity of onerous deed.
41. *Boyd* 1927 SC 414. Latent defect in probativity of onerous deed.

Notarial execution

42. *Hynd's Tr.* 1955 SC (HL) 1. Statutory procedure not strictly observed. (See 1.2.39)
43. *Finlay* 1948 SC 16. Interest of notary in Will; power to charge.
44. Irving 1956 SLT 328. Interest of notary. Deed executed in England.
44a *McIldowie* 1979 SC 271 — Interest of notary in Will — no power to charge.

Holograph writings

45. *Harper* 1938 SC 198. Onus on proof.
46. *Harley* 1957 SLT (Sh.Ct) 17. Holograph will, invalidly attested, held valid.
47. Tucker 1953 SC 270. Partly printed, partly holograph will held invalid.
48. Gillies 1961 SLT 93. Partly printed, partly holograph will held valid.
49. *Campbell* 1963 SLT (Sh.Ct) 10. Partly printed, partly holograph will. Cases reviewed.

Adoption

50. Shiell 1913 1 SLT 62. Holograph docquet subscribed on backing — held invalid; but c.f. 1.2.51.
51. *Campbell's Exors* 1934 SLT 420. Holograph docquet subscribed on backing — held valid.

52. *Craik's Exix* 1929 SLT 592. Improbative will adopted by separate holograph codicil.
53. *Stenhouse* 1922 SC 370. Improbative will in envelope bearing docquet.
54. *Chisholm* 1949 SC 434. 'Adopted as holograph'.

1.3 Delivery of deeds

The need for delivery

1. *Gibson* 1976 SLT 94. Undelivered feu disposition.
2. Life Association of Scotland 13 R 910. Deed not delivered at granter's death — held undelivered.
3. Walker's Exor. 5 R 965. Deed in favour of donor's wife undelivered. Held donor not divested.
4. *Connell's Trs* 1955 SLT 125. Bond to trustees of wife of donor.
5. Clark's Exor. 1943 SC 216. Delivery of testamentary writing does not prevent subsequent revocation.
6. McManus's Tr. 1978 SLT 255. Deed to wife of donor in the hands of his agent, but intimated to her — held not sufficient to infer delivery.
6a. Clark's Exor 1982 SLT 68. Disposition improperly executed but delivered to the grantor's Agent did not, per se, constitute homologation.

Acts amounting to delivery

Registration

7. Linton 1928 SC 209. Registration in sasines in names of donees held sufficient to imply delivery.
8. *Cameron's Trs* 1907 SC 407. Registration in sasines in name of donor as trustee for donee.
9. Tennent 7 M 936. Registration in Books of Council and Session is ordinarily equivalent to delivery.
10. I. R. v. Wilson 1928 SC (HL) 42. Registration in books of Company in name of donee as a factor implying delivery.'

Intimation

11. *Carmichael* 1920 SC (HL) 195. Intimation to donee.
12. Allan's Tr. 1971 SLT 62. Intimation to donee equivalent to delivery.
13. Clark's Trs. 1972 SLT 190. Intimation to agent for donee equivalent to delivery.
14. *Kerr's Trs.* 1974 SLT 193. Intimation to agent for donee equivalent to delivery — 1.3.12 and 1.3.13 discussed.
14a. Clark Taylor & Co. Ltd. 1981 SLT 308 — Intimation — whether contractual obligation, as 'continuing intimation' to obligee, equivalent to delivery.

Possession of deed

15. *McAslan* 21 D 511. Deed held by donee.
16. *Mair* 12 D 748. Deed held by common agent.
16a. *Lombardi's Trustee* 1982 SLT 81. Delivery of Disposition to a common agent who intimated delivery to grantee. Deed held to be delivered.

Acceptance of delivery

17. *Dowie & Co.* 18 R 986. Need for acceptance of delivery.

1.4 Capacity
Tutors, curators and judicial factors
1. I. R. v. McMillan's C.B. 1956 SC 142. Nature of the office of curator.
2. *Leslie's J. F.* 1925 SC 464. Power of J. F. to sell heritage; (but see now 1938 Act S 1).
3. Cooper & Sons 1931 SLT 26. Power of J. F. to sell heritage.
4. *Cunningham's Tutrix.* 1949 SC 275. Tutor's power of sale.
5. *Bristow* 1965 SLT 225. Curator's power to purchase.
6. Barclay 1962 SLT 137. Curator may still require power from the court to sell heritage, not for the purpose of giving title, but to exclude claims by beneficiaries.
7. *Lothian's C. B.* 1927 SC 579. Whether sale at variance with terms or purposes.

Trustees
8. Darwin's Trs. 1924 SLT 778. Whether sale at variance with terms or purposes.
9. *Campbell* 1958 SC 275. Petition to court under nobile officium for power of sale.
10. Horne's Trs. 1952 SC 70. Petition by English trustees to court under nobile officium for power of sale; retrospective sanction of earlier sale not granted.
11. Fletcher's Trs 1949 SC 330. Petition to court under Trusts Acts for power to purchase heritage.

2.3 Descriptions
(See also: 2.9 Possession, 4.1 Vassal's implied rights, 7.1 Voluntary transfer)
Adequacy of description
1. *Macdonald* 1914 SC 854. Description in general terms.
2. *Houldsworth* 1910 SC (HL) 49. General description. (See 7.1.18).
3. *Johnston's Trs* 1925 SLT 124. General description.
4. *Cattanach's Trs* 11 R 972. Inept description by reference. (See 1.2.17).
5. *Murray's Tr* 14 R 856. Inept description by reference.
6. *Maclachlan* 25 SLR 734. Lost plan.
7. *Matheson* 5 F 448. Description by reference at Common Law.

Conflicting terms
8. *Currie* 16 R 237. Boundaries and measurement inconsistent.
9. *North British Railway v. Moon's Trs* 6 R 640. Written description and plan inconsistent.

Subjects conveyed
10. *Hay* 1909 SC 554. 'Right and interest'.
11. *Gordon* 13 D 1. Parts and pertinents.
12. *McKendrick* 1970 SLT (Sh.Ct) 39. Salmon fishings — need for conveyance.
13. Munro Ferguson 8 SLT 326. Salmon fishings; illustration of express grant.
14. Nisbet 7 R 575. Fixtures and fittings.
15. *Jamieson* 3 F 176. Fixtures and fittings.

Bounding title
16. *Reid* 7 R 84. 'Bounded by the lands of A'. (See 2.9.39).
17. *Lord Advocate v. Wemyss* 2F (HL) 1. 'Bounded by the sea'. (See 2.4.4.).
18. *Brown* 8 F 534. Extrinsic evidence to identify boundary. (See 2.9.38).
    (And see also 2.9.35 to 2.9.46).

Particular boundaries

19. *Strang* 2 M 1015. March fences.
20. *Gibson* 7 M 394. 'Bounded ... along the Water of Leith' — boundary was medium filum.
21. *Menzies* 4 F 55. River. (See 4.1.84).
22. *Magistrates of Hamilton* 1929 SC 686. River.
23. *Magistrates of Ayr* 25 R 1184. Public road.
24. *Houstoun* 1911 SC 134. Public road.
25. *Louttit's Trs* 19 R 791. Private road. (See 7.1.99).
26. *Boyd* 1907 SC 912. Lane; conflicting titles; actings of parties.
27. Campbell 1896 4 SLT 79. Bounded by a gable wall excludes the wall.
28. *Hetherington* 7 F 706. Line of trees.
28a.*Gray* 1979 SLT (Sh.Ct) 17. Mutual wall. (See 3.3.18).

2.4 Reservations

Minerals

Title to minerals

1. Bain 3 M 821. Coal — constitution of title by reservation to the Superior.
1a. *Hamilton* 9 M (HL) 98. Reservation of coal and limestone with right to sink pits.
2. *Hamilton* 12 R (HL) 65. Reservation of right to work.
3. Cadell 7 F 606. Minerals under foreshore — charter of novodamus, not reserving minerals, sufficient title to the vassal.
4. *Lord Advocate v. Wemyss* 2 F (HL) 1. Minerals under sea.
5. *Millar* 1910 SC 618. Competing titles — possession of surface.
5a. Fleeming 6 M 782. A disposition of a bare superiority does not carry minerals previously reserved to, and owned by, the disponing superior. But c.f. 7.1.135 Orr.

Subject matter of reservation

6. *Caledonian Railway* 1910 SC 951 (and 1911 SC (HL) 72). Fireclay a mineral in 1856.
7. Magistrates of Glasgow v. Farie 15 R (HL) 94. Ordinary subsoil clay 2 or 3 feet below the surface is not a mineral; and see 2.4.13 N.B. Railway Co.
8. Linlithgow 1912 SC 1327. Shale was not a recognised mineral in 1818 but would now be.
9. *North British Railway v. Budhill* 1910 SC (HL) 1. Sandstone not a mineral in 1845.
9a. Caledonian Railway 1912 SC (HL) 9. Whether freestone is a mineral is a question of fact — relevant factors discussed.
10. *Borthwick-Norton* 1947 SC 659. Sand. (See 2.9.26).

Right to work, and to support

11. *Buchanan* 11 M (HL) 13. Right of surface owner to prevent mineral working.
12. White 10 R (HL) 45. The normal right of support may be excluded by express provision.
13. *North British Railway Co. v. Turners* 6 F 900. Nature of obligation to support.
14. *Barr* 6 F 524. Support of existing buildings.
15. *Neill's Trs.* 7 R 741. Support of building later erected.

Other rights reserved

16. *Scottish Temperance etc.* 1917 SC 175. Reservation of power to build on ground disponed. (See 2.5.29).
17. *Wemyss Water* Trs 1924 SLT 162. Reservation of trout fishings.

2.5 Conditions of tenure

Distinction between real and personal conditions

1. *Tailors of Aberdeen* 1 Rob. App. 296. Definition of real conditions, and requirements for the creation thereof.
2. *Corbett* 10 M 329. Restriction imposed for 10 years only.
3. *Magistrates of Glasgow* 10 R 635. Obligation to build by a certain date binding singular successors.
4. *Peter Walker & Son (Edinburgh) Ltd.* 1967 SLT 297. Obligation to build by a certain date binding original vassal only.
5. *Marshall's Tr.* 15 R 762. Obligation to build contained in a contract of ground annual not personally binding on a singular successor.
6. *Rodger (Builders) Ltd* 1950 SC 483. Effect of personal contract on singular successor.
7. *Wallace* 1960 SC 255. Effect of personal contract on singular successor.

Distinction between real conditions and real burdens

8. Tweeddale's Tr. 7 R 620 Nature of personal liability of sub-vassal to oversuperior for payment of over feuduty.
9. *Wells* 1964 SLT (Sh. Ct) 2. Personal liability of a singular successor to implement real condition imposed by disposition.
10. *Magistrates of Edinburgh v. Begg* 11 R 352. Circumstances in which an obligation to pay road money was neither a real condition nor a real burden.

Constitution of real conditions

The fundamental characteristics

11. *Tailors of Aberdeen* 1 Rob. App. 296. Definition of fundamental characteristics. (See 2.5.1)
12. Tweeddale's Tr. 7 R 620. Discussion of fundamental characteristics.
13. *Aberdeen Varieties Ltd* 1940 SC (HL) 52. Condition contrary to public policy cannot bind a singular successor.
14. Phillips 1962 SLT (Sh. Ct) 57. Condition contrary to public policy does not bind original disponee.
15. *Cooperative Wholesale Society* 1975 SLT (LT) 9. Whether a restriction on use contrary to public policy. (See 3.3.46).
15a *Giblin* 1979 SLT (Sh. Ct) 5. Restrictive condition imposed on purchaser void as being in restraint of trade.
16. *Beckett* 1921 2 SLT 33. Shooting rights cannot be constituted by way of a real burden.
17. *Harper* 1940 SLT 150. Fishing rights cannot be constituted by way of a real burden. (See 4.1.111).

Qualifying the infeftment

(i) Obligations undertaken by the vassal

18. *Morier* 23 R 67. Conditions not entering the title.
19. *Robertson* 1 R 1213. Conditions not recorded.
20. *Liddall* 25 R 1119. Condition not recorded.

21. *Campbell's Trs.* 4 F 752. Recorded agreement, 1874 Act S.32 not applicable.
22. *Gorrie & Banks Ltd* 1974 SLT 157. Reference to recorded agreement; 1874 Act S.32 applied.

(ii) Obligations undertaken by superior

23. *Montrose* 1 M (HL) 25. Obligation of relief undertaken by superior in a feu charter may bind successors in Superiority.
24. *Hope* 2 M 670. Obligation of relief undertaken by superior.
25. *Leith School Board* 1918 SC 94. Superior undertaking to insert conditions in subsequent feu charters may incur liability in damages for breach of contract, for failing to do so.
26. *Duncan* 1941 SC 145. Implied obligation on superior to relieve vassal of cost of repairs.
27. *Jolly's Exix.* 1958 SC 635. Circumstances where failure by superior to insert conditions in subsequent titles did not infer liability on superior.

Identification of subjects affected

28. *Anderson* 1915 SC (HL) 79. Description of subjects affected too indefinite.
29. *Scottish Temperance, etc.* 1917 SC 175. Insufficient specification.

Presumption for freedom

30. *Anderson* 1915 SC (HL) 79. Burden not expressly imposed. (See 2.5.28).
31. *The Walker Trs.* 4 F 594. Restriction not expressly imposed.
32. *Kemp* 1939 SC (HL) 6. Particular use not expressly
33. *Russell* 9 R 660. Building not expressly prohibited.
34. Cowan 14 R 682. Further buildings not expressly prohibited; vassal not restricted.
35. *Carswell* 1967 SLT 339. Particular building not expressly prohibited.
36. *Murray's Trs.* 1907 SC (HL) 8. 'Unseemly building'.
36a *Mannofield Residents Pty. Co. Ltd* 1983 SLT (Sh. Ct.) 71. Whether a prohibition against acts injurious to amenity too vague to be enforceable
37. *Porter* 1923 SC (HL) 94. Construction and use.
37a Mathieson 1914 SC 464. Restrictions as to structure do not restrict subsequent change of use.
38. *Hunter* 1964 SC (HL) 95. Surplus words treated as pro non scripto, if unambiguous.

Intention to burden

39. Montrose 1 M (HL) 25. General observations.
40. *Magistrates of Arbroath v. Dickson* 10 M 630. Annual money payments not declared real burdens.
41. *Cowie* 20 R (HL) 81. Residue bequeathed explicity under burden of an annuity.
42. Buchanan 1911 SC (HL) 40. A general bequest of residue, under burden of an annuity, was not sufficient to imply a real burden.

2.6 Servitudes

General

1. *Patrick* 5 M 683. Servitude a real, not a personal right. (See 4.1.112).
2. *Cowan* 10 M 735. Whether obligation personal or real.
3. *Allan* 2 F 699. Whether obligation to repair personal or real; no duty on servient owner to maintain.
4. *McLean* 1976 SLT (Notes) 47. Distinction between servitude and real burden.

5. *Crichton* 1946 SC 52. Servitude or right of property.
6. Safeway Food Stores Ltd. 1976 SLT 53. Servitude cannot be created in favour of a tenant of the dominant tenement.

Salient characteristics
7. Hamilton 1968 SLT (Sh.Ct) 53. Servitude cannot be created where the same person owns both tenements.
8. *Irvine Knitters* 1978 SLT 105. Servitude is for the benefit of the dominant tenement only.
9. *Hunter* 1964 SC (HL) 95. The presumption for freedom. (See 2.5.38).
10. Clark & Sons 25 R 919. If ambiguous, the least onerous construction is preferred.

Constitution of Servitudes
Positive Servitudes
(a) **Express grant or reservation**
11. *Cowan* 10 M 735. Agreement in missives. (See 2.6.2).
12. *Campbell's Trs* 4 F 752. Unfeudalised grant not followed by possession. (See 2.5.21).
13. *Millar* 1961 SC 1. Meaning and extent of express grant of access.
14. *McEachen* 1976 SLT (Sh.Ct) 38. Express grant excludes alternative implied grant.

(b) **Implied grant or reservation**
15. Cochrane v. Ewart 22 D 358 and 4 Macq. 117. Implied grant of servitude of necessity for drainage.
16. *Walton Brothers* 3 R 1130. Implied grant of servitude of necessity — access.
17. Fergusson 1913 1 SLT 241. Implied reservation of servitude of necessity — aqueduct.
18. Shearer 1 F 1201. Circumstances where a right of access held not necessary for reasonable enjoyment.
19. Fraser 1938 SC 506. Circumstances where a right of access was held not to have been granted expressly or by implication.
20. *Alexander* 3 R 156. No implied grant of servitude for shop sign. (See 4.1.52).
21. Murray 1973 SLT (Sh.Ct) 75. No implied reservation of servitude of necessity — water pipe.
21a Central Regional Council 1980 SLT 126. Grant of servitude of aqueductus created by Statute, by implication.

(c) **Acquiescence**
22. Macgregor 2 F 345. An estate factor has no implied authority to create a servitude by express grant or by acquiescence.
23. *Robson* 1965 SLT 381. Laying of pipes.
24. *More* 1967 SLT (Sh.Ct) 38. Common water pipe.

(d) **Prescription**
25. *Scotland* 1964 SLT (Sh.Ct) 9. Constitution of right of access by prescription.
26. *Kerr* 1939 SC 140. Tantum praescriptum quantum possessum. (See 2.9.60).
27. *Carstairs* 1924 SC 380. Tantum praescriptum quantum possessum. (See 2.9.61).
27a *Richardson* 1982 SLT 237. Quality of possession required to constitute public right of way.

Negative Servitudes

28. *Hunter* 1964 SC (HL) 95. Constitution in disposition of servient tenement. (See 2.5.38).
29. *Cowan* 10 M 735. Constitution by agreement. (See 2.6.2.).
30. *Inglis* 4 F 288. Cannot be constituted by implication.

Exercise and extent of servitude rights

31. *Sutherland* 3 R 485. Erecting gate on public footpath.
31a Midlothian D.C. 1985 SLT 36. Servient owner may not encroach unjustifiably on public right of way.
32. Lanarkshire Water Board 1973 SLT (Sh.Ct) 58. The owner of a dangerous bull may be interdicted from grazing it on land adjoining a right of access.
32a *Walker's Exix.* 1973 SLT (Sh.Ct) 77. Occasional access or regular daily use. (See 2.6.40).
33. Fraser 1959 SLT (Notes) 36. Whether planting trees interference with right of pasturage.
33a Central Regional Council 1980 SLT 126. Aqueductus — interference by overburdening by servient owner.
34. *Taylor's Trs* 23 R 945. Prohibition on building to preserve light. Servitude or burden.

Transmission of the right

35. *Royal Exchange etc Ltd.* 1912 SC 1151. Whether singular successor entitled to enforce.
36. *Braid Hills Hotel Co. Ltd.* 1909 SC 120. Whether singular successor entitled to enforce. (See 7.1.125).
37. *Watson* 1966 SLT (Sh.Ct) 77. Communicating the right to tenant.
38. *Keith* 1977 SLT (LT) 16. Communicating the right, increasing the burden.

Extinction of the right

39. *Millar* 1961 SC 1. Acquiescence. (See 2.6.13).
40. *Walker's Exix.* 1973 SLT (Sh.Ct) 77. Negative prescription — non utendo.
41. Largs Hydropathic Ltd. 1967 SLT 23. Acquisition for statutory purposes may render a servitude unenforceable.
42. Devlin 1972 SLT (LT) 11. By the Lands Tribunal under the 1970 Act S.1(3)(a).
43. *Gray* 1979 SLT (Sh.Ct) 17. A limited right of access is suspended when its purpose ceases. (See 3.3.18).

2.7 Subordinate clauses

Entry

1. *Thomas* 1953 SC 151. Significance of date of entry.
2. *Lothian & Border Farmers Ltd* 1952 SLT 450. Meaning of 'Entry'. (See 2.7.17).

Assignation of writs

3. *Smith* 8 M 204. Effect of assignation of writs. (See 7.3.17).
4. *Porteous* 25 R 563. Effect of assignation of writs.

Assignation of rents

5. Flowerdew 13 S 615. Effect of an assignation of rents as a separate deed in competition with arrestment.
6. Glasgow's Trs 16 R 545. Interpretation of statutory clause.
7. Butter 1912 SC 1218. Interpretation of statutory clause.

Obligation of relief

8. Spottiswoode 15 D 458. Special obligation of relief in a disposition requires special assignation.
9. Montrose 1 M (HL) 25. But not if undertaken by a superior in a feu charter.
10. *North British Railway* 1920 SC 409. Extent of obligation.

Warrandice

11. *Cairns* 9 M 284. Extent of claim.
12. *Leith Heritages* 3 R 789. Warrandice of 'all right title and interest'.
13. Brownlie 5 R 1076, 7 R (HL) 66. Warrandice guarantees only against eviction and does not warrant the particular tenure.
14. *Horsburgh's Trs* 14 R 67. Warrandice from fact and deed guarantees only against acts of the granter himself.
15. Montrose 15 R (HL) 19. A warrandice obligation is strictly construed according to its terms — express absolute warrandice in a gratuitous deed so construed.
16. *Welsh* 21 R 769. Partial eviction. Nature of remedy.
17. *Lothian & Border Farmers Ltd.* 1952 SLT 450. Existing lease not a breach of warrandice.
18. *Christie* 25 R 824. Liability under warrandice persists and continues to bind the original warrantor after the grantee has sold the subjects. (See 7.1.30).
19. *Young* 1909 SC 1340. Warrandice following Articles of Roup. (See 7.1.49).
20. Fraser 1938 SC 506. Warrandice not reflecting prior agreement.

2.8 Infeftment of the vassal

Registration in sasines

1. *Ceres School Board* 23 R 279. In a competition between recorded titles, priority of infeftment determines the preference.
2. *Johnston* 8 SLT 480. Possession without title.
3. *Cameron's Trs* 1907 SC 407. Effect of recording. (See 1.3.8).
4. *Macdonald* 1914 SC 854. Need for adequate description. (See 2.3.1).
5. *Brown* 8 F 534. Indefinite conveyance not a mandate for infeftment. (See 2.9.38).
6. *Swans* 4 M 663. Superior must be infeft — accretion.

2.9 Possession

Positive prescription

General

1. *Scott* 3 RLC 334. Purpose of positive prescription.
2. *Lord Advocate v. Graham* 7 D 183. Working of the positive prescription.
3. Edmonstone 13 R 1038. Possession without title cannot create rights by prescription.
4. *Johnston* 8 SLT 480. Possession without title (See 2.8.2).
5. *Grant* 21 R 358. Rights such as trout fishing cannot be acquired by prescriptive use.

Title

6. *Cooper Scott* 1924 SC 309. Discussion on ex facie validity.
7. Lock 1976 SLT 238. Was the title an express grant, or merely a title habile to found prescription?
8. *Fraser* 25 R 603. Possession on Crown grant disconform to enabling Act. (See 7.4.4).

9. *Hilson* 23 R 241. Title a non domino.
10. *Glen* 9 R 317. Title a non habente potestatem.
11. Ramsay 1909 SC 1441. Which register, county or burgh?
12. *Troup* 1916 SC 918. Not competent to refer to earlier titles in order to make title bounding.
13. *Meacher* 1913 SC 417. Not competent to refer to earlier titles in order to qualify foundation writ.

Whether title habile to carry the right claimed by possession

14. *Auld* 7 R 663. Ambiguity — title to pro indiviso shares, possession of whole.
15. *Nisbet* 1950 SLT 289. 'All rights in any way competent to' the disponers.
16. *Robertson's Trs* 7 F 580. Right of property or right of servitude.
17. *Fleeming* 6M 782. Title to 'superiority' not habile to acquisition of dominium utile.
18. Agnew 11 M 309. No presumption that foreshore is a pertinent without express grant; and prescriptive possession is necessary.
19. *Young* 14 R (HL) 53. Foreshore.
19a *Luss Estates Co.* 1982 SLT 457. Foreshore — barony title.
20. *Stuart* 6 M (HL) 123. 'Fishings'. Salmon fishings. (See 4.1.97).
21. *Zetland* 8 M (HL) 144. Salmon fishings — consolidated title. (See 7.1.147).
22. *Zetland* 11 M 469. Salmon fishings beyond boundaries of associated land.
23. *Farquharson* 1932 SN 28. Salmon fishings — competing titles.
24. *Millar* 1910 SC 618. Minerals, competing titles, both claimants averring possession. (See 2.4.5).
25. *Lord Advocate v Weymss* 2 F (HL) 1. Barony title, minerals under foreshore and sea. (See 2.4.4.).
26. *Borthwick-Norton* 1947 SC 659. Construction; minerals; sand.
27. *Scott* 7 M (HL) 35. Whether rights in lochs were exclusive or common. (See 4.1.90).
28. *Meacher* 1913 SC 417. Whether rights in lochs were exclusive or common. (See 2.9.13).
29. *Stewart's Trs* 1 R 334. Whether rights in lochs were rights of property or of servitude.

Parts and pertinents

30. *Magistrates of Perth* 8 S 82. Possession of island as a pertinent prevailed over express infeftment therein.
31. *Gordon* 13 D 1. Corporeal pertinents cannot be acquired outwith bounding title. (See 2.3.11).
32. *Cooper's Trs* 25 R 1160. Saloon as pertinent of house.
33. Mead 1915 1 SLT 107. Title to a basement flat habile to the acquisition, by prescriptive possession, of a cellar as a pertinent.
34. McArly 10 R 574. Right to retain a signboard on a building established by prescriptive possession.

Bounding title

35. *Cooper's Trs* 25 R 1160. Bounding title prevents acquisition of corporeal property outwith boundary. (See 2.9.32).
36. *Zetland* 11 M 469. Bounding title does not prevent acquisition of salmon fishings beyond boundaries. (See 2.9.22).
37. *North British Railway v Moon's Trs* 6 R 640. Title bounding. Conflict between written description and plan. (See 2.3.9).

38. *Brown* 8 F 534. Title bounding. Identification by reference to extrinsic evidence, separate plan.
39. *Reid* 7 R 84. Identification by reference to extrinsic evidence, adjoining title.
40. *North British Railway v. Hutton* 23 R 522. Particular description with exception, bounding so as to exclude exception.
41. *Houstoun* 1911 SC 134. Title bounding; 'bounded by Quarrelton Street'. (See 2.3.24).
42. *Watt* 18 R 766. Title bounding. Conveyance of attic storey. (See 4.1.55).
43. *Lord Advocate v. Weymss* 2F (HL) 1. Title bounding. Statement of county. (See 2.4.4).
44. *Gordon* 13D 1. Title bounding. Statement of parish. (See 2.3.11).
45. *Nisbet* 1950 SLT 289. Title not bounding (See 2.9.15).
46. *Troup* 1916 SC 918. Title not bounding; not competent to make it so by referring to earlier titles. (See 2.9.12).

Possession

Generally

47. *Robertson's Trs* 7 F 580. Title must support possession. (See 2.9.16).
48. Argyll 1912 SC 458. Title must support possession. Competent to refer to earlier titles to explain possession.
49. *Houstoun* 1911 SC 134. Title must support possession. Competent to refer to earlier titles to explain possession. (See 2.3.24).
50. *Warrand's Trs* 17 R (HL) 13. Salmon fishings, possession relied on to construe express grant.
50a *Fothringham* 1981 SLT 243 and 1983 SLT 444. Salmon fishing — possession not ascribable to title — no prescriptive rights acquired.
50b *Luss Estates Co.* 1982 SLT 457. Whether possession on barony title prescriptive or explanatory. (See 2.9.19a).

Quality of possession

51. *Millar* 1910 SC 618. Possession must be exclusive. (See 2.4.5).
52. *Young* 14 R (HL) 53. Whether possession sufficient to create a title; foreshore. (See 2.9.19).
53. Agnew 11 M 309. Whether possesssion sufficient to create a title; foreshore.
54. *Lord Advocate v. Cathcart* 9 M 744. Whether possession sufficient to create a title; salmon fishings.
55. *Meacher* 1913 SC 417. Whether possession sufficient to create a title; salmon fishings. (See 2.9.13).
56. Maxwell 6 F 245. Possession must be lawful and by legal methods; salmon fishings.
57. *Lord Advocate v. Lovat* 7R (HL) 122. Salmon fishing. Barony title; nature of possession.
58. *Warrand's Trs* 17 R (HL) 13. Salmon fishing. Barony title; possession by rod and line. (See 2.9.50).
59. Roxburghe 6 R 663. Salmon fishings; possession by rod and line is sufficient to maintain an express grant.
59a *Richardson* 1982 SLT 237. Quality of possession required to constitute public right of way. (See 2.6.27a).
59b *Strathclyde (Hyndland) Housing Soc. Ltd.* 1983 SLT (Sh.Ct) 61. Quality of possession required to constitute a public right of way.

59c *Bain* 1983 SLT 675. Competing titles. Use by one party. Extent of use necessary.

Tantum praescriptum quantum possessum

60. *Kerr* 1939 SC 140. Limitation on right of drainage.
61. *Carstairs* 1924 SC 380. Whether access for all, or for limited, purposes.

3.2 Feuduty

Remedies for recovery

1. *Sandeman* 8 R 790, 10 R 614 and 12 R (HL) 67. Discussion of general principles.
2. Tweeddale's Trs 7 R 620. Right of personal action against subvassals. Interest on arrears.
3. *Nelson's Trs* 6F 475. Poinding of the ground.
4. Scottish Heritages Co. Ltd. 12 R 550. A superior previously divested cannot poind the ground.
   (Note: For the personal liability of the vassal and his successors, see 7.1 Voluntary transfer).

Allocation of feuduty

5. *Nelson's Trs* 6F 475 Effect of allocation. (See 3.2.3).
6. *Pall Mall Trust* 1948 SC 232. Allocation under power contained in Charter.
7. Mitchell's Trs 5F 612. Whether superior bound by informal agreement to allocate feuduty.
8. *Moray Estates* 1971 SLT 318. 1970 Act. Objection to amount allocated.
9. *Barr* 1972 SLT (LT) 5. 1970 Act. Allocation on partly demolished building.
10. *Sandeman* 12 R (HL) 67. Effect of irritancy. (See 3.2.1).
11. Cassells 12 R 722. Irritation of the feu annuls the right of the vassal and subvassals without creating any right to recompense for improvements.
12. Ardgowan Estates Ltd. 1948 SLT 186. Use by the Crown for prohibited purpose incurred an irritancy.
13. *Anderson* 1957 SLT 57. Obligation to build without time limit. Purging the irritancy.
14. Glasgow Corporation 1971 SLT (Sh.Ct) 61. Whether irritancy purgeable.
14a *Precision Relays Ltd* 1980 SLT 206. Obligation to build; whether irritancy purgeable as of right or in discretion of court.
15. James Miller & Partners Ltd 1974 SLT (LT) 9. Failure to implement condition within time limit incurred an irritancy, which could be purged.
16. *Maxwell's* Trs 20 R 958. Purging irritancy.
17. *Fothringham* 1950 SLT (Sh.Ct) 25. Superior must irritate the whole feu, not part only.
18. Pickard 1970 SLT (Sh.Ct) 63. Irritancy does not extinguish a statutory burden for the cost of repairs.

3.3 Enforcement of real conditions

(Note: (i) Enforcement by a disponer, and his successors, of real conditions created by a Disposition; and
(ii) The jus quaesitum tertio of co-disponees of part of a feu to enforce the Charter conditions inter se
are dealt with under 7.1 Voluntary transfer).

Title to enforce — of superior and of co-feuar.

1. *Hislop* 8 R (HL) 95. Title of superior and co-feuar compared. No jus quaesitum tertio created.
2. *Nicholson* 1911 SC 391. The requirements for the jus quaesitum tertio. Conditions in titles indicating community of interest.
3. *Johnston* 24 R 1061. Reference to common feuing plan indicating community.
4. *Botanic* Gardens Picture House 1924 SC 549. No jus quaesitum tertio created.
4a *Gray* 1979 SLT (Sh.Ct) 17. No jus quaesitum tertio created. (See 3.3.18).
5. *Turner* 17 R 494. Right reserved to superior to vary conditions excludes implied jus quaesitum tertio. (See 4.1.49).
6. *Lawrence* 1965 SC 403. Express jus quaesitum tertio not invalidated by superior's reserved right to vary.
7. *Smith* 1972 SLT (LT) 34. Power of Lands Tribunal to adjudicate on jus quaesitum tertio.
8. Crombie 1972 SLT (LT) 40. Objection by a benefited proprietor, having a jus quaesitum tertio, to an application for variation of feuing conditions.
9. Eagle Lodge Ltd. 1964 SLT 13. A tenant of the vassal has no standing in a question with the superior to insist on title conditions.

Interest to enforce

10. *Zetland* 9 R (HL) 40. Nature of superior's interest.
11. *Maguire* 1909 SC 1283. Nature of co-feuar's interest.

Loss of interest to enforce

12. *Ewing* 5 R 230. Circumstances in which the actings of a superior did not infer acquiescence.
13. *Macdonald* 1963 SC 374. Actings by superior not inferring acquiescence.
14. *Howard de Walden Estates Ltd.* 1965 SC 163. Actings by superior not inferring acquiescence.
15. *Campbell* 6 M 943. Interest of superior extinguished by acquiescence.
16. Stewart 5R 1108. Circumstances in which the actings of a co-feuar having the jus quaesitum tertio did not infer acquiescence.
17. *MacTaggart* 1907 SC 1318. Acquiescence by co-feuar. Effect.
18. *Gray* 1979 SLT (Sh.Ct) 17. Initial objections not persisted in.

Discharge and variation of land obligations. 1970 Act ss. 1 & 2.

Definition of land obligation

18a Macdonald 1973 SLT (LT) 26. The Lands Tribunal has no jurisdiction to vary a land obligation imposed by statute.
18b Ross & Cromarty DC 1983 SLT (LT) 9. The Tribunal may vary a land obligation notwithstanding pending irritancy proceedings — See also 3.2.15.

S.1 (3) (a) — 'by reason of'

(i) Change in character of land

19. Bolton 1972 SLT (LT) 26. Decline in trade is not.
20. Clarebrooke Holdings Ltd 1975 SLT (LT) 8. Overgrown garden is not.

(ii) Change in character of neighbourhood

21. *Manz* 1973 SLT (LT) 2. 'Neighbourhood'. Pitlochry, not merely its High Street.
22. *Pickford* 1975 SLT (LT) 17. More restricted interpretation. (See 3.3.28).

(iii) Other circumstances

23. *Murrayfield Ice Rink Ltd.* 1973 SLT 99. Decline in skating as recreation etc.
24. James Miller & Partners Ltd 1974 SLT (LT) 9. Drainage problems not amounting to.
25. *Manz* 1973 SLT (LT) 2. Change in local habits in Pitlochry amounting to. (See 3.3.21).
26. Owen 1974 SLT (LT) 11. Change in social habits due to tourism etc. amounting to.
27. Morris & Anr. 1973 SLT (LT) 6. Disappearance of domestic staff amounting to.
28. *Pickford* 1975 SLT (LT) 17. Change not sufficient to justify use of house as a hotel.

(iv) 'The obligation is or has become unreasonable or inappropriate'

29. Bolton 1972 SLT (LT) 26. Reasonableness is not related to profitability.
30. *McArthur* 1975 SLT (LT) 2. Tribunal's discretion to protect 'affected proprietor'.

S.1(3)(b) — Obligation is unduly burdensome

31. *Murrayfield Ice Rink* 1973 SLT 99. S.1(3)(b) applies both to positive and negative obligations. (See 3.3.23).
32. McQuiban & Anr. 1972 SLT (LT) 39. Circumstances in which a restriction against assigning a lease, except as a unum quid, was unduly burdensome.
33. West Lothian Cooperative Society Ltd. 1972 SLT (LT) 30. Circumstances in which an obligation to maintain a ruinous building, requiring pointless and expensive maintenance, was unduly burdensome.
33a Nicolson 1981 SLT (LT) 11 — Time limit for reinstatement — Application for extension of time under 1970 Act S.1.3(b) refused.

S.1(3)(c) — The obligation impedes some reasonable use

34. Solway Cedar Ltd 1972 (LT) 42. Squeezing in one extra house in a small development was not a reasonable use.
35. *Main* 1972 SLT (LT) 14. Proposed use as nursery.
36. Devlin 1972 SLT (LT) 11. Circumstances justifying the discahrge of a servitude of access.
37. Campbell 1972 SLT (LT) 38. Sub-division into flats; application withdrawn after objection of Superior.
38. *Murrayfield Ice Rink* 1973 SLT 99. The applicant must specify a particular proposed use which the land obligation impedes. (See 3.3.23).
39. *Gorrie & Banks Ltd* 1974 SLT (LT) 5. Planning permission not conclusive of reasonableness, but application granted.
40. Bachoo 1977 SLT (LT) 2. Grant of planning permission not conclusive of reasonableness, and application refused.
40a *Scott* 1982 SLT (LT) 18. Application for discharge of restriction on building in garden of sub-divided house refused. Refusal of planning permission indicates that proposed use is not reasonable.

Compensation S.1(4)(i) and (ii)

41. McVey 1973 SLT (LT) 15. Compensation claimed by a superior refused under S.1.4(i).
42. *Robertson* 1976 SLT (LT) 11. Compensation refused under S.1.4(i), following 3.3.41.

43. Blythswood Friendly Society 1976 SLT (LT) 29. Compensation refused under S.1 (4) (i), following 3.3.41.
44. *Keith* 1977 SLT (LT) 16. Compensation refused under S. 1.4 (i) and S. 1.4 (ii). (See 2.6.38).
45. Sinclair 1974 SLT (LT) 18. Application for change of use from dwellinghouse to coffeehouse; compensation claimed by adjoinging proprietor refused.
46. *Co-operative Wholesale Society* 1975 SLT (LT) 9. Compensation granted under S. 1.4 (i) for economic loss.
47. *Smith* 1972 SLT (LT) 34. Compensation granted under S. 1.4 (i) for loss of amenity. (See 3.3.7).
48. *Gorrie & Banks Ltd* 1974 SLT (LT) 5. Compensation granted under S.1.4 (ii). (See 3.3.39).
49. *Manz* 1973 SLT (LT) 2. 'Affected proprietor' has no claim. (See 3.3.21).

Substituted provisions under S.1 (5)
50. Crombie 1972 SLT (LT) 40. Restrictions on type of buildings and screening by trees.
51. *Co-operative Wholesale Society* 1975 SLT (LT) 9. Limitation on use. (See 3.3.46).

Expenses
52. Campbell 1972 SLT (LT) 38. Expenses awarded against applicant on withdrawal of application.
53. *McArthur* 1975 SLT (LT) 2. Expenses awarded to successful objector. (See 3.3.30).
54. *Co-operative Wholesale Society* 1975 SLT (LT) 9. Compensation awarded but no expenses to either party. (See 3.3.46).

4.1 Vassal's implied rights

(See also 2.3 Descriptions; 2.4 Reservations; 2.9 Possession)

Barony privileges (see also Fishings infra)
1. *Lord Advocate v. Cathcart* 9M 744. General principles. Salmon fishings. (See 2.9.54).
2. *Lord Advocate v. Wemyss* 2 F (HL) 1. Minerals under foreshore and sea, various titles. (See 2.4.4.).
3. *Magistrates of Perth* 8 S 82. Prescriptive possession of pertinent on Barony title. (See 2.9.30).

Foreshore and sea
4. Keiller 14 R 191. Express title to foreshore, subject to overriding public rights for recreation by possession from time immemorial.
4.a *Luss Estates Co.* 1982 SLT 457. Whether a barony title habile to include foreshore. (See 2.9.19a).
5. *Smith* 5 F 680. Udal tenure extends to and includes the foreshore, where applicable. General discussion on udal tenure.
6. Agnew 11 M 309. Foreshore, prescriptive possession.
7. *Young* 14 R (HL) 53. Foreshore, 'bounded by the sea'. (See 2.9.19).
8. Crown Estate Commissioners 1977 SLT 19. The public right of navigation in tidal territorial waters does not permit the laying down of moorings on the sea bed.

Parts and pertinents — See 2.9.30 to 2.9.34.

Possession of heritage — See 2.9. Possession: passim

Rights of exclusive occupation — Trespass and encroachment

9. Halkerston M 10,495. Overhanging trees.
10. *Brown* 1977 SLT (Notes) 61. Intrusion of crane into air space.
11. *Houston* 21 R 923. Overhanging building.
12. *Alexander* 3 R 156. Shop sign. (See 4.1.52).
13. Anderson 1978 SLT (Notes) 42. Outside flue affixed to gable; equitable power of the Court to refuse enforcement of proprietor's right to object thereto.
14. *Leith Buchanan* 1931 SC 204. Beaching boats on loch shore.
15. *Brown* 1957 SC 351. Wall encroaching on adjoining land.
16. *Griffin* 1962 SLT (Sh.Ct) 74. Wall encroaching on adjoining land.
17. *Girdwood* 11 M 647. Encroachment; no acquiescence; restoration.
18. *More* 1967 SLT (Sh.Ct) 38. Underground waterpipe. (See 2.6.24).
19. Brown 1973 SLT 205. Straying animals; remedy available to aggrieved proprietor under the Winter Herding Act 1686.
19a *Farquharson* 1977 SLT (Sh.Ct) 22. Straying animals.
20. Paterson 1944 JC 166. Squatters; remedy available to aggrieved proprietor under the Trespass (Scotland) Act 1865.

Common property and common interest

Joint property

21. *Magistrates of Banff* 1944 SC 36. Joint property or common property.
22. *Munro* 1972 SLT (Sh.Ct) 6. Joint property or common property.

Common property

23. *Cargill* 15 S 408. Nature of common property. Multiplication of superiors.
24. *Grant* 8 F 647. Common property and common interest. Exclusion of right of division and sale.
25. *Deans* 1922 SC 221. Common property. Demolition and reconstruction.
26. *Sutherland* 15 R 62. Common property or common interest. Alterations to buildings.
27. Schaw 16 R 336. Rights of individual pro indiviso proprietors; collecting rents.
28. *Lade* 2 M 17. Right of pro indiviso proprietors to sue and defend.
29. Grozier 9 M 826. 2 out of 3 pro indiviso proprietors cannot remove a tenant without the participation of the third.
29a Barclay 1984 SLT 376. An agreement to allow one pro indiviso proprietor to occupy common property does not create a tenancy.
29b Denholm's Trs 1984 SLT 319. If one pro indiviso proprietor is in occupation, the other cannot claim rent or recompense in lieu thereof.
30. D. & S. Miller 1893 1 SLT 262. On the division and sale of common property, one of the several proprietors who has been in possession may recover expenditure on maintenance but may be liable to pay rent.
31. *Morrison* 1912 SC 44. Division.
31a Dickson 1982 SLT 128. Relevance of divorce in an action of division and sale.
32. *Price* 1951 SC 359. Sale of pro indiviso share. Effect on other pro indiviso proprietors. Whether ejection of purchaser competent.
33. *Wells* 1964 SLT (Sh.Ct) 2. Whether obligation to repair personal or real. (See 2.5.9).

Common interest

34. *Grant* 8 F 647. Common interest. (See 4.1.24).
35. *George Watson's Hospital* 11 R 320. Common interest in garden in square. Management.
36. *Donald & Sons* 1923 SC 122. Common interest in public street.
37. *Calder* 13 R 623. Common interest in tenement.
38. *Taylor's Trs* 23 R 945. Prohibition against buildings. (See 2.6.34).
38a *Gray* 1979 SLT (Sh.Ct) 17. Common property or common interest, boundary wall. (See 3.3.18).
38b *Gill* 1980 SLT 48. Common property or common interest, mutual wall.

Common gables

39. *Robertson* 13 R 1127. Common gable, right to recompense, singular successor.
40. *Houston* 21 R 923. Whether wall a common gable. (See 4.1.11).
41. Lamont 2 R 784. The adjoining proprietor is entitled to make vents in a mutual gable.
42. Baird 25 R (HL) 35. Rights attaching to a common gable at common law may be modified or excluded by contract.
43. Jack 3 R 35. One proprietor may not, without consent, remove a mutual boundary wall and erect a mutual gable in its place encroaching on a neighbouring property.
44. *Wilson* 1908 SC 580. Whether a common gable encroaching on adjoining property.
45. *Troup* 1916 SC 918. Common gable resting on garden wall. (See 2.9.12).
45a *Trades House of Glasgow* 1979 SLT 187. Liability for cost of demolition and reconstruction of exposed gable.

Tenement property
Solum, front and rear ground

46. Johnston 4 R 721. An express conveyance of the right in common to the solum, on which a tenement is built, gives no right of ownership in the front area.
47. Barclay 7 R 792. Same circumstances as in 4.1.46.
48. *Boswell* 8 R 986. Express conveyance of background, right to build.
49. *Turner* 17 R 494. Express conveyance of right to solum, proposed alterations thereon.
50. *Arrol* 14 R 394. Whether proprietor can build out over front area.

Main walls

51. *Todd* 22 R 172. Alteration to main wall, no special provision in titles.

Floor and ceiling

52. *Alexander* 3 R 156. Division line between upper and lower floors.

Roofs

53. Taylor 11 M 25. Where the roof of a tenement is not owned in common, the whole roof space and the roof itself belong exclusively to the top floor proprietor.
54. *Sanderson's Trs* 25 R 211. Ownership of roof, conversion of attics.
55. *Watt* 18 R 766. Ownership of roof, extension of attic upwards.
56. *Duncan Smith & McLaren* 1952 JC 61. Maintenance, no provision in titles.
57. *Duncan* 1941 SC 145. Maintenance, partial provision in titles. (See 2.5.26).

Common passages and stairs
58. *WVS Office Premises Ltd* 1969 SLT 254. Ownership of passage, no express provision in title.
59. *Deans* 1922 SC 221. Destruction of common stair, right to rebuild. (See 4.1.25)

Demolition and reconstruction
60. *Smith* 1925 SC (HL) 45. Dangerous building, liability for cost of demolition.
61. *Barr* 1972 SLT (LT) 5. Partial demolition, resulting rights of several proprietors. (See 3.2.9).
62. *Deans* 1922 SC 221. Common stair. (See 4.1.25).

Liability for damage caused by alterations and reconstructions
63. *Thomson* 1958 SC 380. Nature and extent of obligation of support.
64. Kerr 1970 SLT (Sh.Ct) 7. Nature and extent of obligation of support — cf. 4.1.65 and 4.1.66.
65. *Doran* 1971 SLT (Sh.Ct) 46. Nature and extent of obligation of support.
66. *Macnab* 1971 SLT (Sh.Ct) 41. Nature and extent of obligation of support. Nuisance.

Management and repairs
67. *Wells* 1964 SLT (Sh.Ct) 2. Liability for repairs, personal or real. (See 2.5.9).
68. *Deans* 1922 SC 221. Whether repairs necessary. (See 4.1.25).
69. *McNally & Miller* 1977 SLT (Sh.Ct) 33. Whether repairs necessary. 'Majority of proprietors'.
70. Schaw 16 R 336. Discussion on the right of one of several proprietors to collect rents.

Water rights
Surface water
71. *Campbell* 3 M 254. Inferior tenement not entitled to surface water from superior tenement as of right.
72. *Anderson* 1958 SC 367. Inferior tenement must accept natural flow of water from superior tenement.
73. *Crichton* 1946 SC 52. Servitude of water, interference by drainage. (See 2.6.5).
74. Scottish Highland Distillery 4 R 1118. Servitude of dam and aqueduct; interference therewith.
75. McLaren 1971 SC 182. Circumstances where a proprietor may have a duty to maintain his banks to prevent flooding his neighbour's land.

Tidal and navigable rivers
76. *Bowie* 14 R 649. Fishings, express Crown grant.
77. *Buchanan* 9 R 1218. Right to foreshore of tidal river.
78. Lindsay 7 M 239. Mussel fishing in tidal river. Barony title and possession.

Non-tidal, navigable rivers
79. *Wills' Trs* 1976 SLT 162. Right of public navigation.
79a *Scammell* 1983 SLT 462. Right of public navigation.
80. *Campbell's Trs* 1911 SC 1319. Right of public to anchor and moor.
81. *Orr Ewing* 4 R (HL) 116. Private rights in alveus.
81a *Grant* 21 R 358. Fishings in navigable river. (See 2.9.5).

Non-navigable rivers

82. Gibson 7 M 394. Bounded by a river implies ownership up to the medium filum.
83. *Bicket* 4 M (HL) 44. Opposite heritors, operations in alveus.
84. *Menzies* 4 F 55. Opposite heritors, medium filum, main and subsidiary channel.
85. *Cowan* 4 M 236. Upper and lower heritor, operations in alveus.
86. *Hood* 23 D 496. Common interest in flow of water.
87. *Young* 20 R (HL) 76. Pollution.
88. *Macintyre Bros.* 20 R (HL) 49. Pollution. Prescriptive right.
88a. Hardie 1948 SC 674. Operations in alveus interfering with passage of salmon.

Lochs

89. *Macdonell* 8 S 881. Loch surrounded by property of one proprietor.
90. *Scott* 7 M (HL) 35. Competing titles of adjoining proprietors.

Joint or exclusive right.

90a. Menzies 16 D 827. Joint right in loch. Disposition 'with lakes and pertinents'.
91. *Meacher* 1913 SC 417. Competing titles, joint or exlcusive right. (See 2.9.13).
92. *Mackenzie* 5 R 278 and 5 R (HL) 192. One loch or two.
93. *Magistrates of Ardrossan* 14 SLT 349. Loch or stagnum.
94. *Leith Buchanan* 1931 SC 204. Navigation on loch. (See 4.1.14).
94a *Menzies* 3 F 941. Regulation of joint rights of fishing in lochs. (See 4.1.114).

Fishings

Salmon fishings — (See also 2.9.13, 22, 50, 55, 57)

95. Munro-Ferguson 8 SLT 326. Express title.
96. *McKendrick* 1970 SLT (Sh.Ct) 39. Separate tenement. Need for conveyance. (See 2.3.12).
97. *Stuart* 6 M (HL) 123. Crown grant with 'fishings', construction.
98. *Bowie* 14 R 649. Crown grant, tidal and navigable river. Competing public rights. (See 4.1.76).
99. *Lord Advocate v. Cathcart* 9 M 744. Possession on Barony title. (See 2.9.54).
100. *Farquharson* 1932 SN 28. Competing titles. (See 2.9.23).
101. *Warrand's Trs* 17 R (HL) 13. Competing title. (See 2.9.50).
102. *Magistrates of Tain* 15 R 83. Boundaries between fishings.
103. Lord Advocate v. Balfour 1907 SC 1360. Udal Law. Salmon fishings are not inter regalia in Orkney.
104. *Gay* 1959 SC 110. River. Regulation of rights of opposite heritors.
104a *Fothringham* 1983 SLT 444 and 1984 SLT 401. River; medium filium; regulation of rights of opposite heritors.
105. Roxburghe 6 R 663. Method of exercising right.
106. *Lord Advocate v. Lovat* 7 R (HL) 122. Express grant, possession, mode of exercise of right. (See 2.9.57).
107. *Lord Advocate v. Sharp* 6 R 108. Sea fishings exercisable from foreshore, right of access over adjoining land.

Trout Fishing
108. *Don District Board* 1918 SC 37. Nature of the right.
109. *Galloway* 4 F 851. Nature of the right. Lease of fishings.
110. *Johnstone* 1934 SLT 271. Whether right of fishing and fowling a real right or personal privilege. (See 4.1.117).
111. *Harper* 1940 SLT 150. Whether right of trout fishings a servitude or a real burden.
112. *Patrick* 5 M 683. Whether right of angling a right of property, a burden or a servitude.
113. *Wemyss Water Trs* 1924 SLT 162. Reservation of fishings. Whether enforceable against a statutory successor. (See 2.4.17).
114. *Menzies* 3 F 941. Regulation of joint rights of trout fishings in loch.
115. *Meacher* 1913 SC 417. Whether trout fishings in loch owned in common or exclusively. (See 2.9.13).

Game
116. *Welwood* 1 R 507. Nature of right.
117. *Johnstone* 1934 SLT 271. Nature of the right.
118. *Beckett* 1921 2 SLT 33. Shooting rights as a real burden. (See 2.5.16).

5. Heritable Securities

5.2 Pre-1970 Securities

1. Bond and Disposition in Security

Constitution of Security
1. *Bell's Tr.* 12 R 85. Effect on bond of 1696 Act.
2. Smith Sligo 12 R 907. Whether a Disposition expressly in security for future liability was struck at by the 1696 Act.
3. *Alston* 1915 SC 912. Need for precision, interest rate not specified.
4. *Edmondstone* 16 R 1. Security for obligation ad factum praestandum.
5. Church of Scotland Endowment Committee 1914 SC 165. No one can be debtor and creditor in the same capacity in the same obligation.
6. *King* 1908 SC 684. Whether bond extinguished confusione; ranking.

Rights and Duties of Creditor
7. *Gatty* 1921 SC (HL) 1. Whether debtor in default.
8. Arnott's Trs 9 R 89. Bond on superiority; failure by debtor-superior to implement superior's obligations.
9. McNab 16 R 610. Creditor may exercise his various powers concurrently.

Sale
10. Stewart's Trs 10 R 192. Improper procedure invalidating sale. Effect of sale on postponed bondholder.
11. *Nicholson's Trs* 19 R 49. Sale by pari passu bondholder.
12. *Reis* 6 SLT 331. Sale by postponed bondholder, right to assignation of prior bond on repayment.
13. *Morier* 23 R 67. Whether deeds granted by debtor affect purchaser from bondholder. (See 2.5.18).
13a *Cumming* 1928 SC 296. Whether deeds granted by debtor affect purchaser from bondholder. (See 5.2.28)

Summary Diligence

14. *Taylor* 1931 SLT 260. Effect of registered bond.
15. Baillie 21 R 498. Liabilities of creditor in possession.
16. *Campbell* 17 R 661. Creditor in possession is not a singular successor of debtor.
17. *Inglis'* Trs 1911 2 SLT 176. Ejection of debtor.

Foreclosure

18. Sutherland 8 F (HL) 1. Effect of irregularity in procedure on the title of a purchaser.
19. Gatty 1922 SLT (Sh.Ct) 141. Discussion on alleged irregularities in the procedure on foreclosure.

Transmission of Personal Obligation

20. *Fenton Livingstone* 1908 SC 1208. Transmission on death of debtor.
21. *Carrick* 9 R 242. Obligation of relief by a purchaser does not per se imply transmission of personal obligations against him.
22. University of Glasgow 9 R 643. Creditor may enforce personal obligations against original debtor, notwithstanding transmission thereof to a Disponee under the 1874 Act S.47.

Rights and Duties of Debtor

23. *North Albion Pty Investment* 21 R 90. Debtor entitled to assignation on repayment.
24. *Fleming* 1913 1 SLT 386. Circumstances where debtor, repaying, not entitled to assignation.
25. Bruce 1907 SC 637. Creditor not obliged to grant assignation to debtor subject to qualifications.
26. *Cameron* 22 R 293. Implied discharge, marketable title.
27. *Bowie's* Trs 1913 SC 326. Fraudulent discharge, effect on title.
28. *Cumming* 1928 SC 296. Power to feu.
29. *Morier* 23 R 67. Power to feu, effect on bondholder. (See 2.5.18).

Back Letters

30. *Ashburton* 20 R 187. Effect on postponed bondholder.

2. Contract of ground annual

31. Church of Scotland Endowment Committee 1914 SC 165. Debtor and creditor the same person.
32. *Royal Bank of Scotland* 1 Macq. 358. Singular successor not personally liable.
33. *Marshall's Tr.* 15 R 762. Personal liability of singular successor.
34. Murray 18 R 287. A bond was held to be extinguished confusione, but not a ground annual.
35. Healy & Young's Trs 1914 SC 893. Ground annual not extinguished confusione.

3. Pecuniary real burden

36. *Tailors of Aberdeen* 1 Rob. App. 296. General principles. (See 2.5.1).
37. *Cowie* 20 R (HL) 81. Created by notarial instrument. (See 2.5.41).
38. Buchanan 1911 SC (HL) 40. Circumstances where directions in a Will did not indicate an intention to create a pecuniary real burden.
39. *Magistrates of Arbroath* 10 M 630. Intention to burden. (See 2.5.40).

40. *Ewing's Trs* 1923 SC 569. Condition too indefinite to qualify.
41. *Macrae* 19 R 138. Transmission of personal obligation. (See 7.1.124).

4. Ex facie absolute disposition

42. *Union Bank of Scotland Ltd* 14 R (HL) 1. General principles.
43. *Heritable Reversionary Co. Ltd.* 19 R (HL) 43. Effect of sequestration of the creditor.
44. *Ritchie* 1 F 728. Effect on debtor's title.

Rights and duties of creditor

45. Clydesdale Bank Ltd 1909 SC 1405. The creditor may require debtor to accept a reconveyance.
46. *Duncan* 21 R 37. Power of sale; consent of debtor not necessary to fortify title.
47. *Aberdeen Trades Council* 1949 SC (HL) 45. Power of sale, recorded back letter.
48. *Rimmer* 1967 SLT 7. Power of sale, duty to debtor.
49. Lucas 4 R 194. Circumstances in which a debtor was held entitled to interdict a proposed sale by the creditor.
50. *Scottish Property Investment Co.* 8 R 737. Right to eject debtor.
51. *Macintyre* 1967 SLT 95. Conditions of loan, restraint of trade.

Extent of Security

52. *Union Bank of Scotland Ltd* 14 R (HL) 1. Effect of intimation of second security. (See 5.2.42)
53. Campbell's JF 1944 SC 495. Continuing security for interest, bankruptcy of debtor. But see now 1970 Act S.42.
54. *Nelson* 1 R 1093. Security for all indebtedness, stated limit in back letter.
55. *Scottish & Newcastle Breweries Ltd* 1970 SLT 313. Stated limit in back letter. (See 6.1.1).

Liability of creditor

56. *Marshall's Tr* 15 R 762. Liability of creditor; reconveyance. (See 2.5.5).
57. *Liquidators of City of Glasgow Bank* 9 R 689. Prior bondholder in possession. Liability for feuduty.

Rights and duties of debtor

58. *Union Bank of Scotland Ltd* 14 R (HL) 1. Nature of debtor's reversionary right; second security (See 5.5.42).
59. *Ritchie* 1 F 728. Nature of debtor's reversionary right; lease by debtor. (See 5.2.44).
60. *Edinburgh Entertainments Ltd* 1926 SC 363. Nature of debtor's reversionary right; lease by debtor.
61. *McBride* 21 R 620. Title of debtor to sue and defend actions.
62. *Scobie* 1967 SLT 9. Title of debtor to sue and defend actions.

5.3 Standard Securities

1. *UDT Ltd.* 1978 SLT (Sh. Ct) 14. Default. Application to court.
2. *Trade Development Bank v. Warriner & Mason* 1980 SLT 49. Creditor entitled to set aside unauthorised lease.
3. *Trade Development Bank v. Warriner & Mason* 1980 SLT 223. Standard conditions; whether recording of Standard Security form B constituted notice of conditions in an unrecorded minute of agreement; duty of enquiry.

4. *Trade Development Bank v. D.W. Haig (Bellshill) Limited* 1983 SLT 510 Standard conditions. Heritable creditor not affected by personal obligations undertaken by the debtor relating to the security subjects. (5.3.2 and 5.3.3 Distinguished).
5. *Trade Development Bank v. Crittall Windows Limited* 1983 SLT 510. Effect of knowledge of prior personal right on subsequent real security.
6. *Sowman* 1983 SLT 132 and 1985 SLT 65. Ranking. Statutory burden in favour of Local Authority.
7. Prestwick Investment Trust 1981 SLT (Sh. Ct) 55. Default; correct procedure for recovery of possession.
8. Halifax Building Society 1985 SLT (Sh.Ct) 25. Sale by heritable creditor; debtor inhibited; effect of inhibition on the rights of unsecured creditors to surplus on sale.

6.1 Floating Charges

1. *Scottish & Newcastle Breweries* 1970 SLT 313. Extent of security, stated limit in back letter.
2. *National Commercial Bank Ltd* 1969 SLT 306. Extent of security, interest due from date of liquidation.
3. *Libertas-Kommerz* 1978 SLT 222. Whether bond and floating charge assignable by creditor.
4. *Forth & Clyde Construction Co. Ltd.* 1984 SLT 94. Nature of fixed security on appointment of receiver.

7.1 Voluntary transfer *inter vivos*
Contract of sale and purchase of heritage
Constitution of the contract
Form

1. Caithness Flagstone 7 R 1117. Unsigned offer accepted in writing; no resulting contract.
2. *McGinn* 1947 SC 334. Improbative acceptance; covering letter holograph.
3. Gavine's Tr. 10 R 448. 'Adopted as holograph' below the signature effective to constitute a binding offer.
4. Harvey 6 F 511. Circumstances where an individual, illiterate and without separate advice, was held not bound by an offer signed by him 'adopted as holograph'; but c.f. 7.1.5.
5. *Maclaine* 1958 SLT (Sh. Ct) 49 'Adopted as holograph'; effect.
6. Whyte 6 R 699. Acceptance by agents, in proper form, binds the principal.

Consensus in idem

7. *Haldane & Another* 1972 SLT (Sh. Ct) 8. Unilateral undertaking.
8. *Dickson* 10 M 41. No consensus; qualified acceptance.
9. *Heiton* 4 R 830. No. consensus; all conditions not agreed.
10. *Stobo Ltd.* 1949 SC 184. No consensus; 'subject to contract'.
11. Westren 7 R 173. Consensus; purchaser taking possession and making alterations.

Rei interventus and homologation

12. Colquhoun 22 D 1035. All conditions not explicitly agreed, but purchaser carrying out alterations to property.
13. *Secretary of State v. Ravenstone Securities* 1976 SC 171. Whether actings unequivocally referable to informal agreement.
13a *Mitchell* 1936 SC (HL) 56. Homologation of improbative agreement by actings.
14. *East Kilbride Development Corporation* 1953 SC 370. A contract lacking essentials cannot be completed by rei interventus.
15. *Errol* 1966 SC 93. Proof of agreement to found rei interventus.
16. *Law* 1978 SLT 250. Circumstances insufficient to warrant rei interventus or homologation.
16a Clark's Executor 1982 SLT 68. Delivery of improbative writ to granter's agent does not normally constitute homologation; nor would the agent's actings constitute rei interventus.

Essential content

Indentification of subjects

17. *MacDonald* 1 F 68. 'Property known as the Royal Hotel'.
18. *Houldsworth* 1910 SC (HL) 49. 'The Estate of Dallas'. Prior negotiations.
19. *McKendrick* 1970 SLT (Sh. Ct) 39. Whether salmon fishings included in the sale. (See 2.3.12).
20. *Anderson* 1954 SC (HL) 43. Farm and other subjects; prior communings.
20a Murray 1980 SLT (Sh. Ct) 131. Not legitimate to refer to prior negotiations to contradict terms of missives, unless ambiguous.
20b *Russell's Exor.* 1983 SLT 385. Discussion of the rule in Anderson — 7.1.20.

Moveables

21. Nisbet 7 R 575. Vegetables, grapes, etc.
22. Cochrane 18 R 1208. Picture in panel.
23. *Christie* 1949 SC 572. Summerhouse.
24. *Assessor for Fife* 1966 SLT 79. Storage heaters.
25. *Jamieson* 3 F 176. Passing of moveables (See 2.3.15).

Price

26. Stirling 2 S 765. No binding contract if price not fixed.

Date of Entry

27. *Sloan's Dairies Ltd* 1979 SLT 17. Agreed date of entry not essential.
28. *Law* 1978 SLT 250. Date of entry essential (See 7.1.16).
28a *Secretary of State v. Ravenstone Securities* 1976 SC 171. Question whether date of entry would always be implied. (See 7.1.13).
28b *Speevak* 1949 SLT (Notes) 39. 'Entry' and 'Settlement' are contemporaneous. (See 7.1.98).
29. Heys 17 R 381 'Immediate entry' means such early possession as is possible and practicable.

Time Limits

29a *Effold Properties Limited* 1979 SLT (Notes) 84. Condition as to time limit in qualified acceptance did not prevent withdrawal of the acceptance within the time limit.

Seller's obligations

(i) To tender marketable title

30. *Christie* 25 R 824. Seller bound to clear the title.
31. *McConnell* 10 SLT 790. Long lease is not a marketable title.
32. *Bruce* 2 F 948. Decree of irritancy in absence.
33. *Dryburgh* 24 R 1. Undischarged inhibitions.
34. Hamilton 23 D 1033. Title defective; buildings erected in part on an adjoining feu.

Reservation of minerals

35. *Whyte* 6 R 699. Purchaser entitled to resile.
36. *Campbell* 1963 SC 505. Purchaser entitled to resile.
37. *Macdonald* 1 F 68. Purchaser's knowledge; personal bar. (See 7.1.17).
38. *Mossend Theatre Co.* 1930 SC 90. Whether knowledge to be imputed to purchaser.

Burdens

39. *Corbett* 10 M 329. Personal, not real, condition. (See 2.5.2).
40. *Smith* 23 R 60. Undisclosed burden.
41. *Welsh* 21 R 769. Undisclosed servitude. (See 2.7.16).
42. *Cameron* 22 R 293. Undischarged security. (See 5.2.26).
43. Bremner 1911 SC 887. Unallocated feuduty renders title unmarketable.
44. *Armia* 1979 SLT 147. Purchaser not bound to accept undisclosed burdens.
44a *Umar* 1983 SLT (Sh.Ct) 79. Seller bound to disclose all restrictions on title.

(ii) To implement other terms of contract

45. *Bradley* 1966 SLT (Sh.Ct) 25. Closing order an 'outstanding notice'.
46. *Kelly* 1968 SLT 141. 'Notices, etc., under Town & Country Planning Acts...'.
47. Murray 1960 SLT (Notes) 48. Meaning and effect of a condition as to 'unqualified planning permission'.

'Title as it stands'

48. Morton 5 R 83. Observations on effect of this clause.
49. *Young* 1909 SC 1340. No title to 25 sq.yds. out of 383 sq.yds. Purchaser bound to accept title.
50. *Wood* 13 R 1006. Purchaser must accept real conditions in title.
51. *Davidson* 8 R 990. Purchaser must accept undischarged burdens.
52. *Carter* 18 R 353. Purchaser not bound to accept incurable defects.
53. *Leith Heritages Co.* 3 R 789. Effect of obligation 'to put purchaser in the sellers' place'. (See 2.7.12).
54. *Mackenzie* 3 SLT 128. A provision that a purchaser is not entitled to a search does not deprive him of his right to a marketable title.

Right to withdraw or depart from conditions

55. Dewar 1968 SLT 196. Condition as to planning permission c.f. 7.1.56.
56. *Ellis & Sons Ltd* 1975 SLT 10. Condition as to planning permission.
56a *Imry Property Holdings Ltd.* 1979 SLT 261. Whether seller entitled to waive condition.
56b *Gilchrist* 1979 SLT 135. Whether purchaser entitled to waive condition.

(iii) To give possession

57. *Lothian & Borders Farmers* 1952 SLT 450. Tenant in occupation under a lease. (See 2.7.17).

58. Stuart 1976 SLT (Notes) 39. A provision for 'actual occupation' entitles the purchaser to insist on vacant possession of the whole subjects.

(iv) **To grant a valid disposition**

Relationship of disposition to missives

59. *Johnston's Trs* 1925 SLT 124. Terms of description to be inserted in disposition (See 2.3.3).
60. *Equitable Loan Co.* 1972 SLT (Notes) 20. Dispostion not conveying whole subjects sold.
61. *Hay* 1909 SC 554. Sale of 'right and interest'. Seller bound to dispone land. (See 2.3.10).
62. *Cowan* 10 M 735. Servitude to be inserted in disposition. (See 2.6.2).
63. Mackenzie 37 SLR 660. Seller must grant absolute warrandice.
64. *Young* 1909 SC 1340. Warrandice following articles of roup. (see 7.1.49).
65. Fraser 1938 SC 506. Warrandice not reflecting terms of antecedent contract.
66. *Porteous* 25 R 563. Writs (See 2.7.4).

Disposition supersedes prior contract

67. *Lee* 10 R (HL) 91. General principles.
68. *Orr* 20 R (HL) 27. General principles.
69. Butter 1912 SC 1218. General principles.
69a *Winston* 1981 SLT 41. General principles discussed.
69b Hayes 1984 SLT 300. General rule excluded by specific clause in missives to that effect.
70. *Leith Heritages Co.* 3 R 789. General principles. (See 2.7.12).
71. *Anderson* 1954 SC (HL) 43. Reduction of Disposition as erroneous; effect on prior contract. (See 7.1.20).
71a *Russell's Exor.* 1983 SLT 385. If a formal contract does not properly reflect the intentions of both parties, and that can be proved, the Court will correct the error. (See 7.1.20b).
72. *Equitable Loan Co.* 1972 SLT (Notes) 20. Disposition not conveying whole subjects sold. (See 7.1.60)

Effect of disposition on collateral conditions in contract

72a Hayes 1984 SLT 300. Purchaser retaining subjects and claiming damages for breach of collateral obligation; whether quanti minoris.
73. Wann 1935 SN 8. Combined sale and building contract — but disapproved in Winston — 7.1.69a.
74. *McKillop* 1945 SC 166. Combined sale and building contract — distinguished in Winston — 7.1.69a.
75. *Jamieson* 3 F 176. Moveables. (See 2.3.15).
76. *Bradley* 1966 SLT (Sh.Ct) 25. Provisions as to statutory notices. (See 7.1.45).
77. *Winston* 1981 SLT 41. Provisions as to structural condition. (See 7.1.69a).

(v) **To provide clear searches**

78. *Christie* 25 R 824. Seller bound to provide. (See 7.1.30).
79. *Dryburgh* 24 R 1. Obligation to clear the record. (See 7.1.33).

Purchaser's obligations

Payment of price

80. *Rodger (Builders) Ltd* 1950 SC 483. Date of payment. (See 2.5.6).
81. *Prestwick Cinema Co.* 1951 SC 98. Interest on unpaid price.

Purchaser in possession.

82. *Bowie* 1978 SLT (Sh.Ct) 9. Purchaser not in possession; interest.
82a *Chapman's Trs* 1980 SLT (Sh.Ct) 27. Delay in payment of price; whether sellers entitled to claim damages or merely interest.
82b Thomson 1983 SLT (Sh.Ct) 17. Seller not entitled to interst unless purchaser actually in possession.
82c *Tiffney* 1983 SLT (Sh.Ct) 45 and 1985 SLT 165. Seller not entitled to interest unless purchaser actually in possession. Interest not due ex mora.

Effect on purchaser of personal obligations of seller

83. *Ceres School Board* 23 R 279. Unrecorded charter granted by seller. (See 2.8.1).
84. *Davidson* 8 R 990. Burden in a will not made real. (See 7.1.51).
85. *Stodart* 4 R 236. Purchaser barred by knowledge from objecting to right of occupancy.
86. *Rodger (Builders) Ltd* 1950 SC 483. Second purchaser having notice of prior sale. (See 2.5.6).
86a *Trade Development Bank v. Crittall Windows Limited* 1983 SLT 510. Creditor taking real security with knowledge of prior personal obligation — whether affected thereby. (See 5.3.5).
87. *Campbell's Trs* 4 F 752. Personal contract not binding on singular successor. (See 2.5.21).

Breach of contract

Time for implement

88. *Gilfillan* 21 R 269. Valid title tendered too late.
89. *Kelman* 5 R 816. Valid title tendered too late.
90. *Campbell* 1963 SC 505. Where defect fundamental, purchaser not obliged to give time. (See 7.1.36).
91. *Carter* 18 R 353. Circumstances in which purchaser bound to take title tendered late. (See 7.1.52).
92. Kinnear 1936 SLT 574. Defect incurable; purchaser having taken possession and given time, still entitled to resile.
93. *Rodger (Builders) Ltd* 1950 SC 483. Price not tendered at date of entry. (See 2.5.6).
94. Burns 8 SLT 321. Circumstances in which a seller was held not to have given sufficient notice to defaulting purchaser of his intention to rescind and resell.
95. *MacDonald* 1 F 68. Purchaser's objection to title made too late; but cf. 7.1.92. (See 7.1.17).
96. *Crofts* 1927 SC (HL) 65. Instalment purchase; no objection to title until after instalment paid.
97. *Morrison* 1932 SC 712. Purchaser held not barred from objecting until disposition delivered.
98. *Speevak* 1949 SLT (Notes) 39. Seller contractually bound to effect alterations to subjects by date of entry; alterations not completed. Seller held to be in breach and liable in damages; but purchaser not entitled to resile.
98a *Boland & Co. Ltd* 1975 SLT (Notes) 80. Suspensive condition not within power of contracting party to purify.
98b *MacDonald* 1981 SLT 128. Obligation to deliver conveyance of heritable property not imprescriptible.

Purchasers' remedies

99. *Louttit's Trs* 19 R 791. Remedies of purchaser before settlement.
100. *Smith* 23 R 60. Title not marketable; rescission. (7.1.40).
101. *Campbell* 1963 SC 505. Undisclosed mineral reservation, rescission. (7.1.36).
102. *Welsh* 21 R 769. Remedies of purchaser after settlement. (2.7.16).
103. *McKillop* 1945 SC 166. Retention and damages. (7.1.74).
104. *Bradley* 1966 SLT (Sh.Ct) 25. Retention and damages. (7.1.45).
104a Hayes 1984 SLT 300. Retention and damages. Whether quanti minoris.
105. *Steuart's Trs* 3 R 192. Circumstances justifying restitutio after settlement.
106. Hamilton 23 D 1033. Circumstances justifying restitutio after settlement.
107. *Stewart* 17 R (HL) 1. Specific implement, general observations.
108. McKellar 1928 SC 503. Specific implement.
109. *Mackay* 1966 SC 237. Specific implement.
109a *Hoey* 1975 SC 87. Specific implement and damages.
109b *Speevak* 1949 SLT (Notes) 39. Purchaser held not entitled to resile on breach by seller but was awarded damages. (see 7.1.98).
110. *Plato* 1950 SLT (Notes) 29. Specific implement; seller claiming implement impossible.
111. Boag 1967 SLT 275. Seller disappeared. Clerk of Court empowered to execute disposition.

Seller's remedies

112. *Carter* 18 R 353. Action for implement. (See 7.1.52).
113. *British Railways Board* 1971 SLT (Notes) 17. Action for payment.
113a Muir & Black 1981 SLT (Sh.Ct) 68 — Action for payment — whether purchaser's obligations extinguished by the short negative prescription.
114. Inveresk Paper Co. Ltd 1972 SLT (Notes) 63. Rescission.
115. *Rodger (Builders) Ltd* 1950 SC 483. Circumstances not justifying rescission. Disposition to second purchaser reduced. (See 2.5.6).
116. *Johnstone* 1978 SLT (Notes) 81. Rescission — seller's duty to mitigate damages.
117. Commercial Bank 18 R 80. Forfeiture of deposit.
117a Reid 1958 SLT (Sh.Ct) 45. Forfeiture of instalments paid to account of price.
117b *Geo. Packman & Sons* 1977 SLT 140. Impossibility, delay, seller entitled to rescind without notice.

Special disposition of dominium utile

118. *Hyslop* 1 M 535. General principles.

Implied entry

119. Morris 4 R 515. Effect of 1874 Act S.4.

Transmission of vassal's obligations under the Charter

(i) Feu disponed to singular successor

120. Dundee Police Commissioners 11 R 586. Vassal and heirs bound jointly and severally; old vassal liable for future prestations.
121. Marshall 22 R 954. Obligations prestable before disposition granted; continuing liability of old vassal.
122. *Rankine* 4 F 1074. Obligations prestable before disposition granted; continuing liability of old vassal.

(ii) Death of vassal

123. Aiton 16 R 625. Executors renouncing succession not liable for future prestations.
124. *Macrae* 19 R 138. Trustee renouncing succession not liable to implement conditions ad factum praestandum.

Enforcement of conditions imposed by disposition

125. *Braid Hills Hotel Co.* 1909 SC 120. Condition in disposition; title of co-disponee to enforce.
126. *SCWS* 1937 SC 835. Disponer must show interest to enforce.

Enforcement of conditions of tenure by disponees of parts of feu inter se

127. Dalrymple 5 R 847. Original conditions in a single feu charter held to be mutually enforceable by purchasers of parts of feu, inter se.
128. Hill 2 F 799. Charter conditions held mutually enforceable.
129. *Hislop* 8 R (HL) 95. Observations on mutual enforceability. (See 3.3.1).
130. *Girls' School Co.* 1958 SLT (Notes) 2. Charter conditions held not mutually enforceable.
131. *Williamson & Hubbard* 1970 SLT 346. Charter conditions held not mutually enforceable.
132. *Fergusson* 1953 SLT (Sh.Ct) 113. Charter conditions held mutually enforceable.
133. *Smith* 1972 SLT (LT) 34. Charter conditions held mutually enforceable. (3.3.7).

Disposition of Superiority

134. Gardner 3 D 534. Effect of conveyance of a bare superiority.
135. *Orr* 20 R (HL) 27. May carry dominium utile of reserved minerals. (See 7.1.68).
135a Fleeming 6 M 782. A disposition of a bare superiority does not carry dominium utile of reserved minerals.
136. *Ceres School Board* 23 R 279. Carries dominium utile of parts previously sub-feued if prior feu charter remains unrecorded. (See 2.8.1).

Transmission of obligations undertaken by superior

137. Durie's Trs 16 R 1104. Personal obligations undertaken in a mere personal contract to grant a charter do not transmit.
138. *Leith School Board* 1918 SC 94. Failure to insert conditions. (See 2.5.25).
139. *Jolly's Exix.* 1958 SC 635. Failure to insert conditions. (See 2.5.27).
140. *Duncan* 1941 SC 145. Obligation to repair (See 2.5.26).
141. Montrose 1 M (HL) 25. Obligation of relief. (See 2.5.23).
142. *Hope* 2 M 670. Obligation of relief. (See 2.5.24).

Consolidation

143. Bald 2 BLC 210. Consolidation is not effected confusione.
144. Hay 1910 SC 509. Consolidation by prescription; destination in superiority title rules.
145. *Park's Curator* 8 M 671. Effect on dominium utile title and destination therein.
146. Glasgow 14 R 419. Effect on dominium utile title and destination therein.
147. *Zetland* 8 M (HL) 144. Effect on pertinents of dominium utile title.

7.2 Involuntary transfer inter vivos

Inhibitions

General effect

1. *Menzies* 4 D 257. Preference created by inhibition over other creditors.
1a. Murphy's Trustees 1983 SLT 78. Effect of inhibition in an English bankruptcy.
2. *Dryburgh* 24 R 1. Inhibition effective even where no feudal title. (See 7.1.33).
3. Scottish Wagon Co. Ltd 1906 13 SLT 779. Inhibition is negative in nature.
3a McInally 1979 SLT (Notes) 89. Partial recall of inhibition competent.

Effect on heritable creditors

4. McGowan 1977 SLT (Sh.Ct) 41. Inhibition does not prevent sale by bondholder but creates no preference for inhibitor.
5. *Bank of Scotland* 1977 SLT 24. Inhibition does not prevent sale by holder of standard security and creates preference for inhibitor on any surplus as against other creditors.
5a *Abbey National Building Society* 1981 SLT (Sh.Ct) 29. Inhibition creates preference for inhibiting creditor on free proceeds of sale over posterior arresting creditors.
5b *Ferguson & Forster* 1981 SLT (Sh.Ct) 53 — Subjects sold by secured creditors — inhibiting creditor not to be preferred to free proceeds over unsecured creditors. (c.f. 7.2.5a Abbey National Building Society 1981 SLT (Sh.Ct) 29).
5c Halifax Building Society 1985 SLT (Sh.Ct) 25. Nature of preference created by an inhibition.
6. *Mackintosh's Trs* 25 R 554. Inhibition does not prevent debtor discharging a heritable security.
7. Henderson 22 R 895. A creditor, who had inhibited, agreed to a discharge on receiving an assurance as to payment; and was held entitled to enforce that assurance.

Reduction

8. *Mulhearn* 1929 SLT 59. Extent of protection of S.46 of 1924 Act.

Compulsory purchase

9. *Argyll v. LMS* 1931 SC 309. Statutory and Common Law title compared; authorities reviewed.
10. Magistrates of Elgin 11 R 950. Effect of statutory title.
11. Campbell's Trs 1930 SC 182. Effect of statutory title.
12. *Barr* 1972 SLT (Sh.Ct) 63. Statutory title; effect on superior's right to feuduty.
13. *George Heriot's Trust* 1915 SC (HL) 52. Discussion on nature and effect of statutory conveyance.

7.3 Transmission on death

Intestacy

1. *Macrae* 1981 SLT 13. Special service, effect of decree.
2. *Stobie* 1921 SC 894. Special service. Wrong heir served. Effect of decree.
3. Mackay's Exix. 1933 SC 747. General service; validity and effect of decree.
4. *Sibbald's Heirs* 1947 SC 601. General service.
5. McAdam 6 R 1256. 1974 Act S.9. Vesting in the heir.
6. *Robertson* 1978 SLT (Sh.Ct) 30. 1974 Act S.10. Petition for authority to complete title may be presented by an executor.

7. *Fraser* 1978 SLT (Sh.Ct) 5. 1874 Act S.10. Petition for authority to complete title may be presented by a surviving spouse entitled to prior rights.

7a. *McKenzie* 1979 SLT (Sh.Ct.) 68. 1874 Act S.10. Petition for authority to complete title is not competent where the property was last vested in an ex facie absolute disponee.

7b. *Robertson* 1980 SLT (Sh.Ct.) 73. The heir of a deceased heir at law cannot serve as heir in trust under the 1874 Act S.43.

Special destinations

8. *Haddow's Exors.* 1943 SC 44. A destination to A and B in conjuct fee and liferent, for A's liferent and for B in fee, is not a special destination.

9. *Cormack* 1975 SLT 214. Definition of special destintion.

10. *Hay's Tr.* 1951 SC 329. Whether destination revocable.

11. *Shand's Trs* 1966 SC 178. Whether destination revocable; price jointly contributed.

12. *Brown's Tr.* 1943 SC 488. Whether destination revocable; condition of gift.

13. *Munro* 1972 SLT (Sh.Ct) 6. Whether destination revocable; joint or common property. (See 4.1.22).

14. *Perrett's Trs* 1909 SC 522. Revocation; destination created by testator.

15. *Campbell* 7 R (HL) 100. Revocation; destination created by another.

16. *Stirling's Trs* 1977 SLT 229. Revocation. 1964 Act S.30.

16a *Steele* 1979 SLT 228. Effect of survivorship destination on i.v. deed.

16b *Barclays Bank Limited* 1983 SLT 344. Property passing on a special destination is not subject to personal debts of the deceased institute.

Testate Succession

17. *Smith* 8 M 204. Effect of general disposition at Common Law.

18. Thoms 6 M 704. Effect of general disposition mortis causa at Common Law.

19. *Studd* 10 R (HL) 53. Effect of general disposition under 1868 Act S.20.

20. Grant 20 R 404. Effect of general disposition under 1868 Act S.20.

21. *Lawson's Exor.* 1958 SLT (Notes) 38. Estate carried by the will. 'Money'.

22. *Crozier's Tr.* 1963 SLT 69. Estate carried by the will. 'All my other affect'.

7.4 Examination of title

(Note: The headings and cases cited follow generally Burns Practice, 4th Edition, Chapter 10).

Prescriptive progress of titles: (Burns Practice, p.200).

1. *Scott* 3 RLC 334. General principle of positive prescription (See 2.9.1).

2. *Lord Advocate v. Graham* 7 D 183. General principle of positive prescription. (See 2.9.2).

3. *Wallace* 6 F 1093. Title.

4. *Fraser* 25 R 603. Title.

5. *Meacher* 1913 SC 417. Ex facie validity. (See 2.9.13).

6. *Cooper Scott* 1924 SC 309. Ex facie validity. (See 2.9.6).

7. *Troup* 1916 SC 918. Ex facie validity. (See 2.9.12).

8. *Hilson* 23 R 241. Ex facie validity. (See 2.9.9).

9. *Glen* 9 R 317. Ex facie validity. (See 2.9.10).

10. Ramsay 1909 SC 1441. Recording in 'appropriate register' — BRS or GRS? (See now 1973 Act S.15(1) — 'Recording' means recording in GRS.)

11. *Auld* 7 R 663. Title need not be unambiguous. (See 2.9.14).

12. *Troup* 1916 SC 918. Title need not be unambiguous. (See 2.9.12).

13. *Hay* 1909 SC 554. Title must be definite. (See 2.3.10).

14. *Brown* 8 F 534. Title must be definite. (See 2.9.38).

Possession: (Burns Practice, p.204).
See generally 2.9.47 to 2.9.61.
15. *Cadell* 7 F 606. Minerals. Novodamus.
16. *Millar* 1910 SC 618. Minerals, competing titles, possession of surface. (See 2.4.5).

Bounding titles: (Burns Practice, p.205).
See generally 2.9.35 — 2.9.46.

Decree in absence: (Burns Practice, p.206).
17. *Bruce* 2 F 948. Decree of irritancy. (See 7.1.32).

Marketable title: (Burns Practice, p.207).
See generally 7.1.30 — 7.1.44a and 7.1.48 — 7.1.54.
18. *Kinnear* 1936 SLT 574. Giving seller time to cure defects.

Identity of property: (Burns Practice, p.207).
19. *MacDonald* 1 F 68. Parole evidence of identity. (See 7.1.17).
20. *Houldsworth* 1910 SC (HL) 49. Evidence of prior negotiations. (See 7.1.18).
21. *Stobo* 1949 SC 184. 'Subject to contract'. (See 7.1.10).
22. *Sibbald's Heirs* 1947 SC 601. Decree of general service as a title. (See 7.3.4).

Special conditions of title: (Burns Practice, p.208).
23. *Edinburgh Magistrates* 1915 SC 248. Effect of prescription.

Building conditions: (Burns Practice, p.208).
24. *Mackenzie* 3 SLT 128. Failure to implement; effect of stipulation that seller would not provide a search.

Maintenance of roof: (Burns Practice, p.210).
25. *Sanderson's Trs* 25 R 211. Law of the tenement. (See 4.1.54).
26. *Campbell's Trs* 4 F 752. Recorded agreement. (See 2.5.21).
27. *Duncan* 1941 SC 145. Omission of obligation from certain titles. (See 2.5.26).
28. *Magistrates of Banff* 1944 SC 36. Joint and common property. (See 4.1.21).

Reservations and restrictions: (Burns Practice, p.210).
For Reservations see generally 7.1.35 — 7.1.38.
For Restrictions see generally 7.1.39 — 7.1.44a.
29. *McLean* 11 SLT 719. Burden not entering title.

Conjunct and confident persons: (Burns Practice, p.217).
30. McManus's Tr. 1978 SLT 255. 1621 Act. Whether just cause.
30a *Lombardi's Trustee* 1982 SLT 81. 1621 Act. Nature of evidence required to rebut presumption of insolvency. (See 1.3.16a).
30b Hunt's Tr. 1984 SLT 169. Specific averments are required to establish solvency.

Time for objections: (Burns Practice, p.217).
See generally 7.1.88 — 7.1.98b.

Expense of clearing title: (Burns Practice, p.218).
31. *Howard & Wyndham* 17 R 990. General rule.
32. *Cameron* 22 R 293. Undischarged bond. (See 5.2.26).

Effect on purchaser of personal obligations undertaken by seller: (Burns practice, p.305).

See generally 2.5.1 — 2.5.7.; 2..5.18 — 2.5.22 and 7.1.83 — 7.1.87.

33. *Miller* 1949 SC 1. Purchaser entitled to repudiate ineffective lease.
34. *Mann* 1957 SLT 89. Purchaser entitled to repudiate personal right of occupancy.

Effect of negative prescription on personal rights

35. *Skinner* 1953 SLT (Notes) 82. A contractual right to call for a conveyance of heritage is extinguished by prescription.
36. *Pettigrew* 1956 SLT 25. A personal right to heritage is extinguished by prescription.

Settlement obligations

37. *Johnston* 1960 SLT 129. Effect of letter of obligation.
38. *Gibson* 1976 SLT 94. Effect of payment of price in exchange for a letter of obligation only, but no title. (See 1.3.1).
38a Richardson 1 F 145. An obligation by an agent to deliver a discharge of a loan does not bind the principal if the agent embezzles the money.

ALPHABETICAL INDEX OF CASE NAMES

READING LIST

1.1. **Summary of Texts and References**

Basic Texts

Walker's Principles of Scottish Private Law (3rd Edition 1983)
  Volume 3.   Book V.   Chapters 5.1 to 5.24.
  Volume 4.   Book VII. Chapter 7.6.
Burn's Practice Chaps. 1,2,4,5,9 — 35
Halliday The 1970 Act
Halliday The 1974 Act
Halliday The 1979 Act

Statutes (For full title, see below)
1857 The whole Act
1868 SS. 3, 5, 8, 12, 1b, 19, 20, 62, 110, 117-123, 129, 141-143, 163
1874 SS. 3, 4, 6-10, 25, 27-32, 47, 50, 61
1887 SS. 3, 4
1894 SS. 5-11
1924 SS. 2, 9, 11-16, 23-43, 46
1926 The whole Act
1938 SS. 6, 8, 9
1964 SS. 14-20, 36
1970 SS. 1-7, 9-32, 33-43, 45, 46
1972 SS. 1-10
1973 SS. 1-6, 14, 15
1974 The whole Act
1979 The whole Act

Reference Books, Styles, Statutes and Reports
(i) Reference Books

Bell	—	Lectures on Conveyancing (1882) ('Bell's Lectures')
Burns J.	—	Handbook of Conveyancing (5th Edition 1938) ('Burns' Handbook')
Burns J.	—	Conveyancing Practice (4th Edition 1957) ('Burns' Practice')
Craigie J.	—	Elements of Conveyancing — Heritable Rights (1908) ('Craigie's Elements')
Craigie	—	Scottish Law of Conveyancing — Heritable Rights ('Craigie's Heritable Rights')
Craigie J.	—	Conveyancing Statutes 1214-1894 ('Craigie's Statutes')
Erskine	—	An Institute of the Law of Scotland ('Erskine')
Farran C.D.	—	The Principles of Scots and English Land Law (1958)
Gloag & Henderson	—	Introduction to the Law of Scotland 8th Edition 1980 ('Gloag & Henderson')
Gloag	—	Contract (2nd Edition 1929)
Green	—	Conveyancing Statutes (Current Edition)
Green	—	Scots Statutes — Children — Husband and Wife etc. (Current Edition)
Green	—	Encyclopaedia of the Laws of Scotland 16 Vols. (1926-35 with Supplements 1952) ('Green's Encyclopaedia')
Halliday J.M.	—	The Land Tenure Reform (Scotland) Act 1974 ('Halliday's 1974 Act')
Halliday J.M.	—	The Conveyancing & Feudal Reform (Scotland) Act 1970 (2nd Edition 1977) ('Halliday's 1970 Act')
Halliday J. M.	—	The Land Registration (Scotland) Act 1979 ('Halliday's 1979 Act')
Kolbert & Mackay	—	History of Scots and English Land Law
McDonald	—	Conveyancing Case Notes Vols. 1 and 2 ('Case Notes')
Menzies A.	—	Lectures on Conveyancing (Sturrock's Edition 1900) ('Menzies Lectures')
Meston M.C.	—	The Succession (Scotland) Act 1964 (3rd Edition 1982)
Meston & Nichols	—	The Matrimonial Homes (Family Protection) (Scotland) Act 1981
Ockrent	—	Scottish Land Registration (1942)

(i) **Reference Books** (contd.)

Paton & Cameron	—	Landlord and Tenant (1967)
Rankine	—	The Law of Landownership in Scotland (4th Edition 1909) ('Rankine — Landownership')
Rankine	—	The Law of Leases in Scotland (3rd Edition 1916) ('Rankine — Leases')
Ross	—	Lectures on the Law of Scotland (1822) ('Ross' Lectures')
Smith T.B.	—	A Short Commentary on the Law of Scotland (1962) ('Smith's Commentary')
Stair	—	Institutions ('Stair')
Stair Society	—	Volume 1 Sources and Literature of Scots Law (1936)
		Volume 20 Introduction to the History of Scots Law (1959)
Walker D.M.	—	The Law of Contracts & Related Obligations in Scotland (2nd Edition 1985) ('Walker's Contract')
Walker D.M.	—	Principles of Scottish Private Law (3rd Edition 1983) ('Walker's Principles' or 'Walker')
Walker D.M.	—	The Law of Prescription and Limitation of Actions in Scotland (3rd Edition 1981 with 1984 Supplement) ('Walker's Prescription')
Walker D.M.	—	Civil Remedies
Wilson & Duncan	—	Trusts, Trustees and Executors
Wood	—	Lectures on Conveyancing (1903) ('Wood's Lectures')
Young	—	The Law of Planning in Scotland

(ii) **Styles**

Encyclopaedia of Scottish Legal Styles 10 Vols. (1935) ('Styles')
Diploma in Legal Practice — Conveyancing Styles ('Diploma Styles')

(iii) **Conveyancing Statutes**

Royal Mines Act 1424 (1424 c.12)
Leases Act 1449 (1449 c.18)
Registration Act 1617 (1617 c.16)
Real Rights Act 1693 (1693 c. 13)
Registration of Sasines Act 1693 (1693 c. 14)
Infeftment Act 1845 (8 and 9 Vict. c. 35)
Transference of Lands Act 1847 (10 and 11 Vict. c. 48)
Transference of Burgage Lands Act 1847 (10 and 11 Vict. c. 49)
Crown Charters Act 1847 (10 and 11 Vict. c. 51)
Registration of Leases (Scotland) Act 1857 ('The 1857 Act')
Titles to Lands (Scotland) Act 1858 ('The 1858 Act')
Titles to Land (Scotland) Act 1860
Registration of Writs (Scotland) Act 1868
Land Registers (Scotland) Act 1868
Titles to Land Consolidation (Scotland) Act 1868 ('The 1868 Act')
Titles to Land Consolidation (Scotland) Amendment Act 1869
Conveyancing (Scotland) Act 1874 ('The 1874 Act')
Writs Execution (Scotland) Act 1887
Conveyancing Amendment (Scotland) Act 1887 ('The 1887 Act')
Feudal Casualties (Scotland) Act 1914
Conveyancing (Scotland) Act 1924 ('The 1924 Act')
Burgh Registers (Scotland) Act 1926
Conveyancing Amendment (Scotland) Act 1938 ('The 1938 Act')
Public Registers and Records (Scotland) Acts 1948 and 1950
Succession (Scotland) Act 1964
Conveyancing & Feudal Reform (Scotland) Act 1970 ('The 1970 Act')
Redemption of Standard Securities (Scotland) Act 1971
Companies (Floating Charges and Receivers) (Scotland) Act 1972
European Communities Act 1972
Prescription & Limitation (Scotland) Acts 1973 and 1984
Land Tenure Reform (Scotland) Act 1974 ('The 1974 Act')
Community Land Act 1975
Land Registration (Scotland) Act 1979 ('The 1979 Act')

(iii) **Conveyancing Statutes** (contd.)
Law Reform (Miscellaneous Provisions) (Scotland) Act 1980
Matrimonial Homes (Family Protection) (Scotland) Act 1981

(iv) **Reports**

Reid Committee Report	—	Registration of Title to Land 1963 Cmnd. 2032
Henry Committee Report	—	Registration of Title to Land 1969 Cmnd. 4137
Halliday Committee Report	—	Conveyancing Legislation and Practice 1968 Cmnd. 3118
White Paper	—	Land Tenure in Scotland 1969 Cmnd. 4009
Green Paper	—	Land Tenure Reform in Scotland (1972)

1.2. **Authentication of Deeds**
Basic Texts

Burns	Practice Chap. 1
Burns	Handbook Chaps. 2 and 3
Walker	Law of Evidence in Scotland Chaps. 9-11, 16, 17
Walker	Principles Chaps. 1.7 and 4.4
Case Notes	1.2

References

Gloag	Contract Chaps. 10 and 11
Green's	Encyclopaedia Vol. 2SS 651-662 — Blanks in Documents
	Vol. 5SS 1071-1101 — Execution of Deeds
Menzies	Lectures Part 1 Chaps. 1-6
Walker	Law of Evidence in Scotland Chaps. 12, 18, 19, 21, 22
Styles	Vol. 4 Execution of Deeds

Scottish Law Commission — Memo No. 66 (1985) — Constitution of Obligations and Authentication

Statutes
Subscription of Deeds Acts 1540, 1579 and 1584
Execution of Deeds Act 1593
Lyon King of Arms Act 1672
Subscription of Deeds Act 1681
Deeds Act 1696
Blank Bonds & Trusts Act 1696
Forms of Deeds (Scotland) Act 1856
The 1868 Act SS. 20, 139, 140, 144
The 1874 Act SS. 38, 39, 54
The 1924 Act S. 18 and Sch. I
The 1970 Act S. 44
Wills Act 1861
Wills Act 1963
Partnership Act 1890 S.6
Local Government (Scotland) Act 1973 S. 194
The Companies Act 1985 S. 36

Articles

1963 SLT 161	—	The Wills Act 1963
1963 JLS 99	—	The Wills Act 1963
1979 SLT 173	—	Notarially executed Wills

1.3. **Delivery**
Basic Texts

Gloag	Contract Chap. 4
Burns'	Handbook p. 39
Case Notes	1.3

References
Green's Encyclopaedia — Vol. 5 SS 1200-1215 — Delivery of Deeds
Article
1981 JLS 132 and 181 — Delivery of Deeds
1982 SLT (News) 149 — Ownership on Delivery
1984 JLS 400 — Delivery of Deeds etc.
1985 SLT (News) 165 — Ownership on Delivery

1.4.   **Capacity**
Basic Texts
Gloag & Henderson 8th Edition Chap. 6
Case Notes 1.4
References
Burns'   Practice pp. 308 — 323
Green's   Encyclopaedia Vol. 10 SS 55 — 100 Minors and pupils
Walker   Judicial Factors
Wilson   Trusts
Walker's   Principles — Chap. 6.2 Private Trusts
                            Chap. 6.5 Judicial Factors
Scottish Law Commission — Memo. 65 — Capacity of Minors and Pupils
Statutes
Judicial Factors (Scotland) Acts 1849, 1880, 1889
Guardianship of Children Acts 1886, 1925 and 1973
Married Woman's Property (Scotland) Act 1920
The 1938 Act S.1
Succession (Scotland) Act 1964
Trusts (Scotland) Acts 1921 and 1961
Articles
1984 JLS 357 — The Title of a Liquidator
1984 JLS 400 — Delivery of Deeds and the Race to the Register
1985 JLS 20   — Bankruptcy etc. and the Race to the Register
1985 JLS 109 — Insolvency and Title — a Reply

1.5.   **Stamp Duties**
Basic Text
Tolley's Stamp Duties — 2nd Edition 1980
References
Sergeant   —   Stamp Duties
Walker   —   Evidence, Chap. 20
Statutes
Stamp Act 1891
Finance Acts, various

2.   **Creation of the New Feudal Estate.**
2.1.   **Summary of Statutory Developments**
Basic Texts
Walker's Principles   Chap. 5.1 Nature and Classification of Property
                             Chap. 5.2 Land-holding generally — The Feudal System
                             Chap. 5.3 The Sovereign's Paramount Superiority
                             Chap. 5.4 Creation of a New Feudal Estate pp. 49-54
Burns' Handbook   Chaps. 10, 11 and 12
References
Green's Encyclopeadia   Vol. 2 SS 1066-1101 — Burgage
                             Vol. 3 SS 236-296 — Casualties
                             Vol. 3 SS 518-554 — Charter — Feudal
                             Vol. 12 SS 758-863 — Registration and Records
Stair Society   Vol.20 Chap. 14
1976 SLT (News) 257 — Infeftment
Burns' Practice — Chaps. 11, 12 and 16
Statutes
Land Registration Act 1868
The 1868 Act SS. 3, 5-10, 12-15, 17, 20, 21, 100, 138, 141-145, 147, 163
The 1874 Act SS. 4, 15, 16, 18, 20, 21, 22, 23, 25, 26, 27, 28, 32
Feudal Casualties (Scotland) Act 1914
The 1924 Act SS. 8-10, 12, 14, 48
Burgh Registers Act 1926
The 1938 Act SS. 8, 9
The 1970 Act Part I

Statutes (contd.)
The 1974 Act SS. 1, 2, 3
The 1979 Act

Miscellaneous

Reid Committee Report	—	Registration of Title to Land 1963 Cmnd. 2032
Henry Committee Report	—	Registration of Title to Land 1969 Cmnd. 4137
Halliday Committee Report	—	Conveyancing Legislation and Practice 1968 Cmnd. 3118
White Paper	—	Land Tenure in Scotland 1969 Cmnd. 4009
Green Paper	—	Land Tenure Reform in Scotland — 1972

2.2. **The Feu Charter**

Basic Texts

Walker's Principles	—	Chap. 5.4. Creation of a New Feudal Estate pp. 54-76
		Chap. 5.13 — Servitudes
Green's Encyclopaedia	—	Vol. 3 SS 555-647 — Charter, Feudal
		Vol.14 SS 616-671 — Superior and Vassal

References
Erskine Bk. II
Craigie Heritable Rights I. Chap. 3
Burns' Practice Chap. 11, 24
Rankine Landownership Chaps. 5-11, 18, 19, 25-27
Gloag Contract — Chaps. 13, 14, 34
Green's Encyclopaedia Vols. as follows:—

1 SS 104-112	—	Accretion
2 SS 864-897	—	Boundaries and Fences
2 SS 876-987	—	Building Restrictions
7 SS 361-385	—	Fixtures
10 SS 1-54	—	Mines and Minerals
10 SS 1252-1307	—	Parts and Pertinents
13 SS 619-629	—	Sea, Seashore (Part)
13 SS 1215-1267	—	Servitudes
14 SS 246-255	—	Singular Successor
14 SS 677-720	—	Support
15 SS 1107-1125	—	Warrandice
1949 Supplement Appendix	—	Coal Mines

Styles
Vol. 5 Feus
Vol. 5 Fishings
Vol. 7 Mines and Minerals
Vol. 8 Servitudes

Destinations
1984 JLS 103 — Heirs, Executors and Assignees
1985 SLT (News) 57 — Common Property

Articles and Miscellaneous — 2.2 — 2.7

2.3. **Descriptions**
Case Notes 2.3
4 JLS 144 — Letter from the Keeper of the Registers
1966 New Law Journal 1617 — Fixtures and Fittings
1971 JLS 62 — Descriptions in Feu Dispositions
The 1979 Act S.18
(See also Texts and References under Heading 4 — The Estate of the Vassal)

2.4. **Reservations**
Case Notes 2.4
Royal Mines Act 1424
Mines & Metals Act 1592
Petroleum (Production) Act 1934
Coal Industry Nationalisation Act 1946
The Coal-Mining (Subsidence) Acts 1950 and 1957

2.4 **Reservations** (contd.)
Mines (Working Facilities and Support) Act 1966
Minerals — 1975 JLS 205

2.5. **Conditions of Tenure**
Case Notes 2.5
The 1874 Act S.32
1964 SLT (News) 117 — Restrictions on Trade as Conditions in Title
1969 SLT (News) 77 — The Courts and the Conveyancer
2 Conveyancing Review 1 — Restrictions on Use in Dispositions
2 Conveyancing Review 10 — Inherent Conditions of the Feu
2 Conveyancing Review 193 — Personal Rights
1967 JLS 417 — Irritancy as a Real Burden
The 1979 Act S.17
1984 JLS 9 — What is a Real Burden

2.6. **Servitudes**
Case Notes 2.6
2 Conveyancing Review 97 — Servitudes

2.7. **Subordinate Clauses**
Case Notes 2.7
The 1979 Act S.16

Warrandice
1972 SLT (News) 41 — An Aspect of Warrandice
1983 JR 1 — The Scope of Warrandice in Coveyance of Land
1983 JLS 228 — Warrandice and Latent Defects in Heritage

2.8. **Infeftment of the Vassal**

Basic Texts
Walker's Principles Chap. 5.4 Creation of a New Feudal Estate pp. 76-78
Case Notes 2.8

References
Burns' Handbook Chaps. 13 and 18
Green's Encyclopaedia Vol. 4 SS 387-390, 418-431, 449, 457 — Completion of Title
(Parts)
                 Vol.12 SS 804-847 — Registration and Records (Part)
Burns' Practice Chaps. 12 and 18

Statutes
Registration Act 1617
1681 c. 11 (Registration in Burghs)
Real Rights Act 1693
Register of Sasines Act 1693
Land Registers Act 1868
Burgh Registers Act 1926
The 1868 Act SS. 12, 15, 141-145
The 1874 Act S. 54
The 1924 Act SS. 10, 48
The 1979 Act

Articles
2 JLS 29   — The Register of Sasines
3 JLS 217   — The Register of Sasines
1967 JLS   — The Sasine Register
3 Conveyancing Review 108   — Accretion
Infeftment — 1976 SLT (News) 257

2.9. **The Effects of Possession: Prescription**

Basic Texts
Walker's Principles Chap. 5.4 Creation of a New Feudal Estate pp. 78-85
Burns' Practice Chap. 10 (Part)
Case Notes 2.9

References
Burns' Practice Chap. 10 (Part)
Millar Prescription
Napier Prescription
Rankine Landownership Chaps. 1-4
Green's Encyclopaedia Vol. 12 SS 41-88 — Prescription
Walker's Prescription (3rd Edition 1981)
Statutes
Prescription Act 1469
Prescription Act 1474
Prescription Act 1617
The 1874 Act S. 34
The 1924 Act SS. 16, 17
The 1938 Act S.4
The 1970 Act S.8
Prescription & Limitation (Scotland) Act 1973

3. **Superiorities**
Basic Texts
Walker's Principles Chap. 5.5 The Estate of the Superior
Halliday 1970 Act Chaps. 2 and 3
Case Notes 3.2 and 3.3
References
Burns' Handbook Chap. 11
Green's Encyclopaedia Vols. as follows:—

3 SS 555-647	— Charter Feudal
8 SS 968-991	— Irritancies
8 SS 1361-1374	— *Jus Quaesitum Tertio*
14 SS 616-671	— Superior and Vassal

Burns' Practice Chap .13
Gloag Contract Chaps. 13, 14, 37
Halliday's 1974 Act
Statutes
Feuduty Act 1597
The 1874 Act S. 8
The 1887 Act S. 4
The 1924 Act S. 13
The 1938 Act S. 6
The 1970 Act SS. 1 to 7
The 1974 Act SS. 4-7, 15, 19, 21
Articles

1 Conveyancing Review 239	— Redemption or Discharge of Feuduties
2 Conveyancing Review 121	— Irritancy by Over-superior
2 Conveyancing Review 225	— Some Aspects of Allocation of Feuduty
1969 JLS 45	— Superior's Interest to Enforce
1971 SLT (News) 57	— The Lands Tribunal
1971 JLS 281	— Allocation of Feuduty
1973 JLS 109	— The Lands Tribunal for Scotland
1977 JLS 127	— The Lands Tribunal
1976 JLS 364	— Redemption of Feuduty
1979 JLS 282	— Function and Working of the Lands Tribunal in Scotland
1983 JR 137	—*Jus Quaesitum Tertio*
1984 JLS 232	—Rights of Pre-emption

4. **The Estate of the Vassal**
Basic Texts
Walker's Principles Chap. 5.6 — Estate of the Vassal
Walker's Principles Chap. 5.7 — Joint and Common Property
Walker's Principles Chap. 5.8 — The Entailed Estate

Basic Texts (Contd.)
Walker's Principles Chap. 5.9 — The Liferent Estate
Walker's Principles Chap. 5.10 — Teinds, Church, Manse and Glebe
Walker's Principles Chap. 4.39 — Injuries in respect of Heritable Property
Case Notes 4.1
References
Burns' Practice Chap. 16 — Dispositions
Rankine — Landownership Chaps. 9,11,18,24 and 28-33
Green's Encyclopaedia Vols. as follows:

       3 SS 1350 to 1376   — Common Gable
       3 SS 1377 to 1395   — Common Property and Common Interest
       6 SS 1-7   — Division and Sale
       7 SS 1041 -1111   — Game Laws
      10 SS 687-766   — Nuisance and Non-natural Use of Property (Part)
      15 SS 1126-1205   — Water and Water Rights

Henderson/Hogarth — Scottish Planning Source Book (1984)
Jauncey — Fishing in Scotland (1984)
Walker's Principles Chap. 4.39 — Injuries in respect of Heritable Property
Walker — Civil Remedies
Young — The Law of Planning in Scotland
Himsworth — Public Sector Housing Law in Scotland (1982)
Lyall — Air, Noise, Water and Waste : a Summary of the Law in Scotland (1982)
Statutes and Articles

4.1   **Implied Rights**
Trespass and Encroachment
Winter Herding Act 1686
Trespass (Scotland) Act 1865
Civil Aviation Act 1949 S. 40
Salmon and Fresh Water Fisheries (Protection)(Scotland) Act 1951
Joint and Common Property and Common Interest
1 Conveyancing Review   17 — Property Commonly Called Joint
1 Conveyancing Review 105 — The Law of the Tenement
1 Conveyancing Review 143 — Maintenance of Tenement Roofs
1 Conveyancing Review 239 — The Law of the Tenement
1 Conveyancing Review 260 — The Limitations of Common Interest
2 Conveyancing Review 102 — The Law of the Tenement
1973 SLT (News) 68 — Support of Buildings
1980 JLS 141 — Mutual Gable Walls
1983 JLS 472 — The Law of the Tenement
1984 SLT (News) 336 — Regulation of Salmon Fishing
1985 SLT (News) 57 — Common Property
1985 SLT (News) 217 — Salmon Fishing in Troubled Waters
Water Rights and Fishings
Land Drainage (Scotland) Acts 1930 and 1958
Flood Prevention (Scotland) Act 1961
Rivers (Prevention of Pollution)(Scotland) Acts 1951 and 1965
Trout (Scotland) Acts 1902 and 1933
Salmon and Fresh Water Fisheries (Protection) (Scotland) Act 1951
Freshwater and Salmon Fisheries (Scotland) Act 1976
1973 JLS 43, 78, 114, 141, 174 The Law of Pollution in Scotland
Game
Game (Scotland) Act 1772
Night Poaching Acts 1828 and 1844
Day Trespass Act 1832
Ground Game Act 1880
Agricultural Holdings (Scotland) Act 1949

4.2.   **Limitations on the Use of Land**
Statutory Nuisance and Statutory Controls
Housing (Scotland) Acts 1950 — 1974
Prevention of Damage by Pests Act 1949

Statutory Nuisance and Statutory Controls (contd.)
Ancient Monuments and Archaeological Areas Act 1979
Pests Act 1954
Weeds Act 1959
Radioactive Substances Act 1960
Factories Act 1961
Offices, Shops and Railway Premises Act 1963
Rivers (Prevention of Pollution) (Scotland) Acts 1951 and 1965
Countryside (Scotland) Act 1967
Clean Air Acts 1956 and 1968
Housing (Financial Provision)(Scotland) Acts 1968 and 1978
Building (Scotland) Acts 1959 and 1970
Fire Precautions Act 1971
Town & Country Planning (Scotland) Act 1972
Field Monuments Act 1972
Local Government (Scotland) Act 1973
Town & Country Planning (Use Classes) (Scotland) Order 1973
Town & Country Amenities Act 1974
Health & Safety at Work Act 1974
Mines (Working Facilities & Support) Act 1974
Control of Pollution Act 1974
Town & Country Planning (Scotland) Act 1977
Local Government, Planning & Land Act 1980
Town & Country Planning (General Development) (Scotland) Order 1981
Countryside (Scotland) Act 1981
Local Government (Misc. Provisions)(Scotland) Act 1981
Local Government & Planning (Scotland) Act 1982

5. **Heritable Securities**

5.1. **General**

Basic Texts
Walker's Principles — Chap. 5.11 — Real Burdens and Ground Annuals
                      Chap. 5.12 — Securities over Heritage
Halliday — 1970 Act Chaps. 5 — 10
Case Notes 5.2 and 5.3

References
Gloag & Irvine (1897) Rights in Security
Green's Encyclopaedia Vols. as follows:—

1 SS	1	—	50	Absolute Disposition
2 SS	730	—	814	Bond
2 SS	1049	—	1065	Burdens
5 SS	1024	—	1035	Debita Fundi
7 SS	1292	—	1319	Ground Annual
7 SS	1420	—	1453	Heritable Securities
13 SS	777	—	845	Securities

Burns' Handbook Chaps. 4, 20
Burns' Practice Chaps. 14, 25, 27, 29 — 34
Marshall The Companies (Floating Charges and Receivers) (Scotland) Act 1972

Statutes
Bankruptcy Act 1696
Blank Bonds and Trusts Act 1696
Heritable Securities (Scotland) Acts 1845 and 1847
Debt Securities (Scotland) Act 1856
The 1868 Act SS. 117 — 135
The 1874 Act SS. 47 — 49
Heritable Securities (Scotland) Act 1894
The 1924 Act SS. 23, 25, 43
Redemption of Standard Securities (Scotland) Act 1971
Companies (Floating Charges and Receivers) (Scotland) Act 1972
Succession (Scotland) Act 1964
The 1970 Act Parts II & III

Articles

5.2. **Securities before 29.11.1970**
1962 SLT (News) 149 on Campbell's J.F. v National Bank of Scotland
1 Conveyancing Review 5 — The Ex Facie Absolute Disposition
2 Conveyancing Review 129 — The Bondholder's Final Remedy
2 Conveyancing Review 177 — Securities over Reversions of Heritable Property
3 Conveyancing Review 51 — Ex Facie Absolute Disposition in Security of Loans
1967 JLS 32 — Ex Facie Absolute Dispositions — The Fall of the House of Usher
1972 JLS 370 — Secured Loans and Restraint of Trade
1979 JLS 462 — Ex Facie Absolute Dispositions and Their Discharge
1980 JLS 54 — Ex Facie Absolute Dispositions and Their Discharge.

5.3. **Securities after 29.11.1970**
1980 JLS 275 — Ranking of Heritable Creditors
1981 JLS 26 and 280 — Ranking of Heritable Creditors
1983 SLT (News) 169 & 189 — Real Conditions in Standard Securities
1985 JLS 130 and 181 — The Consumer Credit Act 1974
1985 JLS 159 — Bridging Loans and the Consumer Credit Regulations
1985 JLS 222 — The Consumer Credit Act 1974 — Loan Agreements and Standard
Securities

6. **Floating Charges**
Basic Texts
Walker's Principles — Chap. 5.12 — Securities over Heritage
Case Notes 6
Reference
Marshall The Companies (Floating Charges and Receivers) (Scotland) Act 1972
Statutes
Companies (Floating Charges and Receivers) (Scotland) Act 1972
Articles
1981 JLS 57 and 102 — Diligence, Trusts and Floating Charges
1982 SLT (News) 177 — The Registration of Charges
1983 SLT (News) 253 — Floating Charges and Fraudulent Preferences
1984 SLT (News) 25 — The Receiver and effectually executed diligence
1984 SLT (News) 105, 172, 117 — The Nature, Receivership; Floating Charges;
Receivers and Arresters
1985 JLS 242 — Future Assets and Double Attachments

7. **Transmission of the Feu**
7.1. **Voluntary Transfer inter vivos**
Basic Texts
Walker's Principles — Chap. 5.16 — Voluntary Transfer of Land
Chap. 5.18 — Extinction of Interests in Land
Case Notes 7.1
References
Burns' Handbook Chaps. 14, 17
Green's Encyclopaedia Vols. as follows:—

4 SS	500 —	526	Completion of Title (Part)
4 SS	922 —	939	Consolidation
5 SS	1320 —	1369	Disposition (Part)
6 SS	952 —	971	Excambion
13 SS	317 —	451	Sale of Heritable Property (Part)

Stair Society Vol. 20
Burns' Practice Chaps. 9, 16, 19, 23
Gloag — Contract Chaps. 10, 20, 23
Walker — Damages Chap. 12
Statutes
The 1868 Act SS. 5, 8, 141 — 143
The 1874 Act SS. 4, 6, 32
The 1924 Act SS. 8 — 11, 48
The 1979 Act

Articles

1956 SLT (News) 137		
2 Conveyancing Review 165	—	Mineral Reservations and the Unwilling Purchaser
2 Conveyancing Review 193	—	Personal Rights
3 Conveyancing Review 13	—	Situation of Seller under Missives
3 Conveyancing Review 129	—	Remedies for Breach of Missives
1966 JLS 124	—	The *Actio Quanti Minoris*
1966 JLS 264	—	*Rei Interventus* Reconsidered
1967 SLT (News) 231	—	The Reserved Right to Bid
1968 JLS 46	—	Sale by Instalments
1969 JLS 138	—	Division of Large Industrial Units
1969 JLS 70	—	Delayed Settlement
1970 JLS 10	—	Sale of Hertiage
1971 JLS 179	—	The Purchase and Sale of Houses
1972 JLS 315	—	Missives
1972 JLS 316	—	Sale and Purchase of Heritage
1976 JLS 282	—	Conditions in Missives
1978 JLS 277	—	Sale of Heritage — Interest
1979 JLS 485	—	Housebuilders' Missives
1979 JLS Workshop vii	—	Liability to Pay Interest
1980 JLS 17	—	Housebuilders' Missives
1980 JLS W.103	—	A Question of Interest
1980 SLG 68	—	Delay in Settlement
1980 NLJ 171, 195, 219	—	NHBC Scheme Revision
1980 SLG 86	—	NHBC (Scotland)
1981 JLS 414	—	Winston v Patrick in Context
1982 JLS 37	—	Winston v Patrick Again
1982 JLS Workshop 323	—	Recent Authority on Missives
1983 JLS 45	—	The New Missives
1983 JLS 49	—	The Lord Chancellor's Fixtures
1983 JLS 116 & 273	—	Delays in Settlement
1983 JLS Workshop 339	—	Avoiding Winston v Patrick
1984 JLS 103	—	Heirs, Executors and Assignees
1984 JLS 448	—	The Use of Referential Bids in Offers

7.2. Involuntary Transfer inter vivos

Basic Texts

Walker's Principles — Chap. 5.17 — Involuntary Transfer of Land
Case Notes 7.2

References

Burns' Handbook Chap. 19
Burns' Practice Chap. 15
Compulsory Purchase in Scotland — Law Society of Scotland 1983
Graham Stewart — Diligence
Green's Encyclopaedia Vols. as follows: —

    1 SS 298 — 372 — Adjudication
    4 SS 564 — 567 — Completion of Title
    4 SS 607 — 626 and 684 — 686 — Compulsory Purchase
    1949 Supplement — Part 1 Acquisition of Land (Authorisation Procedure)
    (Scotland) Act 1947
    12 SS 736 — 752 — Reduction

Judicial Titles

Statutes

The 1868 Act SS. 59, 62, 129
The 1924 Act S. 46

Articles

1979 JLS 101 Ranking of Inhibitors
1982 JLS 13 and 68 Inhibitions, Securities, Reductions & Multiplepoindings
1983 SLT (News) 145 & 177 — Inhibitions and Company Insolvencies
1983 JR 177 — Prescriptions and foreclosure of adjudications
1983 JLS 495 — Inhibitions and Securities for future advances

Compulsory Purchase
Statutes
Lands Clauses (Consolidation) (Scotland) Act 1845
Railways Clauses (Consolidation) (Scotland) Act 1845
Acquisition of Land (Authorisation Procedure) (Scotland) Act 1947
Town and Country Planning (Scotland) Act 1972
Land Compensation (Scotland) Acts 1963 and 1973
Articles
1956 SLT (News) 103   — Schedule Conveyances
1964 SLT (News) 205   — Schedule Conveyances
1969 JLS 321   — Statutory Conveyances
1971 SLT (News) 47   — Schedule Conveyances and the 1845 Act
1980 JLS Workshop 142 —   Statutory Conveyances
1984 JLS 357   — The Title of a Liquidator
1984 JLS 400   — Delivery of Deeds and the Race to the Register
1985 JLS 20   — Bankruptcy etc. and the Race to the Register
1985 JLS 109   — Insolvency and Title: a Reply
1985 SLT (News) 205   — Compulsory Purchase and the Valuation Date

7.3.   **Transmission on Death etc.**
Basic Texts
Walker's Principles — Chap. 7.6 — Executors & Administration of Estates
Case Notes 7.3
See also under Completion of Title below
References
Burns' Handbook Chaps. 24 — 27
Meston Chap. 8
Currie — Confirmation of Executors
Burns' Practice Chaps. 22, 38, 39, 45
Green's Encyclopaedia Vols. as follows: —
      3 SS 1236 — 1241 — Commissary Court
      4 SS 463 — 499, 549 — 556 — Completion of Title (Part)
      4 SS 812 — 880 — Confirmation of Executors
      6 SS 1116 — 1148 — Executor
      15 SS 1083 — 1097 — Vitious Intromission
Statutes
Confirmation of Executors (Scotland) Act 1823
The 1868 Act SS. 19, 20, 27-50, 101-103, 125-128
The 1874 Act SS. 9, 10, 29, 31, 46
Executors (Scotland) Act 1900
Trusts (Scotland) Act 1961 S.2
The 1924 Act S.5
The 1964 Act SS. 14-22, 30, 36
Law Reform (Miscellaneous Provisions) (Scotland) Act 1968 S.19
Administration of Estates Act 1971
Acts of Sederunt — Confirmation of Executors Amendment 1966
                  Confirmation of Executors 1967
Articles
1979 SLT (News) 257 — Deduction of Title — A Recurring Problem
1984 JLS 103 — Heirs, Executors and Assignees
1984 SLT (News) 133, 180 and 299 — Special Destinations and Liability for Debt
1984 JLS 154 — Debts and Destinations
1985 SLT (News) 57, 92 and 98 — Common Property
Completion of Title and Deeds by Uninfeft Proprietors
Basic Texts
Burns' Practice Chaps. 21, 33, 45 and 46
References
Green's Encyclopaedia
      Vol. 4 SS 432 — 448 and 527 — 548 — Completion of Title (Parts)
      Vol. 5 SS 1370 — 1378, 1433 — 1440 — Disposition (Parts)
Styles Vol. 7. Notice of Title
      Vol. 9. Trusts

Statutes
The 1868 Act SS. 17, 19, 20, 22, 23, 25, 26, 125 — 128
The 1874 Act SS. 31, 45
The 1924 Act SS. 3 — 7
The 1938 Act S. 1
The 1970 Act SS. 12, 48

Articles
1978 JLS 438 — Completion of Title
1980 SLT (News) 257 — Deduction of Title — A Recurring Problem

7.4. Examination of Title

Basic Texts
Burns' Practice Chaps. 10, 13, 15, 19, 24
Case Notes 7.4

References
Greens Encyclopaedia Vols. as follows: —

13 SS 452-478	— Sale of Heritable Property (Part)
13 SS 682-776	— Searches
8 SS 413-445	— Inhibitions
9 SS 719-722	— Litigiosity

Articles

1971 JLS 104	— Enquiries of Local Authorities
1972 SLT 213	— Power of Search
1975 JLS 260	— Letters of Obligation
1977 JLS 212	— Heritable Transactions by Companies
1978 JLS 209 and 306	— A Conveyancing Trap
1979 JLS Workshop i	— Heritable Transactions by Companies
1979 JLS Workshop xxiv	— Inhibition and Search
1982 JLS 13 and 68	— Inhibitions, Securities, Reductions and Multiplepoindings
1984 JLS 369 & 455 and 1984 JLS 75	— The Matrimonial Homes (Family Protection) (Scotland) Act 1981

7.5 A Typical Conveyancing Transaction

Articles
1985 JLS 25 — Repair and Improvement Grants — Breach of Conditions
1985 JLS 155 — Property Enquiry Certificates — The Responsibility of Local Authorities
1985 JLS 159 — Bridging Loans and the Consumer Credit Relations

8. Reform

8.1. Tenure Reform

References
Conveyancing Legislation & Practice (Halliday Report) 1968 Cmnd. 3118

Land Tenure in Scotland	— White Paper 1969 Cmnd. 4099
Land Tenure Reform in Scotland	— Green Paper 1972
1 Conveyancing Review 139	— Conveyancing Reform
9 JLS 152	— Conveyancing Reform Within the Existing System
18 JLS 4 and 8	— Land Tenure Reform

8.2. Registration of Title

Basic Texts
Halliday — The 1979 Act
Notes on Registration of Title — Current Edition — University of Dundee

References
Wood's 'Lectures in Conveyancing' (1903) pp. 44-60
Simpson — Land Law and Registration 1976
Minutes of Evidence. Royal Commission on Registration of Title (1907) (Dunedin Committee)
Memorandum of Evidence to be Submitted by the Council of Law Society of Scotland to the Reid Committee pp. 6-26

Reid Committee Report 1963 Cmd. 2632
Registration of Title to Land in Scotland (Henry Report) 1969 Cmnd. 4137
Registration of Title Practice Book, HMSO 1981

Statutes

The 1979 Act
Land Registration (Scotland) Rules 1980
Commencement Orders —
     No. 1 — S.I. No. 1413 (S.114) Renfrew — 6.4.1981
     No. 2 — S.I. No. 520 (S.68) Dunbarton — 4.10.1982
     No. 3 — S.I. No. 745 (S.   ) Lanark — 3.1.1984

Articles

1964 JLS 285 and 320	— The Torrens System in its Place of Origin Registration of Title to Land in South Australia
1 Conveyancing Review 13	— Registration of Title in England
2 Conveyancing Review 83	— Registration of Title in England
1963 SLT (News) 193	— Registration of Title to Land in Scotland — J.M. Halliday
14 JLS 352	— Registration of Title Pilot Scheme
15 JLS 8	— Registration of Title
1979 JLS 225	— Registration of Title
1981 JLS 219	— Introduction of Registration of Title to Scotland
1982 JLS 109	— Titles to Land — The New System Considered
1984 JLS 172, 212 and 260	— Registration of Title — Comments on the 1979 Act

9.   **Leases**

9.1.   **General**

Basic Text

Walker's Principles — Chap. 5.14 — Licences
                Chap. 5.15 — Leases

References

Aldridge, T.M.	— Rent Control & Security of Tenure, 1966
Bramall, A.	— The Rent Act 1965
Burns'	— Practice Chap. 35
Burns'	— Handbook Chap. 21
Gloag & Henderson	— Chap. 33
Menzies	— Lectures Chap. 29
Paton, G.C.H. and Cameron, J.G.S.	— The Law of Landlord & Tenant in Scotland 1967
Rankine	— Leases
Smith's	— Commentary p. 518 et seq. and p. 887 et. seq
Stair	— Institutions Bk. II 10
Wood's	— Lectures Part 4 Chap. 10
Green's Encyclopaedia Vol. 9 SS 140-248	— Lease

Statutes

Leases Act 1449 c.18
Registration of Leases (Scotland) Act 1857
Hypothec Abolition (Scotland) Act 1880
Removal Terms (Scotland) Act 1886
Heritable Securities (Scotland) Act 1894
Sheriff Courts (Scotland) Act 1907
Increase of Rent and Mortgage Restrictions Act 1920
Conveyancing (Scotland) Act 1924
Rent of Furnished Houses Control (Scotland) Act 1943
Landlord and Tenant Rent Control Act 1949
Tenancy of Shops (Scotland) Act 1949
Long Leases (Scotland) Act 1954
Housing Repairs and Rents (Scotland) Act 1954
Rent Act 1957
Succession (Scotland) Act 1964
Rent Act 1965

Statutes (contd.)
Conveyancing and Feudal Reform (Scotland) Act 1970
Rent (Scotland) Act 1971
Land Tenure Reform (Scotland) Act 1974
Crofting Reform (Scotland) Act 1976
The 1979 Act
Tenants' Rights etc. (Scotland) Act 1980
Rent (Amendment) Act 1985

Articles

1972 JLS 121	— Crofting Law
1979 JLS 191	— The Rent Acts
1979 SLT (News) 249	— Defeating the Rent Acts
1980 JLS 319	— The Tenants' Rights, etc. (Scotland) Bill
1980 SLT (News) 125	— The Tenants' Rights, etc. (Scotland) Bill
1981 JLS W 215, W 223, W 231	— Calculating Fair Rents
1981 SLT (News) 101	— The Tenants' Rights etc. (Scotland) Act 1980 — Part IV
1981 JLS 383	— The Tenants' Rights etc. (Scotland) Act 1980 — Part II
1982 JLS 161	— The Tenants' Rights etc. (Scotland) Act 1980 — Part I

9.2. Commercial leases

References

Ross, M.J.	— Drafting and Negotiating Commercial Leases (Butterworth 1980)
Clarke D.N. and Adams, J.E.	— Rent Reviews and Variable Rents (Oyez 1981)
Aldridge, T.M.	— Letting of Business Premises — 4th Edition

Articles

1976 JLS (Jan) 4	— Irritancies in Leases
1976 JLS (Oct) 368	— Irritability of the Rash Tenant
1977 JLS 20	— Rent Review — A Search for the True Purpose
1977 JLS 309	— Disaster in Leases — Rei Interitus
1979 JLS (Workshop) 38	— Policy Decisions — Analysis of Insurance Provisions in Leases
1979 JLS (Workshop)(xxi)	— Ground Leases — A consideration of pitfalls
1979 JLS (Workshop)(xlv)	— Ground Leases — Further consideration
1979 JLS (Workshop)(v)	— Assigning and subletting
1979 JLS (Workshop)(lv)	— Findings by Arbiters
1979 NLJ 839	— The Lessons of Ravenseft
1980 JLS (Workshop) 117	— Styles Committee Lease
1980 JLS (Workshop) 171	— Comment on Style Lease
1981 JLS 295	— Less Irritating — Scottish Law Commission Memorandum No. 52 — Irritancies in Leases (1981)
1982 NLJ 993	— Drafting Rent Review Clause — A Cautionary Tale
1982 NLJ 677	— Major Structural Repairs
1982 NLJ 786	— Tenant's Right to Remove Fixtures
1983 JLS (Workshop) April et seq	— Rent Review Clauses in Commercial Lease
1983 JLS 519	— The Scottish Commercial Lease: The Way Ahead
1984 JLS 99	— The Scottish Commercial Lease Grows Up
PQLE 'Commercial Leases' Feb. 1983	— Course Papers
Scottish Law Commission Report No.75	— Irritancies in Leases (1983)

9.3. Agricultural Leases

References

Connell	— The Agricultural Holdings (Scotland) Acts 7th Edition
Gill, B	— The Law of Agricultural Holdings in Scotland 1982
The Law Society of Scotland	— Aspects of Agricultural Law

Statutes
The Hill Farming Act 1946
The Agriculture(Scotland) Act 1948
The Agriculture Holdings (Scotland) Act 1949
The Agriculture Act 1958
The Succession (Scotland) Act 1964
The Agriculture (Miscellaneous Provisions) Act 1968
The Agriculture (Miscellaneous Provisions) Act 1976
The Agricultural Holdings (Amendment)(Scotland) Act 1983

Articles
1980 JLS (Workshop) 135 — Style Agricultural Lease
PQLE 'Agricultural Law' Dec. 1982 — Course Papers

1.1 Introduction

As indicated in the Preface to this Volume, these Notes are intended to be used in conjunction with and as supplementing:

> Walker's Principles Book 5 (3rd Edition — Vol. 3)
> My published Conveyancing Case Notes

These three sources, taken together, should be a sufficient general grounding for the Student in the Degree and Diploma Classes of Conveyancing and the Practice of Conveyancing respectively.

I have, in addition, included an extensive Reading List, and further and more detailed information on the Reading List is contained later in this Chapter.

As a general indication of the content and scope of this subject, for the Degree and Diploma Student, I do not think I can do better than quote directly from the Law Society's submission to the Royal Commission on Legal Services in Scotland Volume 1, published in 1977.

'Conveyancing has been defined as 'the art which deals with the transfer of property in writing' (Woods Lectures). The essence of the definition is some form of writing or deed. Wood uses the word 'property' in its widest sense as meaning everything which can be possessed. The expression 'transfer' includes every kind of right relating to such property which can be created, conveyed or extinguished in writing. Such a transfer may be an absolute one of ownership as from seller to purchaser or donor to donee, it may be redeemable i.e. subject to extinction at a future date such as a security or a lease. It includes the preparation of those documents which are preliminary to the actual deed of transfer, such as missives of sale. Conveyancing therefore embraces the preparation of contracts, writs and deeds of every kind, and is not confined to the transfer of heritable property or rights therein. Settlements, trusts, wills, contracts for the purchase or sale of businesses or shares, debentures and loan agreements, leases, leasing or hire purchase agreements, building contracts, contracts of employment, partnership, patent, licence and 'know-how' agreements and indeed every contract or writing of any kind which is preliminary to or in itself creates, transfers, modifies or extinguishes a right or obligation, falls within the work of a conveyancer.

It is of course true that the greater part of the conveyancer's work is concerned with heritable property. This work covers not only the buying and selling of such properties and the preparation of conveyances and securities, but also the preparation of tenancy agreements and leases, deeds granting limited rights such as servitudes or wayleaves, and deeds extinguishing or varying rights or obligations. Further, the conveyancer's duty is not limited to the mere preparation of the deed giving effect to the transaction question. He must be able to advise his client on the effect of the transaction generally, as to the ways of achieving the desired result, the financing of the transaction and its effect on his client's affairs, for example, in relation to taxation, insurances, succession, etc. When acting for a seller of property or the granter of a right, discharge or waiver, he must ensure that his client can give a good title and does not contract to do something which he cannot fulfil or, if the consents of other persons are required, that these can be obtained. When acting for a purchaser or for the person in whose favour the right, discharge or waiver is being granted he must ensure that any preliminary contract is correctly and sufficiently drawn and, by examination of the granter's title, that the granter can grant and that his client will obtain a valid and enforceable title good against all parties and free from any burdens or restrictions prejudicial to his client's interests. He must also ensure that all necessary permissions for the transaction have been obtained from any third party who may have rights in the matter such as the feudal superior, heritable creditor, landlord or over-landlord, or in respect of any statutory requirements or regulations such as planning permission, building regulations, fire certificates, or licensing requirements. Where there are title restrictions the conveyancer may also be involved in an application to the Lands Tribunal to have the restrictions discharged or modified.

The Role of Solicitors in Heritable Property Transactions

In relation to heritable property transactions, the work of the solicitor in Scotland is not confined to carrying out the conveyancing, as the solicitor in Scotland, unlike his English counterpart, is also engaged in the negotiations leading up to the purchase and sale which in England are, with few exceptions, handled by the estate agent. Indeed, the majority of properties in Scotland are bought and sold by solicitors. This fact is undoubtedly to the advantage of the public for, of all the advisers who may or should be involved at one stage or another in the sale of the house such as a surveyor, estate agent, insurance broker, banker, building society or accountant, only the solicitor has the overall knowledge and training to co-ordinate all the various steps and carry through the transaction from the point when the seller first decides to put his property on the market to the point where the purchaser completes the purchase by settling the price, taking possession of the property and recording his title in the Sasine Register. Furthermore, it has already been shown that the solicitor's duty does not stop at the transaction in question. He is also expected to advise his client on the effect which it may have on that client's other affairs and it is only the legal profession which is trained to look at and appreciate the overall picture. This is not to say that the profession is blind to the considerable specialist expertise which other advisers can offer and in many cases the solicitor will advise his client to make use of these services. For example, when selling commercial or industrial property, the client may well be advised to put the sale in the hands of a firm of estate agents specialising in the sale of this kind of property. If this is to be done, the solicitor will consider the client's title and the other aspects of the transaction before instructing the estate agents. On the other hand, the profession is only too well aware of the dangers to the client who instructs someone who has only a limited sphere of activity and is unable to take a broad view of the subject, for example, the client who is persuaded to take out a large endowment policy on the explanation that he will not obtain a Building Society loan unless he does, or where the policy is not suitable for his needs or he cannot really afford the premiums or where the client incurs heavy and unnecessary advertising costs because he has been advised to advertise on four successive days each week, every fourth advertisement being free.

Heritable property ranges from the small tenement flat on the one hand to the large housing development, on the other, from the small shop to the large shopping development, from the single factory to the industrial estate and from the country cottage or smallholding to the large landed estate. The work can, and does, vary enormously from one type of property to another but the difference can be said to be one of degree, for the steps which the solicitor has to take and the considerations which he has to have in mind are normally much the same.'

As the foregoing summary indicates, heritable property includes primarily land and everything affixed to or growing on land such as buildings and trees. It also includes rights directly connected with land such as servitudes.

In contrast, moveable property, which includes both corporeal and incorporeal assets, has no direct connection with land.

These Notes are confined exclusively to heritable property, heritable rights and heritable titles.

There are two main aspects to the law of heritable property:

(i) the substantive law, which is dealt with in some textbooks under such headings as 'Landownership', 'Rights in Security', 'Leases', etc. The substantive law regulates the rights and liabilities of the owner or occupant, on the assumption that his right as such has been properly constituted by the appropriate title.

(ii) Conveyancing, which is primarily concerned with the constitution and transmission of the right of property, (or occupancy) in the form appropriate to the type of property being dealt with. The Conveyance is the traditional document of title by which a right of property in land is transferred from one person to another — hence the term.

As indicated above, all rights to land in Scotland generally require a written title to constitute and to transmit the right. In many cases, rights and liabilities of the proprietor of land are implied at common law but these rights may be varied to a greater or lesser extent by the terms of his particular title; that is, by 'conventional provision'. Therefore, although the substantive law of land ownership is concerned with rights and liabilities of owners and occupiers generally, it is also necessary in each individual case to examine the individual title to the property concerned and consider the particular terms of that title and the extent to which, if any, the title modifies what the common law would otherwise imply. This, in turn, involves the application of conveyancing principles in construing the terms of the documents constituting the title.

So, under the common law of the tenement, as applied to tenement property generally, the proprietor of the top flat is by implication responsible for the whole cost of maintaining the roof. In many cases, however, this common law liability is modified by the terms of the titles to the individual flats in that tenement.

Similarly, the owner of a vacant piece of land has, at common law, an unqualified right to build on or use that land as he pleases. In his particular title, however, he may be prevented from building altogether; or at least limited in his freedom to use land for building or other purposes.

Reading and References.

This is a big subject and there is a good deal of material in Statutes, decisions, institutional writers and textbooks. In the Reading List, I have selected and summarised the principal sources and references for each subject.

The first part (1.1. Summary of Texts and References) includes a general list of recommended text books, references, statutes, and reports.

Note some of the abbreviations there used, which are used thereafter in the Reading List and in the text, e.g. Walker's Principles of Scottish Private Law 3rd Edit. is referred to later as 'Walker's Principles', or simply 'Walker'..

The same applies to a number of common Statutes, particularly the Conveyancing Acts as listed in the List of Statutes, for some of which abbreviated titles are used.

Under the Subject Headings which follow, reading matter is divided into four categories:

(1) **Text.** This lists important basic material with which the student is expected to be thoroughly familiar. Walker's Principles 3rd Edit. Book 5 is the basic text on which these notes rely, with supplementary texts where indicated under various subject heads.

(2) **References.** Under this head are listed some of the more important source references on each topic. These references should be consulted to amplify the text, and when dealing with particular problems.

(3) **Statutes.** Under this head, I have listed most of the more important statutory provisions relating to each topic; but the list does not pretend to be exhaustive.

(4) **Miscellaneous.** Under this head selected Articles, Styles, and other matter are listed.

Case Notes. I have not listed, in the Reading List, any individual cases, although I have included, under each Subject Heading, a reference to the corresponding Subject Heading in the Published Case Notes simply to remind Students of the existence of these Case Notes on individual topics. The Digest of Cases, included after the Table of Statutes at the beginning of this Edition, is reproduced, with minor amendments and additions, from my published Case Notes, for ease of reference.

Text Books. All the material in the Reading List can be found in any university Law Library. For private study, every student ought to have a copy of each of the following:

1. Walker — Principles of Scottish Private Law — 3rd Edit. 1983. 4 volumes; particularly Vol. 3.

2. Green's Scots Statutes — Conveyancing. This volume, regularly edited, updated and annually reprinted, conveniently collects all the current Conveyancing Statutes.

3. Green's Scots Statutes — Husband and Wife, Succession and Trusts.

4. Halliday — The Conveyancing and Feudal Reform (Scotland) Act 1970.

5. Halliday — The Land Tenure Reform (Scotland) Act 1974.

6. Halliday — The Land Registration (Scotland) Act 1979.

7. My own published Case Notes.

1.2. **Authentication**

Reading List p. 1.2

Conveyancing involves the preparation of **written** evidence in competent form to constitute rights or obligations. Is writing essential for this purpose?

The general principle is that, in a court action to establish or enforce a right or obligation, every kind of evidence is admissible to prove the facts and circumstances out of which the action arose. Apart from special cases, the intention of the parties, in any transaction, can be proved without recourse to writing as evidence. But that general principle is subject to a considerable number of exceptions and qualifications.

Obviously, written documents form an important category of evidence; and, in this context, may be classed as Public or Private.

(1) **Public Writings** are documents and records specially prepared by duly authorised officials for the express purpose of preserving evidence in matters of public interest, e.g. Acts of Parliament, Rules of Court, Court Records, Public Registers, such as the Registers of Births, Deaths and Marriages, and so on. See Walker Evidence Chap. 18.

(2) **Private Writings** are documents prepared by individuals either:

(i) because writing is an **essential** to the constitution of the right or obligation; or

(ii) because the parties simply wish to preserve **evidence** of the terms of a transaction, although a written document may not be an essential to the constitution of the right.

There are two types of private writing. The distinction between them depends on the form which the writing takes and the manner in which it is executed.

(1) **Formal Writs.** These are often referred to (not strictly correctly) as 'Probative Writings'. A Formal Writ must comply with strict rules as to form and authentication.

It may be either:

(a) a solemnly attested deed, which implies **sub**scription of the deed by the granter(s) **and** by two subscribing witnesses; **or**

(b) a holograph deed, which means written and subscribed by the granter but not attested; or a deed 'adopted as holograph'.

(2) **Informal Writings.** These include anything whatever in documentary form (written, printed, etc., signed and unsigned), which **fails** to conform to the rules for a Formal Writ.

The distinction is important and relevant when considering whether or not writing is an essential, or is merely desirable as evidence, in any given transaction.

Transactions where writing is obligatory. *(Obligationes Literis).* In a number of transactions, the law **requires** some written document (formal **or** informal), as a prerequisite to the creation of a right or the constitution of an obligation. If there is no written document, no right is created, whatever the intention of the parties may have been. For **most, but not all,** such transactions, a **Formal** Writ is necessary; but there are some special types of transaction, by Statute and at Common Law, where the necessary document need not be a Formal Writ.

(a) **Transactions requiring Formal Writ.**

The **principal** cases, where a Formal Writ is essential, are:

(i) Testamentary Writings and *mortis causa* dispositions generally.

(ii) Titles to heritable property, and any contract or unilateral deed intended to create rights or obligations of whatever kind affecting land, including leases, **except** leases of one year's duration, or less.

(iii) Contracts of Service, of more than one year's duration.

(iv) Assignations of incorporeal moveable rights.

(v) Contracts where the parties have agreed that they will not be bound **at all**, unless and until a formal written contract has been entered into.

(b) **Transactions where Informal Writings will suffice.**

In such cases, writing is still an **essential** to create the right or to constitute the obligation, but it need not be a Formal Writ. In other words, there must still be a written document but the strict rules which apply to the form and authentication of probative writings are relaxed. In this class are:

(i) At Common Law, writings *in re mercatoria* generally, e.g. Bills of Exchange, Promissory Notes, etc.

(ii) Writings statutorily privileged, e.g. the Memorandum and Articles of Association of a Company, where certain formalities are required, but falling short of the Scottish requirements of probativity.

Rei interventus, homologation and adoption

In transactions where a Formal Writ is obligatory, the rule (above stated) is that, if there is no Formal Writ, no right or obligation is created. That rule is subject to two qualifications:—

(1) **Rei interventus and homologation.** This applies only in Contracts. The general principle here is that, where the parties to a contract have reached agreement but the requisite (formal) document is wanting, the subsequent actings of one or both parties **may** create a binding contract. There must be:

(a) Proof of the agreement, which is probably limited to writ or oath; and

(b) Subsequent actings. For *rei interventus,* this means actings by the party seeking to enforce the contract, which proceed upon the supposed contract, which are material, and which materially alter the position of the party so acting. Homologation implies actings by the party seeking to escape from the contract.

(2) **Adoption.** Adoption implies the existence of an informal writing (in a case where Formal Writ is required) coupled with a second, formal document (earlier **or** later in date), referring to and 'adopting' the informal writing, either expressly or by implication.

Proof by Writ or Oath. In certain special types of contract, writing, as such, is not an essential to the **constitution** of the contract; **but** the **fact** of constitution can be proved in Court only by production of a written document (formal or informal); or, if **no** writ is available, then the matter may be referred to the oath of the defender.

If there is no writ, and if, on oath, the defender admits the existence of the contract, his admission supplies the want of writ. If, on oath, he successfully denies it, the pursuer's case fails.

If, in such cases, the alternative of Writ (as opposed to oath) is relied on, then it is relied on purely as a matter of evidence or proof. The written document, as such, is not an essential to the **constitution** of the contract. Examples of this limited class of case, where proof is restricted to writ or oath, are:

(i) Agreements involving Loan.

(ii) Agreements implying Trust. See The Blank Bonds and Trusts Act 1696.

(iii) Innominate and unusual Contracts.

Probativity and Authentication.

Probativity implies that a writing bears *prima facie* evidence of authorship and that no further enquiry is necessary as to the genuine quality of the probative writing. A deed cannot be probative unless it complies with strict rules as to form and authentication. The formal rules are designed to ensure that writings which, in point of form, comply therewith, are genuine. They are, necessarily, a balance of convenience; on the one hand, not so strict or exacting as to make compliance difficult or burdensome; on the other, not so undemanding as to make forgery easy.

Every probative deed is, therefore, divided into two main parts — the **body** of the deed which contains all the operative clauses (i.e. clauses which in themselves give rise to legal consequences); and the authentication of the deed which cannot, in law, add anything to the substance of the operative clauses, but is concerned solely to establish that the deed is the genuine, voluntary and intended act of the granter.

If a writing is probative, it is accepted by the Courts as the genuine and authentic act of the purported granter, without any supporting or corroborative evidence. But probativity is only a *prima facie* presumption; and probative writings are not beyond challenge. If, however, the authenticity of a writing, *ex facie* probative, is challenged, the whole onus of proof lies on the challenger, and it is a very heavy onus to discharge. Unless and until a probative document is successfully challenged (the appropriate process being an Action of Reduction in the Court of Session), the deed must be accepted as genuine and must receive effect. Therefore, no other evidence is required of the rights or obligations which the probative document purports to create or confer, i.e. it proves its own terms.

A writing, which is not probative, is competent evidence but will only be admitted in proof if it is supported, and spoken to, by the oral evidence of a witness on oath; and it can only be treated as an adminicle of evidence. A writing which is not probative cannot, **of itself**, and unsupported, constitute rights or obligations, nor is it conclusive as to its terms.

Formalities of Execution.

Firstly, to summarise the essentials which are still required by law for probative authentication. These requirements are:

(1) Subscription by the parties on the last page of the deed, and on the last page of the Inventory, Schedule, etc., appended thereto; **except** in the case of Testamentary Writings which must be subscribed on **each** page.

(2) Subscription by two witnesses on the last page of the deed but not on the addenda.

(3) Designations of the witnesses, either in the Testing Clause (1681 Act) or appended to their signatures (1874 Act S.38).

(4) A reference, in the Testing Clause, to all alterations in the deed.

Form.

The deed may be written, typed, or printed by any person (granter or otherwise) in any permanent medium, or it may be a photographic representation of any of these. Further, a deed may be partly in one medium and partly in another, e.g. partly printed and partly typewritten.

Today, most deeds are engrossed bookwise, when on more than one sheet, in terms of the Deeds Act 1696. Under that Act, sheets may be single (written on the front only or front and back), or double, folded quarto; each page had to be numbered (abolished by the Form of Deeds (Scotland) Act 1856), and the total number of pages had to be mentioned in the Testing Clause (abolished 1874 S.38). Further, the parties to the deed had to subscribe each **page**; but the witnesses subscribe on the last page only — altered by the 1970 Act S.44.

The Halliday Committee recommended certain changes in the requirements for probativity, now implemented by the 1970 Act S.44, thus:

'Where:

(a) a deed;

(b) an inventory, appendix, schedule, plan **or** other document annexed to a deed,

is subscribed and (where appropriate) sealed on the **last** page' (i.e. of the deed **and** of the inventory **and** of the schedule **and** of the plan, etc.) 'the fact it is not subscribed on every page is unobjectionable.'

But S.44 does not apply to Wills or other testamentary writings.

Additions and alterations (vitiations). It often happens that, due to an error in engrossing or because of later alterations, additional words or phrases have to be added to a deed or are substituted for other words on erasure. Occasionally, certain words or phrases in a deed have to be deleted. Any such additions or alterations on the face of a deed raise an immediate presumption in law that they have been made **after** execution, and are not authenticated by the granter. In law, no person is presumed to have signed an altered document. If such additions or alterations are to receive effect, they must be properly authenticated.

Marginal Additions. If a substantial addition is made to a deed before execution, it will normally be added separately in the margin. This is known technically as a 'marginal addition'. The marginal addition will be signed by the party or parties, but not the witnesses. The practice is to sidescribe in the margin, with the initials or pre-name below the marginal addition and the surname above it; and the marginal addition receives a special mention in the testing clause, the purpose being to show *ex facie* of the deed that the witnesses to the signature on the deed itself also witnessed the signing of the marginal addition. This practice is **not** affected by the 1970 Act S.44.

Interlineations. Minor additions of a word or two can simply be interlined at the appropriate place. Interlineations are not normally signed or initialled, but they must be specially mentioned in the testing clause.

Erasures. In the same way, alterations, erasures and deletions are not in practice signed or initialled, but must be specially mentioned in the testing clause.

Effect. An addition to a deed, whether marginal or as an interlineation, if not authenticated, is held *pro non scripto;* but normally it has no effect on the validity of the deed as a whole. Thus, if a deed contains an unauthenticated marginal addition, the marginal addition is ignored. The same rule applies to words written on erasure, where the words on erasure are not *inter essentialia;* and also to words deleted, **if** the deleted words still remain legible. Thus, a word interlined which is not duly authenticated is simply ignored; the deed receives effect excluding the interlined word(s). Words deleted, if the deletion is not authenticated, are read back into the deed. But if the words written on erasure, or deleted, are *inter essentialia,* or if any deleted words are illegible, then the whole deed may be reduced. If there is any suggestion of fraud, any alteration, however trivial, may result in the reduction of the whole deed.

Blanks in Deeds. Under the Blank Bonds and Trusts Act 1696, a document of debt (except *in re mercatoria*) is void unless the name of the creditor has been inserted, at latest, before delivery. In other cases, the effect of a blank in a deed depends on the nature of the omission. Thus, if the description is omitted from a Disposition, the deed is patently void. Lesser omissions normally have no effect and are simply ignored; but of course they may cause problems of construction.

Addenda. A deed is normally in two connected parts, the body of the deed and the testing clause. The testing clause follows immediately upon the last word of the deed on the final page, and on that page the party or parties, and the witnesses, sign. In practice, for convenience, matter appropriate to the deed itself is frequently relegated to a schedule or schedules annexed to the deed on separate sheets following on the last page of the deed proper. If the schedules are to receive effect as part of the deed (which is the intention), they must also be properly authenticated. In practice, schedules are specially referred to in the body of the deed so as to incorporate them in the deed by adoption; they are signed (on the last page only — 1970 S.44) by the parties (but not the witnesses); and they are referred to in the testing clause to show that the signatures to the addenda have been properly attested. **Each** separate schedule or other addendum must be signed on its last page by the party(ies).

Endorsation. 1868 Act S.140. Where a writ is permitted or directed by Statute to be endorsed upon any deed, additional sheets may be used, but the engrossment of the endorsement must commence on part of the original deed.

Execution by Parties

Some points to note on subscriptions:—

(1) By the Lyon King of Arms Act 1672, superseding earlier Scottish practice, noblemen (and Bishops; but these are 'obsolete' — Drummond v. Farquhar 6th July, 1809 F.C.) may subscribe using their title; all others must subscribe their Christian name, or the initial letters thereof, and their proper surname.

(2) The prefix Mr. or Mrs. to a signature which includes Christian name, or initials, is unobjectionable; but 'Mrs. Smith' or 'Mr. Jones' is bad. Allan 1933 S.L.T. (Sh. Ct.) 2.

(3) Married women in Scotland may sign, using their maiden surname or their married surname; but, if a married woman uses her maiden surname, that should be specially mentioned in the testing clause. Dunlop 2 M.1.

(4) Subscription by initials has been recognised as sufficient, where this was the usual method of signature; 1.2.7. Gardner 5R (HL) 105, and 1.2.8. Lowrie's

JF. 1972 SLT 159. In other special cases, deviation from the strict statutory essentials has been recognised; e.g. a holograph will in letter form signed 'Connie' 1.2.3. Draper 1954 SC 136 and 'lots of love, Mum' — 1.2.4. Rhodes 1972 SLT 98. See Lord Hunter, 'I see no reason to reject … the signature by a familiar or pet name, provided it is proved the writer used to sign letters by that name.'

Note that any such abbreviated mode of signature requires proof; and a deed so signed is not *ex facie* probative.

Witnesses must sign using Christian name (or initial) and surname.

(5) Subscription by mark is wholly invalid for formal deeds, though possibly it may suffice on a writing in *re mercatoria;* — 1.2.5 Morton 1908 SC 171. The same applies to stamps and cyclostyles.

(6) A signature of a party on erasure is unobjectionable — 1.2.6 Brown 15 R 511; but very undesirable.

(7) The signature must be the voluntary, spontaneous act of the granter. Thus, if the writer's hand is guided when he signs his name, that is fatal — Moncrieff 1710 M.15, 936. Similarly, if the signatory inks in a pencilled signature written by another — Crosbie 1749 M.16, 814. The hand may be supported, if held above the wrist — Noble 3R 74, but this is to be avoided except in extreme emergency, because the witnesses may not remember exactly what was done; and there is serious risk that the deed may be reduced. If a person is physically incapable of signing, then the alternative of notarial execution is always available.

(8) Blindness does not *per se* prevent a person from validly executing a deed as a **party,** provided he can sign his name; and, if he does himself sign the deed, it need not have been read over to him. Obviously, it is always better to adopt notarial execution on behalf of a blind person — Ker 15 S 983.

Attestation

The rules for subscription by witnesses (attestation) are statutory, under The Subscription of Deeds Act 1681 which, with the Deeds Acts 1696, forms the foundation of the modern testing clause.

The 1681 Act, as judicially interpreted, and brought up to date by later legislation, applies thus:

(1) **Parties.** The Act applies generally to all writs and to all parties; but its requirements have been modified by Statute in a variety of special cases, e.g.: —

Corporations. A Corporation is a legal person and exists as such separate and distinct from its individual members. Obviously, it cannot sign, but every Corporation has a Common Seal. The Seal is normally used to authenticate any document to which the Corporation is a party, but it can only be so used if duly authorised by the person(s) responsible for the administration of that Corporation. As evidence that the use of the Seal is duly authorised, the normal practice is that the deed is sealed with the Common Seal and signed by one or more authorised officials of the Corporation. The identity of the signatories varies according to circumstances.

Limited Companies. By far the commonest type of Corporation encountered in practice is the Company incorporated under the Companies Acts. Provision is normally made in its Articles of Association both for the use of the Common Seal and for the execution of documents under Seal. This provision differs widely in Articles of Association of different Companies. The following is a typical style:

'The Directors shall provide for the safe custody of the Seal which shall only be used by the authority of the Directors or of a Committee of Directors authorised by the Directors in that behalf and all Instruments to which the Seal shall be affixed shall be signed by a Director and shall be countersigned by the Secretary or by a second Director or by some other person appointed by the Directors for this purpose'.

Apart from the special provisions in the Articles, however, the Companies Act 1985 S.36 contains certain over-riding provisions for the execution by Incorporated Companies of contracts and deeds. Sub-Sections 1 and 2 deal with Contracts and require no comment. Sub-Section 3 deals with deeds, and reads:

'A deed to which a company is a party is held to be validly executed according to the law of Scotland on behalf of the company if it is executed in accordance with this Act or is sealed with the company's common seal subscribed on behalf of the company by two of the directors or by a director and the secretary and such subscription on behalf of the company is binding **whether attested by witnesses or not.**'

A deed by a Company is, therefore, validly executed, either:

(a) If executed in accordance with the Act. This means presumably execution in accordance with the Articles of the Company; **or**

(b) If sealed with the Common Seal and signed by two Directors or by a Director and the Secretary of the Company. In the latter case, witnesses are unnecessary. For a definition of Secretary, see the Companies Act 1985 S.283.

These provisions apply **only** to a Company which is a going concern. When a Company goes into liquidation, the powers of the Directors are vested in the liquidator. Any deed granted by the Company after liquidation is sealed with the Common Seal and subscribed by the liquidator alone. His signature must be attested. (But see, *contra,* Halliday 1979 JLS Workshop (iii) and comment thereon at (xlvii)). The safer view is that witnesses to the liquidator's signature are necessary.

Chartered Companies. If a Company is incorporated by a special Act of Parliament or by Royal Charter, such Act or Charter prescribes the mode of execution and must be referred to.

Regional and District Councils (formerly Cities, Burghs and County Councils). Execution by these bodies is now governed by the Local Government (Scotland) Act 1973 S.194. Any deed sealed with the Common Seal of the Council and subscribed by two Members of the Council and the proper officer of the Council is validly executed, whether attested by witnesses or not. A Local Council has the option of adopting the provisions of this Act or of adopting special administrative provisions in its own local Act. For Dundee, under comparable earlier legislation, there was a local Act entitled 'Dundee Corporation (Consolidated Powers) Order Confirmation Act 1957'. Section 14 read:

'Charters, etc., ... shall be good, valid and effectual if subscribed, with or without Seal, by any two Members of the Corporation and the Town Clerk whether attested by witnesses or not'.

(2) **Number of witnesses.** 'Witnesses' means **two** witnesses. See 1.2.14 Ferguson 1959 SC 56 — the ordinary rule of Scots Law applies, requiring corroboration of any fact by two witnesses.

(3) **Qualification of Witness.** At Common Law, any male over the age of puberty (14 years) and *compos mentis* is a competent witness. This is now extended to females over 14 years of age by the 1868 Act S.139. There are certain exceptions, viz.:

(a) A blind person is never a competent witness (cf. subscription by parties); and

(b) A party to a deed cannot competently witness the signature of another party to the same deed.

On the other hand, there can be no competent objection in Scotland to an instrumentary witness on the ground of interest, undue influence or bad character; although the oral testimony of a witness in Court may be discounted or rejected on such grounds. Thus, one spouse may witness the other's signature; and a beneficiary named in a will may act as a witness, although in neither case is this recommended.

In terms of the 1681 Act, the witnesses **must then know** the granter of the deed but this is reasonably interpreted. Introduction at the time by a mutual acquaintance suffices. The essential test is that the witness shall have credible information as to the identity of the granter.

Only **subscribing** witnesses shall be probative, i.e. each witness must sign. Where a deed is written bookwise, then under the 1696 Act each witness signs on the last page on which the deed ends and the testing clause begins. This still applies, even if there are addenda to the deed.

(4) **Signatures of witnesses.** The rules which apply to the signature of a party apply generally to signature by witnesses, but with witnesses mere initials or mark can never suffice.

It is normal practice, although not strictly necessary, for a witness to add the word 'witness' after his signature; or it can be added in another hand. The purpose is, firstly, to show that the witness knew why he was signing; and, secondly, to protect the witness against any possible risk that his signature might involve him as a party to the deed and to the obligations contained in it.

(5) **Designations of witnesses.** Witnesses must be designed in the deed. This is an additional precaution against fraud as well as preserving a permanent record in the body of the deed of the identity of the witnesses, should they require to be traced. The designation of the witness must be sufficient to identify him beyond reasonable doubt. Thus in 1696 'Indweller in Edinburgh' was deemed a sufficient designation but would not suffice now — Grant M. 16913.

Under the 1681 Act, the designations of the witnesses had to appear in the body of the writ. For the purpose of this and other Acts, information in the testing clause is taken as information in the body of the deed, but subject to this qualification that the testing clause cannot legitimately contain anything which purports to add to or qualify the operative clauses in the body of the deed; 1.2.27 — Blair v. The Assets Co. 23 R. (HL) 36. Walker's Principles Chapter 1.7. page 86 suggests that an operative provision in a testing clause is valid, and refers to Chamber's Trustees and Gibson's Trustees. Lord Gordon's opinion in Chamber's Trustees is contrary to the later House of Lords decision in Blair, and must be considered overruled. In 1.2.28 Gibson's Trustees 1931 SLT 22, the addition was a holograph addition to a typed codicil, written before subscription and followed again by the words 'In witness whereof'. The Court held that the testing clause commenced at the second 'In witness whereof'.

By the 1874 Act S.38, it is now no objection to the probative character of the deed that the witnesses are not named or designed in the body thereof (or in the testing clause thereof — note the distinction between body and testing clause now recognised by Statute) provided always that, where the witnesses are not so named and designed, their designations shall be appended to or follow their signatures.

The witnesses must still be **designed,** under Section 38; but the effect is to render a formal testing clause unnecessary.

Under Section 38, the designation need not be written by the witnesses themselves.

(6) **Function of witnesses.** On the function of witnesses, the Statutes are silent. In the ordinary case, their true function is merely to attest, i.e. to provide evidence by their signature to the deed that the signature of the party which they attest is the genuine, voluntary signature of that party.

Thus, a witness need have no knowledge of the nature or content of the deed which he attests, because he speaks only to authentication. But the witness must know why he signed, i.e. that he is 'attesting' a signature, and the granter of the deed must know that the witness is present, as a witness, for the express purpose of attesting his signature.

Granter and witnesses perform their respective functions of mutual consent. On the one hand, a witness otherwise competent cannot be compelled to sign as such; on the other hand, a witness otherwise competent cannot properly sign unless, at the time, he has the consent of the party whose signature he attests. If the witness does not have such consent, and if he signs notwithstanding, then (although the deed is *ex facie* probative) it is open to reduction, although the granter of the deed may be personally barred from reducing it on that ground, as explained below.

The witnesses must know the granter, but that is not enough in itself; they must be satisfied that the signature on the document which they attest is the authentic signature of the granter. On this last point, the 1681 Act is express. Two situations are envisaged. Either:

(a) the witnesses must see the granter adhibit his signature. If so, there is apparently no express statutory time limit within which the witnesses must sign; or

(b) at the time when the witnesses subscribe, the granter must acknowledge his signature. This is reasonably interpreted and does not necessarily mean that, as the witness actually signs, the granter must acknowledge; but in practice, in **either** case, no interval of time should elapse between signature or acknowledgment by **party** and **signature** by **witness**.

One witness may see the granter sign and another hear him acknowledge. Or the granter may acknowledge his signature separately to two witnesses at different times. The acknowledgment need not be verbal.

The same two witnesses may attest several signatures to a deed. If all the parties sign together, the same two witnesses require to sign once only; if several parties sign at different times, the same two witnesses should sign again on each occasion.

(7) **Time Limits.**

It is certainly fatal to a deed if one, or both, of the witnesses fail to sign before the deed is registered for preservation, or is founded on in Court. The same rule applies where a witness signs after the consent or mandate from the granter of the writ has been withdrawn; See 1.2.25 — Walker v. Whitwell 1916 SC (HL) 75.

The Testing Clause

Prior to 1874, a Testing Clause was essential in order to incorporate in the writ certain information then required by Statute. Since 1874, the only information statutorily necessary is the designation of witnesses; and this may be appended to their signatures. If, therefore, there are no vitiations in a deed, a Testing Clause is not obligatory. But, in practice, certain information over and above the strict statutory requirements is invariably inserted; and, even if the S.38 alternative is followed, a shortened form of Testing Clause is almost always used.

Some points on Testing Clauses:

(1) The Testing Clause must commence on the deed, i.e. the words 'IN WITNESS WHEREOF' which introduce the Testing Clause must appear on a page which also contains part of the operative clauses of the deed, however short that part may be. Parties and witnesses must **all** subscribe on that page; otherwise the subscription of witnesses is not on the last page **of the deed,** and fails to comply with the 1696 Act. But this only applies to deeds written bookwise, **not** to deeds on one sheet — See 1.2.14 — Ferguson 1959 SC 56.

(2) The pages of the deed and all addenda are normally numbered (not essential since 1856); and the number of pages is mentioned in the Testing Clause (not essential since 1874).

(3) Addenda and marginal additions are always mentioned in the Testing Clause; and the same applies to all vitiations.

(4) **Capacities of parties.** Sometimes a party signs a deed in two or more capacities, e.g. as Trustee and as an individual. If so, then arguably he ought to sign the deed twice. If he signs once only, that is accepted in practice as sufficient if his dual capacity is specifically referred to in the Testing Clause, e.g. 'subscribed by me, the said AB as Trustee foresaid and as an individual'. But, if a party to a deed signs it once only and there is no such reference in the Testing Clause, he would find it extremely difficult later to maintain that he had signed in one capacity but not in the other.

(5) Where (as often happens) there is a discrepancy between the name of a party (or witness) and the signature of that party (or witness), this should be mentioned in the testing clause. So, if a witness Alan Bell Smith signs simply 'A. Smith', his **full** name should be given in the Testing Clause, adding 'subscribing with his usual signature 'A. Smith''.

(6) **Date and place of execution.** Neither is essential by Statute or Common Law, but both are always included. The place of execution may be relevant, e.g. in Wills — see The Wills Act 1963. The date of execution is often necessary for Stamp Duty purposes, and may otherwise be relevant.

(7) **Errors in the Testing Clause.** If an error is made in the Testing Clause, e.g. erasure, interlineation, etc., the error should be declared at the end of that clause.

(8) When and how is the Testing Clause completed? In practice, a deed is engrossed down to and including the words 'IN WITNESS WHEREOF'. These words indicate that the operative clauses have ended and that what follows is the testing clause only; that is a precaution to prevent the risk of additional clauses being added to the deed after it has been signed. Bell in his Lectures (and Burns in Green's Encyclopaedia Vol. 2 S.660. — Blanks in Deeds) recommends that the deed should be taken further, and that, before it is signed, the Testing Clause should be partially completed so as to include the number of pages and all vitiations, etc., leaving only the date and place of execution and the names of the witnesses to be filled in after signature. This prevents the possibility of spurious alterations being made **after** execution and being **apparently** duly authenticated by declaration in the Testing Clause, **also** added after execution. But this suggestion, though excellent, is rarely adopted in practice. In any event, that part of the Testing Clause dealing with place and date of execution and the designations of the witnesses cannot be filled in until after execution. Some interval must therefore elapse; it may be only an hour or two or it may be some weeks, but the interval should always be kept to the minimum if a deed is to be signed by several parties, because completion of the Testing Clause is part of the solemnity of authentication. This is stressed in 1.2.25 Walker 1916 SC (HL) 75 although it is recognised that, by long custom, the strict rules in this respect are not applied. Thus, in Blair 6 S.51, a 32-year interval did not invalidate the deed.

Under the 1874 Act S.38, witnesses' designations may be added at any time before the deed is founded on in any action or is registered for preservation. The same rules apply to completion of the testing clause. Death is no bar to adding designations or completing the testing clause — see Opinion of Lord Dunedin in 1.2.25 Walker 1916 SC(HL) 75 which does not support the view expressed in Walker's Principles Chapter 1.7. page 83 that the testing clause may **not** be completed after death. Even where a deed has been registered, or has been founded on, uncompleted, there is a remedy and the defect need not be fatal, — 1874 Act S.39 and 1.2.31 Thomson's Trustees 6 R 141; but, of course, the deed is not *ex facie* probative.

Notarial Execution or Vicarious Subscription.

At Common Law, a writ was sufficiently authenticated if the seal of the granter was affixed, without subscription; and the granter himself was not required to affix his own seal. This could be done for him. Therefore, questions of personal capacity or incapacity presented no problem in the authentication of a document. The presence of the seal on a document sufficiently authenticated it, and it did not matter by whose hand the seal was affixed. Subscription is a **personal** matter, and it must be the voluntary spontaneous act of the granter himself. The Subscription of Deeds Act 1540, which first introduced subscription as an essential solemnity, also made provision for the execution of documents vicariously by a Notary Public on behalf of a person who could not sign his own name. The requirement of that and later Acts have now been wholly superseded by the 1924 Act S.18 and Schedule I for any deed executed after 31st December, 1924.

The points to note in this Section are: —

(1) The Act refers to **any** deed of whatever nature.

(2) The Section is permissive ('any deed, etc., **may**'). In other words, in the case

of blind persons, this procedure is optional and the Section does not alter the rule that a blind person may validly execute at his own hand; but in the case of incapacity there is no effective alternative.

(3) The official who signs vicariously may be:—

(a) As regards any writ a Law Agent, Notary Public, or Justice of the Peace. Law Agent is defined in the 1924 Act S.2, (6), thus 'Law Agent shall mean and include Writers to the Signet, Solicitors in the Supreme Courts, Procurators in any Sheriff Court and every person entitled to practise as an Agent in a Court of Law in Scotland' (Solicitors (Scotland) Act 1949). Notary Public is defined in the 1868 Act S.2. as a Notary Public duly admitted to practice in Scotland. Justice of the Peace is not defined and presumably covers a Justice anywhere in the United Kingdom.

(b) As regards testamentary writings only, in addition to the foregoing, the Parish Minister acting in his own Parish or his assistant and successor so acting. (See also Church of Scotland (Property and Endowments) Amendment Act 1933, S.13, for some slight modifications here).

(4) The Official must know the granter or have credible evidence of his identity.

(5) The granter **must** be blind or unable to write.

(6) He **must** declare his disability.

(7) The deed **must** be read over to him.

(8) He **must** give authority, visible or audible, to the signing of the deed on his behalf.

(9) At that point, the official signs the deed using his own, ordinary signature. In testamentary deeds, he signs **each** page; for other deeds, the 1970 Act S.44 applies, and signature on each page is strictly unnecessary, but certainly desirable. In all cases, he must write a holograph docquet **in his own handwriting** on the last page of the deed, which he subscribes, adding his qualification and designation. **Note** that, on the last page, the official's signature to the docquet authenticates the whole page, i.e., he does not require to sign the last page twice. (See note to Schedule I).

(10) The whole of the foregoing procedure must be carried out entire, as a single continuous process, in the presence of the granter and of the two witnesses, who then sign the deed, in the ordinary way, on the last page only. For a cautionary case, see 1.2.39 Hynd's Trustee 1955 SC (HL) 1. A Solicitor read over a Will to the testator and signed it in his presence and in the presence of two witnesses, employees of the Solicitor. He did not add his docquet at the time nor did the witnesses then sign. The Solicitor and the two witnesses then all returned to his office, and one-and-a-half hours later the Solicitor added the docquet and the witnesses then signed. The Will was held invalidly executed.

The Docquet.

The form of docquet to be written on the deed by the Official is prescribed in Schedule I to the 1924 Act, thus:—

Docquet where granter of deed is blind or cannot write.

'Read over to, and signed by me, for and by authority of the above named AB **(without designation)** who declares that he is blind **(or** is unable to write) all in his presence, and in presence of the witnesses hereto subscribing.'

CD, Law Agent, Edinburgh.
MN, witness
PQ, witness

The docquet **must** be holograph; it will not do to type it on the deed in advance.

There are some notes to Schedule I which give directions as to signatures, etc.

Interest of the Notary.

Although there is no reference to this in 1924 Act S.18, the Official, who signs vicariously, is not permitted to have any patrimonial interest whatever, actual or potential, in the provisions of the deed. That rule is absolute and is most strictly applied. If ignored, the deed is invalid and reducible. The leading (modern) case is — 1.2.43 Finlay, 1948 SC 18.

Informality of Execution.

Prior to I874, the standard rule was that, if any of the strict requirements for probativity was not complied with, then the deed was inevitably improbative.

If the transaction was one of the *obligationes literis,* this carried the inevitable consequence that the whole transaction was invalidated. Thus, prior to I856, it was a statutory requirement that each page of a deed should be numbered and that the number of pages should be mentioned in the testing clause. Failure to number any one page of a deed, or to mention the number of pages, totally invalidated the whole document.

The position has been improved in two ways:

(a) Under the 1874 Act S.38, and earlier provisions, certain of the old meticulous requirements have been abolished; e.g. numbering of pages etc.; and

(b) By the 1874 Act S.39, even if a deed does not comply in all respects with the remaining statutory requirements, it is now possible to petition the court under this Section for a declarator that the Deed is probative, notwithstanding some 'informality of execution'. Note, however, that the 1874 Act S.39 applies only to 'informalities'. The Section cannot be used to cure serious defects in the solemnity of execution. Thus, it is an essential statutory requirement that a subscribing witness must either see the granter sign the deed or hear him acknowledge his signature. If a witness signs without having done either of these, the deed is invalid; and that invalidity is more than a mere 'informality'. Therefore, the deed cannot be declared probative under this Section.

The Effect of ex facie probativity

A deed may appear, *ex facie,* to be probative, if it bears to be subscribed by the granter and by the necessary two witnesses, and the testing clause has been completed. Nonetheless, the deed may be a nullity because there has been some radical defect in the solemnity of execution which is not a mere informality and is thus not curable under Section 39, e.g. where one witness has neither seen the granter subscribe nor heard him acknowledge the signature. That is the standard rule. It is subject to two qualifications:

(i) A deed which is *ex facie* probative must receive effect unless and until it is set aside by a Decree of Reduction. The onus always lies on the challenger to prove the want of due authentication, and very clear proof will be required. It is not sufficient, in an Action of Reduction on this ground, to produce one of the witnesses to the signature who merely says he cannot remember, e.g. seeing the granter sign. Very convincing evidence from the witnesses will be required. Nonetheless, if it can be shown **conclusively** that a witness did not properly subscribe as a witness, the deed, although *ex facie* probative, may be set aside and invalidated by a Decree of Reduction.

(ii) Even although the challenger may prove that the deed was not properly signed and should therefore be invalidated under the previous rule, the challenger may himself be personally barred from founding on that invalidity. Thus, if A signs a loan document and hands it to the creditor apparently duly attested by two witnesses, and obtains a loan in exchange, A cannot then turn round and say that the deed is improperly executed, with a view to invalidating the loan document. A is personally barred from founding on such latent defects in authentication.

Privileged Writings

The statutory rules for probative writings summarised above apply generally to all situations and all types of deed; but there are certain circumstances, and certain types of deed, to which, at Common Law, the statutory provisions have been held not to apply.

Such writings are termed 'privileged writings'. The commonest illustrations of privileged writings are:

(1) Holograph Writings

A writing which is wholly in the handwriting of and is subscribed by the granter is holograph. It is privileged to this extent, that attestation of the signature is unnecessary at Common Law, and so the statutory provisions summarised above do not apply to it. Holograph writings differ from solemnly attested deeds in this important respect, that the onus of proving a holograph writ to be genuine lies on the party founding on it, and not on the party who challenges its authenticity. In contrast, where a writing is solemnly attested according to the statutory rules, the onus always lies on the challenger to prove that the deed is not in fact probative although *ex facie* it appears to be so; and that is a heavy onus to discharge.

However, if a holograph writ can be proved to be written in the handwriting of and subscribed by the granter or is admitted so to be in a court action, then it does have all the qualities of a probative writ, in that it proves its own terms and serves as formal writ for the purposes of the *obligationes literis.*

The privilege is extended to deeds which are not written in the granter's own hand but which he has 'adopted as holograph'. If these words are written by the granter in his own hand at the end of the document and if he then also subscribes, the document is deemed to be wholly holograph.

Similarly, documents in themselves improbative can be given the qualities of probativity by being 'adopted' in another probative writing.

For specialties which arise with documents partly handwritten and partly printed, see 1.2.49 Campbell 1963 SLT (Sh.Ct.) 10.

(2) Writings in re mercatoria

This covers a wide variety of documents in everyday commercial use. They are privileged in that they may receive effect although they do not comply with the statutory requirements for solemn execution.

(3) **Writs executed abroad**

The general rule of International Law, applied in Scotland, is that any deed executed abroad will receive effect here if executed in accordance with the required formalities in the place of execution.

The rule is most commonly applied in the case of Wills, and Powers of Attorney.

As to Wills, there is now a statutory reinforcement and modification of the Common Law under the Wills Act 1963.

Titles to heritable property in Scotland form an exception; they **must** conform to the Scottish requirements of probativity, regardless of other factors.

1.3. Delivery.

Reading List 1.3.

In a number of important transactions, the law requires a formal written document to effect that transaction. But the mere fact that a party has executed a formal written document does not automatically bind the party in terms of that Deed. In most cases, something more is required to make the writing obligatory on the granter; and that further requirement is delivery of the Deed into the hands of the grantee, or its equivalent. So, with limited exceptions dealt with below, the standard rule is that any Deed, whether onerous or gratuitous, becomes effective, irrevocable, and binding on the granter only if it is delivered; and, similarly, that the grantee thereunder cannot enforce that writ against the granter unless and until he has taken delivery thereof.

It follows that, particularly in the case of gifts and other gratuitous transactions, delivery is a vital element in completing the rights and obligations of the parties. Perhaps rather surprisingly, no formal legal act or procedure is required to effect delivery. In all cases, delivery is a question of fact and intention.

In practice, difficulties do not often arise. A deed is normally delivered simply by handing it over physically to the grantee or his agent, either gratuitously, or, in the case of onerous deeds, in exchange for the consideration thereunder. The fact of physical handing over, coupled with intention to make the deed operative, is of itself sufficient delivery. Similarly, a deed is **not** delivered by physical handing over of a deed if accompanied by a covering letter, which says: 'You are to hold the accompanying deed as undelivered'. This is quite a commonplace qualification when physically parting with a deed.

But, occasionally, a doubt arises as to whether or not a deed is to be treated as delivered in particular circumstances. In these cases, there are certain presumptions, arising out of the surrounding circumstances, but in all cases rebuttable. The presumptions may be summarised thus:

1. Presumptions arising from the custody of the deed.

(i) **Deed held by grantee.** Where a deed, gratuitous or onerous, is held by the disponee or grantee thereunder, this raises a **strong presumption** that the deed was delivered and is, therefore, operative. But mere possession of the deed alone does not *per se* imply delivery; in doubtful cases, it is necessary to establish *animus* or intention.

(ii) **Deed in the hands of an Agent.** Frequently, in practice, deeds are delivered and accepted, and held, by Solicitors or other Agents. The rule is that the Agent is equivalent to the party whom he represents.

(iii) **Deed in hands of Common Agent.** If, as often happens, a common agent acts for granter and grantee (e.g. the family Solicitor acting for father and son as donor and donee) the fact that the common agent holds a deed, which apparently effects donation, raises no presumption one way or the other. In such cases, therefore, it is very important to establish delivery by other means; e.g. a separate letter confirming the fact of delivery and a signed acknowledgement thereof.

2. Equivalents to delivery.

(1) **Registration.** There are two main types of registration which may or may not raise presumptions, according to circumstances. These are:

(i) Registration for publication in Sasines. Registration of a deed in Sasines is the final step in perfecting the real right of a disponee of heritage. It follows that, if A, as owner of a heritable property, dispones that property to B, and thereafter the Disposition is recorded in Sasines on behalf of B, the disponee, this necessarily raises an almost irrebuttable presumption that the deed has been delivered.

See 1.3.11 Carmichael 1920 SC (HL) 195 for the ordinary case. But compare 1.3.8 Cameron's Trustees 1907 SC 407 for a specialty, where title was taken in name of A as Trustee for his daughter B, and was recorded on A's behalf; recording was not sufficient to establish delivery as between A and B.

The same principles would apply on Registration of a title under the 1979 Act.

(ii) Registration for Preservation in the Books of Council and Session. In this case, registration does not create rights. The only purpose is to avoid the loss of the principal Deed. As a result, Registration for Preservation is less significant than Registration for Publication. See 1.3.9 Tennent. 7M 936.

(2) **Intimation to the debtor in an obligation.** When an incorporeal moveable right is assigned, the assignee completes his title by intimating the Assignation to the debtor in the obligation. Intimation here is equivalent to registration in the Register of Sasines in the case of heritage. In exactly the same way as with heritage, **intimation will normally infer delivery.**

(3) **Intimation to Donee.** This too may imply Delivery. For some recent cases involving liability to death duties, which underline the importance of delivery in completing a transaction see Case Notes 1.3.11 *et seq.*

Deeds not requiring delivery.

Contrary to the general rule, certain deeds do not require to be delivered in order to become effective. The principal cases are:

(i) **Testamentary Writings.** Delivery is never necessary; and, even if a testamentary deed is delivered to the beneficiary, that does not make it irrevocable nor confer any enforceable rights on the beneficiary *inter vivos.* See 1.3.5 Clark's Exor 1943 SC 2I6.

(ii) **Bilateral Contracts.** A contract becomes immediately binding, once executed by all parties.

Acceptance of delivery.

The grantee is not normally obliged to accept delivery; he has the option to accept or reject it. But apparently, a deed may be delivered so as to bind the granter even although the grantee may be unaware of its existence. Therefore, although delivery is conditional upon acceptance by the grantee, that condition is resolutive and not suspensive. See 1.3.17 Dowie & Co. 18 R 986 and 1.3.12 Allan's Tr. 1971 SLT 62.

1.4. Capacity.

Reading List 1.4.

On the general question of capacity, and its effect on the ability of a person to contract see Gloag & Henderson 8th Edition Chapter 6.

Broadly speaking, the same general principles apply to the ownership of, title to, and disposal of, heritable property.

Capacity and Power. In addition to capacity, the party must also have power to make contracts. In the case of individuals acting for their own beneficial interest, if such an individual has capacity, he also has, by necessary implication, power to deal with his proprietary rights in any way. If, however, a person acts in a representative capacity, such as a Trustee, or as an agent, the Trustee or agent may have capacity but may lack power. If so, any Deed granted by him is voidable.

Domicile. In relation to capacity, the question of domicile may be significant. The general rule, which applies to Scottish heritage, is that the *lex situs* determines whether or not a person has capacity to deal with his heritable property in Scotland. See Anton — Private International Law — p. 392 e.s. But that general principle is hedged about with certain limitations and qualifications. So, in the case of minors, there is some support for the view that the *lex domicilii* may determine the capacity of a foreign **minor** to deal with Scottish heritage.

Clearly, in such cases, the ideal rule is to ascertain the position under both systems of law, *lex situs* and *lex domicilii;* and only to act in reliance on a deed by a person domiciled abroad if that deed is valid under both systems.

Further, where a person acts in a representative capacity in reliance on statutory powers, e.g. trustees, Corporations, etc., their powers are necessarily limited by the relevant statutory authority in their own jurisdiction. Scottish Acts, e.g. the Trusts (Scotland) Acts, etc., have no application in such cases.

Title. The question of title is distinct and separate from the question of capacity and power. The case of trustees is typical. The constituent deed, i.e. the Deed of Trust, must itself be valid before the trustees can act. But, in addition, the trustees must themselves be capable of acting, which does not depend on the terms of the deed, but on personal factors; and they must also have power to act with reference to the trust assets which, again, involves different considerations. The technicalities of title will be dealt with later.

Particular Scottish problems.

1. **Trustees.** The case of trustees is taken first because some of the rules applicable to trustees apply also in other comparable cases, e.g. tutors and pupils, etc.

Capacity. The individual trustee is generally subject to the same rules as to capacity as is any individual. So, a person who is insane cannot effectively deal with his own property; and, although he may validly be appointed as a trustee, he cannot effectively deal with Trust assets.

Title. Normally, there is a Deed of Trust (or its equivalent, e.g. Confirmation-dative) which constitutes the Trustees' title. That deed must, of course, be intrinsically valid in itself. It may take various forms, and, in relation to *mortis* *causa* trusts, there are now special rules, supplementing the Common Law position, under the Succession (Scotland) Act 1964. In *inter vivos* trusts, assets of various kinds may pass to the trustee under the constituent deed or by separate conveyance or transfer; *mortis causa,* assets pass to the trustees either directly under the constituent deed, or, since 1964, indirectly by virtue of Confirmation. In certain circumstances, with both *inter vivos* and *mortis causa* Trusts, the trustees may later acquire assets during the course of administration of the trust. And, in all cases, they may also dispose of trust assets. In addition, during the course of administration, there may be supplementary trust titles in the form of Deeds of Assumption and Conveyance and Minutes of Resignation of trustees, and Decrees of Appointment of new trustees by the Court, etc. In any given trust, there may therefore be a whole series of formal deeds which, together, make up the title of the trustees for the time being to a particular asset in the estate.

Sale of Heritage. At Common Law, trustees had no implied power to dispose of heritage conveyed to them by the truster. Instead, the necessary implication was that any such heritable estate was to be retained by the trustees for the ultimate benefit of the beneficiaries. Thus, if A died leaving a Will conveying his whole estate to trustees, including heritage, the Trustees had a title to that heritage and capacity to deal with it; but they had no power to sell or dispose of it, except in terms of the Will. This rule could be displaced in the following ways:—

1) **Express power of sale.** The truster might competently confer on his trustees an express power of sale; and this express power is still regularly met with in practice in Deeds of Trust. For a typical illustration, see Burns' Practice p. 802 and Elder's Forms of Wills p. 165.

'My trustees......shall have power .... to sell or otherwise realise the trust estate or any part or parts thereof, heritable and moveable.'

2) **Implied power.** The Trusts (Scotland) Act 1921 S.4. provides that, in all trusts, the trustees have power to do certain acts, provided that the act is not at variance with the terms or the purposes of the trust; and any such act, when done, is as effectual as if the Trust Deed had contained an express power to that effect. These powers in S.4., include:—

'(a) to sell the trust estate or any part thereof, heritable as well as moveable ...

(k) to grant all deeds necessary for carrying into effect the powers vested in the trustees'.

There are further powers in S.4. e.g.:— (b) to grant feus of heritage, (c) to grant leases, (d) to borrow money on security, and (e) to excamb (or exchange) land.

S.6. prescribes the method of sale, which may be by public roup or private bargain.

Prior to the 1961 Act, in all cases when dealing with trustees, a purchaser had to examine not only the Trustees' title to satisfy himself as to its intrinsic validity, but, in addition, he had to consider the purposes of the Deed, and the powers of the trustees thereunder, to see whether or not they had power of sale. Otherwise, he might find himself with an invalid title.

The Trusts (Scotland) Act 1961 S.2. has improved the position of the purchaser, although it does not in any way alter the strict rules as to trustees' power of sale. The sole purpose of the section is to protect the purchaser and to spare him the necessity of enquiring into trustees' powers. Note the following features of this section:

(i) It applies to any of the powers in the 1921 Act S.4., not **merely** sale of heritage.

(ii) If, after 27/8/61, the trustees exercise one of the implied powers in S.4., e.g. sale, the validity of the sale, and of the purchaser's title, cannot be challenged by any person merely on the grounds that the sale is at variance with the terms or purposes of the trust.

(iii) If trustees are acting under the supervision of the Accountant of Court S.2. only applies if the Accountant of Court consents. This applies only in special cases, e.g., a *curator bonis* selling heritage for an incapax ward.

(iv) The section does not in any way affect the relationship between trustees and beneficiaries. Thus, trustees who sell, *ultra vires,* may now confer a valid title and the purchaser is no longer concerned with their powers; but, in so doing, they lay themselves open to an action for breach of trust, at the instance of an aggrieved beneficiary.

3) **Power granted by the Court.** If the Deed of Trust contains no express power, and no effective power is implied under S.4., Trustees may not sell unless specially authorised by the Court under the 1921 Act, S.5. Prior to the 1961 Act, such Petitions to the Court were commonplace, and are still competent and not unusual. Undoubtedly, however, petitions under S.5 are less frequent than they were pre-1961, when purchasers were scrutinising trustees' titles, and challenging their powers. Note that the Petition in this case is not concerned with matters of **title**; but only with power of sale. Provided the trustees have power (express, implied or from the Court), the purchaser is not further concerned to consider whether or not the power is being properly exercised. An improper exercise of the power would not in any way invalidate the purchaser's title.

Purchase or acquisition of Assets. The same problem does not here arise, in that a person selling any asset, heritable or moveable, to trustees has no duty whatever to consider, or enquire into, the powers of the purchasing trustees. If, having sold to trustees, it turns out that the trustees do not have power to purchase, the trustees cannot rescind the contract nor retract in a question with the seller. Contrast the position of a purchaser from trustees without power of sale, prior to 1961; his title was open to reduction, and, if reduced, he lost the property. If trustees do make an unauthorised purchase, they have implied power to resell — see Mackenzie Stuart — The Law of Trusts p. 237.

On the other hand, as between trustees and a beneficiary, the trustees can only properly purchase any asset, heritable or moveable, if they are duly authorised by:—

(i) Express powers of purchase, or investment, in the Deed of Trust, which often are expressly conferred.

(ii) Implied powers under the Trusts (Scotland) Act 1921, now substantially supplemented by the Trustee Investments Act 1961.

(iii) The Trusts (Scotland) Act 1961 S.4. which empowers trustees to acquire an interest in residential accommodation in Scotland or elsewhere, if it is reasonably required as a residence for a beneficiary. This power to purchase is, under the 1961 Act, added as one of the implied powers in the 1921 Act S.4., now S.4.(l)(ee). It is, therefore, competent to petition the Court, under the 1921

Act S.5., for authority to **purchase** heritage — see 1.4.5. Bristow 1965 SLT 225 where, in special circumstances, a *curator bonis* applied for special powers to purchase under this Section. The petition was dismissed as unnecessary on the basis that the curator did have implied power; but, as in other similar cases, Lord Cameron stated 'It may well be that curators will decide to err on the side of caution in determining whether to seek the Court's authority for the exercise of such a power as is sought here, or to act at their own hands.'

Foreign Trusts. The foreign trust which you will commonly come across in practice is the English trust. Remember, that Trust Law in England differs radically from Trust Law in Scotland. In particular, the Trusts (Scotland) Acts 1921 and 1961 have no application whatsoever to an English Trust. But, on the basis of international comity, the Court of Session in Scotland will exercise its *nobile officium* to make an order in a foreign trust, if required. Therefore, English trustees may petition the Scottish Court under the *nobile officium,* but not under the 1921 Act S.5., for, *inter alia,* power of sale. The Scottish Courts must then consider how English law views the powers of trustees in relation to the sale of immoveable property.

For a typical case, see 1.4.9 — Campbell Petitioner 1958 SC. 275, where the Court granted power of sale to English Trustees, but declined to include, in the order, an English provision regulating the exercise of the power. Lord President Clyde: 'It is clear that, as this is an English trust, the Trusts (Scotland) Act 1921 does not apply ... and it is equally clear that, as the English Court does not operate in Scotland, an application to this Court is necessary to enable the trustees to give the purchaser of Scottish subjects a good marketable title.' Note, particularly, that the 1961 Act S.2. applies only to **Scottish** trusts. It does not protect a purchaser from e.g. English trustees; and so a purchaser must still satisfy himself that English (or other foreign) trustees do have the requisite power to deal with Scottish heritage under the proper law of jurisdiction of the trust.

The same considerations apply where English trustees purchase Scottish heritage, but again, with this difference, that, in such cases, the seller is not concerned with the powers of a purchasing trustee after the transaction has settled. In all such cases, it is as well to take advice from a lawyer practising in the jurisdiction of the trust.

2. **Pupils and minors.** A pupil is a girl under 12 or a boy under 14. A minor is a child, no longer a pupil, but still under 18.

Pupils. A pupil has no powers and so cannot acquire or dispose of any property, heritable or moveable. But a pupil has by law, or may have by appointment, a tutor or factor to administer his affairs. The tutors are the father and the mother, jointly, and the survivor, with power to either to act alone and independently, — The Guardianship Act 1973.

The tutor-at-law and tutor-dative, and the factor *loco tutoris* are also trustees within the meaning of the Trusts (Scotland) Acts 1921 and 1961. This removes some earlier problems in that, prior to the 1961 Act, it was always arguable that a sale by a tutor was, by implication, contrary to the terms or purposes of the tutor's trust, because the main purpose of the tutor is to preserve the estate of the ward. However, in 1.4.4. — Cunningham's Tutrix 1949 SC. 275, a Petition by a mother as tutor of her pupil child for authority to sell the child's heritage was dismissed as unnecessary on the footing that the heritage was held simply as an investment; but the point was made in this case, that there would be no such implied power where the heritage was in the nature of a family estate or family residence.

As between the tutor and the pupil, these rules still operate as before; but the powers of the tutor are now of no concern to a purchaser who is covered by the 1961 Act S.2. (see above). But remember that certain categories of tutor act under the supervision of the Accountant of Court; and the consent of the Accountant in such cases is necessary for S.2. to protect the purchaser.

The position of the tutor-at-law and tutor-nominate differs from that of a trustee, in that the property of the pupil is held, and the title is taken, in name of the pupil child. Accordingly, the pupil, and not the tutor, is the feudal owner of heritage, and is the registered proprietor both of heritage and of moveables. The tutor merely acts as an administrator and will make up title in name of the pupil child, not in his own name, as tutor. However, if a factor *loco tutoris* is appointed by the Court, then according to Burns' Practice p. 309, the factor will make up title in his own name, and not in name of the ward.

Purchase of heritage by a tutor is probably fairly rare; but may arise under 1961 Act. S.4., which authorises purchase of heritage for a beneficiary's residence — see Bristow Supra. Further, a pupil may, e.g. inherit heritage under the Will of a deceased testator. In all such cases, the pupil is represented by his tutor in the transaction and the consent of the tutor is essential; but title would be made up, in each such case, in name of the pupil child, and not in name of the tutor-at-law.

Minors. The position here is quite different. The minor does have power to act subject to:

(i) the consent of his curator if he has one; and

(ii) the possibility of reduction by the minor, in the *quadriennium utile,* of any transaction completed during his minority.

The father and mother jointly and the survivor are curators-at-law; with power to either of them to act independently or alone — The Guardianship Act, 1973. A *curator bonis* may be appointed by the Court and is answerable to the Accountant of Court. Apparently, although the curator has the powers of a trustee, and may consent, e.g. to a sale by the minor of his heritage, the curator's consent is not sufficient, of itself, to prevent subsequent reduction of the sale in the *quadriennium utile.* So, where property is purchased from a minor, even with the curator's consent, the purchaser's title is not unchallengeable; and the same applies where property is sold to a minor. Admittedly, in many cases, particularly where the curator consents, the risk of a successful challenge is exceedingly remote. Nonetheless, the risk is there. Thus, Burns states (Practice p.310) that no one should readily be recommended to deal with a minor, and cannot be compelled to do so. The 1961 Act S.2. does not protect a person transacting with a minor; and the risk still remains.

3. Judicial Factors.

A J.F. may be appointed by the Court in various circumstances to safeguard and administer an estate, both heritable and moveable.

The Decree or Act and Warrant appointing the J.F. operates as his title to the estate coming under his control but with this specialty that, if there is a known and living ward, e.g. a pupil, the Act and Warrant does not operate as a title to divest the pupil and invest the J.F. Instead, the title remains vested in the ward, but the J.F. has power to administer and deal with the asset in the ward's name.

As to powers, a J.F. is a Trustee for the purposes of the Trusts Acts; and the 1961 Act S.2 applies to protect a purchaser in dealings with a J.F. See above. But a J.F. acts under the supervision of the Court and the Accountant of Court must consent to the exercise of the statutory power e.g. of sale. Failing that consent, a purchaser is not protected under the 1961 Act S.2.

4. Corporations.

Every statutory and chartered Corporation enjoys powers conferred on it by the relevant Statute or Charter, and these should be consulted in all cases.

The commonest Corporation which you will deal with in practice is the Company incorporated under the Companies Acts. Every such Company must have a Memorandum and Articles of Association. In the objects clause of the Memorandum, the Company's powers and the limits of those powers are defined; and the Articles prescribe the mode in which those powers may be exercised. Thus, the Memorandum of every incorporated Company will, in practice, include a power to the Company to acquire and to dispose of property of all kinds, and to borrow on the security thereof. If the Memorandum does not contain such a power, then any such act of acquisition, disposal, etc., may be *ultra vires* of the Company, although with a trading company power to acquire and dispose at least of certain kinds of assets, and power to borrow, are **probably** implied. See General Auction Co. -v- Smith 1891 3 Ch. 432, an early English case confirming that a Company has an implied power to borrow.

The power to sell and purchase and to borrow are, in practice, always included in the Company's Memorandum. In contrast, the power of a Company to guarantee borrowing by some other person, and to grant security therefor, is often omitted from the Memorandum of the Company. This, in recent years, has created problems in the case of Groups of Companies where the parent company borrows for the benefit of the whole Group on the footing that the subsidiary companies will guarantee the parent company's borrowing and grant security therefor. Frequently, this involves an alteration to the Memorandum of the subsidiary company to incorporate that express power.

It may also be necessary to distinguish objects and powers in the Memorandum of Association of the Company. So, in re Introductions 1969 1 AER 887, a company had an express power to borrow in its Memorandum. To the knowledge of a loan creditor, money ostensibly validly borrowed under this power was used for a purpose which was patently *ultra vires* of the objects in the Company's Memorandum. **Held** that the creditor could not rely on debentures issued by the company which were intended to secure that borrowing.

If a Company purchases or sells property, heritable or moveable, without the requisite power in its Memorandum, then the transaction is invalid at Common Law and cannot be ratified. But, under the European Communities Act 1972 S.9. (now the Companies Act 1985 S.35), this *ultra vires* rule has been altered for the benefit of a third party entering into a contract with a Company in good faith; the Company is now deemed to have the appropriate objects clause in its Memorandum. Thus, where A purchases property from a Company, the

Company has **implied** power to sell, even although there is no express power in its Memorandum. But this only applies to the *bona fide* purchaser for value who is genuinely unaware of the absence of the requisite power in the Company's Memorandum. Thus, if A had **actual** knowledge that the Company had no power of sale in its Memorandum, he would not be acting in good faith, would not be protected, and the sale would be reducible. However, there is no obligation whatsoever on A to investigate the Company's Memorandum; and, by failing to investigate, he does **not** put himself in bad faith. In this instance, therefore, the third party purchaser or seller has no 'duty of enquiry'.

For a typical objects clause in a Memorandum of Association of a Company, see Palmer's Precedents p. 303:

'To purchase, take on lease or in exchange, hire or otherwise acquire, any real and personal property and any rights or privileges which the Company may think necessary or convenient for the purposes of its business.'

And at p. 310:

'To sell, lease, mortgage or otherwise dispose of the property, assets, or undertaking of the Company or any part thereof for such consideration as the Company may think fit.'

For the exercise of these powers, a typical clause in Articles of Association might read:

'The business of the Company shall be managed by the Directors who ... may exercise all such powers of the Company as are not, by the Act or by these regulations, required to be exercised by the Company in general meeting ...'

The power to borrow is often limited by the Articles to a stated maximum; but a *bona fide* lender whose loan exceeds the limit is protected by the 1972 Act S.9 (now the Companies Act 1985 S.35).

In the case of any Corporation, property is acquired, and the title taken, in name of the **Corporation**; and is held by the Corporation *socio nomine.* Of necessity, however, all contracts and deeds relating to the Company's assets must be entered into and granted by the Directors. The mode of execution of a deed by a Company (under seal and signed by Directors) has been dealt with.

Liquidation.

A Company may be wound up voluntarily, either in a members' or in a creditors' liquidation; or it may be wound up compulsorily by the Court. In all cases, a liquidator, or joint liquidators, is or are appointed. In contrast to the sequestration of an individual (see below), liquidation does not divest the Company of its assets; but an Order or Resolution for the winding up of the Company has the effect of suspending the powers of the Directors and, by Statute, the liquidator is invested with comparable powers. In particular, the liquidator may, without the sanction of the Court, sell both heritable and moveable property belonging to the Company by public roup or private bargain. A deed granted by a Company in liquidation runs in name of the Company, but the fact of liquidation is referred to; and the deed is executed by the liquidator in place of the Directors.

5. Sequestration.

Where an individual goes bankrupt and is sequestrated, a Trustee in sequestration is appointed by the Court. His position is analogous to that of a Judicial Factor.

But he is appointed under special procedure, and with special powers, under the Bankruptcy (Scotland) Act 1913. The following sections are relevant here:

s.70. The Order of the Court appointing the Trustee in sequestration is termed an Act and Warrant. Under this Section, the Act and Warrant is the Trustee's title to the whole estate of the bankrupt. Contrast the position here with liquidation. In a sequestration, the bankrupt is divested of his whole estate, heritable and moveable, which vests in the Trustee.

ss.97 to 102 define, in detail, the vesting of the estate in the trustee in sequestration; and different effects are prescribed in these sections, depending on the nature of the estate, thus:

s.97(1) deals with vesting of the moveable estate in the trustee; and puts the trustee in the same position as if the bankrupt's moveables had been made over to the trustee by the mode of transfer appropriate to moveables;

s.97(2) deals with vesting of heritable estate in Scotland in the trustee and describes the statutory effect of the act and warrant as a title to the bankrupt's heritage;

s.97(3) deals with vesting of real estate in England and elsewhere and makes similar provision for such estate as for heritable estate in Scotland;

s.97(4) deals with contingent rights and vests these in the trustee;

s.98 deals with the vesting in the trustee of assets later acquired by the bankrupt, e.g. when someone dies after the bankruptcy, leaving a Will under which the bankrupt inherits. That inheritance vests in the trustee under this section; but a further petition is necessary.

s.99 provides machinery for excluding from the sequestration assets wrongly included therein, e.g. where the bankrupt held an asset, ostensibly as his own but of which he was in fact a trustee. The trustee in sequestration may take possession of that asset; but has no title thereto, since trust assets do **not** pass to the trustee in sequestration. Under this section, the beneficiary could recover that asset from the trustee in sequestration;

ss.100 to 102 deal with certain technical aspects of vesting, in certain technical situations;

ss.103 to 107 define the effect of sequestration on proprietary rights generally and **ss.108 to 116** deal with the position of the trustee in sequestration *vis-a-vis* heritable creditors.

Parts of this statutory code, and in particular the sections defining the inter-relationship of the trustee in sequestration and of heritable creditors on heritable estate of the bankrupt, are applied to liquidations by the Companies Act 1985 S.623.

For a discussion on some of the problems which arise out of these vesting provisions in sequestrations, and related problems in liquidations, see Articles in the Reading List.

6. Partnerships.

In Scotland, a firm has a distinct legal *persona,* in contrast to an English firm which is simply a number of individuals trading together. But the legal status of a Scottish firm is **not** equivalent to a Corporation. A Scottish firm may own, hold and deal with moveable property in *socio nomine.* It may also be the beneficial owner of heritage, but it is impossible to take a title to land in name of a firm. Instead, title must be taken in name of trustees acting on behalf of the firm. The partners normally (but not necessarily) act as trustees. Prior to the Trusts (Scotland) Act 1961, this could cause problems in partnership titles; but, since that Act, a *bona fide* purchaser for value has no concern with beneficial ownership and can safely take a title from the trustees for a firm. Nonetheless, problems can still arise. In particular, if heritage was purchased many years ago by a firm and the title taken in name of the then partners as trustees, all the original partners may now be dead, with a resulting lapsed trust, which produces a technical difficulty in the title.

7. Unincorporated Associations.

Any Association which is not incorporated may beneficially own heritable property but cannot take the title in its own name. It must always act through the medium of trustees. Since 1961, this does not normally present any significant problem not already mentioned; but again lapsed trusts are not unusual.

In appropriate cases, the 1868 Act S.26 and/or the 1874 Act S.45 may be used when taking a title in name of trustees for the association to ensure continuity of infeftment.

1.5. Stamp Duties.
Reading List 1.5.

Stamp Duty is a form of Imperial Taxation. You will find in Wood's lectures, at p.103, a short account of the origins and development of this particular tax. All the older taxing provisions have been consolidated and re-enacted in two principal Acts, The Stamp Act of 1891, which imposes the duties, and The Stamp Duties Management Act 1891 which deals with administration. It is the former Act, as subsequently amended, with which we are chiefly concerned.

As in the case of an Imperial Taxation, the law relating to Stamp Duties is *positivi juris;* and the relevant Acts are always strictly construed in favour of the taxpayer. This principle has been frequently explained and applied in other spheres of taxation. So, in applying the Stamp Act (or amending Finance Acts), there can be no room for ideas of principle or equity. The Act may operate as a hardship in some cases and not in others; but that is irrelevant. The sole question is 'Does the strict wording of the Act impose a liability or not?'.

This leads to a further point. Stamp Duty is only payable when expressly imposed in terms of the relevant Act. Sometimes you will find that it is possible, by framing a document in **one** way, to avoid paying Stamp Duty which would be chargeable on that document were it framed in another way. Provided that the writ as framed achieves its purpose, and that there is no concealment or distortion of the facts, it is perfectly legitimate so to frame it that Stamp Duty is altogether avoided or perhaps is payable at a lesser rate. But, of course, there must never be any attempt to **evade** the tax by mis-statement.

The principal charging Act, The Stamp Act 1891, has been frequently and extensively altered by subsequent Finance Acts. It is divided into three parts.

Part I contains the charging section, which imposes the duty on certain specified documents arranged alphabetically in the First Schedule, and also contains some general regulations.

Part II amplifies the First Schedule.

Part III contains miscellaneous provisions.

Scope of the Act. The Act imposes duties on documents; no document, no duty. 'The thing which is made liable to duty is the instrument'.

Method of Payment. The duty is paid by way of impressed stamps, which involves the lodging of the document with the Revenue for stamping. The use of adhesive postage stamps for small fixed duties was abolished several years ago.

Time Limits. As a precaution against evasion, every document (if liable) must have the Stamp Duty impressed thereon within thirty days after execution. In practice, where there are several parties to a deed, the time limit runs from the date on which the last party signed.

Sanctions. To ensure that in every case the duty is paid when due, two separate sanctions are imposed:

i) that a document which is not duly stamped is not admissible as evidence in any civil action; and

ii) that any document not timeously stamped incurs a penalty **over and above** the duty due, when eventually presented. The **penalty** is normally £10, plus unpaid duty, with interest. But this **may** be remitted in whole or in part.

These two provisions are essentially complementary. The effect, with certain limited exceptions, is **not** to render an unstamped document invalid, because (with few exceptions) any document may be presented out of time for stamping. But if so, then the second **proviso** operates, and a penalty is payable in addition to the duty. The result is that, if you ever have to found on an unstamped document in any action, the Court will not reject it out of hand, but will insist that it be properly stamped, before considering its terms; and that of course means payment of duty, plus penalty.

Fines are imposed:—

i) For intent to defraud.

ii) On persons who execute or issue or negotiate unstamped documents.

iii) For refusal to stamp.

iv) On persons who give effect to unstamped documents, e.g. Registrars, official and private, bankers, etc.

It follows that a writ which is insufficiently stamped will not be accepted for registration, nor as a link in title by any agent. Nor will the Revenue, for Income Tax and other purposes, accept a writ as effective unless it is stamped. This, in practice, is sufficient to ensure, in a great number of cases, that stamping is timeously effected.

Basis of Assessment. Two methods are used to arrive at the actual duty payable on any particular document. The method to be adopted in any case may depend purely on the nature of the document, **or** on the nature of the document and the purpose for which (or the circumstances in which) it is intended to be used. The methods are either a fixed duty of a stated amount for the particular document regardless of the value of the property to which it relates; or *ad valorem* duty, calculated as a percentage on the amount involved. A Disposition (a Conveyance) may carry either fixed duty of 50p, or *ad valorem* duty calculated by reference to the price paid for, or the value of, the property conveyed; it will depend on circumstances which mode of fixing the duty applies.

To deal now with particular instances, being cases which you will meet commonly in practice.

1. Fixed duties.

The old fixed duties of 2d. and 6d. (pre-decimalisation) were abolished by FA.1970.

Many other fixed duties have been abolished by the Finance Act 1985.

The fixed duty of 50p applies in a variety of cases, e.g. a conveyance or transfer, other than those expressly charged with duty under the Act. A conveyance is usually charged *ad valorem.* The fixed duty applies to transfers vesting property in new Trustees, transfers of assets to residuary legatees under a Will and other like conveyances which are exempt from *ad valorem* duty.

2. Ad valorem duties.

Ad valorem duties are (as a general rule) fixed, not according to the **type** of document, but according to the nature of the transaction. And there are different **scales** of duty for different kinds of transaction. Thus the standard rate of *ad valorem* duty on sale and purchase is 1% (until recently 2%). The amount of duty depends on the amount involved in a particular transaction, **or** the value of the property dealt with.

(1) Conveyance on Sale.

This includes every instrument and every decree of Court whereby any property is, **on sale**, transferred to a purchaser. 'Property' includes not only land and heritable property generally but also any interest in land and all incorporeal moveable property and rights, e.g. stocks and shares, vested interests in trust estates, goodwill of a business, book debts, and incorporeal rights generally.

'Sale' necessarily involves some element of consideration, and it is on the value of the consideration on which (as a rule) the amount (and the rate — see later) of duty is based. In the ordinary case, where the consideration is a lump sum in cash, no difficulty arises. But consideration need not be in one single payment, nor need it be in cash.

So, property may be transferred in exchange for an allotment of shares; the consideration is then the actual value of the shares at that time.

Again, pre-1974, the consideration could be represented by annual or periodical payments. If the total period did not exceed 20 years, the consideration is the whole amount which is or may be payable during that period. Where it exceeded 20 years, it is the whole amount which will or may become due in the first 20 years. Thus, in the ordinary case of a Feu Charter before the 1974 Act, the consideration was normally an annual feuduty in perpetuity; so, 20 years' feuduty was taken as the consideration. Feuduty can no longer be charged post 1/9/1974, so this no longer applies to Scottish land titles. Where there is a lump sum payment, **plus** annual payments — as often happened — the two must be aggregated.

The deed on which the duty is charged is normally the conventional document whereby the actual transfer is effected, e.g., on sale of land, the Disposition; on sale of stock, the Transfer. But, in many cases, other documents are found liable under this head because they in fact effect a conveyance on sale, though not in conventional form. The emphasis is on the nature of the transaction, not on the nature of the deed.

Partnership Agreements and dissolution agreements, where one partner buys or sells a share in a business, often in fact operate as conveyances on sale, and are chargeable accordingly; but this does not apply in every case. Again, receipts may operate in the same way, e.g. a receipt for purchase price of goodwill, no document being **required** to vest the goodwill in the purchaser. A contract for sale of goodwill may also be so liable — see below. **But** if there is no written contract **and** no receipt, there is no duty payable.

Agreements for sale are normally charged as agreements and not as conveyances on sale, if by law some formal document must follow thereon to vest the property in the purchaser. So, in the simple case of the purchase of a house, missives of sale cannot give the purchaser a valid title — a Disposition is also required. The Missives are exempt from duty, and the Disposition attracts *ad valorem* conveyance on sale duty.

But if the agreement covers other property for which no vesting document is required, it may be liable to *ad valorem* duty *quoad* that other property. This is expressly provided, under Section 59 of the Stamp Act as amended, which renders such agreements liable in respect of any equitable estate or interest, or any interest in property except land; goods; stocks and shares; and ships. So, in the sale of a business, it may be necessary to allocate the price between the various items acquired, e.g. land, goodwill, stock-in-trade, etc., and to pay duty on the Missives in respect of certain of these items — e.g. goodwill, fixed plant and machinery (where not heritable, since heritable plant passes under the Disposition); benefit of contracts; book debts; cash on deposit (not cash in Bank, by concession, nor cash in hand); patents, etc.

Rate of duty.

The rate of duty in the original Stamp Act 1891 for all Conveyances on Sale was 10/- per £100 of consideration. There have been frequent alterations to the basic rate in subsequent Finance Acts. Although of no significance now from the point of view of stamping a deed, it is important to know the various rates of duty from time to time in force in the past when examining a heritable title, because one of the things you have to check is that each writ in the title is properly stamped.

When the rate of duty was first increased in 1910, there was a special exemption in respect of Conveyances (other than transfers of stock or marketable securities) where the consideration did not exceed £500; provided always that the Conveyance contained a clause certifying that the transaction thereby effected did not form part of a larger transaction or of a series of transactions in respect of which the total consideration exceeded £500. In such a case (i.e. under £500), the Stamp Duty remained at 10/- per £100; above that, and for transfers of stock, £1 per £100.

This system of exemptions has been repeated in subsequent Finance Acts. The current rate of duty and all earlier rates in force under previous Finance Acts are given in the Diploma Styles, together with the style of the Certificate of Value.

In all such cases, to qualify for the exemption or for the reduced rates from time to time in force, the deed must contain the Certificate of Value. If the Clause is not included, the full rate of duty is exigible, no matter how small the consideration. If omitted by mistake, the Revenue will accept an endorsed Certificate signed by the parties to the Deed.

The Clause certifies that 'the transaction hereby effected does not form part of a larger transaction or of a series of transactions in respect of which the amount or value or the aggregate amount or value of the consideration exceeds (a stated limit)'. This is designed to prevent evasion of duty by breaking down a single large transaction into a number or series of smaller transactions, e.g., on a purchase of heritable property for £60,000, 4 conveyances, each at a consideration of £15,000 would each be *prima facie* exempt. **But** in such a case, the Certificate could not truly be signed.

On the sale of a business, cash and stock-in-trade can be left out of account. FA 1958 S34(4).

What constitutes a larger transaction or a series of transactions, in terms of the Certificate? Clearly, any single sale at a single price constitutes a single transaction for the purpose of the Finance Acts; that single price cannot be broken down in order to benefit from a reduced rate. The same would apply to a single contract for the purchase of several heritable properties each at a separate stated price.

A series of transactions is more difficult to define. There is no Scottish authority but there is an English case, Cohen 1937, 1.K.B.478. The facts were that a purchaser acquired several separate lots of real estate at an auction; this was held not to constitute a larger transaction or a series of transactions under the Acts. The test seems to be whether the transactions in question were inter-related and inter-dependent; and, if not, the transaction qualifies for exemption.

Note, also, that the exemption and reduced rates do not apply to transfers of stocks and shares or other marketable securities. But **do** apply to other transfers and assignations, e.g. Partnership, reversions, etc.

Excambion

Where two properties are exchanged, whether by Contract or Excambion or by two separate conveyances, the stamp duty is 50p regardless of value. If one party makes an additional cash payment to the other to equalise the values, conveyance on sale duty applies only to the cash payment; and the exemptions and reliefs are available for that cash payment.

Charities

Conveyances or transfers to charities are now exempt from Stamp Duty under F.A.1982.

(2) **Mortgage Duty.** Abolished under FA 1971 from 1/8/71.

Duty was chargeable under this head in every transaction involving the **loan** of money, present or future, where there was some formal document containing an obligation on the part of the debtor to repay a capital sum.

(3) **Leases.**

There are special *ad valorem* scales of duty for leases, depending on the duration of the lease and the rent. Note that frequently an Agreement for lease, which effectively creates the relationship of landlord and tenant and is often not followed by a formal lease, is liable to duty on the appropriate Lease Scale. The Lease itself (**if** one follows) is exempt.

(4) **Certain other transactions** attract special scales of *ad valorem* duty, e.g. Company documents for Capital Duty.

Voluntary Dispositions.

There was no provision in the Stamp Act for *ad valorem* duty on gratuitous Dispositions and transfers of property by way of gift. But by Finance Act 1910 S.74, duty was imposed on any conveyance or transfer operating as a voluntary disposition *inter vivos,* as if it were a conveyance on sale, the value of the property conveyed being taken as 'consideration' in assessing the duty. In other words, a voluntary disposition became a hypothetical sale, and all the provisions as to duty on 'conveyance on sale' applied, including the recent amendments in the rates of duty referred to above, and the exemptions and reliefs on values under the relevant limits.

The scope of this provision extended not only to simple gifts *inter vivos,* but also to voluntary settlements, to the exercise of a power of appointment, to release of life interests, etc.

It also covered any conveyance (other than a conveyance to a purchaser or other person in good faith and for valuable consideration) where, in the opinion of the Revenue, the consideration was inadequate, and the conveyance conferred substantial benefit on the transferee. This prevented evasion of duty by spurious sales to donees at 'give away' prices.

The value of the property was the basis of the charge to duty.

Except in the case of marketable securities, the conveyance or transfer qualified for the exemption from duty and for the reduced rates of duty, provided the deed included the appropriate Certificate of value. The Finance Act 1910 S.74 is repealed and *ad valorem* duty is no longer payable on *inter vivos* gifts, under the Finance Act 1985, as from 26th March 1985.

3. Exemptions.

The Stamp Act 1891 (First Schedule — End) lists certain documents as wholly exempt from any Stamp Duty. The principal are: —

1. Transfers of Government Stock. This extends even to voluntary conveyances; and

2. Testamentary and *mortis causa* dispositions and settlements.

Finance Act 1949 created certain further exemptions.

Again, the various heads in the First Schedule to the Stamp Act confer specific exemptions in certain cases under that head, and this practice is followed in the various Finance Acts amending it or imposing new duties.

Certain special exemptions from existing duties have been introduced by Finance Acts to relieve inequities, e.g. Finance Act 1949 exempting certain documents from 6d. duty and FA.1970 abolishing certain duties, e.g. 2d., 6d. on Agreements, etc. FA.1971 also abolished several *ad valorem* duties; e.g. Bond or Covenant; Mortgage; etc.; and FA. 1985, which abolished several of the remaining fixed duties.

Finally, quite apart from the Stamp Act and Finance Acts, there are a large number of miscellaneous Acts which confer special exemptions from Stamp Duty in special cases.

Apart from these special exemptions, certain documents require no stamp duty because there is no head of duty to bring them into charge. Thus, Stock and Share Certificates are not liable, nor a simple IOU.

4. Miscellaneous and General.

Before leaving this subject, there are certain general and miscellaneous matters which I wish to touch on briefly.

Firstly, some general points as to assessment of duty in certain cases.

1. **Double operation of a Deed.** Where two separate and **unrelated** deeds or instruments are both embodied in a single document, two stamps are obviously required, and in any event this is covered by Stamp Act S.3, e.g. a disposition (conveyance on sale) with Minute of Consolidation (Deed) endorsed. Two stamps were required until 1985 when Deed duty of 50p was abolished.

Under S.4., if a **single** deed effects two or more principal (though related) purposes each of which would, independently, attract duty, it must be separately stamped for each separate matter, or purpose. So, until 25th March 1985, a Deed of Assumption and Conveyance appointing new Trustees was stamped £1, being 50p as an Appointment and 50p as a Conveyance. The 50p fixed duty on appointments was abolished by the Finance Act 1985. The fixed duty of 50p still applies to a conveyance. Accordingly, the duty on a Deed of Assumption and Conveyance is now 50p. But it has been observed judicially that 'all that is required is that the instrument should be stamped for its **principal** object, and that stamp covers everything accessory to this object'.

2. **Deed answering more than one description.** This applies in a variety of cases, e.g. an Assignation of a Bond may also be a voluntary Conveyance *inter vivos,*

and, if so, attracted conveyance on sale duty. This still applied post-1971 until 25.3.1985, when duty on voluntary dispositions was abolished, although the head of charge 'Mortgage Duty — Assignations' was abolished by FA 1971. In all such cases, the Revenue can claim duty under one head only, and as a rule will always claim the larger duty. But where a Deed is specifically chargeable under one specific head, that duty is exacted, though the Deed might be liable to greater duty under some more general head. So, until 25th March 1985, the duty on a Charter of Novodamus was always 25p under its specific head, though it is also a Deed (50p); and a Conveyance (50p). The first two fixed duties are now abolished. The Charter of Novodamus is now liable to 50p as a conveyance.

3. **One transaction effected by several Deeds.** It often happens that, for the completion of a **single** transaction, several Deeds are necessary. *Ad valorem* duty is paid on one Deed only; the others are stamped with fixed duty, usually 50p as a Deed, or Conveyance. But if the *ad valorem* duty is less than 50p (rare) all are stamped *ad valorem.*

Adjudication.

The Revenue, if required, will adjudicate the Stamp Duty on any document, and in certain cases adjudication is obligatory. If adjudicated and duly stamped, the document is impressed with a further stamp, in addition to the duty, called an Adjudication Stamp. That is then **conclusive** evidence that the proper duty has been paid. This has two distinct advantages in that (1) it settles the question of duty with the Revenue once and for all, and (2) any person to whom the deed is subsequently produced is bound to accept it as properly stamped.

There is a general obligation under the Stamp Act 1891 S.5. to set out all material facts relevant to stamping in the body of the deed, and where this is done, adjudication is normally unnecessary. But if the case is complicated, or if there is any doubt as to the head under which the deed is chargeable, then adjudication is appropriate. The normal method of initiating an appeal against an adjudged duty is by Stated Case in the Court of Session.

Despite the general obligation of disclosure, however, it is permissible to omit relevant facts provided there is no intent to defraud. But in that case, adjudication is almost always essential; and all the relevant facts must then be placed before the Revenue.

Adjudication was obligatory in the case of voluntary Conveyances (and in any event is essential for the assessment of value in most cases) and is still required in certain other special instances.

The deed is lodged for adjudication with an abstract or full copy within the time limit for stamping, together with such documents and information as may be relevant.

Denoting Stamps. There are two common examples.

(a) **Duplicate Denoting Stamp.** Where a deed is executed in duplicate, the principal is stamped with the appropriate duty.

If this is 50p or less the duplicate is also stamped with that duty and no Denoting Stamp is required — **each** deed being *ex facie* sufficiently stamped. Where the duty on the principal deed exceeds 50p, the duplicate **may** be stamped 50p, only; in addition, to show *ex facie* that it is sufficiently stamped, it is impressed with a Duplicate Denoting Stamp.

As from 1st August, 1976, the practice has been altered by omitting, from the counterpart deed, stamps showing the amount impressed on the original. Instead, the Duplicate Denoting Stamp will simply say:

'Duplicate or counterpart — original fully and properly stamped.'

(b) **Duty paid denoting stamp.** A Deed may, on the face of it, appear liable to a larger duty than that actually impressed, but in fact the principal duty has been stamped on some other deed, e.g. a **formal** Lease following an **Agreement** for Lease, the **latter** bearing the *ad valorem* duty; the Lease is exempt (formerly a fixed stamp of 6d. only) but, as *ex facie* evidence that this is sufficient, it is also impressed with this stamp to show the duty paid on the Agreement.

In neither case does the denoting stamp act as an adjudication stamp and is **not** conclusive evidence that the Stamp Duty impressed on the other document is in fact the correct duty.

2. **Creation of the new Feudal Estate.**

Reading List 2.1.

2.1. **Summary of Statutory Developments.**

(1) **Summary of position in 1844 — Charter and Sasine.**

First, to consider briefly the formalities involved in the creation of the real right in land as they had developed by 1844. The main features in this development, were:

1. The introduction of written title, called the Charter.

2. Improper investiture; and the giving of sasine through the hand of the bailie or agent.

3. The Instrument of Sasine, as a record both of the terms of the title and of the facts of symbolic delivery; and

4. The introduction of Registration for publication.

Thus, by 1844, the constitution of a real right by subinfeudation required:

1. Delivery of a **Charter** from the superior, embodying a **precept** of Sasine (or Mandate for infeftment), followed by **symbolic delivery** of the land itself, on the ground, out of the hands of the bailie into the hands of the new vassal (or his agent), all of which was recorded in the **Instrument of Sasine** prepared by the **Notary Public**; and

2. Recording of the **Instrument**, within sixty days. Under the Real Rights Act, 1693, the real right only emerged at the moment of such registration, and not before.

On registration, the Instrument of Sasine was minuted, engrossed in the Register, and returned to the presenter duly certified as registered.

(2) **Sasine and Infeftment after 1845.**

Between 1845 and 1868, an initial series of Conveyancing Statutes simplified and modernised the system of land tenure. These were consolidated in 1868. Further reforms were introduced in 1874 and 1924 but, by and large, the fundamental feudal principles of tenure remained unimpaired. The new simplified procedures and writs 'merely introduced shorthand means of expressing what was formerly stated at length, but made no difference in the import of the clauses or the true principles on which our feudal system is based'. 2.3.10 — Hay 1909 SC 554 — per Lord Dunedin.

Since 1964, however, we have been gradually moving away from the original Common Law forms and procedures, thus:

(i) The Succession (Scotland) Act, 1964, completely altered transmission of heritage on death.

(ii) The Reid Committee Report on Registration of Title to Land of 1963 (Cmnd.2032) followed by a further Report on Registration of Title by the Henry Committee in 1969 (Cmnd.4137) recommended, and made detailed provision for, legislation completely altering the old land registration system, now implemented by the 1979 Act.

(iii) The Halliday Committee Report on Conveyancing Legislation and Practice of 1968 (Cmnd. 3118), recommended a large number of reforms. The Report has, in part, been implemented by the Conveyancing and Feudal Reform (Scotland) Act 1970, which completely altered the law of Heritable Securities and made other major changes to the law of land tenure.

(iv) In a White Paper produced by the Labour Government in 1969 'Land Tenure in Scotland — a Plan for Reform' (Cmnd.4099), and in a Green Paper produced by the Conservative Government in 1972 'Land Tenure Reform in Scotland', further major reforms are discussed; and these were in part implemented by the Land Tenure Reform (Scotland) Act 1974, altering the law on subinfeudation and on feuduty.

As the Green Paper correctly points out, the principal remaining features of the feudal system in Scotland are the obligations placed on vassals:

(i) to pay an annual feuduty in perpetuity; and

(ii) to observe conditions and limitations on the use of land, which in many cases the superior alone has power to enforce.

After referring to the Reports above noted and to the 1970 Act, the Green Paper then explicitly reiterates the Government's expressed intention to 'carry out a major reform of the system of land tenure in Scotland and abolish feuduty'. The purpose of publishing the Green Paper was to outline the principal features of this proposed reform, and to throw up certain problems and questions for discussion before legislation was introduced.

The Conveyancing Acts.

The main purpose of the series of Conveyancing Acts, commencing with the Act of 1845 was simplification, in part by providing short clauses with a long statutory interpretation which would serve for practically all situations; and in part by eliminating unnecessary steps in the procedure. But all this was achieved within the framework of the Feudal System and the fundamental principles of Tenure remain unaltered. Cf. Green Paper. 'The Government considers that, in these circumstances, the major reform of Land Tenure ... must involve the abolition of feudal tenure. It is important, however, that this should be carried out in a way which is fair to superiors and vassals alike ... and that the good points of the present arrangements should be preserved so far as possible ...'

The Conveyancing Acts fall conveniently into two parts:

(1) The initial series. Between 1845 and 1868 there were a number of Statutes, each making further amendments to the system; all of which are now consolidated and re-enacted in an Act of 1868 called Titles to Land (Consolidation)(Scotland) Act 1868. Such consolidation, while convenient for the practitioner, is a little confusing for the student because it blurs the process of gradual statutory development;

(2) Since 1868, the Consolidation Act itself has been radically amended by a number of subsequent statutes, principally the Conveyancing (Scotland) Act 1874, 1924, and 1938; the Succession (Scotland) Act 1964; the Conveyancing and Feudal Reform (Scotland) Act 1970; the Land Tenure Reform (Scotland) Act 1974; and the Land Registration (Scotland) Act 1979. But there has been no subsequent consolidating Statute.

The main simplifications in the Acts 1845-1868 were:

i) Abolition of symbolic delivery on the ground.

ii) Direct recording of conveyances in the Register of Sasines in place of the recording of the Instrument of Sasine, which, as a result, disappears.

iii) The introduction of the Warrant of Registration.

iv) The reorganisation, in 1868, of the registration system by abolishing the old Particular Registers of Sasines maintained in each of the separate County Districts and by centralising all registration for publication in the General Register of Sasines in Edinburgh except the Burgh Registers. The General Register is now divided into County Divisions.

The Titles to Land (Consolidation) (Scotland) Act 1868 ('The 1868 Act').

This Act consolidates all the foregoing provisions and a number of other earlier ones as well. Originally, it formed a comprehensive statutory conveyancing code but was fairly quickly amended and has now been largely superseded by later legislation.

It suffices to mention at this stage the following Sections of this Act:

i) S.5. and 8 with Schedule B, which authorised short clauses for conveyances.

ii) S.141 to 143 which deal with direct recording of conveyances and the Warrant of Registration.

iii) Note, particularly, a provision in S.15 to the effect that a conveyance, when recorded, has the same legal effect **as if** a conveyance in the old form had been followed by the recording of an Instrument of Sasine. This is termed 'the system of equivalents', often adopted in this and other Conveyancing Statutes. The general effect is that a new or shorthand method or formula introduced in a later Act is equated to the position under the earlier rules.

Specific Reforms.

The later Conveyancing Acts made various changes on particular matters affecting subinfeudation which I now want to deal with under subject headings. These matters include:

1. **Burgage.** Burgage was originally a distinct and separate tenure within the feudal system applicable to lands within the Royal Burghs, and was always separately treated in the Conveyancing Acts. Thus, Burgh Registers were introduced separately for Burgage under an Act of 1681; and the 1868 Act makes separate provision for burgage and non-burgage property.

Since 1874, however, burgage has been assimilated with feu farm tenure by:

(1) **1874 Act S.25** which provides for the abolition of the distinction between burgage and feu farm; and

(2) **The Burgh Registers (Scotland) Act 1926,** under which, by a gradual process, Burgh Registers have all been absorbed into the Register of Sasines. The last such separate Register closed in 1963.

2. **Subinfeudation.** Subinfeudation was often expressly prohibited in a Feu Charter and any such prohibition was binding on the vassal. But such prohibitions can no longer be enforced; and can therefore be ignored in any title. 1938 Act S.8.

3. **Casualties.** Casualties were due *ex lege,* the actual casualties exigible depending on the nature of the tenure. But the nature of the casualty might be (and often was) varied by the express terms of a Feu Charter. This was known as taxing the casualty. The point of taxing casualties was to substitute casualties definite in amount, or in point of time (or both), in place of the indefinite casualties due *ex lege.*

All casualties, *ex lege* and taxed, have ceased to be exigible as a result of:

(1) **The 1874 Act SS.4, 15, 16, 18, and 23;** and

(2) **Feudal Casualties (Scotland) Act 1914.**

From a practical point of view, the result is that in examining a title, you can altogether ignore the question of casualties, except in so far as the parties have agreed to commute the casualty by payment of additional feuduty, in which case there had to be an Agreement setting out the amount of the additional feuduty payable, recorded in the General Register of Sasines under the Acts above cited.

4. **Reddendo.** The reddendo to be rendered by a vassal to his superior might take various forms, including military services, watching and warding, hunting and hosting, agricultural non-military services, known as carriages and services, and feuduty which might be payable in cash or in kind. All services have disappeared and all feuduties are now expressed in money sterling under:

1. The 1874 Act SS.20 and 21;

2. The Feudal Casualties (Scotland) Act 1914. S.18;

3. The 1924 Act S.l2.

Until 1974, it was still competent to provide for a permanent increase or permanent reduction in the amount of feuduty payable, such increase or reduction to take effect on a definite date or on the happening of a definite event. Any such provision in a pre-1974 Deed is still effective.

Finally, the 1974 Act provides:

S.1.(1) No deed executed after 1.9.74 shall impose any feuduty. But a deed so executed which contains a grant on tenure remains effective. So feuduty goes, but tenure remains **meantime.** A later Act has been promised totally abolishing tenure.

S.1.(2) If a deed so executed **does** impose feuduty, that does not invalidate the deed; but the feuduty clause is unenforceable.

S.21. There is no contracting-out of these provisions.

S.2. Makes a similar prohibition on other perpetual outgoings, e.g. ground annual, in respect of tenure or use of land, **excluding** rent and repairs provisions.

Further, under SS.4-6; feuduties generally other than unallocated feuduties are redeemable, voluntarily or on sale or compulsory purchase; and this applies to other like annual payments. For details, see Chapter 3 — Superiorities.

5. **Warrants of Registration.** The 1924 Act made some technical changes in the form of Warrant, simplifying the provisions of the 1868 Act. There is no change in principle.

Summary of Position at the present day.

What we have so far done is to consider the historical origins and Common Law development, and later the Statutory development, in the process of subinfeudation as a method of perfecting a real right in land. The position as we now find it to-day, resulting from the developments above referred to is:

(1) Agreement by the parties which is incorporated in the formal vesting document, viz., the Feu Charter. The form of this we will consider shortly but note at this stage that no precept or mandate for infeftment is now required.

(2) The Charter is duly (i) **executed,** (ii) **delivered** to the vassal, (iii) **stamped** with the Inland Revenue stamp.

(3) **The Warrant of Registration** in the modern form is then endorsed in name of the vassal, and is signed by him or his Agent.

(4) The Charter, duly stamped, is then presented at the Register House in Edinburgh either:

(a) with Warrant of Registration endorsed thereon, for recording in the appropriate Division of the General Register of Sasines; or

(b) with a Land Registration Application Form 1, for registration of the title in the Land Register, if the land lies in an "operational area" — see Chapter 8.2.

No further procedure is required. Assuming that the Charter itself is intrinsically valid, then registration of the Charter in name of the vassal **completes the infeftment** of the vassal and **perfects his real right.**

As a result, infeftment and sasine have lost their old meaning. An infeft proprietor now means a proprietor who has perfected his real right in the subjects by the recording in the Register of Sasines of an appropriate written title. Nonetheless, by this Charter, the vassal obtains his grant of land and establishes his right on **tenure**, to which the basic feudal rules still apply. He is the vassal holding of and under the grantor, his superior, for payment of a reddendo or return (pre 1.9.74) and subject to the conditions in the Charter — the 'incidents of tenure'.

Registration of Title.

Logically, it would obviously have been better to reorganise the Land Registers as part and parcel of a major Land Tenure Reform. Originally, it was proposed first to complete the Tenure Reform and thereafter to introduce the new system of Registration of Title. But Land Tenure Reform is a controversial matter and will take a considerable time to work out and agree. Registration of Title, on the other hand, is not controversial and a scheme was already worked out for this in detail in the Henry Committee Report. In the result, Registration of Title has been introduced, before the major final reforms to Land Tenure, by The Land Registration (Scotland) Act 1979. In outline only at this stage, the new Registration of Title system involves the guaranteeing of each individual property title by the State on the same general lines as the English system of Registration of Title. In contrast, under the present system of registration, deeds are recorded in Sasines; but the Keeper accepts no responsibility whatsoever for the accuracy or validity thereof.

To convert the existing registration system from Registration for Publication to Registration of Title will not be completed before 1990. The present proposal is to apply registration gradually across the country district by district over a period of years, as in England. The County of Angus is not scheduled to convert to a Registration of Title system until about 1987.

Once a County or District has been declared a Registration of Title district, each property is converted from Registration for Publication to Registration of Title only on sale; so that, inevitably, within each district, properties only gradually convert to Registration of Title.

In the result, although we now have a Registration of Title Act on the Statute Book, it may be 20 or 30 years before 90% of the properties in Scotland have been converted from the present registration system.

The final stage in the Reform of Land Tenure is apparently still under active consideration; or at least it was so by the previous government. But the ultimate form of the revised tenure is still undetermined. Several of the more important points have already been legislated for piecemeal in the 1970 Act and the 1974 Act. Future progress inevitably depends on parliamentary time available.

2.2 **The Feu Charter.**

Reading List 2.2.

Form.

A Feu Charter, in its standard form, is unilateral. It runs in name of and is executed by the superior alone. It contains in essence:

the identification of the parties;

the consideration;

the identification of the subjects in the hands of the vassal;

the tenure; and

some subordinate matter such as (either by express provision or since the 1979 Act by implication) the right to Title Deeds, etc., rents, relief and warranties as to title. It may be sub-divided, into:

 (i) The narrative, or inductive, clause or clauses;

(ii) The operative clauses, which may again be sub-divided into the dispositive clause, which rules, and subordinate clauses, conferring rights ancillary to the main or dispositive clause; and

(iii) The testing clause.

Content.

Taking these various elements in the Charter in more detail:

1. **Narrative Clause.** The standard content of the narrative clause is:

(i) **Granter.** The name and designation of the granter will be given followed by a description of his status, normally 'heritable proprietor of the subjects and others hereinafter disponed' which implies that the granter is beneficial owner and infeft. There are a number of variants to meet special cases.

If the Feu Charter is to be effective as a title to the vassal, then the granter of the Feu Charter (the superior) must have title and capacity to grant it.

(a) **Title.** It is not necessary that he is the beneficial owner; he may, for example, hold the property as Trustee or in some other representative capacity. If so, it **may** be relevant to consider his powers (e.g. if he is a Trustee). **But** he must have the **legal** title, to enable him effectively to convey; and, whatever his capacity, he must be infeft.

If a proprietor, uninfeft, grants a Feu Charter to a vassal who then records it, the result is that the vassal, although having a title on the Record, does **not** have the real right. He does have a valid personal title enforceable against the superior who granted the Charter; and with this advantage that, if the superior later completes title in his own person by whatever means and so obtains an infeftment in the subjects feued by the Charter, this has the effect of validating the vassal's title by the principle of **accretion**. On this principle, the vassal's title is validated retrospectively and, further, in a competition with other competing claimants to the same property it takes preference at the date of the vassal's infeftment, not at the date of the superior's later infeftment.

(b) **Capacity.** Mere title and infeftment are not enough, standing alone. The granter of the Charter must also be capax. See Chap 1.4.

(ii) **Consentors.** In addition, for various reasons, it may be appropriate, although not very usual, for a party or parties to consent to the Charter in which case they are also named and designed in the narrative clause and the reason for their consent is there stated. Consents in other writs (e.g. Dispositions) are common.

(iii) **Consideration.** It is usual but not essential (cf. English Law) for a Conveyance to set out explicitly the consideration. In the case of a Feu Charter executed on or before lst September, 1974, the consideration was normally feuduty ('and other prestations afterwritten' which includes e.g. implement of various obligations by the vassal). The feuduty had to be in Sterling money, but it might be of any amount, with a provision for a permanent increase or decrease. There might be, in addition, a grassum or lump sum payment. No feuduty may now be created — 1974 Act S.1 if the Charter was executed after 1st September, 1974 (subject to limited transitional provisions).

2. Operative Clauses. These include:

The Dispositive Clause. This is the main or ruling clause in the Conveyance. The remaining operative clauses are subordinate to it. Its essential elements are:

(a) **Words of Conveyance.** The Charter replaces actings on the ground by way of symbolic delivery. To be effective, every conveyance, including Feu Charters and Dispositions, must contain clear words expressing an immediate present transfer (or **conveyance**) of the right to the disponee. Thus, a mere agreement to convey was not (and is not) a valid title to heritage. It merely creates a personal obligation on one contracting party to convey property to the other contracting party; but the word 'dispone' has ceased to be a *verbum solemne* — 1874 Act S.27.

(b) **Identity of grantee and the destination.**

Capacity. Subject in certain cases to the consent of some other person (e.g. tutors for pupils), there is now no legal bar arising out of nationality, domicile, residence, age, sex or capacity to prevent or disable anyone from owning heritage in Scotland. This includes both natural and legal persons; but partnerships and other unincorporated associations are excluded from this general rule. They cannot sustain the feudal relationship, and may hold heritage only through the medium of trustees.

Plural disponees. In Scotland, heritage may competently be conveyed to, and held by, several persons. There is no legal limit on the total number. If there are two or more co-proprietors, then they hold either as joint proprietors or as proprietors in common. The distinction between these two types of ownership may be explicitly set out in the Charter e.g. to A and B equally as *pro indiviso* proprietors each of a one-half *pro indiviso* share. This clearly indicates a right of common property by express provision. Each of A and B have an absolute right of ownership in one half undivided share of the property. But the same result may be **implied** from the relationship of the co-proprietors *inter se,* whether that relationship is disclosed on the face of the Conveyance or not. But some care must be taken in construing the terms used which tend to be ambiguous and have different meanings in different contexts.

Joint Property. Joint property vests as a single undivided unit in two (or more) persons, no one of whom has any absolute beneficial or exclusive right to an aliquot or severable share of the subjects. Instead, each has a joint right in the whole subjects along with all his co-proprietors 'not merely *pro indiviso* in respect of possession but *pro indiviso* in respect of the **right**'. Lord Moncreiff 4.I.24 — Grant -v- Heriot's Trustees 8 F.647. Joint property is appropriate in the case of trustees or other persons holding in a fiduciary or representative capacity. But the right also occurs in cases where the several proprietors are united by some contractual or **quasi**-contractual bond, e.g. partnership, where the **firm** is the beneficial owner. It is not normally appropriate to several co-owners, each having an absolute beneficial right in his own person; although in 4.1.22 Munro 1972 S.L.T. (Sh.Ct.) 6 by virtue of special clauses in a disposition, three beneficial owners were held to be joint proprietors. But this decision has rightly been criticised — see 1985 SLT (News) 57.

One of several joint proprietors cannot separately dispose of his joint interest in the property to a third party; and, on his death, his right and interest in the joint property automatically accresces to the survivor(s). No deed or other procedure is required to vest the joint property exclusively in the survivor(s).

Common Property. Here, each of the several proprietors has an absolute, unrestricted beneficial right to a fractional or aliquot share of the whole property so long as it remains undivided. The relative size of his share (i.e. the amount of the fraction) may be stated expressly in terms of the titles; the shares of owners in common are not necessarily equal; but, failing any express statement in the title, the implication is that all co-proprietors own equal *pro indiviso* shares. One of several co-proprietors, owning a *pro indiviso* share, may dispose of that *pro indiviso* share without consulting his co-owners or may burden it with debt; and on his death, the *pro indiviso* share passes to his representativess and does not, in any circumstances, **by implication** accresce to the remaining co-proprietors.

A right of common property may arise simply because several separate persons come to be interested in the same undivided property, as beneficial owners, whether by joint purchase, succession or otherwise. It also often arises in special cases, e.g. tenements.

Common Interest

In certain special situations, separate proprietors of separate tenements (cf. *pro indiviso* proprietors), though owning separate properties, are nonetheless united by a common interest which entitles each of these several proprietors to object to **certain** acts by any other proprietor which may interfere with the comfortable enjoyment of his property.

This body of rules is known generally as the law of Common Interest. The significant difference between the restrictions arising out of property owned in common, and arising out of common interest, is that, in the first case, the individual has, at most, a right to a share only, and not the whole, of a particular property; whereas, with common interest, each individual owns the full and exclusive right of property in his own land, subject only to special restrictions for the benefit of his neighbours. These restrictions need not appear in his title, but are implied by law.

Destinations. There are 2 forms:

(i) **A general destination.** In this case, the property is conveyed, simply, to the named vassal and 'to his heirs and assignees whomsoever'. In view of later developments, the general destination to 'heirs and assignees whomsoever' is now commonly expressed as 'successors and assignees' or 'executors and assignees'. Whatever form of words is used, it now adds nothing, and, if omitted, would have no adverse effect. In fact, it is normally included in any conveyance or other common law deed; but cf. the statutory form of Standard Security.

'I grant a standard security in favour of the said C.D.'. There is **no** destination; and under the 1970 Act S.11(1), a Standard Security operates to vest the interest in the grantee. There is **no** reference to heirs or successors, since that is inevitably implied.

(ii) **The special destination.** This was a device, of ancient origin, frequently adopted to circumvent limitations on the free power of *mortis causa* disposal. Typically, and in its simplest form, the feu was disponed on a special destination 'to A (designed) whom failing' (or 'on his death') 'to B (designed)'; or, commonly, 'to A and B (both designed) and to the survivor of them and to the heirs and assignees whomsoever of the survivor'. In considering the rights of the parties to a destination (e.g. in the illustrations A and/or B) a number of technical and complex rules may have to be taken into account.

For some problems which the special destination creates, see Chap 7.3.

All valid reasons for resorting to the special destination in a conveyance of land disappeared under the 1868 Act S.20; but the device still continues to be used as **one** method of controlling the devolution of a heritable property on the death of the proprietor for the time being. A much commoner method (and a preferable one) is to arrange for the devolution of the property through a Will or other general *mortis causa* deed; and the use of special destination is now generally discouraged. See 7.3.10 — Lord President Cooper in Hay's Trustee -v- Hay's Trustees 195I SC 329.

Finally, the feu is disponed 'heritably and irredeemably', which establishes:

(a) that the vassal's right is inheritable (i.e. transmissible *mortis causa*) as of right in perpetuity. But this has always been so in Scotland; and

(b) that the vassal's right is an absolute and irredeemable one. Cf. Heritable Securities where the debtor as proprietor, having pledged his land in security by conveyance to the creditor, may nonetheless **redeem** his land on payment of the secured debt.

Both elements are implied, if not express, and the phrase, though invariably included in any conveyance, is strictly redundant.

To illustrate these various points by a practical example, a typical narrative clause in a Feu Charter may read:

''I AB (design) heritable proprietor of the subjects and others hereinafter disponed (who and my successors as proprietors of the *dominium directum* of the said subjects are hereinafter referred to as ''the Superiors'') in consideration of the sum of £   paid to me by CD (design) and of other feudal prestations hereinafter contained have sold and do hereby, at the request and with the consent and concurrence of the said CD as is testified by his signature hereto, in feu farm dispone to and in favour of the said CD and his wife Mrs. XY or D residing with the said CD and the survivor of them and the successors and assignees whomsoever of the survivor heritably and irredeemably ALL and WHOLE ...''

The description, reservations (if any), burdens and subordinate clauses then follow — for the content of these clauses see the remainder of this Chapter.

2.3. Descriptions.

Reading List 2.3.

A Conveyance of land, to be valid, must properly and distinctively identify the subjects conveyed. This applies alike to Charters and to any other special conveyance, including the disposition. Complete lack of identification completely invalidates the Conveyance; this occasionally occurs, for technical reasons, in a blundered description by reference.

The part of the dispositive clause which so identifies the subjects conveyed is termed the **description**. There are two aspects to descriptions:

(i) Given that a heritable property is to be conveyed, how do you set about identifying it in the Charter?

(ii) Assuming that land has been conveyed in a Charter containing a description, what is carried to the vassal under that description?

The vast majority of titles in Scotland deal primarily with land as the subject of the Conveyance, other rights being carried to the grantee as incidental thereto. But this is not necessarily so in every case, since a variety of incorporeal heritable rights are capable of separate infeftment. Such rights include, generally, all the *regalia minora,* teinds, and certain other rights. By contrast, certain rights associated with heritable property can never be severed from land and can never be held separately on a separate infeftment. Contrast salmon fishings which can be separately held on a separate title, and trout fishings which cannot be so held.

Further, land or buildings may be divided both in the vertical and in the horizontal planes. Therefore, any given surface area of land can be sub-divided into **any** number of smaller separate surface areas, each held on a separate title; and in the horizontal plane, land can be divided into layers or strata, each layer or stratum being held on a separate title by separate infeftment. The same applies to buildings, both vertical and horizontal division being permitted within a building. But there are practical limits. So, the Keeper using his common law discretion refused to record souvenir plot titles, on the footing, *inter alia,* that each plot was not 'separately identifiable by description or plan'. (Keeper's Report 1969); and, for registration of title, this is now statutory by the 1979 Act S.4 (2)(b).

Whatever the nature of the property (or right) to be conveyed, the general rule in all cases is that, in a Conveyance, any words which are sufficient to identify the subject matter of the Conveyance are in themselves an adequate description. There are no *verba solemnia,* there are no Statutory formulae for an identifying description and no hard and fast rules at Common Law. But that general principle falls to be applied in accordance with the following general rules:

(i) **The Extent of the Grant.** Land is described in a Conveyance in terms of two dimensions only i.e. in the horizontal plane, by reference to surface features only; it is nonetheless normally implied that this carries to the disponee everything *a coelo ad centrum* i.e., all sub-adjacent minerals and sub-strata to the centre of the earth and everything above the surface, including air space indefinitely upwards.

(ii) **Separate Tenements.** As explained, land and buildings can be divided vertically and horizontally, the resulting divisions each being capable of separate infeftment and known as separate tenements. **Some**, but not **all**, heritable rights are also capable of separate infeftment as separate tenements, e.g. salmon fishings. The rule is that each separate tenement must be separately and specifically described (or properly referred to) in a Conveyance. Otherwise, it will not pass to a disponee.

Thus, a Conveyance of **land**, described as such, will **not** carry automatically to the disponee the right of salmon fishings — see 2.3.12 — McKendrick -v- Wilson 1970 S.L.T. (Sh.Ct.) 39. A farm was conveyed 'with parts and pertinents', but no reference was made to salmon fishings to which the disponee laid claim. **Held** that, as the title did not **expressly** include salmon fishings, the action by the disponee must be dismissed.

As a result of this rule, a separate lease of salmon fishings has always been regarded as competent and as binding a singular successor of the landlord. On the other hand, a lease of trout fishings has always been regarded as purely a personal contract, not running with the land. This rule is altered, but only *quoad* Leases, by the Freshwater and Salmon Fisheries (Scotland) Act 1976 S.4, in terms of which a lease of freshwater fish (i.e. trout) in inland waters for more than one year will bind a singular successor of the landlord and thus, for this limited purpose, is created a *quasi* separate tenement.

So also with discontiguous areas of ground. Suppose A owns a plot of ground with a house on it. He also owns an allotment, 50 yards away on the other side of the public road. These are separate tenements. A conveyance which describes the house and garden would not normally carry the allotment as well; special reference to the allotment is required. Similarly, a Conveyance of land **will** automatically carry to the disponee all sub-adjacent minerals, unless and until the minerals are severed from the surface and held on a separate title. Thereafter, the minerals having become a separate tenement, they must be separately conveyed.

(iii) **Fixtures.** Corporeal things are heritable or moveable according to their physical state. The general rule is that, when moveable things are affixed to land, they lose their moveable character and become heritable by accession. This is summed up in the Latin brocard, *inaedificatum aut plantatum solo, solo cedit.* When moveables have become heritable in this way by physical annexation, then on a conveyance of land, described as such, fixtures pass to the disponee without express reference thereto. Thus a Conveyance of land automatically carries to the disponee all buildings thereon, all fixtures within the buildings, growing timber and the like. In practice this is an area, both on contracts and on subsequent conveyances, where disputes frequently arise; and the question of fixtures should always be carefully considered.

(iv) **Implied or Inherent Rights.** A Conveyance of land, described as such, automatically carries to the disponee certain natural and ancillary rights. It is, therefore, unnecessary in any description of land expressly to define, describe or refer to rights in this category. This class of right includes, **typically, but not exhaustively:**

(a) **Exclusive Possession.** This entitles the disponee to prevent trespass or encroachment by the superior or third parties within his boundaries.

(b) **Unrestricted User.** In practice, the theoretical unrestricted right of user is now severely limited by a variety of statutory provisions of general application, and by conventional provisions in particular cases.

(c) **Support.** The disponee is entitled to require his neighbours, laterally and vertically, to support his land, unless that right is expressly varied in the titles.

(d) **Access.** A Conveyance of land carries, by implication if not expressly, the right of access to the disponee.

Certain of these rights may be varied or negatived by the express terms of the Conveyance. But in the absence of any express provisions, they pass automatically on a conveyance of the land.

(v) Special Cases.

(a) **Tenements.** The ownership of heritable property in Scotland, including buildings, may be split laterally in strata and vertically within a single building. This longstanding rule has tended to encourage, in Scotland, the development of flatted tenements within Burghs in which several flats on several floors are owned outright (not merely tenanted) by several independent heritable proprietors. Clearly, this is a situation in which each owner is peculiarly vulnerable to prejudice from the actings of his neighbour.

Very often (but not by any means universally, especially in older titles,) the rights and obligations of the owners of individual flats in a tenement are regulated, *inter se,* in great detail in their respective titles. But, where no provision is so made (or where the provision so made is not exhaustive) then (or to that extent at any rate), the law in Scotland **implies** certain rights and obligations, based on common interest and in this context known as the law of the tenement. Very briefly, and in outline, the rules are:

1. Each flat-owner has an exclusive right of property in the air space within his flat; and may use it as he pleases, subject to the common interest of other owners in the tenement.

2. The owner of a ground-floor flat has an exclusive right of property in the *solum* of the tenement, below his flat, and in the front area and the back ground *ex adverso* thereof; but subject to the common interest of other proprietors which allows any one of them to prevent the use of the *solum* or front and back ground in a manner injurious to the amenity of the objector's property, e.g. building thereon in such a way as to exclude light.

3. In each individual flat, each proprietor owns the enclosing walls, except where these separate him from an adjoining property in which case they are mutual. This applies both to gables and to internal division walls. But each such proprietor must **uphold** his main walls in order to afford support to proprietors above him. Note particularly the **positive** obligation to maintain. In the case of common gables, there are cross rights of common interest between the whole proprietors of all houses in each tenement on either side of the gable, to prevent interference with the gable so as to render the building unstable.

4. As between upper and lower flat, the floor/ceiling are notionally divided along an imaginary line drawn along the centre of the joists. But again, neither party may interfere with or weaken the joists to the detriment of the other.

5. The roof and the space between the ceiling and the roof beams belongs to the top floor proprietor (or **severally** to two or more top floor proprietors); but again, they are bound to maintain the roof (so far as it covers their individual houses) in order to afford protection to the floors below them. This is the most serious burden, as a rule, short of demolition.

6. The common passage and stair in the tenement, the *solum* of such passage, etc., and the enclosing walls thereof, are **common property** vested in the whole proprietors of the several flats in the tenement served by that passage and stair (but no others) as *pro indiviso* owners.

119

7. The cost of repairs to **common parts,** the cost of demolition of the whole tenement and the cost of rebuilding will be divided equally amongst all proprietors. Any one proprietor may insist that the others conjoin with him in rebuilding a destroyed or demolished tenement. In such rebuilding, the rights originally enjoyed must be preserved.

Note particularly a very important difference in effect between a right of common property in e.g. a main wall (either by the law of the tenement where the common wall is mutual or by express provision in the titles) where no operation can be carried out without the consent of all proprietors; and a main wall owned by a particular flat owner, and **not** owned in common, where any operations may be carried out on that main wall (e.g. converting it into a shop front) **provided** other proprietors are not endangered by these operations. The law of the tenement does not impose absolute liability. Proof of negligence, in commission or omission, is required.

In practice, in modern titles, the law of the tenement is substantially excluded by express provision in the title to each separate flat, as follows:

The conveyance to the disponee includes a right, in common with the other proprietors:—

i) to the *solum* on which the tenement is erected, the front ground and back green, and boundary walls thereof, the roof, main walls and gables, rhones, and down pipes, and all pipes, drains and cables serving the tenement in common.

ii) of access for repairs.

It then imposes on each proprietor a real burden for payment of:—

i) a share (equal, by feuduty or by rateable value) of repairs to all items held in common.

ii) a share of the feuduty, unallocated.

and it will usually contain:

i) a declaration that a majority of proprietors (how determined?) may carry out repairs, often through a common factor.

ii) a declaration that the back green, washhouse, etc., shall be used, in common, only for washing and drying clothes and for no other purpose.

For a typical style, see Burns Practice p. 351.

(b) Water Rights.

(i) Surface Water.

Surface water, and water percolating underground, which, in each case, is not confined in a definite bed or channel, may be appropriated by the owner of the land. This rule operates even if, by such appropriation, the owner interferes with the legitimate enjoyment of his neighbours, so there is no Common Interest in this case. Further, each neighbouring proprietor is bound to accept the natural flow of water from an adjoining property in its natural state; and the neighbour cannot complain if the natural flow is artificially interrupted by some other proprietor on whose land the water falls or flows.

(ii) Rights in rivers and streams.

a) **Tidal and navigable rivers.** The *alveus* or bed of all tidal water is vested in the Crown as is the foreshore, subject always to the public rights of navigation and fishing.

b) **Non-tidal, navigable water.** Here, in contrast, the *alveus* and banks belong to the riparian proprietors but again subject to the public right of navigation. The individual proprietor cannot use the *alveus* in such a way as to interfere with that right.

(c) **Non-navigable streams and rivers.** In this case, if the land extends across both banks, so that the stream runs through the land conveyed, the whole *alveus* or *solum* of the river vests automatically in the disponee. If the stream forms a boundary, there is a presumption that the *alveus* or *solum* vests in the disponee, but to the *medium filum* only.

But, despite this several right of ownership in the *alveus,* all proprietors of land through (or along) which the stream flows, from its source to its mouth, are united together in a common interest, to preserve their individual rights in the flow of water in its usual channel, undiminished in quantity and without any deterioration in its quality. Any one riparian proprietor may object if any of these rights is imperilled through the operation of any other riparian proprietor; but he must show actual or probable interference with his rights, arising from some such operation. If his rights are not interfered with in any way, then he has no cause to object. Subject to that common interest, each individual riparian proprietor is entitled as of right, and without express provision in his title, to appropriate the water in the stream (a) for primary purposes, i.e. for domestic use and for animals; and (b) for secondary uses, but only if he does not interfere with the enjoyment of others.

Every riparian proprietor enjoys an absolute right to fish, as a natural incident of ownership, for any fish except salmon. Salmon fishings are a separate heritable right and require a separate conveyance. But the **methods** of fishing are controlled by Statute, under the Trout Acts 1902 and 1933 and the Salmon, etc., Acts 1828 to 1976. The right to fish for trout, etc. ('white fish') may vest in one riparian proprietor to the exclusion of the other but, it would seem, cannot vest, as a separate and independent heritable right, in someone who is not the owner of land adjacent to the stream (or loch).

d) **Lochs.** The same general principles apply to lochs as apply to non-navigable rivers.

Recent provisions have been made, under the Freshwater and Salmon Fisheries (Scotland) Act, 1976, for the preservation of fresh water and salmon fisheries in Scotland by means of Protection Orders to be made by the Secretary of State if he is satisfied that this will increase the availability of fishing in inland waters, and provision is made for policing by wardens, etc., with fines for contravention.

Game.

Game, like fish, are *ferae naturae,* and, therefore, *res nullius.* The term 'game' includes a variety of animals, variously defined in various Statutes. Nonetheless, mere ownership of land carries with it by implication the right to take or kill all kinds of game on that land as a natural incident of the right of property. It is a right personal to the landowner, as landowner, and not inherent in or necessarily associated with the use or occupancy of land. Therefore, where land is let to an agricultural tenant or for other purposes, there is no implication that the tenant has the right to take or kill game.

Under the Ground Game Act of 1880, an agricultural tenant now has, by Statute, the right to kill rabbits and hares on the subjects of lease; and there is no contracting out of the provisions of this Act.

The right to take game may be the subject matter of a valid lease; and, possibly, particularly where the lease is a lease of land with right to shoot thereover, it may come within the provisions of the Leases Act 1449 and so transmit against a singular successor. But it would seem technically impossible to constitute a right of shooting over land as a separate and independent heritable right or as a burden on land.

Infeftment. In the ordinary way, a Feu Charter or other special conveyance operates of itself as a mandate for infeftment by *de plano* recording. This is only so if the Conveyance contains a description 'recognised in Scots Conveyancing, e.g. general or particular description or a description in statutory form'. See 2.3.1. — Macdonald -v- the Keeper of the Registers 1914 SC 854. But want of such a description does not render a conveyance invalid, **provided** the subjects are identifiable, e.g. by description in general terms. Such a conveyance cannot, however, be recorded of itself; Notice of Title is needed to supply the want of description if the grantee is to become infeft. Typically, before the Succession Act 1964, heritage passed to Trustees under a Will which described the property in general terms, thus, 'the whole means and estate, heritable and moveable, real and personal which shall belong to me at my death'. A Will in this form was a valid general Disposition and, as such, operated of itself as a title to the Trustees but it was **not** recordable in GRS. Since 1964, heritage vests in Executors by confirmation thereto; and Confirmation is also for practical purposes a general disposition, not recordable *de plano.*

Methods of Description.

(1) **General Description** (not to be confused with a description in general terms, **nor** with a general disposition). Under this method, the subjects are identified simply by name, and no attempt is made to define the property by reference to physical features on the ground. Such descriptions are common in older titles, but are not now normally employed in a conveyance of new. The identification of the property so conveyed, and its limits, are determined by possession following on the title, and by the operation of the positive prescription. But, clearly, it may often be extremely difficult to identify precisely on the ground the extent of the subjects conveyed under this form of description, and this is often a major problem when examining older titles.

(2) **Particular Description.** Under this method, the subjects conveyed are identified by actual physical features on the ground, whether these features be natural or artificial. This is the method now normally used in practice where land is first conveyed as a separate tenement. Obviously, the variety of possible circumstances is almost infinite and there are no hard and fast rules; but any particular description will, or may, contain the following elements:

(a) The name or postal address of the property, with a reference to the Parish and County; but none of this is necessary, provided the location of the property is clear.

(b) Identification of the boundary line or boundary feature on each side of the property; but very often only **some** of the boundaries are so described. For this purpose, natural or artificial features are used where appropriate, e.g. walls, streams, roads, etc., and the length of each such boundary is normally given. This may raise difficulties as to the actual extent of the property conveyed in relation to that boundary feature. Thus, where property is described as **bounded,** on one side, **by** a wall, it is assumed that the whole wall is excluded altogether **on that particular wording.** *Contra:—* Where the words used are '**enclosed** by a wall', the presumption is that the whole wall is included. Where the boundary is a public road, the presumption is *medium filum*; but '**bounded by** a road' **ex**cludes the whole road, at least if supported by plan and/or measurements — 2.3.24 — Houstoun -v- Barr 1911 SC 134. See also Burns Practice p. 328; but cf. 2.3.22 Mags. of Hamilton 1929 SC at p. 694 — 'bounded by a public road' includes it to *medium filum.*

Contra:— 'bounded by the Water of Leith' (a non-tidal stream) included the stream to the *medium filum,* even in the face of measurements, which were held not to be taxative, in 2.3.20 - Gibson -v- Bonnington Sugar 7 M.394.

For the presumptions which apply for various other features on the ground, see Burns Practice pp. 327 to 329. Any such presumption can be altered by express provision in the deed, e.g. bounded, on the north, 'by the southern face of a wall' or 'by the northern edge of the road', or 'by the mid-line'.

(c) The superficial area may or may not be stated, in imperial or metric measure.

(d) **Plans.** A plan is not essential to supplement a written particular description; but, even in the simplest case, it is always desirable. Normally, the plan is not embodied in the Deed but is appended as a Schedule, being referred to and adopted as part of the Deed by a reference in the description; and as such it is signed and referred to in the Testing Clause.

It is perfectly competent, and increasingly common, to describe properties simply by reference to a plan, **without** incorporating any written description in the Deed. See Article 1971 JLS. 62. But, normally, the Conveyance contains both a written description **and** a reference to the plan in support of it. The disadvantages of relying solely on a plan are:—

i) that it is comparatively easy to alter a plan fraudulently, but difficult so to alter a written description; See 1959 JLS. 144. Letter from Keeper; and

ii) that, until 1934, no record of plans appended to Deeds was kept at the Register House. Since 1934, plans up to a certain size (28" x 22") are photographed and appear on the Record Volumes, but, even so, the photographed plan does not show colourings. This means that, if a description depends solely on a plan (or on colours on a plan), and the principal Deed is then lost (as may happen), the title might well be rendered invalid. To get over this difficulty, statutory provision was made in the 1924 Act S.48 for the lodging of **duplicate** plans in the Register House which are then permanently retained there. The duplicate plan is signed in the same way as the deed and docquetted with reference to it, viz., 'This is a duplicate of the plan annexed to a Feu Charter by ... etc.'; and it is referred to in the Testing Clause. The deed itself with principal plan annexed is, of course, returned to the ingiver. This provision has not been very much used. For a lost plan case, see 2.3.6. — Maclachlan. 25 SLR.734. For some details as to plans in Register House practice, see a note from the Keeper at 1968 SLT. News 22.

Part and Portion Clause. Any piece of ground which is conveyed for the first time as a separate heritable unit, and particularly described as such, normally forms part of a larger area of ground already held on its own title in name of the disponer. It is customary, although not essential, to link up the new particular description with the previous titles by a 'part and portion' clause. This simply repeats, in the most convenient form (normally a description by reference) the description of the larger property, of which the subjects (now described for the first time as a separate unit) form part.

Repugnancies and Ambiguities.

Information in a particular description may be duplicated, e.g. written boundaries and plan, or measurement, which carries with it the possibility of some conflict or discrepancy. Thus, property may be described as 'bounded on the north by an **existing** stone wall along which it extends for One hundred feet or thereby'; but it turns out on inspection that **the wall** is only eighty feet long. Or again, property may be described in a written description by reference to physical features 'all as delineated and coloured pink on the plan annexed'; but, when the written description is related to physical features on the ground, it may turn out that the area delineated and coloured pink on the plan is not the same area. In the ordinary way, discrepancies of this type will not invalidate the Deed. Instead, rules have been developed in the reported cases for reconciling such discrepancies. These you will find discussed in Rankine, Land Ownership Chapter 6. and Green's Encyclopaedia 2.872.

Everything depends on the particular title and particular circumstances but some **general** rules emerge from the cases:

1. If, in the deed, there are written boundaries with stated measurements, and these conflict with a plan annexed, the plan will normally be treated as demonstrative and the written boundaries rule.

2. If, in the deed, there are written boundaries without measurements, and these conflict with a plan **containing measurements**, the plan will normally be preferred. But the deed may declare expressly that the plan is 'demonstrative only and not taxative'

3. The deed may contain written boundaries with stated measurements, which cannot be reconciled on the ground, e.g. 'bounded by a wall along which it extends 100 ft' and, on checking the wall, it is found to be 70 ft. only. If the **written** description of the boundary feature is clear and specific, the **measurement** would be rejected, and the written description is **taxative**.

4. In the converse case where the written boundary is clearly stated and is greater than the stated measurement, the written boundary again will rule, and the **smaller** measurement would not be held to limit the grant, e.g. 'bounded by a wall running from the road to the southeast corner of the tenement at 5 King Street a distance of 100 ft.' which turns out to be 200 ft. on the ground.

(3) **Description by Reference.** In this method of description, there is no specific identification of the property conveyed. Instead, to identify the subjects, a previous recorded Deed containing either a general or a particular description is referred to. Therefore, with limited exceptions, this form of description is only suitable for a Conveyance which transmits to the disponee a separate tenement which is already held on a separate title and is already separately described as such in a prior title. There are **three** types of description by reference (though not always oo roforred to in the textbooks) which are:

(a) **Description by reference at Common Law.** In older Conveyances, it was normal to find the description of the property **repeated** in each **successive** Conveyance of that property. But it is now accepted that, at Common Law, it never was necessary to repeat, word for word, the previous description of the property conveyed. Instead, the property could be identified (or described) in a Conveyance simply by reference to some prior writ which itself contained an identifying description. For a description by reference **at Common Law** (as opposed to description by reference at Statute — see below), there are no settled rules except the over-riding principle that the words used must be sufficient to identify the property. This means that the writ referred to for description must be identifiable. In practice, however, this method of description is seldom relied on and, instead, the next method should always be employed.

(b) **Statutory Description by reference.** The relevant statutory provisions are the 1874 Act S.6l, the 1924 Act S.8 and 1924 Act Schedule D. Under these Sections and Schedule, the requirements for a valid statutory description by reference can be summarised thus:

(i) The Deed referred to may be a Deed of any type, provided it contains a **particular** description and has been recorded in the appropriate Register of Sasines.

(ii) The description by reference must:

(a) state the County (for burgage, the Burgh **and** County) in which the property is situate — 1874,S.61. This has **not** been altered by the introduction of Regions and Districts.

(b) specify the prior Deed referred to for description in terms of the 1924 Act Schedule D.

The basic requirements are not itemised in the Act or Schedule; but normally a description by reference should specify:

The type of Deed referred to, e.g. Feu Charter.

The parties, without designations.

The date of the deed — but is this necessary?

The Division of the GRS.

The date of recording.

The Book and Folio — if otherwise there would be ambiguity which is rare. See 1924 Act S.8(3).

See especially Notes 1 and 4 to Schedule D for further detail.

Nothing more is required; but it is normal to preface the statutory description-by-reference with a short identifying description (usually the postal address). See 1924 Act Sch. D. Note 2.

By the 1874 Act S.61, such specification and reference to the prior recorded Deed in any Conveyance, etc., are equivalent to the full insertion in that Conveyance of the particular description contained in the prior Deed referred to.

These are the rules for a statutory description by reference and in practice they should always be strictly followed, when framing new descriptions. But you will sometimes find, when examining a title, that a description by reference in one of the existing deeds does not comply in some respect with the statutory rules. The question then is whether the deed is valid or not, and in deciding this question there are three main considerations to keep in view:

1. The strict **statutory** essentials are a particular description in the prior deed, specification of the County (and Burgh), the Register, the date of recording and a reference to the prior deed in such terms as shall be sufficient to identify it on record. Omission of County, which is common, or of Register, is clearly fatal. But an error in the date of recording, e.g. wrong day of month may not be, if the deed can be clearly identified notwithstanding. And the same applies to e.g. minor errors

in the names of parties. An error in or omission of the date(s) of the deed (not the date of recording) is never fatal, except in very exceptional cases (e.g. two deeds, same parties, same recording date, no Book and Folio Number, and different dates).

2. Even if the error is sufficiently serious to disqualify the description under Statute, it may nevertheless be a valid description by reference at Common Law; such a description has always been competent, and in the past was not infrequently employed for 'eking out a generalised or incomplete description'. The statutory facilities do not exclude it, or render it invalid in any way; they merely provide a convenient alternative with statutory sanction. As stated above, the exact requirements for a valid Common Law description by reference are not defined. See 2.3.5. — Murray's Trs. 14 R 856., 2.3.7. — Matheson 5 F 448., 2.3.4. (1.2.17) — Cattanach's Trs. 11 R 972.

3. Even if the description by reference has been so hopelessly bungled that it is invalid **as such**, both under Statute and at Common Law, it may still contain sufficient in itself to constitute a general description, in terms sufficient to identify the subjects. Here very little will suffice. The normal short introductory words will certainly serve in most cases, e.g. 'All and Whole that dwellinghouse and pertinents No. 10 Glebe Road, Dundee' standing alone are an adequate general description of a detached dwellinghouse. Again if a deed contains only a bare reference, without identifying words, to a deed itself containing a description by reference that is not a valid statutory description. But if the deed referred to contains anything which could amount to an identifying description, that will be valid at Common Law.

(c) **Description by general name.** This is simply another method of description by reference, although not usually so described. In view of the statutory provisions for description by reference later introduced (as above), it is now virtually obsolete. In the case of Barony or Regality Titles one general name, at Common Law, sufficed to describe several separate subjects. The same effect could be achieved at Common Law in any Crown Grant by including a Clause of Union. A statutory equivalent was introduced for **any** estate by the 1858 Act, re-enacted and consolidated in the 1868 Act S.13. But, as you will see when you consider the provisions of that Section, the essential requirements for a description by general name are more onerous than the requirements for a description by reference; and the latter is, therefore, now almost invariably used in preference.

In practice, with a modern description, there is often a combination of two or even all three of the foregoing methods of description, e.g.

'ALL and WHOLE the farm and lands of Nether Mains in the Parish of Strathmartine and County of Angus' (a general description) 'being the subjects delineated and enclosed within the red line on the plan annexed and signed as relative hereto' (a particular description) 'which subjects hereinbefore disponed form part and portion of all and whole the subjects in said Parish and County particularly described in and disponed by a Disposition by John Smith in my favour dated Seventh and recorded in the Division of the General Register of Sasines for the County of Angus Twelfth both days of August, Nineteen hundred and Fifty-nine' (a description by reference).

Addenda to the Description. In any heritable Conveyance, in practice, it is normal to find (appended at the end of the description of the property) certain additional incidentals, varying in number and nature according to the nature of the property conveyed. Sometimes, such addenda do materially add to the main description, e.g. in the case of separate tenements in the form of incorporeal rights such as salmon fishings where, following on a description of a landed estate, you may find some such right as:

'Together with the salmon fishings in the River Isla, bounding the said subjects hereinbefore disponed on the north and west sides, but only up to the *medium filum* thereof *ex adverso* of the said subjects hereinbefore disponed;'

For reason already examined ('Separate Tenements') if salmon fishings are to pass with a conveyance of land, they must be expressly described; accordingly, this addendum to the description forms a material addition to the subjects conveyed.

So also new servitude rights and privileges, typically free ish and entry, or access, drainage and other like rights materially add to the description of the land.

In other cases, standard and typical addenda in fact add little or nothing to the description of the subjects. Thus, in practice, you will normally find in any Conveyance four typical addenda, which are:

(i) '**The teinds** of the said subjects, so far as I have right thereto.' Teinds are a separate tenement and, strictly, require a separate Conveyance; therefore, in feudal theory, this addendum is necessary if teinds are to pass under the Conveyance to the disponee. But, in fact, teind and stipend have ceased to be of any practical significance and no practical harm is done if the reference to teinds is omitted. In any event, they probably would now be held to pass by implication.

(ii) 'The whole parts, privileges and pertinents of and effeiring to the said subjects hereinbefore disponed.' The exact implication of the term 'parts, privileges and pertinents' is nowhere clearly defined. The general principle has already been mentioned above, viz.:— that all implied rights inherent in the ownership of the land pass automatically on a Conveyance of the same; *per contra,* separate tenements must be separately identified and conveyed. It is, therefore, unnecessary, and adds nothing, to itemise or list implied rights in a Charter or Disposition. The term 'parts, privileges and pertinents' is a general phrase wide enough to embrace all the normal implied rights. Any right not ordinarily implied must be distinctly specified; otherwise, the disponee could not lay claim to it. Therefore, the parts and pertinents clause normally adds nothing but is nonetheless normally included as an addendum. In rare cases, some weight may be placed on the presence of a 'parts and pertinents' clause; for this, see 'Prescription'.

(iii) 'The whole fittings and fixtures in and upon the said subjects hereinbefore disponed.' Again it is doubtful whether this can ever add anything. If the fittings, etc., are heritable in law they pass *sub silentio*; if moveable, delivery and not a mere conveyance is required to transmit the right therein to a disponee. See Lord Kinnear: 7.1.25. Jamieson 3 F.176.

(iv) 'My whole right, title and interest in the subjects disponed' is implied in an onerous conveyance.

Description by Exception

As a general rule, in practice, you always use the most convenient method of describing any particular subject. Suppose that you acquire an acre of ground area X by Feu Charter containing a detailed particular description; later you sub-feu one-half acre, area Y, again by Feu Charter containing a particular description. You are left with area (x-y), the remaining half acre. Now the whole area X is already particularly described, and so is the lesser area Y. The remaining area

X-Y is nowhere particularly described as such. Supposing you sell it; there are two alternatives:

(a) that X-Y may be particularly described (in the Conveyance following on your sale) by boundaries, measurements, etc., and plan; or

(b) much more simply by describing it as the whole area X by reference under exception of subjects Y, also by reference. The form is suggested in 1924, Sch. D. Note 3. This is one example of ground first conveyed as a separate entity where a new particular description is not necessary.

Descriptions in Registration of Title

As you know, registration of title is map based. With limited exceptions, every title sheet (and therefore every land certificate) will include a plan which is an excerpt from the Ordnance Survey Plan of an appropriate scale coloured to indicate the registered property. Therefore, every description, at the date of first registration, whatever its form has been in the past progress of titles, must at that point be translated onto the Ordnance Survey Map. Obviously this will to some extent affect conveyancing practice both before and after registration of each individual title.

For an instructive Article on Ordnance Survey plans, see 1981 JLS Workshop p.245.

1. Pre-registration Practice

In an Operational Area, the Deed which induces registration of title in each case is the first sale by way of Disposition, Feu Charter or Lease of the property after the commencement date. The statutory requirement is that the purchaser, vassal or lessee under such a writ must apply for registration of title; and is barred from recording his Disposition, Charter or Lease in the Register of Sasines to procure a real right.

So far as Registration Practice is concerned, the Deed inducing registration need not itself contain a particular desription, need not constitute a bounding title, and need not contain a plan. Further, if the Deed does contain a plan, it need not be exact and to scale nor on the Ordnance Survey, nor on one of the Ordnance Survey recognised scales of 1/1250, 1/2,500, 1/10,000.

Nonetheless, at the time of application for registration, the applicant must provide the Keeper with sufficient information on the property to be registered to allow him to translate that information on to an Ordnance Survey Map. **But** the information required for this purpose can be given separately from the Title Deed itself.

Accordingly, prior to first registration of the title, there is unlikely to be any significant change in conveyancing practice except that, as a matter of convenience, parties may tend increasingly to use Ordnance Survey Maps of appropriate scale to identify the property conveyed.

Boundaries. Registration of title produces a problem in relation to boundaries which we do not experience at present in Scotland in that, on the 1/1250 scale (the largest), boundary features such as walls are represented by a single black line, and it is impossible to represent such features diagramatically on the Ordnance Survey so as to show whether the boundary lies on one or other side thereof or on mid-line. To get over this difficulty, the Land Certificate incorporates a system of arrows to indicate where the boundary line lies in relation to particular boundary features. An arrow across the boundary line indicates the mid-line thereof i.e. that the boundary feature is mutual. An arrow pointing at one or other face of the boundary feature indicates that the boundary line is on that side of the feature. See Note on Land Certificate.

This is, however, the Keeper's practice; and it is unlikely that the practice of using arrows will commend itself to the profession, meantime, at any rate, when preparing individual title plans. We will probably still continue, where appropriate, to draw plans on a sufficiently large scale to show the boundary line of any individual feature; or rely on a verbal description for that purpose.

One standard exception to the rule that registration of title is map based will be the tenement flat or part of a building separately conveyed. In this case, the postal address and a verbal description of the location of the flat in the tenement will suffice. In addition, where appropriate, the Keeper will plot the *solum* of the tenement and the front and back ground, if any, on an Ordnance Survey map incorporated in the title sheet and Land Certificate.

Again, this is unlikely to produce any change in current conveyancing practice.

If no visible feature exists on a particular boundary, the Keeper proposes to indicate this by a dotted line on the plan; and the plan will carry a legend, thus:

'The boundary shown by dotted lines has been plotted from the Deeds. Physical boundaries will be indicated after their delineation on the Ordnance Map'

At a later date, when the boundary features have been constructed on the ground, and then plotted on the Ordnance Survey Map, they will then find their way on to the title sheet.

2. Registered Land

This implies that the title has already been registered in the Land Register. Therefore:

(i) The property will already appear on the Master Index Map in the Land Register and will have an individual title plan in its title sheet, all on the appropriate Ordnance Survey scale; and

(ii) A title number will have been allocated to that property on the title sheet.

Therefore, any subsequent transfer of the whole of the property can be simply and precisely effected by reference to the title number.

e.g. 'ALL and WHOLE the dwellinghouse known as One Graham Road, Dundee, being the subjects registered under Title Number ANG 1697.'

Nothing more is required. In particular, note:

No reference is required to any prior recorded deed — cf. Description by Reference.

No addenda are necessary — they are all set out in the title sheet.

No part and portion clause is necessary — the part and portion element is all dealt with by reference to the Index Map.

There is no need to refer to burdens, as these are already set out at full length in the burdens section of the title sheet.

If, alternatively, part only of One Graham Road was to be disponed — a particular description would be required in the Disposition in implement of that part sale, in order to identify separately the part of the property being given off for the first time as a separate heritable unit. The practice is still to develop but, one assumes, that, in a Disposition of part of the registered title, the Disposition will proceed substantially as at present, with a written description of the boundaries and a reference to a plan. But, bearing in mind that there will already be in existence in the title sheet an accurate Ordnance Survey plan, the particular description may be much more simply accomplished than at present, by reference to that Ordnance Survey map.

In any event, whatever method is adopted to identify the separate part, it will have to be followed with some such short reference as:

'being part of the subjects registered under Title No. ANG 1697'.

2.4 Reservations.

Reading List 2.4.

Where a conveyance contains a reservation, this implies that a right which, under the description, would ordinarily be conveyed to the disponee, is by express reservation excluded from the conveyance, and retained by the granter/ disponer.

This is always competent, subject to the proviso that a right can only be thus reserved to the disponer if it is capable of separate infeftment as a separate heritable right on a separate heritable title, i.e. as a Separate Tenement.

A clause of reservation is, therefore, strictly speaking, part of the description since it defines some thing or right which is to be excluded from the major or larger thing conveyed. In practice, however, reservations tend to be treated in the same category as burdens; because by far the commonest reservation in a conveyance in practice is a reservation of minerals which usually contains elaborate burdens clauses regulating the working of the minerals for the protection of the surface owner.

As a matter of standard practice, reservations of minerals to the disponer, which in the past were very common in Feu Charters, define the thing reserved by reference to its physical substance; and do not attempt to describe geographically the reserved minerals in the same way in which land is described. Accordingly, a typical clause of reservation of minerals qualifying a conveyance of land reads (Burns Practice p. 243):

'Reserving always to the superiors all stone, iron stone, shale, and all metals, mineral substances and things in or under the subjects hereby feued with full power by themselves or through lessees or others to work and carry away the same ...'

Where a Conveyance contains a clause of this kind, it qualifies the implied rule that the Conveyance of land carries to the disponee everything *a coelo ad centrum* and excludes from the Conveyance everything falling within the categories of things defined in the reservation; in this case, that would include stone, iron stone, shale and 'minerals'. In other typical clauses, the thing reserved is 'minerals' alone, without any specific narration of particular types of minerals or again other types of mineral may be separately specified and identified by name.

Note that, while minerals are often severed from the surface by way of reservation in a Charter, it is equally competent for the owner of surface and sub-strata to convey the minerals on a separate feudal title as a separate heritable right, or 'separate tenement'.

Note also the general rule that, where minerals have once become severed from the surface (whether by reservation or by express conveyance of the minerals), thereafter a transmission of the surface will **not** carry the minerals; and to that extent the ordinary rule that a Conveyance carries everything *a coelo ad centrum* is modified.

Definition of Minerals. Clearly, since the accepted method of defining minerals in a reservation or conveyance thereof, is by reference to their physical substance and by using such terms as 'minerals' (or 'Mines and minerals'; or 'quarries, mines and minerals', etc.) rather than describing their geographical location, it becomes necessary to consider (for the purpose of defining the thing conveyed or reserved) what the terms mean.

Note, firstly, three specialities:

(1) Mines of gold, silver, and lead are *regalia minora,* and a conveyance of land does not by implication carry such minerals. By The Royal Mines Act 1424, they remain vested in the Crown; but the Crown is bound to make a grant of such minerals to the owner for the time being of the *dominium utile* of the surface, on payment of l/10th royalties — The Mines and Metals Act 1592.

(2) Coal and associated minerals. Under the Coal Industry Nationalisation Act 1946, all coal and certain associated minerals, wherever situated, and whether being worked or not, are now vested in and managed by the National Coal Board. Accordingly, a conveyance of land no longer carries coal. This has made a good deal of the law regarding minerals in Scotland of academic interest only.

(3) Petroleum and Natural Gas are vested in the Crown under the Petroleum (Production) Act 1934. The Board of Trade (now the Secretary of State for Energy) have power under the Act to issue licences to work, as they are doing at present, onshore and offshore.

It follows that the term 'minerals' or 'mines and minerals' cannot include the above substances. As to what else the terms include depends, to some extent, on surrounding circumstances.

The word 'mineral' 'is of flexible meaning, to be construed very generally if there be nothing in the deed or in the surrounding circumstances to control this construction.' (Rankine Landownership p. 171).

Rights of Parties. Normally (but not necessarily) the rights and obligations of the surface owner and of the mineral owner or lessee who is to work the sub-adjacent minerals under reservation, are set out in detail in the relevant title. These clauses normally cover three main points, viz: —

(i) The nature of the reserved right. There are two possibilities, viz.: that the right reserved is: —

(a) an express right of property in the minerals, which carries with it by implication the right to work them and carry them away; or

(b) a privilege or servitude of working the minerals.

It is recommended that in every case a right of property should be reserved rather than a mere servitude or privilege of working, since under the latter right the person working the minerals may not enjoy the right to use the resulting shaft or gallery as a pipe-line for transporting minerals extracted from adjoining properties.

(ii) The right to work. The method of working is normally laid down in the title.

(iii) Right of support. A landowner is inherently entitled to support, both lateral and vertical from adjoining proprietors of land abutting his boundaries and from the owner of sub-adjacent minerals. The mere fact that minerals have passed into the ownership of another person does not of itself in any way limit or derogate from the surface owner's right. So far as mineral reservations are concerned, the right of support extends to and includes land in its natural state and (subject to possible qualifications) buildings erected on that land and existing at the date of reservation.

The right of support of land in its natural state is a natural right of ownership; the right to support of buildings already erected at the date of severance of minerals from surface is said to be in the nature of a right of servitude, the surface being the dominant tenement and the minerals the servient tenement on the footing that the mineral owner knew, when the minerals were reserved, of the existence of these buildings and therefore must take them into account in any subsequent operations for the extracting of the minerals. But buildings increase the weight on land, and therefore increase the burden of support. Following the ordinary rule of servitudes, the surface owner is not entitled to increase this burden of support; and the mineral owner may not be bound to provide support for buildings **subsequently** erected unless there was a plain implication from the terms of the title at the date of severance that the erection of buildings was within the contemplation of the parties. But this rule is subject to these qualifications:

i) the servitude right of support of buildings even if not expressed or implied from the terms of the title, may be acquired by prescription; and

ii) if the surface owner can demonstrate that the subsidence is in no way attributable to the extra weight of buildings later added to land, and that the surface in its natural state would have subsided anyhow, he can claim damages for subsidence damage to his buildings as being damage naturally and immediately consequent upon damage to the land in its natural state. The onus is wholly on the surface owner.

The mineral owner is not under any duty to refrain from excavations altogether, leaving the whole sub-strata in the original state; if this were so, then severance of minerals from the surface would be of no practical importance. Instead, his duty is to refrain from carrying on his mineral operations in such a way that the surface is (or will probably be) damaged thereby. Admittedly, this **may** result in an absolute bar on mineral working in certain circumstances, e.g. where the top and sub-soil is of such a kind and the mineral operations are of such a kind, that, taken together, the surface is bound to come down. But this will be a question of facts and circumstances to be considered in each individual case. As a result, if the surface owner has reason to believe that the operations of the mineral owner will inevitably bring down the surface, he has the right, by interdict, to prevent the mineral owner from carrying out any such operations. In any **other** case, his remedy is damages for injury caused, each recurrent subsidence creating a fresh ground of action.

This is only a very brief summary of some of the complex rules which control the relationship between surface and mineral owners. All or any of these general rules may be expressly varied in terms of the respective titles and in practically all cases there is some degree of variation. Further, in certain special cases, the ordinary rules have been varied by Statute. e.g. National Coal Board, under The Coal Mining (Subsidence) Act 1957, must execute remedial work (or pay therefor) in respect of any damage caused to property after passing of the Act by coal mining operations; and must pay compensation for personal injury or death caused by subsidence. For typical clauses, see Burns' Practice pp. 243-4, and the Styles.

2.5. Conditions of Tenure.

Reading List 2.5.

A conveyance of land (by Charter or Disposition) carries with it to the disponee certain implied rights, which include, *inter alia,* the right to make what use the proprietor pleases of his land, including the right to exhaust, convert or destroy the substance of his ground, surface, subsoil, minerals, etc., in any way, but subject always to certain implied restrictions which are imposed on the proprietor by Common Law or by Statute, either for the benefit of adjoining proprietors or of the public generally; and possibly, but not necessarily, subject also to such restrictions as have effectively been imposed on the proprietor by agreement, either as conditions in his title or as conditions in the nature of servitudes.

What we are concerned with here are the obligations and restrictions imposed on the vassal by express provision in the Feu Charter, as conditions of his tenure, which limit and qualify the vassal's right in individual cases, for the benefit of his superior, and in certain cases his neighbours.

Commonly, such conditions are prescribed, as conditions of the tenure, in a Feu Charter; but may also competently be imposed by other means.

In the Charter, such conditions are normally imposed on and bind the vassal; but occasionally a Charter includes a condition binding on the superior and his successors.

Standard Classification of Conventional Conditions.

According to Erskine, the conditions in a Feu Charter ('conditions of tenure') fall into one of three categories.

(1) **Essentials of the Feu.** These are conditions without which the feudal relationship cannot exist; and include:

(i) the tenendas, by virtue of which the **tenure** is created, and the superior's radical right to the *dominium directum* preserved; and

(ii) Reddendo or feuduty, the annual return or consideration for the grant; but, by the 1974 Act S.1.(1), no deed may now impose a feuduty. Any deed executed after 1st September, 1974, which contains a grant of land in feu, takes effect as if there were a feuduty therein. The point of this provision is to negative the Common Law feudal principle by virtue of which a feudal grant, to be valid, must contain some return by vassal to superior as consideration for the grant, whether it be a money feuduty (as it now always is) or, in older Charters, a return in kind.

(2) **Natural Obligations.** These are conditions implied by law; and include Casualties (pre-1914) and Warrandice. No express provision need be made, in which event the law implies a certain legal result. But, by express provision, the implied legal result may be expressly varied in terms of the Charter.

(3) **Accidental or Conventional Obligations.** These include a wide variety of conditions and restrictions which may be imposed on the vassal by Charter. They are not essential to the relationship of Superior and Vassal, nor to the tenure; and they are never in any circumstances legally presumed or implied. Therefore, if any such condition is to be effective, it must be expressly set out in the Charter. Such conditions are often referred to under the general heading of 'Building Conditions' but include a number of conditions of other types as well.

Such conditions are normally imposed by the superior on his vassal:

(a) to secure the feuduty; obviously, a plot of land with a house on it is better security for feuduty than a bare plot of land. For Charters post 1.9.74, this now of course no longer applies. But also,

(b) to preserve amenity. This serves a double purpose, viz.,

i) maintaining the value of the feu as security for feuduty (again no longer applicable for post 1.9.74 charters); and

ii) maintaining the general amenity of the neighbourhood in order to maintain the value of adjoining land still belonging to the superior, for future feuing, or for the benefit of neighbouring proprietors.

Real and personal conditions. As between superior and vassal, the Feu Charter is a Contract. Any conditions which it contains are enforceable, on the basis of the contractual relationship which the Charter establishes between original superior and original vassal. But any vassal may now freely alienate his feu without the consent of the superior. Accordingly, if building conditions are to be of any practical value to the superior, he must be able to enforce them not only against the original vassal but also against successors of the vassal, singular and universal, as future proprietors of the feu in perpetuity; and the right of enforcement must be available not only to the original superior but also to his successors, singular and universal, in the estate of superiority. In other words, such conditions must attach to the **land** rather than to the original vassal personally, and must run with the land. **But**, if a condition in the Charter is to run with the land in this way, then it must satisfy certain fundamental requirements. A condition in a Charter which fails to satisfy these requirements may, and probably will, bind the original vassal personally and his universal successors; but it will **not** run with the land, so as to bind singular successors. For a general discussion on the distinction between real and personal conditions and the implications of that distinction, see 2.5.4. Walker v Church of Scotland General Trs. 1967 SLT 297.

Broadly speaking, a condition is valid as a **personal** condition if it is enforceable under the ordinary rules of Contract.

But any condition in a Feu Charter or other title is not normally intended merely as a personal condition; but is intended to operate as a permanent condition, running with the land, and effectively binding on, and enforceable against, a singular successor in perpetuity, regardless of changes in ownership. Conditions or burdens running with the land must be further sub-divided into two separate categories.

(a) **Real conditions.** Such conditions may occur **either** in a Feu Charter, where they are commonly referred to as conditions of tenure, or in a Disposition as conditions of the grant. There cannot be 'conditions of tenure' in a Disposition because no new tenure is created. To qualify as a real condition, a number of strict rules must be complied with, detailed later.

Further, if the condition occurs in a Disposition, then to qualify as a real condition it must be imposed for the benefit of adjoining property.

(b) **Real burdens.** Any condition imposed in a title which does not qualify as a real condition may qualify as a real burden and as such may run with land.

Both real conditions and real burdens may be positive, *ad factum praestandum* or for payment of a sum of money; or negative in the form of prohibitions, normally against the use of the property for specified purposes.

The importance of the distinction between real conditions and real burdens lies in the manner of enforcement and the resulting liability of the proprietor for the time being of the burdened subjects. The importance of this distinction is not always fully appreciated; and has tended to become blurred because of the habit of referring to all conditions running with land (whether real conditions or real burdens) as 'real burdens'.

For a general discussion, see 2.5.9 — Wells v New House Purchasers Ltd. 1964SLT Sh.Ct. 2, and cases there cited.

Mode of enforcement of real conditions. Here again, there is a distinction between **real** actions (including **real** diligence) and **personal** actions (including personal diligence) as the vehicle for enforcement of such conditions. This distinction is not always clearly stated in earlier texts; but is clearly set out in Walker. Chapter 5.4. page 61.

Broadly speaking, a **personal** action in this sense is an action founded on a particular or **personal** obligation undertaken by a particular person and therefore normally involves a **contractual** undertaking.

A personal action is directed against the obligant himself and no other person.

Ignoring land altogether for a moment, take the case of a simple contractual obligation by A to pay a sum of money to B on a particular date. A is the debtor, B the creditor. If A fails to pay, B can enforce by personal action against A. The procedure is a summons at the instance of B served on A narrating the terms of the obligation and concluding for payment. If decree is granted, A the debtor is personally liable to B the creditor for the whole sum contained in the Decree; and his whole estate, heritable or moveable, can be attached by B (through the process of diligence) in satisfaction of the debt.

A real action, on the other hand, is an action founded on a **real right** in property; the element of Contract does not enter into it at all. There is no question of personal obligation. But any action, real or personal, must have a defender; it is not possible in Scotland to raise actions against inanimate objects. Therefore, any real action is personal in this sense, that it is directed against a particular person, being, in the case of real conditions, the proprietor for the time being of the subjects burdened or affected by the pursuer's right. But, in setting out the averments in a real action, it is unnecessary and irrelevant to aver **contractual** relationship between pursuer and defender; the important averments are the pursuer's real right of action and the defender's real right in the property. Typical real actions are adjudication and poinding of the ground. Decree in such a real action entitles the pursuer to recourse against the particular property affected by the decree; but he has no recourse by diligence or otherwise against any other assets of the defender.

It was this distinction between real and personal actions which was the essence of the dispute in Wells v New House Purchasers Ltd. above. In certain circumstances, a condition in a title may involve substantial liability; and possibly this liability may exceed the value of the property. If the condition gives rise to a personal action against the proprietor for the time being, the value of the property *vis-a-vis* the limit of liability is irrelevant. The debtor's whole estate, including the property affected, can be attached. If, however, the condition gives rise to a real action only, then the value of the property **is** relevant, since, in effect, this is the limit of the pursuer's claim.

A real condition (or condition of tenure), occuring in a Feu Charter, is enforceable as between the original superior and the original vassal on the basis of Contract. Further, in feudal theory, there is a recurring personal Contract between successive proprietors in the superiority on the one hand and successive vassals in the *dominium utile* on the other hand. This originates from the feudal method of transmitting the vassal's right in the *dominium utile* by renewal of investiture and public entry with the Superior involving direct participation on his part.

The **principle** of entry with the superior still applies. The result is that, in any feu, the superior for the time being is deemed to be in direct contractual relationship with the vassal for the time being, just as though both of them were original parties to the Feu Charter. On this basis, the Superior always has a right of **personal** action against his vassal for the time being to implement any condition of tenure in the original Charter which has become real. Further, in certain circumstances, a condition of tenure may **also** be enforced by real action. This always applies in the case of feuduty; it **may** apply in the case of other burdens as well.

Where a real condition occurs in a Disposition, then as between disponer and disponee any such condition is enforceable on the grounds of Contract. But a Disposition creates no new tenure between disponer and disponee. When the original disponee transmits his right of property to a singular successor, the theory of recurring personal contract has no application as between the original disponer on the one part and the singular successor of the disponee on the other part.

So, A dispones to B by Disposition containing real conditions; A and B are in contractual relationship; the Disposition is their Contract; and on the basis of that Contract, A can enforce the conditions in the Disposition by **personal** action against B. Suppose B dispones to C; there is no actual or notional contractual relationship between A and C. None the less, such conditions, if duly constituted as real conditions in the Disposition, **may** be enforced by personal action in a question between the original disponer and singular successors of the original disponee (A and C in the illustration).

In Wells above, the resulting relationship is described as 'a continuing reciprocal relationship between the creditor and the debtor' or 'a continuing relationship associated with the property between the creditor and the debtor in the obligation'; and in such cases, where there is 'a direct proprietary interest in the property in the persons seeking to enforce the obligation', the person in right of the obligation may enforce it by personal action. But the actual basis of this right of personal action is not really satisfactorily explained.

Where a condition in a title (Charter or Disposition) is a **real burden** as opposed to a real condition, this will normally imply personal liability on the **original** vassal or **original** disponee; but, with limited statutory exceptions, no personal liability will transmit against singular successors. Therefore, where the property has transmitted, the creditor in the real burden (superior or original disponer) can enforce the burden against the singular successor by real action only, or by real diligence only.

He can never, in such circumstances, sustain a **personal** action against a singular successor. But he has this advantage, that a properly constituted real burden **for money** gives an absolute and indefeasible preference to the creditor. A real burden of a negative character, e.g. prohibition against certain uses, can always be enforced by interdict. A real burden *ad factum praestandum* may be more difficult to enforce.

Constitution of real conditions. Real conditions and real burdens, whether constituted by a Charter or by a Disposition, must satisfy several strict requirements. These have to be kept firmly in mind when drafting real conditions or real burdens for a heritable title. Otherwise, the condition may effectively bind the original vassal or original disponee personally, but will not transmit against a singular successor. For practical purposes, this is virtually useless in the majority of cases. We are therefore always concerned, when drafting conditions for a Charter or Disposition, to ensure that the conditions do qualify as real conditions or real burdens.

A simple illustration serves to underline the point.

A grants a Disposition to B containing conditions by which he hopes to regulate construction of buildings on the subjects and the use thereof. By an oversight on the part of the draftsman, he fails to make them effective as real conditions or real burdens. On delivery of the Disposition from A to B, B is contractually bound to observe the conditions. Therefore, initially, the conditions are immediately effective in that, if B is to build on the subjects, he must comply therewith by virtue of his contract.

Suppose B wants to build on the property but wants to breach the conditions. He forms a small private company at the cost of about £100 and conveys the property to the company which is, in feudal terms, a singular successor of B. If the conditions of the Disposition from A to B are personal only and not real, the company is not bound in any way by mere personal conditions and could build as it pleased on the property. Further, depending on the terms of the Disposition, there may be no comeback by way of an action of damages or otherwise against B for disponing the property to a company without imposing burdens thereon.

Since private companies are easily, quickly and cheaply formed and very flexible in practice, any personal condition could be avoided by this sort of device with great ease.

Hence the emphasis on making conditions and burdens **real**.

1. **The fundamental characteristics of real conditions**, (which are not required for real burdens):

(a) There must be an element of permanency.

(b) There must be an inherent connection with the subjects disponed.

(c) There must be a natural connection between the condition and the purpose of the Deed.

2. **The inherent characteristics** — these apply both to real conditions and to real burdens alike:

(a) The condition must not be illegal, *contra bonos mores* nor contrary to public policy.

(b) The condition must not be vexatious or useless.

(c) The condition must not be inconsistent with the nature of property conveyed.

3. **Qualification of an Infeftment**. Again this applies to real conditions and real burdens alike:

(a) Deeds **executed** before 5/4/1979.

(i) The condition must appear at full length in the dispositive clause of a **conveyance** e.g. Feu Charter, Disposition, etc.; **or** there must be a valid reference, in the dispositive clause of a conveyance, to a Deed of Conditions already recorded under the 1874 Act S. 32.

(ii) That conveyance, containing the burden or the reference, must **itself** be recorded in the Register of Sasines.

(b) Deeds **executed** after 4.4.79 — See 1979 Act S.17

(i) As in (a) (i) and (ii) above; **or**

(ii) a Deed of conditions must be recorded in the Sasines Register or in the Land Register, where appropriate, which of itself immediately constitutes a real condition or real burden, unless that deed itself expressly otherwise provides.

In practice, when constituting real conditions or real burdens, the possible limited exceptions to this rule are ignored and one ensures in all cases that the condition **does** enter the infeftment and **does** appear at full length on Record.

The exceptions occur in such cases as:—

i) 2.5.23. Montrose IM(HL)25, and 2.5.24. Hope 2M670 — conditions affecting successors in a superiority; and

ii) 2.5.19 Robertson 1R1213 — the only reported case where a condition which did not enter the Record in the title of the vassal disponee was nonetheless held to be real — but this decision has been severely criticised — see 3.3.1 Hislop 8R(HL)95.

4. **The subjects affected must be clearly identified**. This applies to real conditions or real burdens.

5. **A real condition or real burden must be expressed in clear and unambiguous terms**. This introduces the familiar rule requiring precision for the proper constitution of real conditions and real burdens.

As a particular application of this rule in the case of real burdens, the creditor in a real burden must be clearly identified.

6. **There must be an evident intention to burden the property,** not merely to burden the disponee personally — again this applies both to real conditions and real burdens alike.

Of the above rules, the most important from the point of view of **drafting** is in para. 5 above — the need for precision. This is the rule in relation to which most difficulties arise in practice and on which there is most argument as to whether or not a condition in a title is effective in a question with a singular successor. See particularly Burns' Practice p. 225 to 231; and the Case Notes under headings 2.5 — Burdens; and 3.3 — the Estate of the Superior — enforcement of conditions. In Burns' Practice at p. 230 under the heading of:—

'Substance and Expression of the Restrictions'

Burns formulates three rules viz.:

 (i) the presumption for freedom;

 (ii) precision;

(iii) the difference, in the case of buildings, between restrictions on what may be built and restrictions on the use of the buildings after they are built.

In fact, although Burns then deals with each of these rules in turn and cites different cases in support of each, they all amount to the same thing viz:—

If you want to create a condition which binds singular successors, it must be couched in clear and wholly unambiguous terms.

Any ambiguity will be construed in the least onerous manner and for the benefit of the proprietor. If there is any area of the law in which a 'strict construction' is favoured, it is in this field, as the reported cases show.

It is useful and instructive to consider the actual wording in the following cases, most of which are cited in Burns and digested in the Case Notes, as illustrating various pitfalls.

See Case Notes 2.5.28 — 2.5.38, for examples.

Enforcement Clauses. Various provisions are inserted in the Charter to ensure that the conditions in the Charter are duly constituted as real burdens on the feu and that, if they are breached, the superior can take punitive action against the vassal. The enforcement clauses typically include:

(a) Provision for registration of the Charter. This may occur in the destination, or as a burden in the dispositive clause. The effect is to limit the validity of the Charter as a warrant for infeftment to a stated time, say six months from the date of delivery. If not recorded within that period, then the vassal is denied his real right. The objective is to ensure that the Charter is recorded, so that the burdens become real burdens on the feu. In one way, this is less important than might at first appear, in that, if a Charter remains unrecorded and if the benefit thereof is transmitted, as an unrecorded personal title, to an assignee or general disponee, he is bound (even although he is a singular successor) by all the conditions in that unrecorded Charter. 'So long as the title remains personal, an heir or assignee must take it subject to the burdens which were binding on the original disponee in respect that he cannot both plead the personal title and repudiate its conditions.' Craigie, Elements p.50. But it is undesirable that the title should be left in that state. Hence this clause.

(b) Further special provision for registration of burdens. The vassal normally takes infeftment by recording the Charter and, under the preceding clause, he must do this within six months.

Under normal registration practice, the Charter when presented for registration will be recorded entire unless it contains a clause of direction; and the superior can ensure that it does not. **But** the vassal **may**, if he prefers, complete his title by recording, not the Charter but a Notarial Instrument or Notice of Title. If he does so, then it is possible for him to omit the burdens in the Charter from the Notice of Title, and thus to exclude them from his infeftment. In that case, they do not become real burdens on the feu for reasons stated above. Clearly, this is undesirable, and the Charter therefore normally contains a provision designed to ensure that the burdens will enter the Record at full length as a qualification of the vassal's infeftment.

(c) Subsequent reference to burdens. The practical rule is that a burden created as a condition of tenure in a Charter, which has become real by registration in Sasines, continues in perpetuity until discharged, even although the Charter and its burdens may not be referred to in subsequent transmissions of the feu. But it is thought that a burden in a Disposition may be worked off, and may cease to apply, if omitted from the title and infeftment for the prescriptive period, now ten years; or at least by the negative prescription of 20 years. See King 1908 SC 684 at p. 687 — Lord Guthrie Ordinary, re. Ground Annuals.

As a precaution, and to ensure that burdens do persist in perpetuity, it is customary both in the Charter and in a Disposition to require the vassal for the time being, when disposing of his feu, to repeat or at least refer to the Charter for its burdens in terms of the 1874 Act S.32. Notwithstanding the obligation normally imposed on a vassal requiring him to refer to the original Feu Charter for burdens in any subsequent transmission of the subjects, there are certain express statutory modifications to this obligation in the 1924 Act S.9.

Firstly, notwithstanding an obligation on the vassal to refer to burdens, such a reference to burdens is unnecessary in any heritable security.

Secondly, if a required reference to burdens has, inadvertently, been omitted from a particular title, that omission can be cured, and any resulting irritancy avoided, if :—

(i) a reference is now made in the current title to the omitted writ; or

(ii) failing that, if a special memorandum is recorded in Sasines, expressly referring to the omitted writ. 1924 Act Sch. E provides the form.

(d) Declaration of real burdens. No *voces signatae* are required to constitute real conditions or real burdens; but there must be an evident intention that the subjects should be burdened rather than the vassal personally. This can best be achieved by an express provision that all burdens and conditions are to be real burdens upon and affecting the feu in perpetuity; and an express provision of this kind is commonplace.

(e) Irritant and resolutive clauses. If the vassal fails to observe a condition of the Charter, he may, by express provision therein, forfeit the feu to the superior — a very stringent penalty for non-compliance. Express provision is required except for non-payment of feuduty.

The enforcement, variation and discharge of feuing conditions is dealt with in Chapter 3.3.

2.6 Servitudes.

Reading List 2.6.

Real Conditions and Real Burdens can be imposed only *in gremio* of a conveyance (Charter or Disposition) to a disponee, or by a Deed of Conditions under 1979 Act S.17. Otherwise, the proprietor of land cannot, by agreement or unilateral grant, impose a real burden on his own land for the benefit of his superior or a neighbour. But servitudes can be so created; and for this reason Walker, quite logically, treats servitudes as a separate heritable right in Chapter 5.13. But, in practice, servitudes are normally created *in gremio* of a Charter or Disposition and are dealt with here, in the context of the Charter, with particular emphasis on the similarities and points of difference between Servitudes and Real Conditions.

A servitude is a conventional condition running with lands. In brief, a servitude is created for the benefit of a proprietor of land — the dominant tenement — and entitles the dominant owner to exercise certain rights on or over an adjoining piece of land — the servient tenement. From the point of view of the landowner, there is little difference in practical effect between a real condition in the title, and a servitude. Both derogate from the absolute quality of his ownership; both entitle some other party to exercise a right or enforce a restriction affecting the landowner as such. But in law, there are certain important distinctions, both as to constitution of the respective rights and as to their nature.

Classification — Positive and Negative Servitudes. The distinction is important because the mode of constitution differs for each type of right. Positive servitudes entitle the dominant owner to enter on the servient tenement and exercise the servitude right actively thereon or thereunder. Negative servitudes (principally light and prospect) merely entitle the dominant owner to restrict the use of the servient tenement. So, a positive servitude may be actively possessed or enjoyed; a negative servitude cannot be.

Salient characteristics of Servitudes.

1. There must be two separate tenements, or estates in land, the dominant and the servient, and they must be adjacent, though not necessarily actually contiguous.

2. The person entitled to exercise the servitude is so entitled, not **personally** as an individual, but as owner of the dominant tenement. The benefit of the servitude may not be separated from the dominant tenement; nor may the benefit of it be communicated to someone other than the owner (or occupier) of the dominant tenement.

3. While a servitude necessarily infringes on, and derogates from, the absolute freedom of the servient owner, it must nonetheless be consistent with his right of property; in other words, it cannot be so extensive or so burdensome that the servient owner is entirely precluded from using his land.

4. The presumption for freedom operates here, as with real conditons; and here implies —

(a) that the servitude must be duly constituted.

(b) that, in cases of ambiguity, the least onerous result is preferred.

(c) that the dominant owner must exercise the right *civiliter,* in the least burdensome manner.

(d) that the servient owner is limited in his freedom of use only to the extent necessary to allow of the proper exercise of the servitude. So, with a servitude of way, the servient owner may use it himself, may erect unlocked gates, or, in rural areas, if the exact line is not defined precisely, may alter the line to another route equally convenient.

5. The servient owner must suffer or permit a restriction on his freedom of use of his property at the instance of the dominant owner. But (with possibly one exception, *oneris ferendi*) there can be no positive obligation on him to do or execute any act or thing. His role is purely passive.

The various types of servitude right are all of long standing, well defined and well established, and are natural incidents to the proper enjoyment of heritable property. The same, or counterpart, rights exist in other systems (cf. English 'easements' and 'profits a prendre'). But, nonetheless, they are a feudal anomaly, inconsistent with the established principles of tenure in that, in **some** cases, written title is not necessary for their constitution, and sasine (or infeftment) is **never** necessary. Nothing need enter the GRS. In contrast, at common law, real conditions run with lands only if they occur in a conveyance, qualify an infeftment, and enter the record.

As a result, the class of negative servitudes is now closed and will not be further extended. And the Courts are very slow to recognise as a positive servitude any right not already so categorised. But new positive servitudes remain a possibility; and the quality of existing servitudes may be extended, e.g., a servitude of carriageway now normally includes use by motor vehicles.

Positive Servitudes

They may be constituted in three, or possibly four, ways:—

(a) **By express grant, or by express reservation,** in the titles of the persons acquiring the dominant or servient tenement respectively. So, in a Feu Charter, the superior may expressly confer on the vassal a right of access over other land of the superior or he may reserve a right of access to himself, or to a third party, over the vassal's property. Alternatively, positive servitudes may be constituted by mere written agreement (**not** a title) between the servient owner and dominant owner; or by a unilateral Deed of Servitude granted by the servient owner. In all cases, the deed must be probative; or, if improbative, be followed by *rei interventus.* In no case need any deed enter the record (although in fact it is always **desirable** to record it).

Where the deed containing the servitude is a feudalised title to the servient tenement and the servitude qualifies the servient owner's infeftment, nothing further is required; the dominant owner may exercise the right, or not, as he pleases; and only the operation of the negative prescription can (as a rule) deprive him of his right. But, where the deed is **not** recorded (or if recorded, is not a title but, for example, a mere agreement), then the dominant owner **must** in addition enter into possession of the servitude right (i.e. he must commence, and continue, to exercise his right) in order to make it effective against singular successors in the servient tenement.

Possession is required as an alternative to publication in the General Register of Sasines to ensure that, by possession and public enjoyment, the existence of the servitude is made known openly, and can be ascertained, from inspection of the property; in this way, a purchaser of the servient tenement is protected. But this is, in practice, a haphazard and uncertain method of discovering burdens which may be very onerous and can altogether frustrate the intentions of a purchaser.

Where the right is **not** contained in a feudalised title, then probably it must be a known servitude. But, where the deed is a feudalised title, then the right, if not in an exact category of known servitude, may yet be recognised as a servitude right, provided it qualifies the infeftment and has all the salient characteristics of a servitude right.

Again, with express grant or reservation of servitudes, as with reservations and burdens in titles generally, the grant of servitude will be strictly construed in favour of the servient tenement. The terms of the grant must be definite and there must be a definite intention to create a servitude running with the lands. But there are no statutory forms or any necessary words of style.

(b) **By implied grant or implied reservation.** An implied servitude can only be created when the two tenements, dominant and servient, have previously been owned by the same proprietor who has disposed of one (or both) of them, and in so doing has omitted to express such servitude rights as are either absolutely necessary or, in certain circumstances, reasonably necessary for the proper enjoyment of the subjects disponed, thus:

(i) Rights **absolutely** necessary to the use or enjoyment of the dominant tenement (servitude of necessity).

Suppose, for example, A sells to B land completely surrounded by other land of A, but gives B no express right of access; a **grant** of servitude of way will be implied. Also, if A disponed the **other** land to B, retaining the landlocked subjects without reserving to himself access in B's disposition, a **reservation** of a servitude of access is implied for A's benefit. It is **easier** to establish such a servitude, by **constitution** (or grant) in a conveyance over the retained remainder of the subjects, than by **reservation** in a conveyance of the 'servient' part. 2.6.17 Ferguson 1913 1 SLT 241.

But they may arise in **either** way. Or

(ii) Rights necessary for the proper, comfortable enjoyment of the dominant tenement. The extent, and limits within which servitudes may be constituted in these circumstances, are less certain.

The general principle seems firmly established in Cochrane -v- Ewart 4 Macq. 117. This case involved the continued use, following subdivision of a property, of a pre-existing drain serving the dominant and passing through the servient tenement. 'Where two properties are possessed by the same owner, and there has been a severance, anything which was used and which was necessary for the **comfortable enjoyment** of that part of the property which is **granted** '(i.e. the part sold and disponed)' shall be considered to follow from the grant.'

Compare 2.6.21 Murray 1973 SLT (Sh.Ct) 75. The owner of a group of buildings **sold** one of them, together with a small area of ground. Unknown to the purchaser, a water pipe ran under **the subjects of sale**, supplying main water to the remaining buildings **retained** by the seller. In the Disposition in favour of the purchaser, there was no reserved right to maintain this pipe.

The Sheriff rejected an argument that an existing main water supply was necessary for the reasonable enjoyment of a dwellinghouse on the footing that plenty of dwellinghouses in Scotland have no main water; and that the property in question was capable of being used as a house without a mains supply. To reserve a servitude right for this mains supply pipe clearly derogated from the grant in favour of the purchaser which requires an express reservation, except in cases of necessity. Since there was no 'necessity' in this instance, there could be no implied reservation of the necessary servitude right. In the result, by failing to reserve an express servitude right, the seller was deprived of his existing mains water supply.

This case confirms the general statement of principle, in Green's Encyclopaedia 13.1236, that a servitude under this head (necessary for comfortable enjoyment) can only be created by implied **grant** for the benefit of the dispon**ee**; but can never be created by implied **reservation** for the benefit of the dispon**er**.

If, in Murray, the facts had been reversed, and if the water mains serving the sold property had passed through the retained property, it might have been possible to establish a servitude by implication for the benefit of the **disponee.**

In 2.6.14 McEachen 1976 SLT 38, A owned and occupied a dwellinghouse with land attached. He sold and disponed the dwellinghouse and part of his land to B. In the Disposition, A conveyed to B the benefit of all rights of way, etc., in general terms; and specifically conferred on B a servitude right of access to the house by a road leading thereto from the public road across the remainder of A's land, the route being coloured blue on the attached plan.

It later transpired that, when A himself had occupied the house, he had also taken access thereto by a second route over the retained land, but in the Disposition no right was conferred on B to use this second route. Following on the sale, A closed the second route, leaving the first route open. B objected, claiming access to the dwellinghouse by **both** routes.

Held that, since a right of access had been specifically conferred in the purchaser's title by the first route, this by itself automatically excluded the possibility of any implied right of access by the second route.

There is a discussion in this case on the requisites for a servitude of access necessary for convenient and comfortable enjoyment. Clearly, there could be no question here of a servitude of **absolute** necessity, since there was an alternative access route in the title. The Sheriff Principal reviews the authorities at Page 4I and concludes:

'I find it difficult to presume an intention to create by implication a right of way in a case where the proprietor took pains to provide for access to the property disponed by making an express grant of a right of way.' He then distinguishes Cochrane -v- Ewart on the grounds that, in that case, the title was silent as to the mode of access; and follows 2.6.19 Fraser -v- Cox 1938 SC 506.

(c) **By the operation of prescription.** Until 1976, the period of possession required was forty years, with added years for non-age and disability. As from 25th July, 1976, the period is now twenty years in all cases.

The person claiming the right must be infeft in the dominant tenement; and he must show possession of the right, as of right, throughout the full period. Possession is not only proof that the right exists but also proof of the measure and extent of the right; it defines the dominant (and probably the servient) tenement affected by that right and the degree, and way, in which the right may be exercised. *Tantum praescriptum quantum possessum.*

(d) **Acquiescence.** '**It does appear** that, in certain circumstances, a servitude or some similar right' (sic) 'may be created by acquiescence' (Bell's Principles 947);

and there is authority for the view that in some cases singular successors in lands will be bound by the acquiescence of their predecessors. 2.6.22 Macgregor -v- Balfour 2F 345. This has been stated to occur when the thing acquiesced in is visible and obvious, especially where it is of such a character or cost as to be inconsistent with its having been allowed merely during pleasure.

In 2.6.24 More -v- Boyle 1967 SLT (Sh.Ct.) 38. four cottages in a row were served by a common water main running through each garden at the rear of each house. The main burst and was repaired by A, the first proprietor in the row of four. The other three owners declined to pay a share of the cost. So A cut off their water. It then transpired that none of the titles contained any reference to the common pipe, which had been 38 years *in situ*; and there was no right of servitude in the titles, by implication or by prescription. The Sheriff seemed inclined to the view that a servitude right to maintain the pipe had been established by acquiescence.

Note, however, that in this case the common pipe was laid by the original builder while all four plots were in his ownership. By the time each plot was sold, the common pipe was covered and invisible; and it is very doubtful if any of the four original purchasers knew of its existence. If they did, they may have acquiesced. If not, where was the 'acquiescence'?

Possibly, in this case, the right may, alternatively, have been constituted **by implication** in the four original Dispositions.

In 2.6.23 Robson 1965 SLT 381, there clearly was acquiescence, and nothing else. The owner of the allegedly dominant tenement, apparently with the agreement of the servient owner, laid pipes through the servient property for drawing water. The right to lay pipes was not contained in the titles nor established by any formal Deed of Servitude. Later, the servient owner requested the dominant owner to remove the pipes. **Held** that the servient owner, having acquiesced in the laying of the pipes, was personally barred from requiring their removal. Note in particular the comments of Lord Kissen at p.386/387 on the effect of acquiescence in such circumstances.

The indications are that, if personal bar is so established, the effect thereof will transmit against singular successors in the Servient tenement. Rankine — Personal Bar p.55.

Negative Servitudes.

These may **only** be constituted by title, or by **express** grant or by agreement in writing. The writing must be probative; **but** need **not** enter the record.

With a negative servitude, there cannot be any active exercise or enjoyment of the right until the servient owner actually contravenes his servitude obligation. So, with negative servitudes, there **cannot** be any possession; writing alone is therefore sufficient, whether recorded or not, to establish the right. So nothing may show, on record or from inspection of the property, that a negative servitude exists.

Transmission of the right.

It is inherent in the nature of a servitude that, once properly constituted in any of the ways indicated above, it runs with the lands so far as the **servient** tenement is concerned and will continue to affect it no matter into whose ownership it may pass. A servitude is, therefore, effective not only against the original owner of the servient tenement but against his heirs and singular successors whether they have prior notice of the right or not, and whether they acquire the whole, or part only, of the servient tenement. For example, a servient tenement subject to a right of way is later sold in fifty lots as a building estate; all fifty lots remain servient (if the right of way is through each lot).

So far as the dominant owner is concerned, the right subsists for the benefit of the dominant tenement. Two results follow:

(a) singular successors, as owners of the dominant tenement, require no express assignation of the servitude; mere title to the dominant tenement entitles them to exercise or enforce it; and

(b) the servitude cannot be divorced from the dominant tenement so as to benefit someone other than the owner of the dominant tenement. So the dominant owner cannot assign the right to a third party. In fact it is doubtful whether, in certain cases, the dominant owner can communicate the benefit of the servitude right to feuars and tenants, and if so to what extent. Clearly, to communicate a servitude of fuel to **several** purchasers on the break-up of an estate materially increases the burden and would be objectionable; less so, in the case of access or way; not so at all, in e.g. stillicide from a tenement roof when flats are sold individually, with common right, or interest in the roof.

See 2.6.37 Watson v Sinclair 1966 SLT (Sh.Ct.) 77 and 2.6.38 Keith v Texaco 1977 SLT (LT) 16.

Interest to enforce

With real conditions generally there must be interest to enforce — the superior's is assumed, a co-feuar must aver it. Similarly, with servitudes, the dominant owner must have an interest, but the rule now **seems** to be, logically, that the dominant owner need not prove or aver his interest; it is up to the servient owner to show that the dominant owner has no interest to enforce. 2.6.35 — Proprietors of Royal Exchange v Cotton 1912 SC 1151.

Extinction

A servitude, once constituted, will subsist until extinguished.

Methods:

1. **Express discharge**, by the dominant owner, normally (not necessarily) recorded. It must be probative.

2. **Confusio.**

3. **Prescription.** Under the 1973 Act from 25/7/76, the period has become 20 years **absolute** without any addition for non-age or disability. With positive servitudes, the period runs from the last active exercise of the right by the dominant owner; with negative servitudes, it runs from the date when the servient owner first does some act inconsistent with the servitude right.

4. **Acquiescence, etc.** Acquiescence or other evidence of abandonment by the dominant owner may operate to extinguish servitudes within the **prescriptive** period; the same applies on such a change of circumstances that the servitude becomes redundant.

5. **Compulsory Acquisition** of servient tenement. See under 'Compulsory Purchase'. Chap.7.2.

6. **Discharge** by the Lands Tribunal, under the 1970 Act. Part I — see below. Chap. 3.3.

Public Rights of Way.

A servitude exists for the benefit of an adjoining dominant tenement. A public right of way exists for the benefit of the public, between and connecting two public places. It may be of the same degree as the servitude right of way, i.e. footpath, horse road, drove road or carriage road. It may be constituted by express grant, but in the great majority of cases, public rights of way exist by virtue of prescriptive possession for the full prescriptive period of 20 years. It may be lost by disuse for the full prescriptive period; or by a lesser period of disuse coupled with actings by the servient proprietor which are inconsistent with the existence of the right and which are unchallenged over a period of time, of lesser duration than the prescriptive period.

Public rights of way may be vindicated by the general public, or by public bodies such as Local Authorities and Rights of Way Societies.

2.7 **Subordinate Clauses.**
Reading List 2.7.
In a Charter, the subordinate clauses include (a) clauses peculiar to the Charter or other Feudal Grant; and (b) subordinate clauses common to any conveyance of land, including a Disposition which creates no tenure.

The two clauses peculiar to a Feudal Grant are:

(1) **Tenendas.** This is the clause which, reflecting the phrase 'in feu farm dispone' in the dispositive clause, indicates the manner of holding, and clearly stamps this writ as a conveyance on tenure. In its standard form, it reads 'to be holden the said subjects of and under me and my foresaids as immediate lawful superiors thereof in feu farm fee and heritage forever'.

(2) **Reddendo.** This clause, also essential for a proper Feudal Grant, and peculiar to Feudal Grants, sets out the *reddendo* or return to be made by the vassal to his superior as the consideration for the Grant. As we have seen above, since 1924, feuduty had to be stated as a fixed amount of sterling money payable at fixed terms. But, in older Charters, the *reddendo* might take various forms, and in addition the clause normally set out the taxed casualties or duplicands.

Now, under the 1974 Act S.1., no feuduty may competently be created in a deed executed after 1st September, 1974. But:—

i) Tenure may be validly created without **any** *reddendo* — not even 1p. is required.

ii) A purported *reddendo* does not invalidate the whole Charter — it is simply unenforceable.

iii) If a binding contract to feu was entered into pre 8th November, 1973 (Green Paper Date) **and** the Charter is executed pre 8th November, 1975, a feuduty may validly be constituted. 1974 Act S.7. But the deed must contain, *in gremio* or endorsed, a memo to that effect, in the form of Schedule 4.

The remaining subordinate clauses are **not** peculiar to feudal grants but until 1979 were common to all types of conveyance, although in a Feu Charter the clauses take a special form.

In the original form of Feu Charter, all these clauses received lengthy and detailed treatment; in the modern form they are considerably abbreviated. The abbreviated forms now in use are statutory, first introduced by the 1847 Act and re-enacted in the 1868 Act S.5, S.8, and Schedule B.1. Each short clause authorised in S.5 receives a lengthy and detailed interpretation in S.8.

In fact, the forms in Schedule B.1 are primarily designed for use in a Disposition, not a Charter; and in the Feu Charter some adaptation of the statutory clauses is normal.

(1) **Entry.** Sch. B.1. 'With entry at the term of Whitsunday 198 '. This clause determines the date at which the Charter takes effect, to pass the *dominium utile* to the vassal. (See 1874 Act S. 28, for **implied** dates, if this clause is omitted.) For a discussion on the inter-relationship of date of execution, date of delivery, date of entry and date of registration in Sasines, see 2.7.1. Thomas v Lord Advocate 1953 SC 151. Disposition of land as a gift i.v.; signed, 4 May, delivered 6 May, date of entry 15 May, 1945; donor died 12 May, 1950, **more** than five years (the Estate Duty gift period) after delivery, less than five years after entry. Was Estate Duty payable under F.A.1894.S 2.(1)(c)? **Held** (Lord Mackintosh dissenting q.v.) that, by delivery, the deceased had completed the gift outwith the period.

(2) **Assignation of Writs.** Under the present system of registration for publication, recording of the appropriate writ in the Sasines Register is a prerequisite to the real right; but, by recording the appropriate title, the disponee thereunder establishes his real right if, but only if, the recorded title is itself valid and proceeds upon a valid prior progress of titles. The mere fact that A. holds land on a recorded title is not, *per se,* conclusive evidence of his right; some enquiry into a) the antecedents of that recorded title and/or b) possession for the prescriptive period, is always necessary. Therefore, every disponee, whether under a Feu Charter or under a Disposition, normally has an interest in the prior titles in order to maintain his own right. If these titles are not delivered to him (as they may not be), then he must have the right to call for production or exhibition of the prior titles when required.

On sub-infeudation (as here), the superior is not wholly divested; he retains the *dominium directum* which is, in law, a right to land, albeit burdened with the vassal's right under the Charter. The superior, therefore, in practice, retains all prior titles; and the only writ delivered to the vassal is his Charter. The purpose of this clause in the Charter is to confer on the vassal a right to call for production of the superior's titles, when need arises.

Sch. B.1. 'And I assign the writs and have delivered the same according to Inventory'. For the reason stated above, this is unsuitable for a Charter, and the Charter clause reads, instead: 'And I assign the writs, but to the effect only of maintaining and defending the right hereby granted;'

For deeds executed after 4th April, 1979 — the date of passing of the Land Registration (Scotland) Act 1979 — the assignation of writs clause need no longer be included in a Feu Charter and, if omitted, the Charter implies:—

 (i) an assignation to the vassal of all prior Title Deeds and Searches, to the effect of maintaining and defending him in the feu; and

 (ii) that the Superior is obliged for that purpose to make the Title Deeds and Searches furthcoming to him on all necessary occasions at the vassal's expense.

(3) **Assignation of Rents.** Sch. B.1. 'And I assign the rents'. The vassal under the Charter may himself enter into personal possession and occupation of the subjects conveyed to him and usually does so. Alternatively, having acquired the right of property under the Charter, he may part with possession of the property for a term of years to a tenant under a temporary arrangement known as a Lease, in virtue of which, *inter alia,* the proprietor becomes entitled to an annual rent from the tenant. If the Lease is to be valid, the proprietor must himself be infeft. If the feu is sold and disponed to a disponee, that does not automatically bring the Lease to an end; but the disponee becomes entitled to the rents in place of the disponer. It is the person infeft for the time being who is entitled to rent; and rents follow infeftment. Accordingly, the assignation of rents clause in a Conveyance is not necessary to confer a title on the disponee to collect rents; but it does serve to determine the basis of apportionment of the rent payable by the tenant, as between disponer and disponee with reference to the date of entry.

In deeds executed after 4th April, 1979, the assignation of rents clause need no longer be included and, if omitted, the Charter itself implies an assignation to the vassal of the rent payable in respect of the feu, if any.

(4) **Obligation of Relief.** Sch. B.1. 'And I bind myself to free and relieve the said disponee and his foresaids of all feuduties and public burdens'. By S.8, this imports

an obligation to relieve of all feuduties due to the superior and all public parochial and local burdens due from or on account of the lands conveyed, **prior to the date of entry.** In other words, as between granter and grantee all out goings are apportioned at entry. The Clause is not suitable as it stands for a Charter, because so far as feuduty is concerned, the granter/Superior will **remain** liable for the feuduty due by him to **his** superior — (the over–feuduty) — in all time coming.

If he feus his whole property, he may have to redeem the over-feuduty, if allocated. 1974 Act S.5. 'Obligation to grant a conveyance' includes a Feu Charter.

In deeds executed after 4th April, 1979, no express clause of obligation of relief is necessary and, if omitted, the charter itself implies an obligation on the Superior to relieve the vassal of feuduty payable by the Superior to his own Superiors in perpetuity; and of all other ground burdens up to the date of entry.

(5) **Warrandice.** Walker Chapter 5.4 page 74 and Chapter 5.16 page 305. In any transaction for sale and purchase of heritage, there are two stages; first, completion of the contract, and second, delivery of the conveyance to the purchaser against payment of the price when the purchaser takes actual possession; the rights and obligations of the parties differ at each stage. On completion of the contract, the seller's obligations are briefly to give a good title, possession, and a clear search. If at **that** stage the purchaser finds that the seller cannot fulfil any of these obligations, his remedy is rescission of the contract and an action of damages for breach thereof. But once the conveyance has been delivered and the transaction completed, the seller's only remaining obligation is warrandice against eviction; it is then too late for *restitutio in integrum* or for rescission. If, **after** completion, the purchaser **then** discovers some defect in the title or some impingement on his possession, he cannot then reduce the contract, and return the property to the seller. His only action is for damages *quanti minoris,* and it is on the seller's warrandice that this action is based.

In its absolute form, the warrandice obligation represents a **personal** guarantee by the disponer that he will indemnify the disponee against any loss or damage which the disponee may suffer owing to a diminution in the value of his real right arising out of:

(i) complete eviction of the disponee from the whole subjects, or partial eviction from part, owing to a defect in the title; or

(ii) a real burden, or other adverse real right, affecting the subjects, actually made effective against the disponee, which he was unaware of at date of delivery of the disposition — 'constructive partial eviction'.

Warrandice is necessarily, and of its nature, a **personal** guarantee only; and of course, as with any personal obligation, the value of the indemnity to the purchaser depends entirely on the financial stability of the seller and his ability to pay. Thus warrandice by a disponer who later has become bankrupt, although it infers an obligation to indemnify the purchaser to the extent of his loss, may well in fact be worthless. That, however, is a risk which the purchaser must take; he cannot ask for more than the seller's warrandice; he cannot insist that the obligation be fortified either by security or by a third party's guarantee, **except** by express provision in the Contract of Sale and Purchase, which is rare.

The warrandice obligation does **not** indemnify against loss or damage which the grantee may suffer from any cause, other than actual or constructive eviction by an adverse real right.

The existence of a feu right would found a claim in warrandice, since the disponee would be excluded from *dominium utile.* Similarly, servitudes will found a claim, if patrimonial loss can be demonstrated. Leases, on the other hand, will not normally found a claim — See 2.7.17 Lothian and Border Farmers Ltd. v. McCutcheon 1952 SLT 450.

In every case, the disponer's obligation is to indemnify. He is not obliged to take any steps to put the title right, nor can the disponee claim *restitutio in integrum.* This is most strongly emphasised in 2.7.16 Welsh v. Russell 21 R 769. In that case, after completion of the purchase of a house and garden, a right of way was later established across the garden by an adjoining owner. Founding on warrandice, the disponee sued for the present value of the whole subjects, offering to reconvey them as they stood to the seller; in other words, he sought restitution, not indemnity. **Held:** that, in cases of partial eviction, the purchaser's right under warrandice was limited to indemnification for the loss sustained.

Extent of Claim. Warrandice is indemnity and the *quantum* of any claim must therefore be calculated on the basis of the actual pecuniary loss suffered by the purchaser. In cases of total eviction, it is settled that, if the value at the time of eviction is greater than the price paid, then warrandice covers the excess and is not limited to the original price. Thus, if A buys land for £100 and builds to the value of £10,000 on it, A can (if evicted) claim £10,100, not merely the original £100. The converse case, where the value at eviction is less than the original price, is not settled; but presumably, only that value could be recovered. In cases of partial eviction, the *quantum* of the claim is the amount in money terms by which the adverse right diminishes the value of the property. If the adverse right is, e.g. a Bond for an exact amount, no question arises; the sum in the Bond is the amount claimed. In other circumstances, it is a question of valuation.

Degrees of Warrandice. The extent or degree of warrandice to be undertaken by the granter of a deed varies according to circumstances. In every heritable conveyance, warrandice is almost invariably expressed. But, if no warrandice is expressed, then in every case some degree of warrandice will be implied. To omit the clause of warrandice altogether does not therefore mean that the granter gives no warrandice; in the result, a **higher** degree of warrandice may be implied against him than that which he would have undertaken or been obliged to undertake had the clause been expressed in the deed. The nature of the transaction and the capacity of the granter will normally determine what degree of warrandice is appropriate in any particular case. But, of course, it is always open to the parties to agree to specialties to meet special circumstances.

1. **Absolute Warrandice,** the highest degree, indemnifies against loss arising from any defect in the title **or** any adverse right, not attributable to the act or neglect of the grantee. Absolute warrandice is implied in onerous transactions, i.e. sale for adequate price.

2. **Warrandice from fact and deed.** Here the granter is bound to indemnify the grantee against loss arising from any act or deed, past, present or future of the granter himself. He is **not** liable for any defects **not** personally attributable to him. This degree is implied where the consideration is not a full one; and probably also where the granter acts in a representative capacity only. Certainly, in the last case, this is the degree of warrandice always expressed for, e.g. Trustees, thus — 'I as Trustee foresaid grant warrandice from my own facts and deeds only'. It would

be unfair if a Trustee were personally liable to indemnify for all defects, because he has no patrimonial or beneficial interest in the price; but in onerous transactions, the beneficiaries are also taken bound in absolute warrandice.

3. **Simple Warrandice.** Here the granter is liable only for future voluntary deeds adverse to the grantee's right. It carries no indemnity against past acts of the granter, nor against future acts in implement of a prior binding obligation. It is implied in all gratuitous transactions; if expressed, the term used is 'I grant simple warrandice', or 'I grant warrandice, but only against all voluntary acts and deeds hereinafter to be executed or done by me', and this, or fact and deed warrandice, is normally expressed in any gratuitous deed.

Combined degrees. It is quite common for two degrees of warrandice to be combined expressly in a deed. The normal clause in an onerous deed by trustees exemplifies. 'And I as Trustee foresaid grant warrandice from my own facts and deeds only and I bind the trust estate under my charge and the beneficiaries therein in absolute warrandice'.

Consenters. Pure consent alone will not normally imply warrandice in any degree against the consenter; but, where the consenter is conjoined in the operative clause, some warrandice will probably be inferred, at least simple warrandice, possibly more according to the nature of the consent; consenter's warrandice should always be express — usually fact and deed will serve, sometimes absolute is required.

The Statutory Clause. 1868 Act, S.5. and Sch. B.1. This Clause in the Schedule is 'I grant warrandice'. The interpretation of that Clause in S.8. implies

'... unless especially qualified ... absolute warrandice as regards the lands and writs and evidents, and warrandice from fact and deed as regards the rents ...'.

This means —

1. Absolute warrandice as to title, which we have just discussed.

2. The same for the title deeds. In other words, the granter warrants that the whole progress of titles is good and sufficient to maintain the grantee in possession in terms of the dispositive clause of his conveyance. It is not necessarily an absolute warranty that each individual writ is wholly valid according to its terms. This distinction is drawn in 2.7.13 Brownlie v. Millar 7 R (HL) 66 (and see 5 R 1076).

3. The rents are warranted from fact and deed only. The rents are assigned, as we have seen. In any assignation of a debt the degree of warrandice implied is fact and deed only and *debitum subesse* — that the debt subsists and is owing. There is no guarantee that the debtor is solvent or that he will pay; if that were inferred, the granter would be in the position of guarantor to all the tenants. In practice, it means that the leases are valid and are effectually assigned, for what they are worth. (*debitum subesse* is implied. Menzies 179).

If no warrandice is expressed, it will be implied in one degree or another, according to the nature of the transaction and capacity. The converse also holds, viz.: that where warrandice is express, it will entirely supersede whatever obligation would otherwise have been implied by law. And, further, any express warrandice is strictly interpreted according to its terms. This may have unfortunate results. Thus, the use of the statutory clause 'I grant warrandice' is not appropriate in a gratuitous conveyance; fact and deed is the most that should be given, more often simple warrandice only; but if 'I grant warrandice' is so used, it will receive full effect. On the other hand, where fact and deed warrandice only is given in an onerous disposition, that is all that the grantee can later found on, although, had no warrandice been expressed, then absolute warrandice would have been implied.

Qualifications of Warrandice

In an onerous conveyance, the statutory clause is almost always used but it may require qualification. One example — Trustees — has already been given; a similar qualification is appropriate in any conveyance granted by someone **not** the true beneficial owner.

Where there are adverse rights subsisting at the date of conveyance of which the purchaser is aware and which he is to accept (e.g. servitudes, leases, bonds, etc.) all such rights must be excepted from warrandice to prevent any possibility of future claims against the granter.

Transmission

It is settled that the assignation of writs clause in a Conveyance passes on the benefit of existing warrandice obligations to the grantee under a Conveyance. Probably, this passed by implication on a Disposition alone without assignation of writs before the 1979 Act; but this is now implied by Statute under the 1979 Act S.16 (1).

(6) Certificate of Value for Stamp Duty.
See Chap. 1.5.

(7) Consent to Registration

(8) Testing Clause

2.8 Infeftment of the Vassal.

Reading List 2.8.

The mere fact that a Charter is prepared containing all the requisite Clauses does not, of itself, operate to confer any right on the vassal and imposes no obligations on the granter thereof. Before the vassal can perfect his real right and become infeft, a number of further steps are necessary. The further elements involve:

1. **Authentication** — See Chapter 1.2.

A Feu Charter is a formal writ relating to land. It must be probative, and proper authentication will involve:

(a) Execution of the Charter on each page by the superior; or on the last page under the 1970 Act.

(b) Subscription by two witnesses to the superior's signature on the last page of the deed;

(c) The insertion in the deed (normally in the Testing Clause) of the names and addresses of the witnesses.

(d) In addition (although this is not all legally necessary), the testing clause contains some further information including the number of pages of the deed, schedules, plans, etc., a reference to any alterations, marginal additions, etc., in the deed in order properly to authenticate them, and the date and place of execution.

2. **Delivery** — See Chapter 1.3.

The mere execution of the deed by the granter does not, of itself, immediately create binding rights and obligations. So long as the deed remains in the possession of the granter or under his control, it is inoperative; to make it operative, it must be delivered to the vassal.

3. **Stamp Duty** — See Chapter 1.5.

The Feu Charter is, for Stamp Duty, a Conveyance on sale by superior to vassal and is liable to *ad valorem* conveyance on sale duty. With appropriate Certificate of Value, it qualifies for exemption.

Special provision applied before the 1974 Act to the Feu Charter, where the consideration took the form of or included a feuduty. The consideration for Stamp Duty was the total sum of feuduties which would become payable within the 20 years following the date of the deed, plus the *grassum* (if any).

4. **Registration in Sasines.** Mere delivery of a Feu Charter, although essential to the vassal's right, does not of itself operate wholly to divest the superior nor to perfect the vassal's real right in the subjects. Instead, delivery of the Charter merely confers upon the vassal a valid personal title to the *dominium utile* only, of itself a mandate for infeftment and assignable as such by general disposition (and pre-1970 also by special assignation), binding on the superior and on the universal successors of the superior in the superiority in the same way in which a Contract would be so binding. But, until the next step is taken, the vassal's right remains personal as opposed to real and cannot prevail in a competition with a singular successsor of the superior. To convert his personal title into a real right, good against the world, the vassal must complete his infeftment by registration in Sasines. See 2.8.1. Ceres School Board -v- McFarlane 23 R 279, for an illustration of the general principle 'that a singular successor takes the lands free from the personal obligations of his predecessor and unaffected by burdens not appearing on the Records'.

Even on recording of the Charter, the superior still retains his title to the *dominium directum* — See Chapter 3.1. In contrast, the granting and recording of a **Disposition** fully divests the granter thereof who has no remaining or continuing interest in the subjects disponed; and no tenure, nor any equivalent relationship, is created as between disponer and disponee.

Since 1858, the Charter or Disposition operates of itself as a mandate for infeftment by *de plano* recording in the Register of Sasines. Before a writ can be so recorded, it must satisfy certain requirements (see 2.8.4. — Macdonald -v- The Keeper of the Registers 1914 SC 854) which, briefly, are:

(a) that the writ is probative;

(b) that it is properly stamped;

(c) that it is appropriate to the Register of Sasines, i.e., that it deals with an estate in land;

(d) that it contains an identifying description. See generally, Macdonald above;

(e) that it carries the statutory Warrant of Registration.

Warrants of Registration.

The 1858 Act, when abolishing the Instrument of Sasine, also introduced as a new requirement that the conveyance when presented for registration should carry a Warrant of Registration endorsed thereon, authorising the Keeper to record the writ. In terms of the 1858 Act, the Warrant must identify the person taking infeftment and must be signed by him or his authorised Agent.

When, in 1868, all Land Registers were centralised in Edinburgh, a further statutory requirement was added to the Warrant of Registration, in that from 1868 onwards the Warrant must also direct the **Division** of the Register in which the writ is to be recorded.

The 1868 Act S.141 provides, as to Warrants, as follows:

1. **All** deeds and writs of every sort must have a Warrant; and this applies both to writs to be registered in the General Register of Sasines and in the Burgh Registers.

2. All Warrants must specify (which meant in 1868 name and design) the person on whose behalf the writ was recorded and the Division of the General Register of Sasines or the Burgh Register.

3. The Warrant must be signed by the person requiring registration or by his Agent.

The Section then referred to four forms of Warrant adapted to meet various circumstances; but these forms are in turn superseded by the 1924 Act S.10 and Schedule F which supplies a single new composite form of Warrant capable of being adapted to a variety of circumstances. The principal amendments in the 1924 Act are:

1. It is no longer necessary to design a party in a Warrant; he is referred to simply as 'within-named' provided he is designed in the writ itself;

2. Where the Conveyance being recorded contains a destination to several persons and the survivors, or to Trustees *ex officiis* and to their successors as Trustees, the effect of that destination is impliedly imported into the Warrant, without any express reference thereto. Thus, in a Disposition in favour of 'A and B and the survivor of them', the Warrant of Registration simply refers to 'A and B' without reference to survivorship; but the survivorship element is impliedly imported into the Warrant for the purposes of their infeftment.

The Form of Warrant in Schedule F now reads —

'Register on behalf of the within-named A.B. (or on behalf of A.B.) (Designation) in the Register of the County of G. (or in the Registers of the Counties of G, H, and J).

AB.

W.S., Edinburgh,

Agent.'

The Schedule has five notes for guidance in particular cases. The subject matter of these notes is:

1. A variation on the standard form of Warrant referring to a clause of direction.

2. A variation on the standard form of Warrant dealing with combined registration in Sasines and B. of C. and S.

3. A simplification in the case of Trustees, who no longer need set out at full length their fiduciary capacity; but instead insert, in the Warrant, the words 'as Trustees within mentioned'.

4. A variation on the standard form of Warrant to meet one special case, where a writ is recorded along with certain other writs endorsed on it. We will come to this later.

5. A variation on the standard form of Warrant to meet the case where several related writs are recorded together; but this no longer applies, Assignations of unrecorded conveyances having been abolished by the 1970 Act S48.

Note that, as a necessary result of statutory provisions relating to Warrants, the Warrant is the limit of the infeftment. Thus, where a Feu Charter is granted in favour of 'A and B' and is recorded with Warrant of Registration 'on behalf of the within-named A', without reference to B, A. is infeft but B. is not, even although the Charter in favour of B appears on the record.

Accordingly, following on delivery and stamping of the Feu Charter or Disposition, the disponee will endorse a Warrant of Registration thereon and he or his Agent will sign it. The Deed is then presented physically (by hand or by post) at the Register House in Edinburgh; entered in the Presentment Book; later minuted in the Minute Book; copied; and finally returned to the ingiver. His infeftment dates from the date of, and is effective as at the date of, presentation for registration. At that date, the vassal or Disponee is infeft and has established his real right.

The Effect of Infeftment.

Registration is an essential pre-requisite to the creation of the real right. But, in a system of registration of deeds as opposed to a system of registration of title, the mere fact that a deed has been recorded in Sasines is not an automatic guarantee of its validity nor does it necessarily follow that, because the vassal has recorded his Charter, he necessarily has the real right. He has an indefeasible real right if, **but only if**, his Charter derives from a superior whose title is in turn valid and unchallengable. But a defect in the superior's title is not cured by registration of the vassal's Charter; and the Charter may later be reduced, notwithstanding that it has been recorded, if it later turns out that the superior's title was invalid.

Exactly the same principle applies to a Disponee on recording his Disposition.

5. **Registration of Title.** Under the Land Registration (Scotland) Act 1979, registration of deeds in Sasines will be gradually superseded over a period of years and will be replaced by registration of the title. Registration of Title involves a different principle in that, on registering the title, the Keeper of the Registers then guarantees the validity of the Title for the benefit of the applicant registering the same. The same general principles continue to apply viz. that, on delivery of a Charter or Disposition of land in a registration district, the disponee must then register it. Unless and until he does so, he holds on a personal title only; and registration has the effect of converting that personal title into a real right. But the quality of the real right obtained by the disponee on registration of the title differs significantly in certain respects from the real right obtained by him on the recording of a Deed in the Register of Sasines under the present system.

See generally Chapter 8.2.

2.9 The Effects of Possession
Reading List 2.9.

'Sasine' in its original sense involved physical symbolic delivery on the ground. The last traces of Sasine in this sense disappeared in 1858; and, since then, the real right in land has come to depend solely on title. Delivery (other than delivery of the appropriate **title,** which is not the same thing) and subsequent possession of heritage are no longer relevant factors. Thus, A, (infeft in the lands of X on a valid progress of titles) has delivered by post to B. (then resident in Hong Kong) a Feu Charter by A. to B. of the lands of X, in usual form. As between A. and B., delivery of the Charter completes the transfer of the *dominium utile*; and, of itself, confers a valid personal title on B. By posting the Feu Charter from Hong Kong to the General Register of Sasines in Edinburgh, with Warrant of Registration thereon, B. converts his personal title into a real right; and, at the moment of recording, his real right is perfected, notwithstanding that B. still remains in Hong Kong and that the property remains unoccupied for the next thirty years. At the end of that period, B. still has the real right unimpaired, subject only to one possible qualification — see Prescription below.

But possession of heritage may be significant in three ways:—

1. **Possessory Remedies.** See Walker Chapter 5.6. page 100. But the reduction in the period of the positive prescription to 10 years has rendered these remedies largely academic.

2. **Bona Fide Possession.** See Walker Chapter 5.6. page 101.

3. **Prescription.** The general principle is that mere lapse of time, of itself, may operate to create, modify or extinguish rights or obligations in land, or impose limitations on the mode of enforcement thereof. Two applications of the rule apply to heritable titles, namely, the positive prescription which applies **only** in the case of heritage, and the long negative prescription (formerly the negative prescription) which applies generally to all rights involving a debtor/creditor relationship, whether relating to heritage or moveables.

The positive and long negative prescriptions now rest wholly on statutory provision, as interpreted by judicial decision.

All earlier statutory provisions have recently been repealed entire by the Prescription and Limitation (Scotland) Act 1973, with effect from 25th July, 1976. The 1973 Act therefore now provides a complete and self-contained statutory code for both the positive and the long negative prescriptions. However, the old law is to a large extent re-enacted in the 1973 Act, albeit with some significant modifications; and, in the result, the basic underlying principles of earlier legislation on both prescriptions are substantially preserved. Therefore, many of the cases decided under previous statutory provisions still remain relevant to the new code.

Under the 1973 Act, the period of the positive prescription in most cases is now ten years, but remains at twenty years in certain special cases dealt with below. The period of the long negative prescription is twenty years in all cases.

Positive Prescription.

The positive prescription operates actively to create, enlarge, or fortify rights in land which did not previously exist or which, previously, were at least open to challenge.

In feudal theory, all land belongs to the Crown. Therefore, at Common Law, in order to establish a good title to land, it is essential to trace back the title to an original Crown grant and to produce all the links in title intervening between the original Crown grant and the present proprietor. These links must, in themselves, be valid and sufficient to transmit the right. In almost every case, this would involve enormous labour; and the result might well be inconclusive. The original object of the 1617 Act was to secure the *bona fide* proprietor in possession against spurious challenge; but the emphasis has shifted and the main object of the modern legislation on the positive prescription is to limit the period of research and enquiry, in any particular case, to the title, in the progress, last recorded more than 10 years ago; and to declare that such title, so recorded, is absolute in the person of the possessor, no matter what other competing titles may be produced against him. Note the two separate elements. There must be, firstly, a title; and, following thereon, possession for a period. In the result, the rule stated above that title alone, without delivery or possession, confers real rights, suffers a qualification to this extent that, **in a competition**, where two competing parties can both produce titles and infeftment in the same subjects, the one who can prove possession, in addition, for the 10-year period will be preferred.

If title **and** possession for the prescriptive period **do** coincide, all enquiry into the *initium possessionis,* and into the validity of prior titles, is altogether barred. It does not matter that the basic title originated from someone who had no right to grant it (*a non domino,* or *a non habente potestatem*). It does not matter that the original title was granted in bad faith. Indeed, the basic title may have been, and often is, granted, *a non domino,* with the sole purpose of possessing thereon for the prescriptive period in order to create a real right in the subjects to which, prior to the granting of the Disposition, the possessor had no colourable right or title.

In one of the leading early cases on prescription, you will find this dictum (much quoted), viz.:

'It is the great purpose of prescription to support bad titles. Good titles stand in no need of prescription'. 2.9.1 - Scott v. Bruce Stewart 3RLC 334. This proposition is perfectly correct, so far as it goes. **But**, since a **bad** title can be validated by prescription, a bad title **may** prevail in a question with a title originally good on which possession has not followed. Accordingly, a **good** title **may** require possession following thereon to **maintain** it if (or to the extent to which) it conflicts with another competing title.

The positive prescription has two important practical consequences:

(i) Prescription cannot cure a title which is itself *ex facie* invalid or which is forged. With these two exceptions, a title initially defective from whatever other cause is validated and put completely beyond challenge by possession for the necessary period. So, if A occupies land without any right or title thereto, he can grant a Disposition of that land in favour of himself and record it in the Register of Sasines. If he continues to occupy that land for ten years thereafter, then, on the expiry of the ten-year period, the Disposition, which he granted in favour of himself and which was originally totally invalid, becomes valid and unchallengeable; and the true owner of the land, whoever he may be, is no longer able to reduce the Disposition, as he could have done initially, and so loses his right of property altogether.

(ii) In many cases, the description in a title is indefinite or ambiguous, in that the description is not precisely bounding on all sides. In such cases, the extent of the land contained in that title is defined by possession for the necessary period.

However, for reasons explained above, the positive prescription requires both title and possession. If, therefore, the description in an existing title is precise and bounding, possession of land beyond those precise boundaries cannot be founded on or referred to that title, in that the possession on the face of it contradicts the title. Hence the importance of the distinction between bounding titles and titles which are not bounding.

A bounding title in this context is one where the description so precisely defines all the boundaries of the land that the exact extent of it can be ascertained from the title itself.

Where the title is so bounding, corporeal property, e.g. land and buildings, etc., cannot be acquired by prescriptive possession beyond those boundaries; but incorporeal rights, e.g. a servitude right of access, or right of fishings, may be acquired beyond the boundaries.

Now to consider the **quality** of the title and the **nature** of the possession which are necessary to satisfy the statutory rules.

(1) Earlier provisions.

Until 1976, the basic Act was The Prescription Act of 1617 (C.12) which provided, in outline, that possession of land, following on infeftment therein, for forty years, continually and together, peaceably and without lawful interruption, secured the right and title of such possessor beyond challenge, whatever the nature of any competing title may be, unless the title on which he possessed was a forgery. The infeft proprietor in possession had to produce, as the basis of his prescriptive right, a Charter on which infeftment had followed, or an Instrument of Sasine following on a retour of service or a writ of *clare constat.* The period (or periods) of minority of the person(s), against whom prescription is pleaded, were not counted in computing the forty-year period.

The nature of the title on which the prescription proceeds, and the period of possession, were redefined in the 1874 Act S.34; but that, in turn, was repealed and re-enacted by the 1924 Act S.16. The 1924 Act provided that any *ex facie* valid, irredeemable title to an estate in land, recorded in the appropriate Register of Sasines, was to be sufficient foundation for prescription under the 1617 Act; and, further, that possession following on such recorded title for the space of **twenty** years, continually and together and peaceably, without any lawful interruption, should be equivalent to possession for **forty** years under the 1617 Act. Further, no deduction or allowance was to be made on account of years of minority. This period was further reduced to ten years by the 1970 Act S.8, except **quoad** foreshore and fishings vested in the Crown. The 1924 Act and 1970 Act had no application to servitudes or public rights of way or other public rights, for which the prescriptive period remained forty years.

(2) The 1973 Act.

Three distinct but parallel provisions are made in the 1973 Act for three separate cases dealt with in Sections 1, 2 and 3, thus:

S.1. This applies to interests in land generally, and covers, *inter alia,* all proprietary rights held on recorded titles and recorded leases, but **not** servitudes.

S.2. This deals with unusual special cases where, for technical reasons, the title has not been recorded, e.g. allodial land, unrecorded leases, etc. as in S.2(2)(b) and (a) respectively.

S.3. This deals exclusively with servitudes.

The general principle of each of the three Sections is the same, viz.:

If in any given case the owner (and his predecessors in title, if any) have possessed a heritable property or exercised a heritable right for the appropriate period following on the appropriate title, then on the expiry of the period, the validity of the title or right is put beyond challenge. But the detail differs in each of the three Sections to take account of the different nature of the title, and of the property or interest in each case.

1973 Act. S.1. Interests in Land: General.

This section is modified for Registration of Title by the 1979 Act S.10. So far as Sasines titles are concerned the provision here takes this form:

S.1(1) If:

(a) an interest in land has been possessed by the reputed owner (and his predecessors in title, if any), for a continuous period of **ten** years, openly and peaceably; and

(b) that possession was founded on, and followed, the recording in GRS of a Deed sufficient in its terms to constitute a title to that interest,

then, on the expiry of that ten-year period, the validity of that title so far as relating to that interest is exempt from challenge except on the grounds that the deed is *ex facie* invalid; or was forged.

S.1(2) The Section applies to any interest in land, the title to which can competently be recorded. Obviously, this covers all proprietory interests and recorded leases as stated above; but, by virtue of the definition in S.15, interest in land here specifically excludes servitudes, which are specially dealt with in S.3.

Possession

In terms of S1(1)(a) there must have been possession for a continuous period of ten years (or twenty years under S.1(4)), which has been:

'Openly, peaceably and without any judicial interruption.'

In one special case, under S.1(4), possession must be for twenty years, not ten years. This is where the right claimed by possession is a right to the foreshore or to salmon fishings as against the Crown, as owner of the regalia. This only applies as between the proprietor claiming the right, and the Crown. Thus, if the Crown has granted salmon fishings on a Crown Charter to a Crown vassal who in turn sub-feus on a Charter which refers to fishings but not 'salmon fishings', and if the sub-vassal possesses the **salmon** fishings on that title for **ten** years, he has a good claim to the salmon fishings as against his superior. The superiors right as against the Crown is established by the plain terms of the title and requires **no** possession to validate it.

This requirement as to possession is then further amplified by Section 4 dealing with interruption, by Section 14 dealing with the computation of the period, and by the definitions in S.15.

The possession may be natural, by actual physical occupation on the part of the proprietor claiming the right; or it may be civil, by actual occupation on behalf of the owner by his tenants. S.15(1).

In either case, 'possession' implies *animus,* i.e. it must be either in the belief that the occupant is in possession as of right, or with the intention of establishing a right. Possession in *mala fide* counts. But none of this is statutory.

The possession must be in support of and consistent with, the title, not 'in the teeth of the title'. See above, with particular reference to bounding titles.

The possession must be exclusive, and sufficient in extent to support the right claimed by it. The extent and nature of possession vary according to circumstances.

Under S.1(1)(a) the possession must be for a continuous period of ten years (or, S.1(4), twenty years) 'openly, peaceably and without any judicial interruption'. As to continuity, the term 'continuous' is interpreted *secundum materiam*. Thus, it is not necessary, in order to establish a right to salmon fishing by prescription, to show that the claimant has fished continuously, 24-hours-a-day throughout the ten-year period (or twenty-year period in a question with the Crown); nor, in the case of a right of way, that someone has walked continuously over it throughout the twenty-year period. On the other hand, mere occasional acts of apparent possession will not serve. There must be regular and continuing acts throughout the period.

Further, the possession must be open and peaceable, not clandestine or in the face of opposition.

If the possession is physically interrupted either because, for a definite period, the possessor excludes himself from possession or is excluded by another, that will interrupt the prescription and the period would have to start to run again entire from the date when possession was resumed. The same effect follows on judicial interruption, i.e., where a competing claimant has raised an action to exclude the possessor from his possession.

1973 Act S.2. Interests in Land: Special Cases.

Almost identical provision is made in this Section for special and very unusual cases where, for technical reasons, the title is not recorded or is not recordable.

In contrast to S.l, under S.2 possession is founded on and follows the execution of a deed (whether recorded or not) which is sufficient to constitute a title to that interest. Note particularly that the initial title need not be recorded. But, in all these cases, the necessary period of possession is, under S.2(1)(a), twenty years, not ten years as in S.l.

1973 Act S.3. Positive Servitudes and Public Rights of Way.

Under this Section, alternative provisions are made for the establishing of servitude rights by prescription, taking account of the special nature of a servitude right.

Thus, under S.3(1), possession of a servitude for twenty years following on the execution of a deed will establish the right beyond challenge, subject to the same exceptions as are provided in S.1. The deed must be sufficient in its terms to constitute the servitude either by express provision therein or by necessary implication.

Alternatively, under S.3(2), if a positive servitude has been possessed for twenty years, without reference to any written deed, the existence of the servitude as so possessed is exempt from challenge. This simply re-enacts, in a modified form, the former rule that positive servitudes can be created either by deed followed by possession or by mere possession. It underlines the peculiar feature of servitudes with particular reference to prescription in that, here, a **written title** is not necessary, and nothing need appear on the Record. In contrast, under S.1, possession **must** follow on a **written recorded** title; and under S.2, a **written**, though unrecorded, **title**.

A similar provision is made in S.3(3) under which a public right of way is established by twenty-year possession. See 2.9.59a Richardson 1982 SLT 237.

Further, under S.3(4), possession of servitudes means possession of the servitude right by any person in possession of the dominant tenement.

The Long Negative Prescription

This is dealt with in the context of Examination of Title in Chapter 7.4.

3.1 Superiorities.
Reading List 3.

Immediately before the Feu Charter is granted, the granter (the superior) stands at the foot of the feudal ladder, which reaches up, rung by rung, through his superior and his oversuperior, each holding on tenure of and under the Crown as ultimate or paramount superior. In his position at the foot of the feudal ladder, the superior, immediately prior to the granting of the Charter, owns the *plenum dominium,* and is in physical occupation of the *dominium utile* of, *inter alia,* the subjects which are now to be feued to the new vassal under the Feu Charter. (In practice, the superior normally owns a good deal more land besides). By the granting of the Charter, the superior is **not** divested. Instead, retaining his title to the land, he grants certain rights therein for the benefit of his vassal; but his title is now burdened with the subaltern rights of his vassal which he has created for the vassal under the Charter. The superior's title is, and remains, essentially a title to land — his own original title to the *dominium utile* — with the same characteristics *quoad* trans-missions, securities, etc., as any ordinary *dominium utile* title. So, where there have been successive sub-feus of the same land since the original Crown grant, the resulting position is that several separate persons in law own the same land, on separate titles, each for his own separate interest of vassal in the *dominium utile* at the bottom of the ladder, superior, over-superior, etc., upwards to the Crown.

Immediately after the Feu Charter is granted, as a result of which the vassal acquires his right to the *dominium utile,* a new and additional feudal estate has been created. The superior, granting the Charter, remains within the feudal framework. Thus, the Crown feus to A. who thus becomes a vassal of the Crown, holding land of and under the Crown as paramount superior. If A. sub-feus to B., a new feudal estate is created of and under A. In the result, the Crown now has as its immediate vassal, A., and as its sub-vassal B. In other words, there are now sub-adjacent feudal estates of and under the Crown in the same land. **Therefore**, if B. then feus to C., a third feudal estate is created of and under B. holding under A., holding under the Crown. And so on downwards *ad infinitum.* However, for practical purposes, B. when sub-feuing, is divested in this sense, that, having feued and thus parted with the *dominium utile,* he can no longer enjoy physical occupation of the land itself. That right has passed to his vassal C. as owner of the *dominium utile.* In lieu of his right to physical enjoyment of the land itself, however, B., as superior, acquires certain new rights by virtue of the Charter B to C which he did not previously enjoy. It is these new rights which in sum make up the *dominium directum* and comprise in substance the estate of the superior, although in form that estate remains a right and title to land. Walker Chapter 5.5. page 86 states — 'when he grants a feu ... he thereby **retains certain rights** in the lands'; but the strictly correct feudal position is that, when granting the Charter, the superior **retains the lands** themselves, but **grants** certain irredeemable rights therein to his vassal.

These remaining and emergent rights of the superior, which arise as a result of the granting of the Charter, in essence comprise:—

(i) a right to enforce conditions of tenure as against the vassal, for the time being, in perpetuity but subject to variation or discharge by the Lands Tribunal under the 1970 Act;

(ii) a right to collect feuduty in perpetuity, but subject to redemption under the 1974 Act.

In practice, the superior may also retain other rights e.g. salmon fishings in or related to the land conveyed, and minerals thereunder, etc. Rights of this kind, so retained, are not properly speaking rights of the superiority at all. They are, instead, elements in the original *dominium utile* which have been separated from the *dominium utile* feued to the vassal and retained. The superior thus retains the actual physical enjoyment of these retained elements for his own benefit. To illustrate: —

A. owns four acres. He may sub-feu one acre to B., retaining his right of *dominium utile* in the remaining three acres. That retained right in the three acres is not one of the rights of the superiority in any sense. Instead, A. has simply split his *plenum dominium* into two parts, one acre and three acres; and of these two components, he has sub-feued the one-acre part, but not the three-acre part.

In exactly the same way, if A. owns four acres, he may sub-feu all four acres to B., but reserve to himself the minerals. In that illustration, the minerals are not one of the rights of the superiority, as such. Instead, the superior has split the *plenum dominium* into two components, surface and sub-adjacent minerals, and has sub-feued the surface only, retaining the *dominium utile* of the minerals.

Therefore, to treat reservations of this kind as part of the **resulting** estate of the **superior**, is not strictly accurate. However, in practice, minerals are often so regarded, because they are so frequently reserved in the Feu Charter.

3.2. Feuduty.

Until 1.9.74 feuduty was *inter essentialia,* a necessary element in any feudal grant; and has all the qualities of a real condition and of a pecuniary real burden. It affects the whole feu and every portion of it. The superior is already infeft when granting the feu; he requires no further or additional infeftment, beyond his original title to the lands, in order to secure for himself the benefit of this real burden. His right is reserved out of the grant to the vassal, and to the extent of that reservation he remains infeft on his original title. Accordingly, his right to feuduty necessarily antedates, and is preferable to, any rights, absolute or in security, created by or deriving from the vassal.

Again, a feudal grant constitutes a recurring personal contract between successive superiors and successive vassals in the respective estates of *dominium directum* and *dominium utile.* The contract is completed by the vassal's acceptance of the Charter; he and his successors in the feu thereby become personally liable, by way of personal action at the instance of the superior, for implement of the feudal prestations. Once the contract is so constituted, the vassal cannot escape from or renounce it.

On the death of the vassal before the 1964 Act, the heir-at-law became personally liable though not bound to take up succession. Post-1964 Act, the executors confirming to the feu become similarly bound.

On sale to a singular successor, the obligation to pay feuduty passes to him, and, **when certain conditions are fulfilled,** the original vassal ceases to be liable for feuduty subsequent to the date of transfer.

Arising out of these two distinct elements — personal contract and real burden — the superior has a variety of remedies for **recovery** of feuduty if the vassal fails to pay on the due date.

1. **Personal Action.** This is the ordinary action for payment of a debt arising *ex contractu.* The action lies against:

(a) the original vassal **and/or** his successors, (subject as above);

(b) the sub-vassals of the vassal himself, i.e. where the vassal has in turn made sub-feus. Each sub-vassal is personally liable to the over-superior but only to the amount of the feuduty due to his own superior (the debtor vassal); and

(c) the tenants of the vassal, to the amount of their rents.

Where sub-vassal or tenant is, by personal action, forced to pay feuduty to the superior in this way, he has a right of relief against the vassal.

2. **Hypothec,** for last and current feuduty, preferable to the landlord's hypothec, over moveables on the feu. This remedy is very rarely used by superiors, because other remedies are available.

3. **Poinding of the ground.** This is a real diligence available to the creditor in **any** real burden. Under it, he can attach all the vassal's moveables **on the feu** and those of **tenants** to the extent of unpaid rents. It covers all arrears, unless the vassal is sequestrated. The superior is, in that event, entitled to recover by this process only the current feuduty and **one** year's arrears.

4. **Adjudication.** See Chapter 7.2 for detail.

All these remedies are **alternative**; the superior may select whichever suits him best. The **whole** feu is burdened; so the superior may proceed, as above, against the whole, or he can select any particular part of it which best suits his purpose. Suppose A feus 10 acres to B; B builds a house on one acre and sells the house and one acre to C. B retains the nine acres, which remain unbuilt upon. Both B and C are each personally liable for the **whole** feuduty; and C's property (possibly the only part of any worthwhile value for a real action by the superior) is liable (e.g. by poinding of the ground) for the **whole** feuduty.

The superior is entitled to exercise all or any of these remedies *ex lege;* there is no need to make express provision for them in the Charter.

Irritation of the feu; or *irritancy ob non solutum canonem.* This is **not** a remedy for recovery of unpaid feuduty. But it is the superior's ultimate sanction. The modern Feu Charter in practice always contains building conditions and restrictions which transmit, as real conditions, against singular successors; and until 1.9.1974, had to include a provision for *reddendo,* which is also a real burden on the feu.

The superior is always entitled to **enforce** building conditions, and to recover feuduty, by way of the remedies already mentioned.

In support of, and as an alternative to, these remedies, the modern Feu Charter also invariably contains clauses known as the irritant and resolutive clauses which provide that, on failure to observe any of the building or other conditions, or on failure to pay feuduty, the vassal's right created by the Charter is rendered void and becomes forfeit; whereupon the *dominium utile* is to revert to the superior, as if the Charter had never been granted.

In addition to the conventional irritancy, but for non-payment of feuduty only, the superior has a **statutory** right to irritate the feu under an old Scots Act, The Feuduty Act 1597 (c.250), even although the Charter contains no conventional irritancy clause. This statutory remedy became available when the feuduty had fallen two years in arrears. The conventional irritancy clause normally (but not necessarily) repeats this statutory two-year-arrears provision.

But, by the 1974 Act S.15, no action of declarator may now be raised, after 1.9.74, unless at the time the feuduty is 5 years in arrears. This applies both to the statutory irritancy and to conventional clauses, whatever their terms.

On irritation of the feu, the right which the vassal acquired under the Feu Charter, and the relationship of superior and vassal thereby created, is extinguished. The *dominium utile,* which passed to the vassal under the Charter, reverts to the superior just as if the Charter had never been granted. Further, any real rights deriving from the vassal are extinguished along with the vassal's right; and this includes the rights granted by the vassal to his own sub-feuars, heritable creditors, and tenants. The *dominium utile* reverts into the hands of the superior as it stands at the date of irritation; accordingly, the superior, on irritation, becomes entitled to all buildings and other erections on the feu and all heritable plant and machinery. No compensation is payable by the superior to the vassal, regardless of the value of the feu, buildings, etc. See 3.2.1. — Sandeman -v- Scottish Property Investment Co. 1885 12 R (HL) 67 — cf. 3.2.18. — Pickard -v- Glasgow Corporation 1970 SLI (Sh.Ct.) 63.

Clearly, this is a very stringent remedy. There are various statutory provisions designed to prevent oppression of the vassal himself, of his sub-feuars, creditors and others deriving right from him.

In the first place, under the Feuduty Act, 1597, and also under any conventional irritancy clause (notwithstanding provision in that clause to the contrary), the superior cannot irritate the feu except after judicial process, taking the form of an Action of Declarator *ob non solutum canonem.*

To protect the interests of persons deriving right from the vassal, it is provided by Statute that such an Action of Declarator must be served not only on the last entered vassal, but also on sub-feuars, heritable creditors, and others who, at the date of the raising of an Action, appear to have some real right in, or security over, the *dominium utile* as disclosed in a 20-year Search.

Special provisions also apply to the finality of the Decree — See 1887 Act S.4. & 1938 Act S.6.

Purging the Irritancy.

By virtue of the 1887 Act S.4., it is now competent in all cases to purge the irritancy, and to escape from the effect of irritation, by payment or performance at any time before the Extract Decree is recorded. Further, in the case of failure by the vassal to observe an obligation *ad factum praestandum,* the Court (on cause shown) will normally allow the vassal a reasonable period within which to implement the breached condition. Duncanson 15 S.L.R. 356.

In practice, irritation of the feu is rare because the effect, on the vassal, is so severe. But nonetheless, it is the ultimate sanction *in terrorem* which must always be taken into the reckoning.

For a recent case involving irritancy for failure to complete buildings within a time limit and a parallel application to the Lands Tribunal for a variation of that condition, see 3.2.15 — James Miller & Partners Ltd. 1974 S.L.T. (L.T.) 9. The application was refused and so, presumably, decree of irritancy was duly granted in the Sheriff Court; but that is not reported.

Compare 3.3.18(b) Ross & Cromarty District Council 1983 SLT (LT) 9. Superiors raised an Action of Irritancy for breach of feuing conditions. The vassal applied to the Lands Tribunal for a variation; and the Superiors moved the Tribunal to sist the application. The Tribunal refused the Superior's request, and granted the application, leaving it to the Court of Session to determine whether or not an impurgeable irritancy had meantime been incurred.

Allocation of Feuduty.

This involves some specialities. Feuduty is a *debitum fundi.* It is a real burden secured upon the whole of the feu and every part thereof. Suppose that A feus 10 acres to B for a feuduty of £100 per annum. That feuduty is a real burden on the whole 10 acres; and A, as superior, can proceed against the whole 10 acres, or any part thereof, if the feuduty is not paid. Suppose that B builds 10 houses, each with one acre of ground and sells off each house to a separate purchaser. Each such house remains liable to the superior, A, for payment of the whole feuduty of £100 per annum. If the whole feuduty is not paid, A can proceed against the individual owner of one particular house for recovery of the whole. In particular, the superior is not affected by, and has no concern with, the apportionment of the *cumulo* feuduty of £100 in the respective dispositions of the 10 individual houses.

The same general principles apply to building conditions and restrictions. Such conditions are real burdens on the whole feu and every part thereof. Suppose, in the previous illustration, that the Feu Charter in favour of B contained a condition under which the vassal had to maintain 10 houses on the feu in all time coming.

Suppose one house burns down. The proprietor thereof collects his insurance money, leaves the country and makes no effort to rebuild it. In the last resort, refusal by a vassal to observe feuing conditions involves irritation of the feu. In this illustration, refusal by one proprietor to rebuild his house involves the other 9 proprietors in the risk of forfeiture.

Until the 1970 Act, the liability of a proprietor of part of a feu could only be limited with the sanction or consent of the superior. The appropriate process is allocation of feuduty. When a proportion of the original *cumulo* feuduty has been validly allocated on a portion of the original feu, the proprietor of that portion is, thereafter, liable only for the proportion of feuduty so allocated; and, so far as conditions are concerned, while his proportion remains subject to the original feuing conditions in the Charter, he is no longer affected by failure to observe those conditions on other portions of the feu. The resulting position is, substantially, as if the portion of the feu on which feuduty has been allocated had been the subject of a separate Feu Charter. Clearly, the superior's position is adversely affected by allocation, in that the burden of collection is increased and his remedies are restricted. A superior would, therefore, normally only **agree** to an allocation of feuduty subject to augmentation.

If the feuduty is not allocated, and if one of the proprietors of a portion of the feu has paid the whole feuduty to the superior, he has a right of relief against the proprietors of the other portions and may call on the superior to assign his remedies for recovery (Burns Practice p.266); but this is never satisfactory.

Prior to the 1970 Act, there were three ways in which an allocation of feuduty might be obtained by agreement of the Superior:

(i) Express provision in the original Charter. Where, at the time of the granting of the Charter, a split-up of the feu is envisaged, as on a building estate, it is quite common for the parties to agree, by express provision in the *reddendo* clause, that the vassal, at his own hand, may subsequently allocate portions of the *cumulo* feuduty on parts of the feu. To avoid prejudice to the superior, this power is conferred on the vassal subject to certain restrictive conditions which normally include (a) the permitted amounts of feuduty, and permitted areas on which the same may be allocated; and (b) conditions which must first be satisfied before the allocation can be made — normally completion of buildings on the portion of the feu on which feuduty is to be allocated, followed by sale of that portion to a purchaser.

Any allocation made by the vassal which complies with these conditions is a valid allocation and binds the superior. Any purported allocation by the vassal which does not comply with these conditions is not binding on the superior. See 3.2.6. — Pall Mall Trust -v- Wilson 1948 SC 232.

(ii) Charter of Novodamus. This is perfectly competent but not now normally used for allocations.

(iii) Memorandum of Allocation. This is a simple statutory method of obtaining an allocation, and may take one of two forms:

(a) Endorsed Memorandum. By the 1874 Act S.8, the vassal may obtain a Memorandum in the form of 1874 Act Sch. B endorsed on his own title, whether before or after the recording thereof, signed by the superior or his agent but not requiring to be formal or tested.

(b) Separate Memorandum. By the 1924 Act S.13, the same result can be achieved by the **recording** of a separate, **formal**, Memorandum signed by the superior himself.

Either Memorandum is, by Statute, binding on 'all having interest', presumably all **future** proprietors of *dominium directum* and *dominium utile* and others having a real right therein; but **not** on existing heritable creditors who do not consent to it.

These are the formal methods by which an Allocation may be obtained; but an allocation **may** be inferred from the actings of the superior. See 3.2.3. — Nelson's Trs. -v- Todd 6 F 475 and 3.2.6. — Pall Mall Trust -v- Wilson 1948 SC 232.

Statutory Allocation. 1970 Act SS.3 to 6.

In practice, feus and buildings are very often split without any formal allocation of feuduty being obtained; but liability for the *cumulo* feuduty is informally apportioned (the term ''allocated'' is often used, misleadingly), in the respective dispositions, amongst the owners of the individual parts, e.g. a tenement of 6 flats subject to a feuduty of £30. The flats are all sold separately; and each disponee is taken bound, in his disposition, to pay £5 of the *cumulo* feuduty. But this is no concern of the superior and is not of his doing. He continues to collect £30 in one sum from the original owner of the whole tenement and his successors — usually, the purchaser of the last flat to be sold. He in turn collects £5 per annum from the other 5 flat-owners.

The superior plays no part in these arrangements. He is usually quite unaware that individual flats have been sold, and knows nothing of the purchasers of individual flats nor of the apportioned feuduty.

Note also that, in the illustration, 6 x £5 = £30 which exactly equals the *cumulo* feuduty. Often, in practice, the sum of the apportioned feuduty exceeds the *cumulo.*

The **salient** points of the 1970 provisions are:

1. The procedure is **alternative** to existing procedures, by Minute, etc.
2. **Any** proprietor, whose feuduty is not allocated, may serve a **notice** on:
   (a) the superior; **or**
   (b) his agent.
three months before the next term of payment (usually Whit. or Marts.)

3. The form of notice has been prescribed by The Allocation of Feuduty, etc. (Form of Notice) Regulations 1971. It is very brief, and simply states:
   1) the name of the Superior.
   2) the amount to be allocated.
   3) the part of the feu on which allocation is made — **but** no formal description is required.
   4) the name of the owner thereof.

Objection by Superior.

Allocation may prejudice the Superior for reasons already stated. The Act protects his position by providing that, if the Superior **objects** to the **amount** proposed to be allocated on the portion of the feu, he has the right to apply to the Lands Tribunal. In 3.2.8. — Moray Estates Development 1971 SLT 318 a Superior objected to a Notice on the grounds that 'it was not known that the amount of the portion of feuduty specified in the Notice of Allocation has been apportioned', etc. The Inner House, on a stated case from the Lands Tribunal, **held** that, since the Superior could not check the validity of the amount, **without investigation**, he was **entitled** to object.

Proceedings before the Tribunal.
Note the following points:—

1. **Only** the superior can apply to the Lands Tribunal, never the vassal. S.4(1). Any objection must be lodged within twenty eight days of receipt of the notice.

2. The **only** ground of application is objection to the **amount** to be allocated. S.4(1). (But see Moray Estates Development above).

3. On application to the Tribunal, notice must be given by the **Tribunal** to all interested proprietors, and may be given to others at the discretion of the Tribunal. S.4(2).

4. The Tribunal **must** then allocate a portion of the feuduty on **every** portion of the feu. S.4(1). The onus lies on the Tribunal to investigate the title in order to determine how the *cumulo* feuduty may be fairly allocated on the whole.

5. The Tribunal will **not** normally disturb the existing basis of apportionment, and there will normally be no rearrangement of apportioned feuduties under this procedure. But:

i) Under S.5(2), the total allocated feuduties must **not** exceed the *cumulo;* and

ii) Under S.4(1), the Tribunal is to allocate in such manner as they consider reasonable; which **may** produce different amounts on allocation compared with the informal apportionment, e.g. in a tenement, if the apportioned feuduties add up to more than the *cumulo.* For a curious case, where the Tribunal did reallocate apportioned feuduties on what they considered to be a more equitable basis, see 3.2.9. — Barr -v- Bass Ltd. 1972 SLT (LT) 5. A tenement had been partially demolished. It comprised a public house, a betting shop, and 15 houses. The Tribunal were pressed by the objecting Superior to ignore the actual apportionment in the titles, and to allocate substantially the whole on the pub and shop, and nominal amounts only on the demolished houses. They refused to do so, but did not stick to the apportioned amounts in the title either. The interesting concept emerges of a feu-duty allocated on a cube of air without surrounding walls or roof. 'The interests of co-feuars whose dwellinghouses have been demolished will still subsist under feudal tenure.' But the Tribunal's President concedes that 'if the Tribunal allocates feuduty on non-existent houses' (some of whose owners had disappeared) 'the superior is likely to incur loss on those allocations.'

6. An Order, when given by the Tribunal, supersedes all existing informal apportionments and invalidates any Notice of Allocation given under the Act, however long before. S.5(3) and (4). But any prior formal allocation by the **superior** is unaffected.

7. An Order by the Tribunal **need not** be, but normally is, recorded in the Register of Sasines.

8. An Order by the Tribunal takes effect at the next term occurring not less than three months after the date of the Order.

Effect of Allocation by Notice or Order.
In all cases, the allocation effected by Notice or Order is as if there had been a duly recorded Memorandum of Allocation under the law in force prior to the Act — S.5(5). In addition, under S.5(1), when feuduty has been allocated, that portion

of the feu on which allocation is effected 'shall, in relation to the rights and obligations of the proprietors of the remainder of the feu, be treated as if it had **never** formed part of the *cumulo*'.

Ground Annuals.

The same provisions, *mutatis mutandis,* are applied to ground annuals under S.6.

Contracting out.

By S.7, any agreement or other provision, however constituted, is void, in so far as it purports to exclude or limit the operation of any of the provisions of SS.3 to 6.

Redemption of Feuduty.

Voluntary Redemption. — 1974 Act S.4.

Every vassal is now **entitled** to redeem an allocated feuduty by giving Notice to the superior **and** paying the redemption price at or before any term of Whitsunday or Martinmas. S.4(1) and (2). The redemption price is the cash amount required to purchase a holding of 2 1/2% Consols. sufficient to yield the annual amount of feuduty.

Unallocated Feuduty — S.4(1) and (3)

Under S.4(7), feuduty includes any *cumulo* feuduty which is **un**allocated and any part of a *cumulo* feuduty which **has been** allocated. Suppose A owns a flat in a tenement and, in the titles, £5 of the *cumulo* feuduty of £30 is **apportioned** on that flat, but not allocated. A may redeem the *cumulo* feuduty of £30 voluntarily but not his own apportioned £5 alone. This is no great hardship, in that any proprietor can now serve a Notice of Allocation **three months prior to the term** and allocate the £5 on his flat, which he can then redeem. On the other hand, if A sells his flat subject to an unallocated feuduty, there is no obligation whatever on him to redeem; and that feuduty will continue to subsist indefinitely.

Professor Love, in an Article in 1976 JLS 364, takes the view that, on a correct construction of the Act, unallocated feuduty may be redeemed voluntarily, but not compulsorily. This view is not, however, generally held.

Effect of Redemption. S.4(3)

The **only** effect of redemption is to extinguish future liability for payment of the annual sum. Otherwise, the tenure is totally unaffected. So, voluntary redemption (and the same applies to compulsory redemption) is not equivalent to the purchase of the *dominium directum.* There is no actual or deemed consolidation of *dominium directum* and *dominium utile;* and all the conditions of tenure, including irritant and resolutive clauses, **other than** the *reddendo* clause, continue to be enforceable in perpetuity. Therefore, if the object of redeeming feuduty is to extinguish the conditions of tenure rather than to get rid of the annual payment, then a contract to purchase the superiority and a Disposition thereof under the old rules is the appropriate method, followed by consolidation; and for that purpose a somewhat higher price may have to be paid than the current going price of Consols. See later under Consolidation. Chapter 7.1.

Heritable creditors on the superiority. S.4(5).

Redemption of feuduty (voluntary or compulsory) has no adverse effect on heritable creditors on the *dominium utile* and they need not be consulted.

On the other hand, it does have a very adverse effect on heritable creditors on the superiority in that, by redemption, the total value of the superiority can disappear without the creditor being paid anything. So, by these provisions, heritable creditors on superiorities might be seriously prejudiced. To prevent this, S.4(5) provides that redemption is not to prejudice the rights of existing heritable creditors who are not parties thereto. In other words, in a question with heritable creditors, unless they consent, redemption is ineffective.

With voluntary redemption, the result seems to be that the feuduty would revive for the benefit of non-consenting creditors, but the Act is silent on this point.

The practical effect is that no one should redeem a feuduty without being satisfied that there are no securities on the superiority. Admittedly, the superior is bound to indemnify, and this is made explicit in the Act; but if the superior meantime has gone bankrupt, or disappeared, then the vassal is bound to be prejudiced.

Compulsory Redemption of Feuduty. — 1974 Act S.5.

When a feu is conveyed for valuable consideration (i.e. on sale), the feuduty is **automatically** redeemed. This does not apply, however, on any other type of disposal, e.g. on gift, on death, or in security; none of these events trigger off compulsory redemption. S.5(I).

Compulsory redemption applies:

i) Where the Contract of sale was completed on or after 1st September, 1974; or

ii) If there was **no** Contract of Sale (which is rare), then on the date of entry on or after 1st September, 1974.

The redemption date in all these cases will normally be the actual date of entry, whether, at that date, a Disposition has been delivered or not; but by S.5(2), if entry is given before the date of the Contract, which is rare, then the redemption date is the **subsequent** date of the **Contract** (or disposition if there is **no** Contract).

Unallocated Feuduty. S.5(I2)

There is no compulsory redemption, under S.5, on the sale of part of a feu on which no part of the *cumulo* feuduty has been allocated.

Suppose there is a tenement of six flats which has a *cumulo* feuduty of £30 payable thereon. Before 1st September, 1974, a flat (or more than one) has already been sold on a separate title to a separate purchaser without allocation of feuduty but with £5 of feuduty apportioned on that flat. The same flat is later sold by its owner after 1st September, 1974. Since the feuduty is not allocated, there is no obligation on the seller to redeem, and the feuduty continues in perpetuity.

Suppose there is a single feu, subject to a single feuduty, which is sold entire after 1974. Feuduty is compulsorily redeemable. But if the same property is sold in parts, under separate contracts (even although to the same person) with an apportionment of feuduty on each portion, there would seem to be no obligation to redeem; and, instead, the apportioned feuduty would continue in perpetuity. So also if, prior to sale, A, the seller,conveys part of the feu to a nominee, with an apportionment on that part.

If, on lst September, 1974, a flat in a tenement had already been sold, **and** if feuduty had been allocated on that flat; and if the flat is later sold, feuduty on that flat **is** compulsorily redeemable. In the same situation, however, if the proprietor of the remainder of the tenement later sold a further flat, apportioning part of the remaining *cumulo* feuduty on the flat so sold, there would be no obligation on him to redeem the whole or that part of the feuduty.

Remember, however, in relation to these illustrations, that allocation of feuduty may arise by implication. Suppose, again, there is a tenement of six flats with a *cumulo* feuduty of £30. One flat is sold, and feuduty of £5 apportioned thereon in the Disposition. The owner of that flat can now give notice and obtain an allocation of feuduty on that flat under the 1970 Act; and in many cases has done so. By implication, the remaining £25 of feuduty would be allocated on the remaining 5 flats as a whole. Therefore, if the whole remaining 5 flats in the tenement were sold on a single contract to a single purchaser, a feuduty of £25 is **allocated**, by implication, and is therefore compulsorily redeemable.

Procedure on redemption. S.5(6)

Where compulsory redemption takes place, the feuduty is automatically deemed to have been redeemed on the redemption date. S.5(1). And that applies, **whether or not notice has been given** to the superior and **whether or not payment has been made.** (Contrast voluntary redemption under Section 4, where feuduty is redeemed **only** if due Notice and payment has been made.)

However, to avoid prejudice to the superior, **the redemption money**, and arrears of feuduty, **remain a real burden** on the feu until Notice is given. To release the feu from that real burden, the seller or purchaser must give Notice to the superior under S.5(6) and Schedule 2. The Notice runs:

'Take notice that, in terms of S.5 of the 1974 Act, the feuduty of £   per annum exigible in respect of (here describe) as at   1974, will be deemed to have been redeemed at that date by reason of entry having been taken to the said subjects under an obligation to convey by (the name of the seller) dated

When two months have elapsed from the date of the giving of that Notice (or from the date of entry if later), the feu is then automatically disburdened of the real burden for redemption money and arrears of feuduty; and the superior automatically loses his real security therefor. Obviously, this is a serious matter for the superior; and he can only prevent it happening and retain his real security, if

(i) He raises an action against the seller for payment of the redemption money and arrears of feuduty.

(ii) Having obtained Warrant to Cite the seller, he then applies to the Court for an Order continuing the real burden for such additional period as is reasonable to enable the superior to recover the amount due to him.

(iii) He records that Order in the General Register of Sasines.

The whole of the foregoing must be completed within the two-months' post-redemption period. S.5(8). If so, then the real security for redemption money may continue beyond the two-months' period; if not, real security is lost altogether.

Even if the real security is so continued, the superior may not recover the amount due from the purchaser unless the Court is satisfied that he cannot reasonably practicably recover from the seller. S.5(7).

Heritable Creditors. S.5(10.)

The same rules apply here as on voluntary redemption; and heritable creditors on the superiority are not to be prejudiced by compulsory redemption. But the effect is not expressed and is not clear. Arguably, under S.4, payment to the Superior of redemption money without a creditor's consent is not 'due payment' for the purposes of S.4(3) and so there is no effective redemption. But under S.5(I), on sale, redemption is immediate, automatic and unconditional. What rights have non-consenting creditors under S.5(10)? Does the redemption money remain as a real burden for their benefit, under S.5(5)? The Act is wholly silent.

Apportionment

Nothing is said in the 1974 Act about apportionment. But presumably, the Apportionment Act 1870 applies, so that the current feuduty running from the last term to the redemption date is deemed to accrue from day to day and is apportionable accordingly. (This may occasionally occur with voluntary redemption, e.g. annual feuduty at Whitsunday; redeemed at Martinmas. But, **normally,** feuduty is payable at the redemption date.)

Superior's Receipt.

With voluntary redemption, Notice and payment are both necessary elements in redeeming the feuduty; and there is a statutory form of receipt. With compulsory redemption, the feuduty is redeemed whether **or not** Notice is given **or** payment made, and, as a result, there is no provision for a statutory receipt. But, looking to the terms of S.5(6), evidence of payment is desirable. Note, again, the different effect. With voluntary redemption, feuduty **itself** continues as a real burden until the redemption money is paid; with compulsory redemption feuduty itself is at once extinguished **on sale,** regardless of payment.

Compulsory Acquisition.

Special provision is made in Section 6 for compulsory acquisition of land by e.g. Local Authority. The same general principle applies as on sale. Feuduty is automatically redeemed. But, in this case, the Acquiring Authority as purchaser, not the seller, is responsible for payment to the superior of the redemption money.

Further, if part of a feu is acquired, the feuduty in relation to that part is redeemed, although no formal allocation had previously been made thereon. (Contrast private sale of an unallocated portion which does not bring about redemption.)

Apparently, the same rules apply to ordinary voluntary acquisition, **without** a Compulsory Purchase Order, by an Authority possessing compulsory powers.

The Acquiring Authority, not the seller, has the duty to give Notice to the superior; and the Acquiring Authority, not the seller, is personally liable for payment of the redemption money.

But S.5(5) - (9) do **not** apply. So the redemption money in this case never becomes a real burden and the Superior need not take any action against the Authority to protect his position. Instead, under S.6(5), in all cases the Authority:

(a) **must** give Notice **before** the redemption date, which is the date when the Authority takes entry under Notice to Treat, or the vesting date under a general vesting declaration; and

(b) is personally liable for the redemption money and interest.

Over-feuduties.

Over-feuduties are totally ignored in the Act. There seems to be no doubt that they are redeemable, voluntarily; or compulsorily on a sale of the superiority.

So, on sale of a **superiority,** you **must** now redeem the over-feuduty; and you may redeem voluntarily at any time.

But what effect does redemption of feuduty by a vassal have on the over-superior?

Since tenure continues after redemption, the **over**-superior's rights in a question with his vassal (the mid-superior) and the sub-vassals are unimpaired.

Suppose A feus 3 acres to B for £50. B in turn sub-feus 3 separate acres to each of X, Y and Z, each for £25. B then has a surplus of income over outgoings of £25. So long as this continues, there is no risk to X, Y and Z, in that if B defaults, X, Y and Z pay £50 to A direct; and their combined feuduties are more than enough to cover the total due to A.

But suppose X, Y and Z all redeem their respective feuduties of £25 each, paying the redemption money to B.

B is not obliged to pass on the redemption monies to A, **nor** to redeem his £50 feuduty to A in whole or in part.

So B must continue to pay £50 to A, though now drawing no income from X, Y and Z.

Suppose B stops paying A. Under the existing law, A has two remedies against the sub-feuars:

i) Recovery from X, Y and Z to the extent of their unpaid feuduties. **But** their feuduties have been validly redeemed, and so they have no liability.

ii) Irritancy. When B is 5 years in arrears with his feuduty to A, A may irritate the feu. B would then forfeit his title and the titles of X, Y and Z would fall as well. So sub-feuars are **indirectly** liable to over-superiors in this way, even after redemption.

3.3. Enforcement of Real Conditions.

If the superior wishes to enforce a condition of tenure against the vassal for the time being, there are two essential elements, namely, (a) he must have a **title** to enforce the condition, and (b) he must, if challenged, be able to demonstrate **interest** to enforce the condition. The same principles apply to any other person (e.g. co-feuars with the *jus quaesitum*) seeking to enforce a real condition as against the owner of the burdened subjects.

(a) Title to enforce.

As between superior and vassal, title causes no problem. The original Charter is a contract between the original superior and the original vassal, constantly renewed between successors in the superiority and *dominium utile,* on the feudal theory of recurring personal contract. Accordingly, the superior's **title** to enforce feuing conditions is his title to the *dominium directum,* which is in form a title to land and carries with it, *sub silentio,* the title to enforce conditions in the vassal's Charter generally, whether as real conditions or real burdens. See Lord Dunedin in 3.3.2. Nicholson -v- The Glasgow Blind Asylum 1911 SC 391:

'The **title** of the superior to enforce a restriction contained in a vassal's title is always to be found **in that title**, because it begins as a Contract between the original superior and the vassal and continues as between succeeding superiors and succeeding vassals by virtue of the tenure which, in the case of each succeeding vassal, binds him by the Contract.'

Again, as between superior and vassal, the general rule is:

i) that conditions in a Feu Charter are strictly a private matter between the superior and the vassal for the time being. No one can compel the superior to insist on feuing conditions in a question with his own vassal, if the superior himself does not so choose; and

ii) no one other than the superior can so enforce feuing conditions.

But, in certain special circumstances, a situation may be created as a result of which adjoining feuars who derive their title from the same superior may acquire a **title** to enforce conditions in the Charter of a neighbouring co-feuar. This right of enforcement, when so acquired by a co-feuar, is based on the contractual principle of *jus quaesitum tertio,* viz: —

'An obligation imposed by a Contract is *jus tertii* to third parties, and they have no right to enforce it' ... but the rule 'suffers an exception where it is shown that their object was to advance the interests of a third party. That may create a *jus quaesitum tertio,* which will give the third party, or tertius, a title to sue'. Gloag & Henderson 8th Edition pp.101-2. Since the Charter is fundamentally a contract, the rule has been applied to conditions of tenure.

The **title** of a co-feuar, as a third party, to enforce feuing conditions in the Charter of his neighbour can only arise if superior and vassal have actively agreed to this in that original Charter:

and therefore there must be some evidence in the deed itself,' (i.e. the charter) 'that it is intended that the restriction shall be enforceable by a tertius'. 3.3.2. Nicholson -v- Glasgow Blind Asylum 1911 SC 391.

To illustrate this by an example, suppose that A grants a Feu Charter to B; A then grants a second Feu Charter of an adjoining feu to C. A, the superior, is in direct contractual relationship with B, and with C, both being his vassals. But there is no relationship, conractual, feudal or otherwise between B and C *inter se*. A, as superior, can enforce feuing conditions against B and against C. But B has no title on the grounds of direct Contract to enforce the conditions in C's Charter against C; there is no contractual relationship between B and C. If B is to have the right to enforce the conditions in C's charter, this can only be on the basis of *jus quaesitum tertio*; and that *jus quaesitum tertio* must arise out of, and be based on, the terms of the Feu Charter by A to C. There is nothing else on which it can be based. Further, the Feu Charter by A to C must, by express provision, or by clear implication, confer the *jus quaesitum tertio* on B. This means that A, the superior, and C, the vassal, when adjusting the terms of the Charter, must have agreed, expressly or by implication, that B, a tertius, is to be entitled at any time in the future to step in and enforce the Charter conditions in a question with C, although at the time B was not a party to the Charter.

If, however, B in the illustration can establish his *jus quaesitum tertio,* on the basis of the Feu Charter A to C, B's title to enforce feuing conditions against C, once so constituted, is a separate and distinct title, independent of the title of the superior to enforce the feuing conditions.

Thus, Lord Watson in 3.3.1 Hislop v. McRitchie's Trustees 8 R (HL) 95 states, 'It is necessary to keep in view that, when the feuar has a *jus quaesitum tertio,* his title and that of the superior to enforce common feuing conditions are independent and substantially different rights. The title of the superior rests upon contract, a contract running with the estate of superiority and burdening the subaltern estate of the vassal. The right of the feuar, though arising *ex contractu,* is of the nature of a proper servitude, his feu being the dominant tenement'.

Clearly, the right, or absence of right, in one proprietor to enforce conditions in the other's title may be very material to his enjoyment of that property. Similarly, it is very material from the point of view of a proprietor whose title contains burdens, to know whether the superior alone can enforce those burdens against him or whether not only the superior but also neighbouring feuars on the basis of *jus quaesitum* have a right to enforce those conditions against him. And there have been a number of reported cases.

In what circumstances, then, is a *jus quaesitum tertio* conferred upon a tertius? Firstly, certain conditions precedent must be satisfied which are:

(1) The feuars must both or all hold of the same superior; and

(2) The condition, which a tertius seeks to enforce, must be properly constituted as a **real** condition.

Given these conditions precedent, there are two ways in which it is said the *jus quaesitum tertio* may be created. These are:

(i) by express provision in the **respective** Charters. Typically 'the feuars and the superior's other feuars shall be entitled to enforce against each other the conditions and restrictions expressed in their respective Feu Charters for the protection of the amenity of the neighbourhood'. Such clauses are common. See 3.3.6 Lawrence v. Scott and Others 1965 SC 403, for a typical illustration.

(ii) 'When the **whole** titles of the co-feuars manifest an intention that a *jus quaesitum tertio* will be created, by a mutuality of title inferred from an undertaking by the superiors to insert similar restrictions in each feu, or by reference to a common plan' per Lord Guthrie in Lawrence v. Scott *supra* and cases there cited. This is always a difficult question and, if the *jus quaesitum tertio* is to be created by implication in this way, there must be a very clear inference in the titles that this was the intention. Thus, it is not enough that neighbouring feuars hold of the same superior on titles containing similar or even identical conditions. Again, a *jus quaesitum tertio* cannot be created by implication if there is a power reserved to the superior to alter the conditions of the Charter. See 4.1. 49 Turner v. Hamilton 1890 17 R 494; but this does not apply to those cases where the right is expressly conferred by express provisions in the Charters. See Lawrence v. Scott *supra.* On the other hand, a reference to a **common** feuing plan in several Charters as containing (common) restrictions generally implies mutuality; similarly, where the superior undertakes to insert **identical** conditions in other future Charters, **and where this has been done**. A *jus quaesitum tertio* would normally, in these circumstances, be inferred.

A third method is suggested by some authorities viz: an agreement between co-feuars that each may enforce the other's title conditions — see Burns' Practice p.228 and Stevenson 23 R 1079 at p.1090, per Lord Kinnear. But is this truly a case of *jus quaesitum* rather than a direct contractual relationship? In any event, such agreements were not often used because it was doubtful whether such an agreement could effectively bind singular successors. But this doubt is removed in appropriate cases by the 1979 Act S.17.

(b) Interest to enforce

A **title** to enforce Charter conditions (whether by the superior or by a co-feuar based on the *jus quaesitum tertio*) is an essential pre-requisite; but mere title alone is not enough. In addition, the superior or co-feuar must have an **interest** to enforce the condition. In relation to interest, there is a significant difference between the position of the superior and the position of a co-vassal.

The superior's title to sue is contractual; and the general rule of contract is that one party to the contract cannot successfully sue for implement of contractual conditions if his motive is vexatious and if he has no legitimate interest to sue. But he need not **aver** his interest which is presumed; and the onus lies on the defender to prove (if he can) that the legitimate interest (which presumably the superior originally had to enforce the Charter conditions) now no longer exists. See 3.3.10 Earl of Zetland v. Hyslop 9R (HL) 40 *'prima facie,* the vassal in consenting to be bound concedes the interest of the superior; and the onus is upon the vassal to allege and prove that owing to some change in circumstances any legitimate interest which the superior may have had in maintaining the restriction has ceased to exist'.

The nature of the superior's interest is not defined; but it is settled that his interest need not be patrimonial, involving financial loss.

In contrast, a co-feuar seeking to enforce a Charter condition on the basis of *jus quaesitum tertio,* must aver his interest; and his interest must be patrimonial. See 3.3.11 Maguire v. Burgess 1909 SC 1283. Burgess established a *jus quaesitum tertio* to enforce a restriction in a neighbouring title which limited the buildings thereon to dwellinghouses only. The owner of the neighbouring feu proposed to erect a Roman Catholic Church. In the proceedings, Burgess failed to aver and could not prove **partimonial** interest; and on that ground failed. But the superior could have insisted that a condition of this kind be observed.

Loss of interest to enforce

Since interest to enforce is an essential element in the enforcement of conditions of tenure, it follows that a superior or co-feuar who lacks or has lost his interest to enforce is barred from compelling compliance. Loss of interest occurs in three typical situations:

(i) Where, in withholding consent to a variation or discharge of a condition of tenure, it can be shown that the superior is acting *in mala fide* or oppressively, or capriciously. So, in 3.3.9 Eagle Lodge Ltd. v. Keir & Cawder Estates Ltd. 1964 SLT 13, the superior withheld his consent to a variation in Charter conditions, except upon payment of £1,000. The vassal argued that, by **suggesting** a monetary consideration for a waiver, he had either demonstrated his lack of interest or put himself *in mala fide*; but the point was not decided. In similar circumstances in the later case 3.3.24 Howard de Walden Estates Ltd. v. Bowmaker 1965 SC 163 the superior asked for a payment of £1,250 as consideration for his consent; the defender did not press the argument that in so doing he was *in mala fide*. And in any event see Lord Guthrie, 'The fact that the superiors demanded a sum of £1,250 in consideration of their consent ... does **not** indicate a change of circumstances showing a loss of interest'.

(ii) Where, owing to change of circumstances in the neighbourhood, it can be shown that restrictions in the title have ceased to have any content or meaning and accordingly the superior has lost all interest to enforce a condition which is useless to him or to anyone else. This may occur where there has been a general abandonment of the whole plan of development owing to supervening circumstances; where, for example, 'the superior had permitted a continuous and systematic departure from the conditions of feu' as in 3.3.15 Campbell v. Clydesdale Banking Co. 6M 943. Contrast 3.3.13 Macdonald v. Douglas 1963 SS 374, where a feuar proposed to convert a private house into a licensed hotel, in the face of a charter condition prohibiting use for any purpose other than as self-contained villas. The charter expressly conferred a *jus quaesitum* on co-feuars. On the grounds of certain other minor departures from that condition in other Charters, the vassal argued that the character of the area had so changed as to extinguish the interest to enforce it; but the Court refused to accept that argument. Similarly, in 3.3.14 Howard de Walden Estates Ltd. supra, the point is expressed thus: 'The Court has always required, in the absence of acquiescence, clear evidence of a loss of all residential character before it will regard the conditions imposed in the titles as devoid of any content. In my opinion, the present case is very far from any such situation'.

(iii) Acquiescence. Where a superior, otherwise entitled to enforce a feuing condition, has acquiesced in encroachments on or deviations from the feuing conditions, he may become personally barred from seeking, any longer, to enforce them. His interest is thus extinguished. As to the nature and quality of acquiescence see Rankine Personal Bar, Chap. 4. And note particularly,

(a) the superior's acquiescence must be deliberate, in the full knowledge that the feuar is in breach and that he as superior has a right and title to object. Mere silence, looking on, without objection, is not enough; the superior's acting must amount to positive tacit consent.

(b) acquiescence to the breach of a particular condition in a Charter does not *per se* imply loss of interest to enforce any **other** condition in the Charter; see 3.3.16 Stewart v. Bunten 5R 1108.

(c) acquiescence by the superior in a prohibited use in the past may not prevent him from objecting to the continued future use for that purpose by the feuar, unless the feuar has with the superior's acquiescence expended large sums of money; see 3.3.3 Johnston v. Walker's Trs. 24 R 1061. 'Structural alterations made in breach of building conditions, in the knowledge of and without objection by those having right to object, cannot after completion be pulled down. But the mere use of a dwellinghouse in a manner contrary to the title, however long permitted in the past, cannot have any efficacy as to the future'.

(d) 'A singular successor, with express or plainly implied notice, is fixed with the consequence of his author's acquiescence'. (Rankine: Personal Bar p.62 and 3.3.17 MacTaggart v. Roemelle 1907 SC 1318). But the singular successor will be no **further** bound than his author; and **may** be less so.

Co-feuars

All the foregoing rules as to loss of interest apply equally to a co-feuar who has a *jus quaesitum tertio* to enforce conditions in his neighbour's title. He, too, may be personally barred from insisting on conditions, by loss of interest. But on the final point (iii), there is a distinction between the effect, on a superior, of past acquiescence and the effect thereof on a co-feuar. Acquiescence by the superior in a breach, by one feuar, of a feuing condition does not **necessarily** imply loss of interest to enforce the **same** condition in the Charter of other feuars in the area. (See 3.3.12 Ewing v. Campbell 5 R 230 and 3.3.6 Lawrence v. Scott 1965 SC 403); but 'generally speaking, if the **superior** allows the act of the first offender to pass, he must either have willingly allowed it or he must have conceded that all legitimate interest to stop such acts has gone'; 3.3.17 MacTaggart v. Roemelle 1907 SC 1318. Whereas a co-feuar, having acquiesced in a breach by one co-feuar, may still object, later, to the **same** act of contravention by another co-feuar if, in the circumstances, it is more damaging to his own amenity; see again MacTaggart v. Roemelle, 'it is much more difficult to affirm that the quality of the superior's interest differs as regards each instance (of contravention) than it is to do so in the case of a co-feuar'. (Per L.P. Dunedin at p.1323).

The title of the vassal, based on *jus quaesitum tertio,* is independent of the superior's title. Therefore, acquiescence by the superior in a breach of Charter conditions cannot bar the vassal from objection; and vice versa. (See Lawrence v. Scott supra).

Variation of Feuing and other conditions

Feus are perpetual. The rights created for the vassal, and the obligations undertaken by the vassal, in the original Charter continue in perpetuity. At Common Law, neither superior nor vassal may, unilaterally, alter or vary these rights or obligations. But, fundamentally, the relationship of superior and vassal is contractual. It is, therefore, open to the parties to **agree** together to a variation of the terms of the Charter. Further, in certain circumstances, the estate of superiority and (more commonly) the estate of *dominium utile* may be extinguished and cease to exist.

The superior's consent

There are two necessary elements to the enforcement of feuing conditions by superior against the vassal, namely, title and interest.

The superior's **title** to enforce certain categories of feuing condition can be, and in the past has been in certain cases, altered by Statute, e.g. as to carriages and services, and as to prohibitions against subinfeudation.

By the Housing (Scotland) Act 1966 S.189, and earlier enactments, the vassal might, unilaterally, apply to the Sheriff for a variation of a building restriction which prevents sub-division of a dwellinghouse. (Repealed on 29.11.70 by the Conveyancing and Feudal Reform (Scotland) Act 1970 S.52(3) and Sch. 11).

Otherwise, broadly speaking, a variation in the superior's title to enforce feuing conditions was, until 1970, always a matter of active agreement by the superior. But, under the 1970 Act Part I, the vassal may now apply to the Lands Tribunal for a variation of a feuing condition. The Tribunal may discharge the condition *de plano* or vary the Charter by substituting a new condition in its place.

The superior may however also lose his **interest** to enforce a feuing condition owing to change of circumstances in the neighbourhood; owing to his acquiescence; or where the vassal can demonstrate that the superior's consent to a variation in a feuing condition is withheld oppressively or capriciously. This still applies, post-1970, rendering the condition unenforceable so that application for variation under the 1970 Act may be unnecessary. But the superior's interest to enforce need not be patrimonial and it could, and can, be difficult to prove loss of interest, thus often impeding development.

The consent of third parties.

The superior may have agreed to a variation of a feuing condition; or he may be personally barred, through loss of interest, from objecting to a breach, by a vassal, of a particular building condition or restriction; or, the estate of *dominium utile,* with its rights and its feuing conditions, may by merger have ceased to exist. But the *jus quaesitum tertio* to enforce feuing conditions is not in any way affected by subsequent actings of the superior. Thus, an adjoining feuar, with the *jus quaesitum,* can continue to insist on a feuing condition notwithstanding that the superior has agreed to waive it. The existence of the *jus quaesitum* (where it exists) usually means that, even if the superior is willing, a variation by agreement — of superior and of neighbouring feuars — is a practical impossibility.

Charter of Novodamus

Where the superior does agree to an alteration in the building conditions or restrictions, or to an alteration in the feuduty, the appropriate feudal process is for the vassal to surrender his feu into the hands of the superior. The *dominium utile* having then merged with the *dominium directum,* all existing feuing conditions are extinguished. Originally this operated *confusione,* although it has more recently been held that *confusio* does not apply. Technically, as a preliminary to the granting of a Novodamus, the superior should be reinvested; but by Statute this is made unnecessary; 1887 Act S.3. The superior is then in a position to make a new grant of the original feu to the vassal, on new conditions. This new grant differs from an **original** Feu Charter in that it represents the renewal of an existing investiture. The writ is therefore called a Charter of Novodamus; and proceeds, in outline, in the following form:

'I, AB (design), immediate lawful superior of the subjects hereinafter disponed, considering that (here narrate the reason for the granting of the Charter) Do Hereby of new give, grant, dispone and forever confirm to CD (design) and his heirs and assignees whomsoever, heritably and irredeemably, ALL and WHOLE ...'

The Charter then proceeds with a description of the subjects, the burdens, as contained in the original Charter with such variations as have been agreed, and the usual formal feudal clauses. Some adaptation of these clauses (in particular, the warrandice clause) will be necessary to take account of the special circumstances under which this Charter is granted. The superior will normally grant warrandice from fact and deed only, or simple warrandice only.

The provisions of the 1974 Act S.1, which prohibit future feuduties after 1/9/74 cannot be circumvented by using a Novodamus to increase, or create new, feuduty, and any purported increase is unenforceable.

Further, if a Novodamus is granted with reference to two or more feuduties, the effect must not be to increase the total amount payable. Otherwise, the purported increase is unenforceable. See 1974 Act S.3.

Minute of Waiver

The Charter of Novodamus, although the correct and recommended feudal method for varying conditions (and indeed the only competent method for imposing new conditions or for effectively altering *reddendo*) is somewhat elaborate and expensive. In practice, where no new or varied condition is to be imposed upon the vassal but where the parties have simply agreed that the superior will not insist on a particular feuing condition, it is common to incorporate such a variation in a Minute of Waiver. This is shorter and cheaper than a Charter of Novodamus. But, at Common Law, it is a mere personal agreement between superior and vassal which does not affect the title or real right of either of them.

In the result, the Minute of Waiver was, at best, positive evidence that the superior had acquiesced; but went no further than that. It was therefore not suitable for effecting a variation of certain kinds of conditions; nor for imposing new conditions or additional feuduty.

However, by the 1979 Act S.18, the Minute of Waiver has acquired a new significance.

Under that Section, the terms of any deed recorded in the Register of Sasines, whether **before or after** the passing of the Act, by which a 'land obligation' is varied or discharged, shall be binding on the singular successors of the person entitled to enforce that land obligation, and on the singular successors of the person burdened by that land obligation. But new conditions cannot competently be imposed by this device.

For this purpose, 'land obligation' has the same meaning as in the 1970 Act.

1970 Act SS. 1 and 2 — Variation and Discharge of Land Obligations

Under these two Sections, a new judicial body, the Lands Tribunal, was established and given powers to vary or discharge feuing conditions and servitudes, which have either become obsolete, or which frustrate development, because:

(a) the Superior refuses to agree to variation, or will only agree at a price; and/or

(b) in some cases (**not** all), adjoining feuars have the *jus quaesitum tertio*. To obtain agreement from a large number of co-feuars (and indeed even tracing them, in some cases) may prove impossible, even although the superior may be willing to co-operate.

1. What conditions can be varied or discharged?

The Act provides for the judicial variation of 'land obligations' which are defined in S.1(2). To qualify for variation, the obligation must satisfy the following requirements:

(i) It must be an obligation 'relating to land'.

(ii) It must be enforceable by a proprietor of an 'interest in land', *qua* proprietor. He is referred to in these Sections as the 'benefited proprietor' — S.2 (6). Under that Section, an interest in land means any estate or interest in land capable of being owned or held as a separate interest, and to which a title may be recorded in the General Register of Sasines.

The definition clearly includes:

(a) The superior or landlord;

(b) A neighbouring feuar, if he has the *jus quaesitum tertio,* but not a neighbouring feuar without that right;

(c) The owner of the dominant tenement in relation to servitudes.

The Tribunal probably do not have power to determine whether or not a 'land obligation' was originally validly created; nor to grant an order which is purely declaratory of subsisting rights and obligations — see 3.3.34 Solway Cedar 1972 S.L.T. (L.T.) 42 and 3.3.46 C.W.S. v. Ushers 1975 S.L.T. (L.T.) 9.

The Tribunal have power to determine who is a benefited proprietor in this sense — 3.3.7. Smith 1972 (L.T.) 34., and 3.3.46 C.W.S. v. Ushers 1975 S.L.T.(L.T.) 9. If an application is made for variation of a burden which is conceded to be a 'land obligation', then all **subsidiary** questions of entitlement to enforce fall within the Tribunal's jurisdiction.

In very many cases, neighbouring proprietors are materially affected by a proposed variation of feuing conditions, but do not qualify as benefited proprietors within the meaning of the Act. The significance of this is that a benefited proprietor always has a right to be heard before the Tribunal and to state his objection — S.2 (2) and to claim compensation. A proprietor who does not qualify as a benefited proprietor **may** be heard, in the discretion of the Tribunal, as an affected proprietor; but cannot appear as of **right**, and cannot claim compensation.

(iii) Under S.1.(2) the obligation must be one which is binding on a proprietor *qua* proprietor of:

(a) Another interest in the same land; e.g. as between superior and vassal, or

(b) An interest in **other** land; e.g. as between adjoining proprietors.

Such a proprietor is referred to in these Sections as the 'burdened proprietor'; where property is held on an *ex facie* absolute Disposition, the expression includes both the creditor and the debtor in that obligation — S.2 (6).

The second paragraph of S.1 (2) further defines a land obligation as including certain familiar categories of burden, e.g. future and contingent burdens, obligations to contribute towards or defray some expense, negative restrictions on use, and servitudes. But this really adds nothing to the substance of the Section.

Clearly, S.1. (2) embraces:

(i) all ordinary building conditions and restrictions in a Feu Charter, Disposition, or Contract of Ground Annual.

(ii) all leasehold conditions, if the Lease is recordable (whether or not recorded); but see below for some exceptions.

(iii) Servitudes, but **not** wayleaves or other similar agreements for the benefit of some person (e.g. the Gas Board) who is **not** an adjoining proprietor.

Certain special obligations set out in Schedule 1, are expressly excluded and cannot be varied under S.1., viz:

(i) Feuduty and similar annual ground burdens.

(ii) Mineral obligations generally.

(iii) Certain Crown benefits.

(iv) Leasehold conditions in occupation leases and tenancies of crofts, even although recordable.

Further, by decision in 3.3.18a — Macdonald 1973 S.L.T. (L.T.) 26, conditions imposed directly by Act of Parliament cannot be varied.

Under S.2 (5), any condition (otherwise variable) which was created within two years immediately preceding the Application, cannot be varied. Further, the Tribunal are unlikely to agree to vary relatively recent conditions of longer duration, except for compelling reasons.

2. Who may vary?

The only person who can apply for a discharge or variation of a land obligation is 'the burdened proprietor'.

3. In what circumstances will a land obligation be varied or discharged?

The Tribunal is empowered to vary or discharge a land obligation, on being satisfied that, in all the circumstances, one of three alternative situations has arisen as provided for in S.1 (3).

The three alternative situations in S.1 (3) are strictly alternatives, and are not mutually exclusive *inter se.* It is up to the applicant to demonstrate that he comes within one or other of the three alternatives; and he may set about it by picking one of the alternatives which suits his case or, if he prefers, he can bring his application under two, or all three, heads in this Section. If so, then the Application may well be refused under one or two of the three alternative heads, but granted under the third. See, typically, 3.3.35 Main (1972 SLT (LT) 14.

The three alternative provisions in S.1 (3) are as follows:

S.1 (3)(a): That, by reason of changes in the character of the burdened land, or in the neighbourhood, or other material circumstances, the obligation is or has become unreasonable or inappropriate. See Halliday — 1970 Act, pp. 21-27 for an analysis of cases. A typical case under this head would be a restriction limiting the use of a building in a town centre to a dwellinghouse only, where, with the passage of time, surrounding properties generally have been converted to commercial uses as offices and shops.

S.1 (3)(b): That the obligation is unduly burdensome compared with any benefit which would result from its performance e.g. a positive obligation to build (or, more likely, **rebuild**) a stone wall 10 ft. high, where a brick wall 6 ft. high would serve equally well.

S.1 (3)(c): That the existence of the obligation impedes some reasonable use of the land. This is the commonest ground of application, either alone or in conjunction with (a) and/or (b). From the reported decisions of the Tribunal, the following points emerge under this head:

(i) The Tribunal will not consider whether the obligation impedes some **abstract** or hypothetical use. The **applicant** must put forward, and found on, a specific, proposed use which is impeded. 3.3.31 Murrayfield Ice Rink 1973 S.L.T. 99.

(ii) It is not enough for the **objector** to show that the land can be used for **some** reasonable use, e.g. the existing use. If an alternative, prohibited, use is proposed by the applicant, the Tribunal must consider it under S.1. (3)(c) — Smith supra, and in the Inner House, unreported; and Main supra.

(iii) The fact that Planning Permission has been granted is persuasive, but not conclusive.

Logically, the fact that Planning Permission has **not** been applied for, or has been refused, while adverse, is not necessarily fatal.

(iv) The grant or refusal of other forms of Permission or Licence, e.g. Liquor Licences under the Licensing Acts or Betting Office Licences under the Betting, etc., Act 1963 will also be taken into account in the same sort of way by the Tribunal.

(v) It is not enough for the applicant merely to show that a particular proposed use is reasonable in relation to the property in question. The whole circumstances, and in particular the effect on adjoining properties, whether they be benefited or not, should be taken into account. Main supra.

There is a fairly large area of overlap between the three alternative grounds of application in S.1 (3)(a), (b) and (c). As indicated above, many of the reported Applications have been brought under all three heads or under two of them.

4. Compensation. S.1 (4)

Compensation may be awarded to a benefited proprietor, (superior or co-feuar, etc.,) in one of two alternative cases; but not under both heads. Only a **benefited** proprietor may claim; an **affected** proprietor has no entitlement to compensation. The grounds of claim are:

(i) Compensation for any substantial loss or disadvantage resulting from the variation or discharge. This covers:

(a) **Loss of Amenity** — See 3.3.7 Smith supra where the Tribunal granted an Application to vary tenure conditions so as to permit a dwellinghouse to be used as a Licensed Hotel, with an extension of the building for that purpose. There was resulting loss of amenity to neighbouring feuars who had the *jus quaesitum tertio* and were therefore benefited proprietors. Compensation was awarded for depreciation in the market value of the adjoining houses. Contra, 3.3.35 Main where, again, benefited proprietors claimed for loss of amenity but, in the circumstances, the Tribunal held that there was no loss in permitting a sub-basement to be used as a nursery school; and

(b) **Economic loss,** e.g. loss in trading receipts to a public house resulting from the discharge of a restriction against sale of liquor in the title of an adjoining shop, so as to allow for an off-sales certificate there. 3.3.46 C.W.S. v. Ushers 1975 SLT (L.T.) 9.

If the Tribunal discharges a restrictive condition, the superior, obviously, can no longer expect to be paid for granting a Waiver of the discharged condition. There is thus a potential loss of revenue to a superior when applications are granted by the Tribunal. The superior is not, however, entitled to compensation for this loss of potential revenue under S.1 (4)(i).

Note, particularly, that the Tribunal may refuse to vary or discharge a land obligation on the grounds specified in S.1 (3)(c) if, in their opinion, 'due to **exceptional** circumstances related to amenity or otherwise, money would not be an adequate compensation for any loss or disadvantage which a **benefited proprietor** would suffer from the variation or discharge'.

(ii) Compensation to make good the reduced consideration originally payable for a feu because of the presence in the title of restrictive conditions. In other words, where the superior insists on e.g. a prohibition against sale of liquor, he may get a lesser feuduty for his feu in the first place, because of insisting on that condition. In that situation, if the condition is removed, it is equitable that the superior should get compensation. The onus lies on the superior to establish that the feuduty was originally fixed below the free market value — 3.3.21 Manz 1973 SLT (L.T.) 2, where the superior failed to demonstrate this and so no compensation was awarded. Compare 3.3.39 Gorrie & Banks — 1974 SLT (L.T.) 5, where the superior satisfied the Tribunal that a reduced feuduty had been charged in the original Charter and so was awarded compensation which was calculated by capitalising at the date of variation the difference between the original feuduty and what the feuduty would originally have been, at **full** market rate, assuming no restriction in the title.

5. Variation or Discharge

In addition to their powers to award compensation, the Tribunal have some discretion in relation to variation or discharge. They may either discharge the condition *simpliciter,* **or** in **their discretion**, under **any** of the alternative grounds of application, they may prescribe a substituted provision; but the applicant then has the opportunity of rejecting the proposed variation and continuing the *status quo.* This facility has frequently been used, as reported cases show.

When the Order takes effect (see below), any substituted condition can be enforced as if it were an original condition in the original deed.

The Tribunal's power under the Act is limited to varying land obligations; they cannot, in the process of variation, impose a new or extended burden on adjoining land in which the burdened proprietor has an interest, e.g. by removing a restriction on the **burdened** land and in the same process creating or enlarging a servitude right of access over **other** land **not** owned by the burdened proprietor, in order to facilitate a new use of the burdened land. 'Only the **burdened** proprietor may apply, and only ... to have burdens varied or discharged; he may **not** apply, directly or indirectly, ... to have any additional burden placed on any (other) land'. 3.3.23 Murrayfield Ice Rink supra.

6. Effect of the Order.

The Order will be recorded; and, when recorded, 'it shall be binding on all persons having interest'. Even if not recorded, it presumably binds any party to the proceedings; but not singular successors.

7. Procedure.

The procedure is outlined in S.2 and supplemented in detail by Rules promulgated by the Tribunal, — the Lands Tribunal for Scotland Rules 1971.

4. The Estate of the Vassal
Reading List 4, 4.1, 4.2.

The whole of this topic is treated systematically by Walker Chapters 5.6 to 5.10; and most of the ground has been covered already in outline in Chap. 2.3. Descriptions to both of which reference is made.

4.1 Implied Rights.

Walker Chapter 5.6 opens thus: 'The grant of a feudal charter in favour of a vassal confers on him the *dominium utile* or actual beneficial rights in the whole tract of ground comprehended in the description of the lands conveyed, or held to be carried by the conveyance, though not especially mentioned, together with all parts and pertinents of the land on the surface, such as buildings, woods and waters, or under it, such as minerals *a coelo usque ad centrum,* but under exception of regalia, unless expressly granted, and of any heritable subjects expressly reserved by the superior'. When dealing with descriptions in the Feu Charter, I have summarised the rights and benefits, which pass to the vassal *sub silentio* by virtue of the conveyance of the land alone. The purpose of these Chapters in Walker is to amplify that summary, and to spell out in detail the nature of these implied and inherent rights. In particular, I would remind you at this point of the rule as to separate tenements, which I explained in the context of descriptions, namely, that certain, but not all, heritable rights are capable of separate infeftment as separate tenements on a separate title, e.g. salmon fishings; and that each separate tenement must be separately and specifically conveyed to a disponee in a Charter or Disposition. Otherwise, such separate tenements do not pass to the disponee. In contrast, rights which are implied or inherent in landownership do pass automatically and require no separate or specific reference in the conveyance.

Of the matters dealt with by Walker in Chapter 5.6., the following points are selected for special comment here:

1. **Barony privileges.** For a short explanation of the nature of the Crown Grant of Barony and Regality, see Walker Chapters 5.4 page 54 and 5.6 page 99. The significant feature of a barony title in this context is in relation to the acquisition, by prescription, of rights not specifically conveyed by the Crown Charter creating the barony.

In the ordinary case, salmon fishings, being a separate tenement, must be separately conveyed; and the complementary rule is that, to acquire a right to salmon fishings, then you must either have: —

(a) an express conveyance in a Crown Charter of salmon fishing (*cum piscationibus salmonium*) with or without an attendant grant of land; or

(b) a conveyance (charter or disposition) either from the Crown or from a subject superior 'with fishings', ('cum piscationibus') followed by **possession** of the necessary quality for the prescriptive period, which still remains at 20 years under the 1973 Act S 1.(4) in a competition with the Crown. See Chapter 2.9.

Note particularly that, in such cases, a specific reference to 'fishings' in the title is essential; and, if absent, possession for however long a time is of no avail, because it is possession without a title. See generally Farquharson v. L.A. 1932 S.N.28. **But** the barony title is specially favoured in that possession of salmon fishings on a barony title alone, without reference therein to 'fishings', is sufficient to establish a title by prescription.

The same special privilege applies in other like cases, e.g. the foreshore. See 2.9.18 Agnew. 11M 309.

2. **Parts and pertinents.**

I have covered this already in Chapter 2.3. Descriptions.

3. **Possession of heritage** — Walker e.s. deals with two aspects of possession: —

(i) **The effect of possession on title.** I have already dealt with this, in the context of the infeftment of the vassal in Chapter 2.9. where it more naturally belongs.

(ii) **The right of exclusive occupation and use** — This inherent right implies an absolute right to prevent trespass or encroachment by any person or any thing, e.g. buildings, trees and animals, but with the following general exceptions:

(a) Mineral and other reservations, whether by Statute (e.g. coal, petroleum, etc.) or in the titles.

(b) Burdens and servitudes in the titles, e.g. rights of access, aqueduct, grazing, fuel, feal and divot.

(c) Public rights of way.

(d) In certain situations (e.g. emergency), trespass may be justified; and, in certain instances, persons are entitled to enter upon land with statutory sanctions.

4. **Support.**

This inherent right of ownership has been dealt with briefly when dealing with mineral reservations, in Chap. 2.4.

5. **Rights in Buildings.**

6. **Rights in Minerals.**

7. **Timber.**

All these three (5, 6 and 7 above) are components of land which pass *sub silentio* as *partes soli* with the exception, of course, of matters reserved and excepted in earlier titles and by statutory provision. This has been dealt with under Descriptions in the Charter, in Chapters 2.3 and 2.4.

4.2 **Limitations on the use of land.** Walker Chapter 5.6 page 118.

The limitations imposed on individual owners by conditions in or affecting their individual titles have been dealt with already in Chapters 2.5 and 2.6.

But landowners generally are also subject to restraints at Common Law and, increasingly comprehensively, by Statute in their implied right of unrestricted user.

(1) **Common Law Restrictions on use.**

(i) **Liability for injury to person or property — Culpa.** Walker Chapter 4.34 page 599.

Certain acts, or omissions, by a proprietor of land, are regarded by the law as innocuous in themselves; but if the landowner (or occupier) in the doing of such an act or in such an omission, is negligent or reckless and as a result damage is caused to some other person or property, then he is liable in damages. But, in the absence of negligence or culpa, there is no liability on the landowner (or occupier) who is free to act as he pleases, and in particular no one can prevent him from carrying out, on his land, any such innocuous act.

(ii) **Nuisance.** Walker Chapter 4.39 page 660.

In certain circumstances, however, the law regards certain acts by the heritable proprietor as noxious in themselves, in that an act in this category inevitably interferes with the legitimate enjoyment by a proprietor of neighbouring property or inevitably causes inconvenience or injury to the public at large. In these cases, generally grouped under the heading of 'Nuisance', the doing of the act itself is illegal, whether or not there is negligence or fault in the actual execution of it; and the heritable proprietor can be restrained or prevented from any such act by his neighbours or, possibly, by the public at large. He will also incur liability for any demonstrable damage caused to a neighbour or the public. There are a number of such acts which are nuisances at Common Law; and a large number of further acts have become statutory nuisances.

(iii) **Aemulatio Vicini.** Walker Chapter 4.39 page 665.

Actings of a kind which, in the ordinary way, are lawful and unobjectionable, may nonetheless be validly objected to, and the proprietor so acting may be interdicted, if his sole or primary motive is malice or spite towards his neighbour.

The three foregoing principles are all applications of the Law of Delict, and have been dealt with elsewhere in Scots Law.

(2) **Statutory Controls.**

See Reading List 4.2.

With increasing frequency and comprehensiveness, in recent years, statutory controls of various types have been introduced affecting land, some of which may affect a purchaser. The following are **some** of the more important areas where such controls exist and in regard to which investigation on behalf of a purchaser is, or may be, required. The rule of *caveat emptor* will apply, unless suitable provision has been made in the antecedent contract. This underlines the need **either** for **prior** enquiry before a contract is concluded; **or** for the making of suitable provisions as to the statutory controls in the contract of sale and purchase. See later under Ch. 7.1.

1. **Town and Country Planning**

This is just a reminder of some of the more important points in relation to town and country planning which may affect a purchaser of heritable property.

No attempt is made here to deal in detail with the law of town and country planning.

Background

Statutes. The principal statute at present governing town & country planning in Scotland is the **Town & Country Planning (Scotland) Act 1972** which largely — but not entirely — consolidated the law at that date. The 1972 Act has since been amended and extended, principally but not by any means exclusively, by the **Local Government (Scotland) Act 1973** (new planning authorities), the **Town and Country Amenities Act 1974** (conservation areas), the **Town & Country Planning (Scotland) Act 1977,** in certain respects the **Local Government, Planning and Land Act 1980** and the **Local Government & Planning (Scotland) Act 1982.** Planning law is however in a practically continuous state of change. Legislation covering related areas (*e.g.* housing, highways) may also be relevant in dealing with planning matters. The above statutes however, together with regulations made thereunder, form the legislative framework of planning in Scotland.

Regulations. The principal regulations include the **Town and Country Planning (General Development) (Scotland) Order 1981** (830/1981 — referred to as 'the GDSO') which came into effect on 3rd August 1981 and the **Town & Country Planning (Use Classes) (Scotland) Order 1973** (1165/1973 — referred to as the 'UCO'). There are numerous other regulations and orders covering in detail specific aspects of planning procedure.

Most (if not all) procedural matters are dealt with by regulation. (See the relationship for example between s.22 1972 Act and article 8 of the GDSO).

History

Town and country planning in Scotland goes back to 1919; but, for practical purposes, the Town and Country Planning (Scotland) Act 1947 provides the basis for the modern system of planning. The history of the planning system from that Act to the 1972 Act does not really concern us, with the exception of the development planning provisions which may still have considerable relevance in connection with the purchase of heritage and which are referred to below. The old style system of Development Planning was superseded by providing in the 1972 Act for a new system of Development Planning in Scotland which took effect following the 1973 Act on the reorganisation of local government in Scotland as from May 1975.

Development Planning is only one of the two main roles of planning authorities. The other is development control, and forms the more negative side of land use planning. This has developed similarly over the years, and again the 1972 Act contains the basic provisions.

Post-1973 Act Planning Authorities.

The Secretary of State for Scotland has overall responsibility for town and country planning in Scotland, exercised principally through the Scottish Development Department, while the actual administration is carried out by the planning authority as defined in the 1972 Act. Planning authorities and their respective functions and responsibilities are outlined in Part IX of and Schedule 22 to the 1973 Act as amended by the 1982 Act. Over much of Scotland the planning functions are divided between Regional and District Councils — in Central, Fife, Grampian, Lothian, Strathclyde and Tayside regions. In these regions the Regional Council is the regional planning authority responsible for regional planning functions and the District Councils are the district planning authorities with the responsibility for district planning functions. In these regions, there is a concurrent two-tier system of planning. The councils in the Highland, Borders, and Dumfries and Galloway Regions and the 3 Island Areas (Orkney, Shetland and Western Isles) are general planning authorities with responsibility for all planning functions in their areas.

The basic division of functions between the two tiers of planning authority derives from the areas they respectively serve. The interest of the regional planning authority is more general and less detailed (at least in theory) than that of the district planning authority in respect of the latter's area. There can be difficulties in interpreting where spheres of interest and enforceability end. In general, however, the regional planning authority is responsible for survey and structure plans covering its area and has certain reserve powers in respect of district planning authorities in its area. The district planning authority has responsibility for local planning and development control (i.e. the granting of planning permission and the enforcement of planning control) amongst other matters.

Pre-1972 Act Development Plans.

Under the 1947 Act every planning authority (which, by and large, meant every Large Burgh and County Authority in Scotland) was charged with the duty of preparing a Development Plan for its planning area. That plan, once prepared, then had to be reviewed every five years.

The Development Plan was to comprise —

1. A map of the area.
2. A policy statement and survey report in support of the map.
3. A series of detailed plans for each individual area.

It would disclose, *inter alia,* the manner in which, or purposes for which, particular areas are to be used, e.g. for housing, commercial, education, etc.; and the stages by which development is to proceed.

For this purpose, the Development Plan was to include sufficient maps and statements to illustrate all the proposals for the future development within a 20-year period. It would normally:

(i) define the sites or proposed sites of roads, buildings, and public open space,

(ii) allocate (or 'zone') areas for particular types of development,

(iii) define comprehensive redevelopment areas for special, and usually urgent, reconstruction.

(In Dundee there were two stages — 1964 to 1969, and 1970 to 1984, followed by a third unspecific stage beyond 1984).

Designations under the old style Development Plans clearly may still be of concern to a greater or lesser extent to a purchaser and enquiry should always be made of the planning authority, although in most cases the old style Development Plans will by now be superseded by those made under the 1972 Acts. As a precaution, a purchaser will normally make his offer conditional upon there being no adverse planning implications in the Development Plan (which will refer to either the old style or the new Development Plan), by the inclusion of a clause such as 'There is no existing designation ... order or notice or other matter ... affecting the subjects of sale or amenity thereof under ... any statutory enactment.'

Post-1975 Development Planning.

Structure Plans

The intention of the new system is to separate policy planning from the detailed land use planning of an area. (The old-style Development Plans comprised very detailed land use directions). The regional planning authority will consider the policy implications for its whole area and will have produced, firstly, a Regional Report (which sets out policies, programmes and proposals, and will indicate development planning priorities), and, secondly, a Structure Plan for its area. The Structure Plan is the more important planning document and comprises a written statement supplemented by diagrams setting out policies for development and land use. Considerable preparatory study and discussion is required before the Structure Plan can be prepared; and the approval of the Secretary of State is then required. The majority of Structure Plans have now been approved.

Local Plans.

Detailed land use planning will be contained in the Local Plans, which are the responsibility of the district planning authorities. They will consist of a written statement and a map or maps. They will either cover a specified, and usually a fairly restricted, area (such as a village or part of a town) or they may take the form of a subject plan (such as recreational uses of land). They are not to be inconsistent with relevant provisions of the relevant Structure Plan, though they do not need to await approval of the latter. Once approved (and normally the approval of the Secretary of State is unnecessary) Local Plans will offer detailed guidance to developers and purchasers.

The Development Plan for an area will therefore, in due course, comprise the Structure Plan and one or more Local Plans.

Advisory Plans

These do not have statutory effect and may consist of a statement of policy (perhaps to be found in the planning authority's minutes) or a more formal document (such as a proposed Local Plan which has not yet entered the consultation process). Such advisory plans do, however, offer guidance to a planning authority's views, and should be given consideration.

Development Plans and Control.

It should not be assumed that an individual application for planning permission will receive automatic approval simply because the application appears to fall within the guide lines set out in a Development Plan. Each application requires to be considered on its own merits. The Development Plan simply outlines the planning authority's considered view and offers guidance. There may be many reasons why an application for planning permission is refused. Normally, however, an application which lies within development plan guidelines should not be refused on policy grounds, e.g. a planning authority should not refuse an application for a house in an area which has been indicated in an approved Local Plan as suitable for residential development on the grounds, for example, that this use is not appropriate. But it does happen (c.f. Highland Regional Council and developments in the Spey Valley, where the Local Plan appears to have been ignored by the regional planning authority) though it should provide a good basis for appeal.

Development and Development Control.

The 1972 Act operates by imposing a statutory control on all development of land. Development is defined in the 1972 Act S.19(1) as:

(1) '... the carrying out of building, engineering, mining, or other operations in, on, over or under land, or

(2) the making of any material change in the use of any buildings or other land'.

Certain of these expressions are defined in the Act, which also provides for modification in certain cases, both as to what constitutes development and as to certain categories of development which do not require planning permission. Generally speaking, however, before land (which includes buildings or structures) may be developed, planning permission for that development must be obtained from the appropriate planning authority (the district or general planning authority).

Unless and until planning permission is obtained, it is unlawful to carry out any proposed development on land, unless, by statute, permission for that development is not required.

Permitted development.

In terms of the 1972 Act and Regulations made thereunder (particularly the GDSO) certain minor developments do not require planning permission.

Examples of types of permitted development which commonly occur in practice, and which are authorised under the 1972 Act S.19(2) include:

(i) the maintenance, improvement or other alteration to a building, affecting **only** the interior and not **materially** affecting the external appearance;

(ii) the use of any building or land within the 'curtilage' of a dwellinghouse for any purpose incidental to the enjoyment of that dwellinghouse as such;

(iii) the use of land, or buildings thereon, for agriculture or forestry;

(iv) a change of use of land or buildings which is authorised by or falls within any of the use classes specified by the UCO.

The GDSO lists in Schedule I (relating to article 3 of the Order) 22 separate classes of permitted development. Many of these are generally of little relevance to the individual purchaser or developer, but classes I, II, III and IV are important to the practitioner. Thus, under the GDSO:

Class I — development within the curtilage of a dwellinghouse (not including a flat) is permitted within certain tolerances without planning permission being required.

Class II — sundry minor operations are permitted without permission — e.g. erecting fences within certain prescribed dimensions.

Class III — certain changes of use are permitted — see below.

The Use Classes Order.

The current order is the Town and Country Planning (Use Classes) (Scotland) Order 1973, which prescribes 17 separate classes of use e.g.

Class I — use as a shop (with special exclusions);

Class II — use as an office for any purpose;

Class III — use as a light industrial building etc.

The UCO defines various expressions (these definitions assist in interpreting the classes) e.g. shop — 'a building used for the carrying on of any retail trade or retail business wherein the primary purpose is the selling of goods by retail ...', and goes on to specify certain businesses which are deemed to be shops (e.g. a post office, a hairdresser's shop etc.) and some which are not so classed (e.g. an amusement arcade etc.).

'Office' is defined, and includes a bank, a building society office, estate agents office etc.

The UCO is not a comprehensive listing of all possible uses of land but merely catalogues certain types of use. Some uses are not included in any of the classes (e.g. a betting office).

Within any of the classes so specified in the UCO a change of use is not considered as development and therefore does not require planning permission. For example if a shop, (Class I) is used as a butcher's shop, the owner (or a purchaser) may change its use to a grocer's or an ironmonger's shop; but may not change its use to a chip shop, nor to a bank, or a building society office etc.

Similarly a building used as a bank which comes within Class II (office), may be changed to a building society office or an office of any other kind, but may not be used as a shop without permission having first being obtained.

In some cases, planning permission is not required for a change of use between classes: there are cases where, in effect, the proposed use is less detrimental than the previous use — see Class III of Schedule I of the GDSO. In general however, **any change of use between** classes constitutes development.

Application for Planning Permission.

An application for planning permission is made to the district or general planning authority on a form obtained from that authority. The authority may seek additional information from the applicant about the proposed development. A fee is payable at the time of submission of the application. Notice must have been given of the application and the correct certificates duly completed. The certificates are normally printed on or accompany the form.

Intimation of every application (with very limited exceptions) must now be given either to neighbouring proprietors or to the public in general. Every application must now be notified to 'persons having a notifiable interest in neighbouring land' (article 7 GDSO) **unless** notification has been made in terms of the 1972 Act S.23 or S.24. This provision was introduced in the GDSO to meet one of the major criticisms of the earlier legislation in that, before this provision was introduced, many applications for planning permission did not require intimation to neighbouring proprietors; and as a result many applications were granted, either for change of use or for structural development, without the prior knowledge of adjoining proprietors who in many cases were materially affected.

In the case of applications under the 1972 Act S.23 — the so called 'bad neighbour' applications (1972 Act S.23 and Schedule 2) — these must be advertised in the press and notified to neighbouring proprietors in terms of article 7 before the planning authority may entertain such an application. If the applicant is not the owner of the whole of the site of the proposed development, notice of the application must be served on the owner (1972 Act S.4).

Planning authorities may also give public notice of certain other applications (e.g. in conservation areas or of public interest) and seek representations before dealing with the application. It should be noted, however, that, while a planning authority must 'take into account' representations made to it, neither these, nor an objector's strongly held views, can derogate from the right and duty of the planning authority to take whatever decision it feels correct in all the circumstances.

Consideration of an application.

Under S.31 1972 Act every planning authority is obliged to maintain a Register of applications for, and of grants of, planning permission, which is **public** and may be consulted at any time during working hours. Planning authorities will by the nature of the size of their area or their organisation have adopted different procedures for dealing with planning applications. S.56(1) 1973 Act provides for powers to be delegated by the authority to a committee, a sub-committee or an official and the majority of straightforward planning applications will be dealt with under delegated powers. Certain authorities may hear representations in respect of particular applications, certain may only be prepared to consider written representations. The decisions of the planning authority must be recorded in the minutes of that authority.

Determination of application for planning permission.

A planning authority must issue its decision on a planning application within (normally) two months of submission of the application. It may, however, if necessary consultations are numerous or if the application is of more than ordinary importance, seek the applicant's consent for an extension of this period. If no timeous decision is issued, the applicant has a right of appeal on the grounds of a 'deemed refusal'. A determination must be issued in respect of each application.

The planning authority may refuse an application, or may grant it unconditionally, or subject to stated conditions which the applicant or the developer must observe. In the case of a grant of permission, this may, depending on the application, be for outline permission (i.e. a decision in principle, leaving the reserved matters (article 1, GDSO) for later approval) or for detailed permission (allowing the development to be commenced without further planning approval being required).

Appeal

If no timeous decision is issued, if the application is refused, or if the application is granted subject to conditions which the applicant considers to be unacceptable, the applicant has a right of appeal to the Secretary of State for Scotland which must be exercised within six months. The applicant has the right to have his appeal heard at a public local inquiry but the vast majority of appeals are dealt with on the basis of the written submission procedure. This procedure allows each side to present a written statement of its position and avoids the delay and expense inherent in the public local inquiry. Following the 'closing of the record' in the written submissions procedure, or the completion of the report following upon the public local inquiry, the decision on the appeal is then taken: in the vast majority of cases by a Reporter (a Scottish Office Official) who has the necessary power delegated to him. The principal parties (usually the applicant/appellant and the planning authority) must agree to adopt the written submissions procedure, otherwise a public local inquiry will be held. In the case of a major application, or one which has generated considerable local concern, a public local inquiry will almost certainly be held.

No one, other than the principal parties, is entitled to make oral representation at the public local inquiry as of right; but normally all relevant and non-repetitive evidence will be heard, and there is nothing to prevent written representations being made by any interested party.

Planning Permission.

Under the 1972 Act S.30, any planning permission which has been granted enures for the benefit of the land; and so it may be used by the proprietor for the time being, as singular successor of the original applicant, without any formal assignation or transmission thereof.

The 1972 Act SS.38 and 39 require any development normally to commence within five years from the date of the granting of permission. Where outline permission has been granted, application for detailed permission (or for approval of reserved matters) must be made within three years of the outline permission; and the development must normally commence within five years of the outline permission being granted.

There is a power (seldom used) in the 1972 Act S.51 to allow a prospective developer to apply for a determination as to whether or not planning permission is required. In practice, an applicant in this situation would make a straightforward application for planning permission.

Outline Planning Permission

If an applicant intends to build a house on a particular plot of land, he lodges an application for planning permission and, with it, detailed plans showing the layout of the house and details of the building itself. Permission may be granted with or without modification. If the applicant intends to develop a housing estate with, say, 200 houses, it would obviously be a very laborious job to lodge detailed layout and building plans for each plot, which, in the end of the day might prove to be abortive in that the planning authority might not approve what was proposed. It is, therefore, competent, under S.39 1972 Act to apply for 'outline planning permission' (often referred to as planning permission in principle) indicating the general intention without specifying all the detail of the proposals for which planning permission is, ultimately, required. Outline planning permission implies that the developer has approval in principle for his proposals but must submit detailed applications for each phase of the development, all of which requires permission in detail.

Enforcement of Planning Control

The corollary of a system of controlling land use is the means of enforcing that control. This is provided principally by the enforcement notice procedure contained in 1972 Act Part V as amended by the 1982 Act. New regulations — the Town & Country Planning (Enforcement of Control) (Scotland) Regulations 1984 — have now come into effect.

Where a proprietor or occupier of the land either:

(i) carries out development without permission; or

(ii) fails to comply with the conditions subject to which planning permission was granted,

a breach of planning control has occurred. The remedy available to the planning authority is to serve an enforcement notice (1972 Act S.84) stating the breach and specifying the steps required to be taken to remedy this. The planning authority has discretion as to whether or not to serve an enforcement notice and cannot be compelled to do so by, for example, an affected neighbour.

The procedure is statutory and detailed. In Scotland there is no prescribed form of notice, although a specimen form is now given in SDD Circular 6/1984.

A right of appeal lies within 28 days to the Secretary of State for Scotland and the grounds of appeal are specified in the 1972 Act S.85. See also the 1980 Act and the Fees Regulations.

The planning authority have power also to serve a stop notice which, unlike the enforcement notice, may come into effect following service (1972 Act S.87).

Any unauthorised development may be controlled by an enforcement notice with certain exceptions being, generally, development which has been carried on for some time although unauthorised.

Unauthorised development consisting of an operation in contrast to a mere change of use (see 1972 Act S.19) or a failure to comply with conditions subject to which planning permission for an operation was previously granted or a change of use of a building to a single dwellinghouse become immune from enforcement procedure if more than four years have passed since the date when the breach first occurred. In the case of unauthorised development consisting of change of use (except as above stated) this is now immune from enforcement procedure if the change of use commenced before 31st December, 1964.

This immunity from enforcement is important; but unauthorised development which has become immune from enforcement as a result of the statutory provisions is not equivalent to an authorised development for which planning permission has previously been obtained. Therefore, any purchaser should always confirm very carefully that the current use of the property is the authorised use. For this purpose, it may be prudent to check the original use of the property on 1st July, 1948 (the date of commencement of the current planning system). The permitted use of any given property is clearly critical to a purchaser. In many cases, no problem arises and there is no need to make special enquiry, e.g. dwellinghouse clearly used as such for 40 years; or factory recently erected after planning permission obtained. But it is always prudent to make the necessary enquiries.

Certificate of Established Use.
In any case of serious doubt, the matter can be resolved by obtaining from the planning authority a certificate of established use, in terms of S.90 1972 Act. If the planning authority refuse to grant the certificate applied for, their refusal may be appealed to the Secretary of State for Scotland.

Additional Controls
Section 50 Agreement. A planning authority may enter into agreement with any person having an interest in land such as would allow him to bind the land for the purpose of restricting or regulating development of that land. The agreement would normally be recorded in the Register of Sasines and can then be enforced by the planning authority against the owner for the time being. The principal benefit of such an agreement (from the point of view of the planning authority) is that it enables binding conditions to be enforced regulating the development of land which may be of a financial nature or which may not be conditions which could be attached to a grant of planning permission with any certainty of their being enforceable (S.50 1972 Act).

Orders under 1972 S.42 and 49.
The planning authority may, in terms of SS. 42 and 43, revoke or modify a planning permission previously given; and, under S.49 may require a proprietor to discontinue an existing use or to alter or remove any existing buildings or works. These powers are infrequently used.

Special Controls
Listed Buildings (1972 Act SS.52/56, 92/87).
The Secretary of State is required to compile a list of buildings of special architectural or historic interest — listed buildings — throughout Scotland, and may amend the list from time to time. Generally speaking, a listed building cannot be demolished or altered without consent of the planning authority or the Secretary of State for Scotland and, in addition, in the case of demolition, until notice has been given to the Royal Commission on the Ancient and Historical Monuments of Scotland.

The primary control which the planning authority has over listed buildings is by means of the listed building enforcement procedure (S.92) but there is a power of prosecution in S.53. Essentially the form of a listed building enforcement notice is as for the normal enforcement notice although the statutory references etc. are different. Further controls are available to a planning authority in the form of a repairs notice (S.105) and, in the case of a building which is not actually listed but which is considered to be of special architectural or historic interest, a building preservation notice (S.56).

Trees (1972 Act SS.57/60, 98/99).
The planning authority are empowered to make tree preservation orders on a single tree or groups of trees, or woodlands, prohibiting without consent the cutting down of listed trees and for securing replanting. Provisional orders are competent. The order is recorded in the Register of Sasines.

Advertisements (1972 Act SS.61/62, and 101).
The control of advertisements is dealt with by the Town and Country Planning (Control of Advertisements) (Scotland) Regulations 1984.

Waste Land (1972 Act S.63).
The planning authority may require the owner to take steps to improve the amenity of waste land.

2. Compulsory Purchase.

Finally, under Part VI of the 1972 Act, there is an elaborate code for the compulsory acquisition and appropriation of land for various planning purposes, subject, of course, to payment of compensation to the expropriated proprietor. Power is given elsewhere also to various authorities and utilities to acquire land compulsorily for the purposes of their functions. This is discussed below in Chapter 7.2.6.

3. Building Control.

In terms of the **Building (Scotland) Acts 1959 and 1970,** and regulations made thereunder virtually all building operations anywhere in Scotland come under the supervision and control of the local authority and require a building warrant.

4 The Countryside (The Countryside (Scotland) Acts 1967 and 1981).

Rights of way and access to the countryside generally are dealt with under an elaborate statutory code. In particular, an agreement or order, describing the property affected, may be recorded in the Register of Sasines and, when so recorded, is effective against singular successors in that land. It is possible, under this code, that public rights of way may be imposed on the landowner when none previously existed in which case compensation is payable.

5. Ancient (Scheduled) Monuments.

The Ancient Monuments and Archaelogical Areas Act 1979 will in due course supersede the provisions of earlier legislation, such as the Field Monuments Act 1972 in dealing with the preservation of 'monuments'. S.17 provides for agreements to be made between the Secretary of State or the local authority and the owners or occupiers of any monument to ensure preservation, and allows the possibility of compensatory payments. Such agreements are to be recorded in the Register of Sasines and can accordingly be enforced against singular successors. Sections 1 and 2 of the Conveyancing and Feudal Reform (Scotland) Act 1970 do not apply to such agreements.

6. Fire Precautions.

The Factories Act 1961, The Offices, Shop and Railway Premises Act 1963 the Fire Precautions Act 1971 and the Health and Safety at Work Act 1974 impose obligations on owners and occupiers of buildings used as factories, shops, hotels and boarding houses, and for public entertainment to comply with fire regulations, and if necessary to adapt their premises. This can be a very awkward and expensive matter for any builder or developer. Often, when applying for a Building Warrant for very minor adaptations, onerous fire requirements are imposed. This frequently happens following on the purchase of a property and may be a major deterrent to a purchaser.

In all these cases, it is illegal to use the premises unless a valid Fire Certificate has been issued and is still in force. The Fire Authority are given the necessary powers of inspection. If the owner (or occupier) fails to comply with any remedial action prescribed by the Fire Authority, the Fire Certificate may be cancelled.

7. Public Health, Housing, Civic Government and Roads Acts.

These Acts make detailed and elaborate provisions for numerous matters relating to sanitary conditions, housing, streets and drainage, and ruinous and dangerous properties and nuisance.

To some extent, they are superseded by more recent statutory codes on e.g. pollution, waste disposal, sewage, etc.

They have been further amended in detail and applied to the reorganised local authorities by the Local Government (Scotland) Act 1973.

In the context of examination of title, it is relevant to mention the undernoted items especially, since these are occasionally encountered on a sale and purchase of heritage, and may cause problems.

Repairs to houses.

Housing (Scotland) Act 1950 S.7., as amended.
Housing (Scotland) Act 1969 S.24.
Housing (Financial Provisions)(Scotland) Act 1978.
Civic Government (Scotland) Act 1982.

Under the 1969 Act, if the Local Authority is satisfied that any house is in a state of serious disrepair, they may serve notice on the person having control of that house, requiring him, within a reasonable time, to execute works specified in the notice in order to bring the house up to a standard of reasonable repair. If the property is purchased subject to such a notice, the onus lies on the purchaser to carry out the work. The rule of *caveat emptor* applies.

Under the 1969 Act ss.24 (2) and 25 the Local Authority may themselves carry out the necessary work, if the owner fails or refuses; and recover the cost from the owners.

In terms of the 1969 Act S.25, the Local Authority may make a Charging Order burdening the property with the cost. The order is recorded in the Register of Sasines and transmits as a real burden, preferred to all other charges. It takes the form of a 30 year annuity of an amount calculated to repay the cost incurred over that period. Notwithstanding the statutory wording, such securities are postponed to heritable securities recorded prior to the date of the recording of the Charging Order — see 5.3.6 Sowman 1983 SLT 132, affirmed on Appeal 1985 SLT 65; but cf. 3.2.18 Pickard 1970 SLT (Sh.Ct.) 63 where a local authority recorded a Charging Order on certain heritable property. The owner thereof acquired the superiority and, three years later, obtained a Decree of Irritancy of the feu for non-payment of the feuduty. He then argued that the irritancy extinguished the title to the *dominium utile* and, with it, extinguished the preference created by the recording of the Charging Order. The Sheriff held that, the burden having been imposed under statutory powers and in the public interest, the Superior remained liable.

Note that there is now no provision in this legislation which requires the Local Authority to pay regard to the estimated cost of the works or to the value of the house on completion of the works, as there was in the 1950 legislation. In practice, however, Local Authorities do not normally act unreasonably in this respect.

In respect of **repairs notice procedure** this has been made more effective in relation to repairs in tenement buildings because the 1978 Act has broadened the definition of 'house' and the effect is now to bring within the scope of repairs notices the owners of non-residential premises in tenements and similar buildings. Under the amended procedure each owner of premises within such a building should receive a notice referring to defects for which that owner would have some responsibility, even if this is only a partial responsibility. Failing collective action by the recipients, if that is necessary, for example, to secure common repairs, and subject to appeal to the Sheriff, the Local Authority may itself undertake the necessary repairs after the expiry of the specified period which must not be less than 21 days. The expenses incurred by the Local Authority may be apportioned amongst the owners of premises in the building concerned, and retrieved (by charging order if appropriate) from the person having control of the premises following service of a notice. In a building containing a number of houses, or houses and other premises, expenses will be apportioned for recovery from the owners responsible. This apportionment extends to owners of commercial premises in a tenement building where a due share of repairs falls to be allocated against such premises. Repairs grant from the Local Authority might be available to the owner(s) of the houses in disrepair and is available without a financial means test if the repairs in question are classed by the Local Authority as 'substantial and structural'. (Article 3 of the Housing (Disapplication of Financial Hardship Provision for Repairs Grant) (Scotland) Order 1982 made under the proviso to section 10A(3) of the Housing (Scotland) Act 1974 inserted by paragraph 31(a) of Schedule 3 to the Local Government and Planning (Scotland) Act 1982). Grant would not be available to owners of commercial premises on whom a repairs notice had been served but S.9 of the 1978 Act obliges a Local Authority to offer a loan towards the cost of repair works provided an application is made and the Authority are satisfied that the applicant could meet the expense of a loan.

The 1982 Act sections 87-98 give Local Authorities a number of functions in respect of the safe and efficient upkeep of private property. Such functions are in most cases exercised by the issue of notices requiring the carrying out of repairs, etc., within a certain time. Notice powers would clearly be ineffectual unless the Local Authority had reserved enforcement powers enabling them to step in and take action where notices were ignored. Sections 99-109, therefore, provide enforcement powers enabling the execution of works in the owner's default and the recovery of expenses incurred in so doing. Section 106 provides for appeals against any requirement of any notice served under any provisions of this Part, or against the amount of any associated expenses.

Closing Orders and Demolition Orders.

Housing (Scotland) Act 1966 S.15 as amended by Housing (Scotland) Acts 1969 S.17 and 1974 Sch. 3.

Housing (Financial Provisions)(Scotland) Act 1978 S.10

If the local authority is satisfied that a house or houses do not meet what is termed the tolerable standard and ought to be closed, demolished, or improved, then they make either a Closing Order or a Demolition Order or an Improvement Order.

The tolerable standard is defined in Section 14 of the 1974 Act. To meet this standard, the house or houses must satisfy a number of conditions, e.g.:

(a) they must be structurally stable;

(b) they must be free from rising or penetrating damp;

(c) they must have satisfactory lighting, ventilation and heating, piped hot and cold water and a toilet etc.

Under the 1966 Act, the appropriate Order is

(a) where the house not meeting the required standard forms part only of a building, a Closing Order. The effect of this is to prohibit the use of the house for human habitation as from a date specified in the Order; and any tenant must remove by that date; or

(b) where the building in question comprises only the house in question or a number of houses, but no other accommodation, (e.g. shop), all of which fail to meet the tolerable standard, the Local Authority make a Demolition Order requiring the building to be vacated within a period specified, and further requiring that the building thereafter be demolished within a period of three months from the date when the building is vacated.

In practice, these periods are often extended, sometimes for a considerable time, while tenants are rehoused.

The owner of a house then has the option either of carrying out repairs necessary to bring the house up to the tolerable standard in which case the Closing Order or Demolition Order can then be removed; or of leaving the property as it is in the case of a Closing Order or demolishing in the case of a Demolition Order. In many of these cases, the Local Authority take over the tenement from the owner at a nominal figure and carry out the work themselves; but the Local Authority have no obligation so to do.

Under the 1966 Act S.22, if a Demolition Order is not complied with, the Local Authority may themselves demolish and recover the cost from the owner. Under

S.30, they may then make a Charging Order for a 30 year annuity on the property, to secure payment of the cost of any works over the 30 year period. The 1969 Act Sch. 2 regulates the form and recording of the Order.

If property is purchased subject to a Closing Order or a Demolition Order, the effect transmits against a purchaser.

Improvement Orders. Section 10 of Housing (Financial Provisions) (Scotland) Act 1978 introduced S.14A of the Housing (Scotland) Act 1974, which provides a new procedure for Local Authorities to use in respect of a house which fails to meet the tolerable standard. Hitherto there had been no way of compelling improvement of a single sub-tolerable house which needs rehabilitation but which should not be demolished. It is useful to have available the Improvement Order in cases which otherwise would have been the subject of Closing or Demolition Orders because there was no other choice. An Improvement Order in the prescribed form requires the owner to carry out works within 180 days to bring the house up to standard. The owner has a right of appeal against the order to the Sheriff. The house may be acquired by the authority by agreement or, if necessary, by compulsion to secure enforcement.

There is no requirement, under the provisions referred to above relating to Orders for repairs or Closing or Demolition Orders, or Improvement Orders, involving the registration of any writ in the Register of Sasines; so a purchaser will not be put on his guard by a Search over the property. He has to make enquiry of the Local Authority direct to see whether or not any such Order has been issued or is pending.

Improvement Grants. Since the Second World War, Government Grants have been made available to individual owners or certain tenants for improving the standard of houses generally. The scheme is operated through District and Islands Councils. The amount of the Grant and the conditions attaching to Grants are laid down by Statute but have varied substantially over the intervening period. Under the present arrangements, as undernoted, an Improvement Grant is available according to circumstances and the individual local authority scheme for half the approved expenditure to a maximum of £5100 of Grant (1983) or three-quarters of the approved expenditure to a maximum of £7650 of grant.

Conditions of grant are made real burdens on the property by the recording in the Register of Sasines of a Notice of Payment of Improvement Grant describing the property and specifying the conditions to be observed with respect to the house.

The Scheme was first introduced for houses generally under the Housing (Scotland) Act 1950 and was later extended and amended by:

The House Purchase and Housing Act 1959
The Housing (Financial Provisions) (Scotland) Act 1968
The Housing (Scotland) Act 1969
The Housing (Scotland) Act 1974
The Housing (Financial Provisions) (Scotland) Act 1978
The Tenants' Rights Etc. (Scotland) Act 1980 and
Local Government (Miscellaneous Provisions) (Scotland) Act 1981
The Local Government and Housing (Scotland) Act 1981.

The period for observance of conditions is 5 years (by the 1974 Act) at the moment.

Under the 1974 Act, an Improvement Grant can normally be obtained in two circumstances:

(a) A Standard Grant. 1974 Act S.7. In this case, the Local Authority is obliged to give an Improvement Grant for providing certain standard amenities. The standard amenities include a bath or shower, wash basin, sink, w.c., and hot and cold water supply.

For a Grant under this head, the Local Authority must be satisfied:

(i) that the house will be provided with **all** the standard amenities for the exclusive use of the occupier;

(ii) that the house will meet the tolerable standard (see below); and

(iii) that the house will be available for use as a house for ten years.

(b) Discretionary Improvement Grants for improving existing dwellinghouses to a high standard or for converting properties into flats. In this case, the Grant is payable only in the discretion of the Council who may refuse to make a Grant 'on any grounds that seem to them sufficient'.

The Local Authority must be satisfied that the house, when improved, will provide satisfactory housing for such period and conform to such requirements as to construction, condition and services and amenities as may be specified from time to time by the Secretary of State; and the rateable value must not exceed the prescribed limit.

The following conditions apply generally to Grants under (a) and (b) above:—

(i) the house must not be used for any purpose other than a dwellinghouse;

(ii) the house must not be occupied by the owner except as his main residence;

(iii) all steps must be taken to secure the maintenance of the house in good repair.

The provisions as to Notices of Payment of Improvement Grant and the recording of the same in the Register of Sasines are now contained in the 1974 Act S.9(9) as amended. The Local Authority is required to record in the Register of Sasines a Notice in the prescribed form specifying:

(a) the conditions attaching to the Grant;

(b) the period for which the conditions are to be observed; and

(c) the provision of Schedule 2 regarding repayment on breach of the conditions.

Notice of Payment of a repairs grant will also appear in the Register of Sasines.

The tolerable standard is defined in Part II of the 1974 Act. In terms of S.14, a house meets the tolerable standard only if:

(a) it is structurally stable;

(b) it is free from damp;

(c) it has satisfactory natural and artificial light, ventilation and heating;

(d) it has an adequate supply of water;

(e) it has a sink with hot and cold water;

(f) it has an exclusive w.c. within the house;

(g) it has effective drainage;

(h) it has satisfactory cooking facilities;

(i) it has satisfactory access to all external doors and outbuildings.

Housing Action Areas — 1974 Act S. 15-36

District Councils are empowered to declare certain areas 'Housing Action Areas'. In such areas, the Council have power to secure that work is carried out to bring houses in that area up to a specified standard, being not less than the tolerable standard. But in all such cases, Improvement Grants can be obtained of up to 75% of approved expenditure with a ceiling of £7,650 (or 90% = £9,180 in hardship cases) in contrast to the normal 50% £5,100 limit (1983).

Notes:

William Hodge & Co. Ltd., 36 North Frederick Street, Glasgow (041-552-2248) publish a list of forms available in connection with improvement/ repairs grants, demolition and closing orders, and housing action areas.

See Also: 'Public Sector Housing Law in Scotland' by Chris Himsworth. Published 1982 by The Planning Exchange, Bath Street, Glasgow.

House Grants — Categories

(Note: The percentages and financial limits given below are regularly amended by S.I.)

Improvement Grants

Cover a wide range of works needed to raise the standard of a house.

By virtue of S.5(1A) of the 1974 Act and orders made thereunder, there are now two kinds of grant:—
  (i) priority 75%   (ii) non priority 50%

Maximum grant amounts would be:—
  75% of £10,200 i.e. £7,650   or   50% of £10,200 i.e. £5,100

Rateable Value Limit.

The rateable limits for each District are set out in the Housing (Limits of Rateable Value for Improvement Grants and Repair Grants) (Scotland) Order 1985.

If works are for a disabled occupant the rate is 75% and rateable value limit is disapplied.

If the house is in a Housing Action Area the rate is 75% and could be up to 90% if financial hardship is shown by a means test.

No instalments of grant unless applicant is an owner/occupier.

There can be a repairs element in the grant in priority cases.

Standard Grants

For providing those standard amenities lacking in a house, 50%.
Grant maximum is 50% of £2,275.

A very basic grant covering the provision of a fixed bath or shower, a hot and cold water supply, wash-hand basin, sink, w.c.

Fixed maximum grant amounts for each missing amenity.

Repairs Grants

For repair works which, if neglected would threaten the future useful life of the house. Normal repair and maintenance does not qualify (e.g. electrical rewiring, double glazing). Level, 50%. The maximum grant is £2,400.

BUT there is a financial means test unless the grant —
1. is for renewal of lead piping (see below)
   or
2. the works are regarded by the Council as substantial and structural.

Rateable value limit also applies..

Lead Piping Renewal

Dealt with as a type of repairs grant.

Covers the cost of providing a lead free supply at the drinking tap provided the Council is satisfied there is a health risk.

Grant maximum is 75% of £4,800 i.e. £3,600.
No financial means test.
No rateable value limit.
Sample to be arranged first by Environmental Health Department (£10 plus VAT).
House must be otherwise up to standard.

Loft Insulation

Covers loft insulation and also the insulation of water tanks and pipes in lofts, and uninsulated hot water tanks wherever they are located.

Two categories:—
(i) Standard grant is 66% of the cost or £69 whichever is the less.
(ii) Special needs grant is 90% of the cost or £95 whichever is the less.

To qualify for special needs
1. the applicant must either be a man over 65 or woman over 60 and
2. be receiving a supplementary pension or allowance or a rent or rate rebate or rent allowance or
3. the applicant or a dependant living in the same household be receiving a mobility allowance or attendance or constant attendance allowance or
4. the applicant be in possession of a DHSS-provided 3 or 4 wheeled vehicle or be in possession of a private car maintenance allowance.

Streets, pavements and sewers

Roads and streets may be public or private, in the sense that they are either open to the public or under private control. Roads and streets may however also be public or private in relation to the liability to maintain, in that a street which is open to the public as a public thoroughfare may nonetheless be maintainable by private individuals, normally the frontagers on that street. The authority now responsible for roadways is the Regional Council as roads authority. A road or street does not pass automatically to the Regional Council unless and until on application by an interested party the Council has agreed to take over the road or street. It will probably do so if and when the owner or frontagers make up the street to the required standard at their own expense. Thereafter, the Council will assume liability for maintenance.

The same applies, generally speaking, to foot pavements and sewers in public streets. The liability to make up and maintain rests with the individual frontagers according to the length of their frontage. This is, therefore, a relevant point of enquiry when examining title to see whether there is any liability on the purchaser for making up or maintenance.

The burden of making up a public street can be very heavy, particularly with corner properties having a road on two sides.

Under the Roads (Scotland) Act 1984 the Council have power to require frontagers to make up a street, failing which the Council themselves make it up and charge the frontagers with the due proportion of the cost. Normally, this would coincide with the liability in the title; but, if not, title liability is ignored and over-ridden by this provision.

8. **Health & Safety at Work Act 1974.**

Some of the provisions of the foregoing Acts are amended or superseded by the Health & Safety at Work Act 1974.

Under Section 4 of this Act, a person in control of premises is statutorily bound to take such measures as are reasonable to ensure that the premises, and means of access thereto, are safe.

Under Section 5, any person having control of premises is statutorily obliged to use the best practicable means to prevent emission of noxious or offensive substances.

Under the Act, a Health and Safety Commission is set up, whose principal function is to carry out the general purposes of the Act; and there is power to make Regulations on various matters.

9. **Environmental Controls.**

(i) **The Clean Air Acts 1956 and 1968 and Orders made thereunder.**

This Act deals with air pollution and imposes controls on emission of smoke, dust, grit and fumes, and other forms of air pollution. In particular, local authorities are empowered under the Act, by statutory order to be confirmed by the Secretary of State, to declare areas within their districts to be 'smoke control areas' in which, subject to certain exemptions and limitations, the emission of smoke, or of smoke of certain qualities, from chimneys is an offence. (No significant amendment has been made in the Control of Pollution Act 1974).

(ii) **Noise.**

The Control of Pollution Act 1974, Part III replaces the noise nuisance provisions of the Public Health Acts, and the Noise Abatement Act 1960, making new provision for controlling noise from construction and other works. Noise abatement zones may be designated; the local authority must then record in a register noise levels which are not to be exceeded, and may serve noise reduction notices. The Secretary of State may make regulations regarding noise from plant or machinery, and approve codes of practice for minimising noise.

(iii) **The Rivers (Prevention of Pollution) (Scotland) Acts 1951 and 1965.**

As the name implies, these Acts deal with river pollution. River Purification Boards are set up under the Acts to prevent pollution and a code is laid down for the control of pollution, reinforcing and largely superseding the Common Law code. The Control of Pollution Act 1974, Part II, replaces most of the provisions of these Acts, extending existing controls to nearly all inland and coastal waters. The Secretary of State is given wide powers to make regulations for the protection of water, as to precautions by persons having custody or control of poisonous, noxious or polluting matter, and for prohibiting or restricting the carrying on of activities in particular areas. Registers of consents, analyses etc. are to be kept for public inspection, with provision for public notice. There are new provisions about pollution from vessels and on-shore sanitary facilities. Care is required, and enquiry should be made, when any existing drainage or sewage is not direct into a public sewer.

(iv) For various other controls see *inter alia*:

(a) Radioactive Substances Act 1960 — re. Keeping and disposing of radio active substances.

(b) Control of Pollution Act 1974 Part I — re. Deposit and disposal of waste.

(c) The Pests Acts 1949 and 1954 — re. Control of vermin and creation of clearance areas.

(d) The Weeds Act 1959 — re. control of **some** noxious weeds.

10. **Local Acts**

Under earlier legislation, now repealed, local authorities were entitled, if they wished, to introduce their own statutory code, imposing a variety of environmental controls by private Act of Parliament. Such local acts replaced, in the individual local authority area, equivalent general legislation dealing with the same matters under a variety of earlier Acts.

Several of the larger local authorities took advantage of this facility. Such legislation covered, typically, streets, buildings, sewers and drains; and a variety of licensing matters. Under the Civic Government (Scotland) Act 1982, these private local acts of parliament have already been or will shortly be wholly repealed and will cease to have effect.

4.3 The Entailed Estate.

The Entail was a device for securing the devolution of heritage on a predetermined line of succession in perpetuity. The aim was to preserve the family estate intact. The Entail was created by a Charter or Disposition containing an elaborate Special Destination which, under the statutory sanction in the Entail Act of 1685, was made irrevocable by the use of special further clauses in the deed, known as the cardinal prohibitions of entail, **and** by recording the deed in the Entail Register in addition to registration in Sasines.

The cardinal prohibitions provided, in essence: —

(i) A prohibition against disposing of the entailed estate in whole or in part;

(ii) A prohibition against creating any heritable security on the entailed estate; and

(iii) A prohibition against altering the destination in the original Deed of Entail.

These three prohibitions were supported by irritant and resolutive clauses, the effect of which was, in brief, that, if the heir of entail in possession attempted to breach any of the cardinal prohibitions, he immediately forfeited his right to the entailed estate for the benefit of the next heir.

The strict application of these prohibitions was gradually relaxed by the Entail Amendment Acts during the 18th and 19th centuries. Finally, by the Entail Amendment Act of 1914, no new entails may now be created and for this purpose the Entail Register is closed. The Register remains open, however, for other purposes, in particular for the registration of Instruments of Disentail.

Any entail validly created prior to the 1914 Act is still effective as an entail, and the cardinal prohibitions still receive effect, unless and until the heir of entail in possession disentails, which he can now do, under the 1914 Act, in any circumstances if he is major and capax but **possibly** subject to the obtaining of certain consents. The entail destination continues to control succession, even **after** disentail. See, for illustration 7.3.16 Stirling's Trs. 1977 SLT 229.

Almost all entailed estates have now been disentailed and the Entail is rapidly becoming of historical interest only.

4.4 The Liferent Estate.

Liferent and fee are recognised in Scots Law as two distinct and separate rights which can co-exist concurrently in the same property. The detail has already been dealt with in Succession and Trusts; and, in particular, the distinction has been drawn between the older form of liferent, the Proper Liferent, created by direct conveyance of heritage; and the Improper Liferent, created through the medium of a trust, whereby the liferented property, heritable **or** moveable, is conveyed to Trustees, and held by them for the liferenter's use and enjoyment. We are concerned here, briefly, with the Proper Liferent only.

Heritable property can competently be conveyed to A in liferent and to B in fee. Under that conveyance, A takes an immediate vested right of liferent and is entitled to the beneficial enjoyment of the property during his lifetime, to the total exclusion of B. But B also takes an immediate vested right of fee in the property, as absolute proprietor, subject only to the over-riding interest of the liferenter. On the older view, and for practical purposes his proprietary right of fee can be regarded as burdened with the liferent. Accordingly, B takes the property as disponee and institute; and takes infeftment as such. **But** his possession and enjoyment is postponed until the liferenter's death. A, as direct or proper liferenter under the same conveyance, also takes infeftment in liferent, since a proper liferent of heritage is regarded in Scotland as a heritable right capable of separate infeftment. So, in effect, this conveyance is a mandate for two simultaneous and concurrent infeftments, the one in liferent and the other in fee; and it may be and usually is recorded with Warrant of Registration on behalf of A and B for their respective interests.

Where there is a conveyance in this form, infeftment of A, the liferenter, is essential if the right of the liferenter is to be properly constituted as a burden on the property, and to be enforceable against singular successors of B as the proprietor in fee. But the liferent infeftment goes no further than that, and confers no higher right on the liferenter. Accordingly, a liferenter, infeft, is not in the position of vassal or absolute owner. Instead, his right is very similar to that of a tenant under a recorded lease, occupying the property free of rent but with certain obligations as to outlays and repairs.

4.5 **Teinds, Church, Manse and Glebe.**

Before the Reformation, (1560) teinds formed a standard and substantial inherent burden on land for the benefit of the Church (cf. tithes in England). After the Reformation teinds in the great majority of cases passed into the ownership of the landowner on whose property they had formerly been a burden; but soon became subject to a new, but lesser burden known as a stipend, a fluctuating annual burden based on the price of corn.

The present position is now regulated by the Church of Scotland (Property and Endowments) Act 1925. The purpose of the Act is to remove old anomalies and to standardise stipend payments. Under the Act, the standardised stipend has become automatically a real burden on the lands (**not** on the teinds) in favour of the Church of Scotland General Trustees; and is called Standard Charge. It is preferred to all other real burdens, except the incidents of tenure, and is recoverable by the Church of Scotland General Trustees in the same way as if it were feuduty. Where the teinds are held on a separate title from the lands by a third-party titular, which occurs very occasionally, the heritor is empowered (S.17) to deduct the Standard Charge in accounting to the titular for free teind.

Where the standardised stipend is under £1, it is compulsorily redeemed under the 1925 Act.

Standard Charge (not Stipend) is redeemable on sale under 1974 s.5; or voluntarily under the 1925 Act.

There are also various administrative provisions in the 1925 Act, including provisions for allocation of Standard Charge between various parts of the subjects burdened with it, e.g., on the breakup of a large estate.

Broadly speaking, Standard Charge can be ignored in urban properties; in rural properties it may form a substantial impost.

As to title, the technical rule (with qualifications) was that teinds, being a separate tenement, require a separate express conveyance. So, one of the standard addenda to a conveyance was, and to some extent still is, 'together with the teinds'.

Probably in all cases, this conveyance of teinds would now be held to be implied; and in any event, with standardisation of stipend, teinds have no value and no relevance.

Stipend and Standard Charge are inherent burdens on land; and nothing appears in the title to disclose the burden, except in cases where, on the break up of an estate, stipend or standard charge is apportioned in the dispositions to purchasers of parts.

5.1 Heritable Securities — General.
Reading List 5.1, 5.2, 5.3.

The normal rule in Scotland is that a debtor's **whole** estate, both heritable and moveable, is liable for payment of his **whole** debts. If, therefore, A lends £1000 to B, the debtor, without security, A can enforce repayment of his loan by the appropriate diligence out of any of the assets, heritable or moveable, belonging to B at the time of enforcement. But, when A calls for repayment, B may have no assets; and so, in the result, A gets nothing. Or B's assets may prove insufficient to repay the debts of A and others in full; and in bankruptcy, no **one** creditor has any preference over another. A creditor may however acquire a preference by taking security under which, as a matter of contractual arrangement, the creditor annexes a specified asset of the debtor, in advance, at the date when the debt is contracted, and retains his nexus on that asset until such time as the debt has been paid.

The nature of the property determines the method by which an effective voluntary security can be created. So far as heritage is concerned, the cardinal common law principle of an effective voluntary security is that a **real** right in security in a particular heritable property must **vest** in the creditor. Written title, followed by infeftment, is essential to create a real right in land; and this rule applies to heritable securities as it applies to proprietary rights. Accordingly, to create an effective security on heritage at Common Law, it is necessary either (a) that the sum secured should be properly constituted as a real burden on a particular heritable property, as a qualification of an infeftment in name of the debtor; or (b) that a real right in the security subjects should be conveyed to, and vest in, the creditor, by the recording in Sasines of a title in name of the creditor. Such a conveyance to the creditor may take one of two general forms, viz., (a) a conveyance to the creditor expressly for the purpose of securing payment or repayment of a debt (an *ex facie* security deed); or (b) a conveyance to the creditor which is ostensibly (*ex facie*) an absolute conveyance of the right of property without reference to the security element, thus apparently vesting the property in the creditor as **owner**.

Broadly speaking, then, the creditor at Common Law has a choice of three available methods for securing his indebtedness, viz. —

(a) By creating a real burden in the debtor's title for the benefit of the creditor; typical illustrations are pecuniary real burden and the ground annual in the older form;

(b) By infeftment of the creditor expressly in security; typically by a Bond and Disposition in Security; and

(c) By infeftment of the creditor on an *ex facie* absolute title as though he were owner; typically by an *ex facie* absolute Disposition.

All these methods were in common use up to 29/11/70; and each had certain advantages and certain disadvantages. Under the 1970 Act, securities can no longer be created by methods (b) or (c) (and possibly (a)); and a new form of security, the Standard Security, is introduced in this Act to replace the older forms of Deed. But any such security effectively created pre 29/11/70 in the old form remains valid until discharged.

When considering the forms of security used before 1970, and their effects, two main points must be kept in mind: —

(i) A real burden securing payment of a sum of money is of its nature a mere burden on, and a qualification of, the debtor's infeftment. It is, therefore, affected by the rule, already examined, under which such burdens, to be effective, must be precisely stated. This means that the sum secured must be definite and ascertainable on the face of the title. Under a Bond and Disposition in Security and equivalents, the creditor takes infeftment but expressly in security; and, for the application of this rule, a Bond is treated as a burden. Accordingly, only precise and definite amounts could be secured by Bond and Disposition in Security. But an *ex facie* absolute Disposition, being in form a proprietary title and not a mere burden or security, was not affected by this rule, and was not treated as a burden for this purpose.

(ii) The Bankruptcy Act, 1696 (c.5) provides that a heritable security is ineffective to secure a preference for the creditor for any debt contracted **after** the date of the creditor's infeftment. This Act applied generally to pecuniary real burdens and to the Bond and Disposition in Security, etc., on which the creditor is expressly infeft in security. It had no application to the *ex facie* absolute Disposition since, under that form of security, an absolute right of property is apparently conferred on the creditor, not merely a security. As a result, the Bond and Disposition in Security was not available to secure future and fluctuating debt although, by special statutory provision, a Cash Credit Bond which is akin to a Bond and Disposition in Security can secure future indebtedness, up to definite limits.

5.2 Heritable Securities before 1970
Reading List 5.2.
The Bond and Disposition in Security.

In this form of security, the relationship of debtor and creditor and the form of security document are largely statutory. The relevant provisions are:

1868 Act S.118 which authorises the use of a statutory form, supplied in Schedule FF no. 1 and lays down the statutory effect.

1868 Act S.119, containing an elaborate interpretation of the Schedule FF clauses, S.119 being in turn substantially amended, and supplemented, by:

1874 Act SS.47 to 49.

1894 Act: the whole Act.

1924 Act SS.25 to 43.

1970 Act Part III. SS.33 to 43.

The statutory form (1868 FF.1) contains two separate and distinct elements, namely, the Personal Bond which operates to constitute the debt and establish the debtor's personal obligation; and the Disposition in Security, which operates as a Conveyance of the security subjects, in security, in favour of the creditor.

(i) The Personal Bond.

This follows the standard form of Personal Bond, often used without security to establish indebtedness. The Personal Bond has already been dealt with in Scots Law and its general import is clear. See Walker's Principles Vol. 2 p.437.

(ii) The Disposition in Security. The statutory form runs on as follows:

'And in security of the personal obligation before written, I dispone to and in favour of the said CD and his foresaids heritably, but redeemably as aftermentioned, yet irredeemably in the event of a sale by virtue hereof, ALL and WHOLE (here follows the description); and that in real security to the said CD and his foresaids of the whole sums of money above written, principal interest and penalties; and I assign the rents; and I assign the writs; and I grant warrandice; and I reserve power of redemption; and I oblige myself for the expenses of assigning and discharging this security; and on default in payment I grant power of sale; and I consent to registration for preservation and execution; In Witness Whereof'

Note:

(i) The conveyance to the creditor is expressly redeemable except on the happening of one event, namely, sale, in which event, **only**, the conveyance to the creditor becomes irredeemable.

(ii) The conveyance is expressly in security of the obligations set out in the Personal Bond.

(iii) The security subjects are described exactly as in a special disposition but no reference to burdens is necessary. 1924 Act. S.9(1).

By virtue of the Disposition in Security in this form, the Bond was recordable in G.R.S.; but the creditor's infeftment following thereon was not an absolute, but a limited, infeftment in that the debtor can compel the creditor to reinvest him, on repayment of the sums due under the Bond.

If however the debtor defaults and the creditor sells under his power of sale, then the conveyance to the creditor becomes irredeemable and the Bond and Disposition becomes in effect equivalent to an absolute Disposition to the creditor, on the strength of which he is then in a position to convey the security subjects to the purchaser.

Ranking of loans inter se.

The Bond is a mandate for the creditor's infeftment. Infeftment is essential to constitute the creditor's real right and, unless and until the creditor has perfected his real right, (i.e. until the Bond is recorded) he has no effective security.

Because of the limitations in the dispositive clause and because the creditor's infeftment is initially redeemable, the recording of the Bond does not divest the debtor. Instead, the Bond is treated merely as creating a real burden on the debtor's title, and accordingly he can subsequently deal with the security subjects as infeft proprietor, either by way of a subsequent real security in favour of a second creditor or by absolute Disposition of the proprietary right to a singular successor from him. But the creditor under the Bond having taken infeftment, the subsequent actings of the debtor cannot adversely affect the rights secured to the creditor by his infeftment. Therefore, any subsequent conveyance by the debtor, in security or absolutely, is necessarily subject to the infeft creditor's prior rights.

By the combined effect of the 1617 and 1693 Acts, real rights in land are preferred strictly according to priority of infeftment. This rule applies to security rights as it applies to proprietary rights. Suppose A, as infeft proprietor, grants a Bond and Disposition in Security to X recorded in 1960; a second Bond and Disposition in Security to Y recorded in 1965; and a third Bond and Disposition in Security to Z recorded in 1970. X has the first infeftment in security, and takes an absolute priority over Y and Z; similarly Y is preferred to Z. If the property is sold on A's default, X is therefore entitled to payment in full of his principal, interest and penalties before Y can take anything; and similarly Y is paid in full before Z can take anything. This order of preference amongst heritable creditors *inter se* is termed ranking; and their ranking *inter se* is prior or postponed, strictly according to the respective dates of infeftment.

But, in certain cases, two or more creditors fall to be ranked not prior and postponed *inter se,* but equally *pro rata* in proportion to the respective amounts of their several loans. This is termed *pari passu* ranking. Where two or more creditors rank *pari passu,* they share *pro rata* in the proceeds of any sale. *Pari passu* ranking may be constituted in various ways which include:

(i) **The 1868 Act S.142. and 1979 Act.** If two or more Bonds are received by the Keeper of the Registers on the same day they are deemed to be recorded simultaneously and, therefore, rank *pari passu.*

(ii) **Two or more lenders.** Normally, the personal obligation to repay is in favour of a single creditor; but it is equally competent in a single Bond to incorporate several obligations to repay in favour of several creditors. If this is done, **and** if the Bond is then recorded on behalf of the several creditors at the same time, they are all simultaneously infeft and all rank *pari passu.*

(iii) **Subsequent partial assignation.** The priority of a heritable security is established as at the date of its recording. If the original creditor later assigns the whole Bond to an assignee, the assignee completes his right by recording the Assignation. If the creditor, fraudulently, grants two or more assignations of the **same** Bond to different assignees, then as between these competing assignees the preference *inter se* would normally be determined strictly according to the order of recording of the respective Assignations. But, as between any such assignee and a third party deriving right from the debtor, the assignee has the benefit of the preference established by the original recording of the Bond, and ranks accordingly.

A single Bond may competently be assigned in part, or in several parts to several assignees. If so, such assignees rank *pari passu inter se;* but again, in a question with third parties deriving right from the debtor, each several assignee enjoys the benefit of the preference established by the original Bond, *quoad* his portion thereof.

Ranking Clauses. The ordinary rules of ranking may be varied by express ranking clauses in one or several (contemporaneous) Bonds. But, if a Bond to A has been recorded and contains no express reference to ranking, a clause in a Bond in favour of B, recorded later, purportedly ranking B's Bond prior to A's, is ineffective. Priority of infeftment rules.

Reserved Powers. It is perfectly competent, in a Bond, and common, for the debtor to reserve to himself certain powers which, otherwise, he would not or might not be entitled to exercise. There are two typical cases:

(i) **The power of redemption.** The right to redeem is implied but the mechanics are statutory. The statutory short clause reads 'And I reserve power of redemption' which is interpreted in the 1924 Act S.25(1)(c) and S.32, (entirely superseding equivalent provisions in the 1868 Act S.119). The object of the statutory clause is to protect the debtor who, in the ordinary way, duly and punctually pays interest and, when required, tenders repayment of the principal sum and expenses. This provides machinery for discharging the Bond and clearing the Record if the debtor tenders repayment and the creditor cannot or will not grant the appropriate formal discharge. See S.32 and Schedule L.

(ii) **Power to feu, etc.** The debtor, by granting the Bond, has not divested himself; he has merely burdened his title. Accordingly, he can thereafter competently feu, dispone, etc. But any Feu Charter or other deed which he may grant is necessarily subject to the prior preference established by the creditor on the recording of his Bond unless the debtor has expressly reserved to himself in the Bond an express power to the effect that, on granting a Feu Charter, the *dominium utile* of the ground thereby feued will be released from the creditor's security. Normally, the creditor will agree to the insertion of such a reserved power in a Bond only subject to certain conditions which qualify the power, and which must be strictly observed. If not, then Feu Charters purportedly granted by the debtor in exercise of this power will not in fact release the feu from the security. See 5.2.28 Cumming v. Stewart 1928 S.C. 296.

On such feuing, the *dominium directum* remained vested in the creditor and subject to the security. He thus acquired the superiority right in lieu of *dominium utile* and, at normal feuing rates, this was at least of some substituted value for the creditor. Now, under the 1974 Act, feuing remains competent but there cannot be a feuduty. Therefore, future superiorities will have no security value. So, presumably, this device will die out.

Creditor's rights and remedies

The creditor's principal right under the Bond and Disposition in Security is to receive repayment of the principal sum in loan when he calls for it in terms of the Bond (or in terms of some collateral agreement or 'back letter' qualifying the terms of the Bond); and, in the meantime, so long as the principal remains unpaid, he is entitled to regular half-yearly payments of interest at Whitsunday and Martinmas. The debtor is under corresponding obligations.

The only concurrent right of the creditor, while interest is being regularly paid and payment of the principal has not been demanded, is to insure the security subjects against loss by fire to an amount necessary to cover his interest therein and to recover the premiums from the debtor (assignation of rents clause and 1924 Act S.25.(1)(a)).

He has no other powers except on the debtor's default. In particular, since the debtor retains his title and is left in possession, the creditor has no right to interfere with the management of the property or to transact with tenants where the property is let; nor, being a mere security holder, has he any liability to the superior or others in respect of the security subjects.

If, however, the debtor defaults, i.e. fails to pay interest when required or to repay the principal sum when required, or goes bankrupt or grants a trust deed, the creditor is **then** entitled to exercise a variety of remedies against the debtor which include:

(i) **Personal action and summary diligence.** As we have seen, the debtor's personal obligation is distinct from the security element. Under the Personal Bond, the creditor can sue the debtor in an ordinary personal action for payment of principal and interest; and, by virtue of the clause of consent to registration for preservation and execution, he can do summary diligence against the **original** debtor. (For successors, see below).

(ii) **Entering into possession.** Notwithstanding the apparent effect of the creditor's infeftment following on the dispositive clause and the assignation of rents clause, the creditor is not entitled to physical possession of the security subjects nor to deal with tenants and collect their rents unless and until the debtor has defaulted. Thereafter, unless the debtor consents, the creditor must establish his title to rents and to possession by judicial process, which is known as an action of maills and duties. Procedure is regulated by the 1894 Act S.3 and Schedules.

When in possession (either by process or by consent) the creditor **then** acquires additional powers, but also incurs certain new liabilities. His powers are contained in the 1924 Act S.25 and the 1894 Act SS.6 and 7.

In a question with third parties, the creditor in possession incurs the liabilities of proprietor and is, therefore, personally liable to implement feudal prestations and may be liable in damages for injury resulting from defective premises.

(iii) **Poinding of the ground.** This is a real diligence which entitles the creditor in any real security to attach and sell corporeal moveables **on the ground** belonging to the debtor or his tenants or vassals, but not goods of third parties, with a view to satisfaction of the indebtedness out of the proceeds of sale.

(iv) **Sale.** The statutory clause in Schedule FF1 reads 'and on default in payment, I grant power of sale'; and this receives an elaborate interpretation, now, in the 1924 Act S.25(1)(d) and SS.33 to 42 as amended extensively by 1970 Act SS.33 to 38.

This being an express *ex facie* security document, there is no **implied** power. If the creditor is to have power of sale, this must be expressly conferred as it is under this clause, and the power can only be exercised in accordance with strict statutory rules contained in the 1924 Act, as amended. If these rules are not observed, then there is no valid sale and the purchaser cannot be given a good title.

The statutory procedure is elaborate and detailed, and the detail has been altered substantially by the 1970 Act Part III.

For the detail of this procedure see Halliday 1970 Act Chap. 5. Only the salient features are mentioned here.

As a preliminary point, power of sale is available to any bondholder, whether his Bond be prior or postponed; but with this qualification, that a postponed bondholder exercising the power of sale **must** have regard to the rights of the prior bondholder, and the sale is subject to, and cannot in any way prejudice or over-ride, those rights. *Pari passu* bondholders as a rule must concur; otherwise, they fall to be treated as prior bondholders by the selling bondholder, subject to a statutory exception which will be noted later. But the selling bondholder need have no regard to postponed bondholders or to other postponed rights, subject to a general over-riding duty to act reasonably. The essential features of the sale procedure are:

(i) **Notice.** To initiate the sale procedure, and put the debtor in default, the creditor must serve a Notice (1924 Act Schedule M) requiring payment of the capital sum with interest and expenses within three months of its date. (1924 Act S.33).

(ii) **Expiry of Notice.** The three-month period of notice must elapse before any further step is taken, unless with the agreement of the debtor under S.35. The Notice itself is effective for 5 years.

(iii) **Mode of Sale.** 1924 Act SS.36 to 40 and 1970 Act SS.35 to 37. The object of the 1924 Act (and its predecessors) was to prevent oppression of the debtor. Detailed provisions are therefore made in these Sections regulating the procedure to be followed by the creditor after the three-month period of notice has expired. These strict rules have been to some extent relaxed by the 1970 Act, and in particular the creditor may now sell either by public auction or by private negotiation, 'at the best price that can be reasonably obtained'. But he must still advertise in specified newspapers, for specified periods, and adhere to a specified timetable, all prescribed in detail in SS. 36-39.

Purchaser's title. Assuming the subjects to have been duly sold, by roup or privately, by the selling creditor, he is then required to furnish a marketable title to the purchaser. This involves two elements, namely, (1) giving the purchaser a valid and irredeemable proprietary title and (2) ensuring that the property is disburdened of all subsisting heritable securities.

(1) **Proprietary Title.** In terms of the dispositive clause of the Bond itself, sale having taken place, the selling creditor's title has *ipso facto* become absolute and irredeemable. Accordingly, *quoad* title, the Bondholder is in the same position as if the Bond had been a special Disposition in his favour. And accordingly the Bond becomes a proprietary writ. The next step is for the selling creditor to dispone the security subjects to the purchaser by ordinary special Disposition, narrating the circumstances.

In addition, the purchaser will, of course, have to be satisfied that the sale procedure was carried through strictly in accordance with the statutory formulae and, in particular, he will require:

(i) Evidence of service of the Notice. 1924 Act S.34 makes suitable provision for such evidence.

(ii) Evidence of advertisement. The new 1924 Act S.38(4) (formerly 1924 S.38(5)) again makes provision for suitable evidence. i.e. copy advertisement, certified by the publisher.

Strictly speaking, if the purchaser is satisfied with the validity of the prior title and with the sale procedure, the Disposition by the selling creditor in his favour is all that he requires to validate his title. But this is a statutory procedure and any defect, however trivial, may invalidate the sale, whereupon the purchaser's title becomes reducible by an aggrieved debtor or postponed creditor, etc. As a further protection to the *bona fide* purchaser for value from a selling bondholder, special statutory provision is made under the 1924 Act S.41 as amended by the 1970 Act, which excludes any challenge of the purchaser's recorded title on the grounds that the debt had ceased to exist (unless the purchaser knew that) or on the ground of any irregularity in the sale procedure. Under the 1868 Act S.119 the selling creditor is empowered to bind the debtor in absolute warrandice in the Disposition in favour of the purchaser, and to oblige the debtor to corroborate the same.

(2) **Disburdening the Subjects Sold.** The purchaser is entitled to a clear record. The seller must clear it of all subsisting securities. Prior bondholders are not affected by the sale. Therefore, prior bondholders must be paid in full by the selling creditor out of the sale price, against which they grant Discharges. These Discharges clear the Record of these Securities. But there still remains the selling creditor's own Bond; and possibly **also,** a) *pari passu* and b) postponed Securities.

a) **Pari passu Bonds.**

Where there is a *pari passu* Bond, the selling bondholder must obtain the consent of the *pari passu* bondholder to the sale. Otherwise, he will have to treat the *pari passu* bondholder as ranking prior to him. The selling bondholder can now compel the co-operation of an unco-operative *pari passu* bondholder under statutory procedure in the 1894 Act S.11.

b) **Postponed Bonds.**

The selling creditor prepares an account of his intromissions and produces it to a Law Agent; and the Law Agent then prepares a Certificate of Surplus (or of no surplus) in the form of Schedule N of the 1924 Act. The Certificate is then recorded in the Register of Sasines; and such recording, together with the recording of the Disposition in favour of the purchaser, of itself disburdens the Record of the seller's Bond (unless assigned to the purchaser in corroboration) and of all postponed Bonds. The Assignation of the Bond in corroboration and fortification of the purchaser's title is another device to protect a *bona fide* purchaser against the possibility of challenge of his Disposition. If that Disposition is reduced because of some technical defect in the procedure (now improbable, looking to the terms of the 1924 Act S.41 but still a possibility) the purchaser loses his title. As some compensation, the debtor's Bond is assigned in corroboration; and the creditor at least has the benefit of the heritable security. He would, of course, probably also be entitled to claim against the selling creditor under warrandice.

Re-exposure and Foreclosure.

In dealing with sale procedure, I have assumed that the property was duly sold. That may not happen. The selling creditor then has three possible courses to follow. He may either opt for: —

(i) **Re-exposure.** There were special provisions for periods of advertisement etc., in the 1924 Act S.38(4); but now, under the new S.38, all periods are the same; or

(ii) To abandon the sale and continue as he was, probably in possession drawing the rents. This is always unsatisfactory but may continue indefinitely; or

(iii) **Foreclosure.** This is a statutory remedy introduced under the 1894 Act S.8, but again with considerable limitations and restrictions to prevent oppression. The purpose is to allow the creditor to take over the security subjects as his own property in part satisfaction of the debt. The pre-requisites which must first be satisfied are:

(a) That the property has been exposed for sale by **public roup,** and no purchaser has been found.

(b) That the **last upset** price did not exceed the combined total of all prior and *pari passu* Securities; and the seller's own Security **excluding** expenses.

Subject to these pre-requisites, the selling creditor may then petition the Sheriff for a Decree finding that the debtor's right of redemption is forfeit. The Extract Decree may be recorded, and on being so recorded the Bond is converted into an absolute title for the benefit of the creditor, as from the date of recording. Recording automatically disencumbers the land of all **postponed** securities; but prior and *pari passu* securities are wholly unaffected by foreclosure. They therefore remain enforceable against the foreclosing creditor. A *bona fide* purchaser for value taking a title from the foreclosing creditor is protected, and his title made indefeasible, by the 1894 Act S.10, comparably with the provision in 1924 Act S.41(2).

Collateral effects of exercise of power of sale.

Sale is **one** of the creditor's remedies. It is alternative to any other remedy. Accordingly, even although sale procedure may have been initiated, the creditor may take any other action open to him under any of his other available remedies. In particular, sale does not exhaust or limit the personal obligation; so, if the proceeds of sale are insufficient to repay the selling creditor in full, he can still proceed by personal action against the debtor for the balance of the indebtedness. There is no question in Scotland of the debtor's liability under a heritable security being limited to the value, or proceeds of sale, of the security subjects.

Pecuniary real burden — Walker Chapter 5.11 page 156.

Under a Bond and Disposition in Security, the creditor obtained his real right by active infeftment following on a special disposition in his favour operating as his mandate for infeftment. The real right created for the benefit of the creditor under a pecuniary real burden is secured in a different way, and is based on the principle that any conveyance of land may create real burdens as a qualification of the disponee's infeftment. Such burdens may be *ad factum praestandum* or for payment of a sum of money.

Note, in particular, that the creditor in a pecuniary real burden has no separate infeftment in his own person; and indeed there is no writ on which he could take an infeftment. He therefore has no separate title to the security.

The pecuniary real burden suffered from serious disadvantages compared with the Bond and Disposition in Security. It operates as a *debitum fundi,* and as such entitles the creditor to poind the ground or to adjudication; but he has no power of sale; he cannot enter into possession; and he has no personal obligation from the debtor.

For these reasons, this form of Security was rarely employed.

Contract of Ground Annual — Walker Chapter 5.11 page 158.

This is another method by which a pecuniary real burden could be created and secured on land prior to 1/9/74. It has this distinctive feature, that the cash payments secured are annual payments in perpetuity with which the land becomes burdened, instead of capital sums, which produced a result very similar to feuduty under a Feu Charter. The fundamental difference between feuduty and ground annual is that, under a Contract of Ground Annual, no feudal tenure is created, and therefore there is no equivalent to the relationship of superior and vassal between the parties to it.

Primarily, a Contract of Ground Annual is a conveyance on sale by seller to purchaser, the purchase price being fixed as an annual sum instead of a capital payment. As a **secondary** element, the Contract of Ground Annual creates a *debitum fundi* on the land conveyed, firstly by way of a reserved real burden *in gremio* of the dispositive clause; and secondly by way of a reconveyance to the seller in security. It thereby secures to the seller, as disponer, and to his successors, payment in perpetuity of the agreed annual sum. The writ is bilateral in form, as is the Feu Contract. The selling proprietor is the disponer and creditor thereunder; the purchaser becomes debtor in the Ground Annual payments.

Grounds Annuals can no longer be created after 1/9/74 by the 1974 Act S.2. Nor can existing ground annuals be varied so as to increase the annual burden — 1974 Act S.3. For practical purposes, the Contract of Ground Annual is therefore now obsolete and will never again be used. But existing pre-1974 ground annuals continue in perpetuity until redeemed by agreement or under the 1974 Act SS. 4 to 6. In contrast, subinfeudation continues, albeit for no feuduty.

The distinctive feature of the Contract of Ground Annual in its modern form is the inclusion of certain further clauses designed to improve the security of the creditor and the creditor's remedies in the event of default. These further clauses include:

(i) The debtor's personal obligation. Merely to constitute a real burden does not, of itself, constitute a personal obligation on the debtor. In terms of this clause, the debtor/disponee expressly undertakes the personal obligation of payment of the annual sums, and so becomes personally liable.

(ii) A Disposition in Security. Under this clause, the debtor/disponee, to whom the subjects are conveyed in the main dispositive clause, reconveys the security subjects to the original disponer/creditor, but in **security** only for payment of the annual sums. This reconveyance by the debtor/proprietor in favour of the disponer/creditor is similar in form to the form of conveyance in a Bond and Disposition in Security. The effect is to re-invest the disponer/creditor in the subjects conveyed, but in security only, with the attendant advantages of such reinvestiture which are conferred by the subordinate clauses appropriate to a conveyance in security.

On completion of the writ, both disponer and disponee take infeftment with two separate Warrants of Registration. The debtor/proprietor takes infeftment as disponee, in order to perfect his real right of property in the subjects conveyed to him; the disponer/creditor takes infeftment on the reconveyance in his favour in security, in order to perfect his security right.

In the result, the remedies available to a creditor under a Contract of Ground Annual in the modern form are:

(i) Poinding of the Ground.

(ii) Maills and Duties, in virtue of the assignation of rents clause in the reconveyance in favour of the creditor.

(iii) Personal action and summary diligence. Note, however, that the personal action is available only against the original debtor and his universal successsors. It will not transmit against singular successors in the property.

(iv) Adjudication.

(v) Irritancy, under the conventional clause and under a statutory provision in the 1924 Act S. 23(5). In the case of the Ground Annual, the irritancy takes the place of power of sale.

While no new ground annuals may now be created, there are any number of existing Ground Annuals still subsisting; and these will only gradually disappear on redemption under the 1974 Act.

Transmission, Restriction and Discharge.
Change of Debtor.

As we have seen, there are two elements in the ordinary heritable security, viz.,

(a) **Real security.** The creditor's preference is established at the date of creation of the real right. But the debtor is not divested and can deal with the property subsequent to that date, or the security subjects may transmit on his death or on sequestration. **But,** any such transmission of the debtor's right is subject to, and does not in any way adversely affect, the creditor's real remedies, e.g., sale.

(b) **The Personal obligation.** It is usual, in addition to real security, to obtain the debtor's personal obligation for payment or repayment of the indebtedness. The personal obligation binds the original debtor for payment thereof, without reference to the value of the security subjects; and subsists so long as the sum secured remains unpaid, notwithstanding that the debtor may have parted with the subjects in the meantime.

A singular successor who acquires heritable property subject to a heritable security does not, at Common Law, incur any element of personal liability, although he cannot prevent the creditor from exercising his real remedies on the property.

Suppose then that A owns heritage subject to a Bond and Disposition in Security which he sells to B without paying off the Bond. B is to take over the loan. Some years elapse. B then defaults. The creditor can still sue A on the personal obligation, but cannot sue B by way of personal action; alternatively, the creditor can exercise his power of sale and recoup himself out of the proceeds, which does not affect A, the original debtor. If A has to pay, he may have a right of relief against B, but this does not affect the creditor.

This is unsatisfactory, and in practice it is unusual for a purchaser or disponee to take over a loan in this way. Instead, the loan is normally paid off and the disponee borrows of new. But, if taking over the loan is the arrangement between the parties, then the disponer A would normally wish to be relieved of personal liability; and the creditor would normally release him only if he gets the personal obligation from B in lieu. The creditor is not, in any event, bound to release the original debtor. The personal obligation can be made to transmit against a singular successor in two ways:

(i) Bond of Corroboration. This is a separate Deed in terms of which the disponee expressly undertakes personal liability.

(ii) The 1874 Act S.47, as amended by the 1924 Act S.15 and Schedule A2. The object of this provision is to render the Bond of Corroboration unnecessary. The combined effect of the Sections is:

(a) Where the disponee takes by succession, gift or bequest, he incurs personal liability up to the value of the subjects taken by him.

(b) Where the disponee takes by conveyance (other than on succession, gift or bequest), the Disposition in his favour **may** contain an express undertaking by the disponee of personal liability in lieu of the separate Bond of Corroboration. A statutory form is provided in Schedule A2.

Neither of these methods operates to release the original debtor from **his** personal liability. A separate personal Discharge is required. Any such Discharge is without prejudice to the transmitted personal obligation. 1874 Act S.47. It is not recordable.

Change of Creditor.

The creditor's right in a heritable security is, **primarily,** a right to payment of the debt with, **secondarily,** certain additional real remedies for enforcing payment. As such, it is, of course, an asset of commercial value and, like any debt, it may be transferred to a purchaser or donee *inter vivos;* and on the death of the creditor it transmits, as an asset in the estate, to his successors.

Transmission Inter Vivos.

There are some special features here which distinguish transfer *inter vivos* of a heritable security from transfer of an ordinary debt, because, in addition to his right to payment, the creditor has real security over the lands constituted by infeftment. The actual method of transfer varies in detail according to the nature of the security.

(i) **Bond and Disposition in Security.** The old common law Disposition and Assignation has been replaced by a short and simple statutory form of Assignation under 1924 Act S.28 and Schedule K, as amended by 1970 Act Schedule 10, by which the sum in loan and the benefit of the security is transmitted to an assignee.

The statutory Assignation (1924 Act Schedule K1) is a mandate for the infeftment of the assignee by *de plano* recording of the Assignation with Warrant of Registration thereon on his behalf. On such recording, although the Assignation contains no description of the security subjects, and no *de praesenti* conveyance thereof, nonetheless the assignee is then infeft in the security subjects; and is otherwise in all respects in the same position as the original creditor under the original Bond *quoad* real remedies and the personal obligation of the debtor.

(ii) **Contract of Ground Annual.** Again, there are simplified statutory forms, here under the 1924 Act S.23(1). And again a simple Assignation is appropriate in the form of Schedule K2; but with this difference that it is necessary in the case of an Assignation of a Contract of Ground Annual to describe the lands. The effect of the Assignation is set out in the 1924 Act S.23, in terms of which, briefly, the assignee is in exactly the same position *quoad* debtors in the Ground Annual as was the original creditor under the Contract.

(iii) **Pecuniary Real Burdens.** Prior to 1874, the benefit of a real burden was transferred by simple Assignation, coupled with intimation to the debtor; and recording of the Assignation in the Register of Sasines was not appropriate. This is because, with pecuniary real burdens, the creditor has no infeftment. But the rule was altered by the 1874 Act S.30 which provides that the recording in Sasines of an Assignation is to take the place of intimation to the debtor as the criterion of preference. This produces a curious anomaly. The original creditor has no infeftment and no recorded title in his own person; but the assignee can record his title, although by such recording he does not become infeft. For transmission of pecuniary real burdens, the 1924 Act provisions for the Bond and Disposition apply, as modified by the 1924 Act S.43 and Sch. K. Note 4.

Transmission mortis causa.

See Chap. 7.3. — Transmission on Death.

Discharge

(i) Bond and Disposition in Security.

A modern form of discharge is now prescribed by the 1924 Act S.29, which provides that any Bond may be effectually renounced and discharged **and** the land therein effectually disburdened of the same, in whole or in part, by a Discharge in the form of Schedule K3 to the Act, duly recorded.

In practice a formal Discharge is almost invariably employed to disburden the security subjects. But very much less in fact will serve, and there are other circumstances in which property may be disburdened of a subsisting security, viz.:

(i) **Redemption.** Under the debtor's power of redemption and related procedure, without the intervention of the creditor, the Record is cleared. 1924 Act S.32.

(ii) **Confusio.** This is a rule of general application to obligations in Scots Law and applies where the same person in the same capacity becomes both the debtor and the creditor in an obligation. The effect, *quoad* heritable securities, is that the security is absolutely extinguished and cannot be revived.

(iii) **Prescription.** A heritable security, being essentially an obligation for payment of a sum of money, is extinguished by the running of the long negative prescription, notwithstanding the infeftment of the creditor. In practice, payment of interest by the debtor normally regularly interrupts the running of prescription which rarely runs its full course.

(iv) **Payment.** 'An infeftment in security may be extinguished by payment or discharge of the debt' per Lord Kinnear in 5.2.26 Cameron 22 R 293 where part of a sum in loan was repaid but no formal Discharge was granted. The remaining balance of the loan was later discharged by a formal partial Discharge which referred expressly to the earlier partial repayment; **held** that the Record was clear of the whole Bond.

(ii) **Pecuniary real burden.** The same applies as for Bonds under the 1924 Act S.43 and Schedule K Note 4.

(iii) **Ground Annual.** At Common Law, a Ground Annual is perpetual and does not fall to be discharged. But, occasionally, Ground Annuals are expressly made redeemable; and, of course, debtor and creditor may **agree** at any time to capital redemption of the annual sum. In that case, the Ground Annual may be discharged by a similar form under the 1924 Act S.23(2) and Schedule K4. The same general principles apply as apply to the Discharge of a Bond.

Voluntary and Compulsory Redemption under the 1974 Act SS.4 — 6. Exactly the same provisions are made, under these sections, for the voluntary and compulsory redemption of ground annuals as are made for feuduties; and the earlier comments on feuduty redemption apply here also, *mutatis mutandis.* So the formal discharge is now rare.

Restriction

A heritable security creates a real burden on the whole of the security subjects and on every individual part thereof. Thus, if a tenement of flats is bonded by the owner for £2,000 and one flat is later sold, the sold flat remains liable as real security for payment of the whole debt. The creditor, following on such sale, may then in his option exercise his power of sale over the sold flat alone and satisfy his debt out of the proceeds; or he may proceed against the whole, or other parts, of the tenement.

As a result, no purchaser will take a title to heritable subjects forming part of a larger whole where the larger whole is subject to a subsisting security. In such a case, the debtor may pay off the whole loan and have the Bond discharged, which undoubtedly clears the Record and renders the title marketable. But this may be inconvenient to the debtor on a sale of a small portion only of the larger whole. So, as an alternative, a debtor frequently bargains with the creditor in such circumstances for the release by the creditor of the sold portion, on such terms and conditions as the debtor and creditor mutually agree. Where such a release is arranged, it would be inappropriate for the Bond to be discharged; if that were done, the creditor would lose his security for the remaining outstanding loan. Instead, the sold portion can be taken out of the creditor's security by two methods, viz.:

(i) Deed of Restriction. This is a separate formal Deed granted by the creditor. The 1924 Act S.30(1) provides that the security constituted by a Bond may be restricted as regards any portion of the land thereby conveyed by a Deed of Restriction in the form of Schedule K5; and on such Deed of Restriction being recorded, the security shall be restricted to the subjects described in the Bond under exception of the land disburdened by the Deed of Restriction.

(ii) Instead of using the separate Deed of Restriction, it is competent and effective if the creditor consents to the Disposition in favour of the purchaser of the portion sold. A clause is inserted in the narrative of the Disposition to the effect that the creditor agrees to release the subjects disponed from his security, which disburdens the part so disponed.

Future and Fluctuating Debt

Before the 1970 Act and in terms of the Bankruptcy Act 1696 (C.5), a heritable security was effective only to secure sums advanced prior to the creditor's infeftment thereunder. In simple cases, this provided no problem. But, clearly, cases arise in practice where the parties find it very convenient to have a heritable security covering future and fluctuating debt. This is typically and obviously necessary in any ordinary business, running on overdraft, particularly in view of the rule in Clayton's Case (de Vanes v. Noble 3 RLC 654). You will remember that, under that rule, if A has an overdraft of £2,000 which he secures by Bond and Disposition in Security; and if he then operates on that account by paying in £100 each month and drawing out £100 each month, each payment-in is ascribed as a partial repayment of the original £2,000 overdrawn, and each drawing-out of £100 is a new loan. So that after 20 months, although his overdraft is still £2,000, the whole of it is represented by drawings since the date of the security. If, therefore, the security was by way of Bond and Disposition in Security, these drawings would be struck at by the Bankruptcy Act 1696 (c.5) as new indebtedness, and would not be secured. Yet in substance, there has been a continuing security for a continuing loan of £2,000.

Prior to 1970, there were two standard ways in which the provisions of the 1696 Act could be avoided, to secure future and fluctuating debt, namely, by Cash Credit Bond and by *ex facie* absolute Disposition. Both methods are now imcompetent and have been replaced by the Standard Security, under the 1970 Act. In the case of Companies, a third method was made available by way of Floating Charge, under the Companies (Floating Charges) (Scotland) Acts 1961 and 1972. These provisions are now repealed and re-enacted in the Companies Act 1985 SS.410-424.

1. Cash Credit Bonds. Under the Debt Securities (Scotland) Act 1856, a Bond and Disposition in Security may be given as security for cash credit, (i.e. a running account) provided that the principal sum in loan, and interest, is limited to a definite sum; such definite sum took the form of a stated amount of principal plus 15%, (representing three years' interest at 5%). The infeftment on any such security is declared, by this Act, to be equally valid and effectual as if the whole sums advanced on cash credit had actually been advanced by creditor to debtor prior to the date of the creditor's infeftment.

The only special features of the Bond for Cash Credit and Disposition in Security were:

(a) That, in the Personal Bond, it was normal (but not necessary) to provide expressly for a method of fixing the balance due at any given date on the running Cash Account, and the personal obligation is adapted accordingly, e.g. —

'Declaring that a stated account, with a Certificate thereon signed by the Secretary of the Company, shall be sufficient to ascertain and constitute a balance and charge against me and that such a stated account shall sufficiently ascertain and fix the amount of interest chargeable on the said advances which shall have been made on the said Cash Account as aforesaid'.

(b) The Disposition in Security, and in particular the clause declaring that the conveyance is in real security, is adapted to meet the limitations imposed by this Act.

Apart from these specialities, the Cash Credit Bond is in essence a Bond and Disposition in Security and the same rules for assignation, restriction and discharge apply as apply to an ordinary Bond.

The Bond of Cash Credit is, of its nature, specially adapted for use by Banks or Finance Companies who keep running Accounts with clients. It is not suitable for private lenders. In practice, it was not commonly used.

2. Ex facie absolute Disposition.

The security document on which the creditor took his real right in security, in this case, was a Special Disposition granted by the debtor in favour of the creditor by which, on the face of it, the debtor conveyed to the creditor the absolute and unqualified right of **property,** (not **merely** a right in **security,**) in the subjects thereby conveyed, just as if the transaction were a conveyance on sale. In particular, there is nothing in the Disposition to disclose the security element; in terms of the narrative, it bears to be 'for good and onerous causes and considerations'; the dispositive clause is 'heritably and irredeemably'; and there is no power of redemption reserved to the debtor, nor anything equivalent to it. The creditor perfected his security by recording the Disposition, with Warrant of Registration, in the Register of Sasines; and no other writ, (as a rule,) entered the Record to qualify or explain the true relationship between the parties.

As a result, the immediate effect of the recording of the Disposition was feudally to divest the debtor, and invest the creditor, with the *plenum dominium* in the subjects thereby conveyed.

But, notwithstanding this resulting **feudal** position, the transaction remained in substance, as between debtor and creditor, a **security** transaction and it was, therefore, standard practice, and in the interests of both parties, to establish that relationship, and regulate the terms thereof, by a collateral agreement, qualifying the terms of the *ex facie* absolute Disposition.

From the point of view of the creditor, the collateral Agreement was **desirable** in order

(i) to establish the **personal** obligation of the debtor (the Disposition itself creates only **real** security);

(ii) to establish the terms of loan, including interest and repayment of capital; and

(iii) to a lesser extent, to constitute certain other obligations on the debtor.

From the point of view of the debtor, he has parted with his property on an absolute title which empowers the creditor to act as if he were the absolute proprietor. The resulting relationship between debtor and creditor is in its nature fiduciary; with the result that, under The Trusts Act, 1696 (C.25,) the presumption is that the *ex facie* absolute Disposition is what it appears to be; and accordingly the debtor can only establish the true relationship by reference to the creditor's writ or oath. The collateral agreement serves to establish this relationship in the appropriate form.

Naturally, the terms of Back Letters vary substantially, depending on circumstances. They may be relatively short and brief; or they may be very lengthy, as in the case of most Building Societies. Whatever form the Back Letter takes, its salient features will normally include:

1. An express acknowledgment by the creditor that he holds the subjects in security, either for advances to a stated limit, or for all future advances without limit, plus interest and expenses, and any other indebtedness to be incurred by debtor to creditor.

2. A personal obligation by the debtor to pay, or repay, the indebtedness, including the rate of interest and term(s) of payment, etc.

3. A time bargain, binding one or both parties not to call for repayment, or repay, within a time limit.

4. Express undertakings by the debtor:
(a) to pay all outgoings;
(b) to keep the property in repair;
(c) to observe the conditions of tenure;
(d) not to let the security subjects;
(e) to insure;
(f) to pay all expenses.

5. Express powers for the creditor, which include power of sale (although this is unnecessary) and power to insure, (again unnecessary).

6. A reserved power of redemption to the debtor, on payment in full of the indebtedness.

7. A consent to registration for preservation and execution.

Such agreements are normally bilateral, formal and tested. For reasons which we will shortly examine, the Back Letter is not normally recorded, although it may be.

Creditor's rights and liabilities.

Because the terms of the security document conceal the true nature of the transaction, the creditor's position *vis a vis* third parties **not** deriving right through the debtor is significantly different from his position *vis a vis* the debtor.

(a) **In a question with third parties.** The debtor, by the *ex facie* absolute Disposition, has clothed the creditor with the *indicia* of ownership. He must take the consequences of that act. This implies that third parties are entitled to transact with the creditor as if he were in fact the beneficial owner, with the result that the creditor can, without the debtor's consent, sell the subjects and confer a valid and unchallengeable title on a purchaser who is acting in *bona fide* for value without notice of the debtor's rights. Since the Back Letter is not normally recorded, a purchaser relying on the Record does not normally have such notice.

If the Back Letter is recorded, which is rare, then some textbook writers state that this imports a real limitation on the creditor's infeftment. Certainly, recording of the Back Letter gives notice to anyone dealing with the creditor that his title is a security title only. But it is now settled by 5.2.47 Aberdeen Trades Council 1949 S.C.(HL)45, that the recording of the Back Letter does not deprive the creditor of his implied power of sale and will only affect the purchaser to the extent, **if any,** to which the Back Letter prescribes restrictions on the creditor's rights to sell — e.g. requiring Notice, etc., as with the Bond under Statute.

Since the Back Letter is rarely recorded, and since, in any event, the creditor's power of sale is almost always unrestricted, a purchaser is very unlikely to be affected thereby.

But the creditor, having agreed to accept a title which, in form, conveys the right of property to him, with the attendant advantages of such a title, must also accept the liabilities inherent in ownership. Accordingly, third parties are entitled to rely on the form of title; and, in particular, the *ex facie* absolute disponee becomes liable for all feudal prestations, including payment for feuduty and obligations *ad factum praestandum* in the title. He may also incur liability, as owner, to third parties having claims arising out of the defective state of property, etc. (in so far as these fall on the owner rather than the occupier). He has a right of relief against the debtor for any liability so incurred.

(b) **In a question with the debtor.** The creditor's rights and obligations *vis a vis* the debtor, and parties deriving right from the debtor, are regulated, not by the nature of the title, but by reference to the substance of the transaction. For practical purposes, the creditor is regarded as a Trustee for the debtor and, subject to the preference established for the creditor by the recording of the *ex facie* absolute Disposition and to payment or repayment of the indebtedness thereby secured, he must account to the debtor or his representatives for his intromissions with the security subjects and must, on repayment, denude in favour of the debtor or his representatives.

This inherent qualification of the creditor's absolute right in a question with the debtor and those deriving right from the debtor will transmit against the personal representatives of the creditor, e.g. in bankruptcy or on his death; the Trustee in bankruptcy or Testamentary Trustee acquires right to the security subjects, but on the same terms, *vis a vis* the debtor, as the creditor himself enjoyed. See 5.2.43 Heritable Reversionary Co. Ltd. 19 R (HL)43.

It follows that, in a question with the debtor, the creditor is bound to act reasonably. Therefore, although he has an absolute power of sale, and can confer a valid title on a purchaser, he is not entitled, as between himself and the debtor, to exercise that power unreasonably and will be liable in damages if he does so. Further, although the debtor cannot challenge the purchaser's title, he may, if he acts in time, prevent the creditor from proceeding to a sale, by interdict.

These equitable principles which control the relationship of debtor and creditor may be modified or supplemented by the terms of the Back Letter. 5.4.48 Rimmer and Anor. v. Thos. Usher & Son Ltd. 1967 SLT 7 is typical and illustrative. 'The creditor is entitled to sell and in recovering the amount due to him he acts *in rem suam,* but he is also *quasi* trustee for his debtor...' He must not in exercising his power of sale 'do so unfairly and without due regard to the interests of the debtor'. And a provision in the Back Letter allowing 'sale by private bargain, with or without advertisement at such price and on such conditions as the creditor thinks proper' (a usual clause) does **not** relieve the creditor of his common law duty.

If the debtor defaults, he can be removed and the creditor may enter into possession, simply on the strength of his *ex facie* absolute title; and on the strength of that title can deal with tenants as if he were owner.

The extent of the security. It is well settled that an *ex facie* absolute Disposition is not a 'heritable security'. As a result, the Bankruptcy Act 1696 (C.5) and the Debt Securities (Scotland) Act 1856 have no application. Further, since the creditor's title does not create an encumbrance or burden, but is in form a proprietary title, the rule as to precision in regard to real burdens is inapplicable. An *ex facie* absolute Disposition is, accordingly, an effective security for future and fluctuating debt; and will afford effective security to the creditor for all indebtedness however incurred unless (**as is rare**) the terms of the Back Letter are taxative and limit the security to certain specific sums only. For a recent case where the Back Letter was considered by Lord Fraser to be taxative see 6.1.1. Scottish & Newcastle Breweries. 1970 SLT 313. In the Back Letter, the security was stated as covering an advance up to the maximum limit of £1800. Lord Fraser thought this taxative. See also Burns' Practice p.482: 'If the Back Letter declared that property was to be held in security of present and future advances up to ... a certain limit, it might more readily be held that anything beyond that limit ... was not secured'.

The creditor, therefore, has a continuing and covering security for all indebtedness, present and future, either to the stated limit or without limit. That is the normal rule. It is subject to the following qualifications:

(i) If the Back Letter is recorded. The precise effect of the recording of the Back Letter is not settled; but it is probably the case (and safest to assume) that the recording of the Back Letter limits the amount secured to the lesser of either: (a) The amount actually advanced at the date of recording of the Back Letter; or (b) The stated limit in the Back Letter; (this **may** be the limit anyway. See Scottish & Newcastle Breweries above).

(ii) Where the debtor has transferred his reversionary right, absolutely or as further security, and the transfer by the debtor is intimated to the creditor, this then limits the security of the creditor to the amount actually advanced at the time when intimation was made, without reference to any limitations in the Back Letter. If, therefore, the creditor subsequently makes any further advance, such further advance is unsecured. See 5.2.42 Union Bank v. National Bank 14 R(HL) 1 below.

From 29/11/70, this becomes statutory. The 1970 Act SS.13 & 42 provide that, where the creditor in an *ex facie* Disposition has received notice of the creation of a subsequent security over, or of the subsequent assignation or conveyance of, the same interest in land **which is recorded in G.R.S.**, the creditor's preference is restricted to present advances, interest and expenses, **and** future advances which he is **bound** to make under his loan agreement. Mere recording of the later deed is not, *per se,* Notice; but judicial conveyance **is** Notice.

Transmission of the creditor's right. The creditor's right is heritable. It is an estate in land, but it is not a heritable security within the meaning of the Conveyancing Acts. Therefore, the abbreviated statutory forms of Assignation, etc., which are available for heritable securities are not appropriate for transmitting the creditor's interest under an *ex facie* absolute Disposition.

Inter vivos, the creditor may transmit his interest to a new creditor by Disposition of the security subjects in favour of the new creditor, (**not** disclosing the security element), coupled with a separate Assignation of the debtor's personal obligation in the Back Letter. It is probably incompetent to attempt a partial transfer of the creditor's interest, and in any event this is unknown.

Mortis causa, the interest of the creditor in the security subjects transmitted, pre-1964, as any other heritable estate, being always heritable, although the benefit of the personal obligation might be a moveable asset in the creditor's estate.

Under the 1964 Act, the **whole** benefit of the security **and** the personal obligation now passes to and vests in the executors of the deceased creditor, if included in the Confirmation. — See Chap. 7.3. below.

The nature of the debtor's right.
Prior to 5.2.42. Union Bank v. National Bank 14 R (HL)1, it was generally accepted that, because of the form of *ex facie* absolute Disposition, the result was to divest the debtor completely and to leave him with no remaining or residual right which he could subsequently deal with. But it is now settled, following on that case, that whatever the state of the original title may have been, whether or not there is a Back Letter, and whether or not that Back Letter is recorded, the debtor, notwithstanding the absolute quality of the Disposition in favour of the creditor, retains a right to call for a reconveyance analogous to the right of redemption of the debtor under a Bond. This right is in the nature of a *jus crediti* only, a *jus ad rem,* but nonetheless a right in the nature of a right of property, heritable by nature, descendible on death, and transmissible *inter vivos* by the debtor either by way of sale to a purchaser or by way of further security to a second creditor. Any such transmission is, of course, subject to the preferable right of the first *ex facie* absolute disponee which he established by the registration of his Disposition in Sasines. This remaining right of the debtor is termed, generally, the debtor's radical, or reversionary, right; and it may be a right of considerable value.

In a later case, 5.2.44 Ritchie v. Scott I F 728 Lord Kinnear suggests that, in certain circumstances, the debtor, notwithstanding the granting of an *ex facie* absolute Disposition, retains a residual real right in the security subjects; and is, therefore, not completely divested, feudally, by the granting of the *ex facie* absolute Disposition. This opinion seems to be approved in the subsequent case 5.2.60 Edinburgh Entertainments v. Stevenson 1926 SC363. For a full discussion, see Article by Professor Halliday in the Conveyancing Review Vol. 1 p.5. See also 5.2.62 Scobie & Ors. v. W. Lind & Co. Ltd. 1967 SLT 9, for a discussion on the nature of the debtor's right in a question between the debtor and third parties, where it was **held** that a debtor, originally infeft, but divested *ex facie* absolutely, retained a title to sue in an action by him to prevent infringement by a third party. (Red Court Hotel v. Burgh of Largs l955 SLT (Sh Ct)2. distinguished, but **in fact** disapproved).

In considering the nature of the debtor's reversionary right, in the light of these decisions, it is necessary to bear in mind two factors which affect the position, viz.:

(i) The state of the original title. In the simplest case, the debtor, when granting the *ex facie* absolute Disposition, was already infeft. In other words, he started off with a real right, and then conveyed the property to the creditor. But very often in practice the security was constituted at the time when the debtor acquired his right of property; and, to save expense and to eliminate unnecessary writs, the practice was that the selling proprietor, with consent of the debtor, conveyed the property directly to the *ex facie* absolute disponee. In such cases, the debtor had no title at all; and was never infeft. There is an intermediate case where the debtor, without infeftment, but holding on e.g. a general Disposition, conveyed to the *ex facie* absolute disponee, deducing his title. Here, he had **title** but no **infeftment**.

(ii) Recording of the Back Letter. Normally, as has been stated, the Back Letter is not recorded, but it is recordable (in the majority of cases) and occasionally is recorded. It is generally accepted that the recording of the Back Letter imports real limitations into the creditor's title; and this in turn may affect the quality of the debtor's right.

Sale or Second Security by Debtor.

Whatever the nature of the debtor's reversionary right may be, it is transmissible. If the debtor sells his reversionary interest, he grants a special disposition of the property in favour of the purchaser in normal form, and, in addition, the Disposition incorporates a clause assigning to the disponee the debtor's radical (or reversionary) right, and his right to call for a reconveyance from the *ex facie* absolute disponee. If the debtor grants a second security, he may do so either by a second *ex facie* absolute Disposition, in similar form to the foregoing; or by Bond and Disposition in Security (at least Burns so maintains, irrespective of the state of the debtor's title; Practice p.484) or by a Standard Security.

The disponee from the debtor, in order to complete his title, will in practice —

(a) Record the Disposition in the General Register of Sasines. 1970 Act S.13; and

(b) Intimate the Disposition to the first *ex facie* absolute disponee. Intimation is the appropriate method of perfecting a real right to any incorporeal right which has been assigned — in this case, to the debtor's reversionary right. Intimation creates a preference for the assignee at the date of intimation, just as registration creates a preference at the date of recording.

The same principles apply to a second creditor's security.

The effect of an intimated Assignation on the extent of the security has already been noticed above.

On the death of the debtor, his right is heritable and transmits as such. This now creates no problem following on the Succession (Scotland) Act 1964. The executors confirm to the reversionary right.

Leases by the Debtor.

The validity of a Lease depends on the validity of the landlord's title and the landlord must be infeft. Clearly, an infeft *ex facie* absolute disponee can grant a valid Lease. Clearly, also, if the granting of the *ex facie* absolute Disposition does not feudally divest the debtor, who remains infeft, then the debtor on the strength of his original title can grant valid Leases. But the Courts have held, in several cases, where the debtor is left in possession, that he has an implied mandate from the creditor to grant effective Leases, which will be valid whether or not the debtor retains an infeftment in his own person. This principle seems well settled, although of very doubtful logic.

Discharge

Since the *ex facie* absolute Disposition is not a 'heritable security', the statutory form of Discharge appropriate to heritable securities is not suitable to discharge this form of security. Instead, at common law, nothing less than a full formal conveyance (or reconveyance) served to divest the creditor and reinvest the debtor with the security subjects. The reconveyance is, in form, a special disposition, with all the normal clauses.

In addition, the debtor is entitled to a Discharge of the personal obligation constituted by the Back Letter.

The debtor is always entitled to a reconveyance, on payment of all indebtedness. Further, the debtor is bound to accept a reconveyance when required by the creditor; and if he refuses to do so the creditor may invoke the assistance of the Courts in order to complete his divestiture, normally with a view to avoiding continuing liabilities.

Clearly, a short form of discharge, rather than a full reconveyance would save time and effort, in drafting and revising, although *quoad* title the reconveyance is entirely effective.

So, the 1970 Act, S40 (1) provides that a **discharge** (Sch. 9), separate **or** endorsed on the *ex facie* absolute Disposition, shall, from the date of recording, disburden the subjects 'to the extent that it is the subject of the security, and vest the land **in the person entitled thereto,**' as if there had been a reconveyance.

But who is the person entitled thereto? This may be clear from the titles, but some further investigation will normally be required. There is no provision in the form for indicating the identity of the 'person entitled'.

Under S.40(2), the old procedure remains competent.

The form provided in 1970 Act Sch 9 runs:

'I, AB (designed) hereby acknowledge that the disposition granted by CD (design) (or by EF (design) with consent of CD (design)) in my favour recorded G.R.S. on   , although in its terms *ex facie* absolute, was truly in security of an advance of £   ; and that all moneys intended to be secured thereby have been fully paid. IN WITNESS WHEREOF: '

By Note 3, to the Schedule, deduction of title is competent, where the granter is uninfeft. No deduction of title is envisaged for the grantee.

5.3 The Standard Security
Reading List 5.3.

Under the Conveyancing and Feudal Reform (Scotland) Act 1970 Part II (SS. 9 to 32 and Schedules 2 to 7), the whole law of heritable securities in Scotland has been fundamentally changed from and after 29th November, 1970. It is now no longer competent to use the traditional forms of heritable security (including the Bond and *ex facie* absolute Disposition) and, in lieu, the Act provides a new form of heritable security, known as the Standard Security, which must now be used for **all** types of security transaction, and which replaces **all** existing traditional forms.

The background to this major innovation on the law of securities is set out in the Halliday Report Chap. 8, paras. 102 to 106 q.v.

Only the main points of this recent legislation are dealt with in these Notes because:

(i) The 1970 Act Part II and Schedules 2 to 7 contain a comprehensive, intelligible and more or less self-contained code.

(ii) Walker Chapter 5.12 gives a detailed narrative summary of the main provisions of the 1970 Act and Schedules.

(iii) Halliday — 1970 Act, in Chaps. 6, 8 and 10 deals extensively with all the new legislation, and some resulting problems; and in Chaps. 7 and 9, Halliday deals with Practice and Procedure in relation to the new Standard Security. These chapters also include a wide range of styles.

1. **The new forms of Security.**

S.9 **authorises** the use of the new forms of Standard Security; styles are provided — Form A and Form B in Schedule 2. S.9 further provides that the Standard Security is now to be the **only** competent medium for securing any 'debt' by way of heritable security over any 'interest in land'.

The new Standard Security in either form can be used for any **other** purpose for which a heritable security could have been used pre-1970. The Bankruptcy Act 1696 (which renders heritable securities of no effect for future debt) and also the Common Law rule which requires that a real burden for money must precisely state the sum due, are not to apply to a Standard Security. This releases the Standard Security from the two limiting factors which effectively prevented a Bond from being used to secure future or fluctuating debt. Therefore, in contrast to the Bond and Disposition, the Standard Security (although *ex facie* a security Deed) is an all-purpose security, covering fixed or fluctuating, present or future, monetary **or other** obligations.

2. **Exclusion of other forms of security.**

The use of the new form of security is made obligatory by S.9(4). If a deed is granted to secure a debt over an interest in land which is **not** in the form of a Standard Security **but which contains a Disposition or assignation,** then it is void as a Security. If such a deed has been recorded, then the grantee is bound to clear the Record. **But,** under S.31, this does not apply to, nor affect, the validity of any heritable security (**including** the e.f.a. disposition) recorded **before** 29th November, 1970.

The word 'debt' covers
i) payments of every kind, **other than** feuduties and ground annuals or other periodical sums payable in respect of land, and

ii) obligations *ad factum praestandum.* (S.9(8)(b)). So, until 1.9.74 feuduty and ground annuals could be 'secured' by Charter etc. being excluded from the restrictive terms of S.9(3). They can no longer competently be created under the 1974 Act.

Under S.9(7), the Bond and Disposition in Security continued in use for Local Authority Loans under the Small Dwellings Acquisition Acts; but S.9(7) has now been repealed by the Tenants' Rights Etc. (Scotland) Act 1980.

3. The pattern of the new legislation.

The Standard Security, in both its forms, and the supporting legislation, is clearly modelled on the Bond and Disposition in Security and on the legislation authorising the use of the statutory form of Bond. There are, however, some significant points of difference and a number of innovations and improvements on the old law and on the old form previously used. The following points in the new legislation merit special comment:

(i) Style of Deed.

Both forms provided in the 1970 Act, Form A and Form B, are *ex facie* security documents in contrast to the *ex facie* absolute Disposition; and therefore more closely resemble the Bond and Disposition in Security than the *ex facie* absolute disposition.

Form A closely resembles the Bond and Disposition in Security, in that it contains an undertaking to pay; but with this significant difference that, in Form A, the obligation may cover not merely fixed advances already made, but also future or fluctuating advances, to a stated limit or advances of indefinite amount without limit.

S.10(1) provides an elaborate interpretation for the short Form of Undertaking incorporated in Form A; it does not apply to Form B.

Form B, in contrast, although *ex facie* a security document, does not contain *in gremio* any personal obligation or undertaking whatsoever. Instead, it simply refers to the debt or obligation constituted in a collateral document, equivalent to the Minute of Agreement qualifying an *ex facie* Disposition, which itself constitutes the personal obligation and defines the undertaking to repay. There is **no implied personal obligation in Form B.**

(ii) Statutory effect of new forms. Under S.11(1), when recorded, the Standard Security operates to vest the heritable subjects in the creditor as **security** for the performance of the Contract to which the Security relates. Feudally, the effect is the same as if, under former law, the debtor had granted a Bond and Disposition in Security. So, the debtor is not divested, retains his real right (if infeft), and can deal with the subjects as *ex facie* proprietor. The creditor is a mere *ex facie* creditor and (unless in possession) incurs **no** personal liability for feudal prestations.

(iii) Standard Conditions. This is an innovation. Every Standard Security embodies, by statutory implication under S.11(2) the standard conditions contained in Schedule 3, with or without such variation as the parties may agree. These conditions operate both in relation to Form A **and** Form B. Note, particularly, that those conditions in Schedule 3 which relate to power of **sale,** or **foreclosure,** and to the **exercise** of any of those powers, **cannot** be varied. The power of redemption may only be varied to the limited extent prescribed in the Redemption of Standard Securities (Scotland) Act 1971.

(iv) Variation. Except as noted in (iii), the terms of a Standard Security including a Standard Condition may be varied, by agreement, at any subsequent date, under

S.16. This applies even where the condition to be varied (e.g. rate of interest in Form A) appears in the Security itself, and so on the Record; but in that case the Deed of Variation must itself be recorded.

(v) **Ranking.** S.13 deals with the ranking of a Standard Security. The principal ranking still depends, of course, on priority of infeftment; and is determined by the date of recording of the Standard Security. S.13 provides that the Security is restricted to existing advances already made (with interest and expenses) at the date on which the creditor **receives notice** of the recording of a subsequent Security or Conveyance; but his Security also covers any future advances, not yet made, but which the creditor is **bound to make** in terms of the security documents.

(vi) **Assignation, Restriction and Discharge.** SS.14, 15 and 17, and Schedule 4, Forms A, B, C, D and F.

Broadly speaking, the same provisions are made, and the same forms are used, as for a Bond and Disposition in Security under the earlier law; and, when so used, these forms have, broadly speaking, the same effect as they do in a relation to a Bond.

Redemption, Sale and Foreclosure.

Preliminary

The 1970 Act S.32 provides that any earlier statutory provisions relating to a Bond, unless excluded in Schedule 8, shall apply to a Standard Security. **Most** of the earlier Bond provisions are so excluded; and new separate provision is made in Part II of the Act for the comparable position under a Standard Security. **But,** there are still some important provisions carried over from Bonds to Standard Securities, particularly in relation to the creditor's powers. Further, by S.20(1), a creditor's powers on default at Common Law are preserved. In the result, some of the powers of the creditor are set out explicitly in Part II; some are set out in the Standard Conditions in Schedule 3; and some are carried over, by implication from Common Law and from the 1868 Act, 1874 Act, 1894 Act, and 1924 Act. Further, certain of the powers in the Standard Conditions apparently conflict with the Act. Thus, Standard Condition 10(4) provides that a creditor in possession 'may let the security subjects or any part thereof'. **But,** this apparently unfettered power is restricted by S.20(3), on the same lines as existing powers under a Bond. The result is somewhat confusing.

The principal provisions which are carried forward and which apply to the Standard Security (**not** being excluded in Schedule 8), include:

1868 Act S.117. So the Standard Security is moveable in the succession of the creditor, except for legal rights.

1868 Act SS.120, 126 and 127 — Completion of Title. Thus, the title of the creditor under a Standard Security may be completed during his lifetime by recording *de plano* in the GRS with Warrant of Registration; and is available to his successors, if he dies before the Standard Security has been recorded.

1874 Act S.47 and 1924 Act S.15. These two Sections deal with the transmission of the personal obligation of the debtor on sale by, or death of, the debtor.

1894 Act SS. 3 and 4, dealing with procedure for entering into possession by action of maills and duties; and 1924 Act S.26, dealing with the comparable position where the Security includes a superiority. These provisions are not excluded and so apply to the Standard Security.

1894 Act S.5, which entitles the creditor to eject a debtor in actual occupation.

1924 Act S.40. Sale of the security subjects in lots.

1924 Act S.41. Protection of purchasers; but a new subsection (2) is added by S.38.

(i) Redemption.

S.18, Standard Condition 11 in Schedule 3 together with Schedule 5 reproduce, closely but with some differences in detail, the 1924 Act provisions for redemption of a Bond.

(ii) Default by the Debtor.

Broadly speaking, under a Bond and Disposition in Security, there is only one default, namely, failure to pay principal and interest when demanded. So, as a preliminary to the exercise of the creditor's power of sale, the creditor must serve notice requiring payment, to put the debtor in default. On the expiry of the three months' period of notice without payment, the creditor can exercise his power of sale; and, meantime, can exercise certain other remedies including entering into possession.

With the Standard Security, in contrast, there are **three** default situations envisaged, which are outlined in Standard Condition 9, and amplified in detail in SS.19 to 24 of the Act, thus:

1. **9(1)(a).** Where a Calling-up Notice in respect of the Security has been served and has not been complied with.

S.19 prescribes the statutory provisions for notice, which substantially re-enact, with some important differences in detail, the comparable provisions for Notice calling up a Bond and Disposition in Security in the 1924 Act SS.33 to 35. In particular, the period of notice under a Standard Security is now two months instead of three months for the Bond.

2. **9(1)(b).** Where there has been a failure to comply with any other requirement arising out of the Security.

This would apply where, for example, the debtor had failed to pay interest on the due date or had failed to maintain the security subjects in good repair. For this default situation, SS.20 to 23 provide the statutory procedures to be followed by the creditor.

This default provision is entirely new. There is nothing comparable in the 1924 Act. Note that under 9(1)(a), service of the Notice is required to **create** default. Under 9(1)(b), the debtor is in default automatically by mere failure to comply. This would normally entitle the creditor to serve a Calling-up Notice. But he may (as an alternative to calling-up, where appropriate), serve on the debtor a Notice of Default, calling upon the debtor to remedy his default, (e.g. failure to repair, etc.) within a period of **one** month. Failure to comply with an effective Notice of Default entitles the creditor to exercise the power of sale, his power of carrying out repairs and his power of foreclosure; but it does **not** entitle him to enter into possession.

The Notice of Default may be objected to under S.22(1) by application to the Sheriff who adjudicates thereon. In contrast, the Notice calling up the Security under 9(1)(a) is not open to objection in this way. Therefore, although the calling-up Notice requires a two-month period following thereon in contrast to the one-month period following on the Notice of Default, the calling-up Notice may prove a quicker remedy in the long run because it is not open to objection.

Probably the best advice in many cases, where appropriate, is to serve both Notices, calling-up and default; and this is recommended by Professor Halliday.

3. **9(1)(c)**. Where the **proprietor** of the security subjects has become insolvent. There is detailed definition of 'insolvency' in Standard Condition 9(2).

In this case, again, default is automatic; but the creditor acquires no powers unless and until he applies to the Court under Section 24; or, alternatively, serves a calling-up Notice or a default Notice. In terms of Section 24, where the debtor is in default under Standard Condition 9(1)(b) or Standard Condition 9(1)(c), the creditor may apply to the Court for a warrant to exercise any of the powers available to the creditor under 9(1)(a).

Some agents take decree in **every** case as a precautionary policy.

The creditor's powers

Standard Condition 10 then **outlines** the creditor's remedies on 'default' as so defined. These include: i) sale, ii) entering into possession, iii) carrying out repairs, iv) foreclosure. But Standard Condition 10 is a summary or outline only of what the creditor may do on default. You have to look at the Act as well to find out, in detail, exactly what the creditor's powers are, and the restrictions on those powers.

(i) **Sale**.

The statutory provisions for sale under a Standard Security are commendably simple and brief. Instead of the elaborate detail in the 1924 Act (which still applies in Bonds, and still remains elaborate, notwithstanding the amendments in Part III of this Act), the 1970 Act S.25 simply provides that the creditor may sell **either** by private bargain or by public roup. In **either** event, it is his duty to advertise the sale and to take all reasonable steps to ensure that the price, at which the security subjects are ultimately sold, is the best price that can be reasonably obtained. Nothing more is required. In particular, there are **no** provisions prescribing period or number of advertisements, newspapers, place of sale, upset price, etc., as in the 1924 provisions.

Procedure — SS.26 and 27

The procedure following on sale differs from procedure on sale under a Bond and Disposition in Security in certain important respects.

(1) **Clearing the Record**. Prior creditors must grant discharges exactly as for the Bond and Disposition in Security. As to other securities, the creditor is still bound to account to the debtor for his intromissions; but there is no Certificate of Surplus or No Surplus. Instead, the Record is to be cleared of all *pari passu* and postponed securities, merely by the recording of the Disposition in favour of the purchaser, bearing to be in implement of the sale.

(2) **Application of Proceeds**. S.27 lays down the order of application of the proceeds of sale; which are (a) expenses; (b) prior creditors; (c) the creditor's own security and *pari passu* securities *pro rata*; (d) postponed creditors; (e) the balance to the person entitled to the security subjects. There is a proviso which allows for consignation but only in the event of doubt.

In contrast, under a Bond and Disposition in Security, consignation is automatic and essential for obtaining the necessary Certificate of Surplus.

(3) **Pari Passu Creditors**. The old rule requiring consent by *pari passu* creditors is abolished for the Standard Security by 1970 Act SS.26(1) and 27(1).

(ii) Entering into possession.

(1) Standard Condition 10(3) empowers the creditor, on default, to enter into possession and receive the rents and feuduties; but a decree of Maills and Duties or its equivalent is required, unless the debtor consents.

(2) **Granting Leases.** Under Standard Condition 10.(4), the creditor in possession 'may let the security subjects'; but is limited in this power by the 1970 Act S.20(3) to leases for 7 years, except with consent of the Sheriff (cf. 1894 Act S.7. Here, there is **no** maximum limit). He also has the debtor's rights of management and maintenance, if the property is already let.

(iii) **Carrying out repairs, etc.** Standard Condition 10(6) empowers the creditor, when the debtor is in default, to effect necessary repairs, or reconstruction or improvement, and to enter on the subjects for this purpose. This is wider than the equivalent power under 1924 S.25(1)(a). There are no statutory limitations on this right; and, in particular, the creditor need **not**, first, be lawfully in possession.

(iv) Foreclosure.

The whole existing foreclosure code is excluded, but, in substance re-enacted, for Standard Securities under 1970 Act S.28. The statutory requirements are:

1) Exposure for sale by Public Roup at a price not exceeding the security, and all prior and *pari passu* securities;

2) Expiry of 2 months from first exposure;

3) Application to the Sheriff served on the debtor **and** the proprietor **and** any other heritable creditor disclosed by a 20-year Search;

4) The Sheriff may:

i)   allow time to pay; not exceeding 3 months;

ii) order re-exposure, with power to the creditor to bid;

iii) grant decree of foreclosure, declaring the right of redemption extinguished;

5) On recording the decree under 4) iii) above:

i)   the right of redemption is extinguished;

ii) the subjects are disburdened of the security and all **postponed** securities. But prior and *pari passu* securities are unaffected. The creditor may redeem these as the debtor might have done;

6) The debtor's personal obligation to the foreclosing creditor is not discharged;

7) The creditor's title is unchallengeable on grounds of irregularity in procedure.

Poinding of the Ground. This common law remedy is also available if desired.

The Consumer Credit Act 1974

Under this Act, loans below the statutory limit (presently £15,000) are "regulated agreements" which have to comply with certain statutory requirements. The Act applies whether or not the loan is secured; but Standard Securities in favour of Building Societies generally and certain other specified creditors are exempt from the provisions of the Act. Securities in favour of Banks are not, however, exempted.

For a discussion on the provisions of the Act, and the requirements of the current regulations, see an Article in 1985 JLS 130.

6. Floating Charges.
Reading List 6.

The fundamental principle of a heritable security is that a real right in the security subjects vests in the creditor. Such real rights are created either:

(a) By an active infeftment in the person of the creditor, e.g. by the recording in Sasines of a Bond and Disposition in Security or an *ex facie* absolute Disposition; or

(b) By the effective creation of a real burden, as a qualification of a simultaneous infeftment in the security subjects.

Every such heritable security necessarily affects a **particular** heritable property. It becomes effective **only** when a writ relating to that particular property enters the Register of Sasines; the date of registration is the criterion of preference and of ranking; and the security subsists on the security subjects until it is later actively discharged. The result is that, as with proprietary rights, the General Register of Sasines is the measure of, and the index to, all security rights affecting heritable property in Scotland.

In the case of companies **only**, this fundamental principle has been radically altered by the Companies (Floating Charges) (Scotland) Act 1961, later repealed and re-enacted by the Companies (Floating Charges and Receivers) (Scotland) Act 1972, now consolidated in the Companies Act 1985. The provisions for Floating Charges and Receivers are re-enacted in SS.462-485; and the registration provisions in SS.410-424.

Under the 1961 Act (now the 1985 Act), following English precedent, a new type of security known as a Floating Charge was introduced into Scotland.

Creation of the Charge. The 1985 Act applies **only** to 'an incorporated company (whether a company within the meaning of the Act or not)'. '**Incorporated**' excludes partnerships, etc., but guarantee and unlimited companies are included, and also companies registered outside U.K. Any company may create an effective security for any debt or obligation, including guarantees. The method is to grant a Floating Charge over all (or any part of) the property, which may from time to time belong to the company ('be comprised in its property and undertaking'). This includes, *inter alia,* heritable property in Scotland. In the case of Scottish Companies, under the 1961 Act, a Floating Charge could only competently be created by an Instrument of Charge in **statutory form**, as set out in the First Schedule to that Act. But the statutory form was dispensed with in the 1972 Act, and there is now no prescribed form of charge.

Effect of the Charge. The benefit to the creditor of the security effected by the Floating Charge is limited, under the Act, in the following ways:

(a) **Property affected.** Under the 1985 Act, a charge may be created either:

(i) on the whole property; or

(ii) on a specified part of the property (e.g. 'all heritable property in Scotland').

In contrast, under the 1961 Act, the charge affected all property other than assets specifically excluded from the charge, which could prove cumbersome. Note that, in either case, (notwithstanding the reference to 'property **from time to time** comprised in the property and undertaking of the company'), the Floating Charge in fact only attaches to those assets, actually owned by the company at one or other of these dates, viz.:

(i) on the date of commencement of winding up; or

(ii) on the date when a Receiver is appointed.

In the case of a **partial** Charge, only those assets comprised in the specified part of the property at such date are attached.

Thus any asset owned by the company but disposed of before such date escapes from the Charge; and any such asset not owned by the company at the date of creation of the Charge, but subsequently acquired and still owned at such date comes within the Charge.

(b) **Registration.** A Floating Charge has no effect unless and until the Instrument creating it has been registered in the Register of Charges. This was a new Register set up in Scotland under the 1961 Act and is kept by the Registrar of Companies. Detailed provision is made in the 1985 Act SS.410-424, for registration of Charges in this new Register; and, in particular, time limits are prescribed to meet various circumstances.

In the case of a **Scottish** company the Floating Charge must be registered within 21 days of its date. If not so registered, it is **void**, as against the liquidator or any other creditor; the only remedy is to petition the Court to allow late registration. The same rule applies to any company incorporated outside **Great Britain** which creates a Charge on property in Scotland.

Until 22nd December, 1981 companies registered in Scotland, having a place of business in England, were treated exactly as if they were companies registered outside Great Britain and had to register Floating Charges over their assets in both the Scottish and English Registers. Since that date, the registration requirement has been altered so that Floating Charges only have to be registered once in the register of Charges appropriate to the situation of the Registered Office of the company concerned (which was the rule for English companies prior to that date). See Companies Act 1981, and now Companies Act 1985 S.410 and S.396.

It is further provided in the 1985 Act S.462(5) that a Floating Charge, although registrable in the Register of Charges, does not require to be registered in the Register of Sasines nor in the Land Register, even if heritable property in Scotland is included in the property affected by the charge.

(c) **Ranking.** The property is attached by the Floating Charge **subject to** certain preferential claims, including the rights of any person who has effectually executed diligence on the property, and any person holding a fixed or Floating Charge ranking prior to the Charge in question.

Three possibilities are covered in the 1985 Act S.464(4):—

(i) A Floating Charge in competition with a fixed security arising by operation of law, e.g. hypothec. In this case, the fixed security **always** has priority.

(ii) When there are express ranking clauses. Ranking as between a Floating Charge and a voluntary fixed security (**not** arising by operation of law) and between two or more Floating Charges may be regulated by express ranking clauses, thus:

The Instrument of Charge may and usually now does prohibit the creation of:
a) any fixed security; or
b) any Floating Charge
having priority over, or ranking *pari passu* with, the Floating Charge which the Instrument creates.

The Instrument of Charge may regulate the order of ranking, *inter se,* of the Floating Charge and any other specific charge, fixed or floating, present or future. **But** a pre-existing charge is not affected by such a provision, unless it contains a corresponding clause.

(iii) Where there is **no** operative ranking clause, then:

(1) a fixed security which has become **real** (e.g. by registration in Sasines) **before** the Floating Charge **attaches to the property** (i.e. on winding up or appointment of Receiver) ranks before a Floating Charge, even although the latter is first registered.

(2) two or more Floating Charges, if and when they attach property of the company, rank according to their respective dates of registration.

Note that, under this provision, future **fixed** securities with prior ranking can be prohibited. So, on taking **security** from a company, always search the Register of Charges. But a subsequent fixed security, so prohibited, is not voided, merely postponed. And the Charge cannot prohibit outright **disposal** by the company. So a search in the Register of Charges is not necessary on **sale** except for the purpose of disclosing whether or not a Receiver has been appointed. The appointment of a Receiver instantly converts a Floating Charge into a fixed security, the effect of which will transmit against a purchaser of any heritable property of the company.

(d) **Variation.** A new provision in the 1972 Act S.7 (now the 1985 Act S.466) allowed for alteration of the terms of a Floating Charge, once granted. This was not competent under the 1961 Act with unfortunate results on additional lending. (For a comparable difficulty in relation to fixed securities and its solution — see below).

Alteration requires a deed executed by the company, the creditor and any other fixed or floating creditors affected by the variation; and the deed must be registered if it makes **certain** alterations, e.g. by ranking clauses, or by releasing property or increasing the amount secured.

(e) **Effect of Floating Charges on Property.** If, in accordance with the foregoing requirements, a Floating Charge does effectively attach property at the date of winding up, or of appointment of Receiver, then it has effect as if the Charge had become, at such date, a **fixed** security over the property to which it has attached in respect of the principal sum in loan and interest due and to become due thereon — the 1985 Act, S.463(1), S.469(7) and S.470(6).

Special provisions as to fixed securities. Floating Charges represent a substantial innovation in the law of heritable securities in Scotland. In particular, nothing need enter the Register of Sasines; and the Charge attaches to future-acquired property not in the ownership of the Company at the date of creation of the Charge. Further, property is automatically released from the Charge if disposed of prior to liquidation, or appointment of Receiver.

But the 1961 Act also made an important **and unexpected** innovation with regard to conventional heritable securities in Scotland. Under the new Companies Act provisions introduced by the 1961 Act (now the Companies Act 1985 S.410), a **fixed** charge created after the date of passing of the Act must also be registered in the Register of Charges, failing which it is void in a question with the liquidator. In **this** context, fixed charges include any charge on land, wherever situate, or any interest therein, including a charge created by Bond and Disposition in Security or by *ex facie* absolute Disposition, and, now, Standard Security, but excluding a charge for rent, ground annual or other periodical sum payable in respect of land. If, therefore, a company grants a Standard Security, it is **not** now sufficient simply to record that Standard Security in the GRS, although this still remains necessary. **In addition**, the Standard Security, to be effective, must be registered in the Register of Charges; and must be so registered within 21 days following on the date of registration in Sasines. Special forms are provided, and the procedure is regulated under the Companies Act 1985.

The *ex facie* absolute Disposition created special problems. The essence of this form of security was non-disclosure of the security element; and publication of that element (e.g. by recording a Back Letter in GRS) might limit the security to sums advanced at date of recording. Nonetheless, the *ex facie* absolute Disposition was a 'fixed security' and, as such, registrable, thus disclosing the security. So the 1961 Act, now the 1985 Act S.414, specially provides that, in the case of *ex facie* absolute Dispositions, registration thereof in the Register of Charges as a **charge** shall not, of itself, 'render the charge unavailable as security for indebtedness incurred after the date of compliance'. In other words, to register the *ex facie* absolute Disposition (which was obligatory under the Act) did **not** give notice of the security element. The same difficulty could **not** arise with a Standard Security because it is *ex facie* a security; and the security thereby created is only limited by subsequent recorded deed — 1970 Act S.13.

Property acquired by a company which is already subject to a charge requires registration of particulars, within 21 days after acquisition; **but** failure does **not** render the charge void.

Petition for Rectification.

If a charge (fixed or floating) is not registered in the Register of Charges within the 21-day time limit, then an application to the Court of Session is competent and necessary for a rectification of the Register. The Court **may** allow the 21-day limit to be extended.

Miscellaneous

Special provision is also made (now in the Companies Act 1985) for various miscellaneous matters including:

i) time limits for registration of Charges created out of the United Kingdom. S.411(1).

ii) time limits for registration of Charges created in the United Kingdom but which include property situate outwith the U.K. S.411(2).

iii) an obligation on every company to make up and maintain its own private Register of Charges, in which are to be entered copies of Instruments creating Charges. This is in addition to, and separate from, the requirement to register in the Companies Register of Charges. The Register of Charges of each individual company is available for public inspection. S422.

iv) suitable entries will be registered in the Register of Charges when property is released from a Charge, by restriction or discharge. The appropriate entry is by Memorandum of Satisfaction, or partial satisfaction as appropriate. See S.419.

Special forms are provided for these various registration requirements under the Companies (Forms) Regulations.

7.1 Voluntary Transfer Inter Vivos
Contract of Sale and Purchase of Heritage
Reading list 7.1

'It is remarkable that there has been no attempt to formulate, in an Act of Parliament, the law on the general subject of sale of Scottish heritable property as has been done in the case of land in England and the sale of goods both in Scotland and in England.' Green's Encylopaedia Vol. 13 S.318.

Contracts for the sale and purchase of heritage are, therefore, governed by the ordinary Common Law rules of Contract. Only the special features of such contracts are dealt with in these Notes.

There are three basic requirements.

1. Form and Authentication.

Since these are **contracts** relating to **land,** they must, under the general rule, be in writing and probative; and they must be bilateral. There are three recognised forms:

(i) A formal, bilateral Contract of Sale and Purchase executed by the parties and attested.

(ii) Articles of Roup, being the appropriate document for sales by auction and constituting a formal tested offer which is completed by endorsation of a Minute of Preference and Enactment, binding the purchaser to the purchase.

(iii) An exchange of missive letters between seller and purchaser or their respective Agents.

Exchange of letters between Agents is by far the commonest method.

A unilateral **undertaking** to convey land **may** bind the granter, but an ostensible unilateral undertaking will normally be construed merely as an offer, requiring acceptance, see 7.1.7 Haldane v. Watson 1972 SLT (Sh Ct). 'I ... undertake to sell to X the flat occupied by me at (address) for £625, when I vacate the flat.' Held: a mere offer. There was no acceptance, and hence no binding obligation.

Missives. In the ordinary case, the purchaser's Agent submits an offer to purchase, in letter form addressed to the seller and adopted as holograph, which is accepted by the seller's Agent, again by letter addressed to the purchaser and again adopted as holograph. But an offer to sell, followed by an acceptance thereof, is equally competent.

Agents. Normally, missive letters pass between Agents who may bind the principal, whether purchaser or seller, if the Agent has special authority. Under the ordinary rule of agency, a contract by an Agent duly authorised on behalf of a disclosed principal binds the principal only, and not the Agent; otherwise, the Agent is bound.

The Agent's special authority need not be in writing; it may be verbal. **But** note that an Agent, when making an offer on behalf of a named principal, warrants his authority, although he does not warrant that his principal is solvent nor that his principal will duly carry out the Contract. Accordingly, if an Agent makes an offer without due authority, he is personally liable in damages to the offeree; and, of course, cannot recover from his alleged principal. Verbal authority, at a meeting or on the telephone, though competent, is often hard to prove; the Agent should normally insist on having authority in writing, from his principal, to avoid incurring personal liability.

The whole of the contract must be probative of the respective parties. In the case of an exchange of missive letters, the contract comprises at least two, possibly more, letters (or their equivalent). Each separate missive must be probative of the party who signs it, by being holograph, adopted or tested. Thus, if a holograph offer is met by a non-holograph acceptance, the Contract is not probative as a whole, and **neither** party is bound. A *fortiori,* a holograph offer, which is accepted verbally or by telegram or telex, does not create a contract. For a general discussion, see 7.1.2 McGinn v. Shearer 1947 SC 334 where an acceptance (not holograph or adopted) of a probative offer was held to be adopted by a holograph covering letter, thus completing the contract.

A letter by a firm, adopted as holograph, must be so adopted and signed by a partner — an assistant, even although duly authorised, will not do. Littlejohn 1974 SLT (Sh Ct) 82.

A contract made by one or both parties furth of Scotland may not require to comply with the strict Scottish formalities provided that it is valid, in point of form, as a contract for sale and purchase of land, according to the law of the place of execution.

Any defect in point of form **may** be cured by *rei interventus* or homologation, for which see later.

2. Content

In addition to the formal requirements, the contract must contain two essentials, namely, proper identification of the subjects of sale and a statement of the price. Given these two essentials, the law will supply all the remaining implied conditions and obligations of seller and purchaser; in practice, many of these conditions and obligations are expressed in the contract in a number of standard supplementary clauses, for which see later.

3. Consensus in idem

The third requirement for a valid contract for sale and purchase is, as in any contract, that the parties should be at one, at least on the main essentials of the contract. Thus, an offer (valid in point of form and content) to purchase heritable property can never be binding on either party if not accepted because, until accepted, there is no competent evidence of *consensus* and hence no contract. Similarly, an offer to purchase identified heritage but without reference to price, which is accepted, would not be binding, again, because of want of evident *consensus.*

The principal application of the rule as to *consensus* in practice concerns the qualified acceptance of an offer. An offer to purchase heritage normally lays down conditions; and others are implied (see below). An unqualified acceptance completes the contract on those conditions. If the acceptor does not agree *de plano* with the whole conditions, express and implied in the offer, he may accept, but subject to qualifying conditions. That acceptance, in turn, binds neither party, unless and until those qualifications are in turn accepted, in proper form, by the original offeror. The acceptance may, in its turn, lay down further qualifying conditions.

If so, then again neither party is bound unless and until those qualifications are accepted *de plano.* In practice , a contract of sale and purchase often comprises several missive letters from seller and purchaser (or Agents) each qualifying to some extent the previous missive letter. It is only when the final qualification has been accepted *de plano* that the contract is complete; and to indicate that this point has now been reached in a series of missive letters it is commonplace (although unnecessary) to embody in the final letter a statement that the party 'holds the bargain as concluded'.

In the ordinary case, any qualified acceptance of a previous offer or acceptance falls to be treated, in turn, as a fresh offer. It is then in the option of the other party to accept or reject those conditions. But this rule does not necessarily apply to a qualified acceptance if the qualifications contained in the acceptance merely state explicitly what, in any event, the law would imply; in that event, an acceptance apparently qualifed may in fact complete the bargain without acceptance of those qualifications.

For an illustration of the former, where there was no *consensus,* see 7.1.8. Dickson v. Blair 10 M 41, where an acceptance of an offer contained an additional condition that the seller would not give a Search, and that additional condition was never explicitly accepted by the purchaser. It was held that there was no *consensus.* For an illustration of the opposite result in relation to sale of Shares, see Tait & Crichton v. Mitchell 26 SLR 573; the same rule would operate in sale of heritage, although there seems to be no reported case.

'Subject to Contract'. This precautionary phrase is commonplace in England but is not much used in Scotland. The object is to prevent the parties being bound unless and until a formal contract is entered into following on a concluded (informal) agreement. The effect in Scotland is not settled; 'the only rules of Scots Law which it appears to me to be possible to extract from past decisions and general principles are that it is perfectly possible for the parties to an apparent contract to provide that there shall be *locus poenitentiae* until the terms of their agreement have been reduced to a formal contract; but that the bare fact that the parties to a completed agreement stipulate that it shall be embodied in a formal contract does not necessarily import that they are still in the stage of negotiation. In each instance, it is a matter of the construction of the correspondence in the light of the facts proved, or averred, on which side of the borderline the case lies'. Lord President Cooper in 7.1.10 — Stobo Ltd. 1949 SC 184.

For a comparable case, see 7.1.11 — Western v. Millar 7 R 173 where a purchaser introduced an element of doubt into an otherwise completed contract by writing 'I will finally arrange it on my return'.

For a discussion on the English situation, see Law Commission Memorandum No. 65 — Transfer of Land. This is a Report on 'subject to contract' Agreements, where the English practice is discussed in detail and commented on. But the Law Commission concludes that, while the existing procedure has drawbacks, it is based on the sound concept that the buyer should not be bound until he has had full opportunity to obtain legal and other advice, to arrange finance, and to make the necessary inspections, searches, and enquiries.

In Scotland, this is all incorporated in the initial contract by appropriate suspensive conditions; and, therefore, 'subject to contract' agreements are not generally used.

Rei interventus and homologation

These are two applications of the rule of personal bar. Neither is peculiar to sale and purchase of heritage; both apply to contracts in general. In practice, however, cases of *rei interventus* and homologation commonly arise out of contracts relating to heritage, in particular sale and purchase and lease, because of the essential requirement that, properly to constitute such a contract, there must be a probative writing.

Suppose that two parties have reached *consensus in idem* for the sale and purchase of heritage but have not embodied that *consensus* in the necessary probative form; or, alternatively, suppose that two parties have negotiated for the sale and purchase of heritage and have reached agreement on the main essentials, although they have not reached *consensus* on every minute particular. In the latter case, the parties may have embodied their imperfect agreement in probative form, or they may not. In any of such cases, the normal rule is that because of want of form, or because of want of *consensus,* neither party is bound, and either party can refuse to proceed. The motive of the party so repudiating the contract is quite irrelevant. The other party has no remedy, no right to enforce the alleged contract and no right to claim damages.

But if, in any of the circumstances outlined above, one of the two parties to the contract, in good faith and in the belief that a binding agreement has been reached, acts on the supposed contract in such a way that his position is materially altered, and if the other party knows of these actings and acquiesces therein, (or if such actings are the natural consequence of the supposed contract), the contract then becomes binding and enforceable by *rei interventus.*

To illustrate: Suppose that A, by holograph letter addressed to B, offers to purchase a house, which he identifies, at a stated price on a stated date of entry. B accepts the offer in unqualified terms, but the acceptance is not probative, being typed, signed but not adopted as holograph. There is no contract and **neither** party is bound. But if, thereafter, A pays part or the whole of the purchase price to B who accepts payment, this at once creates a binding contract on both A and B by *rei interventus,* from which neither party can thereafter escape.

The need for *consensus.* In the ordinary case of sale and purchase, both parties must be at one on every smallest particular; and, if not, neither party is bound. But if actings have followed on an incomplete contract, *rei interventus* may operate to overcome the lack of *consensus* on **minor** particulars; or put another way, such *consensus* may be presumed from the actings. *Rei interventus* cannot, however, operate to overcome lack of *consensus* on any major, material matter. Thus, A, by holograph letter, offers to purchase the west first floor flat at 6 Park Avenue, Dundee, for £5,000, with entry at Martinmas next, with a condition that the property is subject to a feuduty of £10.50, unallocated. B, the offeree, accepts by holograph letter to A, and in his acceptance states 'the unallocated feuduty apportioned on the flat is in fact £10.60'. A does not reply. While matters remain in that state, and if no actings have followed, there is no contract, and neither A nor B is bound. But if A takes possession and pays the price, his actings would constitute *rei interventus* which would overcome the apparent lack of *consensus* on the minor discrepancy in feuduty. In other words, by *rei interventus* an incomplete contract has been made binding. But suppose that B, when replying to A's offer, says 'with reference to your offer of £5,000 for the dwellinghouse 6 Park Avenue, I would accept £6,000 for it'. A does not reply. Here, there is clearly lack of consent on an essential fundamental of the contract, namely price, which normally *rei interventus* cannot cure. But, again, if A took possession and **paid £6,000 (not £5,000)** to B, his acceptance of B's qualification would be implied and, by *rei interventus*, the contract, **with that variation**, would become binding on both parties.

The quality of actings. In order to constitute *rei interventus*, one of the parties to the contract must act:

(i) in the genuine belief that agreement has been reached and in reliance on the supposed contract;

(ii) to the knowledge (actual or presumed) of the other party; and

(iii)in a way which materially alters the position of the party so acting, or produces some change of circumstances, or loss, or inconvenience, although not necessarily irretrievable.

Proof. If *rei interventus* is to operate, there are two essentials: firstly, a contract involving *consensus* on the main essentials, and secondly, actings which **follow** the contract. **Both** these elements require to be proved.

It is settled that actings alleged to constitute *rei interventus* can be proved *prout de jure.* Thus, any evidence may be led to demonstrate the nature of the actings and to relate them to the antecedent contract.

The rules as to proof of the contract itself are less certain. Thus, Walker on Evidence at p. 310 indicates that, in **every** case, the agreement must first be established by writ, or oath, or by judicial admission on record (or by a combination of these), although the writ so founded on need not, of course, be probative.

But Gloag — Contract — at p. 46 makes an apparent exception to the rule in the case of **incomplete** contracts, followed by actings; the same actings (proved *prout de jure*) may be founded on to establish *rei interventus* and to prove that agreement has been reached. This exception is apparently supported in the recent case of 7.1.15 Errol v. Walker 1966 SC 93. But the decision in Errol v. Walker is expressly disapproved by Walker — Contract 13.36 "the decision ... is irreconcilible with principle and precedent ... Facts cannot both create agreement and be actings on the faith of that agreement".

Locus poenitentiae. If a contract for sale and purchase of heritage is constituted by improbative writings, or is incomplete, it is said that there is *locus poenitentiae,* which means that neither party is bound to proceed; or that either party may resile. *Rei interventus* excludes the plea of *locus poenitentiae,* and effectively prevents either party from resiling. But these terms, '*locus poenitentiae*' and 'resile' are also used in a different context as implying the power to escape from a contract, which was previously or otherwise binding, because of some suspensive or resolutive condition which has not been purified, or on account of breach of contract by the other party. In the context of an improbative or incomplete contract for sale and purchase of heritage, the parties may have reached agreement. But there is no binding legal contract whatsoever, and neither party is bound, unless and until there are relevant actings.

Homologation. In cases of *rei interventus*, the party who has acted binds the other party by his actings. In cases of homologation, a party commits **himself** to a contract by his **own** actings, which, accordingly, do not, in this case, require to produce a loss or change of circumstances. Rather, such actings are evidence that the party so acting has agreed to be bound by the contract, i e they are evidence of acquiescence. Thus A, by holograph letter, offers to purchase heritage, which he indentifies, at a stated price on a stated date. And B accepts by improbative letter. Later B, the seller, intimates Notice of Change of Ownership, redeems the feuduty on the footing that the subjects have been sold, enters A as proprietor on the Valuation Roll, and tells the tenant to pay his rent to A, since A is now owner. By these actings, he has homologated the contract. Homologation is less common than *rei interventus,* although not infrequently both *rei interventus* and homologation may be pleaded in the same case, e.g. A pays the price, which is *rei interventus,* B accepts it and gives a receipt, which is homologation by B. Both could be founded on in a subsequent litigation. For a typical illustration, See 7.1.13a Mitchell 1936 SC(HL)56.

Effect of Conditions in Contracts.

1. Suspensive or resolutive.

This distinction is not normally significant in Contracts of Sale and Purchase of heritage in that, in **practically** all cases, every condition in a Contract of Sale and Purchase is suspensive. Therefore, neither party is bound to proceed with the Contract, nor to settle the transaction, unless and until **all** the conditions in the Contract have either been implemented or, by agreement, departed from.

For an unusual case of a resolutive condition see Gilchrist 1979 SLT 135 where the property was purchased subject to a condition to the effect that the contract was subject to the seller obtaining approval, for Dedication of part of the property, from the Forestry Commission. The application for Dedication was then rejected. The purchaser then sought to waive the condition in order to proceed with the bargain, tendering the price in full in exchange for a Disposition **already delivered**. That in itself is very unusual.

Held: that the condition relating to Dedication was resolutive and the bargain accordingly came to an end automatically when the application for Dedication was refused. Therefore, the purchaser was not in a position to waive that condition and proceed.

2. Conditions inserted for the benefit of one party.

The rule above stated, that neither party is bound to proceed until all conditions are satisfied, suffers this qualification, that a condition inserted in a Contract **exclusively** for the protection or benefit of one of the parties may be waived, unilaterally, by that party even if not purified. If so waived, the Contract is then immediately binding on **both** parties. Clearly, it may therefore be very important to determine which, if any, conditions in a Contract can be said to be for the exclusive benefit of the seller or for the exclusive benefit of the purchaser, and therefore capable of being unilaterally waived in this way.

For a discussion and analysis of this problem, see 7.1.56 — Ellis & Sons Ltd. v. Pringle 1975 SLT 10. The facts in that case were, briefly, that an offer to purchase heritage contained, *inter alia* the following condition:

'This offer is conditional on our clients obtaining Planning Permission for the use of the subjects as office premises. Our clients undertake to apply for this as soon as possible'.

The seller accepted the offer, but subject to a qualification allowing the seller to resile from the bargain if Planning Permission had not been obtained by 6th October, 1973.

Before that date arrived, the purchaser unilaterally purported to withdraw the condition in his offer as to Planning Permission and sought settlement of the contract at the stated date of entry, tendering the price in full. Thereafter, Planning Permission which had been applied for was refused; and the seller then refused to complete the bargain. The purchaser sued for implement, claiming that the condition as to Planning Permission was inserted solely for the protection of the purchaser and accordingly that the purchaser was entitled unilaterally to waive that condition and had effectively done so. In argument, the purchaser founded on the earlier case of 7.1.55 Dewar Ltd. v. Blackwood 1968 SLT 196 where, on a similar set of facts, the Court had found in favour of the purchasers.

In this case, however, the Court took the opposite view holding that, in this contract, there was no implied right allowing the purchasers unilaterally to waive the Planning condition which could, therefore, only be waived with joint consent. Therefore, the seller was entitled to resile. In the course of his Opinion, Lord Dunpark classifies contractual conditions in three categories:

1. Conditions which **can** be waived unilaterally. These are principally conditions which cannot in any circumstances be construed as having been inserted for the benefit of both parties. Examples of these are the normal conditions requiring the seller to provide a good title which can only be for the benefit of the purchaser. Similarly, an offer made 'subject to surveyors report on structure' can only be for the benefit of and protection of the purchaser. Such conditions can clearly be waived unilaterally by the purchaser.

2. Conditions which **cannot** be so waived. These include conditions which, although *ex facie* inserted by one party in his own interests, may **also** operate incidentally for the benefit of the other. Thus, if one party makes an offer 'subject to formal contract' and this is accepted, the condition as to formal contract affects both parties and cannot be unilaterally waived.

3. **Borderline cases** which include conditions of such a kind that only one of the parties **normally** would have an interest in that condition but in which the other party **may** exceptionally have an interest. According to Lord Dunpark, on the facts in this case, the planning condition fell into this third category and in the circumstances could not be waived by one party. Of course, as he later pointed out in his Judgement, it is open to the parties to provide expressly in the contract that a condition may be waived unilaterally by one or other of them; and this is often done. It was not done in this case with the result above stated.

Normal content of a contract of sale and purchase of heritage. For examples, see Diploma Styles.

1. **Indentification of the subjects sold**. A formal 'conveyancing' description is unnecessary, and the barest specification or identification is usual. But care is required here, and a full description, possibly with plan, is often desirable and sometimes essential.

(i) **Doubt as to identity**. The true question, where a doubt arises as to the nature and extent of the subjects of sale, is not what the contract says, but rather what the parties intended. Therefore, extrinsic evidence is normally allowed to prove by reference to the advertisement, to prior communings, to meetings of parties on the ground, etc., what the parties thought was being sold and purchased. 'In my view, these negotiations are crucial, and all that passed, either orally or in writing, is admissible in evidence to prove what was in fact the subject of the sale; not to alter the contract, but to identify the subject'. Lord Chancellor Loreburn in 7.1.18 Houldsworth v. Gordon Cumming 1910 SC (HL)49.

(ii) **Separate tenements.** Subject to the observations in the preceding paragraph, the rules which apply in interpreting a description in a conveyance, and which make it obligatory to incorporate, expressly, all separate tenements, also apply to contracts for sale and purchase. Therefore, if separate tenements are the subject of sale and purchase, each tenement should be separately specified; this applies, typically, to such rights as salmon fishing. See 7.1.19 (2.3.12) McKendrick v. Wilson 1970 SLT (Sh Ct) 39 *supra.*

(iii) **Fixtures and fittings.** In the absence of special provision, it is implied in a sale and purchase of heritage, as in a conveyance, that all corporeal heritable property is included in the subjects of sale and all corporeal moveable property is excluded; therefore, the character of a fixture or fitting, whether heritable or moveable, determines whether or not it is included in the price. But of course parties may (and almost always do) make special contractual provision as to fixtures and fittings.

In practice, under this clause, certain items which in any event are heritable fixtures are often included in the contract by express provision (unnecessarily); and, in addition, a large number of other items, principally in the category of fittings, not being heritable by nature and therefore by implication excluded, are by express provision included in the price. For an exhaustive list of items which may or may not be included in the sale by implication under this general head, see Green's Encyclopaedia 7.361-385-Fixtures.

Items which require special provision in the ordinary case include, in addition to the above, television aerials, storage heaters, washing machines, refrigerators, electric and gas fires, and other electric fittings, floor coverings, summerhouse and garden sheds.

Further, in case of sale and purchase of business premises, such as hotels, public houses, shops, etc., or agricultural property, an elaborate clause may be necessary, with a long inventory of items. See Burns' Practice p. 87 and Styles 8 p. 106. It is commonplace, in sale and purchase of business premises, to provide, in addition that certain further corporeal moveables, typically furniture, stock, machinery, etc., shall pass from seller to purchaser at date of entry at a price to be agreed or fixed by valuation. If so, then it should be made clear whether or not the provision is binding on both parties, or optional to both or either of them; the date of take-over should be specified, with a proviso that it is only such items as then exist which are to be purchased, but subject to a proviso that the seller should not unduly increase, nor unduly work down, the stock, etc., prior to that date.

If the items are to pass at valuation, then additional provisions will have to be made appointing the valuer and providing for payment of his fees.

2. **Price.** This is an essential of the contract. It is normally payable in one sum at the date of entry, in cash; but payment of the price by instalments is not uncommon; and sometimes the price is represented in whole or in part by shares or by some other consideration such as an exchange; and occasionally no price is payable. Some special points to note in regard to price are:

(i) **Deposits.** It is unusual, in Scotland, to stipulate for a deposit, except in Articles of Roup, but competent. If there is to be a deposit, then the clause should be carefully framed and should make it clear whether or not the deposit is forfeit absolutely if the purchaser fails to complete. Commercial Bank 18 R 80.

(ii) **Interest on the price.** Interest is due *ex lege* from the date of entry if the purchaser is in possession and if the price is not then paid. This rule applies, even where the delay is mainly or solely due to the fault of the seller.

There is no legal rate of interest; 5 per cent used to be usual, but at the moment, with high interest rates, a higher rate is charged, often linked to Bank or Building Society Rates.

This rule as to interest can be avoided if the purchaser, at the date of taking possession, deposits the whole purchase price in joint names of himself and the seller (or their respective Agents). Following on such consignation, the seller is entitled to the Deposit Receipt interest only. See 7.1.81 Prestwick Cinema 1951 SC 98. As a result, missives often contain an express provision excluding this rule, to protect the purchaser.

In 7.1.82 Bowie 1978 SLT (Sh Ct) 9, the Sheriff Principal held that a purchaser is not obliged to agree to take entry, and to pay the price or interest thereon, unless and until the seller is in a position to fulfil his part of the bargain by delivering a valid disposition. In such circumstances, if the purchaser in his option prefers to wait until the title is ready, no interest runs between the date of entry and the date of actual settlement. If the purchaser fails to pay the price on the due date through no fault of the seller, the sellers ultimate remedy is to rescind the contract and claim damages. See below — Default by Purchaser.

If, however, the transaction proceeds and the price is ultimately paid some time after the due date; and if, in the interim, the seller has retained possession, he cannot claim interest on the unpaid price unless there is an express provision in the missives to that effect. Such provision is now common place. The rule is based on equitable grounds; the seller cannot, in equity, claim to have both the benefit of the property and interest as well. See 7.1.82c Tiffney 1983 SLT (Sh.Ct.) 45, affirmed on appeal 1985 SLT 165.

(iii) **Price by instalments.** Contracts involving payment of the price by instalments over a period of years have been commonplace since the last war, particularly of flats in tenement which are substandard and so fail to qualify for a Building Society loan.

The usual provision is that the purchaser pays a deposit and thereafter a fixed monthly or periodical sum until a certain total is reached. The periodical sum is usually inclusive of interest but need not be. When fully paid up, but not before, the purchaser is given his title. If he defaults, then either:

(a) all sums paid to date are declared to be forfeit, and the seller is expressly released from the bargain and so is free to resell; or

(b) the seller may rescind. He then holds sums paid to date against loss and expenses of resale; but accounts to the purchaser for any balance remaining thereafter.

See 1968 JLS 46, and 7.1.117a Reid 1958 SLT (Sh Ct) 43 where a provision for total forfeiture, as in (a) above, was held to be enforceable and not invalid as a penalty provision.

Complications arise when the purchaser subsells while still paying instalments; or pays up but neglects to take a title; or disappears without trace, leaving the seller burdened with the property and liable for demolition costs (as commonly happens with sub-standard property).

If the total unpaid price is less than £15,000, the contract is subject to the Consumer Credit Act 1974. See 1974 Act S.189 — Definition of 'conditional sale'. Any loan under £15,000 is also subject to the Act. So this arrangement between seller and purchaser is regulated in either form — conditional sale **or** sale and standard security.

3. Entry. A date of entry is not essential to the constitution of a valid contract — 7.1.27 Sloan's Dairies 1979 SLT 17, but is invariably stated. Failing express provision, the 1874 Act S. 28 applies; or possibly immediate entry would be implied.

Does 'entry' imply 'vacant possession'? Walker states that the seller must give actual possession of the subjects, unless this is excluded by the contract, citing Hays 17 R 381. Admittedly, in that case, 'immediate entry' was so construed; but from the outset, actual possession had been a known and accepted requirement of the purchasers. But cf. Walker Chapter 5.16 page 300 'a title tendered is good notwithstanding ... leases usual in such a property'; and Burns' Practice at p. 343 which suggests that leases are unexceptionable failing express provision. Both refer to 2.7.17 Lothian and Border Farmers 1952 SLT 450 as authority (Lease not a breach of warrandice). Certainly, express provision in the contract for actual occupation is desirable, if not necessary. For a commentary on the terms 'vacant possession' and 'actual occupation' and their implication when used in Missives, see 7.1.58 — Stuart 1976 SLT (Notes) 39.

If property is being purchased subject to tenant's rights, it is normal so to stipulate, and to make further provision — see below.

4. Title. It is implied in any contract of sale and purchase that the seller will deliver a valid disposition in favour of the purchaser, and will deliver or exhibit a valid marketable title and clear searches. This implied obligation is normally the subject of express provision in the contract of sale and purchase, usually with a further provision specifying the period of search.

By far the most important question arising under this express or implied obligation on the seller is as to marketable title. A marketable title means a title so clear as to protect the purchaser, not only from actual eviction, but also from the risk of any reasonable challenge; a title, which is so regular in form and so correct in all particulars that no one, later dealing with the purchaser on sale or for security, will take any exception to it on any ground.

This obligation may, of course, be varied by express provision in the contract, of a general or a particular nature. See below for examples. But in the absence of any such provision, the rule carries the following implications:

(i) Exclusive and absolute right of property.
A feudal title satisfies this requirement; but not a leasehold title, even for a term of 999 years. See 7.1.31 McConnell 1903 10 SLT 790.

(ii) Title to whole and identical property.
It will not suffice to tender a title to practically the whole of the property; and the title tendered must cover the identical property referred to in the missives. On this, the purchaser is absolutely entitled to insist, and his motives are irrelevant.

The best illustration is in the case of minerals. In the ordinary way, a conveyance of, or contract to purchase, an area of ground, carries by implication sub-adjacent minerals. But, of course, if minerals have already been severed from the surface, before a sale, the seller's title to the surface does not carry them. In that event, in the absence of special provision in the missives, the title is not marketable and the purchaser is not bound to accept it; and this applies even to urban properties where minerals are not being worked. This rule was recently reaffirmed in 7.1.36 Campbell v. McCutcheon and Another 1963 SC 505. Lord President Clyde: 'In such circumstances, in my opinion, the purchaser is not obliged to take something less than he purported to buy and is entitled to withdraw his offer, as he did.'

(iii) **Burdens and Conditions.**

The purchaser is entitled to the property freed from all burdens and incumbrances affecting the subjects; but subject to this qualification that he must accept a reasonable feuduty (provided that it is allocated). But, of course, since 1st September, 1974, if the feuduty is allocated, it is automatically redeemed on sale and the question does not arise. If the feuduty is unallocated, the title is not marketable and the purchaser cannot be compelled to accept it. This rule has become somewhat unrealistic in view of the provision in the 1970 Act allowing for unilateral allocation by the vassal but, nonetheless, can still cause problems. The purchaser must also, it is thought, accept normal and reasonable conditions of tenure. But much will depend on circumstances. Thus, in the purchase of a vacant lot of ground, an absolute prohibition in the title against building would render it unmarketable. See 7.1.99 Loutitt's Trs. 19 R 791 and Urquhart 13 S 844.

In 7.1.40 Smith v. Soeder 23 R 60, a foreign purchaser, acting without legal advice, was held entitled to resile from a contract to purchase a two-storeyed cottage, when he discovered that the titles contained the typical restriction limiting use to the building of one house only, but also requiring the proprietor thereof not to open up windows in the rear of the house and to leave part of the ground unbuilt on. 'But it can hardly be the law that the purchaser of a house is entitled to resile because the title contains a provision that it shall be used as a private dwellinghouse only ...' Burns' Practice p. 211.

Similarly, in the purchase of a shop, a prohibition against sale of liquor may render the title unmarketable — at least so says Burns' Practice p. 211, referring to 7.1.31 McConnel 1903 10 SLT 790; but in that case, the purchaser explicitly stated his intention to apply for a licence, and the seller stipulated for a further payment on his obtaining it.

But, in 7.1.44a Umar 1983 SLT (Sh.Ct.) 79, following on the sale of a shop, the purchasers discovered, on examining the title, that there was a prohibition against the sale of alcohol on the premises. They objected to the title on that ground. The Sheriff, quoting from McConnel, and following Lord Keith in 7.1.44a Armia Limited, held that the seller was bound to disclose all restrictions which might materially diminish the value of the property, except where the purchaser knew or must be deemed to have known of the restrictions.

Servitudes affecting the subjects of sale are a narrower case; and it may depend, to some extent, on how burdensome the servitude is. See, typically 7.1.102 Welsh v. Russell 21 R 769 where the indications are that a purchaser can object to **any** adverse servitude right, if it detracts from the value of the subjects and if he was not aware of it when making his offer. See also 7.1.44a Armia Ltd. 1979 SLT 147. where a ten foot servitude right of access across the property rendered the title unmarketable.

Variation of the obligation as to marketable title.

There are two ways in which this general rule, whether arising by implication or by express provision in a contract, may be varied or qualified.

(i) Express modification in the contract. This is commonplace and may take various forms, e.g.

(a) Express partial qualification on a particular point, e.g. that the feuduty is unallocated; or that minerals are excluded; or included in the sale, only in so far as the seller has right and title thereto.

(b) A more general qualification, e.g. that the property is sold subject to the burdens and conditions **in the title deeds.** This throws the onus on the purchaser to examine the **title** for himself and to satisfy himself as to the nature, extent and effect of the burdens **therein contained.** But it does not protect the seller against adverse rights not disclosed on examination of the title, e.g. a positive servitude constituted by prescription or by an undisclosed and unrecorded agreement.

(c) A general provision that the purchaser must take the title as it stands; commonly called the *tantum et tale* clause. Such a clause is standard in Articles of Roup, but may be used in missives, although less commonly. It may or may not be coupled with a clause to the effect that the purchaser has satisfied himself as to the identity, extent and particulars generally and to the burdens and conditions affecting the property in the hands of the seller. The language varies. In its ordinary form, it is implied that the beneficial right of property in the subjects of sale (or at least a substantial portion of them) is vested in the seller; but that any curable defect in the title must be put right at the expense of the purchaser, and that the purchaser must suffer any burdens on the property. If, however, the title proves to be incurably bad, or if the seller is unable to show that he has the substantial beneficial right, the purchaser is entitled to resile. 'But, under some present day contracts, the conditions are wide enough and strict enough to compel the purchaser to proceed, even in the second case.' Burn's Handbook p. 180. This proposition is, at best, doubtful, on equitable grounds.

For a typical clause, see Burns' Practice p. 192.

Whatever form the clause may take, a purchaser cannot be barred from objecting to defective Stamp Duty. Stamp Act 1891 S.117.

(ii) Personal bar. The purchaser may have private knowledge, when making the offer, of a subsisting adverse right. If so, and even if there is no reference to this in the contract, the purchaser is not entitled to require of the seller, when the bargain has been closed, something which the purchaser knew, *ab initio,* that the seller could not give him. See 7.1.38 Mossend Theatre Co. 1930 SC 90, where a purchaser, discovering that minerals were not included in the sale (although this was not referred to in the contract), was held entitled to resile. The main ground of argument between the parties was as to whether the purchaser knew, or could be presumed from circumstances to have known, that minerals were excluded from the sale, because in the district all minerals generally were reserved to the superiors in all previous titles. In this case, the facts and circumstances were not sufficient to impute knowledge to the purchaser. But it is implicit in the decision that, had he **known** in fact of the mineral reservation, he could not later have taken advantage of that fact after completion of the bargain, but would have been personally barred from resiling.

5. **Servitudes and Wayleaves serving the property.**

In urban property, mains services normally enter the subjects of sale directly from the public road, which requires no special provision. But occasionally, as in 2.6.24 More v. Boyle 1967 SLT (Sh Ct) 38, services pass through adjoining property. If so, it is important that any such services are adequately supported by servitude rights, and express provision may be necessary. See 2.6.11 Murray 1973 SLT (Sh Ct) 75. A main water supply to part of property retained by the seller, and passing through the part sold, did not justify a servitude of necessity. So the purchaser was free to remove the pipe and the seller lost his main water. Without appropriate provision in the contract, a purchaser of the remaining property from the seller might find himself without main water and without redress against the seller.

6. Feuduty and other liabilities.

As has been said, a reasonable feuduty does not render the title unmarketable. Probably, the same would apply to stipend and standard charge. But again, since 1st September, 1974, where feuduties, etc., are allocated, they are automatically redeemed and do not affect the purchaser. Unallocated burdens must be disclosed to render the title marketable.

Apart from these, the occupier of heritage is subjected to occupier's rates and in appropriate cases there may also be various other liabilities, not of their nature rendering the title unmarketable. These include, in the case of frontagers within burgh, liability for the cost of making up and maintaining roads and foot pavements under statutory provision; in the case of tenement property, a proportionate share of the cost of maintaining the roof, main walls and other common items in the tenement.

It is usual, but of course not essential, to specify the rateable value (on which rates are payable) and the exact amount of feuduty payable, if not redeemable. It is also usual to provide that, apart from the stated feuduty and rates, there are no other charges, annual or otherwise; and to make express provision that the road and foot pavement have been made up and are taken over.

Where this is done, all these matters become, by express provision, conditions in the contract, and any discrepancy between the contractual and the actual liability entitles the purchaser to resile. It is also normal (although probably unnecessary, at least in urban properties) to provide expressly in the contract for the apportionment between seller and purchaser, of feuduty, rates and other outgoings at the date of entry.

7. Planning and other statutory matters.

Heritable property may be adversely affected, in a variety of ways, under the Town & Country Planning Acts, Housing Acts, Public Health and Burgh Police Acts, and various other Acts dealing with or restraining statutory nuisances. See chapter 4.2. None of these things affect the title, as such, and the existence of any of them does not, therefore, render a title unmarketable. Further, apart from marketability of title, where certain obligations are implied, a contract of sale and purchase of heritage is **not** a contract *uberrimae fidei*; and there is no obligation on the seller to disclose any such adverse matter to the purchaser, except under express provision in the contract. Thus, if an offer is made without reference to such statutory matter, the purchaser may later find, after the bargain is closed, that the property is adversely affected by some statutory control.

The maxim *caveat emptor* applies; he is bound to proceed, even although he knew nothing of the existence of any of these matters.

Special clauses may be necessary in special circumstances. A general catch-all clause may be incorporated to protect the purchaser against most known forms of adverse statutory matter.

8. Time Limit.

An offer, when made, remains open for acceptance for a reasonable time, or until withdrawn. It is standard practice to incorporate in an offer a time limit within which the offer must be accepted, failing which it falls. This would not normally preclude withdrawal of the offer before expiry of the time limit, but it may be prudent to be specific on this point.

9. Special Clauses.

There are any number of special circumstances for which special clauses are necessary. I only mention here some typical specialities.

(i) Let property.

Usually nowadays, the purchaser stipulates for vacant possession; but quite often let property changes hands. If so, then special provision in the contract is desirable, specifying:

(a) The rent or rents receivable, and the basis of apportionment thereof;

(b) Whether or not the property is subject to any statutory controls, e.g. rent restriction, registered rents, etc.

(c) The terms of the lease or leases, including duration and landlord's obligations, which may in certain circumstances be quite onerous.

(ii) Flats.

Two questions here are:

(a) What is included in the purchase? The starting point is the law of the tenement, which may of course, be varied in the titles to each flat. The normal Common Law rule is that the ground floor flat gets the *solum,* front garden, and the back ground. It is prudent to make this a matter of express stipulation when purchasing a ground floor flat; although on the Campbell v. McCutcheon argument (minerals) an offer for a ground floor flat necessarily includes *solum* and ground. *Per contra,* there is no general inference that each upper flat carries with it a joint right to the *solum* or to the use of the back green. Cellars and other pertinents should also be separately identified.

(b) Burdens. The roof is the most onerous; and if purchasing a top flat, it is very important to stipulate expressly that the property is burdened with a proportionate share only and not the whole of the cost of maintenance of the roof, in terms of the titles.

(iii) New Houses.

In order to counteract gerry-building in new houses, with consequent loss to innocent purchasers, the National House-Building Council was set up in Scotland on 7th February, 1969. The following points should be noted with reference to this Council:

(a) It is a voluntary body, which builders or developers may join; but they are not obliged to do so. In practice, a very large percentage of builders do belong, and 'almost all new houses' for sale or letting 'are built under the NHBC Scheme' Law Commission Report. No. 40 p. 7 (Civil liability of vendors and lessors for defective premises).

In Scotland, any post-1969 house which is not covered by an NHBC Certificate will not normally qualify for a building society loan unless construction was supervised and is certified by an architect.

(b) A builder's membership of the Council is conditional upon his implementing certain obligatory conditions which include:

(i) That all new houses must conform to NHBC Standards, which are laid down in considerable detail. To ensure this, the Council make regular inspection of buildings in course of construction.

(ii) That the builder, when selling a new house to a purchaser, must, in the contract, offer to enter into an Agreement in the approved NHBC Form HB.5AS(1980) — The Scottish House Purchaser's Agreement.

(iii) That the builder must complete the house according to standards and requirements laid down by the Council.

The Risks

It is perhaps worth summarising very briefly the main areas of risk which a purchaser runs when purchasing new property.

(1) Purchase of an uncompleted dwellinghouse. There are two possibilities here:

(i) **Where there is a contract but no title;** and deposits or other payments have been made, the purchaser may lose the whole or at least part of these payments because of supervening bankruptcy; and will be denied the benefit of the property, which will be disposed of as part of the bankruptcy assets. **Alternatively,**

(ii) **Where the purchaser has a title,** he will not lose the property; but will be left with an uncompleted building, partly paid for, which, in the nature of things, will cost more to complete (by employing another builder) than on the original contract.

(2) Condition of dwellinghouse after completion and payment. The building may turn out to be defective in that:

(a) **minor defects** may show up within a short period after completion which were not evident at completion date; and/or

(b) **major structural defects** may develop, possibly a considerable time after completion;

and in either event, for whatever reason (including bankruptcy) the builder may be unable or unwilling to put matters right.

Cover under the Scheme.

The principal points which concern the Solicitor in relation to the Scheme are:

i) **Is the purchaser covered?**

There are **six** essential conditions:

1. The cover extends to new dwellinghouses only, constructed after 1968, when the Scheme was first introduced in Scotland.

(**No** conversions, **no** shops, etc.)

It includes detached, semi-detached and flatted houses; with garage, boundary and retaining walls, internal footpaths and drains;

It excludes:

i) Roads and footpaths *ex adverso,* and amenity areas, even if the builder is under obligation to complete these as part of a contract. This is not covered by the NHBC Scheme. So road bonds are still essential; but the need for these should soon be superseded by regulations made under the Roads (Scotland) Act 1984 S.17.

ii) Fences.

iii) Lifts.

iv) Swimming Pools.

2. Only private purchasers, if acquiring for their own occupation, are covered; so, a Company buying a new house for service employees does not get the protection of the Scheme. But a purchaser from such a Company may qualify for protection. See Rule 19. Generally speaking, the benefit of the protection transmits to singular successors of the first purchaser without any special assignation or otherwise; but a second purchaser can only claim for defects which first emerge **after** the second purchaser acquired the house. The second purchaser has no rights in respect of **existing** defects which either should have been reported or should have shown up on a survey.

3. The builder (or the developer) must have been on the NHBC Register at the date when the House Purchaser's Agreement was signed.

4. The purchaser must have entered into a binding contract with the builder or developer. So, deposits before missives are completed are not covered.

5. The purchaser must also have entered into the House Purchaser's Agreement.

6. For structural defect claims, the Notice of Insurance Cover must have been issued.

Documentation.

From 1st January, 1980, the documents comprise:

(i) **The House Purchaser's Agreement.**

The main points in the House Purchaser's Agreement are:

The rights conferred by the Agreement are additional to the purchaser's rights at Common Law and under his own Contract with the builder.

The builder warrants that the dwellinghouse has been or will be properly completed in accordance with the NHBC rules and fit for habitation.

The builder warrants to the purchaser that the standard notice of insurance cover will be issued by the NHBC, to protect the purchaser.

The builder warrants that, within two years of completion of the dwellinghouse, he will remedy any defects which emerge in the house; but this is subject to certain limitations and qualifications, with particular reference to wear and tear, shrinkage and special fittings.

(ii) **The Scottish House Purchaser's Insurance Policy;** and

(iii) **A Notice of Insurance Cover** which is an intimation to the individual purchaser that the standard policy has been brought into operation so far as his particular house is concerned.

The cover provided.

The main cover provided by the Policy, against the risks above referred to, includes the following:

(1) Loss before the issue of the Notice of Insurance Cover. This normally means loss to the purchaser before the building is actually completed.

Here, the NHBC indemnify the purchaser against the consequences of the builder's bankruptcy to a limit of £5,000, less 10% of the admitted value of the claim.

(2) Loss after the issue of the Notice of Insurance Cover.

There are two separate Sections here:

(a) **The initial guarantee period,** i.e. two years from the date of the issue of the Notice of Insurance Cover. During this period, the purchaser deals directly with the builder and requires the builder to remedy defects. **But** if the builder fails to satisfy the purchaser and the dispute goes to Court or arbitration, the NHBC undertake to implement any arbitration award, with a 10% discount on the admitted amount of the claim.

(b) **The structural guarantee period,** i.e. after two years but within ten years of completion of the dwellinghouse. During this period, NHBC undertake to pay the purchaser the cost of remedying any major structural defect or subsidence and resulting damage.

The scheme is subject to certain limits on liability but these are now inflation-proofed automatically and increase as average building costs increase.

No special provisions are required in a contract of sale and purchase either to ensure the issue of the Council's Certificate or to ensure its transmission. The only point of enquiry is, prior to the contract, to ascertain whether or not the builder is a Member of the Council. If he is, then all the foregoing automatically follows. If he is not, then comparable provisions must be introduced into the contract in lieu. The terms of the Agreement and Certificate can be used as a style for suitable clauses in a Contract with a non-Member.

Earlier Arrangements

As mentioned above, there are certain limits on the liability incurred by NHBCs. This has always been so; and, in the result, over the past years of inflation, the cover provided under earlier NHBC Certificates has got out of line with the cost of repairs.

To meet this situation, and as an interim measure, NHBC introduced, on 1st October, 1975, a form of inflation proofing top-up cover which could be purchased as an addition to the NHBC Certificate but was not automatically applied to it.

As from 31st March, 1979, however, inflation proof cover has been provided as part of the Scheme; and this is now built into the current Scottish House Purchasers Insurance Policy HB7AS, which carries built-in inflation cover.

This is a point to cover when purchasing a pre-1979 house.

For further details and some comments on the Scheme see an article by K. Swinton in 1980 Scolag at p.211 e.s.

(iv) **Intended development.** Very often, the purchaser has in mind, at the time of his purchase, some immediate or early development. He may be frustrated in two ways, namely:

(a) Restrictions in the title. It is, therefore, normal to stipulate in the offer that the property is free of any conditions and restrictions; or at least any which would effectively prevent the proposed use. Normally, the seller will place the onus on the purchaser by stipulating that, at least *quoad* burdens, the purchaser must take the title as it stands. But at least the purchaser then gets the chance to see what the restrictions are, and possibly he may have to stipulate that the offer is subject to the requisite waivers.

The wording in these Clauses requires some care. See 7.1.44 Armia Ltd. 1979 SLT 147.

There was a condition in an offer in these terms:

'There is nothing in the titles of the said subjects which will prevent demolition and redevelopment.'

On subsequent examination of the title, it turned out that the property was burdened by a servitude of access for adjoining subjects, a building restriction, and a right to build an external stair for the benefit of the adjoining property.

Lord Wylie in 1977 SLT (Notes) 9 held that the existence of these restrictions on title did not constitute a breach of this condition, because demolition and some redevelopment was possible. Redevelopment on the **whole** site was excluded by the servitude and conditions; but the clause in the Contract did not specify redevelopment of the **whole**. But, on appeal, the House of Lords held the title to be unmarketable, and the purchaser was free to resile.

(b) Planning Permission and Building Committee Approval. Almost all development (including Change of Use) is subject to Planning Permission; and any structural work is subject to building regulation. Special restrictions are imposed on Listed

Buildings. There may also be, in special cases, additional special requirements, e.g. the Fire Authorities for various types of property, and special needs under the Licensing Laws, for Public Houses. See generally Chap. 4.2. If Planning and other Permissions cannot be obtained prior to the making of the offer, then the Contract must be subject to the obtaining of these consents. Otherwise, the purchaser runs the risk of finding himself committed to a purchase of property which he cannot use for the proposed development.

(v) **Loan Clause.** It is now increasingly common for the purchaser to make his offer conditional upon his obtaining a loan. Be careful to ensure that the purchaser may resile if he does not get exactly the loan he requires. But when acting for the seller, make sure that he is not kept hanging on too long by an appropriate time limit.

(vi) **Contract to remain in full force and effect, notwithstanding the delivery of the Disposition.** Such a clause inverts the normal rule that the Disposition supersedes the missives. Lee v. Alexander 10 R (HL) 91 and 7.1.25 (2.3.15) Jamieson 3 F 176 'it is not competent to go behind a deed of conveyance which exhausts the subject matter of the Contract'. In fact, in most cases, it does not matter if the missives are so superseded, but there may be special reasons for keeping them in force. If so, such a clause is competent; see 7.1.65 Fraser v. Cox 1938 SC506: 'normally, of course, when a dispute of that kind has arisen, the only document which would fall to be construed, and the only document which the Court would look at, would be the formal Disposition which had been granted and taken. It would entirely supersede all prior negotiations, including the missives themselves ... But I think that it is competent for the parties to agree, before the disposition is granted, that a term which will be included in the disposition shall fall to be construed as it stood in the missives which preceded the disposition and which would normally be wholly superseded by it.' L.P. Normand at p. 515.

Until recently, the general view was that the missives might still be referred to after delivery of the disposition, on any **collateral** matters. See, typically, 7.1.45 Bradley v. Scott 1966 SLT 2(ShCt)55, where a Contract contained a clause that 'there are no outstanding Notices for repairs or Notices to treat issued by the Local Authority'; in fact, a Closing Order had been made, but this was not discovered until after the disposition had been delivered. The seller maintained that delivery of the disposition excluded the purchaser's right to found on this; but the Court held that, as this was a collateral matter, the Contract still remained unexhausted and could be enforced according to its terms, notwithstanding the absence of any special clause to that effect. See also 7.1.73 Wann v. Gray 1935 SN8 where the Court held that a delivered disposition did not bar an enquiry into the nature and conditions of a Contract between the parties, insofar as the Contract dealt with the construction of a building which, again, was a collateral matter not covered by the disposition.

That general view no longer holds. See 7.1.69a Winston 1981 SLT 41.

In that case, the seller of a heritable property had previously constructed an extension, **purportedly** in accordance with a Building Warrant granted by the Local Authority, but in fact it did **not** comply with the Warrant.

When the property was subsequently sold the missives contained the following clause:—

'The Seller warrants that all statutory and Local Authority requirements in connection with the erection of the subjects of sale and any additions, extensions and alterations thereto have been fulfilled'.

The purchaser assumed that the extension complied with the relevant regulations. Thereafter, a Disposition was delivered to the Purchaser; and, as averred by the Pursuer, 'in accordance with normal conveyancing practice, a condition in the nature of Clause 9 (quoted above) contained in the Missives does not appear in the subsequent Disposition of the subjects'. The statement of conveyancing practice is unexceptionable.

The purchaser then discovered that the building was disconform to the Building Warrant. On the wording of the clause in this particular case, the Inner House took the view that Clause 9 did not incorporate any personal obligation on the seller to do anything in the future; but was simply a statement of the state of affairs or of the condition of the property as at the date of the missives. On that view of the clause, the Court further held that the purchaser could found on the warranty in that clause during the contract stage and prior to delivery of the Disposition; but, after delivery of the Disposition, he was barred from claiming damages for a breach of the provisions of that clause.

The Court reviewed the authorities, including the cases quoted above, and, in particular, added an observation to the effect that the circumstances averred did not take the case out of the general rule:— that provisions in an antecedent contract of sale of heritage (including provisions relating to the quality of the subjects) were superseded by the conveyance following thereon. In the process they formally disapproved of the earlier decision in 7.1.73 Wann v. Gray.

Note that the missives in this case, did **not** contain a standard clause to the effect that delivery of the Disposition was not to supersede the missives; and, in the result, Counsel for the Pursuers failed to persuade the Court that this provision was to be implied.

A Clause in the missives 'that, notwithstanding delivery of the Disposition to the purchaser, the missives are to remain in full force and effect', was and is commonplace. There are conflicting views as to whether such a clause in the missives is now effective looking to the decision in Winston; and there is an argument that, to be effective, such a clause must appear in the Disposition itself or in the Settlement Obligation. See 1982 JLS (Workshop) W 339 and earlier Articles there referred to; and 1983 JLS 45. In Hayes v. Robinson 1984 SLT 300, Lord Ross expressed the view, conceded by Counsel, that a clause in the **missives** was sufficient to exclude the rule in Winston, notwithstanding the subsequent delivery of a Disposition not containing that clause.

(vii) Matrimonial Homes (Family Protection) (Scotland) Act 1981.

Under this Act, which came into operation on 1st September, 1982, occupancy rights have been created for the benefit of the 'non-entitled spouse' on the break-up of a marriage. The Act has already been dealt with in Scots Law and it is not intended to describe the provisions here, except as they affect heritable titles.

In the ordinary case, 'non-entitled spouse' will normally be the wife, deserted by her husband, where the title stands in name of the husband alone. Without the protection of the Act, the husband at common law would be in a position to eject her from the matrimonial home. The purpose of the Act is to create overriding rights for the benefit of the non-entitled spouse to allow her to remain in occupation of the matrimonial home; and these 'occupancy rights' transmit against, and are enforceable in a question with, third parties, whether as purchasers or creditors from the entitled spouse who has the title to the property.

Consistent with that general intention, occupancy rights of a non-entitled spouse are overriding interests for the purposes of registration of title.

Whether the title be recorded in Sasines or registered, nothing will appear in the Register of Sasines or in the Land Register, or in the Personal Register, to give warning to third parties of the existence of such occupancy rights. But, under Rule 5 (as amended) of the Land Registration Rules, the Keeper will endorse a note on the Title Sheet that there are no subsisting occupancy rights of spouses of persons **formerly** entitled, if satisfied that this is so. Such endorsements are covered by indemnity. The Keeper, however, gives no assurance as to the current registered proprietor and and anyone dealing with the registered proprietor must make his own enquiries and take the necessary precautions to ensure that there are no subsisting occupancy rights.

In order to protect the *bona fide* purchaser against the possibility of such occupancy rights, any offer to purchase heritable property or to lend on heritable security should include a clause dealing with potential rights under this Act. See Chap. 7.4.

Resulting obligations of seller and purchaser.

In the absence of special provision in the Contract, or to the extent to which special provision is not made, both parties come under certain obligations. These are:

Seller's obligations

(i) To deliver or exhibit a good marketable title. This means a valid prescriptive progress of titles to the whole and identical property included in the missives. It also means that the seller must satisfy the purchaser on all matters expressly, or by implication, dealt with in the Contract in relation to title, e.g. that feuduty is allocated. If, on examination of the title, the purchaser finds some fault with it, then he is entitled, at the seller's expense, to have any such doubt in the title cleared to the extent of an Outer House judgement; but the normal rule as to expenses would apply on appeal.

(ii) To give possession. Further, the seller must tender title and possession timeously. This does not mean that, if title or possession is not available on the actual date of entry, the seller is automatically in default. See 7.1.29 Hays 17 R 381. The term 'immediate entry' in a contract means such early possession as is practicable; and possession tendered four days after the contract date did **not** put the seller in breach. In the ordinary case, the seller will be given reasonable time to implement his obligation, which of course depends on circumstances. But time may be made the essence of the Contract, either expressly or by implication, in which case the purchaser is then entitled to insist on title and possession on the due date, failing which the seller is **immediately** in breach.

Following on an offer to purchase with entry and actual occupation, failure to give vacant possession timeously to seven acres out of a total of 21 acres purchased under missives, was held to be a material breach of contract, entitling the purchaser to resile, even although the occupant apparently had no legal right or title to be there. 7.1.58 Stuart 1976 SLT (Notes) 39. The date of entry in the contract was 16th January, 1974; and the purchaser intimated his intention to resile on 26th March, 1974. There is no suggestion in the Report that the seller should have been given time to secure the eviction of the occupant, notwithstanding Lord Stott's comment, on the strength of English Authority, that it was for the seller to eject the third party 'before completion'.

(iii) To deliver a valid disposition in favour of the purchaser or his nominees, containing absolute warrandice. Note, however, that, notwithstanding this obligation as to warrandice, absolute warrandice is not, in any circumstances, an alternative or substitute for marketable title.

(iv) To deliver or exhibit clear searches (see later under Searches — Chapter 7.4.)

(v) To implement any other **special** obligations in the contract. e.g. to exhibit Planning Permission.

Purchaser's obligations

(i) To pay the purchase price on the due date.

(ii) Possibly, to take infeftment and, therefore, implied entry under the 1874 Act S.4 within a reasonable time so as to relieve the seller of personal liability for feuduty and other feudal prestations. ('Probably' — Walker Chapter 5.16 page 307).

(iii) To implement any other **special** obligations in the Contract. e.g. to obtain Planning Permission within a time limit.

Breach of Contract

Where the seller or the purchaser cannot, or will not, implement their respective obligations, the remedy of the other party is:

(a) Where *restitutio in integrum* remains possible, **either** implement **or** rescission and damages.

(b) Where *restitutio in integrum* is not possible, (i.e. **normally,** after settlement, when the purchaser is in possession) an action *quanti minoris,* based on the seller's warrandice.

Default by the Purchaser

This normally only arises while *restitutio* is still possible, and almost invariably takes the form of failure or refusal by the purchaser to pay the price. The seller may either:

(a) Sue for implement, by an action for payment of the purchase price in exchange for which the seller tenders a Disposition; or

(b) Rescind the Contract, following on which the seller will resell the property at the best price obtainable and thereafter may sue for damages, which will include the difference between the original and the resale price, plus expenses, etc. But in this case the seller must proceed with caution for two reasons, namely:

(i) Time is **not** normally of the essence of the Contract; and, therefore, failure by the purchaser to pay the purchase price on the due date does not entitle the seller immediately to rescind. Instead, the seller must give notice (perhaps fourteen or twenty-eight days) that, if the price is not paid within the period of notice, then he will hold the purchaser in breach. See 7.1.115 (2.5.6) Rodger (Builders) Ltd. v. Fawdry 1950 SC 483. Under Missives, the price was payable on 11th November but the purchaser was not ready to settle on that date. On 25th November, the seller's Agents gave an ultimatum, requiring payment of the price by the 28th, which was not forthcoming. On 28th November, purporting to rescind, the seller entered into a second contract of sale. (In fact, the purchase price was available on the 29th). **Held:** that the Seller had acted too precipitately, and was not entitled to rescind on such short notice.

The 'ultimatum rule' applies to any obligation in a Contract of Sale and Purchase, whether that obligation falls to be implemented by the purchaser or by the seller, if the party has it in his own power to implement that condition or not as he chooses, but has unnecessarily, or unjustifiably, delayed or refused to implement it. In such cases, time is not of the essence of the contract and an ultimatum must be given by the aggrieved party and must expire before he is in a position to rescind.

If, however, neither party is at fault, and if the fulfilment of a condition in the contract depends not on the seller or purchaser but on a third party or on extraneous circumstances, the ultimatum rule is not appropriate. Instead, the rule seems to be that such conditions must be implemented either:

(a) before the date specified in the contract by which the condition is to be fulfilled. In that case, the date must be strictly adhered to and time is in effect of the essence of such a condition; or

(b) where no special date is fixed for fulfilment of a condition, it must be fulfilled before the date for completion of the contract; or

(c) in the absence of either date, (very rare indeed,) any such condition must be fulfilled within a reasonable time.

See 7.1.98a Boland & Co. Ltd. v Dundas Trs. 1975 SLT (Notes) 80.

In 7.1.117b George Packman & Sons 1977 SLT 140, where a long period had elapsed since the date of entry, Lord Stott expressed the view that the seller was entitled to resile without notice; and was not bound first to impose on the purchasers a time limit for performance. See also 7.1.144 Inveresk Paper 1972 SLT (Notes) 63; and 7.1.116 Johnstone 1978 SLT (Notes) 81 for comment on Rodger.

(ii) Measure of damages. The seller must make every endeavour to minimise his loss by reselling the property at the best possible price obtainable. See 7.1.116 Johnstone 1978 SLT (Notes) 81; but need not **anticipate** breach by the purchaser **before** completion date.

Default by the Seller

This can arise, from various causes, both before and after settlement of the transaction.

Before settlement, where *restitutio* is still possible, the purchaser's remedies are:

(i) An action of implement, to have the seller ordained to deliver a valid Disposition, or, failing that, to acquire a title by adjudication. This remedy is, of course, only appropriate where the seller can implement the Contract (i.e. he has a title and beneficial right) but refuses or lacks capacity to implement.

(ii) Rescission and damages. Normally, in an action of implement, there is an alternative conclusion for damages. Where the seller cannot implement the Contract, because he lacks title, this is the only competent remedy. Again, since time is not of the essence of the Contract, notice is appropriate. If the seller fails to implement because of some technical defect in the title which is curable, then the Courts would normally give him time to put matters right; but not where the defect is complete want of title, even although he may be able and willing to do so. See 7.1.36 Campbell v McCutcheon 1963 SC 505 where Lord President Clyde at p.294 distinguishes between **defects** in title and **want** of title for this purpose. In that case, where property had been sold without reference to a reservation of minerals, and the seller then offered to acquire the minerals and convey them to the purchaser, but the purchaser sought to rescind, the Court declined to allow the seller time to acquire the minerals, and held the purchaser entitled to immediate rescission on the grounds of want of title.

(iii) At this stage, while *restitutio* is still possible, it would seem that the *actio quanti minoris* is not competent. Accordingly, the purchaser must either accept the title as he finds it, subject to the curing of curable defects, or he must reject the title and rescind. He cannot **insist** on proceeding with the transaction, but subject to an abatement of the price *quanti minoris;* although in practice this latter device is a common method of settling minor discrepancies between the Contract conditions and the actual state of the property or title. See Article 1966 JLS 124.

2. **After completion** of the Contract, where normally *resitutio* is no longer possible, the only remedy available to the purchaser arising out of the defects in the **title** is under the seller's warrandice which is, in effect, an action of damages *quanti minoris.*

Until the recent decision in 7.1.77a Winston 1981 SLT 41, it was generally believed that on collateral matters, not exhausted by the Disposition, the same result follows, but here not under the warrandice obligation but under the Contract. And so, to this extent, an action *quanti minoris* was thought to be competent, based on the Contract itself. See 7.1.45 Bradley v. Scott 1966 SLT (Sh.Ct.) 25 where, in Missives, the purchaser stipulated that 'there are no outstanding notices for repairs or notices to treat issued by the Local Authority'. The transaction then settled and the purchaser entered into possession. It was then discovered that the basement of the property was subject to a Closing Order. The purchaser claimed damages from the seller who maintained, *inter alia,* that the Missives had been superseded by the Disposition and that a claim for damages was incompetent, being an action *quanti minoris.* The Sheriff held the action to be competent, this being a collateral obligation with which the Disposition was not and could not be concerned.

The decision in 7.1.69a Winston, referred to above, reaffirms the general proposition that the provisions in the missives, including provisions relating to the quality of the subjects, will be superseded by a disposition following thereon and in implement thereof.

In his decision in Winston, however, Lord Wheatley suggests that there may be certain standard exceptions to the general rule, viz.:

(a) provisions in the missives dealing with moveables;

(b) a collateral obligation in the missives which is distinct from the obligation to convey the subjects of sale; and

(c) where, either in the missives or elsewhere, the parties expressly provide that the missives (or certain clauses thereof) are to remain in full force and effect, notwithstanding the subsequent delivery of a disposition.

Accordingly, if the missives contain what is clearly a distinct collateral obligation, and if that obligation has not been implemented at settlement, the purchaser may still insist on it, whether or not the missives contain the special clause. An illustration of such a collateral condition can be found in 7.1.74 McKillop 1945 SC 166, where the contract provided both for the construction of a building and for the sale of the completed property to the purchaser. Subsequent to delivery of the disposition in favour of the purchaser, structural defects developed and the purchaser claimed damages as a result. She was held entitled to do so on the footing that, in claiming damages, she was simply asserting a separate contractual right, distinct from her right to a conveyance of the subjects, in terms of which she was entitled to expect that the seller would have provided her with a building of a certain quality which the seller had failed to do. Based on that breach of a separate and independent contract, the purchaser was entitled both to retain the subjects and to claim damages; but, in awarding damages, the court stressed that this was not a case of an action *quanti minoris* because of the two distinct and separate obligations.

In an earlier case, 7.1.37 Wann 1935 SN 8, there was a contract for the sale and purchase of a piece of ground on which the seller undertook to erect a dwellinghouse in accordance with a certain plan but without any undertaking as to specifications, etc. The purchaser accepted a disposition thereof on completion of the building. Some years later, structural defects developed and the purchaser claimed damages. Apparently, the missives did not contain the special clause preserving the missives after delivery of the disposition. Nonetheless, the court held that the Disposition did not bar enquiry into the antecedent contract and, on that basis, awarded damages. The decision in Wann is expressly disapproved in Winston. If, however, the missives in Wann had contained the special clause preserving the missives after delivery of the disposition, this seems to be the one possible case where the special clause would allow the purchaser to claim damages which, in the absence of the special clause, would not be competent. If so, then it is difficult to escape from the conclusion that an action in this case is, at least arguably, an action *quanti minoris.*

This same question was raise in the recent case of Hayes v. Robinson 1984 SLT 300. In that case, as noted above, the missives contained the special clause to the effect that the whole terms and conditions of the offer, insofar as not implemented or superseded by delivery of a Disposition, were to remain in full force and effect, notwithstanding such delivery.

The particular obligations which the seller had failed to implement were in part representations as to the quality of the subjects at the date of the contract; and in part a failure by the seller to carry out work which he had contracted to carry out in the missives. The first of these obligations would seem to fall squarely within the type of clause referred to in Winston and would therefore not constitute a personal or collateral obligation to do anything in the future, being simply a statement of the state of affairs at a certain date. On the authority of Winston, and certainly in the absence of a special clause in the missives, the purchaser could not have founded on that obligation after settlement.

The second obligation, on the other hand, being of a continuing nature, can be properly described as a collateral obligation in the sense of McKillop above referred to, but Lord Ross seems to take the view that **both** obligations may truly be regarded as collateral obligations; and, on that footing, a claim for damages for failure to implement these obligations could be regarded not as an *actio quanti minoris* but as a claim for damages for breach of a distinct collateral obligation. However, in Hayes, the purchaser himself was in breach and so not entitled to enforce the Contract. In the result, Lord Ross reached the view that it would not be appropriate **at that stage** to decide whether the action was an *actio quanti minoris* (which would not be relevant) or to enforce a collateral obligation (which would be relevant).

The Special Disposition
Reading List 7.1
The creation, by subinfeudation, of a vassal's right to the *dominium utile* and the conversion of the vassal's personal title, represented by the Charter duly delivered, into a real right by registration in the GRS are dealt with in Chapter 2. The process

of subinfeudation can be repeated indefinitely by successive vassals, each such subinfeudation adding another link, downwards, in the feudal chain. The same general principles apply both to the original act of infeudation by the Crown, and to each act of subinfeudation by each successive vassal.

But instead of subfeuing, the vassal, having acquired a real right in the *dominium utile* of land by recording his Feu Charter from the superior, may transfer his real right in the *dominium utile inter vivos* not by way of subinfeudation but by way of substitution or delegation, so that the transferee (or disponee), on acquiring the *dominium utile* from the disposing vassal, takes the place of the disposing vassal and becomes, in his turn, vassal of the original superior on the original tenure.

Such disposal by the vassal may occur in various circumstances, may be effected by various means, and may have a varying result to the transferee. These include *inter vivos* transmission where the property passes from the vassal during his lifetime; or transmission *mortis causa* where the vassal remains proprietor of the property until his death on which event he is necessarily divested. Such transmission may be **voluntary**, *inter vivos* or *mortis causa,* which implies a positive act of disposal on the part of the vassal, by a deed which may be onerous or gratuitous; or involuntary, by operation of law, e.g. on the sequestration of the vassal *inter vivos,* where his property, including heritage, passes to the trustee in sequestration; or, *mortis causa,* where the vassal dies intestate.

Property may so transmit, in one or other of these ways, to a **singular** successor, or to a universal successor. A **singular** successor is, typically, a purchaser from the vassal of his right to the *dominium utile.* A singular successor is liable only for **real** burdens and conditions running with the lands. In contrast, a universal legatory under the Will of the deceased vassal acquires the property as **universal** successor and as such is liable not merely for real burdens and conditions running with the lands but generally for all debts and liabilities incurred by, and personal obligations binding on, the deceased vassal during his lifetime.

In the case of voluntary transmission, written title is essential for reasons already examined, and may take the form of a special disposition or a general disposition. The special disposition is the deed normally used for *inter vivos* transmission, rarely for *mortis causa* transmisssion; its effect is to convey to the disponee a specific property, described and identified therein. Alternatively, the vassal may grant a general disposition of his whole estate in general terms which embraces, *inter alia,* his right to the *dominium utile* of his feu. This form of deed is commonly used for *mortis causa* transmission but rarely used for *inter vivos* transmission.

With involuntary transmission, the right passes automatically on the happening of a certain event, e.g. the appointment of trustee in sequestration; or decree of adjudication; or death intestate. But some written evidence in due form is required to **vest** the right, and constitute the title of the person in right of the property.

Again, with the voluntary disposition, the effect may be to transmit to the disponee the absolute beneficial right of property; or some more limited right such as a right of liferent or a right in security.

Entry with the Superior

If a new feudal estate is created by the Feu Charter, the disponer as superior retains his title to the land, burdened with the subaltern rights of his vassal. Accordingly, he remains liable to his own superior for all the incidents of tenure inherent in his own title, and becomes, by virtue of the Charter to the vassal, entitled to enforce all the conditions of tenure against the new vassal.

Where the vassal transmits his feu to a third party, by delegation or substitution, the disponing vassal is absolutely divested and retains no further title or interest in the subjects conveyed. At the same time, he is (normally) relieved of all **future** liability for incidents of tenure in his own original Charter; he continues to be liable for incidents already prestable. The disponee becomes liable directly to the true superior for all such incidents of tenure (past and future) along with, or in lieu of, the disponing vassal; and, on the feudal theory of continuing recurring contract between superior and each new vassal, the relationship of superior and vassal is of new established directly **and contractually** between the superior and the disponee of the original vassal. As between disponer and disponee, there is no continuing relationship and no new tenure is created, which is relevant when considering the enforcement of conditions created by a disposition.

The substitution of a stranger as new vassal of the superior in this way is, as you will remember, inherently at variance with fundamental feudal principle. The relationship of superior and vassal involves fidelity and service, and accordingly the selection of the original vassal in mediaeval times involved an element of *delectus personae.* As a result, having personally chosen the original vassal, the superior was not bound later to accept as new vassal someone of whom he had not previously approved. Therefore, where the feu was to transmit by disposition instead of by subinfeudation, the superior personally approved, and agreed to accept, the disponee **in place of** the disponing vassal; and in the result, every special disposition on sale by an existing vassal required the sanction and approval of the superior whose active intervention was essential, if the disponee was to acquire a real right. This active intervention involved the public entry of a new vassal with the superior; and, until publicly entered, the new vassal had a personal title only. '**Public** entry' implied that the superior's consent could only effectually be given in the presence of the *pares curiae.*

Originally, the superior had absolute control and could refuse to accept **any** new vassal. But this, of course, created difficulties particularly as to heritable securities; and the rule was gradually relaxed. But it was not until 1747 that the superior could be compelled to accept an outright purchaser as new vassal; and it was not until 1874 that his active participation as consenter was finally dispensed with.

The historical development of transmission of the feu has already been dealt with in Scots Law. You will remember that, prior to the 1845 Act, the disponee obtained infeftment either:

(a) **By resignation,** which involved the surrender by the old vassal directly into the hands of the superior of the *dominium utile,* but for the limited purpose of allowing the superior, thus reinvested, to grant a new Charter in favour of the disponee known as a Charter of Resignation, which was a Mandate for the disponee's infeftment as direct new vassal; or

(b) By a process of spurious or transient subinfeudation, following on a Conveyance containing the **alternative holding** (or obligation to infeft *a me vel de me*). The disponee **in the first instance** took infeftment as vassal on subinfeudation, holding of and under the disponer (*de me*), thus creating a temporary mid-superiority in the person of the seller, interposed between himself and the true superior. At a later stage, the disponee then went to the true superior; became publicly entered with him; and had his specious infeftment **confirmed** by the superior (*a me de superiore meo*), thus eliminating the temporary mid-superiority initially created. The Deed confirming was termed a Charter of Confirmation.

The effect of a Disposition in this form was twofold:

(a) **Immediate real right.** By taking infeftment at once, and ascribing the infeftment to that portion of the obligation to infeft which provided for the holding by the disponee *de me* of the disponer, the disponee obtained an immediate right, technically as vassal of the disponer on subinfeudation; and accordingly the disponer became mid-superior. No casualty was paid. The true superior could not object, since the disponer still remained his vassal.

(b) **Public entry.** In virtue of the procuratory of resignation, the disponee could, if he preferred, proceed at once to public entry and become infeft on the other leg of the alternative holding, viz., *a me de superiore meo;* but this meant that he had to pay a casualty at once, and might be confronted with delays because of defects in the superior's title. If, however, the disponee did proceed in this way, the disponer was immediately and absolutely divested; but the disponee was required immediately to pay the casualty.

Accordingly, in practice, a disponee would normally take immediate infeftment *de me* of the seller; but sooner or later a situation would arise in which it became necessary to enter publicly with the true superior, such public entry being then obtained by Confirmation.

This procedure was, clearly, complicated and cumbersome, and inevitably gave rise to numerous errors and defects in titles. There were a number of statutory provisions between 1845 and 1874 designed to simplify the procedure, already dealt with in Scots Law.

I remind you again here of:

The 1874 Act S.4. This final development represents a complete and radical alteration of the whole system of transmission.

Firstly, by S.4(1), Charters and writs by progress generally, including Charters and Writs of Resignation and Confirmation, are abolished and can no longer competently be granted by a superior. The effect of this sub-section is to render unnecessary the application to the superior for recognition of a disponee as new vassal; and from this point forwards the superior's intervention in transmission disappears.

The **principle** of Public Entry is, however, preserved by S.4(2) which provides (paraphrasing the Section) that every proprietor who is infeft shall be deemed to be, as at the date of registration of his infeftment in the Register of Sasines, duly entered with the nearest superior whose estate of superiority (according to the rules then in force) would have been not defeasible at the instance of the infeft proprietor. Such infeftment is to have the same effect as if the superior had granted a Writ of Confirmation, irrespective of the state of the superior's title or of his capacity.

In other words, on the recording of a title, Public Entry is automatic and, in the process, all temporary mid-superiorities created by the alternative holding have been eliminated and extinguished, being mid-superiorities defeasible at the instance of the infeft proprietor.

Clearly, this has important consequences, viz.:

(i) The alternative holding is redundant and disappears.

(ii) Defeasible mid-superiorities are abolished and cannot now be created.

(iii) Since Public Entry is implied, the casualty became immediately payable on recording; but this is now of no significance.

(iv) The state of the superiority title can never affect a disponee's real right.

(v) There has now disappeared altogether from the Disposition (a) the obligation to infeft *a me vel de me* (the alternative holding); (b) the procuratory of resignation; and (c) the Precept of Sasine. Further, every Special Disposition has become, of itself, a Mandate for Infeftment by *de plano* recording; and on the recording of such Conveyance, without reference to the superior, the disponee perfects his real right and is impliedly publicly entered with the true superior.

But implied entry was liable to prejudice the superior in two ways.

(1) Under the old rules, when a superior publicly entered (i.e. approved and accepted) a disponee as new vassal, he thereby automatically released the old vassal from any continuing liability for feudal prestations. With implied entry, how is the superior to know who is so liable? The 1874 Act S.4(2) provides that, notwithstanding implied entry, the last entered proprietor remains personally liable for feudal prestations unless and until (a) the disponee has recorded his title; **and** (b) the disponer has intimated to the superior the change in proprietorship by a statutory form of Notice of Change of Ownership. See 1874 Act Schedule A. Until (a) and (b) have occurred, the superior may proceed against either the old vassal or the new vassal.

A new situation has arisen with the passing of the 1974 Act, in terms of which feuduty is redeemable, either voluntarily or compulsorily on sale. See Chapter 3.2. If redeemed, there is no continuing liability on the vassal or his successors to pay feuduty from the date of redemption. **But** the whole other obligations of the feu continue and remain enforceable against the old vassal and his successors in terms of the 1874 Act. Therefore, notwithstanding that no feuduty is payable, Notice of Change of Ownership should continue to be given even after feuduty has been redeemed. This applies not only to the sale on which the feuduty is actually redeemed, but also to subsequent sales occurring after that date; but with this difficulty that, as time wears on, it will be more and more difficult to ascertain who the superior is when no feuduty is being paid. Failure to give Notice of Change of Ownership may involve an owner who has sold his property years previously being held personally liable for implement of feuing conditions, e.g. rebuilding ruinous building, etc. See an Article in 1976 JLS 317.

(2) When a disponee was publicly entered as new vassal, it came to be **presumed**, in practice, that the disponer was discharged of any liability for arrears of feuduty. See Marshall v. Callander Hydro. 22 R 954 G.8. Lord Ordinary at p. 963 for a discussion of this rule. The Lord Ordinary comments that the rule was one of practice only and doubts how far or firmly it was established. Did it apply **only** *quoad* the new vassal? Did it apply to obligations *ad factum praestandum*? But the superior could reserve his rights against the disponer, when giving entry. By 1874 Act S.4(3), the rule is reversed; and implied entry does not prejudice claims for arrears of feuduty against the disponer.

Certain further provisions in the 1874 Act S.4(3) and (4) are now obsolete since they refer to casualties, and can be ignored.

The normal rule as between superior and vassal, based on tenure and the recurring personal contract, is that, when the feu transmits by Disposition (i.e. substitution or delegation), the original vassal as disponer, parting with the lands, ceases to be liable to the superior for implementing the conditions of the Charter; and the disponee, as new vassal of the superior, becomes personally liable in his place. Note that this rule applies only to the **feudal** relationship. In other comparable situations, e.g. under the Contract of Ground Annual the disponer and his universal successors remain **personally** liable to the creditor in the obligation; whereas the disponee, although he may take the **land** subject to the real burden, is not **personally** liable himself in a question with the creditor. See 2.5.9 Wells v. New House Purchasers Ltd. 1964 SLT (Sh Ct)2 C.14. For the comparable case of liability under a Contract of Ground Annual, see 5.2.3 Royal Bank of Scotland Ltd. v. Gardyne 1 McQueen 358.

Under the 1874 Act S.4(3) the superior's right to arrears of feuduty exigible prior to the date of entry is preserved. The same principle applies to other obligations and conditions which have already become enforceable before the vassal sells his interest; and the selling vassal remains personally liable for these burdens: see 7.1.121 Marshall v. Callander Hydropathic Ltd. 22 R.954 and 7.1.122 Rankine 4F. 1074.

Form and content of Disposition

The Disposition, like the Feu Charter, is a unilateral writ, running in name of the granter alone and not executed by the grantee. In general form, it closely resembles the Feu Charter and the principal clauses, with some modifications to suit the altered circumstances, are largely the same. **But** under the modern form of Disposition no new tenure is created, and in the result the tenendas and reddendo clauses are inappropriate; and the Disposition contains nothing equivalent in form or effect.

First, to contrast briefly the form of Disposition with the form of Feu Charter. The essentials of the deed are:

(1) The narrative or inductive clause or clauses;

(2) The operative clauses, which again include the dispositive clause (which rules) and subordinate clauses, conferring rights ancillary to the main or dispositive clause; and

(3) The testing clause.

1. **Narrative Clause.** The normal content here is, as in the Charter, granter, grantee and consideration, the consideration being normally, in a Disposition, a lump sum payment. But in the Disposition (less often in the Charter), there are often circumstances, other than sale, which it may be appropriate to narrate as the reason for the granting of the Disposition.

Otherwise, the same considerations apply as to title and capacity as apply to the granting of a Charter. But by a special statutory dispensation in the 1924 Act S3, which we will consider later, an uninfeft proprietor may effectively grant a Disposition, whereas for an effective Feu Charter the Superior must be infeft.

2. **Operative Clauses.** Again, as in the Charter, these include:

(i) **The dispositive clause** of which the essential elements, again, are:

(a) **Words or conveyance.** The only difference here is that the property is not 'in feu farm' disponed, since that implies tenure. But it is disponed to the disponee, with a destination, heritably and irredeemably, as in the Charter.

(b) **Identification** of the subjects conveyed. There are no specialities as to description. In the majority of cases, the Disposition passes on, entire, the property as it stands in the person of the disponer, in which case a description by reference is usual and appropriate. But it is equally competent to convey, by Disposition, part of an original feu; or part of a part, and so on. In that case, a particular description will be necessary and the same rules apply as in the case of the Feu Charter.

(c) **Reservations** are equally competent in a Disposition.

(d) **Burdens.** A Disposition normally contains a reference to a prior writ for burdens, typically the original Feu Charter; and there may be several such writs. In addition, it is competent in a Disposition to impose real conditions on the disponee, either as conditions inherent or as real burdens, the effect of which we have already examined when dealing with burdens and conditions in the Charter. The same general principles apply to real conditions and real burdens inserted in a Disposition as apply to burdens and conditions in a Charter. But Disposition conditions also present special problems, viz:

(i) Enforcement.

A condition of tenure is normally enforceable by personal action against the original vassal **and** all singular successors, on the recurring personal contract principle.

A condition in a Disposition is enforceable by personal action against the **original** disponee and his universal successors on the basis of direct contract. But the Disposition creates no tenure. Are such conditions enforceable by personal action in a question with a **singular** successor of the original disponee?

According to 2.5.7. Wells v. New House Purchasers Ltd. 1964 SLT (Sh Ct) 2 the rule in 5.2.32 Royal Bank of Scotland Ltd v. Gardyne — 1 Macq. 358 only applies to the contract of Ground Annual and similar arrangements where the disponer, as creditor in the obligation, is neither feudal superior **nor** permanently associated with the land which is burdened.

Applying that principle:

(a) If a burden in a disposition is inserted simply to secure a money payment, e.g. a ground annual or the old pecuniary real burden, then the burden is enforceable against singular successors of the original disponee by **real** action only. **But**

(b) If a burden in a disposition is inserted to secure the amenity of an adjoining property, it can be enforced against singular successors by **personal** action. A typical case in this category is a disposition of a flat in a tenement, imposing burdens of maintenance, etc. According to the Sheriff in Wells, the basis of the right of personal action in this instance is the continuing relationship associated with the property between the creditor and the debtor in the obligation.

(ii) Jus Quaesitum Tertio.

If a superior grants Feu Charters to several adjoining feuars, and if certain fairly stringent conditions are satisfied, each feuar may acquire a *jus quaesitum tertio* to enforce the conditions in his neighbour's Charter. Chapter 3.3

In exactly the same way, if A, by Disposition, sells portions of his feu to B, C and D, with the same conditions in each Disposition, B, C and D may acquire a *jus quaesitum tertio* to enforce these Disposition conditions *inter se.* Exactly the same general principles apply as applied in the case of Charter conditions.

In addition, however, these parts of the feu so disponed are normally subject to the burdens in the original Charter which apply to the whole of the feu and every portion thereof. A question then arises whether each of these disponees is entitled to insist on, and enforce, these Charter conditions in a question with a disponee of another portion of the same feu.

Unfortunately, on this point, there is some conflict in the reported cases. Thus,

Lord Watson in 3.3.1 Hislop v. McRitchie's Trs. 8 R (HL) 95 at p.104, states: 'A sub-feuar, or disponee, acquiring a building lot, subject to a particular condition, with notice in his title that the common author', i.e. the superior when granting the Charter 'has imposed that condition upon the whole area, of which his lot formed part, **must be taken**' i.e. by implication 'as consenting that the condition shall be for the mutual behoof of all feuars or disponees within the same area, and that all who have an interest shall have a title to enforce it.'

Therefore, according to this dictum, in the ordinary case, every disponee of a portion of a feu can enforce conditions in the original Charter, in relation to other parts of the same feu. This principle has been so applied in Beattie 3 R 634 and 7.1.132 Fergusson 1953 SLT (Sh Ct) 113, where the *jus quaesitum tertio* of co-disponees seems to be taken for granted.

In contrast, in Campbell 24 R 1142, one disponee was held **not** to have a title to sue in exactly the situation envisaged by Lord Watson in the passage quoted above; and, in somewhat special circumstances, the Court so held in 7.1.130 Girls' School Co. 1958 SLT (Notes) 2.

The point was discussed again recently in 7.1.131 Williamson & Hubbard v. Harrison 1970 SLT 346. In that case, the Charter of 10 Rothesay Place, Edinburgh (granted in the 19th century) restricted the use of that house to a single dwellinghouse only. In 1925, under legislation then in force, the Sheriff authorised sub-division; and the house was then converted into three self-contained dwellinghouses. Later again, it was proposed to convert the ground floor and basement to an office. The proprietor on the first floor objected, claiming that she had a title and interest to enforce a condition in the original Feu Charter in a question with the ground floor proprietor.

The Court held that she had no **title** to object, because, in the Charter, there was nothing to create rights as between the owners of individual portions of the original dwellinghouse. This, of course, was necessarily so since, in the original Charter, sub-division was prohibited. Lord President Clyde emphasises that the original Charter, by prohibiting sub-division, clearly could not have contemplated any mutuality amongst individual owners of portions of the property *inter se.* But that in itself seems quite irrelevant. The question is whether, when the building was originally split up and disponed to the three purchasers from the original single owner, the three purchasers by implication agreed that each of them should be entitled to enforce the Charter conditions as between each other. According to Lord Cameron, since there was nothing **expressed** in the Disposition to indicate that there was to be any such mutuality as between the three individual owners, no one owner had a title to enforce these conditions as against any other; but that is certainly contrary to the view of Lord Watson quoted above, where agreement between original disponees is to be inferred by implication in these circumstances. See also 7.1.133 Smith 1972 SLT (LT) 34, where Lord Watson's dictum in Hislop is quoted and followed.

To illustrate these rules, suppose that A, the owner of one acre, dispones one-half of it to B. The Disposition in B's favour contains a new burden and an obligation on A, the original disponer, to insert the same burden in any subsequent Disposition of the remaining one-half acre. A then dispones the remaining one-half acre to C and in the Disposition in C's favour inserts the same burden. Both Dispositions enter the Record. In these circumstances, B and C, *inter se,* would each have a *jus quaesitum tertio* to enforce the conditions in each Disposition against the other, on the same general principles which apply in relation to co-feuars. Further, if A, when disponing to B and disponing to C, had expressly provided that each Disposition was granted subject to the conditions in the original Charter and that each of B and C, *inter se,* had the right to compel the other to observe the Charter conditions, then again B and C *inter se* would have a *jus quaesitum tertio* to enforce the Charter conditions by express provision in each title.

According to Lord Watson's dictum, each would have that right by implication only and without the need for express provision to that effect, but not according to Lord Cameron in Williamson & Hubbard.

(iii) **The transmission of the title to enforce.** In a feudal grant, this creates no problem. The superior's title to enforce feuing conditions against his vassal automatically transmits with the superiority. Where conditions are created in a Disposition, the position is less clear.

Suppose A owns one acre, with house on it. He dispones one-half acre to B as amenity feu, retaining the house for himself; and in B's title he prohibits any building on that one-half acre in order to preserve his own amenity. That is a condition imposed on B for the benefit of A's remaining property. A later sells and dispones his house to C. Does C have a **title** to prevent B from building on B's half-acre? It now seems settled, in a case of this kind, that C can insist on the condition in a question with B or with singular successors from B. But does C's right spring from *jus quaesitum tertio*? Or is his title to sue based on an assignation from A of A's contractual right to enforce against B, so that C represents A in the contract? If the latter, then C apparently requires no special assignation of A's right of enforcement; it passes *sub silentio* on the disposition of A-C. The difference between these two cases, *jus quaesitum tertio* and implied representation, could be difficult to define in more complex cases, but may be very important. See and contrast MacTaggart v. Harrower 8 F 1101 where there were express assignations of the right to enforce; and 7.1.125 Braid Hills Hotel Co. v. Manuels 1909 SC 120 where, in the absence of express assignation, the point was decided apparently on the basis of *jus quaesitum tertio* for the benefit of the successors in title.

3. Subordinate Clauses.

As already explained, the tenendas and reddendo clauses which feature in the Charter have no place in the modern form of Disposition. Otherwise, the subordinate clauses follow the same **pattern** as in the Charter, but with differences in detail.

As already mentioned, the statutory clauses introduced in Schedule B1 of the 1868 Act authorised by the 1868 Act S.5 and interpreted in the 1868 Act S.8 are appropriate to a Disposition rather than a Charter and less adaptation of the statutory clauses is here required. Dealing in turn with the subordinate clauses which are:

Entry. No speciality.

Assignation of Writs. The statutory clause is 'I assign the writs' but, in virtue of the 1874 Act S.4, this clause has lost much of its technical value. Under Common Law, a disponee is entitled to **delivery** of those writs which are essential to vindicate his right and which relate exclusively to the subjects conveyed. Under this clause, he can call for production of any other writs, should he wish to refer to them, which in any event is probably implied. In practice, this clause was almost always supplemented by detailed provisions dealing with delivery and custody of the writs which are listed in an Inventory of writs appended to the Disposition, to which reference is made in this clause.

The assignation of writs clause is dispensed with in two separate clauses in the 1979 Act S. 16(1) and 16(2), dealing with the Disposition and the Feu Charter respectively, because the position is somewhat different under each type of writ.

16(1) deals with the Disposition; and provides that an assignation of writs is implied in every Disposition. Further, under this Section:—

(a) The disponer must deliver all deeds relating exclusively to the subjects; and must produce any writs which he retains.

(b) The disponee is entitled to call for production of writs from any other custodier.

(c) The disponee is similarly bound to produce to anyone else having interest any writs delivered to him which are common.

Assignation of rents. The statutory clause is 'and I assign the rents'. The clause may require adaptation. But there is no speciality here compared with the Feu Charter. As with the Charter, the clause is no longer necessary under the 1979 Act S. 16(3).

Obligation of Relief. The statutory clause 'and I bind myself to free and relieve the said disponee and his foresaids of all feuduties and public burdens' is normally suitable without adaptation. Again, this Clause is no longer necessary — 1979 Act S. 16(3).

Warrandice. The same rules apply here as in a Feu Charter. The statutory clause, 'I grant warrandice' is normally used, but may fall to be adapted according to circumstances.

Certificate of Value for Stamp Duty purposes. Again, there is no speciality here compared with the Feu Charter.

Infeftment of the disponee. Since 1874, a Special Disposition operates of itself as a mandate for the infeftment of the disponee by *de plano* recording. The same general principles apply as apply in the case of infeftment of a vassal and, in particular, there must be **delivery** of the Disposition to the disponee, the Disposition will be **stamped, Warrant of Registration** will be endorsed and signed, and the Disposition presented to the General Register of Sasines and there recorded to complete the infeftment of the disponee.

Transmission of the Superiority.

On the granting of a Feu Charter, two interests emerge where one previously existed, in that the *plenum dominium* previously held by the superior is split into two elements *dominium directum* (which the superior retains) and *dominium utile* which passes to the vassal under the Charter. When the Charter is granted, the superior is already infeft on a title which includes *dominium utile.* So far as the superior is concerned, no new title is created by the granting of a Charter; instead, his existing title to land and his existing Infeftment become burdened with the subaltern right of the vassal; to that extent **only** is he divested in favour of the vassal. On the strength of his own original infeftment, the superior is entitled to enforce, as against the vassal and successors of the vassal in the feu, all the conditions in the Feu Charter, including payment of the feuduty. In other words, **the title** to an estate of superiority is in essence a title to land; **the beneficial interest** of the superior is to insist on the incidents of tenure as against the vassal.

It follows that, for the transmission of an estate of superiority, the same rules apply as apply to transmission of *dominium utile,* because the estate of superiority is in itself a title to land. An estate of superiority may therefore transmit by Special Disposition which is, in its terms, a conveyance of land, **not** a conveyance of a mere 'superiority', and in the result, it is virtually indistinguishable from a Disposition of *dominium utile.* This can be very confusing, particularly where the titles of the superiority and *dominium utile* of the same piece of land become intermixed.

There are two typical, and different, cases where a superiority may transmit, viz:

(i) The superiority is sold as a commercial investment. In trust law a superiority is a 'narrower-range' Trustee Security, and gives a good return. But because of the changes in the 1970 and 1974 Acts (supra), and because of the trouble and expense of collecting individual feuduties, superiorities are no longer a popular form of investment and are not easy to realise.

(ii) The vassal purchases his own superiority, in order to discharge his liability for feuduty and other obligations in his Charter. The two estates of *dominium directum* and *dominium utile* then merge in the same person, which raises some specialities, dealt with under Consolidation, below.

Specialities of Superiority Disposition.

The only points of difference between a superiority and a *dominium utile* Disposition are:

(a) Narrative. This **may** (but need not) disclose the true position.

(b) Assignation of Rents. 'And I assign the rents **and** feuduties', but, this clause is no longer required — 1979 Act S.16.

(c) Warrandice. The feu rights previously granted to the vassals are excepted from warrandice.

(d) Schedule of Feuduties. Commonly, a Schedule of Feuduties is appended, but is unnecessary.

Since a Disposition of superiority is in form a Disposition of lands, this may lead to some unexpected results, viz.—

(a) Suppose a superior, A, grants a Charter of a plot on a landed estate, which the vassal B forgets or omits to record. The superior later sells and conveys his landed estate to C, a *bona fide* purchaser for value without notice of the vassal's right. C records this disposition of the estate in the Register of Sasines. For the reasons stated, the Disposition is in form a conveyance of **land** and will include the superiority of B's feu as if it were *dominium utile.* Since C is first on the record, B, the vassal, loses his right. See 2.8.1 Ceres School Board v. Macfarlane 23 R 279. This is what Walker means when he says, at Chapter 5.16 page 320, that 'the superiority of lands can be conveyed **only** if the vassal's estate has already been separated from the superiority by Charter and infeftment'. If, prior to infeftment, the superior conveys the lands, then he is conveying *dominium utile,* not a mere superiority, as the Ceres School Board case demonstrates. But there is no rule of law to prevent him from conveying, as Walker's passage might seem to indicate.

(b) Minerals. As we have seen, a conveyance of land carries sub-adjacent minerals, unless these have previously been severed from the surface. Suppose A, owning *plenum dominium* of surface and minerals, feus the surface, reserving minerals, and the vassal records the Charter. The resulting position is that A owns the *dominium directum* in the surface, but retains the *plenum dominium* in the minerals. If he then sells the superiority, the purchaser's title will take the form of a Disposition of land. And if A, in conveying the superiority to the disponee, does not **again** reserve minerals, the Disposition will carry those minerals to the purchaser of the superiority. See 7.1.135 Orr v. Mitchell 20 R (HL) 27, although in the result in that case, from **other** evidence in the deed, the Court **held** that minerals were **not** carried.

Specialities.

(i) Splitting the superiority. The owner of *dominium utile* may divide it into any number of smaller portions and dispose of each separately. **But** a superior may not dispose of the *dominium directum* in such a way that, in the result, one vassal acquires two or more separate superiors.

(ii) Interjection of a superiority. Where a superior has granted a Feu Charter in favour of a vassal, he cannot so manipulate his estate of superiority so as to introduce a mid-superior between himself and his vassal, thus removing the vassal one stage further from the Crown.

The superior in the Charter **may** reserve special power to do either of (i) or (ii), but this is now rare.

(iii) Mixed Estates. Where the owner of a landed estate has feued off portions of it, he still retains intact his original title to the **whole** estate on the principles already explained; but his beneficial interest in part of the estate is limited to *dominium directum* only. He can dispose of his whole remaining interest, both *dominium directum* and *dominium utile,* by a single conveyance of the **whole** landed estate which will effectively transfer both the estate of superiority **and** the *dominium utile* so far as retained. It is unnecessary in such cases to have a separate Disposition of *dominium directum* and a separate Disposition of the remaining *dominium utile.* See Ceres School Board above.

Infeftment of Disponee.

There are no specialities. The disponee requires infeftment, his title being a title to land, and he obtains it by recording the Disposition with Warrant of Registration.

Extinction of the Feudal Relationship.

In modern practice, it very rarely happens that a **superiority** is extinguished. All defeasible mid-superiorities, which were at one time temporarily created by the use of the alternative holding, have now been extinguished by the 1874 Act S.4. Tinsel, or forfeiture, of the superiority is obsolete, as a result of the 1874 Act S.4. Relinquishment of the superiority by the superior into the hands of his vassal, authorised by the 1868 Act S.110, has, rarely (if ever) been used in practice.

But the estate of *dominium utile* is frequently extinguished, by merger with the superiority title, the effect being, in substance and in feudal theory, to disburden the superiority title thereof. This happens in two situations, viz.:

(i) By Irritation of the feu. See Chapter 3.2.

(ii) By Consolidation. Where the same person in the same capacity becomes debtor and creditor in the same obligation, the obligation is automatically extinguished *confusione.* Originally, *confusio* applied to the relationship of superior and vassal; so that, if the superior acquired the *dominium utile* on a separate title, that, of itself, disburdened the superiority title of the subaltern right created by the Charter in favour of the vassal.

But this no longer applies; see 7.1.143 Bald v. Buchanan 2 RLC 210. Instead, where the two separate estates of superior and vassal vest in the same person, they remain separate and distinct. There is no automatic merging or extinction of the subaltern right; and accordingly the superior, having acquired the *dominium utile,* can later dispose of it on the original title, by Disposition; or, retaining the *dominium utile,* can dispose of the superiority as a separate feudal estate.

If the *dominium directum* and the *dominium utile,* as two separate feudal estates, are to merge so as to form a single feudal estate, a further step is required, termed consolidation, which is the legal reunion of two separate, but adjacent, fees in the same land. The effect of consolidation is to restore the estate of *dominium utile* to the superior and to merge it in the superiority title. See and compare 7.1.147 Zetland v. Glover Incorporation 8 M (HL) 144 per Lord Westbury, who maintains that the *dominium utile* is **not** totally extinguished; and contra, L.P. Inglis in 7.1.145 Park's Curator 8 M 671 at p.675 who takes the view that the effect is to extinguish and destroy the *dominium utile.* It follows that, on consolidation, there is, thereafter, only one feudal estate and only one title, namely, the superiority title which (including the destination, if any, therein) thereafter controls the subsequent devolution of the estate.

Consolidation can be effected in three ways.

1. **Resignation ad perpetuam remanentiam (or resignation ad rem).** This is the original feudal method, the vassal surrendering, or resigning, the feu into the hands of the superior. In contrast with resignation *in favorem,* which was a temporary and conditional resignation, resignation *ad rem* implies a permanent and unqualified surrender of the *dominium utile* into the hands of the superior. It was effected either by a Procuratory of Resignation granted by the vassal; or by a Disposition granted by the vassal in favour of the superior, containing, in place of the usual feudal clauses, a Procuratory of Resignation. Since 1858, this clause has been replaced by a short statutory clause 'And I resign the lands and others above disponed *ad perpetuam remanentiam'* which is inserted immediately after the clause of entry in an ordinary form of Disposition.

This method is still available (1924 Act S.11(2)). The superior must be **infeft** in the *dominium directum,* and the Disposition, containing the clause of resignation *ad rem,* must be recorded. There is then immediate consolidation of the two estates.

2. **Minute of Consolidation.** This is a statutory simplification, in two forms, under 1874 Act S.6 and 1924 Act S.11.

By 1874 Act S.6, where one proprietor is infeft in two adjacent feudal estates, he may record a Minute of Consolidation (1874 Act Schedule C) which, when recorded, consolidates the two estates, to the same effect as if consolidation had been effected by Disposition containing the clause of resignation *ad remanentiam.*

By the 1924 Act S.11(1) where an infeft superior acquires the *dominium utile,* he may endorse a Minute of Consolidation on the Disposition of *dominium utile* in his favour before that Disposition is recorded; and on the subsequent recording of the Disposition, with endorsed Minute, the *dominium utile* is consolidated with the superiority, to the same effect as if a separate Minute of Consolidation had been recorded under the 1874 Act S.6. The endorsed Minute can also be used, with the same effect, where an infeft vassal acquires the *dominium directum.*

3. **Prescription.** Since the case of Bald v. Buchanan, *supra,* the mere acquisition by the same person of the two feudal estates of superiority and *dominium utile*

does not, **of itself,** operate an immediate consolidation. **But,** where the same proprietor continues to own both feudal estates for the prescriptive period, it is **presumed** that he has possessed the two estates on the superiority title and that, by prescription, the *dominium utile* is consolidated with the superiority thereof.

The foregoing rules apply not only to consolidation of *dominium utile* with the immediate superiority; but also to consolidation of a mid-superiority with the immediate superiority thereof.

The foregoing rules may suffer some qualification where:

(a) The superiority title is **not** (as is normal) a title to lands, but is merely a title to a 'superiority' or 'estate of *dominium directum*'. Or

(b) The superiority title is entailed.

Since both these situations are now extremely rare, they are not further dealt with here. See further Burns' Handbook pp. 221 and 222.

7.2 Involuntary Transmissions — Statutory Titles.
Reading List 7.2.

The real right is the foundation of ownership; and it is of the essence of the real right that it is secure against challenge from all comers.

In heritage, the real right depends upon infeftment. And, as we have seen, infeftment proceeds upon a Mandate for infeftment, followed by registration of the appropriate writ in the Register of Sasines.

At common law, if the real right is to transmit *inter vivos,* it can only do so on a Mandate for infeftment actively granted by the infeft proprietor which must take the form of a special conveyance (Feu Charter or Disposition) by the infeft proprietor; or, at least, a general disposition by him which satisfies the minimum requirements of the 1874 Act S.27 in that it contains a word or words importing a conveyance or transference or a present intention to convey. Nothing less will operate as a Mandate for infeftment to a transferee.

But this general rule is subject to certain qualifications. In the first place, in certain circumstances, the Courts will intervene to give effect to personal or equitable claims affecting the real right vested in an infeft proprietor. In the second place, by Statute, certain bodies, especially Local Authorities and certain Ministers, are given powers of compulsory expropriation in the national interest, in the exercise of which, failing co-operation by the infeft proprietor, the Acquiring Authority can obtain a valid title under statutory procedure.

1. **Adjudication in Implement.** Walker Chapter 5.17 page 330.

The infeft proprietor may, in various ways, voluntarily undertake obligations which affect his real right in heritage, and may create valid and enforceable personal claims at the instance of some other party. Normally, the infeft proprietor implements such obligations by granting an appropriate title in favour of the grantee; but, if he declines to grant the appropriate title, then the grantee may invoke the assistance of the Courts to supply, by decree, the want of a voluntary Mandate for the infeftment of the grantee without which the infeft proprietor cannot be divested and the grantee cannot perfect his real right.

The appropriate process is adjudication in implement, a form of diligence under which a person in right of land, or for whose benefit a debtor has agreed to grant heritable security, may obtain a title to land or security over land.

Suppose that A, infeft, and beneficially entitled to a heritable property, enters into a contract (valid in point of form and content) to sell his heritage to B. In terms of such a contract, A undertakes to convey the heritage to B, but the contract does not contain 'any other word or words importing conveyance or transference, or present intention to convey or transfer'. Accordingly, while it confers on B a valid and enforceable right to the heritable property, it does not *per se* operate as a title, nor as a Mandate for the infeftment of B. In the ordinary way, following on such a contract, A will convey the property to B. But suppose he declines to do so. B may then raise an action of adjudication in implement against A for implement of the contract of Sale and Purchase, and the decree supplies the want of the conveyance by A to B, and operates in lieu thereof.

The Extract Decree operates as a title, and may be recorded direct in the GRS to complete the adjudger's infeftment, or used, unrecorded, as a link in title. In a competition, the date of preference is the date of recording of the Extract Decree, not the date of the Decree itself. (1868 Act SS.62 and 129, as amended by the 1874 SS.62 and 65).

2. Adjudication for Debt. Walker Chapter 5.17 page 327.

The whole of a man's estate, both heritable and moveable, is liable for payment of his whole debts. As we have seen, a secured debt creates a preference for the creditor at the date of the security; and such creditors obtain, *ab initio,* a nexus on the security subjects and powers of enforcement by e.g. sale. The unsecured creditor has no equivalent, *ab initio;* but can later acquire rights equivalent to those enjoyed by the secured creditor through the process of adjudication for debt. This takes two forms, adjudication for payment and adjudication in security. This type of adjudication differs from adjudication in implement in that the intention here is, **not** to confer an **absolute** title on the creditor, but rather to **secure payment** for the creditor out of the heritable property adjudged to him.

(a) **Adjudication for payment.** This process is competent to a creditor holding a **liquid** document of debt, e.g. a Personal Bond or a Decree for Payment.

Decree, when obtained, is recordable in Sasines; and operates as a judicial conveyance to the creditor of the heritable property adjudged, for payment of the debt, but subject to a power of redemption at the instance of the debtor at any time within ten years of Decree. This ten-year period is the period of redemption, otherwise known as the 'legal'. In the result, the creditor's title under an adjudication for payment is initially a redeemable title, whereas under adjudication in implement the pursuer's title is immediately indefeasible. And at any time within the legal, the creditor can be forced to denude in favour of the debtor if he receives payment of his claim in full. In the result, the creditor has a mere security only, which he cannot convert into cash to liquidate his debt for at least ten years.

(b) **Adjudication in security.** This is competent (but now unknown) where there is no liquid document of debt, in special circumstances only. It differs from adjudication for payment in that there is no 'legal' and the right of redemption persists indefinitely.

3. Bankruptcy and Sequestration — Walker — Chapter 10.1.

Adjudication for debt, although still competent, is rare in modern practice. Instead, it is usual for the estate of the debtor to be sequestrated for the general benefit of the whole body of creditors. Procedure is regulated by the Bankruptcy (Scotland) Act 1913. Sequestration follows on a Petition to the Court, by the debtor or by a creditor, for the appointment of a Trustee to whom the whole of the debtor's estate is transferred. The Trustee holds and administers the estate in trust for the general body of creditors.

For the purposes of title, the Act and Warrant of the Court, confirming the appointment of the Trustee, transfers the whole property of the debtor, heritable and moveable, to the Trustee absolutely and irredeemably as at the date of sequestration; but only so far as belonging beneficially to the debtor.

The Act and Warrant operates as a **general** disposition in favour of the Trustee on which he may (if he wishes) complete title; but not by recording of the Act and Warrant *de plano.* He will normally complete title immediately in order to exclude the possibility of some other party acquiring a valid real right. Thus, if the debtor, prior to sequestration, has granted a Standard Security which has not been recorded at the date of sequestration; and, if, thereafter, the creditor records it **before** the Trustee completes title, the creditor will be secured. Completion of title by the Trustee excludes that possibility.

The Act and Warrant also vests in the Trustee property later acquired by the debtor after the date of sequestration; but in addition, the Trustee **must** obtain a Vesting Order from the Court and **must** record the same in the Register of Sasines within one month of the date thereof. 1924 Act S.44(4)(b) & Sch. O.

Heritable Creditors.

The Bankruptcy (Scotland) Act 1913 also makes detailed provision for the conflict of interest between the Trustee in sequestration and heritable creditors, and confers certain powers, in SS. 108 to 116. Sequestration does not in any way invalidate existing heritable securities nor deprive the creditor thereunder of his powers. Thus, a heritable creditor can sell under the power of sale; the Trustee **may** concur to fortify the title: S.108.

Alternatively, if a secured creditor concurs, the Trustee can sell in his own name. The creditor's consent clears the Record of his own and all postponed securities: S.109. Note that, in this case, *pari passu* creditors are **not** discharged.

If the general body of creditors so resolve, the Trustee alone may sell; and may prevent a heritable creditor from proceeding under his power of sale: S.110. But the price, in this case, must be sufficient to pay off the secured creditor in full, thus fully protecting his interest.

Under the foregoing Sections, the Trustee must sell by public roup. He may, alternatively, sell by private bargain with consent of a majority of creditors, the heritable creditor, and the Accountant of Court.

Under S.116, any creditor may purchase any asset sold at a public roup.

The 1970 Act makes no changes to the foregoing.

Recording of Abbreviate in the Personal Register.

In addition, there are provisions for registration of an abbreviate in the Personal Register dealt with in Chapter 7.4.

4. Reduction — Walker Chapter 8.1 page 267.

A real right in land is secure from challenge against all comers. But the real right only has this characteristic of invulnerability if it has proceeded on, and been constituted in virtue of, a valid antecedent title, or series of titles. As we have seen, the title or series of titles on which the real right is based must be probative writing(s); and one characteristic of a probative writ is that, *prima facie,* it is valid and enforceable according to its terms. This does **not** mean, however, that a probative writing is automatically exempt from challenge. It may be challenged on a variety of grounds including e.g. want of capacity, error, fraud, force, or defect in the solemnity of execution; but the onus of establishing any such latent defect in a probative writ lies on the challenger and not on the person acquiring right thereunder, whose interest is to sustain the writ.

Suppose, then, that A, is infeft in a heritable property as beneficial owner but is insane. He executes a Disposition thereof to B. Any Deed by a person, insane, is invalid from want of capacity; but the Deed may be *ex facie* valid. Suppose this deed is. B records it in Sasines and apparently perfects his real right thereby; and takes possession. A *curator bonis* is then appointed to A. How does the curator recover the property from B as ostensible owner? He must raise an action of reduction against B, the disponee, seeking to have the Disposition to B reduced.

The onus lies on A's curator to establish and prove that A, at the date when the Disposition was executed, was insane; but if he satisfies the Court on this point, then, notwithstanding the apparent probative quality of the Disposition by A, the Court will then grant Decree of Reduction, the effect of which is to avoid and invalidate the Disposition; with the further consequence that all titles following on, and deriving their validity through, that Disposition are also reduced and rendered wholly invalid. In other words, the title to the heritable property in question is restored, by reduction, to the state it was in immediately prior to the granting of the invalid Disposition by A.

Note the difference in effect between a Decree of Reduction and a Decree of Adjudication; the latter operates as an active title, equivalent to a Disposition, in favour of the pursuer. A Decree of Reduction has a purely negative effect, invalidating existing writs.

It follows from what has been said that every heritable title in Scotland is, theoretically, open to challenge at any time on the grounds that any one of the progress of titles is invalidated by a latent defect of the kind described above. In practice, Actions of Reduction affecting heritable titles are rare; and this risk is one which a person dealing with a heritable proprietor on an *ex facie* valid title must simply accept.

As a further protection to a purchaser dealing with a heritable proprietor on the faith of the Record, the 1924 Act S.46 provided that, where a deed, Decree or other writing recorded in Sasines (or forming an unrecorded mid-couple in a recorded title) has been reduced by Action of Reduction, the Extract Decree must be recorded in the General Register of Sasines; and further that the Decree is not pleadable against a third party who has *bona fide* onerously acquired a right to the heritage in question prior to the recording of the Decree in Sasines.

The intention of this Section is, obviously, to extend and enhance the security of a recorded title in a question with *bona fide* purchasers for value. This evident intention, however, has been limited by the decision in 7.2.8 Mulhearn v. Dunlop 1929 SLT 59 where the Court **held** that the Section, in its terms, protected a *bona fide* purchaser acquiring the disputed subjects, but **only** during the short period between the granting of the Decree and the recording of that Decree; the Section did not protect a purchaser who acquired the heritage in question prior to the date of granting of the Decree.

So, in the A - B case above, B (the disponee of the insane A) sells the property to X, a *bona fide* purchaser, who believes the Disposition A - B is valid and records a Disposition B - X before A's curator is appointed. The curator is thereafter appointed and raises an action of reduction to invalidate the 2 dispositions and obtains Decree. X loses the property; but could claim against B under warrandice.

1970 Act S.41.

S.41 introduces a novel provision in regard to discharges of heritable securities. Prior to this Act, if a Bond had been discharged at any time within the last **twenty** years, it was still necessary to examine the Bond, its transmissions, and discharge(s), for intrinsic and extrinsic validity. When the Bond was discharged, say, eighteen years ago, this was patently rather a waste of time. S.41 provides that, where (before or after the passing of the Act) a Discharge has been duly recorded more than **five** years previously, the subsequent reduction of that Discharge (because, presumably, it was improperly granted) is not to affect the title of a *bona fide* purchaser for value; and the 1924 Act S.46 ceases to apply to that Decree of Reduction.

5. Appointment of Trustees, Judicial Factors, etc.

This is another case where, on the application of an interested party, the Court will intervene to appoint a new Trustee on a pre-existing Trust, where for some reason or other the existing Trust machinery has broken down; or to appoint a Judicial Factor to take over and/or administer an estate on behalf of an incapax, missing, or unknown, proprietor. In such cases, the Decree of the Court **either** operates as a feudal conveyance in favour of the Trustee or Factor so appointed, in virtue of which he can make up title to the Trust heritage; **or** it operates as a Judicial Power of Attorney, entitling the Factor to deal with heritable estate in name of an incapax ward. See Chap. 1.4.

6. **Compulsory Purchase** — Walker Chapter 5.17 page 322.

In any developing industrial society, the individual's right of property in land must yield to the over-riding needs and interests of society as a whole. Otherwise, if the individual right of property in land is to be paramount, then any individual owner, by declining to co-operate, can frustrate all manner of developments, typically, railways, canals, trunk roads, water and sewage. Of course, many land owners appreciate this need and are willing to co-operate, when required, in disposing of land to the appropriate authority by agreement. But inevitably there will be cases where, for one reason or another, the landed proprietor cannot or will not co-operate; and to meet these cases it is necessary for the State or certain public bodies to have powers of expropriation, subject always to payment of the appropriate compensation. What we are concerned with here is the effect, in outline, *quoad* title, of the exercise by an appropriate authority of powers of compulsory acquisition of land.

In the exercise of such powers, there are two elements to consider, namely, the **conferment**, by Statute, of the actual power to acquire; and, secondly, the procedure regulating the **exercise** of the power, to prevent oppression and injustice, including regulations for payment of compensation.

Prior to 1845, both elements were normally conferred together on the Acquiring Authority by a single Act of Parliament especially passed for the purpose. But in all such cases the **procedure** became more or less standard; and accordingly, to avoid the necessity of repeating at length, in each separate Act of Parliament conferring **power** to acquire, provisions as to **procedure,** an Act was passed in 1845 known as the Lands Clauses Consolidation (Scotland) Act 1845, which contained a detailed and elaborate procedural code to be adopted in any future Act of Parliament conferring power of compulsory acquisition on an Acquiring Authority, where that was considered appropriate. The Lands Clauses Act has been subsequently modified, and the statutory procedure expanded by later Acts, principally the Acquisition of Land (Authorisation Procedure) (Scotland) Act 1947, the Town and Country Planning (Scotland) Act 1972 and the Land Compensation (Scotland) Acts 1963 and 1973. In England, its equivalent has been repealed, but in substance re-enacted, by the Compulsory Purchase Act 1965, as amended by the Acquisition of Land Act 1981. This does **not** extend to Scotland and, so far, there is no Scottish equivalent; subject to these modifications, the Lands Clauses Act of 1845 still applies.

From the point of view of heritable title only, compulsory acquisition of land implies, in the final analysis, the divesting of an individual heritable proprietor, infeft or otherwise, and the investing of the Acquiring Authority on a feudal title, or its equivalent. This, of course, can always be achieved by conventional means where the proprietor is willing and able to co-operate and where, by arrangement, he conveys his heritage to the Acquiring Authority. In practice, this very commonly happens. But in the majority of cases, the Acquiring Authority urgently requires land for its development and, in practice, it will put in train the compulsory purchase machinery, even although it later acquires land by conventional titles, with a view to the ultimate acquisition, if necessary, of land by compulsory purchase.

The commonest cases of compulsory purchase in modern practice are by a Local Authority for roads and housing purposes.

There are two different procedures, under which the Acquiring Authority can obtain a Statutory Title to heritage in Scotland, though initially the procedures are similar — Acquisition of Land (Authorisation Procedure) (Scotland) Act 1947.

In outline, (and ignoring altogether specialties of which there are any number) both procedures commence in the following form:

(i) **Compulsory Purchase Order.** The Acquiring Authority makes an Order, known as a Compulsory Purchase Order, specifying the land to be acquired, which is published by advertisement and served on owners and lessees. Individual owners are given an opportunity to object, and objections may be followed by a public inquiry. None of this has any effect *quoad* title.

(ii) **Confirmation.** The Compulsory Purchase Order must be confirmed by the Secretary of State (or other confirming Authority). Confirmation must be advertised and affected persons notified, and only then does the Order become final. This has still no effect, *quoad* title.

Thereafter the procedures differ and are dealt with separately:

1. **Ordinary procedure under the Lands Clauses Act, as amended.**

(i) Notice to Treat. This is a Notice, served by the Acquiring Authority on the individual heritable proprietor, intimating the intention to acquire compulsorily and, when served in accordance with the statutory procedure, has the effect of creating a notional binding Contract of Sale and Purchase of heritage between the owner and the Acquiring Authority under which the owner has agreed to sell his land to the Acquiring Authority, and is bound thereafter to convey it in implement of that Agreement, as under any normal Contract of Sale and Purchase. The purchase price is represented by compensation, computed in accordance with statutory formulae. After serving the Notice to Treat, the Acquiring Authority may take possession of the subjects, on 14 days' written notice, under the Acquisition of Land (Authorisation Procedure) (Scotland) Act 1947 Second Schedule para. 3.(1).

(ii) Following on the Notice to Treat, the proprietor may convey the land to the Acquiring Authority, in which case the Conveyance may take one of two forms, namely, a statutory form, as prescribed in Schedules to the Lands Clauses Act, which is known as a Schedule Conveyance; or a Common Law (or conventional) Conveyance such as any heritable proprietor grants in favour of any ordinary purchaser.

Where the title takes the form of a Schedule Conveyance, the effect is not altogether clear; but it has been authoritatively stated that, on the recording of the Schedule Conveyance within the 60-day time limit stipulated in the Act, the Acquiring Authority creates for itself a statutory tenure which extinguishes the relationship of superior and vassal, and in effect renders the property allodial. See 7.2.13. — Heriot's Trust v. Caledonian Railway Co. 1915 3C(HL)52.

Where the Acquiring Authority takes a Common Law (or conventional) Conveyance, it acquires a feudal title just as any individual disponee would do.

(iii) If the proprietor, having been served with Notice to Treat, declines to convey, whether by conventional or Schedule Conveyance, the Acquiring Authority is statutorily empowered to record a Notarial Instrument at its own hand, which, by Statute, has the same effect as the recording of a Schedule Conveyance.

(iv) Where the subjects compulsorily acquired, on a Schedule Conveyance or Notarial Instrument duly recorded under the foregoing procedure, are subject to servitudes, or other real conditions, such servitudes or conditions are extinguished; or, at least, cease to be enforceable in a question with the Acquiring Authority.

2. General Vesting Declarations — The Town and Country Planning (Scotland) Act 1972, S.278 and Sch. 24.

When a Compulsory Purchase Order has come into operation, i.e. after the statutory procedure for compulsory purchase has run its course, the Acquiring Authority may execute a General Vesting Declaration. It must contain a particular description or a description by reference of the land to be acquired. The intention to make a General Vesting Declaration must be published in the Press not less than two months before the vesting declaration is actually made and this is usually done in conjunction with the advertisement of the confirmation of the Order. Immediately on executing the Declaration the Acquiring Authority must intimate its terms to every owner and occupier (except short term tenants) having an interest in the affected land. (paras. 1 - 4).

On the expiry of a period to be specified in the Declaration (at least 28 days) then:

i) the Lands Clauses Act 1845 (those parts adopted by Schedule 24 of the 1972 Act) and the Land Compensation (Scotland) Act 1963 apply as if Notice to Treat had been served on each owner and occupier; and

ii) the land described in the Declaration, and the right to take possession thereof, vests in the Acquiring Authority subject only to short tenancies. Notice to short tenants is required.

The Declaration is to be recorded in the G.R.S.; and thereupon has the same effect as a Schedule Conveyance duly recorded under S.80 of the 1845 Act.

On completion of compulsory purchase, all servitudes and other like rights over the land acquired are extinguished. (Town and Country Planning (Scotland) Act 1972, S.108).

7.3 Transmission on Death and Completion of Title
Reading List 7.3.

We are not here concerned with the substantive rules which determine the beneficial entitlement to property, heritable or moveable, on the death, testate or intestate, of the proprietor thereof. These rules have already been dealt with in Scots Law. What we are concerned with here is the technical machinery by which the person beneficially entitled, on testacy or intestacy, acquires a title and perfects his real right to heritable property passing to him from his deceased ancestor and to which he has succeeded as a beneficiary on the death of the previous proprietor.

Position before the 1964 Act.

Prior to the 1964 Act, there was a fundamental difference in procedure, particularly noticeable on intestacy, between the transmission of heritage on death and the transmission of moveables.

At common law, heritage never transmitted to the executor **as such.** On **intestacy,** heritage transmitted directly to the heir-at-law as the person beneficially entitled, subject to his pursuing the appropriate procedure and procuring the appropriate title. After 1868 and under the 1868 Act S.20, if the deceased died **testate,** heritage passed directly under his will to the beneficiaries or trustees, without any administrative procedure. The will itself operated as their title, as **general disponees.**

In practice, the Trustees appointed by will were normally appointed Executors Nominate as well, and, as Executors, confirmed to and administered the moveable estate; but, *quoad* heritage, Confirmation was unnecessary and inappropriate.

The procedure for making up title differed substantially depending on whether the deceased was intestate, or testate; on whether or not the title contained a special destination; and in the case of intestacy, on whether the deceased was infeft or uninfeft.

1. **Intestacy.** This implied that, in the deceased's title, the destination was to the deceased and 'his heirs and assignees whomsoever', being a general destination.

The procedure which the heir-at-law followed depended on various factors which can best be illustrated by an example. Suppose that A was the original ancestor deceased and intestate. B was the eldest son and therefore, under the old rules, his heir-at-law. C was B's eldest son, and therefore, also under the old rules, B's heir-at-law.

(i) **Assume that A died infeft.** Three alternative courses were open to B, the heir, in whom, by survivance alone, the right to A's heritable estate vested. These alternatives were:

(a) **Special Service.** This was available **only** where the deceased died infeft. B, the heir, presented a Petition for Special Service in the Sheriff Court, describing the property, referring to the burdens, and averring his relationship to the deceased A, to establish his claim as heir-at-law. 1868 Act SS26 - 46.

Decree was equivalent to a special disposition granted by A in favour of B (1868 Act S. 46) and, as such, could be recorded direct (with Warrant of Registration) in the Register of Sasines.

If B died before he had recorded the Special Service Decree, the benefit of the Decree transmitted to his representatives; and the Decree could be used by them as if it were a special but unrecorded Disposition (1868 Act S.46).

(b) **General Service.** Again, B petitioned in the Sheriff Court, but the Petition for General Service did not describe or refer to any specific property. Hence 'General' as opposed to 'Special' Service.

Decree was equivalent to a general Disposition by A in favour of B (1874 Act S.31). The Decree was not recordable in the Register of Sasines, since it contained no identifying description, and indeed no reference to any heritable estate at all; but, as a general Disposition, it was a valid mid-couple, allowing B to take infeftment by recording a Notice of Title, using the General Service Decree as a link. If B did not take infeftment, the benefit of the Decree transmitted to his representatives as if it were a general Disposition in his favour. (1874 Act S. 31).

(c) **Writ of clare constat.** This was the original feudal method — a charter by progress from the Superior renewing the investiture for the benefit of the heir. It was available **only** where the deceased A was infeft. Being in the form of a Charter, containing a description, it was a mandate for infeftment by *de plano* recording. But, if B did not take infeftment thereunder, the benefit of the writ died with him and did not transmit to his representatives.

(ii) **Assume that A died uninfeft.** The only procedure available to B was General Service, Decree having the effect already described above — 1874 Act S.31.

(iii) **Assume that after A's death, B then died with only a personal right.** By 1874 Act S.9, a personal right to A's heritage vested indefeasibly in B the heir, simply by his survivance, without further procedure. If B died, without having obtained a Decree of Service nor having recorded a writ of *clare constat* he had a personal right but no title. B's personal **right** transmitted to his representatives automatically on B's death; and they acquired **title** to A's heritage by a Petition for Authority to complete title, under the 1874 Act S.10.

2. Special Destinations.

Walker Chapter 7.4 page 208 e.s.

Any conveyance of land, e.g. Charter, Disposition, or Heritable Security, may contain a special, as opposed to a general, destination directing the devolution of the property on the death of the initial disponee along a particular line of devolution. e.g. 'to A., and on his death to B, and on B's death to C'; or 'to A and B and the survivor of them'.

The special destination raises problems, particularly:

(a) as to revocability;

(b) if revocable, as to whether or not it has been revoked by some other testamentary writing, e.g. a Will; and

(c) as to completion of title thereunder.

Normally, such destinations are revocable, except for:

(i) contractual destinations, and

(ii) survivorship destinations in gifts.

Failing revocation, the destination still determines the **beneficial** succession; but, since the 1964 Act, apart from special cases, it has ceased to have any effect **quoad** title.

In fact, since 1868, the use of such destinations is increasingly less common because of the facilities provided by the 1868 Act S.20 with reference to Wills; and, with the exception of destinations to husband and wife and survivor, they are rarely met with in practice.

Terms used in Destinations.

A special destination may take the form of a conveyance to a series of named persons, one succeeding to the other, which was rare; or it may restrict the line of devolution by reference to derivative terms, which was common; or it may take the form of a survivorship destination. In the second case, quite a number of terms were used in practice and acquired technical legal meanings, e.g., heir male of the body, etc.

But, whatever form the destination took, all destinations have this in common, that they are embodied in a *de praesenti* conveyance of heritage to a series of persons who take in succession. The person first called in this conveyance was known as the institute; any person called to take in succession to the institute was known as a substitute.

The effect of destinations on the rights of the parties.

In the ordinary case, where the destination in a Disposition takes a simple and typical form, e.g. 'to A and on his death to B', both parties being named and being strangers *inter se,* A is the institute, being the disponee **first** called. When the Disposition is delivered to A, he becomes the immediate and absolute proprietor, in fee, of the subjects thereby conveyed. The Disposition is a mandate for A's infeftment by direct recording in the GRS. The presence, in his title, of the destination-over to B does not in any way detract from, or affect, his unfettered and unqualified right, as absolute proprietor, to dispose of the property by *inter vivos* or *mortis causa* deed, onerously or gratuitously. Any such *inter vivos* disposal by the institute evacuates the destination and wholly defeats the rights of the substitute B; and B has no subsequent claim either on the property itself, nor on the proceeds of sale if A has disposed of it for a consideration.

A also has unfettered power of *mortis causa* disposal which, again, evacuates the destination and defeats the rights of B, provided:

i) that the destination is revocable; and

ii) that A observes certain rules as to revocation of the destination.

But, if A dies without effectively evacuating the destination, then B, the substitute, takes in preference to A's representatives or heirs whomsoever.

As to the foregoing provisos:

i) Revocability.

Where the proprietor of heritage dispones it gratuitously to a disponee or several disponees, the disponer or donor is entitled to dictate the terms of any special destination. Alternatively, in an onerous Conveyance, it is the disponee who dictates the terms of the destination.

Obviously where there are two (or more) disponees who are jointly putting up the price they can, together, dictate the terms of the destination in the Conveyance; and where they **agree** to a special destination (e.g. to A and B **and the survivor)** then, because they are jointly contributing, the element of survivorship introduced into the destination would be held to be a matter of contract between A and B.

Any provision as to devolution of property, taking effect on death, is normally revocable; but a party may competently contract to make a Testamentary Disposition in certain terms, and the contract is enforceable. The net result is that, where a special destination is contractual, the parties to the destination are deprived of their right of *mortis causa* disposal; and cannot, by *mortis causa* deed, evacuate the destination. Their power of *inter vivos* disposal, onerously or gratuitously, is not affected. See Lord Mackay in 7.3.12 Brown's Trustee 1943 SC 488.

In fact, in modern practice, by far the commonest destination is the 'A and B and the survivor' case; and very often, these are in fact contractual, because the parties have jointly contributed. In the result, the only question which in the ordinary way now arises in regard to the interpretation of destinations is whether or not, by being contractual, they are irrevocable at the instance of one or other of the parties to the destination.

Thus, where there is a Disposition of heritable property to 'A and B and the survivor of them' recorded in the Register of Sasines with Warrant of Registration on behalf of A and B, the effect is to vest each of A and B with an immediate and indefeasible right to a one-half *pro indiviso* share of the subjects; and each of A and B is thereupon immediately entitled to dispose of that share *inter vivos*, gratuitously or for onerous consideration.

As to *mortis causa* disposal:

(i) Where the price was **jointly** contributed by A and B, then neither A nor B can by testamentary writing alter the survivorship destination or prevent the survivor from taking the predeceaser's one-half *pro indiviso* of the property. But this does not in any way interfere with the right to dispose *inter vivos* of the one-half *pro indiviso* of each party. See 7.3.11 Shand's Trustees 1966 SC 178.

(ii) Where the price was contributed solely by A, then A can alter the survivorship destination *quoad* his one-half *pro indiviso* of the property. B cannot, by *mortis causa* deed, alter the survivorship destination *quoad* his one-half *pro indiviso* of the property. But either A or B may dispose *inter vivos* of his one-half *pro indiviso*, thus, in effect, evacuating the destination. 7.3.12 Brown's Trs. 1943 SC488.

(iii) Where the subjects were donated by X to A and B and the survivor, then **neither** A nor B can alter the **survivorship** destination by *mortis causa* deed. But again, either can dispose *inter vivos* of his one-half *pro indiviso*: Brown's Trs. supra.

Express additional provisions
The express terms of the destination or express provisions in the deed containing it may modify these rules and further restrict the rights of co-disponees. See Burns' Practice p. 371/2 for some illustrative styles which set out the rights of co-disponees explicitly, and it is thought would receive effect. Burns, however, makes no attempt in these styles to modify or take away the right of the co-owner to dispose of his *pro indiviso* share *inter vivos*. He deals with *mortis causa* disposal only. And it is arguable that, on principle, the *pro indiviso* owner must have this *inter vivos* right.

But see 7.3.13 Munro v. Munro & Another 1972 SLT (Sh.Ct.) 6 where the Sheriff goes further. In this case, heritage had been disponed by a father to his three children, under an arrangement between all parties, the full nature of which is not disclosed in the report. The disposition was in favour of the father in liferent, and the three children equally between them and to the survivors and the last survivor of them, and the heirs of the last survivor in fee. This was followed by an express declaration that none of them might revoke, alter or affect the destination to the last survivor. The Sheriff held that, in the circumstances, the destination created a right of joint ownershiip, and not of common or *pro indiviso* property. Hence, apparently no one of the three children had any *pro indiviso* share which he could deal with *inter vivos* or *mortis causa.* He quotes, with approval, L.P. Cooper in 4.1.21 Mags. of Banff v. Ruthin Castle 1944 SC 36 to the effect that joint property can only exist where the plural disponees are interrelated by virtue of some trust, or contractual or quasi-contractual bond (e.g. partnership), so as to create an **independent** relationship. The Sheriff doubts if this independent relationship is created in this case by the disposition alone; but he finds sufficient in the **surrounding circumstances** to justify his view. 'It is a reasonable **inference** that the common thought was that each child ... should, throughout his life, have the opportunity to live in or return to the family home ... There was, **on my understanding,** a pre-existing agreement to keep the family home open for each of them during their respective lives, and the destination was conceived with this in mind.' If so, why not so provide in the deed; or confer a conjunct fee and liferent? As a result of the terms of the very special arrangement in this case, express and implied, it would seem as if the three children were in effect Trustees under a self-imposed trust for themselves and the survivors in conjunct liferent and the last survivor in fee, and this quasi trust provided joint, not common, ownership.

For a full discussion of the effect of such a destination in various circumstances see 7.3.10 Hay's Trustee 1951 SC 329, and for a criticism of the decision in Munro, see a recent article in 1985 SLT (News) 57.

ii) **Evacuation.** This has been dealt with in detail in Succession. For the modern rule as to evacuation of a destination, see Succession (Scotland) Act 1964 S.30. The **old** rule was that, where the destination was not created by the deceased himself, any Will, earlier or later in date, revoked the destination. Where the deceased himself had been responsible for creating the destination, a Will later in date than the destination **might** revoke it; but only if the two were patently incompatible *inter se.* Otherwise, destination and Will both received effect as the joint testamentary instruction of the deceased.

Now, by S.30 **any** Will executed after 10th September, 1964, revokes a special destination only if it refers to it and **expressly** revokes it. Otherwise, the destination stands.

See 7.3.16 Stirling's Trs. 1977 SLT 229 — No express Clause — no revocation.

Completion of Title under Destinations.

Where the deceased's title contained a Special Destination, not revoked at the death, the property passed, not to the heir-at-law, but to the 'heir of provision' under the special destination.

He in turn required a title which he obtained by serving as heir of provision, in Special or in General, to the deceased institute or substitute.

The Decree of Service, Special or General, had exactly the same effect for the heir of provision as a Decree of Service in favour of the heir-at-law, i.e. it operated as his title. If the Decree were Special, he could record it *de plano*; if General he could complete title by Notice of Title.

In either case, the benefit transmitted to his successors.

Survivorship Destinations. These represent a technical speciality. A Disposition to A and B and to the survivor operates as an immediate *de praesenti* conveyance of one-half *pro indiviso* of the property to each of A and B as institutes, coupled with a substitution of the survivor of them to succeed, as substitute, to the one-half *pro indiviso* vested originally in the predeceaser. Therefore, on the recording of a Disposition to A and B and the survivor, with the Warrant of Registration on behalf of A and B, each becomes infeft in one-half of the property *pro indiviso* and the mandate for infeftment is wholly exhausted.

If B predeceases survived by A, then (in the absence of revocation by B) A takes B's original one-half of the property as substitute; he is therefore heir of provision *quoad* B's one-half. Therefore, you might expect that A would have to serve as heir of provision to B in B's one-half. But, in the case of survivorship destinations, the strict rule was not applied and, in the illustration, A, as survivor, did not require to serve or to carry through any other procedure in order to make up title to B's one-half share. By mere survivance, following on a survivorship destination, A as survivor is vested and infeft in the share of the predeceaser.

3. Testate Succession

The Common Law rule prior to 1868 was that any Disposition, Special or General, *inter vivos* or *mortis causa,* to be effective had to take the form of an immediate *de praesenti* conveyance containing appropriate clauses and, in particular, had to include the magic word dispone. Further, every such conveyance, to be effective, had to be probative according to the strict Scottish rule.

So far as *mortis causa* deeds are concerned, this rule was altered by the 1868 Act S.20, the effect of which was that:

(a) if the **apparent** intention was to bequeath heritage; and
(b) if the Will, in its form, was appropriate to carry moveables; and
(c) if the will was validly executed;

it operated as an effective title to heritable property belonging to the deceased, and was equivalent to a General Disposition.

Thus, any will which referred to 'estate' or 'property, heritable or moveable' or which used other words indicating an intention to deal both with heritage and moveables, and which carried evidence of testamentary intention, was sufficient to carry heritage even although it lacked any form of *de praesenti* or even *mortis causa* conveyance.

It was important, however, to distinguish between three different forms of Will, viz.:

(i) a Will containing an express conveyance to Trustees which they could use as their title but which did not operate as a direct title to the beneficiary;

(ii) a conveyance directly to a beneficiary or beneficiaries, with or without appointment of Trustees, which could be used by the beneficiaries as a direct title to the heritable property, bypassing (as it were) the Trustees or Executors; and

(iii) a Will containing a conveyance to beneficiaries coupled with an appointment of Trustees. In this case, to allow the Trustees to take up the heritage and administer the Estate in preference to the beneficiary or testamentary disponee, the 1874 Act S.46 applied; and specially empowered Trustees, under this form of Will, to make up title and then to deal with the heritable estate as if the Will had contained a conveyance in their favour.

In any of these cases, the general disponee, (Trustee or beneficiary) could use the Will as a General Disposition in his or their favour and complete title by Notice of Title regardless of the state of the ancestor's title — infeft or uninfeft. Alternatively, the Will could be used as an unrecorded mid-couple or link in title for the purpose of deduction of title under the 1924 Act S.3.

By the 1874 Act S.29, any two or more such deeds may validly be used, together, as links in title when deducing title.

The Succession (Scotland) Act 1964.

The 1964 Act S.14 makes two complementary and very important innovations so far as *mortis causa* title to heritage is concerned, viz.:

(i) The Section extends to heritage rules previously applicable only to a moveable succession. At Common Law, the only person who can make up title to the moveable estate on the death is the Executor duly confirmed; and this rule is now applied to heritable property, with limited qualifications as noted below.

(ii) For purposes of administration, heritage **vests** in the Executor, provided always that he has duly confirmed thereto as required by this section but not otherwise.

Confirmation as a title to heritage.

In relation to heritage, the 1964 Act SS.14(2) and 15(1) provide that an Executor is not to be taken as having duly confirmed to heritable property **unless** a description of that heritable property is included in the Confirmation in accordance with the provisions of the appropriate Act of Sederunt. By Act of Sederunt of 17th May, 1966, (Confirmation of Executors Amendment), the requisite description is such a description 'as will be sufficient to identify the property or interest therein as a separate item in the deceased person's estate', i.e. (normally) the postal address. A formal 'conveyancing' description is clearly **not** required.

Assuming the Executor has duly confirmed to heritage belonging to the deceased, the nature and quality of the title conferred on the Executor by Confirmation is defined in S.15. This Section proceeds by applying to heritage generally the limited provisions of the 1924 Act S.5 which applied only to heritable securities where moveable in the succession. The necessary amendments to 1924 S.5 are contained in the 1964 Act S.15 and Schedule 2. The result is that, under the 1924 Act S.5(2)(a), as amended, where the proprietor of any estate in land, which vests in an Executor under the 1964 Act S.14, has died, whether infeft or uninfeft or with or without a recorded title, whether testate or intestate, Confirmation in favour of the Executor which includes the appropriate description shall **of itself** be a valid title to such estate in land. Such Confirmation is also a valid mid-couple for any deduction of title, but is **not** recordable in the General Register of Sasines.

It is not clear from these provisions whether Confirmation is intended to be the **only** effective title to heritage under these provisions. Provided it includes the appropriate description, Confirmation is in itself a valid title equivalent to a general disposition in favour of the Executors; and it is certainly arguable that no other title can competently be used. But the Professors of Conveyancing, in an Opinion delivered in April 1965, took the view that Testamentary Trustees and Executors could use the Will as an alternative link-in-title; and two of them took the view that a legatee could also so use the Will where it contained a direct bequest of heritage in his favour.

The amendment to the 1924 Act S.5(2)(a) also affects Probates and Letters of Administration. But with this difference, that under the 1924 Act S.5(2)(b), Probate or Letters of Administration were deemed to include heritable securities, without actually containing these items; in fact, a Probate cannot 'contain' any items since it carries no Inventory. The intention, obviously, is to make Probate and Letters of Administration valid links in title to Scottish heritage vested in a deceased of English domicile; but some doubt arose as to whether the 1964 Act S.15 in fact accomplished this.

This difficulty is now resolved by the Law Reform (Miscellaneous Provisions) (Scotland) Act 1968 S.19 which provides that S.15(1) of the 1964 Act shall have effect, 'and be deemed always to have had effect', as if it had read —

'provided that a Confirmation (other than an implied Confirmation within the meaning of the said Section 5(2)) shall not be deemed, for the purposes of the said Section 5(2) to include any such interest unless a description of the property ... is included or referred to in the Confirmation'.

This made it perfectly clear that a resealed Probate, etc., operated as a valid link without containing any description or identification of the subjects.

Further, under the Administration of Estates Act 1971, English and Northern Ireland Probates, etc., no longer require to be resealed, but operate automatically as titles to Scottish land without resealing.

Special Destinations and Entails. Special administrative provisions are made by the 1964 Act SS.18, 30 and 36 (2). The effect of S.30 has been noticed already.

Prior to the 1964 Act, there were two peculiar features of heritable destinations. Firstly, such destinations might or might not be revocable. If revocable, and if effectively revoked, the destination was of no effect *quoad* title and instead the property passed to the trustees or legatee under the Will of the deceased. If irrevocable or if not in fact revoked, then on the death of the person in right of the property for the time being, the right of property passed under the destination, but the deed containing the destination did not of itself operate as a title to the successor, except in the case of survivorships. With that exception, the substitute required a new mandate for infeftment which he obtained by service as heir of provision.

By the combined effect of the 1964 Act SS.18 and 36, the administrative position post-1964 is as follows:

(i) If a special destination in the title has been effectively revoked by the deceased, the property is part of his estate and vests in his Executor as if it had been held on a general destination.

(ii) If the special destination has **not** been effectively revoked, then the heritable property does not form part of the deceased's estate. The beneficial interest in the property passes to the substitute next called in the destination. As to title:

(a) if the substitute requires a title (as he does in all cases except in the case of survivorship destinations) the heritable property vests in the Executor by virtue of Confirmation thereto, but only for the limited purpose of enabling the Executor to convey the property to the substitute next called in the destination (cf. resignation *in favorem*).

(b) if the substitute does not require a title, as in the case of survivorship destinations, then the property does not vest in the Executor at all, and he cannot competently confirm thereto. Even if he does confirm, the Confirmation in this case is **not** an effective title.

Similarly, under the 1964 Act S.18(1), all entailed property vests in the Executor by Confirmation but only for the purpose of conveying it to the next heir of entail.

Subsequent transactions by the Executor with heritable property.
There are three possible situations following on a death, viz.:

(i) The Executor is to retain the heritage to which he has confirmed; typically, in a continuing Trust. In this case, the Confirmation is his title. He can use the

Confirmation to expede a Notice of Title and thereby take infeftment as Executor; but he is not obliged to take infeftment; and, instead, can hold the property on the Confirmation as uninfeft proprietor in trust.

He cannot record the Confirmation *de plano* in the Register of Sasines with a view to completing his title.

(ii) The property is to be transferred to a beneficiary. A new and useful shortcut is provided here by the 1964 Act S.15(2). Under the old rule, prior to 1964, where the whole estate was conveyed to trustees with a direction to the trustees to make over heritage to a particular beneficiary, the Will was the trustees' link in title but they then had to grant a formal Disposition in favour of the beneficiary. Now, under the 1964 Act, any such transfer can be effected to a testamentary beneficiary, to a statutory successor, or to a surviving spouse or child claiming legal rights by endorsing a short docquet on the Confirmation (or on a Certificate of Confirmation). A short statutory form of docquet is given in Schedule 1 to the Act. Any such docquet, so endorsed, may be specified as a mid-couple or link in title in any deduction of title, but is not recordable in the Register of Sasines with a view to completing the beneficiary's title.

This procedure is optional, in that it still remains competent to transfer heritage to a beneficiary by Disposition, etc., as before.

(iii) The property is to be sold by the Executor. Confirmation is his title. He may complete title using it as a link or he may dispone as uninfeft proprietor, using the 1924 Act S.3. He **cannot** use a docquet on the Confirmation to give a title to a purchaser.

Protection of Purchasers.

Under the old rules, prior to the 1964 Act where a man died testate, leaving a Will dealing with heritage, a purchaser from the trustees under that Will, or from a legatee, had to satisfy himself that the Will was intrinsically and extrinsically valid and that the seller had a valid title thereunder to sell the property to him. Further, prior to the Trusts Act 1961, in the case of trustees, it was necessary to consider whether trustees had power to sell. If it later turned out that the Will, as a title, was defective in any respect, or if the trustees (prior to 1961) did not have the requisite power, then in any of these events the purchaser's title might later be reduced on the grounds of any such defect. Similarly, when a man died intestate and his heir had served as heir-at-law in special or in general, the Service Decree could nonetheless be reduced within the twenty-year period following thereon, on the grounds that the wrong heir had been served.

As a result, a purchaser only took a title from the deceased's representatives, whether testate or intestate, after careful enquiry into the title; but he was bound to accept the risk of reduction on these grounds. See 7.3.4. Sibbald's Heirs v. Harris 1947 SC 601.

Under the 1964 Act, Confirmation for the first time becomes a title to heritable property. But, as with any other forms of title, Confirmation is open to reduction on a variety of grounds, e.g. that the Will was improbative or otherwise invalid because of want of capacity, fraud, revocation, etc.; or, in the case of a Confirmation-dative, on the grounds that the wrong person had been confirmed, (cf. wrong person served as heir).

Were it not for the provisions of the 1964 Act S.17 then, where a death occurred on or after 10th September, 1964, a purchaser or other person dealing with the title would require to consider the terms of the Will, or the terms of the Petition on which Confirmation proceeded, and the validity and propriety of endorsed docquets, etc. or dispositions to beneficiaries etc. (S.17 is **not** confined to docquets). All such enquiry is rendered unnecessary by the 1964 Act S.17, in the circumstances therein envisaged. The Section provides that, where any person has in good faith and for value, acquired title to an estate in land which has vested in an Executor by Confirmation thereto, whether such person takes his title directly from the Executor or from a person deriving title directly from the Executor, the title so acquired is not open to challenge on the grounds that the Confirmation was reducible or has in fact been reduced; nor can the title be challenged on the grounds that the property has been **conveyed,** by the Executor, to the wrong beneficiary (by docquet or disposition).

The General Disposition as a link-in-title other than on death.

Before considering the completion of title of trustees and executors following on a death, it is convenient here to deal with certain cases where a general disposition may operate as a link-in-title otherwise than on death.

1. Trusts.

(i) **Deed of** Trust. We have noticed already the situation both pre- and post- 1964 where a Will or Trust Disposition and Settlement operates as a direct conveyance of heritage by the deceased to his trustees. Since 1964, Confirmation is the recommended alternative title, but, nonetheless, in the opinion of the Professors of Conveyancing, the Will itself can still be used as a valid link, being a general disposition.

In exactly the same way, although less commonly, a heritable proprietor can grant a general disposition of his whole estate to operate *inter vivos,* e.g. a Trust Deed for Creditors, or, possibly, a general disposition of his whole estate for *inter vivos* trust purposes. But, normally, when setting up an *inter vivos* trust, specific assets are conveyed by special conveyance, rather than by way of a general disposition of the whole estate.

In all these cases, however, where there is a general disposition conveying heritage, the constituent deed operates as the link-in-title to the trustees.

Alternatively, in the case of Wills, it was and is possible for the deceased to convey his estate directly to the beneficiary and the view of two of the Professors is that, in that situation, the Will operates as a valid link. But because of the doubts expressed in the Professors' Opinion, it is now undesirable in any circumstances to use the Will as a link for a beneficiary post-1964. Notwithstanding the direct conveyance to a beneficiary of heritage in a Will, under the 1964 Act the Executors or trustees have power to confirm to that heritage and, if they so confirm, it vests in them and the Confirmation is their title.

(ii) **Deed of Assumption and Conveyance.** The Trustees acting under any Trust, *inter vivos* or *mortis causa,* normally have power to assume new Trustees by virtue of the Trusts (Scotland) Act 1921 S.3; and, under the Act, executors-nominate have the like power. But, in addition to the appointment of new Trustees, the new Trustees will require a **title** to the Trust Assets. The appropriate Deed is, therefore, a combined Deed of Assumption, operating as an appointment of the new Trustees, and Conveyance, operating as a general disposition of the Trust assets in favour of the new Trustees.

It is technically competent, in a Deed of Assumption and Conveyance, to incorporate a special conveyance of heritage, but this is now never done. As a result, the Deed of Assumption and Conveyance operates as a general disposition in favour of the new Trustees and can be used as a link in their title.

In *inter vivos* deeds, the truster may reserve, or may have by implication, a power to appoint new Trustees. Having divested himself of his assets which are invested in the original Trustees, the truster has no power to give a title to new Trustees appointed by him. Thus, by *inter vivos* Deed of Trust, A appoints B and C to act as Trustees and conveys certain heritable estate to them. B and C both then die. A, the truster, then appoints X as Trustee but cannot give X a title. In that situation, X could obtain a title to the Trust Assets from the executors of C, the last surviving Trustee, if they confirm to the Trust Estate, under the Executors (Scotland) Act 1900 S.6 — See below.

The same applies in unusual cases where some third party has the power to nominate new Trustees. This does not give him power to confer a **title** on the new Trustees.

(iii) **Resignation or removal of a Trustee.** A Trustee or Executor-nominate normally has power to resign office, by a Minute of Resignation. This effectively divests the Trustee of his interest in the Trust assets, including heritage, which devolve on the continuing Trustees without the necessity of any conveyance or other transfer by the resigning Trustee — See the Trusts (Scotland) Act 1921 S.20. Nonetheless, it is the custom to include a Minute of Resignation in any narration of links-in-title in a clause of deduction of title, etc. — see below.

Alternatively, in certain situations, the Court may remove a Trustee — see 1921 Act S.23. Removal has exactly the same effect as resignation, and the Decree of Removal would normally be included in the links-in-title.

(iv) **Lapsed Trusts.** If all Trustees on an existing Trust have died, new Trustees must be **appointed** to continue the administration; and in all such cases, the new Trustees will also require a title. The new Trustees appointed in a lapsed Trust may derive their **title** in the following ways:

(a) **1921 Act S.22.**

Where no one has power to appoint new Trustees, e.g. typically, in a testamentary case, where all the Trustees have died without assuming any new ones, then the Court may appoint Trustees under the 1921 Act S.22. In terms of that Section, the Decree appointing the new Trustees had to include a warrant authorising them to complete title; but this requirement as to warrant in the Decree has been removed by the 1938 Act S.1. In the result, a Decree of Appointment, standing alone, operates as a general disposition in favour of the new Trustees appointed thereunder.

(b) **1921 Act S.24**

As an alternative, in the case of certain lapsed Trusts, to avoid the necessity of appointing new Trustees, it is competent for beneficiaries, where the administration in the Trust is complete, to petition the Court for authority to allow the beneficiaries to make up title to the Trust Estate. The situation here envisaged is that A has died leaving a Will in favour of a Trustee B and directing B to make over the residue of his estate to X, Y and Z. B administers the estate but dies before the assets are actually made over; but, at the death, nothing remains to be done except making over the assets. X, Y and Z could then petition the Court for authority to complete title thereto. In such cases, under S.24 of the 1921

Act, the Decree in favour of the beneficiaries operates as a general disposition in their favour.

(c) Where the deceased and the last surviving trustee died before 10th September, 1964, the Executors (Scotland) Act 1900 SS.6 and 7 did not apply — see below for the effect of these provisions. Instead, it was competent, pre-1964, for the heir-at-law of the last surviving trustee to serve as heir-in-trust, either by virtue of express provision in the Deed of Trust itself or under the 1874 Act S.43. In such cases, the heir so serving did so simply for the purpose of providing a **title** to heritage in the lapsed Trust, which he would then convey to new Trustees appointed, by one mode or other, to continue the administration, or directly to the beneficiary absolutely entitled.

This device is still regularly used in cases where the title to property has been taken in name of the partners of, and trustees for, a firm where all the partners have died **before the 1964 Act.** To make up title now to that partnership property, the heir-at-law of the last surviving trustee can serve so as to provide a title for the benefit of the present partners.

Service as heir-in-trust was not available where the Truster died before, but the last Trustee died after, 10th September, 1964, simply because the 1964 Act did not so provide — See Browning 1976 SLT (Sh.Ct.) 87. The procedure has been revived for an heir of provision, (but not for an heir-at-law under the 1874 Act S.43) by the Law Reform (Miscellaneous Pensions) (Scotland) Act 1980 S.6.

(d) If the deceased died after 10th September, 1964, then new Trustees may be appointed by the Court; or title can be made up through the medium of the Executors of the last surviving trustee under the Executors (Scotland) Act 1900 SS. 6 or 7.

Take the case where A died infeft in a heritable property after 10/9/64, testate or intestate.

B confirms as A's Executor and includes A's heritage in the Confirmation, which therefore vests in B as Executor by virtue of Confirmation thereto. Normally, B will deal with A's heritage either by selling it or passing it on to A's successors, by disposition or 1964 Act S.15 docquet. But suppose he fails to do so and then dies. The title to A's heritage lapses on B's death and has to be revived.

The 1921 Act S.22 or S.24 may be invoked — see above.

Alternatively:

i) **Executors (Scotland) Act 1900 S.6.** B's Executor, nominate or dative, if he is willing so to do, may include A's heritable estate, in the Inventory of B's estate, and so in B's confirmation, under a special heading of Estate held in Trust. See Currie on Confirmation 7th Edition Chapter 16 for full details. Such Confirmation allows B's Executor to transfer A's unadministered heritage either:

a) To new Trustees appointed in A's estate; or

b) To A's successors;

but does not confer any further power of administration on B's Executor.

ii) **Executors (Scotland) Act 1900 S.7**

If S.6 procedure is not practicable, anyone interested in A's estate may petition the Sheriff for appointment of an Executor-dative *ad non executa* who, when appointed, may confirm to A's unadministered heritage. The Confirmation *ad non executa* is a valid title; and the Executor *ad non executa* has full power to administer.

2. Judicial Factors.

The Decree appointing a Judicial Factor, prior to the 1938 Act, had to contain a Warrant authorising the Judicial Factor to complete title to the estate coming under his charge as Factor. However, this is no longer necessary by virtue of the 1938 Act S.1, in terms of which any Decree appointing a Factor operates as a general disposition in his favour of all heritable estate coming under his charge. It can, therefore, be used as a link-in-title for the purpose of dealing with that estate.

3. Trustee in Sequestration.

In the case of the Trustee in Sequestration, the Decree appointing him, (the Act and Warrant) vests all the estate of the bankrupt in the Trustee under the Bankruptcy (Scotland) Act 1913 S.97. Accordingly, the Act and Warrant is a general disposition in favour of the Trustee, and can be used as such when dealing with the bankrupt's heritage. There is no obligation on the Trustee to complete his title by recording a Notice of Title; but normally he will do so in order to exclude possible competing titles or securities. In that case, he will use the Notice of Title — see below.

Where, after the date of sequestration, the bankrupt acquires right to other estate, e.g. as a beneficiary under the Will of a deceased testator, this estate also vests in the Trustee in Sequestration automatically by virtue of his original appointment; but, in this case, in addition, the Trustee in Sequestration is obliged to record a Memorandum in the Register of Sasines in the form of Schedule O to the 1924 Act under the 1924 Act S.44(4)(b).

Completion of Title and Infeftment Following thereon.

No real right in land can be created without infeftment; and infeftment implies:
i) written title;
ii) entry with the superior (now implied under the 1874 Act S.4 on the recording of the appropriate title without the necessity for any special feudal clauses); and
iii) registration in the Register of Sasines of an Instrument of Sasine, under the 1617 Act.

Until 1858, in the case of land, (1847 in the case of heritable securities, where the change was made rather earlier) the Instrument of Sasine was the only writ which could competently be recorded; and, in particular, a Feu Charter or Disposition could not itself be recorded in Sasines. This was because, until 1858, symbolic delivery, actual or notional, was an essential element in the creation of the real right; and the only competent evidence that symbolic delivery had taken place was the Instrument of Sasine. Accordingly, the Instrument of Sasine, in addition to defining the subjects and the person procuring infeftment therein, also narrated the Warrant or Warrants on which Sasine proceeded and the act of Sasine.

Under the Titles Act of 1858, the whole notion of Sasine, and the Precept of Sasine, were both abolished; and the special conveyance (Feu Charter or Disposition) became, for the first time, recordable direct in the Register of Sasines for procuring infeftment in the person of the disponee thereunder. As a result, the Instrument of Sasine became redundant; and, in any event, in its old form, was no longer appropriate since it narrated, *inter alia,* the Precept of Sasine and the act of Sasine, which had ceased to be legal requirements.

This major change in the procedure for procuring infeftment created no special problem, where the title took the form of a special, recordable conveyance, (other than problems dealt with by the introduction of the Warrant of Registration — see Chapter 2.8.). In the great majority of cases pre-1868, the title did take this form. But, even before 1858, a general Disposition might, in certain circumstances, form a valid link-in-title. A conveyance of land may operate as a **general** (as opposed to a **special**) Disposition where, *inter alia,* it contains no particularised description, but merely a description in general terms; but one of the essential pre-requisites for registration of the writ in Sasines is that the writ to be so registered takes the form of a special conveyance, containing an identifying description.

After the 1868 and 1874 Acts, it became very much more common in practice for a person to have the right to land under a general, as opposed to a special, Disposition. Such a general Disposition was, undoubtedly, a valid title, but was not of itself recordable *de plano* for the procuring of infeftment. Such cases arose in the following, typical, situations:

(i) Under the 1868 Act S.20, which validated Wills generally as links-in-title. Such Wills were normally in the form of a general Disposition either to Trustees or to a beneficiary direct.

(ii) Under the 1874 Act S.31, which introduced general service (as opposed to special service) as a competent title to the estate of an intestate, who had died infeft; and equated such a Decree to a general disposition.

(iii) Because of the increasing use of Trusts, with a consequent increase in Deeds of Assumption and Conveyance and Minutes of Resignation, not containing any description of the Trust Heritage.

(iv) In the case of heritable securities, because such securities became moveable estate under the 1868 Act, (in the great majority of cases) with a consequent increase in cases where Confirmation, as a general Disposition, operated as a link-in-title, not of itself recordable.

Clearly, to meet cases of this kind which frequently arise in practice, there must be some machinery whereby a person in right of land under a general Disposition, (or its equivalent) can put his title on Record, and so procure himself infeft.

Such provision was duly made, in an elaborate form, in the 1858 Act by the introduction, under that Act, of a new writ, known as the Notarial Instrument. These provisions were re-enacted and extended by the 1868 Act, in particular SS.17, 19, 23, 25 and 125-128. The Notarial Instrument in turn, and to a large extent the foregoing provisions, have been superseded in practice by the 1924 Act.SS.4-6 and the Notice of Title, introduced under the 1924 Act. But the effect of the Notice of Title is equated, under the 1924 Act, to the effect of a Notarial Instrument; and it is therefore necessary in the first place, to look briefly at the 1868 provisions.

The main provisions, in the 1868 Act. relating to completion of title to land, are SS. 17, 19, 23 and 25. SS.125 to 128 deal with heritable securities.

Speaking generally, the Notarial Instrument is a semi-official narrative under the hand of a Notary Public but is a narrative only, simply setting out certain facts, or purported facts, which have been brought to the attention of the Notary. It is **not** an operative deed and does **not** of itself create or confer rights. It merely serves as a necessary and conveneient vehicle for transporting a personal, (or unfeudalised), title to land onto the Record, so as to convert that personal title into a real right, and procure infeftment. On this aspect of the effect of the Notarial

Instrument, see Kerr's Trustees v. Yeaman's Trustees 15 R 520 (the Opinion of Lord Rutherford Clark; ignore the other judgements) and Sutherland v. Garrity 1941 SC196.

In addition to procuring an infeftment for the person on whose behalf the Notarial Instrument is expede and recorded, the Instrument may also have the effect of converting personal and unsecured burdens contained in unrecorded links, such as a Will, into a real burden on the subjects to which the Notarial Instrument relates. See 2.5.41 Cowie v. Muirden 20 R(HL)81, where a testator, in his Will, conveyed his whole estate, heritable and moveable, in general terms to his son B, declaring, in the dispositive clause of that general Disposition, that it was granted *inter alia* under burden of an annuity in favour of the testator's daughter C; and the annuity was declared to be a real burden on the heritage conveyed to B. B, as general disponee, completed title to his father's heritage by recording a Notarial Instrument which, *inter alia,* narrated the above declaration as to the real burden in favour of C. The Court held that the annuity was validly constituted as a real burden on the land; and accordingly that, on the recording of the Notarial Instrument in this case, two real rights emerged, viz., B's real right to the **land** which had belonged to his father, and C's real right in security to the annuity as a **real burden** thereon. Contrast Mackenzie v. Clark 11 SLT 428 where, in similar circumstances, the Notarial Instrument failed to refer to the burden, and thus the annuitant was unsecured.

Notice of Title. In practice, the Notarial Instrument has been superseded, although not abolished, by the Notice of Title, introduced under the 1924 Act. The main purpose of the 1924 Act is simplification. In place of the numerous sections in the 1868 Act dealing, separately, with completion of title to land and to heritable securities, the use of the Notice of Title for completing title to land **and** securities in all circumstances is dealt with in one relatively simple section, S.4; and six forms of Notice of Title, two for land, two for heritable securities other than ground annuals, and two for ground annuals, are introduced, replacing all the various forms of Notarial Instrument under the earlier Acts.

Further, the Notice of Title may be signed by any law agent, not merely a Notary Public. Hence the change of name.

Section 4 provides: 'Any person having right either to land or to a heritable security by a title which has not been completed by being recorded in the appropriate Register of Sasines, may complete his title in manner following.'

Four separate situations are then dealt with under Sub-Sections (1), (2), (3) and (4); and the Section then concludes:

'And on such Notice of Title being recorded, as in this Section provided, the title of the person on whose behalf it is recorded shall be, in all respects, in the same position as if his title were completed as at the date of such recording by Notarial Instrument in the appropriate form duly expede and recorded according to the present law and practice.'

Generally speaking, there are three distinct categories of person who may be said to have a right to land, viz:

1. The infeft proprietor, having a recorded title. Clearly, the Section has no application in his case, because his title is already completed.

2. The uninfeft proprietor whose right is constituted by an active but unrecorded **title,** such as a special but unrecorded Disposition or, much more commonly, a general Disposition or its equivalent. The Notice of Title is available for any such disponee.

3. A purchaser under Missives or a beneficiary in a Trust, although undoubtedly having **right** to land, does not have right to land by **title**. A Contract is not a title, since it contains no words of conveyance. The Trust Deed is a title to the Trustees. It is not (normally) a title to the beneficiary, whose right is a *jus crediti* only, a mere *jus ad rem,* which entitles him to call on the Trustees to denude.

The 1924 Act S.4 makes no distinction between the case where the immediate predecessor in title of the person expeding the Notice was infeft, and the case where he was uninfeft. The procedure under this Section applies equally to either case. Thus A, infeft on a recorded special Disposition, died pre-1964, leaving a Will containing a general conveyance to B. B is a person in category 2 above, and might complete title to A's heritable property by Notice of Title. He is not **bound** to complete title. Suppose in fact, that he failed to do so. He died uninfeft, leaving a Will in favour of C. Again, C is a person in category 2, even although B was uninfeft; and C might complete title to the heritable estate originally belonging to A, again by Notice of Title under S.4.

The 1924 Act S.4(1) and (2) contain two alternative procedures for completing title to land; ('land' is defined in the 1924 Act S.2(1) to exclude securities, but otherwise having the definition assigned to it in the 1868 Act S.3 and 1874 Act S.3, which is very wide). S.4(1) deals with the normal case; S.4(2) provides an alternative for very special circumstances, and is rarely used.

S.4(3) and (4) make comparable alternative procedures available for completing title to heritable securities.

S.4(1) provides: 'A person having **such** right to land may complete a title thereto by recording in the appropriate Register of Sasines a Notice of Title in or as nearly as may be in the terms of form No. 1 of Schedule B to this Act, in which Notice of Title such person shall deduce his title from the person last infeft.'

'Deduction of Title' is defined in S.2(3) as implying the specification (in, *inter alia,* a Notice of Title) of the writ or series of writs (without narration of the contents thereof) by which the person expeding the Notice has acquired right from the person last infeft. In other words, however many unrecorded mid-couples may intervene between the person last infeft and the person now completing the title, the deduction of title starts with the last infeftment and then narrates all the intervening unrecorded links.

Broadly speaking, anything which operates as a **title** to land, *inter vivos* or *mortis causa,* may be used as a link in title in a Deduction of Title for this purpose; and even were this not implied, it is express in terms of the 1924 Act S.5(1) which defines the writs which can be used as links in this context as including any Statute, Conveyance, Decree, or other writing whereby a right to land is vested in, or transmitted to, any person. The definition of 'Conveyance' in the 1924 Act S.2(1)(c) is extremely wide; and the definitions of the same term in the 1868 Act S.3 and the 1874 Act S.3 are expressly adopted for the purpose of the 1924 Act by the 1924 Act S.2(1). The definition is extended to include, not only the principal writs themselves, but also Extracts and office copies, as defined in the 1924 Act S.2(2); for an equivalent provision in the case of Probates and Letters of Administration, see 1874 Act S.51 and 1887 Act S.5.

For an illustration of a Statute operating as a vesting writ for this purpose see the Local Government (Scotland) Act 1973 S.222 and the Local Authorities (Property, etc.) Order 1975 — S.I. 659. Under that Act and Order, heritable property, vested in the old Local Authorities, was transferred to and vested in the new Regional or District Authorities set up under the 1973 Act. But it has been made quite clear by the Law Society Conveyancing Committee and the Scottish Development Department that the combined effect of the Act and Order is simply to give the new Local Authorities a title equivalent to a general disposition. It does not create any infeftment for them. Therefore, when disponing land, the Local Authority must deduce title through the Act and Order.

Compare the Church of Scotland General Trustees Order Confirmation Act 1921 in terms of which property is transferred to the transferees thereunder to the same effect as if Dispositions had been granted **and recorded** in the appropriate Division of the General Register of Sasines. Obviously, in the latter case, the transferees are deemed to be infeft although having no recorded title.

The first form of statutory provision is common; the second is rare.

'Conveyance' includes any general **or** special disposition e.g. pre-1964, a Will, or post-1964 a Confirmation. Suppose A, infeft, grants a Feu Charter or Special Disposition to B. Normally, B completes title by recording the Charter or Disposition *de plano.* He may equally well, if he wishes, record a Notice of Title using the Feu Charter or Disposition as a link, though there is normally no point in so doing.

The normal form of Notice for completing title to land in Schedule B.1 is straightforward. In outline, its content is:

1. A narrative, defining the person expeding the Notice and having the right to the land.

2. A description of the subjects to which title is being made up.

3. Burdens. It is appropriate, in the Notice of Title, to refer to burdens in the usual way.

In addition, however, it may be necessary (although this is extremely rare) to set out at length in the Notice of Title the terms of any real burden or condition running with the land and contained in one of the unrecorded midcouples or links-in-title on which the Notice proceeds. Special provision is made for this in Sch.B.1, in terms of which, in addition to setting out the burden at full length, it is necessary to specify the writ in which the burden appears. See 2.5.41 Cowie v. Muirden 20 R(HL) 81.

4. Deduction of title. This is the clause which complies with the instruction in 1924 Act S.4.(1) to deduce title. It contains three essential elements, viz.

(a) Identification of the person last infeft, by name and designation. Note particularly that he must be **designed**.

(b) A specification of his infeftment. Only the minimum detail is required, normally the division of the Register and the date of the last recorded title.

(c) Deduction of title proper, being the specification of the writ, or writs, by which the person expeding the Notice acquired right from the person last infeft. There may be one, or several. Each writ must be separately specified, giving sufficient information to identify the writ, e.g. the type of writ, the party or parties, without designations, its date, and date of registration; but narration of the content of each writ is unnecessary.

5. Presentment of writs to the official. As already mentioned, under the 1924 Act, the Notice of Title may now be signed by any law agent, not merely a Notary Public. It is generally stated that the agent executing the Notice should have no direct interest therein; but it is quite unobjectionable for a solicitor to expede a

Notice on behalf of a client and this is regular practice. The clause simply states — 'Which last recorded title and subsequent writ(s) have been presented to me YZ (designed), Law Agent.'

The Notice is executed by the law agent, as a formal attested document, and the testing clause added in the usual way.

The writ is then sent to Register House for recording with the Warrant of Registration thereon endorsed and, on recording, the title of the person expeding Notice is completed in accordance with the statutory formula.

As already mentioned, the 1924 Act S.4(2) provides an alternative to S.4(1) for completing title to land in one very special set of circumstances, rarely encountered in practice. Before this alternative procedure can be used for completing title to the land, the following requirements must be satisfied:

(i) There must be in existence a special, but **unrecorded,** Conveyance by the person last infeft; in addition, there may, and usually will, be subsequent unrecorded mid-couples, such as a Will, etc.

(ii) The special but unrecorded Conveyance must be in such a form that it could have been recorded by the disponee thereunder, and, had it been so recorded, would have procured an infeftment for that disponee.

(iii) The special but unrecorded Conveyance is **now** to be recorded along with Notice of Title.

The typical case for which the 1924 Act S.4(2) makes this special provision arises in this way. A, infeft, grants a Feu Charter in favour of B who, before the Charter is recorded, dies, leaving a Will in favour of C. The Charter contains building and other conditions of title, including an obligation on the vassal to record the Charter *de plano,* which is not uncommon. But the Charter has not been recorded, in accordance with this clause, and cannot now be recorded *de plano* since the disponee, B, is dead. Under the 1868 Act S.142 a Conveyance can be recorded only during the lifetime of the grantee. How can C comply with the requirement of the Charter that it should enter the Record? The 1924 Act S.4(2) provides suitable machinery.

Under this alternative procedure, a Notice of Title is prepared in the form of Schedule B.2 to the Act, again executed by a law agent, and this is then recorded in the Register of Sasines, with Warrant of Registration, on behalf of the person expeding the Notice; **and,** along with the Notice, there is also recorded in Sasines the special but unrecorded Disposition, which is docquetted with reference to the Notice of Title form B.2.

The form B.2 differs radically from form B.1 in certain important respects:

(i) Description. All that is required in Form B.2 by way of description is a reference to the special Conveyance in these terms 'All and Whole the subjects disponed by the Disposition (or as the case may be) granted by CD (designed) to EF (designed) dated and recorded in the Division of the General Register of Sasines for the County of Angus **of even date herewith'**.

(ii) Burdens. No reference to burdens in Form B.2 is necessary, because that reference is already contained in the special Conveyance itself. Any burdens contained in any later, but unrecorded, Conveyance operating as a link or mid-couple must, of course, be set out in full. It is very unlikely that this will occur.

(iii) The specification of the last infeftment is not necessary, because the special Conveyance to be recorded along with this Notice is itself granted by, or at least must connect up with, an infeft proprietor.

(iv) The Deduction of Title and Presentment of Writs to the official are modified accordingly.

Otherwise, the general rules for Notice of Title B.1 apply.

Registration. As mentioned above, the Notice of Title B.2 is presented for registration **along with** the special but unrecorded Conveyance. The Warrant of Registration is endorsed on the Notice of Title, and is adapted to meet the special circumstances under Note 5 to Schedule F, in terms of which the Warrant will include a reference to the Disposition entering the Record along with this Notice. There is no Warrant of Registration on the special Conveyance; instead, the special Conveyance carries a docquet, also signed by the recording agent, in terms of Schedule B Note 7 which runs:

'Docquetted with reference to Notice of Title in favour of AB recorded of even date herewith. YZ (designation), Agent.'

The 1924 Act S.4(3) and (4) then make equivalent provision for an ordinary, and special-circumstances, procedure for completing title to a heritable security (or part thereof) which includes a Bond and Disposition in Security, pecuniary real burden, ground annual, and standard security.

S.4(3) applies to any heritable security **already recorded;** for that case, the form Schedule B.3 is the normal form (equivalent to B.1) for Securities other than ground annuals; form B.4 is used for ground annuals and differs from B.3 in that (as in the case of other forms dealing with ground annuals) B.4 contains a description.

S.4(4) applies to unrecorded securities. It provides for the recording thereof, along with the special form of Notice Forms B.5 or B.6, for Securities and ground annuals respectively; c.f. Form B.2 for land.

Finally, the 1924 Act S.6 provides that a Notice of Title expede in terms of the Act is equivalent to a Notarial Instrument expede according to the present law and practice. As a result, for practical purposes, the Notarial Instrument is superseded, although it can still competently be used.

Registration of Title

If the subjects lie in an operational area for Registration of Title, the Notice of Title is no longer used; and instead the uninfeft proprietor (in Category 2 above) simply applies to his Keeper to be registered as proprietor. See the 1979 Act S.3(6).

Deeds by Uninfeft Proprietors.

As a general feudal principle, a Mandate for Infeftment can originate only from a proprietor who is himself infeft; and the same general rule applied also to dealings with heritable securities.

The old rule has now been altered, but with limitations, under 3 different provisions:

(i) **Continuity of Trust Infeftment — 1868 Act S.26 and 1874 Act S.45.** Both these provisions refer to Trusts; and the object is to render unnecessary completion of title of new, in the case of a Trust, on the occasion of the assumption of a new Trustee. The 1868 provision applies only to religious and educational Trusts, where the title to Trust heritage has been taken in the name of office bearers or Trustees for behoof of the Association, and their successors in office. The 1874 provision applies to any Trust, but only where the office of Trustee is conferred upon the holder of that office *ex officio* (or on the proprietor of an estate) and his successors in office (or estate).

In these limited circumstances, when the Trustees have taken an original infeftment, then, notwithstanding subsequent changes in the body of Trustees, there is notionally a deemed continuity of infeftment; and the present Trustees for the time being, (as successors in the office under the 1868 provision, or as the holder of the office or owner of the estate for the time being under the 1874 provision) are **deemed** to be infeft, even although there is no title on the Record in their name. This is a useful, but very limited, provision. It is particularly appropriate in the case of Churches and other similar Associations.

(ii) **Disposition etc. by person uninfeft.** 1924 Act S.3. This is a statutory short-cut available in **all** cases, (not merely in the case of Trusts) to any person having right to land or to a heritable security whose title thereto has not been completed by being recorded in the Register of Sasines. Compare S.4 and **note** the similarity in wording. In other words, the short-cut is available to a person in category 2 of the three categories referred to in the context of the 1924 Act S.4 above, who holds an active title in his favour which is of itself a Mandate for infeftment by expeding a Notice of Title.

In the case of such a person, the Section provides:

(a) In the case of **land,** that the person entitled may grant a **Disposition** (which is interpreted as including a special Disposition, but **not** a Feu Charter or a Bond and Disposition in Security or Lease); if, in such Disposition, he deduces his title from the person last infeft, by incorporating, in the Disposition, a clause of deduction of title in terms of Schedule A (1) then, on such Disposition being recorded, the title of the disponee is in all respects in the same position as if, at the date of recording of the Disposition, the disponee had completed title by recording a Notarial Instrument. Put shortly, an uninfeft proprietor can now dispone provided he deduces title; the Disposition then becomes a Mandate for the infeftment of the disponee by *de plano* recording.

The only significant difference between a Disposition by an **un**infeft proprietor and a Disposition by an **in**feft proprietor is the incorporation of the clause of deduction of title in terms of Schedule A(1); and this clause is identical in form to the clause of deduction of title in a Notice of Title.

(b) In the case of a **heritable security** duly constituted as a real burden on land by having been recorded in the Register of Sasines, the creditor for the time being in right thereof may deal with that security by way of Assignation, Restriction or Discharge, without first completing title, provided, again, that in such Assignation, Deed of Restriction or Discharge, the uninfeft creditor deduces title in terms of Note 2 to Schedule K to the Act, and two alternative methods of deduction of title were provided for dealings with heritable securities.

This provision is further amended by the 1970 Act S.47 and Schedules 10 and 11. The effect of this amendment is that, where the granter of the assignation etc. has a recorded title, no further specification or deduction is necessary. Where the granter has no recorded title, he deduces title from the last recorded title to the security.

Again, under the 1924 Act S.3 when the assignee, etc., records the Assignation containing this Deduction of Title, his title is in all respects in the same position as if he had completed it by Notarial Instrument under the pre-1924 rules.

The same rules applying to dealings with Standard Securities under the 1970 Act.

As a result of this provision, the Notice of Title is far less common than its predecessor, the Notarial Instrument. But completion of title by way of Notice of Title is still commonplace; for one thing, it is generally accepted that you cannot have an effective Feu Charter or Lease, unless the granter is infeft. For another thing, if property is to be retained indefinitely, it may be prudent to complete title for reasons later to be examined.

(iii) **Standard Securities.** (1970 Act S.12) Heritable Securities (not being **dispositions** under 1924 Act S.3) could not be granted by the uninfeft proprietor; but the 1970 Act S.12 allows an uninfeft proprietor to grant a Standard Security, thus: S.12(1) ... 'a standard security may be granted over an interest in land by a person having right to that interest but whose title thereto has not been completed by being duly recorded' provided he deduces title; Notes 2 & 3 of Schedule 2 provide the style of deduction. Note 2 deals with the normal case where A, as uninfeft proprietor, is granting a Standard Security. He inserts a clause of deduction of title **identical** to 1924. Sch. A, **except** that, here, the person last infeft need **not** be designed.

Note 3 deals with the case where the granter has right as proprietor to the reversion of subjects held under *ex facie* absolute disposition. A similar clause of deduction is used. Two cases are covered — (a) Where the granter of the *ex facie* absolute Disposition was himself originally infeft; and (b) where the granter was not originally infeft, but held on a personal title i.e. Category 2. **No** deduction of title is required in the commonest case, where the granter never had a title; but in that case he also assigns his reversionary right. (According to Halliday — 1970 Act 2nd Edition p. 108, he assigns the reversionary right in all three cases.)

The 1924 Act S.5 (Deduction of Title) is applied by S.12(3) to define midcouples or links-in-title.

Assignation of an unrecorded Special Conveyance.

As an exception to the general rule that, before dealing with land or heritable securities, the person in right thereof had to be infeft, it was always competent at Common Law for the person in right of a **special** Conveyance (e.g. Feu Charter or Disposition) who had **not** taken infeftment thereunder, to assign the benefit of that unrecorded Conveyance to an assignee, without himself becoming infeft. The same applied to a heritable security.

This procedure was still available until 29/11/70 under statutory sanction. The 1924 Act S.7 and Schedule C applied both to land and to heritable securities; but were rarely employed.

If the 1924 Act S.7 was used, then the first prerequisite was that there should be in existence a special Conveyance (Disposition, or Feu Charter, or equivalent) in favour of a disponee who might have recorded the same in the Register of Sasines *de plano* to complete his title; but that special Conveyance had not been recorded. The disponee thereunder might transmit his rights under that special Conveyance by assigning the same to an assignee who then came in place of the assignor as if he, in turn, had been the immediate disponee under the special Conveyance itself. Accordingly, this is again transmission of a right to land by way of substitution or delegation, but in the special circumstances outlined above

The 1924 Act S.7 introduced a new short form of Assignation, superseding the old pre-1858 Disposition and Assignation, for transmitting the benefit of a special but unrecorded Conveyance. The Assignation might either be endorsed on the special Conveyance which was being assigned; or it might be an entirely separate writ. Suitable forms of Assignation, endorsed and separate were provided. This situation rarely arose in practice because a special Disposition or Heritable Security would normally itself be immediately recorded. By recording, it ceased to be available as a mandate for infeftment and therefore could not be assigned as such.

Completion of Title.

Where a special but unrecorded Disposition has been assigned under the 1924 Act S.7, the subsequent infeftment of the assignee presented some complicated variations; See Burns' Handbook Ch.16 for detail.

The 1970 Act S.48 abolished the use of this simple procedure and repealed the statutory provisions under which the short forms were made available. So the special assignation of an unrecorded Disposition is no longer competent. But note that only the **special** assignation is struck at. A special but unrecorded disposition etc., may still be assigned by a **general** disposition (e.g. a Will pre-1964) and often so passes. In that case, the grantee must either take infeftment by Notice of Title under the 1924 Act S.4; or use both the General Disposition and the Special but unrecorded Disposition as **un**recorded midcouples, when disponing as uninfeft proprietor under the 1924 Act S.3.

7.4. **Examination of Title.**

Reading List 7.4.

1. **Insurance.** 'The risk passes with the making of the Contract, though the seller remains liable for fault till delivery of possession'. Green's Encyclopaedia following the Latin brocard *periculum rei venditae nondum traditae est emptoris.*

See 7.1.27 Sloan's Dairies Ltd. 1979 SLT 17 — the purchaser acquires a *jus ad rem specificam* at the date of completion of the contract; his right of action is an action for delivery or *ad factum praestandum* and the risk of damage passes from seller to purchaser at the date of the contract.

So, the purchaser should insure the subjects of sale immediately on the completion of the bargain.

2. **Conditions in the Contract.** Certain general obligations in the Contract of Sale and Purchase are implied; several special conditions are often expressed. The first step in examining a title is to read the contract through from beginning to end; and to note all the special conditions and points to look for, when examining the title, e.g. is the feuduty allocated? what is the liability for roof repairs? etc.

3. **Proprietary Title.** The main point to establish is the validity and sufficiency of the seller's proprietary title, i.e. that he has the legal title and the beneficial right. For this purpose, the whole prescriptive progress of title must be carefully examined, starting with the foundation writ. But, for **this** purpose, nothing earlier than the foundation writ need be considered. The points to look for are:

(i) **Foundation Writ.** The quality of the foundation writ has been dealt with in Chapter 2.9. Under the Prescription and Limitation (Scotland) Act 1973, possession must be founded on and follow the recording of a deed sufficient **in its terms** to constitute a title to the interest in land (here — the **proprietary** interest). By such possession the validity of the title is put beyond challenge, except for forgery, or *ex facie* invalidity. Therefore, we are only concerned with the **intrinsic** validity of the foundation writ; extrinsic matters can be ignored. Assuming that the foundation writ is a Disposition, then the points to look for are:

Stamp Duty. The writ must be properly stamped, although insufficiency of Stamp Duty is not a bar to prescription. Where the foundation writ is a conveyance on sale, this simply involves an arithmetical check. In other cases, e.g. a Disposition carrying a 10/- or 50p. Stamp, the facts may vouch the sufficiency of the duty, but in some cases adjudication may be necessary.

Narrative. In a foundation writ, nothing in the narrative can affect the intrinsic validity. See 2.9.6. — Cooper Scott 1924 SC 309 — still relevant to post-1976 foundation titles.

Dispositive Clause. The points to check are:

The disponee and the destination: check this information against the next writ in the progress.

Description. Does this correspond exactly with the Contract; and does it correspond exactly with what the purchaser imagines he has purchased? In all but the simplest case, this requires a physical check on the ground with the client, possibly by a surveyor. Where the foundation writ contains a description by reference, check the description for intrinsic validity and also check the description in the prior writ referred to.

Reservations and Burdens. Note, for reference, all writs referred to for burdens, and note the content of any new reservations or burdens in this writ.

Remaining Clauses. Note any specialities but, in the ordinary case, nothing in the subordinate clauses could affect the **intrinsic** validity of the foundation writ.

Authentication. The writ must be probative.

The Warrant of Registration, and infeftment following thereon, must coincide with the dispositive clause.

(ii) **Subsequent Titles.** Each writ following the foundation writ must then be meticulously checked, whether recorded or not. In the case of each subsequent title, you are concerned with extrinsic as well as intrinsic validity. If the next writ in the progress is e.g. a Disposition granted by the disponee under the foundation writ, the points to check are:

Stamp Duty as above.

Granter. Does he connect up with the prior title?

Narrative. This must be scrutinised in detail and any material facts must be checked by reference to extrinsic sources.

Dispositive Clause. Check the disponee and destination. Check the description, make sure that it coincides with the foundation writ, or, if it differs, whether the differences are in order. Check the burdens clause and note the content of any new burdens. Check all the subordinate clauses, noting any specialities. In particular, check carefully any clause of deduction of title, and vouch it by reference to the links narrated therein.

Authentication, Warrant of Registration and subsequent infeftment will be checked as in the case of the foundation writ.

In addition, there may well be other points which are material in a writ within the progress, although not material in the case of the foundation writ. Typically, questions of capacity are significant, although they cannot affect the validity of a foundation writ. The same applies to e.g. powers of sale of trustees, and so on.

This meticulous check is then repeated for each subsequent writ in the progress down to and including the seller's own title.

If this examination discloses no defect in the title, then the seller has a valid proprietary legal title and the beneficial right.

4. **Burdens.** Establishing proprietary title in this way does not, however, mean that the title is unencumbered. There are two types of burden which may materially affect the property in the hands of the purchaser, viz.

(i) **Real conditions, running with the lands.** If real conditions have been constituted by writs within the progress, their content will already have been noted in the examination of the proprietary title. But, in addition, there may be valid subsisting burdens constituted by writs outwith the progress of titles. These will normally be referred to in the reference to writs for burdens; but a failure to refer to prior writs for burdens, even throughout the prescriptive period, does not extinguish conditions of tenure, although it may extinguish real burdens created by a Disposition; nor will it extinguish a *jus quaesitum tertio.* When considering real conditions affecting the title, the main points to look for are:

(a) **Building Conditions.** All building conditions and restrictions must be read carefully and you must consider whether any of the burdens, being of an unusual or unexpected nature, is objectionable in terms of the Contract (see above under Marketable Title); or is contrary to express contractual provision. Normally, building conditions fall into three categories which are:

i) Conditions *ad factum praestandum.* These include, typically, an obligation to build a house, to enclose and to make up roads, all within a time limit. Failure to comply incurs an irritancy. In the case of old feus, it is normally safe to assume that all such conditions have been duly complied with; but, in the case of recent feus, the standard practice is to require the seller to produce a certificate from the superior that all such conditions have been duly carried out and complied with.

ii) Money payments. These include, typically, payments to the superior for roads; and payments to neighbouring feuars for one-half of the cost of erecting mutual walls or fences. Again, in old feus, it is normally safe to assume that all these payments have been duly made; but, in the case of recent feus, the seller should be asked to produce receipts for all such payments in order to vouch the discharge thereof.

iii) Restrictions on User, etc. These conditions are, of course, continuing. The question is whether they are still being duly complied with. If not, consider (1) whether the consent of the superior to some deviation has been obtained or whether the superior has acquiesced; and (2) whether there is a *jus quaesitum tertio* for the benefit of neighbouring proprietors and if so whether they have consented.

(b) **Reservation of Minerals.** Normally, the original reservation occurs in the original Charter; but this is not necessarily so. As a result, a reservation of minerals can easily be missed.

(c) **Other Conditions.** These include Clauses of pre-emption and redemption again normally (but not necessarily) contained in the original Charter.

Pre-emption

A Clause of pre-emption in a Charter or Disposition entitles the superior, etc., to the first refusal of the feu on sale by vassal, etc. Such a Clause, though possibly still operative, may not be enforceable, according to its terms, because of statutory limitations in the 1938 Act S.9, the 1970 Act S.46; and the 1974 Act, for Dispositions.

In the case of Feu Charters, whatever the terms of the pre-emption clause:

i) the superior must accept the pre-emption offer within 21 days of such offer being made (or less if so provided in the Charter); and

ii) if at any time since 17.5.38 (or possibly only since 29.11.70) a pre-emption offer has been made and not accepted, the right is absolutely extinguished and is never again exerciseable on any later occasion.

By the 1974 Act S.13, the same rule is applied to any clause of pre-emption in any other kind of deed, e.g. Disposition executed after 1.9.74, by adding a new sub-section (3) to the 1938 Act S.9 to that effect.

Redemption and Reversion

A Clause of Redemption in a Charter entitles the superior, normally at any time in his option, to reacquire the *dominium utile,* usually at a fixed price.

Under a Right of Reversion, the *dominium utile* automatically reverts to the superior on the happening of a certain event.

The 1938 Act S.9 does not apply to such clauses and there is no equivalent statutory restriction. But by the 1974 Act S.12, a right of redemption or of reversion created by a deed executed **after** 1.9.74, may only be exercised within 20 years of the deed, if it is exerciseable on the happening of a definite event which is bound to occur (e.g. death) or in the option of the superior.

Otherwise, there is no restriction. So a provision that, if the feu ceases to be used by a Charity for charitable purposes, it will revert to the superior, remains enforceable in perpetuity.

(d) **Feuduty**. A purchaser is entitled, by implication, to an allocated feuduty; and if allocated, redemption is automatic on sale. So no special provision is required in the Contract of Sale and Purchase; but the purchaser is entitled to be satisfied that the redemption price has been paid, **and** that the property is no longer burdened with a real burden for the redemption price.

Accordingly, the purchaser can require from the seller, at settlement, **either** (i) evidence of the redemption price having already been paid, at the time of sale **or** on earlier redemption; or (ii) if the feuduty has not already been redeemed at settlement, an obligation to produce in due course due evidence of redemption.

In either case, evidence of redemption will normally take the form of (i) Superior's Receipt; or (ii) a Copy Notice with Acknowledgment by the superior thereon and a Search continued for a period of two months beyond the date of the Notice (or date of entry, if later).

The point of these alternatives is that if the superior is paid the redemption money (and gives a receipt), then he no longer has a real burden therefor; or if he gives **no** receipt so that there is **no** evidence of payment, (and he is not statutorily obliged to do so on **compulsory** redemption) but if no Order appears in the Register of Sasines within two months after redemption date, then, again, there can be no continuing real burden and so the purchaser is no longer concerned. But remember the rights of heritable creditors.

Alternatively, after settlement, the **purchaser** could give the Notice, to start the two months period running, and continue the Search until two months thereafter.

5. **Heritable Securities**. It is, of course, necessary to ensure that the title is disencumbered of all subsisting heritable securities. The positive prescription does not assist in this case, although the negative prescription is of some help.

The general working rule is:

(a) Go back over the title for the past 40 years and take a note of all heritable securities appearing from the titles (or the Search) as subsisting within the 40-year period.

(b) Check, (from the Search or titles,) which of these have been finally discharged.

(c) Ignore any security discharged more than 5 years ago, because under the 1970 Act S.41, a discharge by the ostensible creditor cannot be challenged, in a question with a *bona fide* purchaser, more than 5 years after recording.

(d) If the security was finally discharged within the 5 year period, then check the original security deed, all transmissions thereof, and the final discharge, all in detail, to ensure a proper and valid discharge.

(e) Any remaining securities are presumably still subsisting, unless they have been effectively restricted. Check the title and search for deeds of restriction or clauses *in gremio* in Dispositions disburdening the subjects thereby disponed, and, if there are any such, make sure that the property has been effectively disburdened of these securities. If the subsisting securities have not been so restricted, then the purchaser's Agents should see and revise draft discharges of the remaining outstanding securities, and take an obligation from the seller's Agents to deliver valid discharges, in terms of the revised drafts, within three to six months after settlement of the transaction.

6. Possession. There are two points here:

(i) **Prescription.** In any examination of title, one relies on the positive prescription. This requires both title **and** possession. The quality and duration of possession have been dealt with in Chapter 2.9. Strictly speaking, it is not enough simply to examine the title in isolation; one should also enquire into the extent and quality of possession over the 10 year period since the date of the foundation writ. But, in practice, evidence of possession is rarely called for by the purchaser, although the seller would require to satisfy the purchaser on this point, if called upon to do so.

(ii) **Vacant possession or subject to tenant's rights.**
This is a point which should be dealt with in the Contract. If the property is purchased with vacant possession, then an inspection of the property will show whether or not vacant possession can be given.

If the property is purchased subject to tenant's rights, the purchaser's Agent should always call for and examine in detail the lease or leases. He does this not only to establish the benefits flowing to the landlord under these leases, but also to satisfy himself as to the obligations incumbent on the landlord, since these benefits and these obligations (unless personal to the original landlord, which they would rarely be) will transmit and be enforceable by and against the purchaser.

7. Searches.
A Search for Incumbrances is essential for the proper examination of heritable title. In **all** cases, two Registers must be searched, namely the Register of Sasines (the Property Register) and the Register of Inhibitions and Adjudications (the Personal Register).

In special circumstances, searches in other Registers may be appropriate, e.g. the Register of Entails; the Register of Rents under the Rent Act in the case of let properties to establish the registered rent(s), if appropriate; Register of Planning Applications etc.

(1) The Property Register. The purpose of a search in the Property Register is:—
(i) to disclose the state of the proprietary title at the date of completion of the transaction; and
(ii) to disclose all incumbrances affecting the property, other than Floating Charges, in each case as evidenced on the Record.

In the Property Register, the Search is directed at a particular heritable property; and accordingly the Search itself opens with a description of the property searched against, normally a particular description or description by reference. The Search is confined to the Division(s) of the G.R.S. in which those subjects are situate, or, where the property was burgage, to the particular B.R.S. **and** the G.R.S. in which the property lies.

Over a given period, which is specified in the Search, the Search discloses all **recorded** writs appearing in those Registers which in any way affect the property. The details of the writs so disclosed are very brief, and, in particular, do not normally disclose conditions and restrictions contained therein. Remember that, in a system of registration of deeds, the property search can only certify that the writs, which it discloses, are the only writs recorded in the relevant Registers which purportedly affect the property during the period of search. It therefore gives notice to anyone dealing with the property that these writs have been recorded and apparently affect the property; but it goes no further. In particular, it is not in any sense a certificate of the sufficiency or validity of the title.

The period, which the Property Search must cover for a proper examination of a title, is closely linked with the positive prescription. Thus, in a purchase of heritage, the purchaser's Agent first satisfies himself as to the validity of the proprietary title. For this purpose, he examines the foundation writ and subsequent progress. In addition to that examination, he must **also** be sure that the writs which he has examined are the **only** recorded writs affecting the property; and for this he relies on the Property Search. Accordingly, if the Property Search is to fulfil its function in this respect, it must go **back** to the foundation writ; and it must cover a continuous period from the date of recording of the foundation writ to completion of the purchaser's title.

In addition to validity of title, the purchaser's Agent is also concerned to ensure that the property is disencumbered. Here, the positive prescription does not assist him. A Bond and Disposition in Security, recorded long before the date of recording of the foundation writ, may still be enforceable. The only way of being absolutely sure that the property is disencumbered is to carry the Property Search back to the original Crown writ. In fact, on grounds of expediency, a shorter period of Search is accepted by the profession; the actual period is arbitrary. A forty-year Search is now recommended in all cases; but this is not necessarily foolproof. Thus, a Bond may have been recorded fifty years ago, and would not be disclosed by a forty-year Search; but the probability is that some writ will have entered the Record relating to that Bond in the past forty years, e.g. Notice of Title, Assignation, Partial Discharge, etc.

As already mentioned, the Common Law obligation on a seller with regard to period of Search in the Property Register is uncertain. Accordingly, the standard practice is to insert, in the contract of sale and purchase, an express obligation under which the seller is obliged to exhibit a Search in the Property Register going back either (a) for at least forty years prior to the present date; or (b) to the date of recording of the foundation writ, if that writ was recorded more than forty years ago.

(2) **The Register of Inhibitions and Adjudications.**
Walker Chapter 1.9 page 111.

This is a purely diligence Register, closely associated with the Register of Sasines, but quite separate and distinct from it and serving quite a different purpose. The General Register of Sasines is a Publication Register, the object being to make known to the public at large the existence, or purported existence, of real rights affecting land; and accordingly, the only writs which are registrable in the Register of Sasines are writs relating to land and identifying particular heritable subjects to which they relate. The Register of Inhibitions and Adjudications, (commonly known as 'the Personal Register') is not concerned with land, nor with titles to land as such. It is only concerned with persons and the personal capacity of persons to grant deeds affecting land. Originally, there were several such Registers; but all these have now been amalgamated together into a single Register under this name. (1924 Act S.44).

The Personal Register is now the only Register for the publication of personal diligence; and, further, **a third party** cannot create any effective bar on the capacity of a heritable proprietor nor prevent him from dealing with heritage unless an entry appears against that heritable proprietor in the Personal Register. This has no application to **natural** incapacity. If a heritable proprietor is insane, or is in pupillarity, he is automatically barred from effectively dealing with his heritable estate, and no entry to that effect appears in the Personal Register.

The law provides equitable remedies for the benefit of persons having valid claims upon heritable property feudally vested in the infeft proprietor. (See adjudication, reduction and sequestration above). But these equitable remedies involve delay. Meanwhile, in the period between the raising of the action and the granting of the Decree, the infeft proprietor remains ostensibly the infeft proprietor and may confer an active title on a *bona fide* purchaser for value who is unaware of the pending action, to the prejudice of the person claiming an interest in the heritable property in question. To prevent such prejudice, immediate interim procedures are available to the pursuer in an action (or a creditor) whereby he can effectively prevent the debtor in the obligation from dealing with heritage. These procedures do not, in themselves, provide an active title for the claimant (or creditor). To be effective, an entry **must** be made against the infeft proprietor in the Personal Register, and it is **only** by making the appropriate entry in this Register that this result can be achieved. There are three different types of entry which can be made with similar results.

(i) **Notice of Litigiosity**.

Heritable property becomes litigious when it is the subject matter of a depending **real** action; (e.g. adjudication or reduction). When heritage is litigious, this implies a prohibition against alienation of the heritage to the prejudice of the pursuer in the action, (or to the prejudice of a creditor who has done real diligence) where the object of that action (or real diligence) is to acquire a title to the heritage, absolutely (or in security). Note that the infeft proprietor is not absolutely barred from dealing with the property, simply because his property has become litigious. He may deal with it, but anyone taking a title from the infeft proprietor has notice of the potential claims upon it; and a title so taken may later be reduced at the instance of the person who has rendered the property litigious.

Originally, the mere calling in Court of a real action affecting heritable title was sufficient publication, and **of itself** rendered the property litigious. But by the 1924 Act S.44(2)(a), no action relating to land shall, *per se,* make property litigious; and, in order to produce a state of litigiosity, a notice in the form of Schedule RR to the 1868 Act must be recorded in the Personal Register. Property only becomes litigious at the date of the recording of such notice.

The notice is very brief.

'8 Nov. 1982. Notice of Summons of Adjudication.

Scottish Co-operative Wholesale Society Ltd., 95 Morrison Street, Glasgow:— Against (1) John Green trading as L.P. Green & Co., formerly 1 Dickson Street, Glasgow, now 9 Pitt Street, Glasgow; and (2) Renfrew Building Society. Signeted 8th November, 1982.

AB, W.S., Edinburgh, Agent.'

Further, by S.44(2)(b), Decree in an Action of Adjudication does not, of itself, make property litigious.

The Notice of Litigiosity has no effect on the proprietor's capacity to deal with **other** heritage; it affects only the heritable property to which the Action relates. But this does not appear on the face of the Register.

Further, litigiosity strikes only at **future, voluntary** deeds: and so cannot bar the subsequent granting of a Disposition of heritage which has been made litigious if it is in implement of a contract dated prior to registration of the notice.

(ii) **Inhibition.**

In any **real** action, the *status quo* may be preserved, and prejudice to the pursuer may be avoided, by rendering the property litigious, through the recording in the Personal Register of the appropriate Notice. A personal action, e.g. for payment of a debt, as opposed to a real action, is not directed at, nor does it directly affect, heritable property belonging to the defender. But the whole estate of the debtor is liable for payment of his **whole** debts; so that the pursuer in a personal action for payment is indirectly interested in heritage belonging to the debtor in that, if he succeeds in his action, he may then have recourse, by diligence, against heritage of the debtor.

In order to protect his potential interest in heritable property belonging to the debtor, a creditor may, by the appropriate procedure followed by the appropriate entry in the Personal Register, inhibit the debtor. The effect of an inhibition is similar to litigiosity, in that, by inhibition, the inhibited proprietor is effectively prevented from granting any **future voluntary** deed affecting **any** heritable estate or interest belonging to him at the date when the inhibition becomes effective. Again, deeds granted by an inhibited party are not, of themselves, void; but they remain voidable at the instance of the prejudiced creditor.

An inhibition is purely negative. It never operates to confer an active title on the inhibitor. And it only affects heritable estate. But an inhibition may confer a certain preference on the inhibitor in a sequestration. For Articles on Ranking, and comment on recent cases, see Reading List 7.2 and 7.4.

There are two alternative procedures:

(a) **Letters of Inhibition.** This procedure is competent only:

i) In execution, where the creditor holds a liquid document of debt; or

ii) In security, where the creditor holds an illiquid document of debt and the debtor is *vergens ad inopiam* or *in meditatione fugae.*

No formal action is necessary; instead, all that is required is to present the document of debt with a Bill in the Petition Department of the Court of Session, which is granted by the Clerk of Court. The form of Letters of Inhibition is statutory under the 1868 Act S.156 and Schedule QQ.

The letters are signeted, and served on the debtor and, thereafter, entered in the Register of Inhibitions and Adjudications. They are effective only from the date of such registration.

(b) **Inhibition on the Dependence.** Where a debt is illiquid, it requires formal constitution by action in the Courts. Letters of Inhibition are not available. Instead, it is competent to include, in the Summons of any Court of Session action concluding for payment, a warrant to inhibit; and where so included, the Summons (after Service on the debtor) may be registered in the Personal Register.

The effect is to inhibit the defender as from the date of such registration. A very useful device.

Inhibition on the dependence is also available in a Sheriff Court Action, and if this benefit is required the procedure is to apply for warrant to inhibit to the Petition Department of the Court of Session, producing the Initial Writ or a certified copy thereof.

Notice of Inhibition. Where the creditor intends to inhibit the debtor by **either** method, he may register in the Personal Register a Notice of Inhibition under the 1868 Act S. 155 and Schedule PP. This is a form of advance warning that an

Inhibition is on the way; but it has no effect whatever unless Letters of Inhibition, or a Summons containing the warrant to inhibit, are subsequently registered within 21 days following on the registration of the Notice. In that event **only,** the Letters, or Summons, date back to the date of registration of the Notice.

(iii) **Abbreviate of Sequestration.**

The effect of an Act and Warrant appointing a Trustee in Sequestration, as a title to the debtor's heritage, has been noticed already. But, in addition, in every sequestration it is **obligatory,** within 48 hours of the first deliverance, to register in the Personal Register an Abbreviate of the Petition and Deliverance. (1913 Act S.44). Such registration has the force of an Inhibition. It, therefore, prevents the bankrupt from disposing of his heritable estate to the prejudice of other creditors, pending completion of title, subsequently, by the Trustee in Sequestration.

Duration of Entries in the Personal Register.

(i) **Notice of Litigiosity.** The effect of such Notice expires:

(a) Five years from the date of registration; or

(b) On the expiry of six months from the date of final Decree in the Action, whichever shall first happen. 1924 Act S.44(3)(a).

(ii) **Inhibition.** An Inhibition is of no effect after the expiry of five years from the date on which it first became effective. 1924 Act S.44(3)(a).

(iii) **Abbreviate of Sequestration.** The effect of the Abbreviate lasts for five years only. It then falls; but, unlike a Notice of Litigiosity or an Inhibition, the effect of the Abbreviate can be renewed by the recording of an appropriate Memorandum, and can be kept in force by subsequent renewals for 20 years. Bankruptcy Act 1913 S.44 and 1924 Act S.44(4)(c).

Apart from the Statutory prescriptions, the effect of any of these entries in the Personal Register can be removed by Discharge at the instance of the creditor or trustee who made the original entry; or may be recalled by the Court. Appropriate Discharge entries are then made in the Personal Register.

e.g.:

'Discharge by said Scottish Co-Operative Wholesale Society Ltd. of said Notice of Summons of Adjudication (registered 8th November, 1982) but only in so far as said Notice relates to the said Renfrew Building Society'.

It is generally accepted that the effect of the statutory prescription is two-fold, viz.:

(a) That, when five years have expired from the date of registration of a Notice or an Inhibition, the debtor/proprietor is released from the effect thereof; and he is then absolutely free from any prohibition against alienation;

(b) That, even if the debtor/proprietor has alienated his heritage during the five-year period, the party in right of the Inhibition or Notice absolutely forfeits his right to reduce the alienation by the debtor/proprietor immediately on the expiry of the full five-year period. (But it is not altogether clear whether the 1924 Act S.44 achieves this second effect).

A Search in the Register of Inhibitions and Adjudications (generally known as 'the Personal Register') is intended to disclose any legal bar which may still be effective against the present proprietor or any predecessor in title within the prescriptive period, in case such a legal bar, (e.g. an Inhibition) might have prevented the proprietor from conveying the property at the date when he conveyed it or might render a title granted by such a person reducible at the instance of a third party.

A Search in the Personal Register is normally combined with a Search in the Property Register, for convenience; but it serves an entirely separate purpose and may be separately instructed. The practical rules governing period of Search and persons searched against in the Personal Register take into account three main factors, namely:

(a) that Inhibitions and Notices of Litigiosity prescribe in five years — 1924 Act S.44; but

(b) that Abbreviates of Sequestration, although they also prescribe in five years, may be renewed by Memorandum.

(c) that extrinsic invalidity (i.e. granting deeds under disability) is cured after ten years by the Positive Prescription.

The practical rule is that all persons having the legal title, or any beneficial right, to the property within the past **ten** years are searched against in the Personal Register, but for a period of five years only prior to the date of completion of the purchaser's title. The 10-year period was formerly 20 years, before the passing of the 1970 Act, reducing the period of the positive prescription. Further, if any proprietor has been searched against for a period of five years prior to the date on which he was divested (which is normal in any sequence of titles), then it is unnecessary to conduct any further search against that person on any subsequent transaction.

(3) **The Register of Charges.** A Search in this Register is only appropriate in the case of **a Limited Company** dealing with heritage. It discloses Floating Charges. It also discloses all Fixed Securities, although these would, in any event, be disclosed by a Search in the Property Register. Accordingly, when a Company is granting a Standard Security, or a Floating Charge, a search in the Register of Charges is **always** required because a Floating Charge **may** competently prohibit the Company from granting any **subsequent** fixed security ranking prior to the Floating Charge. In the absence of such a prohibition, a subsequent **fixed** charge automatically takes priority. Floating Charges rank *inter se* according to their dates of registration.

When heritable property is being sold by a Limited Company, as a going concern, the property is automatically released from a Floating Charge on sale, and no Search is required. **But**, when the Company goes into Liquidation, or when a Receiver is appointed, the Floating Charge becomes a Fixed Security. A Search in the Register of Charges would not reveal the Liquidation of the Company but **would** reveal the appointment of a Receiver which is noted in that Register. The Deed of Appointment of the Receiver is filed in the Company's file.

In the case of liquidation, there is a time lag of anything up to 15 days during which, under Statute, the Resolution putting the Company into liquidation may be lodged; for the appointment of a Receiver the statutory time limit is seven days. Therefore, a Search in the Company Register is never right up to date.

When purchasing from, or lending to, a Company, one should accordingly Search the Company's file in the Register of Companies, not merely the Register of Charges, **and** obtain an assurance from the Seller's Agent (or the Directors of the Company) that the company is not in liquidation, that a Receiver has not been appointed, and that no such action is contemplated. The seller's Solicitor, or the Directors of the Company, should so warrant this **at settlement**. See Article 1977 JLS 334 and 1979 JLS Workshop i. The Purchaser's Agents, in practice, commonly accept such an assurance as sufficient, without requiring an actual search.

If a Search is required in the Register of Charges, then it will normally be from 27th October,1961, which was the date of commencement of this Register; or from the date of incorporation of the Company, if later.

Instructions to Searchers.
In practice, the Searchers are normally instructed by way of a Memorandum for Search, or for Continuation of Search, framed by the seller or borrower and revised by the purchaser or lender. The seller or borrower instructs the Search in terms of the revised Memorandum.

There are two possible cases. Either there already is a Search over the property, brought down to a particular date; in which case that Search would normally be continued. Or, where there is no such Search available for continuation, a new Search must be instructed. But in the latter case, the new Search will normally connect up with some previous existing Search, and this affects the commencing date.

In the case of a new Search, the Memorandum for Search will contain a short description; where an existing Search is to be continued, the Memorandum instructs **that** Search to be continued, and so no Description is necessary.

In addition, the Memorandum will also specify:

(a) The Register, i.e. the Division of the G.R.S. in which the Search is to be conducted; and

(b) The starting and closing date. The starting date will normally be the day after the closing date of the prior Search. Note, however, that, where the previous relevant entry is marked 'grantee's interest not traced' the continuation, or new Search, should start from that date, **not** from the date following. The closing date is not normally known at the time when the Memorandum is prepared. Thus, on sale and purchase, the closing date of the Search will be the date of recording of the Disposition in favour of the purchaser; but the Memorandum is adjusted prior to settlement. In practice, therefore, the closing date is stated as 'the date of Certificate (to include Disposition by A.B. in favour of C.D.)'.

Personal Register
The working practice is:

(i) Make a list of all the parties having the legal title or a beneficial right to the property at any time within the past 10 years.

(ii) Check, on the existing Search, if any of these parties have been searched against for a full five-year period prior to divestiture; and, if they have, delete them from the list.

(iii) The remaining parties now fall to be searched against on this occasion. For this purpose, the Searchers should be given the full names and addresses of individuals.

Specialities:

(a) Trustees or Executors. The practice is to search against them as a body, naming and designing the truster, but not naming individual Trustees.

(b) Firms. The practice is to search against all individual partners as individuals and as Trustees for their firm; and against the firm *socio nomine*.

(c) Heritable creditors. Creditors under *ex facie* securities, e.g. Bond and Disposition in Security and Standard Security, are not searched against in practice; but see Burns' Practice p. 300 — inhibition of heritable creditor prevents effective discharge, if notarially intimated to the debtor; Act of Sederunt 19/2/1680, which **in practice** is ignored. In theory it applies to **any** Bond etc. discharged **within** the 5 year period (1970 Act S.41). *Ex facie* absolute disponees are searched against as having the legal title; and so is the beneficial owner as debtor proprietor for his beneficial interest.

In all cases, the period in the personal Search is for five years prior to completion of the current transaction.

Interim Reports on Search

The Search in the Property Register is made up from the Minute Book and the Minute Book is normally some weeks behind. Clearly, it is not possible to deliver, at the settlement of a transaction, a Search which has been continued right down to date to disclose the Disposition in favour of the purchaser. As a precaution, (which in fact protects **both** sets of Agents) an Interim Report on the Search should always be obtained. This will show, in the Property Register, the writs that the Search will disclose to within some weeks prior to settlement; and in the Personal Register any entries to within 24 hours of the date of Search.

Settlement Obligations

At the settlement of a transaction, the Disposition normally supersedes the Contract. One of the seller's obligations is to deliver or exhibit a Search. The seller can never implement this at the date of settlement, and some delay in producing the Search is inevitable. In addition to the Interim Report, it is therefore usual, at settlement, to require the seller's Agents to grant an obligation undertaking to deliver or exhibit a clear Search; and it is customary to include, in such obligations, implement of any other conditions of the contract which are not fully implemented at settlement, e.g. delivery of a Discharge of a Bond repaid by the seller out of the purchase price, exhibition of Estate Duty Clearance Certificates, etc. But a purchaser is not obliged to agree to this, and his Agent should accept this obligation only with circumspection. Thus Solicitor A acts for the seller of heritage subject to a Bond. The Bondholder has his own Solicitor X. Solicitor A undertakes to deliver a discharge of the Bond. The purchaser's Agent, on the strength of that obligation by A, pays him the full price. A then goes bankrupt. His obligation is worthless, and the property remains **burdened** in the hands of the purchaser, although, within limits, the risk is covered by the Professional Indemnity Insurance Policy — see below.

It may be different if A also acted for the creditor in the security and had ostensible authority to receive repayment of the security; but see Richardson v. MacGeogh's Trs. 1 F 145.

Note that such obligations are always personally binding on Agents. See 7.4.37 Johnston v. Little 1960 SLT 129 and article. 1959 JLS 135 — Settlement obligations. So the purchaser's Agent is relying on the personal integrity and standing of the other Agent; and the Agent granting the obligation guarantees his client to that extent. Again, he should grant such obligations only with circumspection.

Originally, the Letter of Obligation dealt with Searches and, possibly, certain additional items such as Estate Duty Clearance Certificates. It is also common practice to cover production and delivery of e.g. the discharge of a Bond in the settlement obligation. But the purchaser is not obliged to agree to this, for the reasons given above. In that case there are two alternative procedures, either:

i) the seller repays the loan in advance of settlement of the sale and delivers an executed discharge at settlement; or

ii) if the loan is to be repaid out of the proceeds of sale, the practice is to have a tripartite (or multipartite) settlement with the seller, the purchaser and the bondholder all present together. The purchaser passes over a cheque to the bondholder to repay the sum in loan, taking delivery of a Discharge in exchange, and a second cheque for the balance to the seller.

In either case, the purchaser thus obtains immediate delivery of both the Disposition in favour of the purchaser **and** the executed Discharge of the Bond; and there is, therefore, no need for the Letter of Obligation to cover delivery of the Discharge since it is delivered at settlement.

The purchaser is quite entitled to insist that, at settlement, Discharges of all outstanding heritable securities are actually delivered. He is not in any circumstances bound to accept the seller's Letter of Obligation on a matter of that kind, and there are risks in so doing.

In recent years, however, it has become common practice to cover delivery of the Discharge of a Bond, etc., in the Letter of Obligation, at settlement. In addition, the practice has been further relaxed so that nowadays it is a common occurrence for a transaction of sale and purchase to settle between agents before the Disposition is ready for delivery, and in some cases even before the purchaser's Agents have had a proper opportunity to examine the title. Usually, this is because of pressure from the purchaser who wants early possession.

From the purchaser's point of view, his Agents should not settle in these circumstances except by consigning the price in joint names, pending delivery of a Disposition; but the seller will normally not agree to that because, once the price is consigned, the pressure by the purchaser ceases, and the purchaser's Agent tends then to drag his feet. In the result, there is a delay in the seller obtaining the price. Therefore, the seller's Agent will normally only agree to early settlement if the price is paid in full, even although he is not in a position to deliver a Disposition to the purchaser in exchange. As a result, the purchaser's Agent may agree to hand over the price without title but, as a measure of protection, will then insist on, and will normally get, an undertaking by the seller's Solicitor that a Disposition will be delivered to the purchaser in due course. While this practice is now commonplace and works satisfactorily in the great majority of cases, it does involve serious risks for both Agents and parties.

The risks can be summarised thus:

1. **The risk to the purchaser.** The risk here is that, in the end of the day, the seller may prove unwilling or unable to implement the obligation, although contractually bound by the contract to do so. If he is merely unwilling to do so, then the purchaser has a remedy through the action of implement; but this may involve him in considerable delay and expense.

However, the seller may be totally disabled from completing the transaction by supervening circumstances, e.g. bankruptcy intervening. In that case, the property, although subject to a contract, will pass to the trustee in sequestration who can repudiate the contract. The purchaser has no real right but merely a contractual claim against the seller; and the trustee in sequestration is not bound to implement that claim. In the result, even although the purchaser has paid over the price and is in possession, and even although he has a binding contract with the seller and a binding obligation by the seller's Agent to deliver a Disposition, he cannot maintain his position in a question with the trustee in sequestration who can eject him and resell the property to some other purchaser. The purchaser's only remedy in such a situation is to rank in the sequestration and claim damages for a breach of contract; but if, as often happens, there is nothing for the ordinary creditors, then in the result the purchaser has lost his money.

Alternatively,the property could be subject to a heritable security, or several heritable securities, and the seller may have sold at a price less than sufficient to pay off all the creditors in full. In the ensuing delay, one of the heritable creditors gets tired of waiting and exercises his power of sale which, of course, he is perfectly entitled to do, notwithstanding the binding contract of sale and purchase. Again, as a result, the purchaser may lose his money.

The purchaser's position is substantially but not completely protected by the Letter of Obligation as explained, below.

2. **The risks to the parties' Agents.** If the purchaser's Solicitor has explained the position in detail to the purchaser, made the purchaser aware of the risks and has then settled without title on the purchaser's express instructions, the Agent will not be liable. But in many cases, the purchaser's Agent settles without title against the seller's obligation **without** putting the purchaser in the picture. In that case, he is most certainly guilty of professional negligence and would be liable in restitution to the disappointed purchaser.

The purchaser's Solicitor covers himself, to some extent, by obtaining a Letter of Obligation from the seller's Agents undertaking to see to it that a Disposition is delivered in due course. That Obligation is personally binding on the seller's Solicitor. See Johnston v. Little above. If the seller will not, or cannot, implement his bargain, for reasons outlined above, the seller's Solicitor is personally liable under his settlement obligation to the purchaser's Solicitor. So, in effect, the seller's Solicitor undertakes to indemnify the purchaser against loss in the event that the contract cannot be implemented. He is a **guarantor** for the seller.

If the seller's Solicitor is substantial and can pay the purchaser his damages in full, then the purchaser and his Agents are at least able to recover damages, and so to that extent are covered against loss. But note that their only remedy is damages. If, for example, sequestration intervenes and the trustee in sequestration repudiates the contract, the seller's Solicitor cannot offer implement, but damages only in lieu. In most cases, this is reasonably adequate protection; but it could happen that the Seller's Solicitor is also insolvent and unable to pay, in which case the loss would fall on the purchaser or his Agent.

Every practising Solicitor is now obliged to carry Professional Indemnity Insurance under a Master Policy negotiated by the Law Society of Scotland. The liabilities of Agents, both for Seller and Purchaser, are thought to be covered by the Master Policy, but only within certain limits and subject to possible exceptions.

3. **The risk to the seller.** Where the transaction settles in this way, the seller gets the purchase price in full, and his risk is minimal. Nonetheless, there are certain risks. For example, it is possible that, notwithstanding payment of the price, the transaction may not settle in the end of the day. Suppose, for example, that the purchaser has paid over the price against a Letter of Obligation before his Solicitor has fully examined the title, as does happen not infrequently. Thereafter, the purchaser's Solicitor discovers a fundamental defect in the title of which he was not aware when paying over the price. As a result, he repudiates the contract, and claims repayment of the price.

If the unmarketability in title is of a minor nature, it may be that, by paying over the price and taking possession, the purchaser has barred himself from rescinding the contract on grounds which otherwise would have entitled him to do so. See 7.1.17 McDonald v. Newall 1F 68.

But, clearly, there could be certain situations where, because of a major defect in the title, the purchaser is entitled to rescind and claim repayment. Meantime the seller may have paid off heritable securities out of the money paid to him by the purchaser; or he may have purchased another house. In either case, the seller might have difficulty then in finding the money to repay.

Although this procedure has now become commonplace in practice, it should be treated with the greatest caution because of the risks outlined above, which are not by any means remote.

For a cautionary case, see 1.3.1. Gibson v. Hunter Homes Ltd. 1976 SLT 94. Mr Gibson bought a house from Hunter Homes Ltd. which he paid for on 31st October, 1974, and took possession, without getting delivery of his Feu Disposition. Shortly thereafter, Hunter Homes Ltd. went into liquidation before the Feu Disposition had been delivered. Mr Gibson then sued for implement but the Court held, without difficulty, that the house remained the property of the Company, and that Mr Gibson had a mere personal right but no real right therein. As a result, the liquidator was entitled to repudiate the contract of sale to Mr Gibson, as he did, and to resell the property, defeating Mr Gibson's claim in the process. This left Mr Gibson with a claim for damages as an ordinary creditor in the liquidation.

It appears from the Report that the Solicitors for Hunter Homes Ltd. had granted a Letter of Obligation undertaking to deliver a validly executed Disposition, which of course they could not do. Mr Gibson was encouraged by the Judges in that case to institute proceedings against the Solicitors who granted that Obligation, presumably for damages for failure to implement the same. Obviously, this put the Solicitors granting the Obligation in a position of some difficulty, and they may well have had to pay Mr Gibson in full, and then claim as ordinary creditors in the liquidation.

This case underlines the risks both to the purchaser, and to the seller's Solicitors who granted the Obligation.

For some further comments, see an Article by Mr R.A. Edwards in 1975 JLS 260.

8. **Miscellaneous Items.**

According to circumstances, there may be quite a number of other things which affect the validity of the title to a greater or lesser degree, or which impose some restraint on the proprietor, and which may not emerge from mere scrutiny of the titles and the Search. In practice, however, an examination of the title will normally disclose the risk. Some of the more important of these undisclosed items are —

(1) **Want of capacity.** There is no way of telling from the titles if a deed has been granted by a pupil or minor, or by someone insane. Normally the purchaser's Agents accept this risk without enquiry; but it does sometimes happen.

(2) **Forgery.** Again, there is no way of telling, by a scrutiny of the title, whether one of the writs is forged. But again, the purchaser's Agents normally accept the risk.

(3) **Latent defects.** Any writ, or decree, although *ex facie* valid, is open to reduction on various grounds, as we have seen. A typical case is a Decree of General Service

in favour of an heir who later turns out to have been wrongly served. Again, this is a risk which the purchaser is bound to take. See 7.3.4. Sibbald's Heirs v. Harris 1947 SC 601 where L.P. Cooper says, 'the obligation on a seller is to produce an *ex facie* valid prescriptive progress of titles, not to guarantee the purchaser, by Policies of Insurance or otherwise, against every risk of subsequently emerging latent defect. In so far as these risks are taken into account in our system of conveyancing, they have been left to rest on the classical obligation of warrandice, and warrandice is offered here.'

The 1924 Act S.46 provides that a Decree of Reduction is not to have any effect in a question with a *bona fide* purchaser for value who has acquired right prior to the Extract of the Decree being recorded in the Register of Sasines. Presumably, this Section was intended to obviate this risk; but, if so, its intended effect was cut down by 7.2.8. Mulhearn v. Dunlop 1929 SLT 59. See Chapter 7.2.4. Reduction — above.

Some measure of protection is afforded under other statutory provisions, thus:
i) The Succession (Scotland) Act 1964 S.17. Where a person has, in good faith and for value, acquired a title to heritage which has vested in an executor, either directly, or indirectly, from the executor or from someone deriving title from the executor, then his title is not challengeable on the grounds that the Confirmation was reducible; nor on the grounds that the executor should not have transferred the property to a particular beneficiary.

ii) The Trusts (Scotland) Act 1961 S.2. A sale of heritable property by Trustees may be contrary to the terms or the purposes of the Trust, in which case the Trustees have no implied power of sale under the 1921 Act S.4. Until 1961, this meant that, in a question with a *bona fide* purchaser for value, the beneficiary could challenge the title of a disponee who purchased heritage from the Trustees without the necessary powers. Under this Section, notwithstanding the lack of power, a Disposition by Trustees to a *bona fide* purchaser for value is put beyond challenge.

The Section protects only a *bona fide* purchaser for value from the Trustees in a Scottish Trust. It does **not** apply in English or other Trusts. Further it protects **only** the purchaser from Trustees. If the Trustees, mistakenly, convey heritable property to the wrong beneficiary and the beneficiary then sells the property, that sale is not covered by the 1961 Act S.2.

In contrast, if the Executor dispones or transfers the heritage to the **wrong** beneficiary, who **then** sells the property to a *bona fide* purchaser for value, the purchaser is still protected against that defect in title by the 1964 Act. S.17.

(4) **Unrecorded Interests.** As we have seen earlier, the significant feature of a real right is that, in a competition between real right and personal right or title, the real right invariably prevails. Similarly, burdens and restrictions imposed on or affecting a heritable proprietor will not transmit or run with the lands against a singular successor unless they are made real. We have seen this general principle illustrated in various cases, typically, 2.8.1. Ceres School Board v. Macfarlane 23 R 279. In that case, A granted a Feu Disposition in favour of B who entered into possession of the feu but did not take infeftment. Many years later, D, in ignorance of the Feu Disposition by A to B and acting in good faith, took a conveyance from A of the whole estate, and infeftment followed. The Court held, in these circumstances, that D's right to the land was not affected by the prior but unfeudalised Feu Disposition in favour of B.

Again, in 2.5.21 Campbell's Trustees v. Corporation of Glasgow 4 F 752, a heritable proprietor gave certain undertakings to the Corporation, for consideration, which were embodied in a recorded Agreement, but did not enter or qualify an infeftment. The property having later transmitted to a singular successor, he declined to implement the undertakings and was held entitled to do so on the grounds *inter alia*, that the Agreement was merely a personal Contract which derived no efficacy from being recorded in the Register of Sasines and that the recorded Agreement did not create a servitude; accordingly, the obligation did not transmit with or run with the lands.

But, while this general principle is well established, a singular successor may find himself bound by some prior personal obligation undertaken by or affecting a predecessor in title, if he was aware of the existence of this personal obligation when perfecting his real right.

The general principle and its qualification is stated by Lord Gifford in 7.1.85 Stoddart v. Dalziel 4 R at p.236. The facts there were similar to the facts in Ceres School Board, in that A agreed, by verbal Contract, to feu ground to B who entered into possession, built a house on it, and paid feuduty. A then sold the subjects to C who took a title and infeftment. But the facts in this case differ significantly from the facts in Ceres School Board because, in this case, C, the singular successor, was aware of the fact that B was in occupation, that B had built a house, and claimed some sort of right in the feu. In these circumstances and in the light of C's knowledge, the Court held that he was personally barred from founding on his infeftment and real right with a view to excluding or defeating the prior personal right of B.

Lord Gifford, in this case, sums up the principle and its qualifications thus 'The principle is, that a singular successor is entitled to be free from the personal obligations of his predecessor, and to take the subjects unaffected by any burden not appearing on the title or on the Record. But the singular successor only has this right if he was in ignorance of the existence of any obligations or deeds granted by the seller relative to the subjects and if he was in all respects a *bona fide* purchaser, without notice of any right in any third party or of any circumstances imposing a duty of enquiry. In this case, I think the pursuer was bound to make an enquiry.'

This qualification of the general principle, involving personal bar on the part of the singular successor, is illustrated in a later case 2.5.6., Rodger (Builders) Ltd. v. Fawdry 1950 SC 483. In that case, A contracted to sell heritage to B. Later, thinking (wrongly) that B was in default, A purported to rescind the Contract with B and resold the subjects to C, to whom he then disponed them. C recorded the Disposition. But C was aware of the prior Contract between A and B. On enquiry, he was assured by A that the previous Contract had been legally rescinded and, on the strength of that assurance, he went on and completed his title. The Court held that, i) A having unwarrantedly rescinded the contract between himself and B; and ii) C having notice of B's potential rights as prior purchaser, C was then put on his enquiry; and had not sufficiently discharged his duty of enquiry in taking the seller's word for it that the Contract between A and B had been rescinded. Therefore, he was not a *bona fide* purchaser without notice of the prior rights of B and, although he had the first and indeed the only feudal title, he could not prevail in a question with B, the prior purchaser, having a personal right only.

In the result, the Disposition by A in favour of C was reduced, leaving C with an action of damages only against A. The Lord Justice Clerk sums up the principle in rather more fanciful idiom thus, 'C assumed that his title would be safe once the goal of the Register House was reached. But, in this branch of the law as in football, offside goals are disallowed. In certain states of knowledge a purchaser is regarded as not being in good faith and goes to the Register House at his peril. ... C is not allowed to rely on the registration which, in the knowledge which he possessed, he succeeded in obtaining.'

Clearly, from these cases, knowledge creates a personal bar in **some** circumstances, but not in all. It is difficult to define precisely those cases where prior knowledge will create a personal bar and those cases where it will not.

Burns attempts the definition in these terms (Practice P. 306) 'the opinion may be ventured that this rule would apply to (1) any deed, whether sale or security, following a prior unfeudalised sale; (2) a sale following an unfeudalised security; but that it would not apply to (3) a security following on another unfeudalised security, assuming at least that there was no undue haste'.

See also 5.3.2 Trade Development Bank v Warriner & Mason 5.3.3. Trade Development Bank v Crittal, at p.113.

Contrast 2.5.7. Wallace v. Simmers 1960 S.C. 255, where heritage was sold, subject to a prior Agreement conferring a right of occupancy on a third party, not amounting to a Lease, of which the purchaser was aware. Having completed his title, the purchaser was held not to be bound by the prior Agreement as to occupancy, notwithstanding his knowledge of it. Lord President Clyde, having emphasised that the right constituted by the Agreement was a mere personal right of occupancy only, not a liferent, not a servitude and not a real burden, nor capable of being converted into a real right, deals with the general principle in these terms 'From the decisions, it is clear that the exception' (to the general principle) 'only operates where the right asserted against the singular successor is capable of being made into a real right. If it is nothing but a mere personal obligation not capable of being so converted, then the singular successor is not in any way bound or affected by it.'

But this attempt to define the limits of the exception is not altogether satisfactory. Clearly, from the decisions, a singular successor is personally barred in circumstances such as in Rodger (Builders) Ltd. where there was a prior contract of sale and purchase, known to the singular successor. Certainly, in such cases, the right of the first purchaser is capable of being converted into a real right by the granting of the appropriate Disposition. But it is very difficult to distinguish, logically, the facts in Rodger (Builders) Ltd. from the facts in Campbell's Trustees v The Corporation of Glasgow where, again, there was what amounted to an agreement to convey, (for consideration) although admittedly at a future date, which is very close indeed to sale and purchase, since the agreement to convey was granted in exchange for a price. Yet in Campbell's Trustees the agreement, although known to the singular successor because it was recorded and published, was held to be personal and not binding on him.

Similarly, it is quite clear, on authority, that a mere personal agreement, although recorded (prior to the 1979 Act), purporting to impose burdens on A's property will **not** bind a singular successor from A, even although he knows of this obligation; yet the right of the creditor in that intended burden might be made real by the granting of the appropriate title. But now, under the 1979 Act S.17 (Deed of Conditions), S.18 (Variation and discharge of land obligations) and S.19 (Boundary agreement) recorded agreements may bind successors under these special statutory provisions.

(5) **Servitudes.** Both positive and negative servitudes may be duly constituted by a writ which need not enter the Record. Admittedly, in the case of positive servitudes, there must be publication by possession, but this is a very uncertain protection; and for negative servitudes publication and possession are unnecessary. Further, a servitude right may enter the Record in the dominant, not in the servient, title.

(6) **Heritable Securities.** As indicated above, securities recorded more than forty years ago may not be disclosed by a forty-year Search, although the risk is small.

(7) **Terce and Courtesy.** This is a diminishing risk, but nonetheless these rights may subsist and are enforceable against singular successors, although nothing may appear on the Record; but the titles show the risk. However, these rights could emerge, under the old rules, following on **divorce**, not merely on death and here the title does not show the risk. The practice in the past used to be to ask the seller's Agent for an assurance that the title was clear of these burdens; but this is not now done.

(8) **Death Duties.** We are now concerned only with **Estate Duty** where the death occurred **before** 14th March, 1975. See F.A. 1975 S.49.

By F.A. 1894 S.9(1), a rateable proportion of the total Estate Duty applicable to property not passing to the executor as such becomes automatically a charge on the heritage and attaches thereto, without any notice on the Record and without any other procedure; and is preferred to all other charges on the property except those existing at the death. It runs with land, so that, theoretically at any rate, a purchaser might find himself liable for a rateable proportion of Estate Duty payable on the death of a previous owner.

The purchaser is protected by F.A. 1894 S.8(2) and S.11(1). The combined effect of these two Sections is that, twelve years after the death, Estate Duty ceases to be an effective charge on heritage; within the twelve-year period a purchaser is protected from liability by production to him of a Clearance Certificate under S.11 which, when granted, is conclusive evidence that Duty has been paid, and disencumbers the property of the charge.

Where the death occurred on or after 14th March, 1975, Capital Transfer Tax has replaced Estate Duty on the death.

Under F.A. 1975 (now the Capital Transfer Tax 1984), CTT may be payable both on *inter vivos* transfers and on death. Any tax so payable is a charge on the property transferred or held in trust. **But** no heritable property in Scotland is subject to the charge, which therefore cannot affect a purchaser or creditor nor even a gratuitous disponee. See the Capital Transfer Act 1984 S.237(4).

(9) **Charges on Land.** From time to time in the past various pecuniary burdens have been imposed on heritable property in Scotland, which do not show in the titles. Such imposts include:

i) **Teind and Stipend thereon, now converted to Standard Charge.** For the history of teind and stipend, see Green's Encyclopaedia 14.793 to 880 (Teind and Teind Court) and Walker Chapter 5.10 page 152. The present position is now regulated by the Church of Scotland (Property and Endowments) Act 1925. The purpose of the Act is to remove old anomalies and to standardise stipend payments. Under the Act, the standardised stipend has become automatically a real burden on the lands (not on the teinds) in favour of the Church of Scotland General Trustees; and is called Standard Charge. It is preferred to all other real burdens, except the incidents of tenure, and is recoverable by the Church of Scotland General Trustees in the same way as if it were feuduty. Where the teinds are held on a separate title from the lands by a third-party titular, which is very rare, the heritor is empowered (S.17) to deduct the Standard Charge in accounting to the titular for the free teind.

Where the standardised stipend is under £1, it is compulsorily redeemed under the 1925 Act.

Standard Charge (**not** Stipend) is redeemable on sale under the 1974 S.5; or voluntarily under the 1925 Act.

There are also various administrative provisions, including provisions for allocation of Standard Charge between various parts of the subjects burdened with it, e.g., on the breakup of a large estate.

Broadly speaking, Standard Charge can be ignored in urban properties; in rural properties, it may form quite a substantial burden.

ii) **Land Tax (Cess).** This ancient tax has long since ceased to apply in urban properties. In rural properties, it was exigible as a fixed tax up to 1949; but has been completely abolished by F.A. 1963 S.68.

iii) **Income Tax Schedule A (Property Tax).** This was a tax chargeable, not strictly as a tax on property but as a personal tax on the owner of heritable property, as owner, whether in occupation or not. It was abolished by F.A. 1963. SS.16-21.

iv) **Local Rates.** Until 1956, the **owner** of heritage in Scotland paid Owner's Rates; the occupier paid further rates known as Occupier's Rates. This system was changed by the Valuation and Rating (Scotland) Act 1956, since which Act there has been one Rate only, levied by Local Authorities on occupiers. The **owner,** as such, no longer pays any rates at all. The Rates are now divided into Regional and District. Rates are not a burden on land, in the accepted sense, but merely the personal liability of the occupier, who appears as such on the Valuation Roll.

(10) **Conjunct and confident persons.** By the Bankruptcy Act 1621 gratuitous alienation by an insolvent person to a conjunct and confident person is reducible; but the title shows the risk. For a recent illustration, see Hunt's Trs. v. Hunt 1984 SLT 169.

(11) **Unrecorded leases and tenants' rights.** In practically all cases, leases transmit against singular successors under The Leases Act I449. Nothing appears on the Record, and therefore nothing appears in the Search to indicate the existence of such rights. But an examination of the property should disclose the position.

(12) **Occupancy rights under the Matrimonial Homes (Family Protection) (Scotland) Act, 1981.** (**Note:** The 1981 Act, and in particular S.6(3)(e) is to be amended, and new forms will be required under the Law Reform (Miscellaneous Provisions) (Scotland) Bill 1985, now before Parliament.)

This Act came into operation on 1st September, 1982 and creates occupancy rights for the benefit of the non-entitled spouse as described in Chapter 7.3.

When acting for a purchaser or creditor, it is important to ensure that the property is not affected by any occupancy rights; and to bear in mind that the existence of any such rights will not be disclosed either in the Register of Sasines or the Land Register, nor in the Personal Register. As noted above, if the title is registered, the Keeper will state on the Title Sheet that there are no subsisting occupancy rights of spouses of persons **formerly** entitled, if satisfied that this is so. The statement attracts indemnity. It does **not** cover the current proprietor, so that enquiry is still necessary as to his/her position.

Under Section 6 of the Act, the 'non-entitled spouse' may consent to the dealing (by sale or by security) with the matrimonial home; and such consent excludes any subsequent claim for occupancy rights in that matrimonial home. The Secretary of State, by Statutory Instrument (SI 1982 No. 972) prescribed two separate forms of consent, viz:

i) a clause of consent to be inserted in the Deed effecting the dealing e.g. the Disposition in favour of the purchaser from the entitled spouse; and

ii) Deed of Consent as a separate document.

In appropriate cases, either of these prescribed forms should be used, and should comply strictly with the statutory requirements.

Alternatively, the non-entitled spouse may renounce his or her occupancy rights by renunciation under S.6 of the Act.

If there is no 'non-entitled spouse', then the Act provides for an Affidavit which, under SS.6 and 8, protect a third party dealing with the entitled spouse against the possibility of any subsisting occupancy rights adversely affecting the property.

The forms of affidavit and renunciation are **not** prescribed by Statutory Instrument; but the Law Society has provided suitable forms in circulars to members dated 28th July and 5th November 1982, and these forms should be followed in practice.

The recommended forms are reproduced in the Diploma Styles. New forms may be expected shortly — see note above.

Practice.

Some practical points on the effect of the Act on normal transactions include:

1. Title in joint names

Where the title to a dwellinghouse is in joint names, no special action is required, on sale, on purchase, or on granting security because both parties grant the Deed(s); but with two qualifications:

(i) Title in joint names, and Security granted by one of the spouses only, on his or her one half *pro indiviso* share. This is a very unusual situation and will only rarely occur; but if it does, consent of the other spouse would seem to be required.

(ii) Title in joint names, followed by a divorce. If, after divorce, one of the parties to the marriage remains in occupation of the original Matrimonial Home (as may easily happen), and then remarries, the Title may remain in the original joint names. None-the-less, on remarriage the new spouse acquires a right under the Act and becomes a 'Non-entitled spouse'.

The consequence of this would seem to be:

(a) When selling property on behalf of husband and wife, where the title is in joint names, you should confirm with them that they are still the same husband and wife, and that there has been no intervening divorce.

(b) When purchasing property from a husband and wife, the same enquiry should be made of the selling agent, and confirmation obtained from the selling agent that there has been no intervening divorce and no second marriage.

2. Title in one name

i) **Sale.** When selling a dwellinghouse, and when the title is in the name of one spouse only, or in name of one or more unmarried owners then either:

(a) If there is no non-entitled spouse, get an Affidavit to that effect (one from each owner if more than one); or

(b) If there is a non-entitled spouse, get a Renunciation from the non-entitled spouse.

These will be delivered to the purchaser at settlement.

ii) **Security.** When arranging heritable security, either at the time of purchase or as an additional advance, if the title is not in joint names of the spouses, then proceed as in 2(i).

Note:

(i) If the security is granted simultaneously with the purchase, the same Affidavit or Renunciation will serve. But, if the non-entitled spouse is consenting, and has not granted a Renunciation, consent (*in gremio* or separate) is required to the granting by the entitled spouse of a standard security.

(ii) In the case of a subsequent advance, a new affidavit must be obtained (from each borrower if more than one); or the non-entitled spouse must either renounce, or consent to the additional Security.

3. **Purchase.** When purchasing a dwellinghouse:

(a) in all cases where there is no non-entitled spouse, insist on an Affidavit by the Seller to be delivered at settlement and then registered in the Books of Council and Session. No Stamp is required.

(b) in all cases where there is a non-entitled spouse, take a Renunciation or the consent (*in gremio* or separate) of the non-entitled spouse. The Renunciation should be delivered to the purchaser at settlement, and then registered in the Books of Council and Session.

4. **Death**

A question has been raised as to whether or not occupancy rights continue after death; and, therefore, whether an Affidavit/Renunciation should be obtained when purchasing a property from Executors.

According to Nichols & Meston — Matrimonial Homes (Family Protection) (Scotland) Act 1981, Ch. 2.25. occupancy rights automatically terminate on death; but they admit that this is only an implication from the terms of the Act.

It is equally arguable that, if the deceased spouse died testate, the Will is a dealing by the entitled spouse; and, if the Will bequeaths the house to somebody other than the widow or widower, he or she could claim occupancy rights, notwithstanding the death, on the basis of the dealing.

Where the death is intestate, the rights of the non-entitled spouse are protected as prior rights.

The safest course, meantime, may be to assume that a widow or widower, if he or she does not inherit under the Will, may have occupancy rights; and to take the appropriate Affidavit, or Renunciation and consent, in every case when dealing with Executors or legatees other than the surviving spouse. Since this may not show on the confirmation, some enquiry may be necessary, until the position is clarified.

9. **Examination of Superiority and other Titles.**

If the Seller produces, as his title, a Charter (and subsequent writs) recorded within the last 10 years, the Charter is not a good foundation writ, nor is this a valid progress of titles despite a common misconception that a Feu Charter, even if granted within the 10 year period, is of itself a valid title. In any such case, it is essential to examine the superiority title (which, prior to the granting of the Charter, was of course, a title to the *dominium utile)* back to a valid foundation writ recorded more than 10 years ago, to ensure that the superior who granted the original Charter had a valid title to do so. This, in addition, involves examination of the superiority Search.

There are, of course, in most areas, some large superiority titles, typically in building estates, which are well known to Agents from previous examination. In such cases, it may be unnecessary to examine the prior title again on a subsequent occasion, although it is normally necessary to look at the Search.

It is not unusual, in larger building estates, for the Builders' Agents to insert in the Contract of Sale and Purchase an express provision excluding the purchaser's right to examine the superiority title (purely for administrative convenience), but possibly subject to the granting of a Certificate by the superior's Law Agent that the title is valid.

Otherwise, the title to the *dominium utile* by itself, coupled with possession, normally suffices to establish the proprietary title and the burdens on it. But in certain limited cases an examination of titles to adjoining properties may be appropriate or necessary. There are 4 common illustrations.

(i) **Boundary features.** While the proprietor can normally establish possession of the land within the boundaries, he can rarely establish exclusive possession of the boundary feature itself. Suppose, then, that there was a Disposition by A in favour of B in 1970 which disponed the lands of X and described them as bounded 'on the north by the north face of a boundary wall separating the said subjects hereinbefore disponed from other subjects belonging to C, which said wall is erected wholly on the subjects hereinbefore disponed'. On delivery of the Disposition, B enters into possession. It would seem from his title that he is the exclusive proprietor of the boundary wall on the north boundary; and therefore can use it as he pleases, e.g. for a garage, etc. But suppose that, in a Disposition by A in favour of the said C of the adjoining subjects on the north recorded prior to the 1970 Disposition, the same boundary in C's Disposition is referred to as 'the centre line of the mutual wall separating the said subjects hereinbefore disponed from other subjects belonging to me'. Normally, neither B nor C can establish exclusive possession of the boundary feature itself. Therefore, the titles would be conclusive as to the ownership of the boundary feature; and as C's title was recorded before B's, B could not prevail in a competition with C and, accordingly, the wall would be mutual and not B's property. This might frustrate B in some development.

The same sort of problem can occur in other, less usual circumstances, e.g. with fishings, lochs, common property, etc.

(ii) **Tenements.** In the absence of express provision in the titles, the Law of The tenement supplies, by implication, certain rights and imposes certain obligations on tenement proprietors *inter se.* This can, and often does, cause difficulties. Suppose that A in 1970 dispones the top flat in a tenement to B and imposes on B the burden of payment of a one-eighth share of the cost of maintaining the roof, chimneyheads, main walls, and other common items in the tenement. *Prima facie,* this supersedes the Law of the Tenement, (at least *quoad* roof) and limits B's liability for roof repairs to a one-eighth share only.

But suppose that A, when selling off the remaining flats in the tenement, fails to insert any comparable obligation in the Dispositions of the other flats. Since the other titles are silent, the Law of the Tenement will apply in their case; and, *quoad* roof, the Law of the Tenement provides that the top flat proprietor pays the whole cost of maintaining the roof above his flat. Therefore, contrary to what appears in the title, (which is also the **earliest** separate title) B is in fact burdened with the payment of the whole, not merely a one-eighth share, of the cost of roof repairs. This may be a very serious liability.

For a cautionary illustration, see Article I968 JLS 90. A builder disponed a top flat in a new block of eight flats to a purchaser, inserting a clause restricting the disponee's liability for roof repairs to a one-eighth share only and undertaking to insert a similar burden as to roof repairs in the titles of the seven remaining flats. He then went bankrupt. The Trustee in sequestration conveyed the remaining seven flats without any comparable condition. In the result, the purchaser had no right of redress except theoretically, against the bankrupt; but that was valueless. She complained to the Scottish Law Commission, but there has been no change in the Law of the Tenement.

(iii) **New Feus.** Exactly the same problem can arise in new feus, with cross obligations to pay for one-half of the cost of boundary features.

2.5.27 - Jolly's Exix. v. Stonehaven I958 SC 635 is typical. In that case, under a Feu Charter, a feuar was bound to erect, at his own sole expense, a boundary wall which was to be mutual to the feuar and the superior, the superior paying no part of the cost of erection; but in terms of the Charter, the feuar was to be entitled to recover one-half of the cost of erecting the boundary wall from the feuar of the adjoining ground when the same came to be 'feued'. This is a very common type of provision in practice. Later, the superiority of the feu was sold; and later still, the adjoining ground was sold and disponed (but **not** 'feued'). In the Disposition of the adjoining ground, no obligation was inserted as to payment of one-half of the cost of erection of the boundary wall. Since the titles were silent, the disponee of the adjoining ground could not be held liable for the cost; and, because at the time of granting the Disposition, the disponer was no longer superior of the feu, he was held not to be liable in damages. Therefore, the apparent right to recover one-half of the cost of the boundary wall in the feuar's Charter was totally ineffective.

(iv) **Part Disposals, with restrictions on the part retained.** A owns a house and garden, with 1/2 acre spare amenity ground. He sells the 1/2 acre to B, to build a house on. In the contract, and in B's Disposition, A undertakes not to use his own house for any purpose other than as a residence. A then sells his own house to C but without inserting any restriction on use. C converts the house to a licensed hotel; and B cannot prevent C from so doing. See 7.4.29 — McLean v. Kennaway 11 SLT 719 — a right of pre-emption was conferred on a Disponee A of part of a tenement entitling him to acquire the remainder, i.e. it entered the Disponee's title in the G.R.S. The Disponer then sold the remainder, without first offering it to A under the pre-emption. A then sought to reduce the disposition of the remainder to the Disponee thereof but was held not entitled, in that the pre-emption had not been effectually created a real burden on the remainder.

Note incidentally that, in this case, the fact that the pre-emption appeared on the Record, in the title to another property, was held **not** to be public notice thereof, and **not** equivalent to intimation to the Disponee of the remainder, (warning him of the right and putting him on his enquiry). Otherwise, the principle in Rodger (Builders) Ltd. *supra* would have applied.

Note also that, had the right conferred on A been in the nature of a servitude e.g. *non altius tollendi,* he could have enforced it against the successor in the remainder. Indeed, the case was argued on the basis of dominant and servient tenement, but Lord Low rightly rejected that argument.

Despite what may be serious risks in some cases, titles of adjoining property, flats in tenements, etc., are rarely examined in practice by purchaser's Agents.

Negative prescription.

The new long negative prescription reintroduced in its new form by the Prescription and Limitation (Scotland) Act 1973 SS.7-11 may indirectly affect heritable titles. In summary, SS.7 and 8 provide that:

(a) if any obligation has subsisted unpursued for twenty years and not acknowledged by the obligee; or

(b) a right has become exercisable and has remained unenforced for twenty years;

then the right or obligation is altogether extinguished.

Certain rights and obligations are, however, declared to be 'imprescriptable' and are excluded from the operation of these Sections by Schedule 3. The rights which cannot be extinguished by the negative prescription include the following:

(a) Real rights of ownership. This applies only to **real** rights and does not prevent the extinction of mere personal rights or personal titles, See 7.1.98b — Macdonald 1981 SLT 128 — The right to demand delivery of a disposition under a Contract of Sale and Purchase is a personal right and prescriptable. But a right constituted by infeftment can never be lost by non-exercise for however long a time.

(b) Similarly, the rights of a tenant under a recorded lease cannot prescribe.

(c) *Res merae facultatis* cannot prescribe and are not extinguished by non-use.

(d) The right to serve as an heir, and make up title to a deceased's estate, is imprescriptable, and therefore cannot be lost by lapse of time.

Bearing these exceptions in mind, the main cases where the negative prescription affects heritable title are:

(i) Heritable Securities. If no action is taken by the creditor to enforce a heritable security, and no interest has been paid throughout the twenty year period, the obligation and the security is then automatically extinguished and cannot in any circumstances revive. Therefore, by implication, the title is disburdened thereof, although this does not disclose itself on the Record.

(ii) Servitudes. In contrast to *res merae facultatis,* servitudes are extinguished by the long negative prescription. Further, under the 1973 Act, the period is now twenty years in all cases, in contrast to the earlier period of forty years plus non-age etc.

In the case of positive servitudes, the period starts to run from the date when the servitude was last exercised. In the case of negative servitudes, the period starts to run from the date when the negative servitude was infringed without objection. In order to exclude the long negative prescription under the 1973 Act, a relevant claim must have been made, which means either by appropriate proceedings in Court, by diligence or by arbitration.

Alternatively, in the case of obligations, the long negative prescription is interrupted by 'relevant acknowledgment' which means such performance by the debtor as clearly indicates that the obligation subsists or unequivocal written acknowledgment by the debtor or on his behalf. See SS.9 and l0. Deeds *ex facie* invalid or forged are not exempted from challenge by the negative prescription; this mirrors the equivalent provision for positive prescription in SS.1 to 3.

7.5 A Typical Conveyancing Transaction.
Reading List 7.5
Contributed by D.J. Hogarth, Head of Department of Legal Practice, University of Dundee.

1. Introduction

1.1 The Diploma course of Practice of Conveyancing concentrates on the **conveyancing** aspects of the purchase and sale, leasing and charging of heritable property in Scotland. The following note may be useful in indicating the sequence of events in a typical purchase/sale/loan conveyancing transaction from the **solicitors'** point of view, and in identifying at what stage particular matters have to be dealt with.

1.2 For the purposes of this note S (the seller) owns a house at 12 Park Place, Dundee bought in 1978 with the help of a loan from the Invergowrie Building Society: S's title is therefore burdened with a heritable security in their favour. (S's title is set out in more detail in 7.5 Appendix 1).

1.3 P (the purchaser) owns a house in Edinburgh which he has to sell before he can complete the purchase of S's house and the title of P's house is burdened with a security in favour of the Edinburgh Building Society. So far as the sale of P's house and the repayment of the Edinburgh Building Society mortgage are concerned, while P's solicitor will be dealing with these matters at the same time as the purchase of S's house, for the purposes of this note they will be ignored since *mutatis mutandis* (as lawyers are fond of saying) the procedures will be as for the sale of S's house and the repayment of his mortgage. A simplified summary of the various elements of the transactions is given below:

(1) P contracts to purchase a dwellinghouse from S.

(2) P must then:
  (a) sell his own house and repay the loan out the proceeds;
  (b) apply for and obtain a new loan to complete his purchase. He cannot simply transfer his existing loan to his new house.

(3) P completes his purchase using:
  (a) his new Building Society loan;
  (b) the balance of the sale proceeds from the sale of his own house, after paying off his loan.

But, if his own house has not sold in time, P must use temporary bridging finance to tide him over the gap between the date when he pays the purchase price of the new house and the date when he receives the sale price of his existing house. This is often an anxious (and expensive) gap of some weeks or even months. It sometimes happens that P cannot sell his own house; and is forced to re-sell the house just purchased from S. He can avoid this risk only if he sells his own house first before completing a binding contract for the purchase of another house. But, if he sells first before purchasing another house, it may then be difficult to find another suitable house in time before he has to vacate his own house under his contract of sale.

These are hazards inherent in the sale and purchase of a dwellinghouse.

(4) S, on completion of the sale, uses the proceeds to repay his Building Society loan and pay the costs of the sale. S in turn may be purchasing another house in which case he proceeds as P above.

1.4   The purchase/sale transaction and the loan transaction (whether borrowing or repaying the loan) are in each case two separate and distinct transactions; but it is usual for the seller's solicitor to act both for the seller and for his building society (acting thus in two separate capacities) and likewise for the purchaser's solicitor to act both for the purchaser and for his building society (acting again in two separate capacities). This has the benefit both of simplifying the transaction by reducing the number of solicitors involved and of restricting the fees which both purchaser and seller will have to meet.

1.5   Every conveyancing transaction involving heritable property is obviously different, but the basic pattern of each is similar. The note refers to a typical straightforward sale/purchase/loan transaction with no problems — and you can always hope that this will happen in practice! It should not however be treated as anything more than an outline of the steps involved: it is not a guide to be followed indiscriminately in every (or indeed any specific) case.

1.6   In certain respects the practice of solicitors in different parts of the country differs in detail: this note follows the practice in Dundee.

1.7   For a summarised outline of the progress of a conveyancing transaction, based on a paper prepared for the Law Society of Scotland, see edited excerpts annexed at the end of Chapter 7.5.

2.   **Preliminary**
From advertisements to conclusion of missives

2.1   S is moving from the Dundee area for business reasons. He makes an appointment with his solicitor to discuss the sale of his house. At this stage the solicitor's advice will be general, outlining the various steps involved in the sale and the repayment of the mortgage.

2.2   Following their meeting S's solicitor writes to the Invergowrie Building Society to obtain the title deeds of the house (the Society holds them in security of the mortgage) — they are sent on **loan only** by the building society until the outstanding balance of the mortgage is repaid. S's solicitor checks the titles which he receives and if they are incomplete *i.e.* if there is no prescriptive progress or if certain deeds referred to for burdens or for description are missing, he will try to obtain the other deeds which he requires either from the solicitors who hold them (*e.g.* on behalf of superiors) or, if they cannot be traced, by way of quick copies or extracts from Register House.

2.3   S's solicitor requests, from the appropriate local authority or authorities, certificates confirming the position with regard to various matters including for example (i) whether the house is affected by (a) any matters arising under the planning and housing legislation or (b) by any road improvement schemes (ii) whether the road, pavement and main drain *ex adverso* the house have been adopted for maintenance purposes etc. This is usually referred to as 'writing for the usual local authority certificates' without specifying what matters might be covered! (Obtaining the replies may take anything up to 4 or 5 weeks. Verbal inquiries can be made to gain an idea of what the position is likely to be although some Authorities refuse to give verbal information. In cases where there is some doubt as to *e.g.* the planning position, it is sensible to await confirmation in writing of the position).

2.4   S's solicitor will also clear up at this stage any matters in the title which a purchaser will (almost) certainly raise *e.g.* a subsisting right of pre-emption; he will also (depending on the age and type of property) for example, check with the Superior the position regarding feuing conditions and obtain from him a certificate that all feuing conditions except those of a continuing nature have been implemented (*e.g.* that the house, fences, etc., have been completed to the Superior's satisfaction).

2.5 With the title deeds, and having clarified the public land use position, S's solicitor visits S's house to check the boundaries etc., against the title; to inspect the house and garden; to advise on and discuss the price which the house should, it is hoped, fetch; to take instructions on matters such as entry (bearing in mind S's future intentions as to buying another house); to confirm which fixtures, fittings and other moveable items *e.g.* carpets are to be included in the price and which may be for sale separately at an additional price to the purchaser; to confirm the viewing arrangements (*e.g.* by card from the solicitor; by telephoning S; at set times) and to confirm the advertising arrangements etc.

2.6 S's solicitor then prepares a Schedule of Particulars giving full details of the house and confirms the details with S, inserts details of the house in the local Solicitors' Property Centre; and instructs the necessary advertisements in the local/national press.

2.7 P in the meantime has been through the same procedure with his solicitor so far as his house in Edinburgh is concerned. Armed with an indication of the price range which he can afford or at least almost afford, he is looking for a house in or near Dundee. He will take into account the net price he will get for his Edinburgh house — **i.e.** the sale price less the amount required to repay the mortgage and the fees and other costs involved in his move; but bearing in mind the larger mortgage he will be able to afford on the basis of his higher salary. His solicitor has advised him initially to visit the Dundee Solicitors Property Centre and to take the 'Courier' on Tuesdays and Thursdays, the main days when property is advertised.

2.8 P visits S's house, likes it and expresses interest to S: S (having been well briefed by his solicitor) indicates that any offers should be made to his solicitor, that 'considerable interest' — a useful phrase — is being shown, but that in principle the price, date of entry, etc., are acceptable to him. P should not push for a decision, however keen he may be on the house. He should first discuss the purchase with his Solicitor and possibly his Surveyor. Since P wishes to have the house surveyed before he makes an offer or since he will need a mortage to fund, in part, the purchase and the Building Society will require the house to be valued, P (also having been well briefed by his solicitor!) finds out when a surveyor will be able to obtain access.

2.9 S may report P's interest in the house at this stage to his solicitor and give instructions in the event of an offer being received (see below).

2.10 P meets his solicitor, indicates his interest and gives him full details of the house (*i.e.* a copy of the Schedule of Particulars) and any other arrangements provisionally made as to *e.g.* fittings and fixtures, etc. P's solicitor is at this stage generally aware (as a good solicitor should be) of P's financial position so far as buying a house is concerned; S's house is within P's financial reach; there is unlikely to be any difficulty about obtaining a suitable mortgage; P's solicitor therefore telephones (or writes) to S's solicitor 'noting his client's interest' in S's house: the result of this is, or should be, that before S finally concludes the sale of his house, he will allow P a chance of offering to buy it. P's solicitor also enquires whether a 'closing date' has been fixed (*i.e.* a date by which offers have to be in the hands of S's solicitor) and seeks to elicit any other relevant information which he can about *e.g.* the price level likely to be acceptable, the most suitable date of entry etc.

2.11 P and his solicitor then discuss the sale of his Edinburgh house (luckily an acceptable offer has already been made) and the purchase of S's house.

2.12 The price which P should offer is clearly of the greatest importance since, if there are other interested potential purchasers in the market, it will normally have to be higher than any other competing offer; in arriving at the final price to be offered various factors have to be borne in mind however such as the amount of loan which may be obtained (and this will depend both on the property and the borrower's income) and the funds which P can himself raise (probably from the sale of his Edinburgh house). Two competing factors finally are present: P must be advised as to the likely costs of the move (both practical *e.g.* removal costs, new carpets, curtains etc., and legal *e.g.* stamp duty, recording dues, legal fees, cost of survey) but he must weigh the total cost of the move against the fact that he has to move to Dundee and that if he does not manage to buy S's house he will incur further costs in trying to buy another house. P and P's solicitor must therefore consider very carefully the price which P can and should offer, and whether — when the amount is settled on — this is likely to be successful. This is one area where the solicitor's experience and expertise is of particular importance to the client: to buy the house but not to pay over the odds for it! The difficulties of deciding what price to offer in these circumstances should not be under estimated. One of the reasons for odd prices (*e.g.* £20,107 or £35,253) being offered is not basically because this includes some fitment valued at £7 or £3 but so that in theory your client will have a slight edge (of £7 or £3!) over another offer.

Price almost always determines which of several offers the seller will accept. Other factors, such as the date of entry or the personal preference of the seller for a particular purchaser, rarely outweigh the accepting of the highest offer. Except at a public roup, the seller is never obliged to accept the highest, or indeed any, offer.

2.13 Since P cannot (in this case) buy S's house without a satisfactory loan, P's solicitor will advise on the best method of funding the purchase. (It is assumed that P will obtain a loan from his building society, but he may borrow from a bank or other financial institution depending on the property, his financial circumstances etc.). P's solicitor advises P with regard to the amount of loan required and obtains details of P's financial position (*e.g.* salary, wife's salary, outgoings etc.). P's solicitor already has details of the property and of how access can be obtained for a surveyor.

2.14 P's solicitor contacts P's building society and advises them of P's application for a loan, of the property concerned and of how access can be obtained for their surveyor. The building society instruct a surveyor to carry out a valuation survey of the house — this can usually be done very quickly — and advise P's solicitor by telephone of the outcome of the survey and how much they are, in consequence, prepared to lend. The survey is carried out on the Society's behalf, **not** on behalf of the prospective borrower. For this reason, many Solicitors advise the purchaser not to rely on the Building

Society's survey alone, but to instruct an independent survey report which puts the purchaser in a stronger position to claim damages from a negligent surveyor if some structural defect is overlooked at the survey stage. (See notes below.) The society will also, before they make even an informal offer of a loan, have confirmed the other details given by P in the application form (*e.g.* his salary), of the amount of the mortgage they are prepared to advance and when the money will be available.

2.15 P is then in a position to make a formal offer for S's house. He instructs his solicitor to make the formal offer and confirms the price, the date of entry (bearing in mind when the sale of P's Edinburgh house will be completed and when the new mortgage will be available), what is to be included in the price and which (if any) other fittings etc., are being bought separately etc. P's solicitor then writes to S's solicitor offering on behalf of P to buy S's house (a missive or formal offer). The offer will specify the purchaser, the property, the price offered and what is included in the price, the date of entry, and such other conditions as are (or appear to P or P's solicitor to be) necessary or appropriate. (The offer conditions will vary depending on the property and on the circumstances). The offer will usually conclude by stating a time limit by which an acceptance has to be received.

2.16 When S's solicitor receives the formal offer from P's solicitor he 'takes instructions' from his client. (In most cases there will be a number of offers and the client will have to be advised of each and of the conditions which each contain). In this case S confirms that he wishes to accept P's offer and that the price, the subjects, the date of entry etc., are all acceptable to him. S's solicitor checks the conditions of the offer (*e.g.* description and burdens) against the titles and against the local authority certificates which he has by now received. In this case (unusually!) no qualifications need to be made to the offer and S's solicitor send P's solicitor a formal letter accepting the latters' formal offer to buy S's house. The bargain is now struck and missives have been concluded.

2.17 If the offer cannot be accepted unconditionally, S's solicitor will reply by sending a formal **qualified** acceptance to P's solicitor (qualifying P's solicitor's offer in relation to the unacceptable condition(s) and P's solicitor will reply either by accepting these qualifications, or by further amending them; and letters will pass until an acceptable bargain is struck.

2.18 As soon as the bargain is struck, P's solicitor must insure the house in at least the amount of the price either (i) on a temporary policy (ii) by having P's interest noted on S's insurance policy or (iii) by instructing P's building society to insure the house.

Notes:

1) (Paragraph 2.14)

Building societies (or other lending institutions) before making an offer of loan, require, to be satisfied that the property offered as security is of sufficient value, and for this purpose they will instruct a **valuation survey** to be made of the property. This is **not** a **structural survey** whose necessity is a matter for the purchaser and his solicitor to decide. The building society's valuation survey will not necessarily be made available to the prospective borrower (in this case, P). In cases where the house concerned is fairly new and is covered by a NHBC certificate, it may be unnecessary for the prospective purchaser to instruct a structural survey, but where the house is older a structural survey will be sensible. Whether or not a structural survey should be obtained is a matter for careful consideration by the prospective purchaser and his solicitor; and the presumption should be in favour of a structural survey.

The difference between a **valuation survey** (taken for security purposes) and a **structural survey** (to see if the house is structurally sound etc.) is important and should be clearly understood.

If a purchaser is advised or wishes to have a structural survey carried out, it will usually be possible for his solicitor to arrange for the same surveyor as has been instructed by the building society for their valuation survey, also to produce the structural survey; this practice does allow the costs of both surveys (which will be met by the prospective purchaser/borrower) to be kept to a minimum.

2) (Paragraph 2.16)

'Missives' is the comprehensive term for the various letters which set out the bargain for the purchase/sale of property. They must be holograph or adopted as holograph, hence the terms 'formal offer' 'formal acceptance' etc.

3. **Examination of Title**
   (from conclusion of missives to settlement)

3.1 Once missives are concluded, S's solicitor sends to P's solicitor:
   (i) **the title deeds** of the house — which should include a prescriptive progress and all the deeds referred to for burdens and for description together with a Search.
   (ii) **draft Memorandum for Continuation of Search** bringing down the existing Search. If there is no separate search for the house, what is required will be a draft **Memorandum for Search.**
   (iii) **draft Discharge** of the Standard Security granted in favour of Invergowrie Building Society — this deed is drafted by S's solicitor.
   (iv) **draft Letter of Obligation** obliging S's solicitor to deliver (a) a completed Search brought down in terms of (ii) above, (b) a duly recorded Discharge in terms of the draft (iii) above, and (c) any other deeds or documents not available at the time of settlement.

3.2 P's solicitor examines the title offered and writes to S's solicitor requesting exhibition of any deed(s) not exhibited which he (P's solicitor) requires to look at to complete his examination of the title. P's solicitor will compare the title description (and the plan, if any) against the actual property, and will advise P of any discrepancies and of any burdens in the title (whether referred to in the missives or not). P's solicitor also checks the local authority certificates and all other relevant matters (e.g. services to the property) particularly if mentioned in the missives. (It is helpful if some form of aide-memoire is used by the purchaser's solicitor — it avoids any relevant points being omitted from consideration. An example is given in Appendix 2 at the end of Chap. 7.5).

3.3 P's solicitor then raises with S's solicitor any queries or other matters in connection with the titles or the bargain which he considers necessary or appropriate. S's solicitor in response to these requests obtains and furnishes to P's solicitor such deeds or other information as the latter has requested.

(In some cases the seller's solicitor may consider that some of the purchaser's solicitors' requests are less than reasonable, or some of the information requested may be unobtainable or cannot be confirmed; some degree of practical expediency is therefore necessary in dealing with title examination, without however, compromising verification of the title being offered).

3.4 P's solicitor prepares Notes on Title.

3.5 P's building society have in the meantime made a formal written offer of loan to P which he has accepted. P's building society have instructed P's solicitor to act for them in connection with the security documents — this is normal practice, it reduces the fees paid by the purchaser/ borrower and saves time by avoiding the necessity of involving 2 solicitors — and have enclosed drafts of the security documents required.

Note: The security documents will reflect the type of security taken. There will certainly be a Standard Security; but assignation of e.g. life policies may also be required.

3.6 Having examined the title offer, and on the assumption that it is acceptable and that all the queries — the 'observations on title' — have been satisfactorily answered, P's solicitor:
(i) drafts the Disposition by S to P (having confirmed with P the destination to be taken in the deed)
(ii) revises or approves the draft Discharge (paragraph 3.1 (iii))
(iii) revises or approves the draft Memorandum for (Continuation of) Search (paragraph 3.1 (ii))
(iv) revises or approves the draft Letter of Obligation (paragraph 3.1 (iv))
P's solicitor then returns to S's solicitor:
(i) the titles as sent, and
(ii) the revised/approved draft Discharge, Memorandum and Letter of Obligation, and encloses
(iii) the draft Disposition.

3.7 S's solicitor revises or approves the draft Disposition and returns it to P's solicitor.

Note: A draft deed is **approved** if no amendments require to be made to it; it is **revised** if it requires to be amended. Do not however revise another solicitor's draft unless it **requires** to be amended *i.e.* if there is an error or omission which is more than simply a matter of style.

The matters referred to in paragraphs 3.8 all take place at the same time.

3.8 P's solicitor at the same time as dealing with the matters in 3.6 above (i) confirms to P's building society that the title of the house is in order and (ii) requests that the loan cheque be sent to him shortly before the settlement date. P's solicitor also writes to P asking to be put in funds (to the extent of the difference between the purchase price and the building society loan) to allow settlement to take place.

Note: The net proceeds from the sale of P's present house (after deducting his existing building society loan over that house) will be taken into account in the financial calculations made by P's solicitor. The need for bank bridging should be borne in mind — P's solicitor may have to arrange this even if settlement of the purchase of S's house and the sale of P's present house occur on the same day.

3.9 P's solicitor engrosses the Disposition and sends it (along with the revised/approved draft for comparison purposes) to S's solicitor. S's solicitor then sends the engrossed deed to S to sign; S signs and returns the signed deed to his solicitor together with the Schedule of Signing giving the details of signing (the place and date of signing and the names, designations and addresses of the witnesses). S's solicitor retains the signed Disposition.

3.10 P's solicitor at the same time as he engrosses the Disposition, prepares the Standard Security (and any other security documents required *e.g.* assignation of life assurance policy etc.) in favour of P's building society, and sends this to P to sign; P signs and returns the signed deed to his solicitor together with the completed Schedule of Signing.

3.11 S's solicitor engrosses the Discharge and sends it to the Invergowrie Building Society for execution, asking at the same time for a note of the amount required to settle S's loan on the settlement date (*i.e.* the date of entry). The Invergowrie Building Society return the Discharge duly executed with a statement setting out the amount required to settle the loan on the settlement date.

3.12 S's solicitor writes to the Searchers (*e.g.* Register House or private searchers) enclosing the Search and the revised/approved Memorandum for Continuation, and instructs the Search to be brought down in terms of the Memorandum; he also asks for an Interim Report to be prepared as close to the settlement date as possible and for a note of fee to be submitted along with the Interim Report.

3.13 Once the Interim Report is received:
S's solicitor writes to P's solicitor enclosing this together with the Search and a draft State for Settlement (setting out in effect the sums of money due to complete the purchase by P of S's house) accompanied by such vouchers (e.g. rates receipts) as are necessary to vouch the State (these will have been previously obtained from S) and indicating that he is in a position to settle on the due date. S gives a set of keys for the house to his solicitor.

3.14 P's solicitor approves the Interim Report and revises/approves the draft State for Settlement and returns it to S's solicitor indicating that he is in funds to settle as he has now received the loan cheque from P's building society, and a cheque from P or from the solicitor acting for the purchaser of P's Edinburgh house or he has arranged for bridging finance to be available. Note that the Consumer Credit regulations will apply to any bridging loan of £15,000 or less — see 1985 JLS 159.

4. **Settlement**
'the next step is the fee ...'

4.1 P's solicitor has arranged with S's solicitor that they will settle at 11 a.m. on the settlement date. P's solicitor — or more likely the trainee solicitor — arrives at the offices of S's solicitor with a cheque for the amount brought out in the State for Settlement (i.e. the price of the house plus or minus any apportionments of e.g. rates).

In exchange for the cheque S's solicitor hands over to P's solicitor
(i)   the Disposition, signed by S, together with the approved draft (prepared by P's solicitor) and the Schedule of Signing,
(ii) the titles falling to be delivered,
(iii) the executed and attested Discharge with the warrant signed and a covering letter to the Keeper of the Registers,

      (iv) the Letter of Obligation duly signed together with the agreed draft (which draft is after comparison left with S's solicitor)

      (v) the receipted State for Settlement, and

      (vi) the keys of the house.

4.2 P's solicitor then:

      (i) passes the keys for the house to P

      (ii) completes the testing clause of the Disposition and signs the warrant

      (iii) completes the testing clause (if necessary) on the Standard Security in favour of P's building society and signs the warrant, and

      (iv) sends the Disposition, the Standard Security, and the Discharge to Register House for recording (together with in the case of the Discharge the letter to the Keeper from S's solicitor requesting that the Discharge be recorded — this is necessary since, strictly speaking, the Discharge ought to be forwarded to S's solicitor). If the Disposition requires to be stamped, this must obviously be done before it is sent for recording.

4.3 S's solicitor sends the Invergowrie Building Society a cheque for the amount due to repay the loan and in due course S will receive a statement from the society to the close of the account.

4.4 S's solicitor returns any title deeds which he may have borrowed from the other solicitors and cancels or arranges for the cancellation of the house insurance and any bankers order (*e.g.* for monthly mortgage payments). He also advises the Regional Council (as the rating authority) of the change of ownership. Finally, he fees S and remits the balance of the proceeds of sale to him or as he directs.

4.5 P's solicitor confirms the change of ownership to the Regional Council and likewise fees P and accounts to him.

5. **Finale**

Some months later ...

In due course (some months later) Register House returns to S's solicitor the recorded Discharge which in terms of the Letter of Obligation S's solicitor forwards to P's solicitor who acknowledges it and marks the Letter of Obligation (handed over at settlement) as being implemented to this extent. P's solicitor will at the same time receive from Register House the recorded Disposition and Standard Security. P's solicitor will usually at this stage forward the title deeds together with the Discharge, Disposition and Standard Security to P's Building Society (who will retain them) but he may await the return of the Search before doing so (this may take 9 months or longer). The Search is returned to S's solicitor (since he instructed it) who forwards it to P's solicitor. If this is the final item in the Letter of Obligation, P's solicitor marks the Letter as 'implemented' and returns it to S's solicitor. P's solicitor then forwards the Search to be retained along with the other titles to the Building Society.

Note: The above is the procedure in a sale/purchase where a **Disposition** is granted. Where the title granted is a **Feu Disposition,** there are certain differences (though basically the procedure is similar) since the sellers' solicitor prepares the draft Feu Disposition which is sent to the purchaser's solicitor for revisal/approval who then returns it to the former for engrossing.

7.5 **APPENDIX 1**

(Specimen)
INVENTORY OF TITLES
of detached house
12 Park Place, DUNDEE

Property Writs

1. Feu Disposition by Scott Properties Ltd., in favour of John Maclean recorded GRS Angus 25 May 1951.

2. Disposition by John Maclean in favour of Mrs. Helen Smith or Wilson recorded GRS Angus 3 September, 1981.

3. Confirmation in favour of George Wilson as Executor of the late Mrs. Helen Smith or Wilson issued at Dundee 9th July, 1982.

4. Disposition by George Wilson as Executor foresaid in favour of S recorded GRS Angus 15 March, 1983.

Security Writs

5. Bond and Disposition in Security by John Maclean in favour of Rackrent Finance Co. Ltd., recorded GRS Angus 25 May 1951.

6. Discharge of No. 5 above recorded GRS Angus 3 September, 1971.

7. Standard Security by S in favour of Invergowrie Building Society recorded GRS Angus 15 March, 1983.

Searches

8. Search for Incumbrances from 25 May, 1951 to 15th March 1983.

7.5 APPENDIX 2

EXAMINATION OF TITLE Partner......................... 1985

Questionnaire Assistant...................... Date....................

Client...

Property ....

1. **Missives**
   Has the client been sent a copy of the concluded Missives?

2. **Title**
   a. Have you seen and examined a Foundation Writ?
   b. Have you seen and examined **ALL** subsequent links in title?
   c. Are **ALL** these Writs wholly valid?
   d. Have you checked each clause of deduction of title and the mid couples?

3. **Description**
   a. Is the Property **correctly** and **consistently** described throughout?
   b. Does the description correspond with the Missives?
   c. Has it been confirmed by (i) the surveyor **and** (ii) the purchaser?
   d. Has a copy of the plan, if any, been submitted to the client for approval?
   e. Does the Property comprise one site?

4. **Services**
   Has the Property got:
   a. Direct access from the public road?
   b. Main water from the public road?
   c. Mains electricity from the public road?
   d. Main drainage from the public road?

5. **Survey.**
   Is there a Survey Report and have you checked it?

6. **Burdens**
   a. Have you examined **ALL** the writs referred to for burdens?
   b. Are you satisfied that **ALL** burdens have been complied with to date?
   c. Are you sure that there are no unexpected or unusual burdens?
   d. Are you sure that no burden conflicts with the terms of the Missives?
   e. Have you brought the burdens to the attention of the purchaser?
   f. Tenements/divided houses — are the roof repairs mutual?
   g. Top floor flat — do the titles of the lower flats contain an obligation to maintain roof?

7. **Feuduty**
   a. Has the feuduty been validly allocated and redeemed?
   b. If unallocated, does the last feuduty receipt correspond with the Title?
   c. Have you seen a cumulo feuduty receipt?

8. **Searches**
   a. Is the Search clear?
   b. Have you seen a clear Interim Report?

9. **Miscellaneous**
   a. Have all the conditions in the Missives been complied with?
   b. Have you received a satisfactory reply to the Planning, Roads and Sewers etc. letters?
   c. Have you seen a Completion Certificate for any extension or alterations?
   d. Have you got the appropriate Matrimonial Homes Act Forms completed?
   e. Is the garage, if any, covered by N.H.B.C.?
   f. Are all the N.H.B.C. papers in order?

10. **Minerals**
    a. Are there any known or intended workings under the Property?
    b. If so, what provision is made for compensation etc?

11. **Wet Rot, Dry Rot etc.**
    a. Have you seen all guarantee certificates and all relative particulars prior to the Date of Entry?
    b. Does the guarantee require to be assigned?

12. **Draft Disposition**
    a. Is the granter infeft?
    b. If not,
       (i) are you satisfied with the links in title,
       (ii) have you correctly deduced title, **and**
       (iii) have you **designed** the person last infeft?
    c. Is the destination to the disponee(s) correct, according to our instructions?

13. **Attach a Summary of Description, and Burdens, and copy plan** (if any)

7.5 APPENDIX 3

Excerpts from Replies by the Law Society of Scotland to the Questionnaire issued by the Royal Commission on Legal Services, with some editing and comments by the Author, to bring it up to date,

SALE AND PURCHASE OF HERITABLE PROPERTY

Note: It is assumed that the property is not in an operational area for Registration of Title.

1. STEPS IN SALE AND PROCEDURE

3rd Feb

Seller's Solicitor

S.1 Ascertain marital status of client.
S.2 Advise client on transaction, on asking price, and on advertising.
S.3 Obtain particulars of property.
S.4 Prepare particulars, and draft advertisement
S.5 Have particulars and draft advertisement approved by client.
S.6 Instruct Advertisement.
S.7 Lodge particulars in Solicitors' Property Centre
S.8 Write for title deeds held by seller's Building Society.
S.9 Write to Local Authority with planning, road, etc. enquiries (and instruct Interim Report on Search — but see S.33).

7th - 18th Feb

S.10 It is assumed that the property is advertised for two weeks during which time the seller's Solicitor will answer enquiries, give particulars to interested parties, arrange viewing and if necessary show the property and arrange for surveyors to inspect it.

8th Feb

S.11 Check seller's titles received from Building Society — in particular the state of the title with particular reference to Occupancy Rights.
S.12 Write for any necessary prior but undelivered writs. If title in joint names, check that both parties are instructing sale and will sign the Deed. If title in one name, then obtain Consent or Renunciation of Occupancy Rights by non-entitled spouse or an Affidavit by seller if seller is unmarried.

14th Feb

Purchaser's Solicitor

P.1 Discuss proposed purchase with client and ascertain marital status.
P.2 Approach Building Society or Bank for a loan and instruct them to survey the property. (Note: It may be advisable for the client to instruct his own survey as well. See Chap. 7.5.2.14 and Note thereon).

17th Feb

P.3 Obtain results of survey(s) (and instruct specialist survey on wet rot etc. if required).
P.4 Discuss these with purchaser (particularly the cost of repairs, if any, required, and amount of loan). Advise on price and other terms of offer to be submitted to seller's Solicitor.

18th Feb

Seller's Solicitor

S.13 Advise client to fix closing date (since number of interested parties).
S.14 Inform interested parties.

Purchaser's Solicitor

P.5 Arrange bridging finance for balance of price for period 30th March to 15th April. (Note: 30th March is the date of entry in the offer to purchase. The purchaser has already sold his own house with entry on 15th April. Bridging is required to cover the gap of 2 weeks).
P.6 Take instructions to submit offer.
P.7 Frame offer and deliver before closing date.

22nd Feb

Seller's Solicitor

S.15 Receive offers.
S.16 Check these with client's titles.
S.17 Advise client of terms of offers, and discuss which offer to accept. Take instructions on the terms of the offer to be accepted.
S.18 Frame acceptance, qualified if necessary; and send this to successful purchaser's Solicitor.
S.19 Advise unsuccessful purchasers.

23rd Feb

Purchaser's Solicitor

P.8 Receive qualified acceptance.
P.9 Discuss qualifications with client. Make such further enquiries as may be necessary and consider whether further qualifications are necessary.
P.10 Obtain instructions to send qualified or unqualified acceptance, as appropriate.
P.11 Prepare and deliver acceptance.
(Note: P.8 - P.11 apply only if seller's acceptance is qualified).
P.12 Advise client of concluded bargain (unless purchaser's acceptance is qualified).
P.13 Instruct Building Society to arrange property insurance for client; or arrange temporary cover. (Note: Missives now commonly provide that the risk is not to pass until entry, in which case insurance by the purchaser may not be necessary before that date).
P.14 Submit loan application forms to Building Society; or confirm with purchaser that he has done this direct. (Note: It is assumed that the purchaser has an existing endowment Policy which is to be assigned to the Building Society as collateral security).

24th Feb

Seller's Solicitor

S.20 Receive final acceptance.
S.21 Advise client of concluded bargain.
(Note: S.20 - S.21 apply only if seller's acceptance was qualified. If so, and if the purchaser makes further qualifications, the seller's Solicitor proceeds as in P.8 - P.12).

2. STEPS IN CONVEYANCING PROCEDURE

27th Feb.

Seller's Solicitor

S.22 Frame.
   (a) draft Memorandum for Search or Continuation of existing Search;
   (b) draft Letter of Obligation;
   (c) draft Discharge of Building Society Loan;
   (d) draft Retrocession of Life Policy assigned to Building Society as collateral security.

S.23 Send drafts (a), (b) and (c), title deeds, any guarantee Certificates for Wet Rot, Dry Rot eradication works etc. together with any Report and Quotations, any N.H.B.C. documentation, Local Authority Certificates on planning, roads, etc. and appropriate evidence to comply with the Matrimonial Homes (Family Protection) (Scotland) Act 1981, to purchaser's Solicitor (purchaser's Solicitor has no concern with (d)).

S.24 Acknowledge prior titles received from other agents and pay borrowing fee (see S.12 above).

28th Feb - 3rd March

Purchaser's Solicitor

P.15 Acknowledge titles. Examine and make Notes on Title for file. Ensure that appropriate evidence to satisfy Matrimonial Homes Act is with titles if property has been transferred since March 1982.

P.16 Report to purchaser on results of examination of title; ask him to confirm description and send plan, if available; explain import of burdens.
   (Note: This may involve careful checking with client and his Surveyor, and discussions on effect of title conditions in relation to the marketability of the title).
   Also report to purchaser on content of Local Authorty Certificates etc.

P.17 Revise.
   (a) Memorandum for Search or continuation thereof.
   (b) Letter of Obligation.
   (c) Discharge of seller's Sandard Security.

P.18 Frame draft Disposition.

4th March

P.19 Return titles, drafts (a), (b) and (c) and send draft Disposition to seller's Solicitor, make any necessary observations on the title and request further information on Guarantees, N.H.B.C. etc. as required.

7th March

Seller's Solicitor

S.25 Acknowledge titles and drafts.

S.26 Make necessary enquiries to allow observations on title to be dealt with.

S.27 Revise draft Disposition.

11th March

S.28 Reply to observations on title.

S.29 Return draft Disposition.

S.30 Engross Discharge and Retrocession of Life Policy.

S.31 Send these to Building Society for execution.

S.32 Obtain note from building Society of amount required to redeem the seller's loan.

S.33 Instruct Interim Report. (Note: It may be prudent in special cases to instruct an Interim Report before concluding the bargain e.g. in case parts of the property have been sold or feued, or servitudes etc. created. In the ordinary case, this is unnecessary).

15th March

Purchaser's Solicitor

P.20 Receive Building Society instructions.

P.21 Advise client and obtain Endowment Policy (see P.14 above).

P.22 Consider replies to observations on title.

P.23 Engross draft Disposition.

P.24 Send draft Disposition and engrossment to seller's Solicitor.

P.25 Prepare draft Standard Security, Personal Bond, if any, and Assignation of Policy, Consent Form, Renunciation or Affidavit, and undertaking to be given by the purchaser to his Building Society with regard to carrying out repairs, which is a condition of his loan.

P.26 Prepare engrossments.

P.27 Send all security deeds etc. to client with instructions for signature.

P.28 Write to Insurance Company to check no encumbrances on Policy and premium paid to date.

16th March

Seller's Solicitor

S.34 Compare engrossment with draft Disposition.

S.35 Send engrossment of Disposition to seller for signature.

S.36 Return draft Disposition to purchaser's Solicitor.

S.37 Return prior writs to custodier.

S.38 Send Renunciation of Occupancy Rights, if any, for stamping and then registration in Books of Council and Session.

21st March

Purchaser's Solicitor

P.29 Receive confirmation re. Policy from Insurance Company.

P.30 Send Report on Title to Building Society and confirm that the Society is protected against Occupancy Rights.

P.31 Requisition cheque from Building Society.

Seller's Solicitor

S.39 Consider the terms of the Interim Report.

S.40 Submit Interim Report to purchaser's Solicitor.

S.41 Prepare State for Settlement.

S.42 Submit State for Settlement and supporting vouchers to purchaser's Solicitor.

S.43 Advise Rating Authority of change of ownership and apportionment of rates (if not apportioned by Authority).

24th March

Purchaser's Solicitor

P.32 Examine Interim Report and return it.

P.33 Check State for Settlement and return it.

P.34 Advise purchaser of sum required to cover purchase price, fees and outlays, and ask for cheque for balance due (Note: The whole sum may be covered by the Bridging Loan cheque and the Building Society loan).

28th March

Seller's Solicitor

S.44 Receive signed Discharge and Retrocession from Building Society.

S.45 Receive signed Disposition from client.

S.46 Receive keys from client.

S.47 Arrange settlement.

Purchaser's Solicitor

P.35 Receive signed writs from client.

P.36 Receive Building Society cheque.

3. PROCEDURE AT SETTLEMENT

30th March

Seller's Solicitor

S.48 Receive purchaser's Solicitor's cheque.

S.49 Hand over:

 (a) Keys.

 (b) Titles.

 (c) Signed Disposition.

 (d) Letter of Obligation.

 (e) Signed Discharge and selling Solicitor's Letter of Instructions to the Keeper. (Note: Delivery of the Discharge may be covered by the seller's Solicitor's Letter of Obligation).

 (f) Any Guarantee Certificates for Wet Rot, Dry Rot, Eradication Works, Central Heating Maintenance.

 (g) Receipted State for Settlement.

 (h) Evidence to satisfy Matrimonial Homes Act.

Purchaser's Solicitor

P.37 Draw and encash cheque on bridging account and cash Building Society cheque.

P.38 Hand over own cheque for full price as detailed in State for Settlement.

P.39 Check signature on signed deeds and take delivery of items S.49 (a) to (h).

4. MATTERS REMAINING TO BE DEALT WITH AFTER SETTLEMENT

30th March

Seller's Solicitor

S.50 Repay Building Society loan (and record Discharge; if not delivered at settlement).

S.51 Account to client for balance of price, less fees and outlays.

S.52 Intimate Retrocession to Insurance Company.

S.53 Cancel client's insurance.

S.54 Redeem feuduty (if not already redeemed).

Purchaser's Solicitor

P.40 Hand keys to client.

P.41 Stamp Disposition (if applicable) and Renunciation if not done by seller.

P.42 Record:
(1) Disposition.
(2) Standard Security.
(3) Discharge, if delivered at settlement.

P.43 Intimate Assignation to Insurance Company.

P.44 Advise Building Society of settlement and return Completion Particulars Form (if any).

P.45 Instruct client to have an Engineer check that Central Heating Plant is in proper working order at the Date of Entry. Raise any problems with seller's Solicitor immediately.

6th April

Seller's Solicitor

S.55 Receive Feuduty Redemption Receipt (if applicable).

S.56 Send Redemption Receipt to purchaser's Solicitor.

7th April

Purchaser's Solicitor

P.46 Check feuduty redemption (if applicable).

P.47 Mark Letter of Obligation as so far implemented, and advise seller's Solicitor.

P.48 Register Renunciation for preservation (if not done by seller).

11th April

Seller's Solicitor

S.57 Receive duplicate Notice of Intimation from Insurance Company (Retrocession).

S.58 Deliver Life Policy and Retrocession to client.

15th April

Purchaser's Solicitor

P.49 Receive duplicate Notice of Intimation from Insurance (Assignation).

P.50 Receive price of client's present house.

P.51 Repay Bank bridging; account to client for balance; obtain interest certificate for tax purposes and advise client to include interest in his tax return.

15th June

P.52 Confirm repairs completed.

P.53 Instruct Building Society to make final survey and if satisfactory to release retention.

22nd June

P.54 Receive balance of Building Society loan.

P.55 Send cheque for this to client (less additional survey fee).

15th July

Seller's Solicitor

S.59 Receive recorded Discharge from Register House.

S.60 Send recorded Discharge to purchaser's Solicitor.

16th July

Purchaser's Solicitor

P.56　Check Discharge.

P.57　Mark Letter of Obligation and advise seller.

P.58　Send recorded Disposition, Standard Security and other title deeds to Building Society. Indicate those writs which are to follow.

11th Nov

Seller's Solicitor

S.61　Receive Search from Searchers.

S.62　Check this.

S.63　Send Search to purchaser's Solicitor.

12th Nov

Purchaser's Solicitor

P.59　Check Search.

P.60　Return Letter of Obligation marked as fully implemented.

P.61　Send remaining title deeds, if any, and Search to Building Society.

8.1 Land Tenure Reform
Reading List 8.1

As already explained, substantial reforms to the system of land tenure have already been enacted in the 1970 Act, 1974 Act, and the 1979 Act; and a major reform of the law of positive prescription has already been made in the 1973 Act.

For some time past, further major reforms have been mooted, starting with the Halliday Report, and then in the White Paper and, later, the Green Paper, Land Tenure Reform in Scotland, produced in 1972. This is the last official pronouncement on Land Tenure Reform; and some of the reforms outlined in these Papers have already been implemented e.g. the abolition of feuduty, and leasehold reforms.

The major proposal in both the White Paper and the Green Paper, was, however, the total abolition of tenure and dismantling of the feudal system. So far, apart from abolishing feuduty and providing for the redemption thereof, and allowing for compulsory variation of land conditions and compulsory allocations of feuduty in the 1970 Act, no further attempt has yet been made to legislate for this further and major upheaval in the Land Tenure system.

Probably because of the reforms in the 1970 to 1979 Acts and the introduction of Registration of Title, the matter has lost political immediacy, and seems to have dropped out of the legislative programme of both parties. It may be, therefore, that, notwithstanding the proposals in the Green Paper and in its predecessor, the White Paper, each of which, in different ways, mooted total abolition of the tenure system, no further legislation is now in contemplation.

Since the Green Paper is more than ten years old, and nothing has been said by the present Government as to further reforms, I do not propose to explore the position further.

The latest published material on this topic is detailed in the Reading List.

8.2 Registration of Title
Reading List 8.2
The Existing System

For reasons already explained, the Scottish system of registration for publication is a negative or passive system, carrying purely negative sanctions. Within its limitations, the system has operated most effectively for several centuries; but in a negative way by denying the benefit of the real right, and therefore of infeftment, to any unrecorded title. Admittedly, since 1617, a title which has been registered for publication taken together with possession over the prescriptive period, does produce a positive result, in that, by prescription, a registered title may be validated or vindicated; but a considerable lapse of time is always required before the result is achieved.

The principal further disadvantages, which are inherent in the Scottish system of land tenure, (and in other systems as well), are:

(i) **Identification.** Until, perhaps, 100 years ago, it was commonplace to describe properties, particularly rural properties, simply by their name alone, without any attempt to define area or boundaries on a plan. Detailed particular descriptions, usually supported by plan, are now the accepted norm for 'new' properties, but modernisation and elaboration of an inadequate description in an existing title is relatively unusual. Even the modern particular description is very often inadequate and does not precisely define and delimit the subject matter of the grant. Further, deed plans are not always accurate; and Register House has never attempted to correlate plans of adjoining properties in order to make sure that boundaries coincide.

One remedy would be to improve the standard of conveyancing and, in particular, to make it obligatory, in any description of old or new properties, to refer to a plan prepared by a person properly qualified. Normally, a simple two-dimensional plan on one sheet would suffice. For more complex subjects, plans on several sheets, possibly in three dimensions, or showing different elevations, might be required — e.g. for mineral strata, parts of buildings, etc.

Accurate mapping of individual properties on Ordnance Survey Maps, and correlation of individual properties and their boundaries *inter se* on index or master plans, is one of the cardinal features of any system of registration of title; and the introduction of registration of title will cure this weakness in the existing system.

The same criticism applies to the indentification of ancillary rights e.g. servitudes, fishings, the right to enforce burdens, etc. Here, precision, in the nature of things is much more difficult to attain, and registration of title is not such a certain solution.

(ii) **Conditions of Tenure.** Another criticism of the existing system is that the burdens and conditions affecting the title, (and to some extent reservations, although this is perhaps a criticism of the identification system) are difficult to discover and may be uncertain. But at least with our system of registration for publication, any condition of tenure, to be effective, must be recorded in the Register of Sasines; and to this standard rule, there are only very limited exceptions, e.g. in the case of servitudes and leases, where there are other means of discovering the adverse right.

Apart from these limited exceptions, all conditions of tenure are at least ascertainable by searching in the Register of Sasines. Again, registration of title is not the only and necessary cure for this weakness in the system; and other solutions are possible. But registration of title will virtually eliminate this weakness, again subject to certain standard exceptions and qualifications.

(iii) **Heritable Securities.** The same principles apply to heritable securities as apply to conditions of tenure, although, in practice, it is usually easier to ascertain whether or not securities are outstanding than to ascertain the position as to old burdens. Again, registration of title will eliminate all difficulties.

(iv) **Proof of Ownership.** Finally, and most important, in our present system of registration for publication, the mere recording of a title in the Register of Sasines is never in any circumstances a guarantee of the validity of that title nor of the right of the party on whose behalf the title was recorded. Therefore, in every title, some examination of the titles for at least 10 years back is always necessary. Often, such examination is time consuming, repetitive and uncertain. The recent reduction in the period of positive prescription from 20 years to 10 years, (with certain exceptions), has cut down the necessary period over which the title must be examined but does not wholly eliminate examination, nor does it eliminate the risks inherent in the present system of recording.

The only true cure for this defect is a system of registration of title. Under registration of title the State assumes responsibility for registering the ownership of every individual heritable property throughout the country or in defined areas; and, on such registration, issues a Certificate to reputed owners which, when issued, becomes conclusive evidence of title and, therefore, bars all questions as to, and investigation of, antecedent titles. In the process, this eliminates all earlier invalidities or doubtful points and defects in the earlier titles on which the right depends.

After protracted delays, this system of Registration of Title has been introduced into Scotland under the Land Registration (Scotland) Act 1979; but, although the Act has come into operation, the process of registration itself is gradual, and at this date (30th June 1985) the system is actively operating only in the Counties of Renfrew, Dumbarton and Lanark, although it will shortly be extended to Glasgow; and thereafter to other counties on a progressive programme.

The new Scottish Registration system follows, fairly closely, the system of Registration of Title which has been operating in England on a compulsory basis for at least 50 years. But there are significant differences between the two systems, in part reflecting differences in the Land Tenure systems; and in part reflecting ideas which emerged in the preparation of the Reid and Henry Committee Reports. In the result, the Scottish system is a good deal simpler than the English one.

Note, in contrast to our present system of registration for publication, that, in Registration of Title, the role of the Registrar is an active one, in that the Keeper, as Registrar must scrutinise the individual title, must satisfy himself that the reputed owner has a valid title, and must satisfy himself as to identity and burdens affecting the property which he is registering. He must then positively certify that the individual proprietor is indeed the proprietor of that particular property. By so certifying, he makes unchallengeable what was possibly an invalid or vulnerable title.

Note also, in contrast to certain other forms of registration, that the State here intervenes, in the public interest, to certify **ownership**. Compare, in particular, motor vehicle registration where, for fiscal purposes, and also for the purpose of control and law enforcement in traffic offences, every vehicle operating on the public roads in Britain must be registered. But this Certificate issued under statutory authority has no effect whatsoever *quoad* **title**.

1. The Register and the Registrar.

Obviously, a new Register of Title was required. But, in Scotland, this was a relatively simple problem. A comprehensive system of registration already exists, with a central Register House in Edinburgh fully and efficiently staffed with sophisticated techniques for the existing system of registration. The Sasines Register contains, in readily accessible form, a great deal of information which will be translated onto the Certificate of Title on Registration of Title. Logically, under the 1979 Act, the new Land Register is placed under the control of the Keeper of the Registers. It is housed in the same premises as the GRS — Meadowbank House — and the two Registers will work in parallel, and will be closely co-ordinated. But, in Registration of Title, the role of the Keeper alters from a mere passive role in the controlling of intake of deeds for publication to the much more important and active role of examining and adjudicating upon titles presented for registration. In the new system of Registration of Title, he is given a great deal of discretion as to what he registers and more importantly as to what he guarantees.

2. Registration.

For practical reasons, the process of registration of title can only be introduced gradually. It would be quite impossible to introduce it instantaneously for every title throughout the whole of the country.

The original intention was to introduce the new system, area by area throughout Scotland, on a nine-year programme starting in April 1981 with the County of Renfrew. For some years previously, the Keeper had been operating a pilot scheme for this County and a good deal of practical experience had been gained from that pilot. The order of progression originally proposed was:

Year 1 — The County of Renfrew, which has been an operational area from 6th April 1981.

Year 2 — Glasgow, which will become an operational area on 30th September 1985 — see below.

Year 3 — The Counties of Lanark and Dumbarton, also now operational areas — see below.

Year 4 — Midlothian.

Year 5 — Remainder of the central belt.

Year 6 — Angus, Kincardine and Aberdeen.

Year 7 — Ayr, Dumfries and Galloway.

Year 8 — Southern rural areas.

Year 9 — Northern rural areas.

But already the programme has altered, with the substitution of Dumbarton and Lanark for Glasgow in Years 2 and 3 and further deferments in the programme are not unlikely.

Dumbarton is an operational area from 4th October, 1982 (1982 S.I.520); Lanark from 3rd January 1984 (1983 S.I. 745); and Glasgow from 30th September 1985 (1985 S.I. 501).

Once an area has been declared a Compulsory Registration Area in terms of Section 30 of the 1979 Act, ('an operational area') then broadly speaking (for details see later) on any sale of heritage within that area after it has been declared an operational area, the title of the purchaser **must** be registered in the new Land Register.

In urban areas, properties change hands only about once every seven or eight years on average, and much less frequently in rural areas. On that average, it will therefore be at least a further ten years from the date when the area is declared operational until a majority of the titles in that area have been registered.

On this timetable, therefore, one cannot expect to have more than half of all the properties in the northern rural areas on the Register of Title in this century, although admittedly, in Renfrew, Dumbarton etc., 50% to 70% of the properties may be on the Register within the next ten years.

By way of comparison, Registration of Title has been compulsory in England on the same sort of basis since 1925, and they have proceeded, as is proposed here, District by District, although on a much slower programme than ours will be. By 1978, in England, more than 50 years after registration became compulsory, about 75% of the whole of the country was within Compulsory Registration areas; and about 50% of all properties in England had found their way onto the new Register. See 1978 NLJ 131.

Registration of Title is therefore a very gradual remedy for the imperfections which it **eventually** will cure.

3. Certificates of Title.

On receiving an application for registration of a title to a particular property the Keeper examines the whole progress of titles, satisfies himself as to its validity, and then **certifies** that the applicant is the owner of the property identified in the Certificate. The extent and particulars of the property are similarly certified, subject to the burdens and conditions specified in the Certificate; and subject also to certain inherent qualifications which apply to every Certificate.

Therefore, the system of registration embodies machinery for the identification of:
(a) the property and its ancillary rights, with plan;
(b) the burdens affecting the title which include:
   (i) the conditions of tenure;
   (ii) heritable securities;
(c) the owner of the property, with a specification of the nature of his right therein.

All this is contained in the Certificate of Title issued to the owner; and the Certificate exactly reproduces the entries in the Title Sheet maintained in the Register itself.

Again, in our present system of registration, this machinery exists in embryo in the Search sheets maintained in Register House; but, of course, a new format is required and substantial additional information will appear on the Certificate of Title. But, in Scotland, we are a good deal further ahead than, say, in England, where registration of title is superimposed on unregistered titles.

The Certificate of Title almost wholly replaces and supersedes the title deeds; but a reference back to the earlier titles may still be necessary in limited and unusual cases. Therefore, the owner may still have an interest to retain his title deeds.

4. Over-riding interests.

Some interests are too ill-defined or indeterminate to register on individual Certificates; and certain interests are too insignificant to register. In any system of registration of title, this is inevitable. In the result, the legislature has the choice either:

i) of eliminating all such interests in land, so that the Certificate of Title can be a complete and exhaustive record of every single minute item in or affecting that title; or

ii) of permitting these minor and indeterminate adverse rights to co-exist along with the registered title, and to affect the registered land, although they may not appear in the Certificate of Title. In Scotland, as in England, we have adopted the second alternative, and these adverse interests are termed 'over-riding interests'.

Obviously, and ideally, over-riding interests should be kept to the minimum; and the 1979 Act has gone further than the English system in curtailing these adverse rights which affect or 'over-ride' every Certificate of Title, although not explicitly mentioned thereon.

We are already familiar with the general principle of 'over-riding interests' in Scotland on the present system of registration for publication, in the sense that certain rights prevail against the infeft proprietor holding on a recorded title without these rights themselves entering the Register of Sasines. Thus, servitudes, although normally constituted by recorded deed, do not require to enter the Register of Sasines; and the same applies to public rights of way. Nonetheless, these rights prevail against singular successors in perpetuity. So also Leases, under the Leases Act 1449, bind singular successors although not disclosed on the Record.

5. Rectification and Indemnification.

Our existing system of registration is negative in this sense that, unless a title is recorded in the GRS, no real right is obtained. But it does not necessarily follow that recording automatically creates a real right; a recorded title is not beyond challenge. Suppose that A, improperly and without having right or title to do so, dispones land to B who in good faith and for value accepts the Disposition and records it. Suppose the property really belongs to C who has an unchallengeable right and title thereto. The fact that B, in good faith, has recorded a title does not prevent C from attacking that title by an action of reduction. If he successfully attacks B's title and if that title is reduced, then C acquires a title to the property in place of B whose only remedy is an action of damages against A. If A cannot pay, B is the loser. C, the true owner, emerges virtually unscathed.

In contrast, in a system of registration of title, if B has become the registered owner and has taken possession, his registered title is beyond challenge. Even although C may be able to demonstrate beyond doubt that he had a valid right and title to the property registered in B's name, C cannot, as of right, reduce B's title. On the other hand, in certain circumstances a discretion is vested in the Keeper to amend or rectify the Register where it appears to him that a mistake has been made. But in any such case, whether the register is rectified or not, if anyone can show that, as a result of registration or rectification, he has suffered loss owing to fault or negligence on the part of the Keeper, then he can claim compensation from the State. Thus in the A-B-C case above, in a system of registration of title, where A wrongly and without any power to do so transfers his registered title to B (if that were possible), C cannot challenge B's title as of right. He may, however, make representations to the Keeper; and the Keeper in certain circumstances may at his own hand rectify the Register by removing B from the Register and putting C in his place. If he does so, then he may have to compensate B for his loss; if he does not rectify the Register in this way but if C can satisfy him as to the rights which he has lost, then the Keeper would be bound to indemnify C.

Further, under the 1979 Act, the Registrar is not allowed to rectify the Register to the disadvantage of the proprietor in possession; and the Courts cannot so require the Registrar, except in certain specified situations. See the 1979 Act S.9.

The Land Registration (Scotland) Act 1979.

S. 1. This is the formal Section under which the new Register is created known as 'The Land Register of Scotland'. The Register is to be public — cf. England, where the Register is private; and is placed under the management of the Keeper of the Registers.

Throughout the 1979 Act, the word 'register' 'registered' etc., mean the new Land Register and Registration of Title therein.

Commencement — See S.30

Section 1 of the Act, setting up the Register, came into operation on 4th April 1979 under S.30 and is operating under the control of the Keeper of the Registers. The remaining Sections in Parts I and II of the Act, dealing with the mechanics of registration, have been and are to be introduced for particular defined areas of Scotland on the phased programme above referred to. This is to be achieved by Statutory Instrument; and different days have been and are to be appointed under S.30 for different areas, as indicated in the timetable outlined above.

It follows that everything provided for in the Act and referred to in these Notes as regards the mechanics of registration, etc. apply only within an area which has been so declared to be an Operational Area.

'The commencement of the Act' in SS.2-14 therefore means, in relation to each Operational Area only, the date on which it became operational.

S.2 — Compulsory Registration.

Within each Operational Area, and from and after the operational date as fixed in the Statutory Instrument, broadly speaking, every title must be registered in the Land Register when the property is feued, sold or leased on a long lease.

In addition, in limited circumstances, the Keeper may be willing to accept a title on a voluntary registration, but this facility will be sparingly used in Scotland, although commonplace in England.

Once a title to a property has been so registered under this Section, thereafter (but **only** thereafter) every subsequent transaction relating to that property also becomes registrable, e.g., the transfer of the registered interest, a heritable security over the registered interest, a liferent of the registrable interest, and generally any other transaction which affects the registered title.

Further, under S.2(5) the Secretary of State may, at some future date, require certain interests in land, not then registered, to be brought onto the Register, so as to complete registration in a particular area. It is thought that this power will not be used for a very long time to come. According to Halliday — 'Ultimately, in each area, a stage will be reached when a substantial majority of interests in land within the area will have been registered in the Land Register, and it will be desirable to enable the Division of the Register of Sasines for that area to be closed. This sub-Section empowers the Secretary of State to require that interests in land in that area ... be registered'.

S.3. — The Effect of Registration.

The effect of registration is defined in this Section as having the following effects:

3(1) (a). It vests in the registered proprietor a real right in the registered interest as also in any right, pertinent or servitude, express or implied, forming part of that registered interest. The right so vests subject only to:

(i) any adverse entries in the title sheet itself; e.g. heritable securities, conditions of tenure, Notices of Improvement Grants, etc., actually entered in the Title Sheet and Land Certificate; and

(ii) any over-riding interest, whether entered in the Title Sheet or **not**;

3(2) (b). On registration, all rights and obligations entered in the title sheet are similarly made real.

3(1) (c). Registration also 'affects' any registered real right or obligation relating to the registered interest in land.

These three sub-sections, however, are qualified by a proviso to the effect that registration only has these effects insofar as the right or obligation in question is capable, under existing law, of being made real.

Further, under S.3(3), from the date when a particular area becomes an Operational Area, certain transactions have to be registered in the Land Register which, at the moment, do not require to be recorded in the Register of Sasines. In these cases, registration is obligatory and is the only means of making the right or obligation real. These cases, where registration is obligatory, include:

> the right of the lessee under a long lease;
> the right of the udal proprietor and
> the right of a kindly tenant.

In contrast, in any other case, rights can be made real by any other means which are effective at present. Thus under the existing law in non-Operational Areas a short lease is made real, under the Leases Act of 1449, by the granting of a Lease in certain terms, followed by possession by the tenant. If the lease is a long lease, recording is an **alternative** to possession.

But once an area has been declared operational by the Secretary of State, then, on the granting of a long lease (i.e. a lease for more than 20 years), possession ceases to be available as a method of making the right real. The long lease must be recorded, whether or not the landlord's title has been registered. In contrast, under a short lease, possession still makes the right of the tenant real; and there is no question of his having to register his interest to protect himself against a singular successor as registered proprietor.

SS.4 to 6 — The Machinery of Registration.

(1) Registration for Publication in the G.R.S.

Under the 1617 Act, as amended, there is maintained in Edinburgh the General Register of Sasines divided into County Divisions with a Presentment Book, a Minute Book and a set of Record Volumes for each County Division.

The requirements for recording in the Register of Sasines are:

1. A deed in conventional form completed and duly executed is delivered to the disponee, and stamped.

2. A Warrant of Registration is endorsed on that Deed on behalf of the disponee, etc.

3. The Deed, with endorsed Warrant, is then presented, by hand or by post, to Register House in Edinburgh and, subject to certain technical requirements, e.g.

probativity, Stamp Duty, Warrant of Registration, etc., the Deed is then recorded. On recording:—

(a) The Deed enters the Presentment Book, so as to pinpoint the date of presentation and of ranking.

(b) The Deed is minuted, i.e. a short summary of its terms is prepared in Register House for the Minute Book.

(c) The Deed is then photographed (previously copied by other means) and the copy is bound up with the Records Volume and indexed.

(d) A copy of the Minute is entered on the Search sheet for that property.

(e) The Deed is stamped with the Keeper's Certificate showing that it has been through the Register House but nothing more.

(f) The principal deed is then returned to the ingiver.

The Certificate of Registration endorsed by the Keeper on the Deed merely certifies that the Deed has been recorded on a given date, but goes no further than that. In particular, the Certificate does not guarantee the validity or sufficiency of the Deed in any way.

At the date of recording in the Register of Sasines, the disponee may or may not be in possession; and he may or may not be the person properly entitled to the land, in that the Deed may or may not be valid; but, unless the Deed is grossly inept, the Keeper is bound to accept it and record it, although he may raise matters of substance or of detail with the ingiver, as a matter of Register House practice.

(2) Registration in the Land Register.

Under SS.4-6 of the 1979 Act, there are very significant differences in the mechanics of registration in that:

(i) A formal deed in normal form is still required to vest the right in the disponee, although the Keeper may be prepared to allow some shortcuts in the completion of the required formalities.

(ii) No Warrant of Registration is required. Instead, under S.4(1), the vesting deed is sent to the Keeper **along with** an Application for Registration of the title; and the applicant sends the whole of the Title Deeds with that Application. The Keeper examines the title, just as a purchaser would examine it, for validity, burdens, etc.; and may require the applicant to furnish further information, e.g., as to identification of the property, boundaries, servitudes, possession, etc.

(iii) The Keeper will reject the Application if:

(a) the property is not sufficiently described to allow him to identify it on the Ordnance Survey map;

(b) it relates to a souvenir plot;

(c) it is frivolous or vexatious; or

(d) if the title is **already** registered, and if the deed omits to mention the title number.

(iv) On receipt of that Application for Registration, the Keeper notes the date of receipt thereof which is deemed to be the date of registration, i.e. the date of infeftment, **unless** the Application is rejected by the Keeper (as it may be but only on limited grounds) or is withdrawn.

(v) Under S.5, the process of registration of the title includes the following requirements:

in the case of proprietary rights, i.e. resulting from a Disposition, a Feu Charter, etc., the Keeper makes up a Title Sheet to the property (or rather, to the interest being registered). The Title Sheet is a summary of all the salient features in the title to that interest and is dealt with in detail in S.6. The essential content of the Title Sheet comprises:

(a) a description of the property by reference to an Ordnance Survey plan.
(b) the name of the proprietor.
(c) any adverse entries in the Personal Register.
(d) any heritable securities.
(e) any enforceable real right or subsisting real burden.
(f) any exclusion of indemnity.
(g) such other information as the Keeper may think fit to enter.

Further, in terms of S.6(2), the Keeper is empowered either to repeat verbatim rights or burdens, or to summarise these, or to refer to them in the Title Sheet by reference to a previous recorded deed, a copy of which is put up with the Title Sheet for completeness.

Under S.5(4), over-riding interests will also be registered by the Keeper in most cases, if drawn to his notice.

The content of the Title Sheet is set out in detail in the Rules. It contains four parts, viz.:

The Property Section — i.e. the description of the property
The Proprietorship Section — i.e. the identity of the owner
The Charges Section — i.e. heritable securities, etc.
The Burdens Section — i.e. conditions of tenure, etc.

Every Title Sheet will be given a distinguishing number (the 'title number'); and, in any future transaction relating to that title, the number must be quoted.

The Title Sheet is part of the Land Register and is retained permanently by the Keeper. It will be updated from time to time whenever information reaches the Keeper relating to any individual property on his Register.

For each individual owner, a formal copy of the Title Sheet, containing all the same information, will be issued on registration, and it will be updated from time to time as required. In the case of proprietary interests, the copy of the Title Sheet issued to the owner takes the form of a Land Certificate which certifies that he is the owner of the land described in the Property Section.

Lesser interests, such as heritable securities, liferents, etc., are also registrable; but only after the title to the property itself has been registered. Thus, if the infeft proprietor of heritable property in Renfrew sells and dispones it to a purchaser, the purchaser **must** apply for the registration of his title as purchaser.

But if that same owner of property in Renfrew, instead of selling it, grants a Standard Security in favour of a creditor, the Standard Security will be recorded in the Register of Sasines. Registration in the Land Register is not required, and indeed not competent, merely on the granting of Securities, etc.

If, however, the property in Renfrew has been sold and the purchaser has registered his title as purchaser, a Title Sheet will have been prepared in the Land Register and a Land Certificate will have been issued to him. If he **then** grants a Standard Security, the creditor must register that Standard Security in the Land Register and it is then noted on the Title Sheet of that proprietor. In other words, once the title of the proprietor has been registered, every subsequent transaction is registrable in the Land Register; and nothing can subsequently be recorded in the Register of Sasines to affect that title.

As will be later explained, the Land Certificate issued to the Registered Proprietor, and any other writ issued or updated by the Keeper of the Land Register, is guaranteed by the Keeper, with certain exceptions.

Because the Keeper guarantees every registered title, and every subsequent transaction relating thereto, he has to examine the title on first registration, as indicated above, in exactly the same way as the purchaser's solicitor examines the title at the present time on the present system, in order to satisfy himself as to the validity of the proprietary title and the burdens and charges thereon.

If he is not satisfied with the validity of the title, then he will normally register it, but will exclude indemnity either generally or on certain aspects of that title. If there is any exclusion of indemnity, this must be explicitly expressed on the Title Sheet and on the Land Certificates. See below.

The Land Certificate.
The form of Land Certificate, which mirrors the Title Sheet is prescribed in the Rules, Form 6. See Diploma Styles for a specimen. As you will see, the Land Certificate consists of at least eight separate pages and, in addition, there may be incorporated in, or annexed to it, Schedules of Burdens, or copies of whole writs.

The salient features of the Land Certificate are as follows:

Page 1 contains:
 i) the title number;
 ii) the postal address;
 iii) standard information about the indemnity.

Page 2 contains:
(a) a series of boxes for inserting the date up to which the Land Certificate has been updated. As indicated above, the Land Certificate is a document issued to the individual registered proprietor. With limited exceptions, the Land Certificate will have to be produced to the Keeper by the Registered Proprietor on any subsequent transaction affecting the registered interest. The Land Certificate is then made to correspond with the Title Sheet by adding whatever additional information is required.

The successive dates to which the Land Certificate is thus updated will be shown in the boxes provided at the top of Page 2.

(b) a note about over-riding interests. You will find the full definition of over-riding interests in the interpretation section S.28(1). The Land Certificate details the over-riding interests, thus:
i) short leases (i.e. leases of less than 20 years);
ii) long leases where the lessee acquired the real right (by recording in Sasines or by possession) prior to the area becoming operational;
iii) the right of crofters or cottars under statute;
iv) servitudes — although in many cases servitudes will in fact be disclosed on the Title Sheet;
v) public interests generally, except those which, on the present system, require the recording of a deed in the Register of Sasines. This includes e.g. matter affecting property under the Planning Acts, Housing Acts, Health and Safety at Work Acts, Fire Precaution Acts, etc. etc. But a Notice of Improvement Grant which, under the present Housing legislation, requires to be recorded in the Register of Sasines will, under the new system, have to be registered in the Land Register

as a burden on the Title Sheet of the property concerned; and these will not over-ride;

vi) floating charges (whether fixed or not);

vii) public rights of way;

viii) real rights which have become real otherwise than by recording of a deed in the Register of Sasines, e.g. terce;

ix) rights of common interest and common property generally, excluding such rights as have been constituted by recorded or registered deed. Therefore, only the common law rights over-ride under this head.

x) the occupancy rights of a non-entitled spouse under the Matrimonial Homes (Family Protection) (Scotland) Act 1981. See S 6.(4) of that Act.

Page 3 reproduces the plan of the individual property, an essential feature of the system of Registration of Title. It is simply a copy of the relevant section of the Ordnance Survey map and the property in question is outlined with a heavy red line or tinted or otherwise delineated. The title number appears again at the top right-hand corner.

Three scales of Ordnance Survey plan are used.

1/1250 which will be used for all normal urban property. In very exceptional cases, however, the Keeper may produce a special plan on a larger scale if that is necessary to show details.

1/2500 which is the scale to be used for rural properties, farms, etc.

1/10,000 — a much smaller scale for use in hill and moorland properties.

One weakness of the plan system is that, because of limitations of scale, it is impossible in many cases exactly to define the boundary line in relation to the boundary feature e.g. the centre line of a wall, etc.; but the Keeper overcomes this difficulty either by verbal description or by a system of arrows, mentioned below.

Colouring. Different colours will be used in appropriate cases to distinguish different areas or rights.

The next pages reproduce the four sections above referred to, with the individual information for each of these four sections in the standard form.

Page 4 contains: A The Property Section. The Property Section gives the Title Number, the County, the nature of the interest, the nature of the tenure, and a description of the property, primarily by reference to the plan. The verbal description is cut to the minimum.

Ancillary rights, e.g. servitudes of access for the benefit of the property will be added to the description, as additional proprietorial rights.

Page 5 contains: B. The Proprietorship Section, giving the name and address of the proprietor, the date of his registration as such, and a note of the price paid.

Page 6 contains: C. The Charges Section, which lists the **outstanding** heritable securities on the property. Sections B and C will be updated by deletion of spent items and the addition of new entries, without reframing the entire Land Certificate afresh on each registration.

Page 7 contains: D. The Burdens Section. This is the final section of the Title Sheet and will normally be the longest one. For this reason, it is put as the last section of the Title Sheet to allow for additional pages and for the affixing of copy deeds, etc.

In general there are three ways in which conditions of tenure, etc. will be introduced into the Title Sheet, thus:

1. Feu Charter by ... etc. 'Note: Copy in Certificate'.
   This means that a full and complete copy of the Feu Charter referred to in this entry will be attached to the Certificate.

2. Feu Charter etc. ... 'Contains the following burdens'.
   In this case, the terms of the burdens are reproduced verbatim, so that the full original text thereof is copied in the Land Certificate.

3. Minute of Waiver, etc.
   The **import** of the Minute of Waiver is then **summarised** in the entry itself by the Keeper, but is not reproduced at full length. The Keeper guarantees the accuracy of this Summary.

Boundaries

The use of arrows on the Certificate plans and their meaning are described on the last page. The intention is to indicate the actual boundary line as defined in the title with reference to a boundary feature by the use of arrows. As already mentioned, because of limitations of scaling, the Plan of itself cannot accurately show whether the boundary line is, say, to the east or west of an existing wall or along the middle of the line of it. This may be important. To get over the limitations of scaling, the Keeper may indicate by the use of arrows, whether, **according to the titles,** the boundary line lies on one side or other of the physical features on the ground, or along the mid line thereof, as indicated in this note, but the information as given is not guaranteed. Alternatively, this information may be incorporated in the Property Section as a verbal addendum to the written description.

Charge Certificate

The Charge Certificate is the equivalent document issued to the creditor in a heritable security and contains similar entries to those in the Land Certificate. The security document itself is attached to it.

S.7. Ranking

This Section preserves the general principle which applies to recording in Sasines, viz., that, in a competition, priority of infeftment rules; and if there are competing conveyances, by A to B and by A to C, of the same area of ground; and if both are acting *bona fide* and without notice of the other title, the first disponee on Record prevails against the other, whose only remedy is an Action of Damages under warrandice against A.

So, under S.7(2), titles to registered interests, in the Land Register, are also to rank according to the date of registration of those interests.

As between the two Registers, Sasines and Land Registers, again, priority of infeftment determines priority of right, but with qualifications. Thus, A, infeft, grants a heritable security to B which B records in Sasines under the present rule; and, at the same time, A dispones the property to C who applies for registration of the title. If B records the heritable security before C applies for registration, B is preferred. If not, B acquires no real right by his Security but has a personal right of action against A under warrandice.

If, however, in the same situation, A sells land in a Registration of Title area to B and, simultaneously, sells the same land to C; and B and C are both *bona fide* purchasers for value without notice of each other's claim, the two Dispositions to B and C are each registrable in the Land Register.

Under S.3(2) and S.8(4), the Keeper should refuse to record either of these two Dispositions if presented for recording in the Register of Sasines in the traditional way. Suppose, however, that, by oversight, the Disposition A to B entered the Register of Sasines and, later, C applied for registration of his title. In this case, even although B has the first recorded title, the title has been **wrongly** recorded; and, in this case, C would prevail over B.

Rectification of the Register and indemnity to individuals suffering loss.

In contrast to the present system, under Registration of Title, the document of title issued to the registered proprietor is the Land Certificate which in turn exactly reflects the content of the Title Sheet. The Title Sheet and Land Certificate are the creation of the Keeper of the Registers and absolutely determine the rights and obligations of the individual proprietor to the exclusion of the contents of the earlier titles. That being so, there must clearly be, and under S.9 there is, provision for correcting errors or mistakes in the Title Sheet and Land Certificate in relation to individual properties.

Thus, under S.9(1), the Keeper in certain circumstances may, and if so required by the Lands Tribunal shall, rectify any inaccuracy in a Title Sheet which is brought to his notice. **But** this power to rectify the Register is very severely restricted by S.9(3). Under that Section, the Keeper may **not** rectify the Register to the prejudice of the proprietor in possession of the registered interest except in very limited circumstances; and so, with these limited exceptions, the proprietor in possession on a registered title is now immune from the challenge of that title on any grounds whatever.

The Keeper can only rectify the Title Sheet and Land Certificate to the prejudice of the proprietor in possession in the following circumstances:

(i) to note an over-riding interest; but the over-riding interest would, of course, over-ride in any event, whether noted or not. This, therefore, does not truly prejudice the registered proprietor;

(ii) where everyone concerned has consented;

(iii) where the error was caused by the fraud or carelessness of the proprietor in possession — and therefore he has only himself to blame;

(iv) where rectification relates to something against which the Keeper has previously declined to indemnify the proprietor in possession, by an express exclusion of indemnity on the Title Sheet and Land Certificate.

Similarly, on the application of an interested party to the Lands Tribunal or to the Courts, rectification may be ordered; but the Lands Tribunal and Courts are similarly restricted in ordering rectification to the prejudice of a proprietor in possession.

So, under Registration of Title, if a *bona fide* purchaser for value registers a title and then enters into possession of the registered land, his title is **immediately** put beyond challenge and he does not require to possess on that title for ten years in order to validate it. This is a very considerable improvement on the present law of positive prescription, so far as the owner in possession is concerned.

Closely linked with the question of rectification is the matter of indemnity.

Not only does the Keeper guarantee the validity of every title which is registered, subject only to those cases where he excludes indemnity. In addition, where the registered proprietor or a third party can demonstrate that, because of entries made in the Register by the Keeper, he has suffered loss, then he normally has a claim for compensation against the Keeper. This right to indemnity is expressly conferred by S.12 in terms of which any person who suffers loss as a result of:

(a) rectification of the Register;

(b) refusal of the Keeper to rectify the Register;

(c) any error or omission in a Land or Charge Certificate or in other information given by the Keeper in writing, e.g. in a Search,

is entitled to be indemnified by the Keeper.

Clearly, there will be quite a number of cases where, because of known or suspected defects, the title is not marketable; and in these cases it clearly would be impracticable for the Keeper to guarantee the title absolutely. In exactly the same way, where the proprietor under the present system knows that there is a defect in his title, he is at risk if he grants absolute warrandice. In any such case, the Keeper is empowered by S.12(2), on registration, to exclude the right of the registered proprietor to indemnity in respect of anything appearing in, or omitted from, the Title Sheet of that interest, by an express exclusion of indemnity endorsed on and appearing in the Title Sheet and Land Certificate.

Thus, A is the reputed owner of 100 acres. He has an *ex facie* valid title to 95 acres, supported by possession, but not to the remaining 5 acres. He sells and dispones the whole property to B. B applies for registration of the title. The Keeper will register the title to the whole 100 acres; but would exclude indemnity in respect of the 5 doubtful acres. The title to that 5 acres, and the exclusion of indemnity, will be cured in the end of the day by the operation of the normal rules of positive prescription, i.e. possession following on a recorded or registered title for the relevant period.

S.10 — Prescription.

The general principle of Prescription continues to operate under Registration of Title but with certain modifications. The general principle is, as you will recall, that possession on a recorded title for the ten-year period creates rights and eliminates defects for the benefit of the proprietor in possession of that property on that recorded title.

The principal modification arising out of registration of title is that, where a title to property is registered in name of an applicant without exclusion of indemnity, there is no longer any need to rely on the positive prescription to create rights or cure defects. The act of registration itself automatically confers an unchallenge-able title on the *bona fide* applicant, provided he enters into and continues in possession; and there is no longer any ten-year waiting period in that situation.

However, where an applicant for registration of title presents to the Keeper a title which is clearly defective, the Keeper may exclude indemnity, in which case, under the rectification rules, if the invalidity is later established by appropriate action by a competing proprietor, this is one of the cases where the Keeper can rectify the Register to the disadvantage of the proprietor in possession. Therefore, if a title is registered with exclusion of indemnity, it still requires the ten-year prescription to cure that defect. On the expiry of the ten-year period, the proprietor with a registered title excluding indemnity simply applies to the Keeper for the removal of that exclusion, whereupon his title immediately becomes absolute and unchallengeable.

Further, and contrary to what might at first sight appear, a title recorded in the Register of Sasines can still effectively compete with a registered title.

Suppose that, in an operational area, A is already in possession of one acre of ground on a title recorded in Sasines, which either expressly includes, or is habile to include, that acre; but the title to that acre is defective.

Under the present rule, possession on that title for ten years will cure the defect, and give A an absolute right thereto.

Suppose that B acquires an adjoining estate by disposition which expressly includes A's one acre. B registers the title, and so apparently becomes the registered proprietor of A's acre.

If, in that situation, A continues in possession for the ten-year period and so validates his right by prescription, A could then apply to the Keeper for a rectification of the Register so as to exclude A's acre from B's registered title. This is **not** one of the cases where B could object to rectification because, since A is in possession, B, the registered proprietor, is **not** the proprietor **in possession.**

On rectification, B **might** have a claim against the Keeper, but he could not insist on retaining his title to the one acre because, lacking possession, the Register will be rectified against B, to exclude that one acre from B's earlier registration.

In the converse situation, where B registers a title to 100 acres in the Land Register and where, after the date of that registration, A then records a title habile to include the one acre in the Register of Sasines A can never prevail against B on a title recorded in the Register of Sasines because, the 100-acre title having **first** been registered, it is no longer competent to record a title in Sasines which includes any part of that 100 acres under S.8(4). If A is to compete with B, whose title is already registered, A himself must apply for registration of a title to the one acre. In normal circumstances, the Keeper will be prepared to accept that Application and register A as proprietor to the one acre only, even although B is already shown as the proprietor of that acre and 99 more; but, when registering A's title, the Keeper will exclude indemnity.

Under the 1979 Act S.10, if A then possesses on that **registered** title, excluding indemnity, for the ten-year period, he can then prevail against B, and require rectification of the Register in his favour in respect of that one acre because B is not in possession.

9. Leases
Reading List 9.

It is assumed that the reader is already familiar with the general law of Landlord and Tenant; and no attempt is made in these notes to rehearse the general principles which apply to that relationship. All we are concerned with here is, briefly, some points to note on the practical aspects of Leases in everyday practice.

9.1. General Points on Leases

9.1.1 Lease as a real right. At common law, a Lease is essentially a personal contract between the infeft proprietor, in this context 'the Landlord', and a temporary occupant, in this context 'the Tenant', who is permitted by the Landlord, for a limited period of time and for payment of a rent, to enjoy the benefit of the property to the temporary exclusion of the Landlord throughout the duration of the Lease.

This fundamental characteristic of the Lease as a personal contract carries with it two consequences:

(i) **Assignability.**

The selection of the Tenant in most cases involves some element of *delectus personae.* In the result, in the great majority of cases, either by implication or by express provision in the Lease, the Tenant is prohibited from parting with possession of the whole or any part of the subjects of let either by way of assignation of his interest, in whole or in part, or by subletting. This is one feature which distinguishes occupation of property under a Lease from occupation on tenure where, generally speaking, there is freedom of disposal.

(ii) **Transmission.**

Since a Lease is essentially a personal contract, the common law rule was, (and is), that the Lease is not binding in a question with a singular successor of the Landlord because the Tenant has no real right. That common law rule has been excluded, in the great majority of cases, by the Leases Act 1449 C.18.

The principal purpose of this Act was, originally, to give some security of tenure to tenant farmers; but it has since been extended to include Leases of almost every kind of property with very limited exceptions.

The main result of the Act is to create for the Tenant a right to maintain himself in possession in terms of his Lease, when the Landlord dispones the property to a singular successor who takes infeftment as proprietor in his place. As a result of the provisions of this Act, the Tenant is equally entitled to insist on the terms of the Lease in a question with a singular successor as he was with the original Landlord on the basis of contract; and so the Tenant acquires, under this Act, a *quasi* real right which transmits against singular successors for the duration of the original Lease.

As an extension of this principle, by later statutes, Tenants of particular types of property are given much more extensive security of tenure, and certain other rights as well, including, in some cases, the right to continue in occupation at a controlled rent. Two particular cases where statute further controls the relationship of a Landlord and Tenant in this way are dwellinghouses under the Rent Act 1984, and agricultural property under the Agricultural Holdings Acts. These statutory provisions are referred to later in this chapter, under separate headings.

The 1449 Act, in contrast, protects the Tenant strictly according to the terms of the original contract and not beyond. To produce this result, however, the Lease must first satisfy certain basic requirements viz.

(i) It must be in writing and the writing must be probative, except for Leases of less than one year's duration.

(ii) There must be a definite and continuing rent and the rent must not be illusory.

(iii) There must be a definite termination date, however far into the future; and

(iv) The Tenant must have entered into possession. In the case of Leases, taking possession on the part of the Tenant is equivalent to the taking of sasine by the vassal under the feudal system. The Tenant is not, however, so protected during any period of possession prior to the date of entry specified in the lease.

If a Lease is entered into which fails to satisfy these requirements, it may be binding, on the basis of contractual agreement, between the original Landlord and his universal successors on the one hand and the Tenant and his successors on the other; but it will not bind a singular successor of the Landlord. The same applies to a Lease which complies with the above requirements but where the subjects of let are not within the scope of the Act, e.g. salmon fishings. That particular exception has, however, largely been negatived by the Fresh Water and Salmon Fisheries (Scotland) Act 1976 S.4 in relation to Leases of fishings in inland waters.

9.1.2 Rent

As with Feus in earlier days, so with Leases the contractual arrangement between Landlord and Tenant starts off, in the ordinary way, on a strictly commercial basis with the Tenant paying to the Landlord an annual rent of full commercial value. In other words, the Landlord as proprietor receives by way of rent a return on his property equivalent to what he might expect to receive as a return on any other form of investment. But, taking into account improvements to the premises carried out by the Tenant, and the steady increase in property values particularly in periods of inflation, rents tend to diminish in real value to the Landlord with the passage of years, which has two results:

(i) As time passes, the Lease becomes an asset of increasing value to the Tenant, particularly in commercial premises with the build up of goodwill; and

(ii) In modern Leases, this tendency for the rent to get out of line with current rental values is counteracted by the introduction into the Lease of a Rent Review Clause, the effect of which is that, at regular intervals throughout the period of the Lease, the rent is reviewed and may be increased in line with increases in real values.

9.1.3 Possession

So far as the Tenant is concerned, the Lease has two substantial disadvantages compared with ownership of property on tenure viz.:

(i) Firstly, sooner or later, the Lease comes to an end, whereupon at common law, and in the absence of contrary provision in the Lease, the property, with all buildings, fixtures and improvements generally, even although these have been provided at the expense of the Tenant, reverts to the Landlord without any compensation to the Tenant. This, in effect, means that the value of the Tenant's asset is written down to nil at the termination of the Lease.

To some extent this disadvantage can be counteracted either:

(a) by entering into a Lease for a long initial term or by providing in the Lease for an option to the Tenant to renew his Lease for successive terms; or

(b) by providing expressly for compensation for Tenant's improvements.

(ii) Secondly, because of the requirement that, to qualify for the protection of the 1449 Act, the Tenant must enter into possession, a Lease could not be used as security for borrowed money because the essence of any heritable security is that the borrower is left in possession to enjoy the benefits of the property, while the lender has security without actual occupation. Given the requirements of the 1449 Act, a creditor of a Tenant could not obtain security over the Lease except by taking possession of the subjects of let; and in any event that would probably be prohibited either by implication or by the express terms of the Lease itself.

In many cases, the Tenant takes land on a long Lease with the intention of building. If the Lease is for a long enough term, the Tenant may find it economically viable to put buildings on the land even although, at the end of the Lease, the buildings pass to the Landlord without payment. Such Leases were and are commonplace in England. Until recently, in Scotland, building Leases were much less commonly encountered, but, for technical reasons, did regularly occur. In recent urban redevelopments they are now frequently used, particularly in commercial and industrial precincts.

One consequence of this type of Lease is that the Tenant invests substantial sums of money in building, or in improving and fitting out buildings on land, although he is not the owner thereof. Inevitably, in many such cases, the Tenant has to borrow the money required for such development; but, under the 1449 Act, he is not in a position to grant security. Borrowing for development on leasehold land was therefore impracticable, notwithstanding the protection of the 1449 Act.

9.1.4 Registration

These difficulties, which the Tenant on a long Lease encountered, were removed by the Registration of Leases (Scotland) Act 1857. The main purpose of the Act was to permit publication of the Tenant's right by recording of the Lease in the Register of Sasines in place of, or as an alternative to, the publication of that right by the taking of possession.

When registration was first introduced for feudal titles under the 1617 and 1693 Acts, the essential feature of the registration legislation was that recording of a Deed in Sasines became an essential element in the obtaining of the real right. In contrast, under the Registration of Leases Act, registration is optional in this sense that the Tenant may still secure his real right under his Lease simply by entering into possession, without recording any Deed in the Register of Sasines. As an alternative, but strictly as an alternative, he may, if he prefers, record the Lease in the Register of Sasines, in which case he is not obliged to take possession in order to establish his real right under the 1449 Act. In practice, he may, and often will, do both.

The principal benefit to the Tenant of this legislation is that it allows the Tenant, while taking possession, at the same time to grant security on his Lease and to borrow money on that security so as to allow him to develop his leasehold property.

A further effect of the 1857 Act is that, if a Lease is recorded before the Landlord has disposed of the subjects to a singular successor, then no rent is necessary and no definite termination date is required, in contrast to the position where the 1449 Act alone is relied on. Two points must be stressed:

(i) Firstly, even although Leases and transmissions thereof may now be registered under the 1857 Act in the Register of Sasines, the recording of the Lease, or of an assignation thereof, does not create infeftment. Therefore, a Lessee with a recorded Title is still a Tenant holding on a Lease; and, in a question with a singular successor of the Landlord, the Tenant still relies on the provisions of the 1449 Act as amended and extended by the 1857 Act and its amendments. He is in no sense infeft as Tenant, in contrast to the position of a proper liferenter or of an heir of entail in possession; and the recording of his Lease does not to any extent divest the Landlord nor exclude the Landlord from his full proprietary title.

(ii) Leases of short duration of are commonplace. To allow every lease to be recorded in the Register of Sasines, regardless of its duration, would have vastly increased the volume of writs entering the Sasines Register and created a major administrative problem there. Therefore, to prevent overloading of the system , the 1857 Act originally restricted the registration of Leases to those Leases

(a) where the term of the lease was not less than 31 years; and

(b) where the subjects of let did not exceed 50 acres in extent.

The Act has been amended by two later provisions viz:

(i) The 1974 Act Schedule 6 has reduced the necessary term for a recordable Lease to 20 years; and has abolished the 50 acre limit. At the same time, the 1974 act introduced a prohibition against the granting of a long lease of property intended to be used as a dwellinghouse.

(ii) Under the 1979 Act, when an area has been declared operational for the purposes of Registration of Title, then the Tenant under a long Lease no longer has the option either to take possession or to register the Lease. Instead, after the area becomes operational, registration of the Lease in the Land Register is an essential requirement to the obtaining of a real right; and to that extent the 1449 Act is excluded and repealed.

9.1.5 Procedure under the 1857 Act

The provisions and effect of the 1857 Act as amended can be summarised thus:

(1) Any probative Lease of more than 20 years duration may be recorded in the Register of Sasines, either by the original Tenant or by any subsequent assignee. Provision is also made for the recording of a certified copy Lease where the principal is lost — Long Leases (Scotland) Act 1954 S.26; and of extracts in certain circumstances — 1857 Act S.19 as amended by the 1974 Act Schedule 6(6).

(2) In operational areas, any such Lease, or transmission thereof, taking effect after the date when the area became operational must be registered in the Land Register to secure the real right. But this does not apply to securities on Leases already validly recorded in the G.R.S.

(3) The area of the subjects let is now irrelevant — 1974 Act Schedule 6(5).

(4) No statutory form of Lease is provided by the 1857 Act; and any normal conventional form of Lease will serve for the purposes of registration.

The 1857 Act does, however, provide statutory forms of assignation and of renunciation of a Lease; and also provides forms of heritable security over Leases with appropriate forms for assignation and discharge of such securities. The forms have been amended and adapted by the following provisions:—

(i) The 1924 Act S.24.

The general purpose of this Section is to assimilate Lease forms with the forms in use for proprietary rights; and, in particular, for the purposes of any assignation or security writ the subjects of let are to be described in terms of Schedule J to the 1924 Act.

Further, by S.24, all the powers, rights and forms applicable to feudal property are, with necessary adjustments, made applicable to Leases and securities over Leases as if the right of the Tenant thereunder were a proprietary right.

(ii) The Long Leases (Scotland) Act 1954 S.27.
This Section removed certain earlier requirements for the description of the subjects of let, and simplified the forms of writ above referred to.

(iii) The 1970 Act S.32 and Schedule 8.
The statutory modifications introduced by the 1970 Act in relation to heritable securities were applied, by these provisions, to registered Leases in the same way as to proprietary rights; and, in consequence, certain provisions in the 1857 Act dealing with assignations in security etc. were abolished.

As a result of the 1970 Act provisions, heritable securities over Leases are now constituted by Standard Security in either Form A or Form B, using the 1924 Act provisions for description; and otherwise with the same general results as apply to a Standard Security over proprietary rights.

(iv) The 1974 Act SS.8-10 and Schedule 6.
The principal modifications in this Act are, as above noted:

(i) the reduction in the required period of a registerable Lease to 20 years; and

(ii) the prohibition on the granting of long Leases on dwellinghouses.

The 1974 Act also abolished casualties in Leases granted after the passing of that Act; but casualties in pre-existing Leases continue to be exigible.

(5) Where the Lease itself has not been recorded by the original Tenant, it can be recorded by any subsequent Tenant in right thereof for the time being as assignee, by the recording of the Lease together with a Notice of Title, using the Notice of Title Form 2 of Schedule B to the 1924 Act, and specifying the links in title connecting him with the original Tenant. As with the use of that form in other situations, the Notice of Title carries the Warrant of Registration and the Lease carries a docquet referring to that Notice.

(6) Once the Lease has been recorded, whether by the original Tenant or by a successor in the manner above referred to, it can then be transmitted by the Tenant in right thereof for the time being, whether or not he himself has a recorded Title, using the form of assignation provided by the 1857 Act as amended by the later enactments above referred to.

Similarly, the Tenant in right of the Lease for the time being can grant a Standard Security thereon.

(7) The combined effect of the enactments above referred to is that a Lease, on recording, effectively secures a real right for the Tenant thereunder as at the date of recording in a competition with all other recorded titles which enter the Record subsequent to the date of the recording of that Lease.

(8) In the case of unrecorded Leases, where the right transmits by assignation as it may do, subject possibly to the prior consent of the Landlord, the title of the assignee is completed by intimation of the assignation to the Landlord.

In the case of recorded Leases, consistently with the provisions for the recording thereof, the title of an assignee of a recorded Lease is completed by the recording of the assignation in the Register of Sasines; and the recording of the assignation effectively vests the Lease in the assignee to the extent to which the Lease is assigned.

(9) In relation to all the foregoing forms, whether of assignation of the Lease itself or securities thereon, and of renunciation of Leases, the whole Lease may be dealt with, using the forms provided by the 1857 Act as amended in terms of the enactments above referred to.

In that case, it is unnecessary to describe the subjects of let (c.f. the Assignation of a Bond and Disposition in Security or of a Standard Security); and all that is required is to assign the Lease itself thus:

'I AB (Design) IN CONSIDERATION of the sum of   POUNDS (£   ) now paid to me by CD (Design) hereby ASSIGN to the said CD a Lease granted by EF (Design) in my favour of the subjects therein described lying in the County of Angus dated   and recorded in the Division of the General Register of Sasines for the County of Angus on   ; With entry as at   '

Where part only of the subjects of the Lease is to transmit, then a description is required to indicate the part assigned. In that case, the foregoing form is used but with a description of the Lease modified on the following lines:

'but in so far only as regards the following portion of the subjects of lease, viz ...'

The portion assigned is then described or referred to as in Schedule D to the 1924 Act for proprietary writs.

9.1.6 Examination of the Landlord's Title

It is an essential feudal requirement that, for the granting of an effective lease, the Landlord must be infeft, subject only to the rules of accretion which apply to leases as they apply to the granting of a Feu Charter. The facility for deduction of title which applies to the granting of a Disposition and, now, to the granting of a Standard Security, has not yet been extended to the granting of Leases.

Further, not only must the Landlord be infeft as a preliminary to the granting of an effective Lease but, in addition, he must also, of course, have a valid and marketable title.

This is a point which is frequently overlooked by the Tenant's agent when revising the Lease. But it is just as important to a Tenant as it is to a purchaser to ensure that the Landlord granting the lease has a valid title so to do.

Therefore, the solicitor for the Tenant should insist, in the preliminary contract, that the Landlord has a valid and marketable title; and, as part of the procedure on revising the Lease produced by the Landlord's solicitor, the Tenant's solicitor should insist on examining the Landlord's title to assure himself of its validity.

Further enquiry may be necessary e.g. where there is a heritable security, in which case the consent of the heritable creditor may be necessary; or a floating charge, where the same applies.

The Tenant's solicitor should also insist on production of searches in exactly the same way in which a purchaser's solicitor insists on searches before completing a transaction of sale and purchase.

The Tenant's solicitor must also bear in mind that there may be conditions in the title, e.g. restricting the use of the property etc. which apply not only to the ownership of the property by the Landlord but to the use to be made of the property by the Tenant. All writs referred to for burdens must therefore be carefully examined just as in the case of sale and purchase.

Finally, exactly the same principles apply to settlement obligations on completion of a Lease as apply to settlement obligations on completion of sale and purchase.

9.2 Commercial Leases

Contributed by Mr. S. Brymer, Solicitor, Dundee.

Reading List 9.2.

Introduction

The approach to leasehold tenure in general in Scots Law and English Law is fundamentally different. In the Law of Scotland, the question of Commercial Leasing is not really covered and reference is often required to the General Law of Contract. In England, there are a number of Landlord and Tenant Acts and the position is largely governed by Statute. In Scotland, there is no equivalent legislation to the Law of Property and the Landlord and Tenant Acts. As mentioned previously, the main Scottish Statute is the Leases Act 1449 c.18. Naturally, linked to this statutory intervention in England, there is a vast amount of case law on all aspects of the law from both the view point of the Landlord and of the Tenant. These English cases and Articles, however, must be read carefully by the Scottish practitioner who should always remember the different principles often applied in Scots Law. However, within the last two decades, Investment Leases on a Full Repairing and Insuring basis have been introduced into Scotland.

It can now be fairly said that this is an established area of the law of Landlord and Tenant; but notwithstanding, there is still a significant lack of a text book offering practical guidance to a prospective Tenant's Solicitor. In this Section, therefore, it is intended to discuss clauses which often occur in Commercial Leases and as such should be noted and to suggest possible revisals on behalf of the Tenant. Only the major points in a Commercial Lease will be dealt with here but there are a number of other areas in a Commercial Lease which should also be studied carefully by the Tenant.

There are many different types of Commercial Lease e.g. modern shopping centre developments, industrial units etc. Each Lease has its own characteristics and, every clause must therefore be considered fully, and carefully revised.

The Tenant's Solicitor should first carefully read all the documents received from the Landlord before commencing to revise the draft Lease. Under no circumstances, should the bargain be concluded prior to the terms of the draft Lease being agreed by the Landlord and the Tenant. The Tenant's Solicitor should first take a copy of the draft Lease and use this as a working draft. This draft should then be revised and sent to the client with a report. After a meeting with the client, alterations can be made to the fresh draft and forwarded to the Landlord with a qualified acceptance to his Offer to Lease. If then the Landlord refuses to accept certain revisals made by the Tenant's Solicitor, the Tenant can be advised of the consequences of such rejections.

In revising the draft, the Tenant's Solicitor should read it through from beginning to end before making any form of detailed revisal. This is important as many related Clauses are often separated by a number of pages in the Deed. Use of a check-list showing the salient points to look out for could be helpful. If there is a definition/interpretation section in the lease document, it should be studied carefully. The Lease should then be revised where applicable to safeguard the Tenant's interests.

The foregoing is a very brief outline of the general steps to be followed by a Tenant's Solicitor in revising a Commercial Lease. There are a number of important areas which should be given specific mention however.

These are:—
1. Landlord's Title to Lease and Description of Subjects etc.
2. Monetary Obligations of the Tenant.
3. Rent Review.
4. Tenant's Repairing Obligation.
5. Insurance.
6. Alienation.
7. Irritancy.

9.2.1. Landlord's Title to Lease etc.

(a) Sub-leases

The Landlord may himself hold the subjects on Lease. In this case, the Head Lease should be examined in addition to the Head Landlord's title. An important consequence of the Landlord holding title by virtue of a Lease is that, if the Landlord's Lease is forfeited, any derivative rights will fall with it. Sub-tenants in Scotland under Commercial Leases are not protected by the law, unlike the protections available under statute in England. The Tenant should seek to obtain an undertaking from the Head Landlord that if the immediate Landlord's Lease falls, the Head Landlord will grant a new Lease on the same terms for the remaining duration of the original Lease. (This is dealt with further under 'Irritancies').

Heritable Creditors

The premises may be subject to a Standard Security. In this event, it is essential that the Tenant sees a Letter of Consent to the Lease from the heritable creditors in order to satisfy Standard Condition 6. Failure to comply with this procedure could be fatal for the Tenant. 5.3.3 — Trade Development Bank v Warriner & Mason (Scotland) Ltd. 1980 SLT 223.

Planning Permission etc.

Exhibition of all Planning Permissions, Building Warrants, Certificates of Completion and other necessary Permissions and Consents should be requested to satisfy the Tenant that the Landlord has complied with all relevant legislation etc. In addition, the usual Roads and Planning letters should be requested.

(b) Designations of Parties to the Lease

(i) The Tenant

In English law, the continuing obligation of the original Tenant is implied by law — notwithstanding subsequent alienation of the Lease. Such a continuing obligation has to be expressly provided for in a Lease in Scotland. Accordingly, the inclusion of 'Assignees' for example, within the definition of the 'Tenant' should be carefully considered, and any attempt to impose joint and several liability on the original Tenant along with assignees should be resisted. The Tenant's Solicitor should be cautious however, and revise the whole Lease carefully to see if this continiuing obligation has been inserted into the Deed in other places.

Where the Tenant is an individual or a Limited Company, the position is relatively straightforward. However, the case of a firm or a partnership deserves separate treatment. Partnerships cannot own heritage in Scotland, *socio nomine,* but a partnership as such may become a tenant. Some Landlords, however, insist that the individual partners must act as Trustees for the firm. If so, one often finds however that the obligations are deemed to extend to existing partners at the date of commencement of the Lease and to all persons who may subsequently become partners at any time during the period of the Lease. Effectively, the

Landlord is trying to bind future partners of the firm before they even become partners. Such a clause should be strongly resisted.

(ii) Guarantors

A Landlord may well request Guarantors. This request should be resisted by the Tenant. If the Tenant agrees to a Guarantee, the Landlord will try to ensure that it is a worthwhile one. Therefore, in the case of a Limited Company, only a Director being a major shareholder with a certain proportion of the issued Share Capital will be accepted by the Landlord with an obligation that if he leaves the Company, then another similar Guarantor should be obtained. If the Guarantor is a Company, the Landlord will check to ensure that it can competently give Guarantees in terms of its Memorandum and Articles. If the Guarantee is given, the Guarantor's Solicitor should read the definition of 'Guarantor' carefully so as to ensure that there is no possibility of the Guarantee continuing once the original Tenant assigns his interest in the Lease. This is a common fault.

(c) Description of the Leased Subjects.

It is essential that the Tenant obtains the subjects which he thought he was to obtain together with all necessary pertinent rights for their proper use and enjoyment. Careful investigation of plans and the Landlord's title is therefore essential. If a site visit is impossible, the Tenant's Solicitor should obtain a copy of the prospective Tenant's survey report and plans if possible.

There is no reason why a description in a Lease should be any different from a description in any feudal grant. This is not often the case in practice however. In complex office blocks or shopping centres, great care will have been taken when drawing the description of the subjects. As well as the subjects themselves, the Tenant will require all necessary pertinents such as access, use of services etc. Revise this into the Lease if omitted by the Landlord. The reservations made by the Landlord should be noted carefully by the Tenant's Solicitors. It is advisable in fact to incorporate an adequate conveyancing description in the Lease, whether or not the Lease is to be registered. Reference ought also to be made to a Plan — Ordnance Survey if possible.

In many modern Leases, one often finds that the Tenant is leasing no more than the airspace within the unit. In such cases, the Landlord will retain the main walls and roof etc. and will perhaps repair them but recover the cost of so repairing from the Tenant by way of service charge. These points can only be ascertained after careful examination of the draft Lease. Therefore, when dealing with the description of subjects, the Tenant's Solicitor should consider the whole Lease so that he may report to his client on the extent of his holding and the restrictions on it, if any. Such restrictions will normally take the form of reservations to the Landlord of various rights such as the right to lay and maintain services etc. One normally finds such reservations scattered throughout the Lease. It is advisable therefore that a summary be given to the Tenant of all rights which he has in the subjects, whether exclusive or common etc.

(d) Duration.

The date of entry in the Lease should be a definite stated date not earlier than the actual date of entry — howsoever it may be determined. The term of a Lease may vary depending on a number of factors such as the individual characteristics of the Landlord and the Tenant and perhaps the state of the commercial market in the area. If a Lease is to be registered in Sasines, it must be for duration of more than twenty years — twenty years and one day will suffice.

The rates of stamp duty increase by reference to the term of the Lease at seven years, thirty five years and one hundred years (Finance Act 1974 Sch. 11). Therefore, if the desired term is to be for longer than thirty five years, it may be desirable to prescribe an initial term of less than 35 years, with an option to renew, so as to minimise the stamp duty implications for the Tenant. It should however be borne in mind that (i) a Lease for thirty years with an option to renew for a period of twenty five years is chargeable as a Lease for thirty years and not fifty five years. — Hand v Hall (1877) 2EX.D355 and Sergeant on Stamp Duties 5th Edition pg. 149; (ii) when the option is exercised, the instrument used to evidence the renewal will attract ad valorem duty at that time — Rankine on Leases pg. 106 and (iii) the possibility that the option may not be binding on a singular successor of the Landlord should be considered — Paton and Cameron on Landlord and Tenant pages 95-97.

9.2.2. Monetary Obligations of Tenant.

(1) Rent.

The amount of rent to be charged by the Landlord may well have already been agreed by the Tenant before a Solicitor is consulted. The annual rental may be fixed for the initial period of the Lease, say five years, or it may be staged over this period. It is never too late to request a rent free period which benefits the Tenant and may cover his initial fitting out works, if nothing else. The period granted will vary depending on the type of unit involved. An alternative to a rent free period is for the Tenant to commence payment of rental at the date of entry but at a reduced rate for a certain period.

Rent is usually payable quarterly or half yearly in advance. Payment in advance is onerous and the rental period should be kept to the minimum. The Landlord may also provide for rent to be payable by Bankers Order.

The Tenant should not, if possible, agree to forego his common law right of retention of rent. Such a right can be useful to the Tenant in attempting to secure performance of the Landlord's obligations under the Lease. If however there is a Head Lease and the sub-tenant retains rent, the Head Lease could well be irritated thus causing derivative rights (e.g. the sub-lease) also to fall as aforesaid. Therefore, in such circumstances, the Head Landlord may refuse the Tenant's revisal.

(2) Turnover Rent.

This form of rent is common in America. An additional sum over a flat rate rent (which itself is subject to review) is usually paid. This additional sum is a percentage of gross sales over a minimum figure of sales. The machinery for calculating this form of rent should be examined carefully if used in a Scottish Lease.

(3) Interest.

There will undoubtedly be an interest provision either in the rent clause or in a separate clause to which reference is made throughout the Lease. Generally, the rate provided for by Landlords is penal and should be reduced if possible. The reason for a high interest rate is to prevent the Landlord becoming the 'unofficial and unpaid Banker' of the Tenant. If at all possible, the Tenant should not be committed to paying a penal rate of interest and a period of grace before interest becomes due should be requested. Many Leases have a clause providing for liquidate penalty for failure to pay rent when due. This is certainly penal and should be deleted. There may also be other clauses throughout the Lease which contain interest provisions.

(4) **Insurance Premiums.**

If the Landlord insures, the Tenant will be required to pay the premiums on demand. The Tenant will also have to pay any premiums for risks against which he himself must insure e.g. plate glass, public liability etc.

(5) **Rates and other charges.**

Rates will be the responsibility of the Tenant. The other charges should however be restricted, if possible, to those of an annual or recurring nature. Taxes arising out of the Landlord's dealing with the subjects should be excluded along with any rents payable to a Head Landlord.

(6) **Service Charge.**

In many leases, there is a clause allowing the Landlord to carry out certain services for which he can charge the Tenant(s). Such clauses can be very onerous. There are a number of essential points to be considered in the service charge clause. Briefly, however the most important items to be excluded from the cost of the services are —

(i) Damage caused by the insured risks, and

(ii) Damage caused by latent or inherent defects — see infra.

The basis of apportionment should also be investigated, especially if there are unlet units in the development. A sinking fund is usually adopted in service charge situations so as to provide for regular payments from the Tenants towards the ultimate cost of repair. If there is a sinking fund, however, the Tenant must ensure that it is placed outwith the control of the Landlord in order to safeguard the Tenant's position in the event of the Landlord's liquidation.

(7) **Common Charges etc.**

These will be ascertainable following upon an examination of the title deeds. The Tenant's potential liability should thus be calculated prior to conclusion of missives; and

(8) **Expenses.**

It is suggested that it is an outdated feature of the law of Landlord and Tenant that the Tenant must pay the Landlord's legal fees in respect of the preparation of the Lease. Resist this if at all possible. If the tenant must pay these fees, ensure that they are reasonable and properly incurred and that there is no responsibility to pay VAT thereon where the Landlord is registered for VAT purposes. Most certainly refuse to pay the Landlord's Surveyors and other professional advisers' costs in this regard. There may also be expenses throughout the Lease in respect of the service of schedules of repair and applications for consent etc. These are unavoidable. However, the Tenant should provide that these charges must be reasonable.

9.2.3. **Rent Review.**

The object of a rent review clause is to minimise the consequences of inflation on the Landlord's investment. Such a clause allows the Landlord to take account of fluctuations in market value so that the Tenant is paying throughout the duration of the Lease, a rent which equates in real terms with the market rental value of the subjects. Therefore, the rent review clause will have been drafted carefully by the Landlord's Solicitor — possibly in conjunction with the Landlord's Surveyors.

Essentially, a rent review clause provides for the rent to be reviewed after a set period following agreement between the parties. If there is no agreement, the matter will be decided by some independent third party. Clauses are not so straight forward in practice however and there are a number of elements of a rent review clause which require further comment. In this area of the law, Scots Law again has no text books and few authorities and comparisons are often made to English Law examples, of which there are many. For a detailed discussion on rent review clauses in general, reference is made to the Series of Articles in the Workshop of the Journal of the Law Society of Scotland, commencing April 1983 *et seq.* by E. D. Buchanan, Esq.

The following is a summary of some of the major elements in the Rent Review Clause: —

Rent Review Dates.

The frequency of reviews will vary with location, the norm presently being three years/five years. It is essential for a Landlord that these dates are clearly and unambiguously expressed in the Lease. Phrases such as 'in the fifth year of the Lease' are not recommended from the Landlord's or the Tenant's view point.

Older Leases tend to provide for longer periods between reviews. In such cases, the Landlord may well attempt to obtain a premium rent i.e. a higher rent than that which would have been the case had the review interval been less. In other words, the Tenant would be paying a premium rent for the advantage of infrequent rent reviews. Even if accepted, such a clause has the disadvantage however that the market rent may rise dramatically, in which event, the premium would not adequately compensate the Landlord.

In Leases of a longer duration than say twenty five years, it is common to see procedure for a review of reviews. This will probably take the form of an option exerciseable by the Landlord entitling him to review the frequency of reviews or redraft the rent review clause so as to produce a new clause which conforms to the prevailing market practice. Such a clause is really another attempt to protect the Landlord's investment.

Timetable for Review.

(1) Notice.

Certain Leases provide that the rent will be reviewed without the necessity of any form of notice from the Landlord to the Tenant. Many Leases however provide for some form of notice to trigger the operation of the review machinery. As a result, these Leases are drafted to ensure that even if the Landlord fails or omits to serve notice, he may do so at a later term without penalty. However, in England, it is now established by decisions that time is not of the essence in relation to rent review procedure unless the parties expressly so stipulate or it could be inferred from the circumstances that the parties so intended — United Scientific Holdings Limited v Burnley Borough Council and Cheapside Land Development Co. Ltd. v. Messels Service Co. Ltd. (1978) AC904.

This is probably also now the case in Scotland following upon the recent case of Banks v. Mecca Bookmakers (Scotland) Limited 1982 SLT 150. An argument against this principle however, is that the review procedure was agreed in a Contract and that the agreement of the parties ought to be enforced. Cf. Lord Neaves in Stewart v Watson (1864) 2M1414 at pg. 1422. To avoid this argument, therefore, the Landlord's clause may well dispense with the requirement of notice and may contain a declaration that time is not of the essence.

An interesting point arising from the Banks case is the dicta of Lord Grieve where he stated that acceptance of rent at the old rate by the Landlord after the stipulated review date was acquiesence in the situation. The result would therefore be that the Landlord would be barred from insisting on the missed rent review. In light of this decision therefore, Landlords will insert a provision to the effect that demand for and/or acceptance of rent at the old rate by the Landlord after a review date shall not constitute a waiver of the Landlord's right to review.

(2) Counter notice.

Some Leases are drafted so that once the Landlord serves notice of review, the Tenant only has a specified period within which he can object or else be deemed to have accepted the reviewed rental. This can be beneficial for a Landlord but should be avoided by the Tenant who could be faced with an inflated reviewed rental with only a short period to object. If the Tenant omits to serve such notice due to error or administrative failure, he will pay the penalty.

(3) Postponed Reviews.

Failure on the part of a Landlord to initiate the rent review procedure will result in back rent being due. If such a late rent review takes place, it is only equitable for the Tenant that the level of the market rent should reflect the level that would have applied at the original rent review date. In addition, the Tenant should not suffer a penalty when he has not been in a position to pay the increased rent which was unknown. Therefore, the increased rent should be payable only from the postponed date and not backdated to the original rent review date.

Basis for Review.

The next major elements of the rent review clause deal with the various assumptions to be made and the facts to be taken into account in establishing the current market rental value of the subjects. In arriving at the reviewed rental for the subjects, a Surveyor will obtain guidance from the Lease as to what assumptions etc. should be made. These instructions should be clear and unambiguous to avoid dispute. Accordingly, both the Landlord and the Tenant must ensure that the Lease, as agreed, enables their Surveyors, (and in default of agreement the Arbiter or Expert) to establish clearly the market rent of the hypothetical letting of the subjects. The salient matters to be discussed, are:—

(1) Upwards only review.

Most Leases provide for the rent to be reviewed in an upwards only direction. However, this may not be commercially viable, especially in poor market conditions. This has been commented on in England in the case of Stylo Shoes Ltd. v. Manchester Royal Exchange Ltd. (1967) 204 EG 803.

(2) Valuation

There are a number of important definitions and assumptions built into a rent review clause — especially as regards the definition of 'the current market rental value' of the subjects. The most important of these are:—

(i) **Willing Landlord and Willing Tenant** — these characters are assumed as they may not be present in the negotiation. This assumption is consistent with the hypothetical open market assumption. The implication of this assumption was clearly dealt with in the English case of FR Evans (Leeds) Ltd. v. English Electric Co. Ltd. (1977) 36P and CR185. The willing Landlord assumption prevents the actual Landlord from arguing that he would not in fact let the property to the Tenant at the review date e.g. because the market was depressed at that date. The term was initially introduced in England in S.34 of the 1954 Act, presumably for this reason. It also prevents the Landlord arguing that, due to personal difficulties, he could only accept a certain level of rent. The term thus recognises the fact that, with a rent review, a settlement must at some stage and by some means be reached e.g. a notional letting must be effected and there is a rent on which a willing Landlord and willing Tenant would agree.

(ii) **User** — it is a fact that a restrictive user clause will result in the rent available at a review date being less than what would otherwise have been available. This was demonstrated by the English case of Plinth Property Investments Ltd. v. Mott Hay & Anderson (1979) 249 EG 1167CA. To counter this fact, many Landlords attempt to introduce an assumption that notwithstanding the actual use, the use at the review date will be any use within a certain Use Class Order. This should be resisted by the Tenant who should insist upon the review being in the context of the User Clause in the Lease.

(iii) **Duration** — the assumed duration of the hypothetical letting may either be for a period equal to the original term of the Lease or for a period equal to the unexpired term. The former is better for the Landlord in most cases and the latter for the Tenant. Many Leases are now drafted with a compromise based on an assumed duration of either the unexpired residue or ten/fifteen years whichever is the greater.

(iv) **'Lease whether as a whole or in part'** — this is better from the Landlord's point of view although possibly damaging for Tenant if he cannot assign or sub-lease.

(v) **Vacant Possession** — Where a rent review clause provides for the yearly rental value to be assessed on the basis of a letting with vacant possession, a discount may be applied to the rent to compensate for the fact that no rent free period will occur at the rent review. Tenants should beware of the vacant possession assumption where there are sub-tenants. Furthermore, the assumption may also negate the effect on rent of a restrictive user clause as the Courts may hold that if vacant possession is to be assumed at a review date, it is illogical also to assume that only the existing Tenant can occupy the subjects.

(vi) **'Lease on the same terms and conditions of the existing Lease — other than rent and the provisions of the Rent Review Clause.'** The latter part of this assumption is for the benefit of the Landlord. The Tenant should insist upon the Rent Review provisions being included.

(vii) **Rent to be without premium.**

(viii) **Tenant's Obligations** — the Rent Review clause may also provide for the valuation to be on the assumption that the Tenant has performed all his obligations under the Lease.

(3) Disregards for Valuation

The Tenant's Agent should ensure that the effect (if any) on rent of certain matters is not to be taken into account when the Landlord reviews the rent. The inclusion of these disregards is essential. These disregards, which have their origin in English Law in the Landlord & Tenant Act 1954 Section 34, are as follows:—

(i) Occupation by the Tenant or any predecessor in title or permitted sub-tenant of the Tenant;

(ii) Goodwill attached to the subjects by reason of the trade of the Tenant or his foresaids;

(iii) Initial shop fitting works — especially in a shop unit; and

(iv) Alterations or improvements carried out by the Tenant otherwise than in pursuance of any obligation to the Landlord. This is an important disregard as failure by the Tenant to include this in the Rent Review Clause will result in all his improvements being taken into account by the Landlord at the Review Date. This was demonstrated in the case of Ponsford v H.M. Aerosols Limited (1979) A.C. 63. If the Lease is a Ground Lease where the Tenant has paid for and erected buildings on the ground, then the Landlord ought only to be entitled to a revised rent based on his interest in the subjects i.e. the ground alone.

The Landlord may also add that the fact that the subjects have been damaged or destroyed is to be disregarded.

Determination of Reviewed Rental in the event of Dispute

If there is no agreement between the Parties by a given date, the Lease usually provides for the matter to be referred to the decision of some independent person to be agreed between the parties or failing agreement, to be appointed by a Third Party. The usual procedure is by way of a reference to arbitration. However, many Landlords prefer that the matter be referred to an Expert, i.e. a Surveyor having specialised knowledge of the area. The referral to an Expert is designed to accelerate the process of determinating the new Rent. It is arguable however as to exactly how valid the distinction between the Arbiter and the Expert is. Many leases expressly state that the third party is to act as an 'Expert and not an Arbiter'. However, it has been suggested that all such determinations of reviewed rental by an independent third party will be *de facto* arbitration. For a detailed review of this matter, reference is again made to the Articles in 1983 J.L.S. (Workshop) April *et seq.*

Some Landlords attempt to exclude Section 3 of the Administration of Justice (Scotland) Act 1972 where the determination is by an Arbiter. Such a right of appeal to the Courts on a point of law is essential from the Tenant's point of view. The Tenant should also resist any provision that he pays for the independent determination of rent. Each Party should pay their own costs unless the award of the Arbiter declares otherwise.

Miscellaneous Matters

(i) Rent pending determination of Review

If the reviewed rental has not been ascertained by the Review Date, the Landlord may be entitled to assess a Provisional Rent. The Tenant will therefore pay this new rent, which may be high. Such a clause ought to be resisted by the Tenant. If it is to be accepted, there should be an accounting between the Parties upon the determination of the reviewed rental with interest at a high rate if possible. Many Leases provide that the existing rental will continue to be chargeable, however, in such circumstances with the increased sum due by the Tenant as a debt to the Landlords. If interest is to be chargeable on this debt, then the Tenant should attempt to reduce the interest rate as much as possible.

(ii) Counter Inflation Legislation

Many Leases contain clauses dealing with the situation of rent increases being prohibited or restricted in the future by some Statutory Regulations. These clauses are a result of controls imposed in Section 11 of the Counter Inflation Act 1973. It is suggested that these clauses are often unnecessary. The Regulations, if re-imposed will probably only restrict or prohibit collection of increased rentals. Therefore, it will still be competent for the rent to be reviewed on the normal dates in the normal way. Any increase will be payable in whole or in part as soon as the relevant Regulations permit. The Tenant should avoid clauses providing for interim reviews, but, if such a clause must be accepted, the Tenant should ensure that any such review or reviews will contain a valuation based on market values at the original Review Date and not at any later date.

(iii) Memoranda

Once the review has been agreed, that agreement will be incorporated into a formal addendum to the Lease. Try to ensure that the Tenant does not have to meet all the expenses of this. In particular, the Tenant should not meet the Landlord's Surveyors costs.

(iv) Retail Prices Index

Review Clauses often provide for the rent to be increased in accordance with the appropriate increase in the Retail Prices Index between the Date of Entry and the Review Date. However, Landlords and Tenants generally prefer the revised rent to be fixed by real people rather than by an anonymous Index. A major problem with this procedure is that all the indices measure rises in prices and no official index is related to property. Therefore the Tenant should not accept such a procedure.

(v) English Law

As mentioned previously, English Law has had a major influence on the development of the Law of Commercial Leases. There are numerous English Law cases on each of the salient points of the Review Clause. If a lesson is to be learned from this fact it is that Landlords' Solicitors should draft their Review Clauses with care and attention so as to avoid litigation! Although the English Law cases may not always be followed in Scotland it is suggested that they remain of great importance.

9.2.4. Tenant's Repairing Obligation

At Common Law, the position of a Tenant was much more favourable than it is under the usual current commercial provisions. The Institutional writers state that once a Tenant is in possession under an Urban Lease, the Landlord is bound to repair any defect which makes the subjects less than wind and water tight and not in a tenantable condition. Such an obligation is very rarely found in a modern Commercial Lease.

Without proper repair, the Landlord's investment is put in jeopardy. However, the fact that the property is held on lease, so that the maintenance responsibility can be divided between the two parties involved, seems to give scope for endless disputes. In recent years, the clear trend has been for the Landlord to put all the responsibilities on to the Tenant. Many Landlords have taken the view that an undivided repairing obligation reduces the scope for argument. However, there are always situations where a building is or may be converted into multi-occupation and where significant structural work and even external decoration can only be appropriately done by someone with an interest in the whole property. In such circumstances, the cost of these works will undoubtedly be recovered by the Landlord by way of a Service Charge payable by all the Tenants.

Each Lease will differ according to circumstances. Therefore, a Tenant's Agent must read the entire Lease carefully especially the link between the Repairs and the Insurance Clauses. Indeed, a major problem arises where damage is caused to the subjects by a risk for which there is no insurance cover. Accordingly, it is essential to the Tenant that his liabilities should be mitigated wherever possible. The two main areas where such exceptions can be made are as follows:—

(i) Damage by Insured Risks

Generally, the Landlord will insure the subjects and recover the premium from the Tenant. Therefore, there will be a specified list of risks against which the Landlord insures. The Tenant must have sight of this policy or an extract thereof — see infra. To cover the situation where damage is caused to the subjects by an insured risk, an exception should be made to the repairs obligation of the Tenant, so as to provide that such damage should not be repaired by the Tenant. However, this will be further qualified by the Landlord to the effect that such damage will only be excepted where it has not been occasioned by the act or default of the Tenant himself; and

(ii) Latent or Inherent Defects

If at all possible, a similar exception from liability should be made in respect of such defects. However, Landlords generally resist such revisals, taking the view that the Tenant took the subjects as he saw them at the Date of Entry — *caveat emptor*! The defects may have been caused by some negligent design or bad workmanship on the part of the Landlord or his contractors or architects. Accordingly, the defect may have been inherent in the structure of the subjects. If the repairing obligation of the Tenant is not qualified, the Landlord may look to the Tenant to repair such defects at any time throughout the Lease. Some Landlords may agree to carry out such repairs but this should not be regarded as a general rule. Indeed, the clause in the Styles Committee Lease cf. 1980 J.L.S. (Workshop) 117 — on this point is not standard. The Landlord will have his own contractual rights against his contractors etc. as aforesaid whereas the Tenant has no such right of recourse. It is therefore essential for the Tenant to attempt to revise this clause by excepting liability for repairs necessitated by latent or inherent defects. Care should be taken to ensure that such liability is also excepted from the Service Charge, if any, so as to avoid the possibility of the Landlord still being able to charge the Tenant under this provision.

If the Landlord accepts the revisal, a claim should also be made for compensation to the Tenant for any loss or damage caused to him during the execution of the repairs by the Landlord.

Reference must also be made in the Insurance Clause to the exception from liability in respect of inherent defects etc. As already stated, the Landlord will probably reject these revisals. If this is the case, the Tenant should request either that, in the event of such damage the Landlord will assign his rights to the Tenant against the Contractor etc. or conjoin with him in an action for reparation.

Basically however, all Tenants should be advised before taking a lease of subjects, whether new or old, that they should have the subjects surveyed by an experienced surveyor. The survey should be carried out prior to the bargain being concluded (the surveyor can also be asked to comment on the level of rent being sought and the rent review patterns.) Therefore, on obtaining the survey, the prospective Tenant can either refuse to take a lease or negotiate for a reduced rent or reduced liabilities to repair if the subjects are in bad shape — e.g. internal repairing only.

It is quite common for Back Letters to be prepared to the effect that, notwithstanding the terms of the Lease, certain items will not require to be repaired by the Tenants. In addition, a Record of Condition is sometimes placed with the Lease so as to remove any argument as to the condition of the subjects at the commencement of the Lease.

The Tenant's Solicitors should also attempt to reduce the Tenant's repairing obligation by introducing an exception of 'fair wear and tear'. This could be a useful protection for a Tenant of an old building in that it would absolve him of liability to carry out major repairs due to the age of the building.

It is quite common for there to be confusion over what the respective parties have to repair under the Lease. Every Lease will contain an obligation to repair, and the Tenant should consider the Lease carefully so as to ascertain the extent of his obligation, the meaning of the obligation and whether or not this is reasonable.

The definition of the subjects, perhaps elsewhere in the Lease, should be considered carefully in order to discover whether the Tenant is directly liable for repairs to external walls, roof, drains and other services etc. As previously stated, many leases provide the Tenant with no more than a right to the air space within the internal walls with the Landlord maintaining the external walls etc. and recovering the cost by way of a Service Charge. In practice, the Tenant cannot argue against carrying out day to day maintenance or repairs of a decorative nature. However, arguments arise where there are major repairs. In such cases, the definition of the subjects can be critical. If the Title to the subjects in question includes a right of common property or common interest in the roof, such right of ownership forms part of the subjects so that, if the obligation merely says that the Tenant must repair the subjects, the Tenant is liable for the repair of the relevant material parts. However, if part of the subjects or the building of which the subjects form part remains in the Landlord's control or if the Landlord has retained a contractual duty of repair, then he has an implied contractual duty to take reasonable care that his Tenant shall not suffer damage. What constitutes 'reasonable care' in this context has however to be determined by reference inter alia to the Landlord's knowledge of the defect or potential defect which gives rise to a risk of damage.

Repairs/Improvements

Once the Lease has been agreed, there are often problems over the interpretation of the repair clause. The most common argument is as to whether certain works more readily constitute an improvement rather than a repair. There has been much case law on this subject in England, and the position there is that it is always a question of degree whether that which the Tenant is asked to do can properly be described as a repair, or whether it would involve giving back to the Landlord, a wholly different thing from that initially let. in other words the approach in England is to look at the particular subjects, consider the state which they are in at the date of the lease, consider the terms of the lease and then come to a decision as to whether the requisite work can be fairly called repairs. However onerous the obligation, it is not to be looked at in vacuo.

The whole question of what constitutes a 'repair' was dealt with inter alia in the English case of Ravenseft Properties Limited -v- Davestone (Holdings) Limited (1980) 1 QB 12.

It is suggested that the test to be applied in English Law is this: if the work which is done is a provision of something new for the benefit of the occupier, that is properly speaking an improvement; but, if it is only the replacement of something already there, which has become dilapidated, then albeit that it is a replacement by its modern equivalent, it comes within the category of repair and not improvement.

It has been suggested however that there is no such test in Scots Law which would take work of repair, no matter how extensive, out of the Tenant's repairing obligation in the Lease. In other words, in Scots Law, regard should be had to the scope of the rebuilding obligation against the background of the common law doctrine of *rei interitus.* See 1985 JLS 99.

9.2.5. Insurance

As has been previously stated, the Insuring Obligation is the complement of the Repairing Obligation. Basically, the Insuring Obligation is designed to secure that financial resources will be available to restore insured damage and to reinstate the subjects when destroyed by an insured risk. Insurance will either be carried out by the Landlord, with the Tenant normally repaying the premiums or by the Tenant under the supervision of the Landlord who will request sight of the policy and premium receipts etc. Most leases contain an obligation of the former type since Landlords prefer to keep reinstatement under their control. Therefore, the usual arrangement is that the Landlord insures the property and the Tenant refunds the premium or an allocated portion thereof as '*quasi rent*'.

There are two supplementary reasons for this common arrangement viz:

i) the Tenant automatically bears the full cost of increased premiums; and

ii) a refund of premium is not rent, and so attracts no stamp duty.

The main points to be noted are:

(1) **Choice of Insurance Company.**

Normally, the Landlord decides the amount of cover and selects the appropriate Insurance Company. It is therefore essential for the Tenant to have the right at any reasonable time to have sight of the Insurance Policy, or an extract thereof and the Premium Receipts. This will enable the Tenant to check the sufficiency of cover and that the Policy is in force. The Landlord is not likely to accept a revisal allowing the Tenant to alter the Insurance Company if he can find a better quotation. The Insurance Company should be an office of repute. The Tenant's Agent should investigate this matter.

(2) **Extent of Cover.**

The Tenant should consider the definition of 'the insured risks' carefully. The definition may be in a totally separate place in the Lease from the Insurance Clause itself. This definition ought at least to list the minimum risks to be covered. Any discretion in the Landlord's favour to insure against other risks should be limited to other 'normal commercial' risks. The value insured should be no greater or no less than the full reinstatement value with associated fees and loss of rent. This will require constant reappraisal however in order to keep it in line with inflation. Loss of Rent Insurance is designed to provide cover for the Landlord when the subjects are destroyed, in whole or in part, and he is receiving no rent or at the most partial rent. The period of cover is linked to the likely period of reinstatement, this presently being for a minimum of three years. The Tenant will pay the Premium on such insurance.

(3) **Liability in the event of shortfall in Insurance Monies.**

If the Landlord insures, the Tenant should attempt to make the Landlord liable for any such deficiency out of his own resources. Although it would be better to express this in the Lease, the Common Law may in fact provide a remedy for the Tenant where the Landlord has not fully insured. However, many Landlords resist this revisal. As in most matters, it is often a question of commmercial strength as to who wins.

(4) **Damage by Insured Risks.**

If the Landlord has sole control of insurance, it is essential that the Tenant qualifies his repairing obligation with regard to the restoration of insured damage. This emphasises the points made previously when discussing the repairing obligation of the Tenant. If damage from an insured risk occurs, the Insurance Company may, except where the Tenant is one of the insured (*infra*), have the right to enforce the contractual obligations of the Tenant to reinstate the subjects, if this is so provided. Therefore, as previously stated, it is essential to exclude from the Tenant's Repairing Obligation the restoration of insurance damage unless the Policy or claim has been invalidated because of some act or default of the Tenant.

(5) **Insurance in Joint Names of Landlord and Tenant.**

Fire Insurance is a Contract of Indemnity against loss or damage by fire. Therefore, the Insurance Company will have a right of subrogation entitling them, on indemnifying the insured, to be put into the position of the insured and to exercise all rights competent to the insured against third parties in respect of the fire damage. Accordingly, if the Tenant is one of the insured and was responsible for the damage to the subjects, then the insurers would have no such claim because it is generally no answer to a fire policy claim that the damage resulted from the negligence (without fraud) on the part of the insured or one of them.

Many insurance companies now waive their subrogation rights; but it may be prudent to provide for the endorsation of the Tenant's interest on the insurance policy. Possibly, this is tantamount to accepting the Tenant as a joint insured.

The whole question of allocation of insurance monies in the event of destruction of the subjects has been the subject of case law in England. See re King (1963) 1 Ch.459, and Beacon Carpets v Kirby (1984). The position in Scots Law has been discussed in an Article in 1985 JLS 99.

(6) **Rent abatement.**

The provision that a Lease endures notwithstanding damage will be dealt with infra. However, if there is such a provision, the Tenant may well be liable to continue paying rent for a period during which he may not be able to obtain access to the property. This is unacceptable. In practice, the Landlord insures against loss of rent in addition to the usual perils as aforementioned. Accordingly, in the event of damage to or destruction of the subjects, and the Landlord's Insurance Policy not being vitiated in whole or in part or insurance monies being withheld due to the actions of the Tenant, the 'loss-of-rent' insurance monies (designed also to cover any provisions for rent review) will compensate the Landlord during the period when the Tenant's obligation to pay rent is suspended. It is now common for a Lease to provide that the rent is suspended until reinstatement is effected or until the expiry of the loss of rent insurance monies, whichever is the earlier. A Tenant should not accept such a provision without qualification.

A rent abatement provision is designed to protect a Tenant so that he is not obliged to pay rent in the circumstances previously described. It would also be advisable to ensure that service and other common charges are abated with rent. Abatement may be for a period during which the whole or any part of the subjects are destroyed. Therefore, it may be that only a proportion of the rent etc., payable will be abated. It may also be worth considering whether the Tenant ought to attempt to introduce a 'long stop provision' into the Lease which would enable the Tenant to bring the Contract to an end if the subjects are not restored within a specified period. (Landlords do not generally accept this revisal however (see (8) infra).

(7) Reinstatement

There is no general rule as to who should reinstate subjects damaged or destroyed by an insured risk. In theory, under a Full Repairing and Insuring Lease, the Tenant should repair and reinstate the subjects. This is often the case. However, many Landlords prefer to undertake the obligation of reinstatement and thus receive the insurance monies. Indeed, some Landlords declare that it shall be in their option whether or not to rebuild the subjects at all! If the Landlord reinstates, the Lease will normally provide that he shall apply the proceeds of the insurance monies towards reinstatement within a definite period. Do not accept a provision that the Landlord will reinstate with no time limit. It is preferable that a set period of say 3 years, is laid down in the Lease.

If the Tenant reinstates, the Landlord will wish to retain some control e.g. over the type of building/plans to be submitted and approved etc. The Landlord may also provide that the insurance monies will be consigned in joint names in a Bank and only be released upon receipt of the Tenant's Architect's Certificates of Completion. This should be resisted by the Tenant, if possible.

(8) Rei Interitus.

At Common Law, if subjects are destroyed or can be regarded as constructively destroyed through the fault of neither the Landlord nor the Tenant, the Lease comes to an end and the loss is divided equally between the Landlord — who will lose rent, and the Tenant — who will lose possession. An Institutional Investor in the Landlord's interest will not accept this. Accordingly, it has become common in modern Leases to include a contractual provision that notwithstanding damage or destruction, the Lease will remain in full force and effect. Such a provision will often be found in various places in the Lease, most notably in the Repairing and Insurance Clauses.

A Landlord's solicitor will therefore try to avoid the application of the doctrine of Rei Interitus. Indeed, one often finds that as well as stating that the Lease will continue as aforesaid, the Landlord is often successful in stating that the Tenant will be fully liable for repairing, renewing and if necessary rebuilding the subjects if damaged or destroyed by any defect latent or patent.

The Common Law recognises that, while it is possible for parties to bind themselves to perform some particular act no matter what may happen, it is rarely their intention to do so, and that to enforce performance after a material change in circumstances would often be to bind the parties to a contract which they did not intend to make. In other words, the Common Law principle rests on the basic 'frustration' rules.

The Landlord's solicitor may therefore be instructed to combat the application of these principles in whatever way possible — especially if there is a fund involved. Therefore, the Lease will be drafted so as to transfer all obligations onto the Tenant and to give him little room to plead frustration. However, it becomes increasingly difficult to avoid the operation of Rei Interitus in respect of a lease of premises within a larger building, control of the remaining units of which does not lie with the Landlord.

It is suggested that it is now settled that since the case of Cantors (Properties) (Scotland) Limited 1980 SLT 165, in the absence of express or necessarily implied stipulations to the contrary, the effect of total and accidental destruction by fire of the whole leased subjects is that the contract is terminated. It is always, however, open to the contracting parties to provide otherwise. If they do not, then the contract will determine if the subject matter is totally destroyed so that neither party is bound and neither party can compel performance of any of the stipulations to the contract.

(9) **Other Insurances.**

The Tenant may also be liable to insure against a selection of other risks such as public liability, plate glass insurance, loss of licence (if applicable) etc. Exhibition of the policies and or premium receipts will be required by the Landlord.

9.2.6. Alienation.

At Common Law, a Tenant has freedom to assign and sublet unfurnished urban subjects. This right however is severely curtailed in most modern Commercial Leases. Modern clauses are drafted so as to retain control for the Landlord over the original Tenant. In English Law, there is continuing Privity of Contract between the Landlord and his original Tenant for the full period of the Lease. This is not the position at Common Law in Scots Law, and a provision is a Scottish Lease that the original Tenant guarantees the whole terms of the Lease throughout its endurance should, if possible, be rejected. This is essentially an attempt to import into Scottish Leases what is understood to be an implied term of similar Leases in England.

A Landlord will have investigated the financial standing of his original Tenant thoroughly and will be reluctant to release him for a substitute who may not be as acceptable. A feature of the Landlord's control over the identity of his new Tenant may well be that he will insist upon the new Tenant being of 'sound financial standing'. In practice, Landlords' agents use a wide variety of phrases to attempt to obtain such control. (see infra). If there is any doubt as to the financial standing of the proposed Assignee, the Landlord may well request that the original Tenant stand as guarantor for his successor throughout the unexpired period of the Lease. The Tenant, however, should resist this request. His sole interest is to assign the Lease if he can find a suitable Assignee and obtain the Landlord's consent.

(1) **Alienation of Part Only of the Subjects.**

Alienation of part of the subjects whether by Assignation of Sub-Lease, is generally prohibited in a Lease. There are sound reasons supporting such a prohibition unless the subjects are of such proportions that a dealing with part only would be a beneficial enterprise.

(2) **Alienation of the Whole.**

(a) **Assignation.**

Assignation of the Tenant's interest in the whole of the subjects will, almost always by express provision require the Landlord's consent. If there is an element of *delectus personae* in the Lease, consent may well be required notwithstanding the absence of express provision. The matter of consent, and any other restriction on the right of the Tenant to assign the Lease or indeed to sublet the subjects, will be read according to its terms. A simple provision for the Landlord's consent, for example 'but excluding Assignees, legal or conventional, without the previous written consent of the Landlord' gives the Landlord an absolute discretion as to whether to grant or withhold his consent. The most common revisal to such a clause and in fact elsewhere in the Lease is to add the phrase 'which consent shall not be unreasonably withheld'. Due to the lack of Scottish Case Law and reported arbitration decisions on the point however, the effect and meaning of this phrase remains in doubt. Without such a revisal being made, the basic Scottish Common Law position as stated in the case of Duke of Portland -v- Baird (1865) 4M10 — would prevail viz: that the Landlord's power to refuse consent is absolute. In fact, due to the absence in Scottish Law of a doctrine similar to the English Law Privity of Contract Rule, the Landlord may have good reasons as to why he should have full power to decide whether a prospective substitute Tenant is acceptable to him. Basically, however, each case will be decided on its own merits with the onus of proof being firmly on the Tenant. Such a revisal may in fact do no more than provide for the possibility of the question being referred to the objective consideration of a neutral arbiter as a control on the subjective view taken by the Landlord.

Many clauses also lay down detailed qualifications as to the financial standing and suitability etc. of the prospective Tenant. Such phrases may, it is suggested, weaken the Landlord's power to withhold consent if the assignee fulfills these additional qualifications. Such a provision may run e.g. 'not without the written consent of the Landlord, which consent shall not be unreasonably withheld in the case of a respectable and responsible assignee'

From the Tenant's point of view, such a clause will fall to be considered in two stages. If the assignee is not a 'respectable and responsible person' as evidenced by Bank and Trade references, then the Landlord will have an unqualified right to withhold consent. It would only be if the proposed assignee complied with this provision that the Landlord's power to withhold consent would be fettered and could only be exercised if it was reasonable so to do.

(b) Sub-letting

The Landlord may not object to the Tenant sub-letting the whole subjects as he will retain his rights against the original Tenant. He will however insist upon the rent in the sub-lease not being less than the open market rent. Indeed, he may insist on the rent not being less than the rent in the Head Lease. This should be resisted, if possible, by the Tenant especially in a bad economic climate where rents are actually falling. The Landlord may prohibit the sub-tenant from granting further subleases so that he does not become too distant from the actual tenant in occupation. However, this is not a valid objection as he does retain his rights against the original Tenant, and, if that lease falls, all derivative rights from it also terminate. As mentioned earlier however, Landlords will usually expressly prohibit sub-letting of parts.

(3) Assignation to related or associated Companies

If a Tenant is a large multiple company, it may be desirable to obtain the Landlord's consent to an assignation to another company within the same group. Landlords will generally refuse permission unless the original Tenant company or the parent company continues to guarantee the Lease. Otherwise, the Tenant could assign the Lease to an associated company, liquidate that company and thus walk away from its responsibilities under the Lease. The Landlord may also be approached for his consent to the occupation of the subjects by an associated company of the Tenant company. Once again however, this may be permitted only subject to the Landlord having prior notification.

(4) Franchises/Concessions

It is common to find franchises/concessions being offered in large leased subjects such as Superstores. These persons do not have security of tenure as their exact pitch within the subjects may be uncertain. They thus lack particular subjects of let. Landlords usually allow franchises but often impose an upper limit on their number.

(5) Pre-emption

Beware a Lease containing a right for the Landlord to buy back the Lease on the occasion of an assignation. This can delay the sale of the Tenant's interest quite substantially. In general, this clause should be read carefully in order to advise the Tenant of his ability to deal with his interest in the Lease at some time in the future. The clause may also restrict the Tenant from dealing in any manner of way with his interest or the subjects themselves. Such a comprehensive prohibition could also exclude the Tenant's Common Law right to create a security over the subjects, if the lease is recordable.

Finally, if the Alienation clause provides for a rent review on the occasion of an assignation or sub-letting, then it should be deleted. It has been suggested that such a provision is against section 16 of the Land Tenure Reform (Scotland) Act 1974 which prohibited the creation of casualties in Leases.

9.2.7. Irritancy

An irritancy may be legal, imposed by law, or conventional, agreed upon by the parties to a particular contract. The parties to a Lease are free to make any lawful stipulation for the conventional irritancy of that Lease and consequently irritancy clauses vary in form from Lease to Lease. Their stipulations, however, must be lawful.

The only legal irritancy in a Lease is for nonpayment of two successive years rent. Such irritancies are purgeable.

At Common Law, conventional irritancies, unless they merely express what the law implies, are not purgeable once incurred, notwithstanding questions of hardship. A tender of payment after irritancy has been incurred but before declarator comes too late. The Court can grant relief if the Landlord's exercise of his right to terminate the Lease amounts to oppression. In the light of recent Scottish authorities, however, it is apparent that the Courts have interpreted oppressive use or abuse in an extremely narrow way in the context of irritancy of Leases. Thus, irritancy clauses in Commercial Leases will be interpreted strictly according to their terms. Therefore the Tenant must attempt to qualify this otherwise unmitigated power. The position in Scotland should be contrasted briefly with that in England where the law of Landlord and Tenant is largely statutory. Basically, English Law, unlike Scots Law, leans against forfeiture of Leases as a general principle and the Tenant has an equitable remedy of relief. In addition, the Landlord must follow a specified statutory procedure in each case.

Defects in a strict irritancy clause

The main problems for a Tenant in a strict irritancy clause are:—

(i) The circumstances justifying irritancy of the Lease may extend to extraneous occurrences such as the alteration of the financial status of the Tenant due to insolvency as well as to non-implement by the Tenant of his obligations under the Lease.

(ii) The Landlord may apply the sanction of irritancy to any breach, however minor.

(iii) The Tenant has no entitlement to prior warning of an irritancy nor is he given an opportunity to remedy a remediable irritancy within a given period.

Effect of Irritancy on third party interests

The present law not only penalises the Tenant but also third parties whose rights derive from the Tenant's interest under the Lease and whose derivative rights will automatically be affected if that interest is terminated by irritancy.

(a) Heritable creditors

No creditor will lend to a Tenant on security of a Lease unless revisals are made to the irritancy clause or the Landlord gives satisfactory assurances to the Creditor.

(b) Sub-Tenants

If the Head Tenant's lease falls, so do all subleases.

These two cases apart, certain other third parties may have a legitimate interest in receiving notice of a impending irritancy whose effects they may wish to prevent. This may be revised into the draft Lease by the Tenant's Agent. It is suggested that it is only fair, however, that if such parties are to obtain notice, they must have first notified their respective interests to the Landlord.

As a result of pressure for reform, the Scottish Law Commission considered the whole subject of Irritancies in Leases and issued a Report (No. 75) in 1983. This report followed a number of cases in Scotland, the most notable being Dorchester Studios (Glasgow) Limited v Stone and Another 1975 SLT (HL) 153. The recommendations of the Report have now resulted in Clauses 4-7 of The Law Reform (Miscellaneous Provisions) (Scotland) Bill (1985).

In general, the Bill makes provision for two forms of protection for a Tenant against the penal enforcement of irritancies in Leases. The first is a new notice procedure applicable where a Landlord seeks to terminate a Lease on the basis of the Tenant's failure to make any monetary payment due under the Lease (Clause 4). The second, which is applicable to all other conventional irritancies in Leases, is a development of the aforementioned equitable power of the Court to grant relief from abuse or oppressive use of irritancies. Both forms of protection also cover the possibility of breach of a contractual term which is, or which is deemed to be, material as well as a reliance by the Landlord on a conventional irritancy Clause. The bill does not apply to Leases of land used wholly or mainly for residential purposes or to crofts, the subjects of cottars, and other holdings to which the Small Landholders (Scotland) Acts 1886 to 1931 apply.

Clause 4 implements a recommendation of the Commission and introduces a mandatory notice procedure in respect of termination based on the Tenant's failure to make a monetary payment under the Lease. The requirement to give notice applies equally where the Landlord relies on a material breach of contract by the Tenant as it does to the breach of a conventional Irritancy Clause. Subsection (2) of Clause 4 provides details of the notice procedure and the need for a tenant to comply with any notice served in order to obtain protection. The matters to be stated in the notice are listed.

Clause 4 subection (3) stipulates a minimum period of fourteen days for payment of arrears. This must be specified in the notice. Account is taken of the possibility of "days of grace" being permitted. The notice must be served by Recorded Delivery at an address in the United Kingdom.

The provisions of Clause 5 are designed to restrict a Landlord's powers of termination in circumstances other than those covered in Clause 4, by reference to the test of the 'fair and reasonable Landlord'. This test is based on the proviso to Section 26(1) of the Agricultural Holdings (Scotland) Act 1949. All the material facts will be looked at in each particular case. However, no doubt the onus of proof will be firmly on the Tenant. The test is applicable only to the particular circumstances in which a Landlord seeks to rely on the Irritancy Clause. It is not intended to exclude the possibility that in certain circumstances it may be fair and reasonable for a Landlord to resort to irritancy without offering the Tenant an opportunity to remedy the relevant breach. Furthermore, in considering the circumstances of a case, regard will be had as to whether a reasonable opportunity has been afforded to the Tenant to enable the breach to be remedied.

Clause 6 of the Bill provides that the parties to a Lease cannot contract out of any provisions of Clause 4 or 5. The provisions of the Bill, when law, will also apply to all relevant Leases, regardless of their date. However, an exception is made for these cases where a Landlord has, prior to the commencement date of the legislation, given notice to the Tenant of his intention to terminate the lease, whether on the basis of breach of contract or of a conventional Irritancy Clause. The application of the Bill is restricted to an irritancy incurred during the currency of a Lease.

Clause 7 is the interpretation clause which provides that residential leases are outwith the scope of the Bill.

The Bill is, for Tenants, a most welcome, and overdue, piece of legislation. To date, a Tenant's attempt to revise the Irritancy Clause in a Lease has regrettably often been refused. It is however only reasonable that, if a breach is capable of being remedied, albeit late, it should be so remedied, as neither the subjects nor the Landlord's interests will be prejudiced. No protection is, however, offered by the Bill to third parties.

Finally, if the Tenant is a Company, and a Liquidator or a Receiver is appointed, the Tenant's interest in the subjects may have substantial value, which the Liquidator or Receiver may wish to realise for the benefit of the Tenant's creditors by finding an Assignee acceptable to the Landlord. The Tenant's Agent should therefore ensure that a period of time is given to the Liquidator or Receiver so as to enable him so to do, provided always that he undertakes liability for performance of all the obligations of the Lease which may include payment of the rent in arrears as well as rent accruing during the period itself.

The general aim in revising the Irritancy Clause in a Lease has been to produce a Clause which effectively acts as a compulsitor to performance of the relevant contractual obligations rather than as a means by which a Landlord can rid himself of an unsatisfactory Tenant. Clauses 4-7 of the Bill go a long way toward protecting a Tenant from the rigours of Irritancy Clauses. It is suggested, however, that notwithstanding the protections offered by the Bill, the Tenant's Solicitor should, whenever possible, carefully revise the Irritancy Clause, to procure the maximum protection for the Tenant.

9.3 Agricultural Leases

Contributed by W.T. Fraser, M.A., LL.B., Advocate, Aberdeen.

Reading List 9.3.

The Practical Aspects of Letting and Management of a Farm

Foreword

The letting and management of a farm for a client is one of the transactions involving Lease that the Solicitor will not encounter very often unless he is involved in a farming practice. If the Solicitor acts for an estate owner, he may find that he will be more involved with this type of work. Forms of Lease vary greatly but in general are framed with a view to the efficient management of farms whatever type of farm is being considered be it arable, pastoral or whatever. In view of the excess of demand for farms over supply, the provisions of most Leases tend to favour the Landlord. Because the Solicitor framing the Lease acts for the Landlord, most Leases are framed from the Landlord's point of view and indeed this text has been written from this point of view. Most Leases seem to minimise the rights of the Tenant as far as possible. This is perhaps a result of the provisions of the Agricultural Holding Acts which tend to favour the Tenant. In passing, it is confirmed that where a particular Estate is involved it is usual for there to be detailed Conditions of Let attached to the Lease to ensure that the conditions of tenure in regard to entry, payment of rent, management, waygoing and the like are more or less in similar terms. These Conditions of Let are also known as Conditions of Lease, Articles and Conditions of Lease, Regulations and Conditions of Let and so on. The principal is often registered in the Books of Council and Session for preservation. In drafting the Lease of a farm, the Solicitor has to consider not only the common law position but also the legislation on Agriculltural Holdings.

The main statutes dealing with Agricultural Holdings in Scotland are the Agricultural Holdings (Scotland) Act 1949, the Agriculture Act 1958, the Succession (Scotland) Act 1964, the Agriculture (Miscellaneous Provisions) Act 1968, the Agriculture (Miscellaneous Provisions) Act 1976 and the Agricultural Holdings (Amendment) (Scotland) Act, 1983. There are also certain important provisions in what remains of the Agriculture (Scotland) Act 1948.

There are numerous forms of Lease available but the style provided is the style prepared for the Workshop Series of Styles by the Law Society of Scotland.

Where a Solicitor is acting for the Landlord he would wish to follow this style as closely as possible subject to variations for the particular type of farm. However, if the Solicitor is acting for the Tenant there are several changes he would wish to make in this style, if at all possible. In practice, the Landlord would permit very few variations from the Lease prepared for revisal by the Tenant. Before progressing further it is useful to mention that there is an abbreviated style of Lease at Page 272 of the Sixth Edition of Connell on The Agricultural Holdings (Scotland) Acts. Further, under Section 4 of the 1949 Act it is possible *inter alia* to secure a written Lease in terms of the Fifth Schedule to the 1949 Act remembering always that the obligations as to the provision and maintenance of fixed equipment are deemed to be included in any Lease entered into from 1st November, 1948 by Section 5 of the 1949 Act. Lastly, it should be remembered that Section 2 of the 1949 Act provides that where any land is let to a person for use as agricultural land for a shorter period than from year to year, and the circumstances are such that if that person were a tenant from year to year he would in respect of that land be the tenant of an agricultural holding, then the Lease shall take effect with necessary modifications, as if it were a Lease of the land from year to year. This provision can usually be avoided if the Lease for a shorter period than from year to year has the prior approval of the Secretary of state.

Before passing on to the next section it should be remembered that despite the various types of Lease, there are four cardinal elements of a Lease, namely —
1. Parties to the Contract.
2. Heritable subjects let.
3. A consideration for the let and
4. A period of time for which the subjects are let.

9.3.1. Taking Instructions

This is always an important matter for a Solicitor. In the case of Leases, it is not so much the taking of instructions that is important as the imparting of information and warnings to the client at the earliest stage so that he will be quite sure to what he is committing himself. This has the effect of fully informing the client of the position and also protecting the Solicitor.

(1) The client must be informed that the Lease will fall under the protection provided by the Agricultural Holdings Acts which with certain exceptions give the Tenant security of tenure. It is not proposed to go into these exceptions in any detail, but it should be noted that permitted exceptions can be set up under Sections 1 and 2 and 25 (2)(b) of the 1949 Act in certain circumstances, although generally it is not possible to contract out of the security of tenure provisions of the Agricultural Holdings Acts. There are various Contracts which would appear to enable the Landlord to exclude the Tenant's statutory rights, but it is not proposed to deal with these Contracts here other than to say that the most common is the type of arrangement whereby the Landlord controls the position by entering into a Partnership Agreement with the farmer and controlling the termination of the partnership and thereby controlling the termination of the Lease. To avoid the Landlord incurring possible financial liability, it is usual to constitute the partnership under the Limited partnership Act, 1907.

(2) The Landlord must be advised that the rent can only be varied by following the statutory procedure in Section 7 of the 1949 Act as amended by Section 2 of the 1958 Act and the Agricultural Holdings (Amendment) (Scotland) Act 1983 S.2. Further, the variations can only be at certain times, for example at a break in the Lease or at the termination of the Lease. Normally before a rent is varied three years must pass from the commencement of the tenancy, the last increase or reduction or a direction that the rent should continue unchanged. The statutory procedure envisages variation of rent being carried out by Arbiters from the Panel of Agricultural Arbiters prepared by the Lord President of the Court of Session. In each arbitration the appointment is by the Secretary of State for Scotland. There is provision for parties appointing an Arbiter by agreement or to go to the Land Court on Joint Application. In terms of the 1983 Act S.5, an Arbiter's award may be appealed to the Land Court.

(3) If the property is subject to a heritable security the consent of the creditor would require to be obtained. In terms of Standard Condition 6 of the Schedule 3 of the Conveyancing and Feudal Reform (Scotland) Act 1970 the debtor is not entitled to enter into any Lease of the subjects.

(4) The Landlord should also be informed of the fees that are to be charged by the agent for the management of the property, if this is in fact to be done.

(5) The Solicitor should also inform the Landlord whether or not the Solicitor will be obliged to deduct Income Tax from rents.

(6) Whether acting for a Landlord or a Tenant, the Solicitor should advise the client of the importance of having a Record of Holding prepared. There is no obvious penalty for not having a Record prepared but if one is not prepared it means that the Landlord would probably lose rights to claim for dilapidations and deteriorations and the Tenant would lose rights to claim compensation for high farming. If no Record is prepared there is much to be said for the view that the Solicitor should have a letter on file from the client who should give authority for dispensing with a Record after having received the explanation for the reasons for a Record.

(7) Any particular requirements of the Landlord should also be obtained such as prohibition on certain uses of the farm, for example the running of a caravan site or camping site.

(8) It should also be explained to the Landlord that it is possible to vary the clauses imported by statute with regard to liabilities of the Landlord and the Tenant for provision and maintenance of fixed equipment by entering into a Post Lease Agreement in terms of Section 5 (3) of the 1949 Act. In practice, this usually increases burdens on the Tenant. To ensure that Tenant will sign the Post Lease Agreement it is prudent to have some benefit to the Tenant in the Post Lease Agreement.

(9) Where the Solicitor is factoring the farm or the Estate he should obtain authority to instruct repairs up to a certain limit without reference to the Landlord. This will certainly assist in the smooth running of the operation.

(10) It is also advisable to establish exactly what the Solicitor is expected to do with the rents received. Is he to be responsible for repayments to heritable creditors, insurance premiums, rates, etcetera from rents received or is he merely to remit the net proceeds to the client or a Bank or Building Society on receipt?

(11) A transaction sheet should be placed at the front of the client's file mentioning the cardinal elements of the Lease along with the forwarding address of the Landlord, any authority to execute repairs and instructions regarding remitting rents. A copy of the transaction sheet should be passed to the Cash Room.

9.3.2. Selecting a Tenant

Before a Tenant can be found, certain preliminary work requires to be completed. There is usually no diffficulty in finding a Tenant for a farm in view of the circumstances referred to beforehand. The Solicitor will now have to visit the farm to take particulars to be used for framing the advertisement and particulars. It is preferable to advertise for a Tenant in respect that the Landlord is given the widest choice of Tenant and he is able to see the range of rents offered and to obtain a good rent — it is probably the case that he should select a Tenant from the higher rents but not necessarily selecting the highest rent, especially if it is out of line. It is essential that he has a Tenant who will make a success of running the farm. A certain amount of co-operation will be required from the outgoing Tenant and this should be borne in mind.

If there is a heritable creditor, his consent should be sought at this stage. The heritable creditor may in addition provide certain additional forms for signature by the Tenant. When the marketing of the property is put in hand, the advertisement should be in the local press and need only contain particulars of the locality of the farm, its type and size and a note of the houses and steading accommodation as also the date of entry and confirmation that further particulars can be obtained. Some Solicitors charge for these particulars to try and make sure they are only dealing with genuinely interested parties. It is a good idea to advertise at least some four months before the entry date.

The particulars of let should be quite comprehensive and include matters such as

(a) description and situation

(b) type of land

(c) area

(d) plan

(e) number of houses and steading accommodation

(f) services such as water, electricity, telephone, gas and drainage

(g) outgoings such as rates for houses and drainage and also water rates

(h) the type of the tenancy — it is helpful to have a draft lease for perusal by interested parties

(i) the outgoing or waygoing valuations should be listed and it is essential to give a note of the basis of valuation and the method of valuation. In practice, provision should be made for two valuers, one appointed by each party with provision for an Oversman

(j) viewing arrangements should be made. This is where co-operation is required from the outgoing Tenant

(k) details for offering should also be given and if possible there should be a form attached to the particulars leaving space for an offerer to put in the details of himself and his family, the rent, the improvements required by the offerers, the particulars of farming experience, particulars of the present farming system, capital and other resources available, proposals for future use of the holding, the name and address of the Bank Manager, the name and address of two referees and the name and address of the present Landlord, if any

(l) the closing time should also be detailed.

Normally one would find quite a number of persons interested in the property. There seem to be at least two different ways of choosing a Tenant. The first and more usual involves asking for offers of rent and selecting the Tenant from the higher band of offers consistent with the Tenant being able to make a success at that figure. It is important not to necessarily select the highest offerer as this may not produce the most suitable Tenant. It is essential to have a good farmer with sufficient capital and good character. The second and less usual system seems to be to adopt a fixed rent and choose the most suitable applicant from that figure or around that figure. There are other methods and each Solicitor will have his own viewpoint. He should of course discuss the matter fully with his client. The Tenant may wish to be separately advised but if he is not so advised and asks anything about the Lease then he clearly must be supplied with the appropriate information. It is thought, however, that there is no positive obligation on the part of the Landlord's Solicitor to advise the Tenant of his rights as to for instance security of tenure or other matters. Some Solicitors conclude missives of Lease and then have the Lease completed thereafter. Other Solicitors merely take in offers and conclude a Lease with the successful offerer. The Tenant will no doubt wish his Solicitor to revise the Lease and the engrossed Lease should be signed by the Tenant in the presence of two witnesses and completed by the Landlord again in the presence of two witnesses. Thereafter the Deed should be sent to the Stamp Office for stamping.

9.3.3. Terms of Lease — See Style in Workshop 1980 JLS W 135.

Parties — It is essential to correctly name and design the parties in view of the importance of the relationship which is involved.

Destination — It should be noted that the Destination here excludes successors and assignees and sub-tenants, the exclusion of assignees and sub-tenants being declaratory of the Common Law. It is thought that if the Landlord wishes to exclude grazing lets that this should be specified. Successors and not merely legatees are excluded. Legatees can competently be excluded; but the Executors of the deceased Tenant are always entitled to deal with his interest as lessee under the Succession (Scotland) Act 1964 S.16.

Subjects Let — This provides for the area which should now be in hectares and a boundary plan. The boundary plan and also outline plans of the buildings are required for the Record.

Duration — Leases used frequently to be for a period of fourteen years with a break at seven years. There is a tendency now for a ten year Lease with a break at five years or a five year lease or in some circumstances for a Lease for one year only which will be continued by tacit relocation. From the point of view of the Landlord, especially from removal and succession aspects, it is preferable to have a short Lease of, say, six years with a break at the end of the third year. When one reads the other Clauses in the Lease where a Lease is for one year it at least looks unusual.

Rent — It is noted that the Rent refers to periods of possession and not to crops and years so that if the let is a Whitsunday let of an arable farm the rent will be payable six months forehand and if it is a Martinmas let the rent will be payable at the legal term. For reference to forehand, legal terms and backhand rents an 'Introduction of the Law of Scotland' by Gloag & Henderson 8th Edition at Page 452 may be found useful. If possible, the terms Whitsunday and Martinmas should always be followed by a specific date.

Rent Revision — This envisages a revision every five years and this would apply to a Lease for a longer period than five years provided there is a break. Care will have to be taken in using this Clause if the rent revision period is altered to three years.

Minerals — this clause would appear to give a Landlord power to work minerals without actually resuming the land.

Alter marches etcetera — is a useful provision to have in case this may be required.

Resumption — This clause gives a power of resumption for any purpose except for agricultural purposes. No time is specified but the better view is that a Tenant should be given at least two months notice so that he may deal with matters and in particular intimate a claim for compensation for high farming or intention to remove fixtures.

Water — This is a statement of the Common Law position.

Game — Game is reserved and the time for Notice of Claim of damage is for the period of twelve months ending 31st October in each year which is substituted for the calendar year. Further, to avoid having to pay the Tenant compensation for damage by deer, the Tenant is granted permission to kill deer on arable land or enclosed pasture.

Wood and Plantations — This extends the Common Law position and clarifies in detail the position with regard to the use of Woods and Plantations.

Wayleaves — These are reserved, subject to payment for surface damage.

Roads — The right to use roads and means of access are reserved.

Access by the Landlord — This is over and above the Common Law and Statutory rights in the 1949 Act.

Rates — This is a useful Clause to include in the Lease.

Landlord's Obligations to re-instate and re-insure — This is a Clause which the Tenant can call on the Landlord to put into a Lease under the Fifth Schedule of the 1949 Act.

Tenant's Obligations to Insure Crops etcetera — This is a Clause which the Landlord can call on the Tenant to put into a Lease under the Fifth Schedule of the 1949 Act.

Landlord's Obligation for Fixed Equipment — This is a Clause imposed on the Landlord by Statute. The Landlord is also obliged by Statute to carry out his obligations at the commencement of the tenancy or as soon as reasonably possible thereafter.

Tenant's Obligation for Fixed Equipment — This is a Clause imposed on the Tenant by statute. It narrates that the Landlord has carried out his obligations at the commencement of the tenacy or as soon reasonably possible thereafter.

Tenant's Other Obligations — This narrates the detailed obligations incumbent on the Tenant to uphold the fixed equipment under the Lease. These will have to be carefully observed in that a Notice to Remedy certain breaches within a reasonable time can be served on the Tenant under Section 25(2)(e) of the 1949 Act and failure to remedy breaches can result in a Notice of Removal being served on the Tenant. The Tenant has certain important remedies under the Agriculture (Miscellaneous Provisions) Act, 1976 and these should be noted.

Record — Whereas in many cases a Record is not completed, it is a prudent course to follow. Whereas compensation for dilapidations and deterioration would generally depend on a Record being in existence, the right to compensation for improvements does not so depend except where the compensation is for high farming.

Alteration to Fixed Equipment — In carrying out Improvements under Part II of the First Schedule to the 1949 Act the Tenant will have to be particularly careful.

Tenant's Fixtures — This would appear to strike at the Tenant's rights to remove fixtures under Section 14 of the 1949 Act and should be resisted by the Tenant if at all possible.

Stock — The use of the farm is restricted to an arable and/or livestock rearing farm only. There is also a prohibition against breaking up permanent pasture. As the Tenant has statutory rights relating to permanent pasture under Section 9 of the 1949 Act, the permanent pasture should be specified.

Muirburn — This refers to the burning of heather muir, whins or bracken and is covered by the Hill Farming Act 1946.

Camping or Caravanning — This prohibits camping or caravanning. Similar types of prohibition can be entered here such as the restriction of the number of dogs to be kept on a farm.

Market gardening and dairy farming — This Clause ensures that the Landlord does not have to provide for the alteration or provision of or pay compensation for specialised fixed equipment such as for market gardening, commercial flower or vegetable cultivation, dairy farming, pig or poultry production. It does not prevent use of the farm for these purposes.

Last Year — This provides for the cultivation prior to outgo. It also provides for outgoing, waygoing or awaygoing valuation to be taken over from the outgoing Tenant. The items to be taken over are the usual items of grass and clover seeds sown with the clean land grain crop, the grain and the turnips. There does not appear to be value paid for the straw, the first year grasses and ploughing and harrowing of fallow ground. The style of lease does not appear to specify for the method of valuation and this should be specified to avoid difficulty.

Residence on Farm — This is an important clause for a Landlord and it ensures that the farm will be cultivated by a resident tenant with presumably a higher standard of husbandry than by an absent tenant.

Waste Ground — This would not appear to be a usual clause and the question of compensation at outgo would have to be considered.

Irritancy — This permits the Lease to be irritated for bankruptcy, sub-letting, failure to pay rent and certain other matters. This is a dangerous Clause from the point of view of a Tenant and an attempt should be made to alter it if at all possible. In this case, reference should be made to the case of Dorchester Studios (Glasgow) Limited v Stone and Another 1975 SLT (HL) 153 and the new legislation which has been promoted in this matter. The possibility of founding on the principle of Mutuality of Contract in defence should be looked into.

Consideration would also have to be given to the question of whether or not claims for improvements were enforceable.

Removing — Where there was any doubt, the Tenant would wait until a Court Order was made against him. In this connection he should take the appropriate steps against a Notice of Removal by requesting the reference of the matter to the Land Court or arbitration, depending on the circumstances, that is whether the Notice of Removal is given under Section 26 or Section 25 of the 1949 Act. No comments are made on the form of Notice of Removal or the grounds for giving them in these Notes.

Registration for Preservation and Execution — This would be a prudent Clause to include.

9.3.4. Taxation

Income Tax — It should be noted that whereas a Farmer is treated as carrying on a trade and is assessed to Income Tax under Schedule D Case 1 with certain special additional rules, the income from the farm letting is normally charged under Schedule A.

Capital Transfer Tax — To obtain relief for agricultural property from 10th March, 1981, you must either have occupied the property for the purposes of agriculture for at least two years before transferring it, or have owned it for seven years up to that time, with others farming. Rules are relaxed where you inherit the property or where you have replaced one agricultural property by another.

The relief is 50% if you enjoy the right to vacant possession or can obtain this within the next twelve months. Otherwise, the relief is normally 20% (applying to tenanted situations etcetera).

By virtue of the Capital Transfer Act 1984 S.16 the grant of a tenancy of agricultural property is not to be treated as a transfer value if it is made for full consideration.

Value Added Tax — Certain matters are not to be treated as taxable supply and these are set out in the Value Added Tax Act 1983 Schedule 6. The exemptions include the grant, assignment or surrender of any interest in or right over land or of any licence to occupy land. Therefore the sales of lands and rents will not attract Value Added Tax. The exemption does not apply to the provision of hotel or holiday accommodation, facilities for camping in tents or caravans, parking facilities, game and fishing rights, rights to fell timber and storage and mooring facilities for ships and aircraft.

9.3.5. Insurance

Great care must be taken in instructing insurance cover as special problems arise with regard to replacement value of old buildings and in view of the fact that some of these buildings would never be replaced in their original form as they are totally unsuited for farming requirements today.

9.4 Leases of Private Dwellinghouses
Contributed by K.W. Swinton, Solicitor, Dundee.

The letting of houses can be divided into the private sector and the public sector, i.e. where the Local Authority, New Town Development Corporation or Scottish Special Housing Association is the Landlord.

9.4.1. Public Sector Tenancies
It may be noted in passing that until recently there was little legislation relating specifically to public sector tenancies. This has now changed by virtue of the Tenants' Rights etc. (Scotland) Act 1980 Part II. This provides that where the tenancy is a secure one, which covers most Local Authority Tenants other than those in job related accommodation or who have been housed under the Homeless Persons Act, the Tenant has a right to a written lease, to certain security of tenure and there are provisions for succession to the tenancy on the death of the Tenant.

Housing Authorities are also charged with certain duties in relation to homeless persons in terms of the Housing (Homeless Persons) Act.

9.4.2. Private Sector Tenancies
The private sector covers tenancies not in the public sector. The Rent Acts are now consolidated into the Rent (Scotland) Act 1984. The principal features of the Act are security of tenure, transmission of the tenancy on the death of a tenant and systems of rent control.

In terms of S.1 of the Act a tenancy is a protected tenancy where a house is let as a dwellinghouse unless the rateable value exceeded £200 on 23rd March 1965 or if the house was completed after that date and prior to 1st April 1978 on its first being assigned a rateable value thereafter if it exceeds £600 and from 1st April 1985 £1600. The Act covers both unfurnished and furnished tenancies. S.2 provides certain exemptions where the rent does not exceed two-thirds of the rateable value, where the rent includes an element for board or attendance, where it is a holiday let or where the tenant is studying at a specified educational institution.

For there to be a protected tenancy, what is required is the lease of a house or a part of a house as a separate unit and exclusive possession. During the currency of a Lease, a Tenant of a protected tenancy is known as a contractual Tenant. At the end of the contractual period of the tenancy the Tenant can remain in occupation of the property as a statutory Tenant by virtue of S.3.

A statutory tenant may only be removed by the Landlord on the grounds specified in Schedule 2 of the Act which is divided into two parts. Part I contains grounds on which the Court **may** grant possession, and Part II grounds on which the Court **must** grant possession to the Landlord. Additionally the Court may grant repossession if it is satisfied there is a suitable alternative accommodation for the Tenant and it is reasonable to do so. (S.11(1)(a) of the Act).

Part I of Schedule 2 lists ten cases in which the Court may grant possession, such as non-payment of rent, commission of a nuisance, overcrowding etc. Part II of the Schedule provides absolute grounds for repossession. These include where the dwellinghouse was formerly occupied by an owner occupier who now requires it for himself or a member of his family and in various circumstances on the death of a former resident owner occupier; or if the owner occupier has moved to another area and wishes to purchase another house there in connection with a job; or if a heritable creditor is entitled to repossession on grounds of default by the former owner occupier. There are further additional cases for houses required by a Minister; agricultural workers; retirement homes; houses specially adapted for disabled people where the Landlord has some person who satisfies the requirements of disability but the Tenant does not; and a serviceman's home.

A specific type of protected tenancy is a short tenancy governed by S.9. Such a tenancy is for a fixed period between one and five years. A fair rent must be registered for the property at the commencement of the Lease and the Tenant must receive notice prior to the commencement that it is a short tenancy. If these conditions are complied with, the Landlord is entitled to recover possession at the end of the period; if he serves the appropriate notice timeously the Tenant then has no right to stay on as a statutory Tenant and can be removed.

If possession is to be recovered, it is a pre-requisite of any court Action that Notice to Quit is served on the Tenant. The style for the Notice to Quit itself is laid down in the Schedule to the Sheriff Court Act 1907. Appended to the Notice to Quit must be certain prescribed information in terms of S.112 of the Act and S.I.1980/1667 which advises the tenant of his right to remain in the subjects after expiry of the Notice to Quit and that possession may only be recovered on the grounds set out in the Act. The failure to include the prescribed information renders the Notice invalid.

Certain periods of notice are laid down. In the absence of any express provision, the Sheriff Court Act 1907 S.38 provides that the appropriate period of notice required before an action of summary ejection (now encompassed in a Summary Cause action for recovery of possession of heritable property) can be raised is one-third of the term of the lease if for less than four months, and forty days for a lease of four months to one year. This can be contracted out of in terms of the lease, but S.112 of the Act provides for a minimum of twenty-eight days notice in all cases which cannot be contracted out of.

Not only is there security of tenure for the original contractual Tenant; but the tenancy can transmit on the death of the Tenant. S.3 of the Act and Schedule 1 provide that on the death of the Tenant the tenancy may pass to a member of his family. Schedule 1 allows for a second passing of the tenancy on the death of a second person where a member of the family resides with the second Tenant for at least six months prior to his or her death.

Rent Control

The terms of the Lease between the Landlord and Tenant will provide for a rent. If the rent is payable weekly, a rent book or other receipt for rent must be given and the rent book or receipt must provide certain prescribed information as to the Tenant's rights. (S.113 of the Act and S.I. 1980/1671). If the rent is payable monthly, however, these provisions do not apply. The rent contracted for between Landlord and Tenant is not automatically what the Landlord is entitled to recover. Part V of the Act provides for a system of registration of rents. An application for determination of a fair rent may be made either by Landlord or Tenant or jointly. As fair rent levels tend to be somewhat below market level the application is often made by the Tenant. Application is made to the Rent Officer who is required to take into account all the circumstances of the case which will include the age, character and location of the house, its state of repair and the quantity, quality and condition of any furniture provided. There is disregarded any scarcity value attaching to the premises, i.e. the fact that there are more prospective tenants than properties available; and any circumstances personal to the Landlord and the

Tenant. Any defects attributable to the Tenant are disregarded, but want of repair etc. attributable to the Landlord are not.

In reaching the figure for fair rent, reliance may be placed on registered rents of similar properties in the area, and it is also common for landlords to argue on the basis of return on capital value. Either Landlord or Tenant may appeal from the Rent Officer's determination of the fair rent within a period of twenty-eight days of receipt of notice of the same to a Rent Assessment Committee, which will make a determination on similar criteria. Thereafter, appeal lies to the Court of Session on a point of law only. Once registered, the rent will continue to apply to the property indefinitely but after a period of three years application may be made to review the registered rent.

In the event of the registered rent being less than the contractual rent, the Tenant is entitled to have repaid to him, or to deduct from rent payable by him in the future, the excess rent paid by him between the date of application and determination of the rent. If the registered rent is higher than the rent being paid, then the rent can be increased until it reaches the registered rent. The current maximum increase is £104 per annum or 25% of the rent — S.I. 1980/1664.

Part VII Contracts

A Part VII Contract originally was designed to cover furnished lets which were excluded from the protection of the Act. A Part VII Contract will not be held to exist where there is a regulated tenancy. The main condition therefore is the inclusion of a substantial degree of services included in the rent and the right to occupy a dwellinghouse as a residence. (A similar rateable value provision applies.) With a Part VII Contract there is no automatic security of tenure but a Tenant under such a contract can apply to a Rent Assessment Committee who may grant a security of tenure. In doing so they will normally fix a rent. The period of security of tenure is limited to six months and the Tenant may apply for a further extension of this. A Rent Assessment Committee may reduce or increase the rent or approve the rent presently being paid.

Premiums

Part VIII of the Act provides for a prohibition on taking of premiums, that is money given for the grant or assignation of a Lease. The Act contains special deeming provisions so that being forced to acquire furniture in a flat at an inflated price is to be regarded as a premium. Where a premium has been paid, it is recoverable by the party who paid it.

With furnished leases it is common practice to take a deposit as security for damages often amounting to one or two months' rent. It had been argued that doing so might be considered to be a premium, but S.90(3) of the Act provides that up to two months' rent is not to be regarded as a premium.

Under S.22 of the Act offences are created making it a criminal offence to remove a tenant without Court Order or to harass him. In practice however, the police are reluctant to interfere in such cases as they consider these to be matters of civil rather than criminal jurisdiction.

INDEX